Teaching in Inclusive Classrooms

Third Edition

Brian R. Bryant, who left us too soon, provided much of the foundation for the third edition through his authorship on the previous two editions. His work, but more importantly his life, continues to inspire us along with so many others who had the privilege of knowing him.

Teaching in Inclusive Classrooms

Third Edition

Diane P. Bryant

The University of Texas at Austin

Deborah D. Smith

Claremont Graduate University

Brian R. Bryant

The University of Texas at Austin

Sage

Sage

FOR INFORMATION:

2455 Teller Road
Thousand Oaks, California 91320
E-mail: order@sagepub.com

1 Oliver's Yard
55 City Road
London EC1Y 1SP
United Kingdom

Unit No 323-333, Third Floor, F-Block
International Trade Tower
Nehru Place, New Delhi – 110 019

18 Cross Street #10-10/11/12
China Square Central
Singapore 048423

Library of Congress Cataloging-in-Publication Data

Printed in Canada.

ISBN: 978-1-0718-3495-4

Names: Bryant, Diane Pedrotty, author. | Smith, Deborah Deutsch, author. | Bryant, Brian R., author.

Title: Teaching in inclusive classrooms / Diane P. Bryant, Deborah D. Smith, Brian R. Bryant.

Description: Third edition. | Thousand Oaks, California: SAGE, 2025. | Includes bibliographical references and index.

Identifiers: LCCN 2023048357 (print) | LCCN 2023048358 (ebook) | ISBN 9781071834954 (paperback) | ISBN 9781071834947 (epub)

Subjects: LCSH: Inclusive education—United States.

Classification: LCC LC1201.B79 2025 (print) | LCC LC1201 (ebook) | DDC 371.9–dc23/eng/20231102

LC record available at https://lccn.loc.gov/2023048357

LC ebook record available at https://lccn.loc.gov/2023048358

This book is printed on acid-free paper.

24 25 26 27 28 10 9 8 7 6 5 4 3 2 1

Acquisitions Editor: Leah Fargotstein

Content Development Editor: Kenzie Offley

Production Editor: Aparajita Srivastava

Copy Editor: Diana Breti

Typesetter: diacriTech

Cover Designer: Rose Storey

Marketing Manager: Victoria Velasquez

BRIEF CONTENTS

DETAILED CONTENTS

PREFACE

TO OUR READERS

When we wrote the first edition of this textbook, we came together with one main purpose: to help teachers complete their special education and inclusion course *inspired* to teach students with disabilities in inclusive settings and *equipped* to do so effectively. At that time, the increased reliance on accountability systems and high-stakes testing had made apparent the number of students who struggled and who were at risk for school failure. Because the vast majority of students with disabilities spend more than 80% of their school day learning in general education classrooms, meeting the needs of students with disabilities remains a challenge. Unfortunately, even though an increased number of evidence-based instructional procedures have become available, many classroom teachers working in inclusive settings still feel unprepared to meet the challenges these individual students bring to the learning environment. In the prefaces to the first and second editions, we wrote that the text was designed to fulfill what we saw as our two critical responsibilities to our reader; we remain steadfast to those purposes in this updated version of the text:

- To increase knowledge of *proven* practices. A wealth of information exists about instructional practices that are evidence based and effective for students with unique learning needs or disabilities who are learning in inclusive settings. We have worked to make this information accessible to you by analyzing the existing body of research, selecting those practices that have proved to be most effective (and that will be of most help in the teaching situations you will encounter most often), and presenting that information in the context of real classrooms. To that end, our text discussion and supporting features focus on *what works.*
- To improve instructional decision making. The ADAPT Framework that we have integrated throughout this text will help you determine *how, when,* and *with whom* to use the proven academic and behavioral interventions in your repertoire to obtain the best outcomes. The ADAPT Framework will help you develop the "habits of mind" needed to respond thoughtfully and flexibly to the challenges you will meet in your classroom long after your coursework is over.

We hope that by the time you have completed your reading of this third edition, we will have met these responsibilities and you will have confidence in your ability to meet the needs of all students in your classroom. We remain confident that with the appropriate knowledge and tools, all teachers can make a positive difference in the educational lives of students with unique learning needs or disabilities.

ORGANIZATION OF THIS TEXT

We begin with chapters that provide an overview of inclusive education and the delivery of individualized services to students with different learning needs. Chapter 1 examines the meanings of the terms *disability* and *inclusive education,* and the key legislation that has affected the development of inclusive classrooms: The Individuals with Disabilities Education Act of 2004 (IDEA), the No Child Left Behind Act of 2001 (NCLB) and its reauthorization in 2015 as the Every Student Succeeds Act (ESSA), and the Assistive Technology Act of 2022 (the reauthorization of the 2004 ATA or the Tech Act). In Chapter 1, we introduce the concept of the ADAPT Framework and continue that theme *throughout* the book. For example, in Chapter 2 we continue the discussion of the ADAPT Framework by providing examples of how it is applied to individualized education programs (IEPs) and other special services that help teachers meet the needs of their students.

Because children with disabilities represent a very diverse group, in Chapter 2 we explain the variety of unique services that are brought together and individually tailored by multidisciplinary teams to meet each student's educational needs. These teams can include many different professionals—general education teachers, special education teachers, speech/language pathologists, physical therapists, occupational therapists, school nurses, and others—who provide a variety of services. It is not uncommon for three or four (or even more) professionals to work with a single student and their family. It is important for these professionals to collaborate to meet the total needs of the student. Many years ago, this need to collaborate and to communicate with one another set the stage for collaborative consultation, a field that has become increasingly important in the age of inclusion. Consultation is the topic area covered in Chapter 3, which describes how teams of professionals work together to meet the unique needs of all students. Chapter 4 continues the focus on diversity of *all* learners by specifically addressing culturally and linguistically diverse learners and their families. In Chapter 4, we also provide information about children who are gifted and talented and discuss children who are viewed as twice exceptional.

Chapters 5 and 6, respectively, focus on children with the most common disabilities or conditions and children with less common disabilities or conditions. These two chapters are organized by the most recent prevalence data provided by the federal government, reflecting students served through funding provided by IDEA because their educational performance is negatively affected by their disability or condition. For years, autism spectrum disorder (ASD) was considered a less common disability or condition; in this edition, we include it in the most common disabilities or conditions category because more and more children are identified as having ASD. Most common disabilities or conditions, discussed in Chapter 5, are those that teachers are most likely to encounter in classrooms—such as learning disabilities, speech or language impairments, attention deficit hyperactivity disorder (ADHD), ASD, intellectual disability, and emotional or behavioral disorders. In contrast, less common disabilities or conditions discussed in Chapter 6 include such conditions as health impairments, multiple disabilities, developmental delay, physical disabilities, d/Deafness and hard of hearing, visual impairments (low vision and blindness), traumatic brain injury, and deaf-blindness.

Chapter 7 addresses differentiating instruction to promote access to the general education curriculum. This chapter focuses on the steps of the ADAPT Framework and the four categories of adaptations, which are then integrated into Chapters 11, 12, 13, and 14. Chapter 8 focuses on Universal Design for Learning (UDL), assistive technology devices and services, and instructional materials and textbooks. Many textbooks used in content classes such as history and science are written in a way that leaves struggling readers unable to access the important information found on their pages. We examine the role of adaptations and assistive technology as tools that can be used by teachers to promote access, despite the challenges posed by the difficulty level of the textbooks.

In today's schools, students spend considerable time taking tests. The types of tests and their purposes are almost as diverse as the content tested and the students who are assessed. Assessment and the use of student performance on various measures is discussed in Chapter 9. For some students with disabilities, test administration differs from that of their peers, and the differences (and why those differences exist) are discussed in this chapter.

Chapter 10 discusses the importance of creating a positive classroom ematerialsnvironment by communicating effectively with students, arranging the classroom, teaching social skills, and addressing problem behaviors. Finally, in Chapters 11 through 14, we focus on specific content areas: reading, writing, mathematics, and content-area reading and study skills. In these chapters, we present practical, evidence-based strategies for adapting instruction to meet the needs of all students.

SPECIAL FEATURES

- As with the previous edition, two **Opening Challenge** case studies begin each chapter. They describe in some detail a specific teaching challenge at the elementary and secondary level (middle school and high school), which is then revisited throughout the chapter. Students are asked to reflect on their knowledge of the subject matter before reading the chapter and are encouraged to record their responses to Reflection Questions in a journal.

- **ADAPT in Action** sections are integrated in the text discussion in many of the chapters. This illustrative section applies the ADAPT Framework, a research-validated problem-solving approach, to the student and teacher introduced in the Opening Challenge scenarios. In these features, the teacher "thinks out loud" using the ADAPT Framework, thus allowing the reader and teacher to go through the problem-solving steps.
- The Universal Design for Learning (UDL) approach to instruction is integrated in several chapters, through the **UDL in Action** feature, with specific lesson activities as examples of how the principles of UDL can be accounted for as part of instructional design.
- **Working Together** features offer practical advice on how an idea or concept can be taught using a collaborative approach that involves other school professionals and/or family members. Questions are posed for deliberation about how professionals tackle issues together.
- **Instructional Strategies** feature key research-to-practice, classroom-based activities that are relevant to topics in the chapter. Sample lessons for teaching the skills that students need to succeed in each area include the instructional objective, instructional content, instructional materials, a means to deliver the instruction, and methods to monitor student progress.
- **Considering Diversity** features examine various issues from a cultural or linguistic perspective; they illustrate how the diversity of our school populations is related to academic instruction and management.
- **Tech Notes** features provide readers with information about assistive and instructional technologies that can be employed with students who have learning or behavioral problems. Examples from classrooms are used to show practical applications.
- **Multi-tiered systems of support** (MTSS), including both the response to intervention (RTI) model for academics and Positive Behavioral Interventions and Support (PBIS) for the prevention and remediation of social and behavioral problems, is first described in Chapter 2. RTI and PBIS are models that deliver evidence-based tiered instruction as part of the schoolwide approach, which is designed to promote improved academic performance for all students and minimize behavior problems. Those discussions, as appropriate, are continued in many chapters across the book.
- Each chapter closes with a **Summary** section, followed by **Review the Learning Objectives** with answers to help readers review material and assess their understanding of key topics. **Revisit the Opening Challenge** questions return readers to the scenarios presented in the Opening Challenge and monitor their learning of key concepts in relation to the development of the teacher and student scenarios. Examples of professional standards also are included at the end of each chapter.

NEW and Enhanced in This Edition

- **Updated Coverage of Multi-Tiered Systems of Support**

  Since the last edition, the concept and applications of multi-tiered systems of support (MTSS) for academics, response to intervention (RTI) and early intervening, and Positive Behavioral Interventions and Supports (PBIS) have further developed. These systems have proven to be effective in improving both academic and behavioral learning and also in preventing years of school failure. For these reasons, we bring you current concepts about these systems and explanations of how they are implemented using evidence-based practices and high-leverage practices.
- **Current Data About Prevalence and Placement**

  All the data about the number of students identified for special education services through IDEA have been updated and are the most current available. These data guided our organization of the book's content regarding each disability and condition from the most common, discussed in Chapter 5, to those disabilities or conditions that occur less frequently, discussed in Chapter 6. Across the years, where these students are educated—whether in general education classrooms or in more restrictive, separate educational settings—has changed. As a result, current and historic placement trends are now included in the text.

- **Enhanced Focus on Equity and Diversity**
  Across the text, we bring you special features and discussions about the over- and underrepresentation of groups of students from various ethnic and racial groups. We bring you discussions and data about their unequal treatment in the public school systems, and we provide ways to resolve some of these inequities.
- **Enhanced Discussion of the IEP Process**
  Since the publication of the last edition, the Supreme Court strengthened the concept of FAPE, a free appropriate public education, for students with disabilities. The 2017 court case, *Endrew F. v. Douglas County School District*, substantially changed and increased parents' and families' roles in the education of their children. This court decision also changed the roles of teachers and administrators in the IEP process by mandating that the goals stated in students' IEPs be reasonable, yet ambitious. In this edition, we discuss the implications of this court decision and how its criteria are met. We also explain the new component of IEPs that include present levels of academic achievement and functional performance (PLAAFP).
- **New and Expanded Coverage of Gifted Education**
  Because students with unique academic abilities and other talents do not receive services through IDEA, content about them and their education has been moved to Chapter 4. Too many students with special gifts and talents do not receive instructional programs that address their amazing potential, and many of them come from historically underrepresented groups. In addition, most students who are gifted and have disabilities (often referred to as twice-exceptional learners) are overlooked; they, too, are underrepresented among this very special group of learners. In these sections, we bring their situations to your attention and discuss ways schools and teachers can be more responsive their learning needs.

ONLINE RESOURCES

This text includes an array of instructor teaching materials designed to save you time and to help you keep students engaged. To learn more, visit sagepub.com or contact your SAGE representative at sagepub.com/findmyrep.

ACKNOWLEDGMENTS

Thanks to our colleagues who contributed their writing and expertise to Chapter 4, "Culturally and Linguistically Diverse Learners and Families and Gifted and Talented Learners." For the first edition, the late Janette K. Klingner, of the University of Colorado Boulder, wrote sections on culturally and linguistically diverse students, multicultural education, bilingual education, and special education. Margarita Bianco, of the University of Colorado at Denver and the Denver Health Sciences Center, wrote the section on students who are gifted and talented. For the second edition, we are grateful to Sylvia Linan-Thompson for revising the chapter.

Our gratitude goes out to the many reviewers, focus group attendees, and advisory council members who have greatly enhanced this project over the years of its writing. Your thoughtfulness and commitment to the project have made this a better book.

For this edition:

Heather Pease, University of North Florida

Michele Miller, University of Illinois, Springfield

Pamela Schuetz, SUNY Buffalo State University

For the second edition:

Michele Augustin, Washington University in St. Louis

Jill Choate, Fort Lewis College

Amy Freier, Trinity Bible College and Graduate School

Robert Loyd, Armstrong State University

Lorna Sheriff, Stephen F. Austin State University

Annmarie Urso, State University of New York at Geneseo

For the first edition:

Dona C. Bauman, University of Scranton

Nancy Beach, Ferrum College

Judy Bentley, State University of New York at Cortland

Pamela Brillante, William Paterson University

Kimberly Boyd, Virginia Commonwealth University

Melinda Burchard, Messiah College

Nancy G. Burton, Concord University

EunMi Cho, California State University, Sacramento

Su-Je Cho, Fordham University

Hollie C. Cost, University of Montevallo

Susan Courey, San Francisco State University

Aaron R. Deris, Minnesota State University, Mankato

Jason Fruth, Wright State University

Heather Garrison, East Stroudsburg University of Pennsylvania

Terri M. Griffin, Westfield State University

Vicki Jean Hartley, Delta State University

René Hauser, St. Bonaventure University

Jude Matyo-Cepero, University of Nebraska, Kearney

Virginia McLoughlin, St. John's University

Carol Moore, Troy University

Wendy Pharr, Northeastern State University

Jazmine Ramirez, Miami Dade College

Bruce Saddler, University at Albany, SUNY

Thomas Simmons, University of Louisville

Linda Smetana, California State University, East Bay

Shanon Taylor, University of Nevada, Reno

Harriet L. Thompson, Western Governors University

Colleen A. Wilkinson, Medaille College

Jie Zhang, The College at Brockport, SUNY

We are deeply grateful for the expertise, support, and commitment of the SAGE team to see this revision project to fruition. Their belief in us and in this project, from the beginning, has exceeded all reasonable expectations. Many people comprised the team who worked on this book, both the first and second editions. Although we do not know all of them by name, their expertise with their craft is truly evident; to this team we express our gratitude. First and foremost, we thank Leah Fargotstein, acquisitions editor, for her continuing support, advice, wisdom, and patience as this revision journey unfolded and found its way to a wonderful conclusion. Our gratitude is also extended to the entire SAGE team that each contributed in different ways to the development of this third edition: Diana Breti, copy editor; Kenzie Offley, associate content developer; Aparajita Srivastava, production editor; and the many others who behind the scenes help to create an inviting book for students as they prepare to work in inclusive educational settings.

As we did for the first and second editions, we would like to acknowledge the contribution of Dr. Kavita Rao, professor at the University of Hawaii of Manoa, for helping us to create a format for the UDL lessons. Her contributions (e.g., suggesting that we provide information on UDL checkpoints rather than principles; editing our early work) were invaluable, are reflected in this edition, and we appreciate her taking the time to provide excellent guidance and expertise to provide input on UDL.

We would also like to extend a special thanks Kenzie Offley for her wonderful work on the new videos that accompany the third edition. We also thank the teachers and administrators who graciously allowed her to film their schools and classrooms: Principal Lou Lichtl and instructors Jason Brown, Jeff McCann, Brinden Wohlstattar, and Melissa Wood-Glusac at Thousand Oaks High School in Thousand Oaks, California; instructors Jan Evans, Tema Khieu, Lisa Sigafoos, and Mia Tannous at the University of Texas Elementary School in Austin, Texas; and Dedham Public Schools Superintendent Michael J. Welch and instructors Heather Caruso, Paul Sances, and Lisa Walsh of Riverdale Elementary School and Liz Amato, Meghan Armstrong, and Ariel Katz of Dedham High School in Dedham, Massachusetts.

You have a textbook that we hope will inspire you as educators to reach out to all students. You will hear the voices of many as you read and learn numerous, practical ways to work with all students across the grades. We wish you the best!

D. P. B.

D. D. S.

B. R. B.

ABOUT THE AUTHORS

Diane P. Bryant is a professor in the Department of Special Education at The University of Texas at Austin, and a member of the Board of Directors for the Meadows Center for Preventing Educational Risk. Diane served as principal investigator for multiple response to intervention grants from the Texas Education Agency and the Institute of Education Sciences. Diane taught special education classes for many years. She has published articles on instructional strategies for students with learning disabilities in refereed journals such as the *Learning Disability Quarterly, Journal of Learning Disabilities, Remedial and Special Education, Journal of Mathematical Behavior, International Journal of STEM Education, Teacher Education and Special Education*, and *Learning Disabilities Research & Practice*. She is the co-author of three textbooks and three tests.

Deborah D. Smith, emerita professor of the School for Educational Studies, Claremont Graduate University, is a graduate of Pitzer College, University of Missouri, and the University of Washington. Deb received her credential preparation for general education at California State University, Northridge. She has been a professor of special education at the University of New Mexico, Vanderbilt University, and Claremont Graduate University. Deb has authored 20 textbooks and more than 40 chapters and journal articles. She has directed many externally funded projects, including the Alliance Project, the Special Education Faculty Needs Assessment (SEFNA), and the IRIS Center, totaling more than $40 million. She has won numerous awards and has made many international presentations.

Brian R. Bryant lived and worked in Austin, Texas. After working in Maine as a special education teacher (2 years at a K–8 rural school and 1 year at an urban high school), Brian earned his doctorate in special education at The University of Texas at Austin. He then served as director of research for PRO-ED, Inc., for 10 years and served as director of the Office for Students with Disabilities at Florida Atlantic University (where he also served as instructor in the Department of Special Education), as project director of the Texas Assistive Technology Partnership (Tech Act project), and as a private consultant. Brian held an adjunct faculty lecturer appointment in the Department of Special Education at The University of Texas at Austin for many years. For several years, he had an appointment as a research professor and fellow with The Meadows Center for Preventing Educational Risk in the College of Education at The University of Texas at Austin. In addition to his co-authored books, *Assistive Technology for People With Disabilities* (2011) and the current text, Brian was the author or co-author of more than 100 psycho-educational tests, articles, books, book chapters, professional development materials, and other products dealing with remedial education, learning disabilities, intellectual disability, assessment, and assistive technology. His primary research interests were assessment and intervention in learning disabilities and intellectual disability and the exploration of assistive technology applications across the life span. He served as president of Psycho-Educational Services, an Austin-based publishing and consulting company.

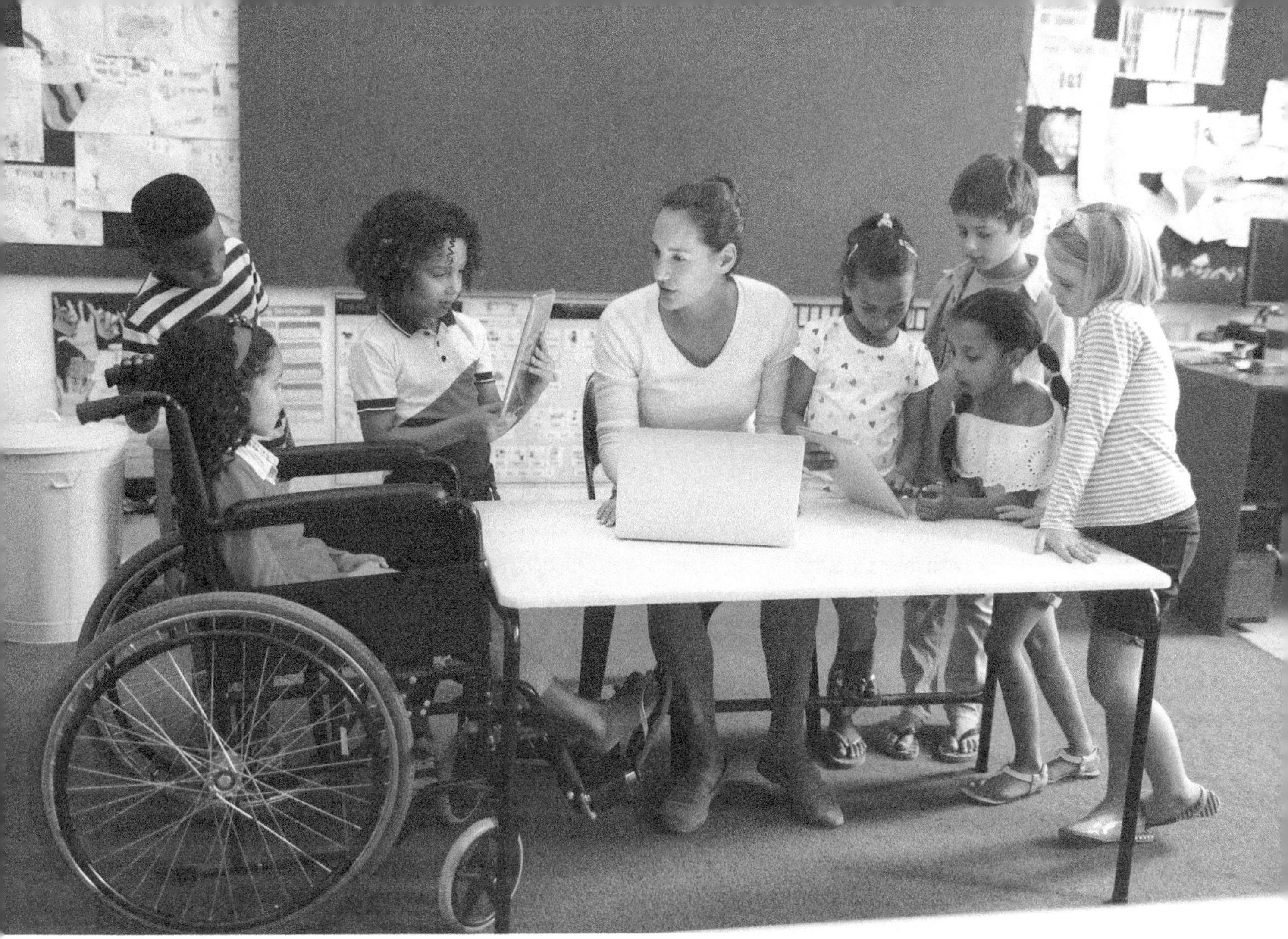

iStock.com/Wavebreakmedia

1 INCLUSIVE TEACHING AS RESPONSIVE EDUCATION

LEARNING OBJECTIVES

After studying this chapter, you will be able to meet the following learning objectives:

1.1 Explain the five steps of the ADAPT Framework.

1.2 Describe four guidelines that should be applied to determine an inclusive education for each student with a disability.

1.3 Identify the nine foundational tenets of special education.

1.4 Explain the history and development of special education.

1.5 Discuss the four different perspectives of disability.

1.6 Identify the 14 special education (disability) categories outlined by the federal government.

Opening Challenge

New Beginnings

Elementary Grades. It is the week before the first day of school. Ms. Thomas, a first-year teacher, sits in her fourth-grade classroom thinking about what it will be like to finally have her own students to teach, her own classroom to organize, and a real paycheck! She remembers spending years in her teacher preparation program, taking many day and night classes, traveling across town to observe classroom after classroom, doing week after week of student teaching, staying up late revising lesson plans one more time, and being so excited when she saw the great scores she and her friends received on the state's competency and certification tests for teachers. Ms. Thomas feels well prepared to assume the responsibility of educating a class of general education students. She has waited so long for this day to arrive; she has wanted to be a teacher since she was in elementary school. Ms. Thomas begins to prepare for the school year with great excitement and anticipation. But as she looks at her class list of 24 students, matching their names with their student files, she is worried. *"The range of their academic skills is so wide; their district's benchmark test scores from the previous year are all over the map. One student has been identified for gifted education, two have IEPs* [individualized education programs] *for reading and math problems, another student has a behavior intervention plan, still another has a 504 plan because of low vision, and three students are English learners. Additionally, two of the boys will continue to receive speech therapy in a group session from the speech/language pathologist twice a week. I haven't heard about special schedules for any of my students yet. It all seems so overwhelming. I wish I could go back and take that inclusion course again!"*

Secondary Grades. Mr. Salazar, a ninth-grade English teacher, is getting ready for his first teaching assignment and the first day of his teaching career. His department has five English teachers, most of whom have many years of experience, and some of whom have offered advice about how to prepare for the first week. He is nervous but knows that his secondary preparation in English is strong and his education classes provided lots of information regarding pedagogy and classroom and behavior management. Student teaching gave him experiences working with students from many different backgrounds, including students from various historically underrepresented groups, a variety of disabilities, and several English learners. He learned about adapting instruction but hasn't had many experiences with people who provide support services to students. Now, he is reviewing the students' folders. *"I am glad for the student teaching experiences because now I have five students with LD* [learning disabilities]. *I have one student who uses an assistive technology device for accessing print. Who is going to help me with this? I took an introduction to special education course but I am still concerned. I have 250 students each day. How am I going to meet the needs of all students?"*

Ms. Smith and Mr. Salazar share similar concerns. They are first-year teachers and although their preparation was strong, they must now apply what they have learned with diverse groups of students. Are they ready for the challenge?

Reflection Questions

In your journal, write down your answers to the following questions. After completing the chapter, check your answers and revise them on the basis of what you have learned.

1. Do you think Ms. Thomas and Mr. Salazar are overly concerned about their students' varied needs? Do you think they are just having first-year-teacher jitters? Why or why not?
2. What advice would you give them about planning for their students with disabilities and for those with other special learning needs?
3. How can they learn more about the special education services their students should be receiving this year?
4. Provide some suggestions to Ms. Thomas and Mr. Salazar to help them be responsive to all their students' needs.

THE ADAPT FRAMEWORK

The ADAPT Framework is a tool for instruction and assessment of struggling learners that reflects proven best practices in the field. The framework will help you develop a mindset for the selection of effective interventions and teaching practices. The framework, discussed throughout this text, reflects and underscores this mindset we want you to take away from your course. You can use its five steps to help you make informed decisions about adapting your instruction to individual students' needs and the tasks all students must complete in school. For now, Table 1.1 gives a quick look at the ADAPT Framework.

TABLE 1.1 ■ Introducing the ADAPT Framework

A	D	A	P	T
ASK "What am I requiring the student to do?"	DETERMINE the prerequisite skills of the task.	ANALYZE the student's strengths and struggles.	PROPOSE and implement adaptations from the four categories: Instructional activity Instructional content Instructional delivery Instructional material	TEST to see whether the adaptations helped the student accomplish the task.

The five steps in ADAPT are as follows: A—Ask, "What am I requiring the student to do?" D—Determine the prerequisite skills of the task. A—Analyze the student's strengths and struggles. P—Propose and implement adaptations from the four categories (instructional activity, instructional content, instructional delivery, and instructional materials). T—Test to determine whether the adaptations helped the student accomplish the task. Thus, different instructional methods might be employed for members of a class who are all learning the same content. The ADAPT Framework assists educators in making an inclusive education more responsive to students' individual learning needs.

INCLUSIVE EDUCATION

The term ***inclusive education*** usually means that students with disabilities access the standard curriculum in the general education classroom. Miscommunication can easily occur when the term *inclusion* is used: Whereas one person might use the word to mean that a student attends a neighborhood school and receives most instruction in the general education classroom, to another it might mean *all* the student's instruction is delivered in the general education classroom. It is easy to assume everyone is truly communicating about where a student should be educated, but it is wiser to be sure everyone is using the same definition before having an in-depth discussion of students' education. To understand the concept of inclusive education better, let's review how it emerged and developed.

Origins of Inclusion

The basic concepts of inclusion and integration of students with disabilities into the public education system have their roots in the original **Individuals with Disabilities Education Act (IDEA)**, then called the Education of All Handicapped Children Act (EHA), a law passed in 1975. Before 1975 many children with disabilities were denied access to public education. To those who were instrumental in developing the original IDEA law, inclusion probably meant that children with disabilities had the right to go to public school and receive a free education. Neither the type of school nor the location where the education was delivered was the focus of those early advocacy efforts.

Even before the passage of IDEA, when education for students with disabilities became required by many states, the nation saw a rise in the number of separate schools (e.g., schools for the blind, or d/Deaf, or—as they were then called—schools for the orthopedically handicapped) built for specific types of disabilities. Such specialized schools increased in number after IDEA's passage in 1975. Real growth also occurred in the number of special classes—sometimes on the grounds of neighborhood schools but often in basements and portable buildings—for this newly included group of students. The first model for inclusive education reflected the idea that, whenever possible, students with disabilities should be included in the public education system and **mainstreamed**, or educated together with peers without disabilities, such as in art, music, and physical education.

Was the creation of segregated programs for these students contrary to the concept of inclusion? Most likely, at that time, the answer to this question would have been a resounding "no." Special schools and special classes offered highly specialized programs to students with disabilities and their families. Some special schools offered facilities and services that are feasible to deliver only when students with similar needs are congregated. For example, when all students with severe physical disabilities in one school district attended the same school, the building included a special therapy pool and full-time services of many professionals like physical therapists, occupational therapists, and speech/language pathologists. When these students attended their neighborhood schools, they were spread across many different buildings and large geographic areas, diluting the intensity of services available to them. Many families believed the potentially negative aspects of segregation were outweighed by the highly specialized services it made possible.

Evolution of Inclusive Education

As time passed, however, dissatisfaction with segregated programs grew. Parents began to question whether separating youngsters from their siblings and neighborhood friends was the best strategy for their education. Decades ago professionals and policymakers were concerned about the **efficacy** of special education programs and practices (Finn et al., 2001; Gartner & Lipsky, 1987). Many of them came to believe separate programs were ethically and morally wrong (Sailor, 1991; Snell & Brown, 2006). In particular, advocates for students with the most substantial and complex disabilities maintain that the benefits of having so-called typical role models (illustrating how children without disabilities behave and interact with each other) that lead to community participation in adult life outweigh the benefit of intensive services that might be more readily available when groups of youngsters needing a particular program are clustered together (TASH, 2022; Turnbull et al., 2020). Across the years, educators' and advocates' thinking about special education and the students it serves evolved. To many, the **least restrictive environment (LRE)**—usually interpreted as access to the general education curriculum in the general education classroom—has emerged as the most critical variable to be considered when decisions about special education placement are made.

Of course, participation in the general education curriculum does not automatically result just because students with disabilities are placed in typical classroom settings. Something special needs to happen. Some of these approaches are less intrusive than others and benefit many learners, those with and without disabilities. One such approach, the **Universal Design for Learning (UDL)** framework, focuses on accessing the curriculum so a broad range of students with very different learning preferences can approach it and learn without an intervention being made especially for them. You will learn more about this framework throughout this text.

Another approach, **assistive technology (AT)**, focuses on helping students compensate for challenges with the instructional situation. The third and most commonly used approach today focuses not on the curriculum but on making adaptations to the instructional situation that match specific students' needs (Danielson et al., 2017; Fuchs et al., 2017). In Chapter 7 and in highlighted themes found in each chapter we discuss differentiating, adapting, and modifying instruction so struggling learners can more successfully access the general education curriculum. In Chapter 8 you also will learn about UDL and AT, both of which can be used to promote access to the general education curriculum. These approaches enable general and special education teachers to work effectively with all students to help them be successful in their classes.

DIFFERENTIATING, ADAPTING, AND MODIFYING INSTRUCTION: MODIFYING ASSIGNMENTS BY ASSIGNING A LOWER-LEVEL TEXT

What is it? Modifying instruction is not the same as making accommodations, differentiating instruction, or adapting instruction. Modifications change the expectations for learning or reduce the requirements of the task. Assessment reflects these changes or modifications.

Example: Mrs. Bowen assigns her sixth-grade class a 100-page novel and asks them to write an essay about plot and character development. However, Miguel has significant learning/language disabilities and according to his IEP requires modifications to such assignments. Mrs. Bowen finds an abridged edition of the same novel for Miguel that is written at a lower level. She asks Miguel to summarize the story and describe the main characters. Her assessment of Miguel's work is adjusted accordingly.

Inclusive Education Practices

As you have read, inclusive education has many different interpretations. The range of interpretations is the foundation for different inclusive education practices. For example, one interpretation of inclusive education is called **full inclusion** using **pull-in programs**, where students receive all educational services in the general education classroom. With this practice, speech/language pathologists would come to the general education class to work with a student who needs speech therapy, rather than removing the student for individualized work. Another interpretation is called **coteaching**, wherein special education teachers come to general education classrooms to work with students needing intervention or share instructional duties across academic content for all students in the class (Friend, 2019; Friend, & Barron, 2020). You will learn more about coteaching in Chapter 3.

A dilemma for parents and educators of high school students with severe disabilities is choosing which is more appropriate or more important: access to the standard high school curriculum leading to a standard diploma, or community-based instruction where on-the-job training, independent transportation, and home management are taught in real-life settings.

iStock.com/Edwin Tan

The **array of services**, or what is often called the special education **continuum of services** (an older term is *cascade of services*), offers additional practices for serving students with disabilities when they are not receiving some or all of their education in the general education classroom. **Pull-out programs** include resource rooms, partially self-contained special classes, self-contained special classes, and special education schools (center schools). For the vast majority of students who receive most of their education in general education classes, the resource room is the option for pull-out special education services. Resource room instruction often consists of small-group instruction focused on areas most in need of intensive intervention. This instruction may occur for 30 to 60 minutes several days a week. However, the number of these classes is shrinking because many students who attend resource room settings now receive most, if not all, of their education in general education classrooms (inclusive settings), thus leaving a reduced number of options available for even short-term, intensive intervention. For example, in the 2019 school year, 95% received at least some portion of their education in general education setting and 64.8% of all students with disabilities—those with mild to moderate disabilities as well as those with severe disabilities—received at least 80% of their education at local public schools in general education classes (Office of Special Education Programs [OSEP], 2022). The participation rates for students with disabilities in general education classes have increased consistently over the past 20 years, and only 4.9% of those students attend separate schools or separate residential facilities today. Clearly, these data reflect current inclusive education practices in public schools.

An additional special education service is available to students at risk for being identified as having a disability. **Early intervening** (not to be confused with early intervention, which refers to services that are designed for young children from birth to age 5 who do have disabilities) was first outlined in 2017 and then in 2022 incorporated into the IDEA regulations. This option is for school age children, particularly children in Kindergarten through Grade 3, who have *not* yet been identified as having a disability but who need additional support to succeed. It allows school districts to use no more than 15% of their IDEA funds to provide such special education services (34 C.F.R. §300.226). The idea is, for example, to prevent reading failure before such problems compound and result in a special education referral.

The Inclusion Debate

At the heart of discussions about inclusive education, particularly full inclusion, is the dynamic tension between free appropriate public education (FAPE) and the least restrictive environment (LRE) possible: the delivery of an appropriate education and participation in the LRE must be responsive to the individual's needs at that particular time. Let's think about how some of these conversations might unfold.

For example, should full-time placement in a general education setting be a goal for every student with a disability, even if doing so means that some elements of an educational program that individuals need to achieve to their full potential would have to be sacrificed? If a high school student has severe disabilities, parents and educators might have to decide which is more appropriate or more important: access to the standard high school curriculum leading to a standard diploma (including science and foreign language requirements) or community-based instruction where on-the-job training, independent transportation, and home management are taught in real-life settings. For some students, full inclusion does not lead to a standard diploma because they do not achieve the criteria for that diploma, even if they participate in a fully inclusive setting with students without disabilities (for more information, see https://tiescenter.org/).

Some scholars argue that full inclusion, where students with disabilities receive all their education in a general education setting, is not sufficient to support those with more severe needs, whether academic, emotional, social, or physical. Other scholars believe all students have a right to fully inclusive educational practices where they can benefit from being integrated into a school setting with their peers and gain a sense of belonging and active participation in the mainstream. Thus, the role of special education services is to support all students with unique learning needs or disabilities in general education classes by designing instruction and applying adaptations that accommodate individual learning needs. The inclusion debate more often includes perspectives and discussions that range along a continuum where professionals and parents embrace the strengths of different inclusive practices and make decisions based on individual students' needs.

Some guidelines can help when challenging decisions are being made about what comprises an inclusive and responsive education for each student with a disability. First, special education placement decisions must be individually determined because services should be tailored to the needs of each student with disabilities. Second, no single answer is possible for all students with disabilities. Third, students with disabilities need an array of services (and placements) available to them for the delivery of individualized education programs that range in intensity and duration. Experts in intensive instruction emphasize that "place" is *not* the most important aspect of a student with disabilities' education; rather, it is that the student receives instruction individually determined by data, delivered by a highly trained teacher, with only one to three students at a time, and be at least four days per week for 45 minutes per session (Danielson et al., 2017; Fuchs et al., 2017). Few professionals or parents advocate either for fully inclusive settings or for fully segregated settings. Fourth, the guiding principle must be based not on placement alone but also on how students can best access the general education curriculum, master academic targets, and develop life skills they need to succeed when they are adults. Next, we introduce you to special education.

SPECIAL EDUCATION

Special education is designed to meet the unique learning needs of each infant, toddler, preschooler, and elementary through high school student with disabilities, and individuals up to the age of 21. This instruction might be delivered in many different types of settings, such as hospitals, separate facilities, and homes, but it is most commonly provided at the student's local school in the general education class with neighborhood friends. Special education reflects a variety of instructional targets: braille for students with severe visual disabilities, manual communication systems for d/Deaf[1] students, social skills training for students with emotional or behavioral disorders, and so on.

General education and special education differ along some very important dimensions. First and foremost, they are designed for students with different learning, behavioral, social, communication, and basic functional needs (such as the need to learn daily living skills). Second, some differences are based in law—what is stated in IDEA and its regulations—and result in key components of special education. Third, general education tends to focus on groups of learners, whereas the special education approach focuses on individuals.

One way to gain a better understanding of special education is to study some of its key distinguishing features. Although we cannot put forth a single description because these services must be designed for each individual's unique learning needs, nine fundamental tenets provide the foundation:

- Free appropriate public education
- Least restrictive environment
- Systematic identification procedures
- Individualized education programs
- Family involvement
- Related services
- Access to the general education curriculum
- Evidence-based practices
- Frequent monitoring of progress

Let's examine each of these features that form the foundation of special education.

Free Appropriate Public Education

From the very beginning of IDEA, Congress stipulated that educational services for students with disabilities are to be available to parents at no additional cost to them. These students, despite the complexity of their educational needs, the accommodations or additional services they require, and the cost to a school district, are entitled to a **free appropriate public education (FAPE)**. Note that Congress included the word *appropriate* in its language. FAPE must be individually determined because what is appropriate for one student with a disability might not be appropriate for another. FAPE provisions emphasize that special education and related services must be designed to meet the unique needs of students with disabilities and prepare them for further education, employment, and independent living (Wrightslaw, 2017). FAPE guarantees, under the 2015 Every Student Succeeds Act (ESSA), that students with disabilities receive a regular high school diploma if they received a standards-based curricular education. This diploma is not aligned to the alternate academic achievement standards, which students with the most significant cognitive disabilities may receive (OSEP, 2017b). However, students with significant cognitive disabilities are still entitled to complete requirements for a high school diploma.

Least Restrictive Environment

Students with disabilities must receive their education in the least restrictive environment (LRE). In other words, special education services are not automatically delivered in any particular place. Today, LRE is often misinterpreted as meaning placement in general education classes. IDEA does not mandate that students with disabilities receive all their education in the general education setting. The U.S. Department of Education, in its 2006 rule implementing IDEA, explains LRE in this way:

> To the maximum extent appropriate, children with disabilities, including children in public or private institutions or other care facilities, are educated with children who are nondisabled; and that special classes, separate schooling or other removal of children with disabilities from regular educational environment occurs only if the nature or severity of the disability is such that education in regular classes with the use of supplementary aids and services cannot be achieved satisfactorily. (71 Fed. Reg. 46539 [2006])

The federal government identifies an array of placements, in addition to the general education classroom, that are appropriate for some students with disabilities. These placements include resource rooms, special classes, special schools, home instruction settings, and hospitals. For some students, exclusive exposure to the general education curriculum is not appropriate. For example, a secondary student with significant cognitive disabilities might need to master **functional skills** or **life skills** essential for independent living as an adult. That student might also need to receive concentrated instruction on skills associated with holding a job successfully. To acquire and become proficient in skills necessary to live and work in the community often requires instruction outside the general education curriculum, outside the general education classroom, and even beyond the actual school site. This instruction is often best conducted in the community, on actual job sites, and in real situations. In fact, **community-based instruction** is a well-researched, effective special education approach (Barczak, 2019; Rowe et al., 2020). Thus, there is no single or uniform interpretation of LRE. A balance must be achieved between inclusive instruction and a curriculum that is appropriate and is delivered in the most effective setting.

Systematic Identification Procedures

To decide which students qualify for special education—those who actually have disabilities—and to determine what that education should be requires systematic identification procedures. National data clearly show that current methods tend to overidentify culturally and linguistically diverse students (e.g., students from historically underrepresented groups, English learners) as having disabilities (OSEP, 2022). For example, American Indian or Alaska Native students are almost four times more likely to be identified as having a disability than all other racial and ethnic groups combined. Although to a lesser degree, Black, Hispanic (the term used by the federal government), and

Native Hawaiian or other Pacific Islanders are also overrepresented in higher incidence categories (e.g., learning disabilities, other health impairments), but not so in categories such as deafness or visual impairments. Interestingly, Asian and White students tend to be underrepresented in special education when compared to their percentage in the general school population. These facts concern federal, state, and local policy makers. Needless to say, educators must be careful of identifying students as having disabilities when they do not, but they also must be certain that students in need of such services actually receive them.

Concern about the traditional school assessments and the resulting education programs have given rise to other methods of identifying which students are in need of extensive special education services. For example, experts in learning disabilities are confident that individualized data-based assessments are essential for students who need intensive interventions (Lemons et al., 2018). We discuss these procedures in greater detail throughout this text, but know that the role of general education teachers in the identification process is evolving and growing.

The first task in the identification process is to ensure that a lack of appropriate academic instruction is not causing difficulties. The next is to collect data about the target student's performance, showing that high-quality classroom procedures do not bring about improvements in academic or social behavior for this particular student. Then, for those students who do not make expected gains with intensified interventions, further classroom evaluations are conducted. The ensuing classroom assessments include comparisons with peers who are achieving as expected, careful monitoring of the target student's progress (through **data-based individualization**), and descriptions of interventions tried, accommodations implemented, types of errors made, and levels of performance achieved (Morris-Mathews et al., 2020). The result of such evaluations may well lead to individual students receiving **intensive intervention**. You will learn about these procedures in Chapter 2.

Individualized Education Programs

At the heart of individualized programs are standards-based **individualized education programs (IEPs)** for schoolchildren ages 3 to 21 and **individualized family service plans (IFSPs)** for infants and toddlers (birth through age 2) with disabilities and their families. Each of these students is entitled to an individually designed educational program complete with supportive (related) services. In some states the guarantee of an individualized education is extended to gifted students as well, but because federal law does not protect gifted students' special education, schools are not required to address those students with individualized education.

IEPs and IFSPs are the cornerstones that guarantee an appropriate education to each student with a disability. The IEP is the communication tool that spells out what should comprise each child's individualized education. Therefore, every teacher working with a special education student should have access to the student's IEP. They should all be very familiar with its contents because this document includes important information about the required accommodations, the necessary special services, and the unique educational needs of the student. You will learn more about IEPs and IFSPs in Chapter 2.

Family Involvement

Educators' expectations of parent and family involvement are greater for students with disabilities than for their peers without disabilities, and the strength of families and their engagement with the school does make a real difference in the lives of their children (Center for Parent Information and Resources, 2019; 34 C.F.R. §300.322, 2017). For example, there is an expectation that parents participate in the development of their children's IEPs and become partners with teachers and schools. Families have the right to due process when they do not agree with schools about the education planned for or being delivered to their children. They are also entitled to services not usually offered to parents of typical learners. For example, parents of infants and toddlers with disabilities (birth to age 2) receive intensive instruction through special education along with their children.

Recognizing the challenges parents often face in raising and educating their children with unique learning needs, advocacy groups and professional organizations have formed over the years to support

Parents and family members of students with disabilities have important roles to play. Linking home and school communities is the responsibility of both families and teaching professionals.

Maskot / Alamy Stock Photo

families and those who work with them. For example, the Learning Disabilities Association of America (LDA) has a long history of advocacy on behalf of individuals with learning disabilities and the professionals and families who work with them. The Arc of the United States is another long-standing advocacy group. Its focus includes ensuring that all students are provided appropriate public education services. CHADD (Children and Adults with Attention-Deficit/Hyperactivity Disorder [ADHD]) is made up of hardworking volunteers who provide support and resources to parents and professionals. The National Federation of Families for Children's Mental Health exists to provide national-level advocacy for the rights of children with emotional, behavioral, and mental health challenges and their families. It works collaboratively with a national network of family-run organizations. In addition, the federal government funds a national network of parent training and resource centers. In additional to one national center, the Center for Parent Information and Resources (CPIR), it makes at least one award for information and supportive services for parents in each state.

Leaders in these organizations, who often are parents themselves, have succeeded in influencing funding at the state and national levels for appropriate educational services for students with disabilities. Parent advocacy groups are very powerful, as shown by their contribution to key court cases resulting in legislation that now protects students with disabilities in all aspects of the educational system.

Related Services

Another important difference between general and special education is the array of services the latter offers to help students with disabilities profit from instruction. **Related services** are the multidisciplinary or transdisciplinary set of services many students with disabilities require if their education is to be truly appropriate. Those services are specified in the student's IEP and can include adaptive physical education (APE), AT, audiology, diagnosis and evaluation, interpretation for the deaf, family therapy, occupational therapy (OT), orientation and mobility, the assistance of paraprofessionals (paraeducators and teacher aides), physical therapy (PT), psychological services, recreation and therapeutic-recreation therapy, rehabilitative counseling, school counseling, school nursing, school social work, speech/language pathology, special transportation, vocational education, and work study (see 71 Fed. Reg. 46539, 2006). For example, in some cases a **paraprofessional**, sometimes called a paraeducator, supports the special education program and works with a special education student in the general education classroom (Biggs et al., 2018). These professionals' services often make inclusion possible because they provide individualized assistance to students with disabilities for extended periods of the school day (OSEP, 2019).

Multidisciplinary teams of related services professionals go into action to meet the individual needs of students with disabilities. The federal government considers the cost of related services professionals—such as school nurses and school counselors—to be covered in part by funding from IDEA (see 71 Fed. Reg. 46539, 2006). You will learn more about related services in Chapter 2 and collaboration with families and paraprofessionals and how to work with students who exhibit unique learning needs or disabilities in Chapter 3.

Most related services specialists are **itinerant**, working at several schools during the same day and at many different schools across the week. Scheduling their time can be complicated, but it is vital to ensure that students with unique learning needs do not miss any educational opportunity. Multidisciplinary teams of experts not only deliver critical services to students with disabilities and their families but also serve as valuable resources to teachers as they strive to meet the needs of each student. Despite the remoteness of a school, the distance a specialist might have to travel, or the shortage of related services specialists, there is no excuse for not making these experts available to teachers and their students with disabilities.

Access to the General Education Curriculum

Another key feature of special education is access to the general education curriculum. Although rising from 62% in 2010, only 73% of students with disabilities leave school with a standard diploma (OSEP, 2022). To obtain a standard diploma students must participate in the general education curriculum and be assessed in the accountability measures (state- and district-wide tests) that monitor all students' progress. Advocates contend that students who receive their education in inclusive general education classrooms are more likely to have greater exposure to the standard curriculum and a better chance of graduating with a standard high school diploma than those students who receive their education in more restrictive environments, such as self-contained special education classrooms. Therefore, when IDEA was reauthorized in 1997 it required that all students with disabilities have access, to the fullest extent possible, to the general education curriculum and its accountability systems.

Of course, access to the curriculum and to a specific place often go hand in hand because the general education classroom is the place where students have the greatest opportunity to access the standard curriculum. The general education curriculum is not appropriate for all students with disabilities, however. Some require an alternative curriculum or intensive treatment not available or not suitable for instruction in the general education classroom. Examples include orientation and mobility training for students who are blind, job skills training in community placements, public transportation instruction, social skills training, physical therapy, and speech therapy for a student who has a stutter. Placement issues, LRE, access to the general education curriculum, and alternative curricular options are not mutually exclusive. Each can be in effect for part of the school day, school week, or school year.

Effective, Evidence-Based Practices

Passage of IDEA in 2004 emphasized that teachers should use instructional methods that are *evidence based.* Two types of effective practices must be implemented in classroom settings. One type, **evidence-based practices**, has been proven effective through systematic and rigorous research. In fact, according to IDEA, there must be documentation that evidence-based interventions were implemented before a student believed to have a learning disability can be referred. The second type, **high-leverage practices** (e.g., praise, systematic feedback), has been proven effective through years of use and success (Brownell et al., 2020–2021). The student's responses to these interventions also must be documented as part of the process of identifying the disability. This data-based individualization process, promoted and endorsed in IDEA, is incorporated into the multi-tiered systems of support (MTSS) framework, which includes response to intervention (RTI) and Positive Behavioral Interventions and Supports (PBIS), which you will learn about in Chapter 2.

EFFECTIVE PRACTICES: FOCUS ON BEHAVIOR-SPECIFIC PRAISE

What is it? Behavior-specific praise, an evidence-based practice, addresses the student or group of students, describes the desired behavior, is delivered immediately after the behavior occurs, and exceeds the use of reprimands at least 4:1.

How is it implemented? Behavior-specific praise can be public, by saying it out loud, or private, by delivering a note to the student or using a nonverbal gesture. It should be age and individual appropriate and not embarrass or stigmatize the individual or group.

Example: "All students at Table 1, thank you for remembering to bring in your homework today!" Or "Jessica, I appreciate your raising your hand to ask a question."

For more on behavior-specific praise, go to the IRIS Fundamental Skill Sheet: https://iris.peabody.vanderbilt.edu/wp-content/uploads/misc_media/fss/pdfs/2018/fss_behaviro_specific_praise.pdf.

We define special education, in part, by its practices, which are more intensive and more supportive than are practices for students without special learning needs. Years ago, researchers identified six common features of effective special education, and these features hold true today (Coyne et al., 2011; Swanson et al., 1999):

1. Validated (using practices proved effective through research)
2. Individually determined (matching teaching procedures to individuals)
3. Explicit (directly applying interventions to content and skills)
4. Strategic (helping students apply methods to guide their learning)
5. Sequential (building on previous mastery)
6. Monitored (evaluating progress frequently and systematically)

Most students with disabilities and most of those with unique learning needs do not require this intensive instruction for all their education. But when their learning is not on a par with that of their general education peers, it is time for action.

Frequent Monitoring of Progress

Even when teachers carefully select evidence-based practices, there is no guarantee individual students will respond positively or sufficiently. For this reason, teachers use **progress monitoring**—a set of evaluation procedures that assess the effectiveness of instruction on skills while they are being taught. The four key features of this approach are that students' educational progress is measured (a) directly on skills of concern, (b) systematically, (c) consistently, and (d) frequently.

One commonly applied method of data-based individualization is a progress monitoring system called **curriculum-based measurement (CBM)**. In this approach, the areas of most concern are measured directly to check progress on the curricular tasks or skills to which interventions are being directed. The foundations of CBM began long ago (Deno, 2003; Foegen et al., 2007) and have been further developed and refined across time (Fuchs et al., 2014; Stecker et al., 2005; Vanderbilt, 2022). These assessments occur often (e.g., weekly) and provide educators with useful feedback, on the basis of which they can quickly modify their instructional approaches. Because CBM results can be used to tailor the special education a student receives, by guiding the selection of practices and monitoring their effectiveness, CBM must not be omitted. You will learn more about monitoring student progress when specific curriculum targets (such as reading) are discussed in Chapter 9. We turn our attention now to discussing the origins of special education.

THE FOUNDATIONS OF SPECIAL EDUCATION

Although many people believe U.S. special education began in 1975 with the passage of the national law we now call IDEA, it actually began more than 200 years ago. The legend of special education's beginnings is not only famous—it's also true. In 1799, farmers in southern France found a young boy living in the woods, and they took this "wild child" to a doctor in Paris. Jean-Marc-Gaspard Itard, the doctor who now is recognized as the father of special education, used many of the principles and procedures of explicit instruction still implemented today to teach this boy, who they named Victor and who probably had intellectual disabilities.

In the early 1800s, Edouard Seguin, one of Itard's students, came to the United States to begin efforts to educate students with disabilities in this country. In fact, these early efforts were taking root across Europe as well. For example, in Italy, Maria Montessori worked first with children with cognitive disabilities and showed they could learn at young ages through concrete experiences offered in environments rich in manipulative materials. Meanwhile in the United States, Thomas Hopkins Gallaudet began to develop Deaf education, and Samuel Gridley Howe founded the New England Asylum for the Blind (later the Perkins School for the Blind). Elizabeth Farrell initiated public school classes for students with disabilities in 1898. Although special education and the idea of educating students with disabilities are not new, they were not uniformly accepted. In the United States, it was another 75 years before education became a right, something all students with disabilities were entitled to receive. You may be surprised to learn, in the next section, that the guarantees in place today were adopted rather recently.

Inconsistent Opportunities

Although positive attitudes about the benefits of educating students with disabilities emerged centuries ago, the delivery of programs remained inconsistent for almost 200 years. In 1948, only 12% of all children with disabilities received special education (Ballard et al., 1982). In 1962, only 16 states had laws that included students with mild intellectual disabilities under mandatory school attendance requirements (Roos, 1970). In most states, these children were not allowed to attend school, and those with more severe disabilities were routinely excluded.

In the early 1970s, Congress studied the problem, and here's what it found (20 U.S.C section 1400[b] PL 94-142, 1975):

- One million of the children with disabilities in the United States were excluded entirely from the public school system.
- More than half of the 8 million children with disabilities were not receiving appropriate educational services.
- The special educational needs of these children were not being fully met because they were not receiving necessary related services.
- Services within the public school system were inadequate and forced families to go outside the public school system, often traveling great distances from their residence and at their own expense.
- If given appropriate funding, state and local educational agencies could provide effective special education and related services to meet the needs of children with disabilities.

Congress realized that special education, with proper financial assistance and educational support, was necessary to make a positive difference in the lives of these children and their families.

Early Court Cases: The Backdrop for National Legislation

The end of World War II ushered in a time of increased opportunities for all, eventually leading to the civil rights movement of the 1960s and to advocacy for people with disabilities in the 1970s. Before then, concerns about unfair treatment of children with disabilities and their limited access to education were being taken to the courts and legislatures state by state. Table 1.2 summarizes landmark state

TABLE 1.2 ■ Landmark Court Cases Leading to the Original Passage of the Individuals with Disabilities Education Act

Case	Date	Issue	Finding
Brown v. Board of Education	1954	Overturn of separate but equal doctrine; integration of Kansas public schools	The case was the basis for future rulings that children with disabilities cannot be excluded from school.
Pennsylvania Association for Retarded Children (PARC) v. Commonwealth of Pennsylvania	1972	Access to public education for students with intellectual disabilities	In the state of Pennsylvania, no child with intellectual disabilities can be denied a public education.
Mills v. Board of Education of the District of Columbia	1972	Access to special education for all students with disabilities	All students with disabilities have a right to a free public education.

and local court cases that paved the way for national special education to be consistently offered to all children with disabilities. After years of exclusion, segregation, and denial of basic educational opportunities, consensus was growing that a national civil rights law, guaranteeing students with disabilities access to the public education system, was imperative.

Next, we review some of the key laws and court decisions that protect students with disabilities. Consider the impact of these court decisions on the lives of students with disabilities and their families.

Laws and Court Decisions That Protect Today's Students With Disabilities

The nation's policymakers reacted to injustices revealed in court case after court case by passing federal laws to protect the civil rights of individuals with disabilities (Florian, 2007). Table 1.3 lists some of the important laws passed by Congress that affect individuals with disabilities. As you study these, notice how one law sets the stage for the next.

TABLE 1.3 ■ Landmark Laws Guaranteeing Rights to Individuals With Disabilities

Date	Law or Section	Name and Key Provisions
1973	Section 504	Section 504 of the Rehabilitation Act of 1973 • set the stage for IDEA and the Americans with Disabilities Act (ADA); • guaranteed basic civil rights to people with disabilities; and • required accommodations in schools and in society.
1975	PL 94-142	Education for All Handicapped Children Act (EHA) • guaranteed a FAPE in the LRE; and • was a landmark civil rights effort for students with disabilities.
1986	PL 99-457	EHA (reauthorized) • added infants and toddlers; and • provided the IFSP.
1990	PL 101-476	Individuals with Disabilities Education Act (IDEA) • changed the name of PL 94-142 to IDEA; • added individualized transition plans (ITPs); • added autism as a special education category; and • added traumatic brain injury as a category.

Date	Law or Section	Name and Key Provisions
1990	PL 101-336	Americans with Disabilities Act (ADA) • barred discrimination in employment, transportation, public accommodations, and telecommunications; • implemented the concept of normalization across U.S. life; and • required phased-in accessibility in schools.
1997	PL 105-17	IDEA 1997 (reauthorized) • added ADHD to the category of other health impairments; • added functional behavioral assessments and behavioral intervention plans; and • changed ITP to a component of the IEP.
2001	PL 107-110	Elementary and Secondary Education (No Child Left Behind) Act of 2001 (ESEA or NCLB) • required that all schoolchildren participate in state and district testing; • called for 100% proficiency of all students in reading and math by 2012; and • called for scientifically based research for programs and interventions.
2004	PL 108-364	Assistive Technology Act of 2004 (ATA, or Tech Act) (reauthorized) • provided support for school-to-work transition projects; • continued a national website on AT; and • assisted states in creating and supporting device loan programs, financial loans to individuals with disabilities to purchase AT devices, and equipment demonstrations.
2004	PL 108-446	IDEA (reauthorized; called Individuals with Disabilities Education Improvement Act [IDEIA]; commonly referred to as IDEA) • required special education teachers to be highly qualified; • mandated that all students with disabilities participate annually either in state and district testing with accommodations or in alternative assessments; • eliminated IEP short-term objectives and benchmarks, except for those who use alternative assessments; • changed identification procedures for learning disabilities; and • allowed any student to be placed in an interim alternative educational setting for involvement in weapons, drugs, or violence.
2008	PL 110-325	Americans with Disabilities Act Amendments Act (ADAAA) (reauthorized) • restored workplace protection diminished by previous court decisions; and • redefined "major life activities" to enable individuals with disabilities to be protected against discrimination in the workplace.
2010	PL 111-256	Rosa's Law • changed the terms *mental retardation and mentally retarded to intellectual disabilities and intellectually disabled* in federal laws.
2010	PL 111-148	The Patient Protection and Affordable Care Act • prohibited exclusion for preexisting conditions; • eliminated caps on benefits; and • prohibited discrimination based on disability and health status.

(Continued)

TABLE 1.3 ■ Landmark Laws Guaranteeing Rights to Individuals With Disabilities (*Continued*)

Date	Law or Section	Name and Key Provisions
2011	PL 99-457 PL 108-446	Individuals with Disabilities Education Act: Part C-Early Intervention Program • allocated funding to states to serve infants and toddlers through age 2 with developmental delays or who have physical or mental conditions that result in developmental delays; and • ensured early intervention services for infants and toddlers with disabilities birth through age 2.
2015	PL 114-95	Every Student Succeeds Act (ESSA) (reauthorized the ESEA) • required all students be taught to high academic standards to prepare them to succeed in college and careers; • ensured annual state assessments that measure student progress toward high standards; • ensured accountability in lowest-performing schools; and • made the following changes to IDEA: • The ESSA removed "highly qualified special education teachers" and included qualifications for special education teachers as holding state certification as a special education teacher or passing the state special education licensing exam. • The ESSA revised the term *limited English proficient to English learner.* • The ESSA clarified that alternative assessments should be aligned with alternative academic achievement standards for students with the most significant cognitive disabilities who cannot participate in regular assessments even with accommodations. Expectations for achievement are modified with respect to the state grade-level academic content but alternative assessments must be aligned to grade-level content (academic) standards. • The ESSA specified that only 1% of students in special education can be given alternative tests. • The ESSA required evidence-based interventions.
2022	S 2401 – 117th Congress (2021-2022)	21st Century Assistive Technology Act (Reauthorization of the Assistive Technology Act of 2004) • Modernizes and broadens the former AT Act • Includes devices such as wheelchairs and screenreaders • Allows for technical assistive services for training and testing out (borrowing) AT devices • Expands assistance to find corporate and private funding to assist with purchases of such equipment and devices

Every Student Succeeds Act

The Every Student Succeeds Act (ESSA) was signed by President Obama on December 10, 2015. The ESSA reauthorized the Elementary and Secondary Education Act (ESEA), which has been a commitment to national education law and equal opportunity for all students for more than 50 years. Prior to the ESSA, under President George W. Bush, the ESEA was reauthorized as the No Child Left Behind Act of 2001 (NCLB). One major goal of NCLB was to raise academic achievement for all students and to close the achievement gap between poor, urban, and rural schools and wealthier schools in middle-class suburban areas. Although the emphasis on school district accountability was important in ensuring a quality education for all students, difficulties were encountered in operationalizing all of the requirements for the implementation of this law. Building on successes of NCLB and recognizing that some changes were needed, the ESSA was enacted to create a law that focused on the goal of fully preparing all students for success in college and careers.

> Disability is a natural part of the human experience and in no way diminishes the right of individuals to participate in or contribute to society. Improving educational results for children with disabilities is an essential element of our national policy of ensuring equality of opportunity, full participation, independent living, and economic self-sufficiency for individuals with disabilities. (OSEP, 2017b)

Section 504 of the Rehabilitation Act

In 1973, Congress passed **Section 504 of the Rehabilitation Act**, intended to prevent discrimination against individuals with disabilities in programs that receive federal funds. Section 504 required public buildings to provide **accommodations**, such as wheelchair ramps, to allow or facilitate access by people with disabilities. This means public schools must provide accommodations to students whose disabilities or health conditions require some special attention in order to allow them to participate fully in school activities. This law set the stage for both IDEA and the Americans with Disabilities Act (ADA) because it included some protection of the rights of students with disabilities to public education and many provisions for adults with disabilities and their participation in society and the workplace. Let's direct our attention now to the law that specifically targets schoolchildren and their families.

Americans With Disabilities Act

Congress first considered the civil rights of people with disabilities when it passed Section 504 of the Rehabilitation Act of 1973. However, after almost 20 years, Congress became convinced by advocates, many of whom were themselves adults with disabilities, that Section 504 was not sufficient and did not end discrimination for adults with disabilities. Congress took stronger measures by passing yet another law. On July 26, 1990, President George H. W. Bush signed the **Americans with Disabilities Act (ADA)**, which bars discrimination in employment, transportation, public accommodations, and telecommunications. Bush said, "Let the shameful walls of exclusion finally come tumbling down." Senator Tom Harkin (D-IA), the chief sponsor of the act, spoke of this law as the emancipation proclamation for people with disabilities (West, 1994).

ADA guarantees people with disabilities access to all aspects of life—not just those supported by federal funding—and implements the concept of normalization across all aspects of U.S. life. Both Section 504 and ADA are considered civil rights and antidiscrimination laws. ADA supports and extends Section 504 and ensures that adults with disabilities have greater access to employment and participation in everyday activities that adults without disabilities enjoy. It requires that employers not discriminate against qualified applicants or employees with disabilities and mandates new public transportation (buses, trains, subways) and new or remodeled public accommodations (hotels, stores, restaurants, banks, theaters) to be accessible to persons with disabilities.

ADA has had a substantial impact on the daily lives of people with disabilities. For example, it requires telephone companies to provide relay services so deaf individuals and people with speech impairments can use ordinary telephones. It is thanks to ADA that **curb cuts** for wheelchairs also make it easier for everyone to use carts, strollers, and even roller skates when crossing streets. For students making the transition from school to adult life, improvements in access and nondiscrimination practices should allow genuine participation in their communities.

Section 504 and ADA also affect the education system, but there are some important differences between those laws and IDEA. Section 504 and ADA incorporate a broader definition of disabilities than does IDEA because they guarantee the right to accommodations even to those who do not need special education services and to those beyond school age. For example, it is under the authority of ADA that college students with unique learning needs or disabilities are entitled to special testing situations (untimed tests, braille versions, someone to read the questions to them) and that schoolchildren with ADHD who do not qualify for special education receive special accommodations.

Like IDEA, the ADA law has sparked controversy. On the one hand, some members of the disability community are disappointed because they still cannot find jobs suited to their interests, training, or skills. On the other hand, many small-business owners claim that ADA requires them to make accommodations that are expensive and rarely used.

Individuals With Disabilities Education Act

Congress found widespread patterns of exclusion, denial of services, and discrimination (Knitzer et al., 1990). Therefore, it decided that a universal, national law guaranteeing the rights of students with disabilities to a FAPE was necessary. The first version of the special education law was passed in 1975 and was called the **Education for All Handicapped Children Act (EHA; Public Law (PL) 94-142)**. (The first set of numbers refers to the session of Congress in which the law was passed, the second set to the number of the law. Thus, EHA was the 142nd law passed in the 94th session of Congress.) Congress gave the states 2 years to get ready to implement this new special education law, so it was actually initiated in 1977. It was to be in effect for 10 years; for it to continue after that time, a reauthorization process was required. After the first 10-year period, the law was supposed to be reauthorized every 3 years, but it has been two decades since its last independent reauthorization.

EHA was reauthorized the first time in 1986. (Congress gives itself a couple of extra years to reauthorize laws so they do not expire before the congressional committee can complete the job of rewriting them.) Congress added services to infants, toddlers, and their families in this version of the special education law. In its next reauthorization, Congress (retroactively) changed the name of the law to PL 101-476, the Individuals with Disabilities Education Act (IDEA), added autism and traumatic brain injury as special education categories, and strengthened transitional services for adolescents with disabilities. In the 1997 reauthorization of IDEA, issues such as access to the general education curriculum, participation in state- and district-wide testing, and discipline assumed prominence. When the law was reauthorized again in 2004, many changes were made in the way students with learning disabilities can be identified. The 2004 version of the law also encourages states and school districts to help all young students who are struggling to read, in hopes of preventing reading/learning disabilities and also getting help as early as possible to those who need it (see 71 Fed. Reg. 46539, 2006). IDEA has not been formally reauthorized since 2004. Instead, as part of the ESSA (2015), changes were made to some provisions of IDEA (see Table 1.2 for a list of some changes).

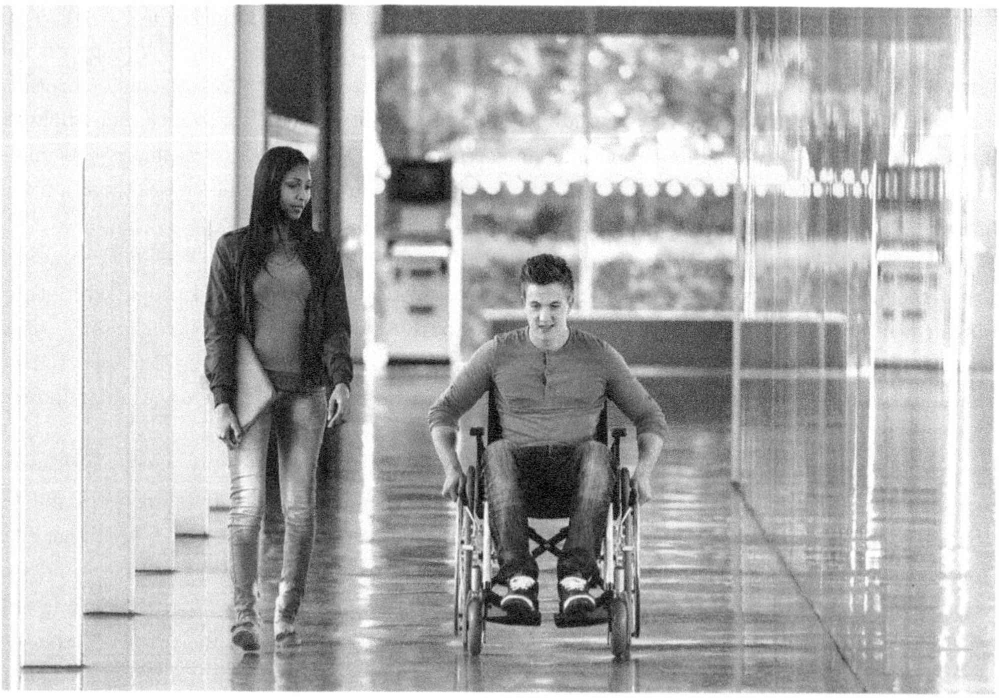

Federal legislation broadly defines disabilities and impairments that significantly limit one or more major life activities, including walking, seeing, hearing, and learning.

iStock.com/vm

Assistive Technology Act of 2004 and 21st Century Assistive Technology Act of 2022

On October 25, 2004, President George W. Bush signed the reauthorization of the Assistive Technology Act of 2004 (ATA, or Tech Act) into law, and in 2022 President Biden signed its more modern reauthorization, which includes more AT devices for older Americans. People with disabilities find this law of growing relevance because they are confident that increased community participation depends, in part, on technology. The term *assistive technology device* was first defined in the Technology-Related Assistance for Individuals with Disabilities Act of 1988 (PL 100-407). In this legislation, AT devices were defined as "any item, piece of equipment, or product system, whether acquired commercially off the shelf, modified, or customized, that is used to increase, maintain or improve the functional capabilities of individuals with disabilities" (Sec. 3). Individuals with disabilities can use technology, whether disability-specific (e.g., braille printers, speech synthesizers, wheelchairs), specialized (e.g., good grip utensils, ergonomic seating), or general (e.g., organizing tools, software including screen readers), to help them become more independent. Both AT acts apply to the education system and the federal legislation; IDEA mandates that IEP teams must consider whether the student needs AT to receive a FAPE. School districts have become increasingly aware that IEP team members need knowledge and skills to make informed AT decisions. Neither act allows for direct funds to be used for purchases; however, it does encourage and assist in locating independent private and corporate funding for such purchases on behalf of individuals with disabilities.

AT is critical to the ability of people with disabilities to participate in the workplace, in the community, and in school; it removes barriers that restrict their lives. For example, AT allows people with hearing problems to go to their neighborhood theaters and hear the movie's dialog through listening devices or to read it via captions. It allows people with physical disabilities to join friends at a local coffeehouse by using a variety of mobility options. It provides text-to-audio translations to those who cannot access printed passages because they cannot see, and it provides immediate audio-to-text translations to those who cannot hear lectures. The potential is limited only by our creativity and innovation.

However, AT is expensive and far beyond many people's budgets, particularly those who are underemployed or unemployed. For both students and adults, both acts offer (through the states' loan programs) training activities, demonstrations of new devices, and other direct services. This law enables students to test equipment and other AT devices both at school and at home before they are purchased. Access to information technology is important and unfettering to all of us, and restricted access to it results in barriers with considerable consequences.

Influential court cases, landmark legislation, and laws related to education and the greater society have paved the way for special education services as we know them today. Let's consider court decisions next.

Court Decisions Defining IDEA

It is the role of the courts to clarify laws passed by Congress and implemented by the administration. (Implementation of IDEA is the responsibility of the United States Department of Education). Although Congress thought it was clear in its intentions about the educational guarantees it believed necessary for children with disabilities and their families, no legal language is perfect. Since 1975, when PL 94-142 (EHA; name was later changed to IDEA) became law, a very small percentage of the children served have been engaged in formal disputes about the identification of students with disabilities, evaluations, educational placements, and the provision of a FAPE. Most disputes are resolved in noncourt proceedings or in due process hearings. Some, however, must be settled in courts of law—a few even in the U.S. Supreme Court. Through such litigation, many different questions about special education have been addressed and clarified. Table 1.4 highlights a few important U.S. Supreme Court decisions.

The issues and complaints the courts deal with are significant, and the ramifications of those decisions can be momentous. For example, a student named Garret F. was paralyzed as the result of a motorcycle accident at the age of 4. Thereafter, he required an electric ventilator (or someone manually pumping an air bag) to breathe and so to stay alive. When Garret was in middle school, his mother requested that the school pick up the expenses of his physical care while he was in school. The district

TABLE 1.4 ■ Landmark U.S. Supreme Court Cases Defining the Individuals With Disabilities Education Act

Case	Year	Issue	Finding/Importance
Rowley v. Hendrick Hudson School District	1982	Free Appropriate Public Education (FAPE)	School districts must provide those services that permit a student with disabilities to benefit from instruction.
Irving Independent School District v. Tatro	1984	Defining related services	Clean intermittent catheterization is a related service when necessary to allow a student to stay in school.
Smith v. Robinson	1984	Attorneys' fees	Parents are reimbursed legal fees when they win a case resulting from special education litigation.
Burlington School Committee v. Department of Education	1985	Private school placement	In some cases, public schools may be required to pay for private school placements when the district does not provide a FAPE.
Honig v. Doe	1988	Exclusion from school	Students whose misbehavior is related to their disability cannot be denied education.
Timothy W. v. Rochester, New Hampshire, School District	1989	FAPE	Regardless of the existence or severity of a student's disability, a public education is the right of every child.
Zobrest v. Catalina Foothills School District	1993	Paid interpreter at parochial high school	Paying for a sign language interpreter at a parochial school does not violate the constitutional separation of church and state.
Carter v. Florence County School District 4	1993	Reimbursement for private school	A court may order reimbursement to parents who withdraw their children from a public school that provides inappropriate education, even though the private placement does not meet all IDEA requirements.
Doe v. Withers	1993	FAPE	Teachers are responsible for the implementation of accommodations specified in individual students' IEPs.
Cedar Rapids School District v. Garret F.	1999	Related services	Health attendants are a related service and a district's expense if the service is necessary to maintain students in educational programs.
Arlington Central School District Board of Education v. Murphy	2006	Fees	Parents are not entitled to recover fees for expert witnesses in special education due process hearings.
Forest Grove School District v. T.A.	2009	Private school tuition reimbursement	Parents are entitled to tuition reimbursement for private school special education services regardless of whether the child had received special education services in a public-school setting and the public school had not provided a FAPE.
Endrew F. v. Douglas County School District	2017	Equal opportunity to achieve success like other kids	The school district argued that the boy who had autism had the right to only a de minimis, or minimal, benefit from the IEP. The Supreme Court unanimously ruled to send the case back to the trial level. The district judge in the case, who had initially ruled in favor of the Douglas County School District, reversed his decision and ruled in favor of the parents of a child with autism.

refused the request. Most school district administrators believed providing so-called complex health services to students was not a related service (and hence not the district's responsibility), but rather a medical service (excluded under the IDEA regulations). In other words, across the country, districts had interpreted the IDEA law and its regulations to mean that schools were not responsible for the cost of health services.

The Supreme Court, however, disagreed and interpreted IDEA differently. The justices decided that if a doctor is not necessary to provide the health service, and the service is necessary to keep a student in an educational program, then it is the school's obligation to provide the related service. The implications of this decision were enormous (Katsiyannis & Yell, 2000). Not only are the services of additional staff expensive—between $20,000 and $40,000 per school year—but it adds increased liability for schools, additional considerations for IEP teams, administrative costs, and the complications of having yet another adult in a classroom.

The case of Endrew (Drew) is very different. In this case, the Supreme Court defined FAPE: what comprises an appropriate education. The crux of the case was that the school district administrators believed that any progress was sufficient, but Drew's parents argued that Drew's educational program outlined in his IEP was inadequate and the court agreed, setting forward that all IEPs must surpass **de minimis** progress from year to year. Although the courts did not precisely define the concept of de minimis, they made it clear that expectations for each student with a disability should be high, progress must be monitored, and parents should be involved in decision making about their child's educational program (OSEP, 2017a).

Next, we focus on the nature of disability as a backdrop for the remaining chapters.

THINKING ABOUT DISABILITIES

Some of you might answer the question, "What is a disability?" by expressing the notion that **disabilities** are absolutes—something an individual does or doesn't have. You might have said the concept of disability is complex and that there are many different perspectives on what it is and what it means to each individual, family, and culture. You might have included in your answer that the intensity of a disability is the result of different conditions or experiences and that the response to it—the intensity of instruction, types of services, and community supports—depends on an individual's unique needs. These answers reflect the idea that individualized adaptations and assistance can reduce the impact of the challenge presented by a disability.

Why did we ask how disability is conceptualized? First, the concept of disability is not as simple as it initially appears. Second, the way people, groups, and cultures think about what it means to have a disability affects the way they interact with people with disabilities, and those interactions, in turn, become events that influence individuals' outcomes (Artiles, 2020; Branson & Miller, 2002; Winzer, 2007). Some responses—such as low or unreasonably high expectations—can have long-term negative results. So, let's think together about various ways to conceptualize the term *disability* and also about how attitudes toward disability can influence students' lives.

Different disciplines, cultures, and individuals disagree about what disabilities are or how to explain them (Artiles, 2019; Skiba et al., 2015). For example, many psychologists, education professionals, and medical professionals describe children and youths in terms of various characteristics, such as intelligence, visual acuity, academic achievement, or behavior. In its *Diagnostic and Statistical Manual of Mental Disorders*, fifth edition (DSM-5), the American Psychiatric Association (APA) describes many characteristics that help to describe or define a condition or a disability because they set the individual apart from what is called normal, typical, or average (APA, 2013). In this common approach, human characteristics or traits are described as a continuum; at one end, very little of the target behavior is observed, and at the other end an unusual amount of the trait is expressed. Here's an example. In DSM-5 the APA (2013) describes ADHD (hyperactivity and impulsivity) as including the following behaviors:

a. fidgets with hands or feet or squirms in seat

b. leaves seat in classroom or in other situations in which remaining seated is expected

c. experiences feelings of restlessness

d. has engaging in leisure activities quietly

e. is "on the go" or acts as if "driven by a motor"

f. talks excessively

g. blurts out answers

h. has difficulty waiting their turn

i. interrupts or intrudes on others (partially adapted from APA, 2013, p. 59)

Note that all the behaviors described in the DSM-5 account of hyperactivity are expected in children to some extent. What identifies hyperactivity is that an individual exhibits "too many" of these behaviors. Now let's think about the reverse situation, when displaying "not enough" or "too few" of the behaviors of concern (e.g., social isolation, withdrawal) leads to the identification of a disability.

Other perspectives can also provide a framework for understanding disabilities and unique learning needs. Let's turn to four different ways of thinking about disabilities:

- The deficit perspective on disabilities
- The cultural perspective on disabilities
- The sociological perspective on disabilities
- People with disabilities as members of a minority group

The Deficit Perspective on Disabilities

The deficit perspective reflects the idea that behavior and characteristics people share are distributed along a continuum, with most people falling in the middle of the distribution, where they make up the average. For example, some people are short and some are tall, but most people's height falls somewhere in the middle; the average of everyone's height is at the center of the distribution. The scores from most human characteristics create such patterns, forming what we call a **normal curve**, like the one shown in Figure 1.1. Because of the way the distribution tends to fall, with the highest number of scores in the middle and proportionally fewer as the distance from the average score increases, the distribution is also referred to as the **bell-shaped curve**.

Suppose we plotted the number of students obtaining each academic achievement score on the graph in Figure 1.1. Few students would obtain low scores, and their scores would be plotted at the left-hand side of the graph. The number of students receiving higher scores increases as we move to

FIGURE 1.1 ■ A Hypothetical Distribution of Scores Creating a Normal or Bell-Shaped Curve

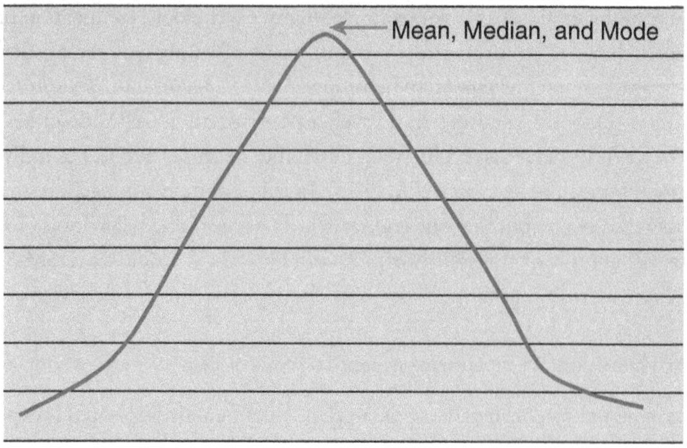

the right until we reach the average or mean score. Somewhere in the middle of the distribution are typical learners, whose behaviors and characteristics represent the average or majority of students. The progressively fewer students who obtain higher and higher scores on the test complete the right-hand side of the distribution or curve. The number of characteristics we can count in this way is infinite, and each individual student probably falls at a different point on each dimension measured. Thus, the unusually tall student might have slightly below-average visual acuity and an average score on the distance they can kick a ball. Clearly the hypothetical average student, or typical learner, does not actually exist—or exists very rarely—because the possible combinations of human characteristics are endless.

Regardless, in mainstream U.S. society, the most common way we describe individuals is by quantifying their performance. Unfortunately, this way of thinking forces us to consider everyone in terms of how different they are from the average, and half the members of any group will be below average. The deficit approach also contributes to the tendency to think about students with disabilities and also marginalized students as deficient or somehow less than their peers, placing them at an unfair disadvantage and not considering more positive approaches to help them succeed (Artiles, 2022).

The Cultural Perspective on Disabilities

A second way to think about disabilities and the people who might be affected does not use a quantitative approach; rather, it reveals a cultural perspective that reflects the diversity of our nation. Alfredo Artiles of Stanford University aptly points out that the United States today includes many different cultures, some of which embrace concepts and values that differ greatly from mainstream ideas. Nonmajority cultures often hold different views of disabilities, and many do not think about disabilities in terms of deficits or quantitative judgments of individuals (Artiles, 2022). The beliefs of teachers and other professionals who work with students are important to understand because different perspectives result in different responses to a disability.

First, education professionals and the families with whom they work might not share the same understanding of disability. Second, they might not have a common belief about what causes disabilities. Knowing this helps us understand why different families approach education professionals differently when told their child has a disability. Because disability does not have a single orientation or fixed definition, it is not thought about uniformly or universally (Skiba et al., 2016). Also, the same individual might be considered different or as having a disability in one culture but not in another. Or, the degree of difference might not be considered uniformly across cultures.

CULTURAL SENSITIVITY AND RESPONSIVENESS: USING EFFECTIVE MODES OF COMMUNICATION WITH FAMILIES

To build trust and supportive relationships with families, it is important to communicate frequently about their child's progress at school to report successes and areas of challenge and to learn of their concerns. But to do so requires knowledge and an understanding of the capabilities available to family members. During the COVID-19 pandemic, this became abundantly obvious. Many families in both rural and urban areas do not have reliable access to the Internet, so messages from school sent via e-mail may not be received. Others may not have texting capabilities. Learn about the families of each of your students in a personal and objective way, find out their communication preferences, and use those perhaps on a daily or weekly basis.

The Sociological Perspective on Disabilities

Instead of focusing on people's strengths or deficits, the sociological perspective views differences across people's skills and traits as socially constructed (Longmore, 2003; Artiles, 2019). The way a society treats individuals, and not a condition or set of traits the individual exhibits, is what makes people different from each other. If people's attitudes and the way society treats groups of individuals change, the impact of being a member of a group changes as well. In other words, according to this perspective what makes a disability is the way we treat individuals we think of as different.

Some scholars and advocates hold a radical view, suggesting that disabilities are a necessity of U.S. society, structure, and values. Years ago, Herb Grossman posited a theory that when societies are stratified, variables such as disability, race, and ethnicity become economic and political imperatives (Grossman, 2002). They are needed to maintain a hierarchical class structure. Classifications result in restricted opportunities that force some groups of people to fall to the bottom. Clearly, this rationale or explanation for disabilities is controversial, but let's see how the sociological perspective might apply to at least one disability. Using this perspective, intellectual disabilities (referred to as mental retardation in the IDEA, 2004; see Rosa's Law in Table 1.2) exist because society and people treat these individuals poorly. If supporting services were available to help every individual when problems occur, then people with intellectual disabilities would not be negatively treated. In other words, if individuals with significant differences are treated like everyone else, problems associated with intellectual disabilities will disappear.

Serious issues have been raised about sociological perspectives on disabilities. Some special education scholars maintain that disabilities are real, not just sociologically constructed, and significantly affect the people who have them no matter how they are treated (Anastasiou & Kauffman, 2017). To these critics, sociological perspectives arise from a need for sameness, in which everyone is truly alike. They contend that this position is dangerous because it (a) minimizes people's disabilities, (b) suggests that individuals with disabilities do not need special services, and (c) implies that needed services can be discontinued or reduced. All three scenarios leave individuals with disabilities vulnerable to diminished outcomes. Whether or not you believe the sociological perspective can be used to explain disabilities, it does explain why people with disabilities and their advocates believe they experience bias and discrimination, just like members of many other historically underrepresented groups. For these reasons, many of the laws that protect children, youth, and adults with disabilities are considered civil rights laws.

People With Disabilities as Members of a Historically Underrepresented Group

The late Paul Longmore—a founder of the disabilities studies movement, former director of the Paul K. Longmore Institute on Disability at San Francisco State University, and also a person with disabilities—maintained that, like other historically underrepresented groups, individuals with disabilities receive negative treatment because of prejudice (Longmore, 2003). The ways in which people are treated by society and by other individuals erect real barriers that influence their outcomes. Many individuals with disabilities believe that this perception of disabilities **handicaps** them by presenting unnecessary challenges and barriers. This belief leads many people to think of people with disabilities as belonging to a historically underrepresented group, much as the concepts of race and ethnicity have resulted in Blacks, Hispanics, American Indians or Alaskan Natives, and Native Hawaiian and other Pacific Islanders being considered part of historically underrepresented groups.[2] Difficult situations occur not because of a condition or disability, but rather because people with disabilities are denied full participation in society as a consequence of their status. In fact, IDEA is often referred to as a civil rights law. This places IDEA in the same category as the Voting Rights Act of 1965, which prohibited discriminatory practices that had denied some citizens their right to vote in state and national elections. The U.S. Department of Health and Human Services (2022) reinforced this concept through its guidance about civil rights protections for people with disabilities who were not receiving health protections during the COVID-19 pandemic.

DISABILITIES DEFINED

We have just discussed four very different perspectives on disabilities. Let's return to more traditional views of disabilities and the conditions that cause them. (We discuss other special learning needs that schools and society do not consider disabilities, including those prompted by giftedness, social and economic inequities, and cultural and linguistic differences, in Chapter 4.)

Causes of Disabilities

One way to organize the causes of disabilities is to divide them into three groups by time of onset, whether before birth, during the birth process, or after birth. **Prenatal** or **congenital** causes occur before or at birth and are often genetic or inherited. Heredity is responsible for Down syndrome and congenital deafness. Diseases and infections in expectant mothers, such as measles and HIV/AIDS, can devastate an unborn baby, and such events are also considered prenatal. **Perinatal** causes occur during the birthing process. They include low birth weight and injuries due to oxygen deprivation, umbilical cord accidents, obstetrical trauma, and head trauma. One common perinatal cause of disabilities is cerebral palsy. **Postnatal** causes occur after birth, and here the environment is a major factor. A few examples of postnatal causes are child abuse and neglect, environmental toxins, and accidents. Another way to consider why disabilities and unique learning needs arise is to classify the reasons in terms of biological causes, environmental causes, and other risk factors. Many of these causes occur during all three periods of onset.

Biological Causes of Disabilities

Heredity is a biological cause of disabilities, as are diseases and health conditions. Thus, a virus that results in a severe hearing loss is considered a biological cause of disability. Seizure disorders such as epilepsy are biological reasons for special healthcare needs, as are diseases such as juvenile arthritis and polio. In Chapters 5 and 6, where we present information about specific disabilities, we will have more to say about some types of conditions that students bring to school.

Environmental Causes of Disability

In addition to biological factors, other situations can cause challenges that result in educational difficulties. Some of these are environmentally based. Many are preventable, but many others cannot be prevented. Toxins abound in our environment. All kinds of hazardous wastes are hidden in neighborhoods and communities. For example, one toxin that causes intellectual disabilities is lead. We can pinpoint (and, you would think, eliminate) three major sources of lead poisoning in the United States today: water pipes made out of lead, lead-based paint, and leaded gasoline. Lead-contaminated water systems, such as the now famous one in Detroit, have poisoned thousands of children. Finally, in 2021–2022, Congress set an ambitious agenda to replace all such lead pipes that deliver water to many neighborhoods. Unfortunately, that effort will take years to accomplish. Neither lead-based paint nor leaded gasoline is sold today, but unfortunately lead has remained in the dirt children play in and on the walls of older apartments and houses where they breathe it directly from the air and household dust, eat paint chips, or put their fingers in their mouths after touching walls or windowsills. Low-income children in the United States have a much higher risk of having lead poisoning, with a result of lowered cognition, than children whose families are more affluent (Marshall et al., 2020). Lead is not the only source of environmental toxins government officials worry about; other concerns include pesticides, industrial pollution from chemical waste, and mercury found in fish (Centers for Disease Control [CDC], 2021).

Other Risk Factors

Other environmental issues can trigger problems for children as well. Asthma, a health condition covered in our discussion of Section 504 in Chapter 2, is the leading cause of school absenteeism and is the leading cause of chronic illness in children (Asthma and Allergy Foundation of America, 2022). Teachers and schools can reduce problems with asthma through the use of simple interventions. For example, asthma is often triggered by exposure to specific allergens. For some students, the chance of an asthma attack is reduced when the classroom is free of chalk dust, plants that generate pollen or mold, cold and dry air, smoke, paint fumes, and chemical smells. For others, the fur of classroom pets can cause an episode. Clearly, exposures to toxins are preventable, and the effect of a condition can be reduced.

Categories of Students With Disabilities

Nationally in 2019, almost 6.5 million children and youths ages 6 to 21 and an additional 806,319 children ages 3 through 5 received services through IDEA (OSEP, 2022). For school-age children ages 6 to 11, this number reflects 12.7% of the resident population and for students 12 to 16, it represents 12.2%. The federal government describes 13 disability-specific categories that (the original IDEA law described deafness and hard of hearing as two separate special education categories) can be used to qualify infants, toddlers, preschoolers, and young students eligible to receive special education services. It also described a 14th category for young children, developmental delay, that does not require a specific disability identification. This action allows states and school districts to use the term *developmental delay* for children birth to age 3 (IDEA Part C, 2004) and children ages 3 through 9 (IDEA Part B, 2004) who have delays in physical development, cognitive development, social or emotional development, or adaptive (behavioral) development. However, young children can be identified with a specific disability if they have a diagnosed condition (physical or intellectual) that is identified early in their lives. Children under the age of 3 might also be identified as at risk for developmental delays, bringing them intervention services early and preventing or reducing the impact of their delayed behaviors. In Chapters 5 and 6, we discuss each of the disability categories, including their prevalence rates.

Within these categories are many conditions. For example, stuttering is included as a speech impairment, ADHD is included in the category of other health impairments, and Tourette's syndrome is included in the emotional disturbance category.

People think about these **special education categories**, or disabilities requiring specialized educational responses, in different ways. First, the names for these categories differ slightly from state to state, and parent and professional groups do not necessarily prefer the terms. Second, some categories—such as deafness and hard of hearing—are often combined. And categories are often ordered and divided by **prevalence**, or the size of the category: **high-incidence disabilities** occur most frequently and **low-incidence disabilities** occur the least often. States and local school systems tend not to use this demarcation system. One reason is that some people mistakenly think incidence or prevalence relates to the severity of the disability. Remember, however, that all disabilities are serious, and mild to severe cases occur within each special education category. Check carefully to see how your state views these determinations about prevalence.

Some students exhibit problem behaviors and need exemplary teachers. How do federal laws distinguish between students who exhibit problem behaviors and students with attention issues or learning disabilities?

iStock.com/skynesher

Table 1.5 shows an overview of the 14 special education categories used by the federal government and most states and the different ways they are referred to in school settings. IDEA requires states to use these disability areas to qualify children and youths for special education services. Figure 1.2 shows the prevalence data for each special education category. We provide more detailed information about each of these special education categories or disabilities in Chapters 5 and 6.

TABLE 1.5 ■ Special Education Categories Explained and Ordered by Prevalence

Federal Term	Other Terms	Comments
Specific learning disability	Learning disabilities	Includes reading, language, writing, and mathematics disabilities. Includes dyslexia, dysgraphia, dyscalculia.
Speech or language impairments	Speech disorders or language disorders; communication disorders	Includes articulation, fluency, and voice problems.
Other health impairment	Health impairments; special health-care needs	Under IDEA, it includes ADHD.
Autism	Autism spectrum disorder (ASD)	DSM-5 defines ASD that it previously identified with five subcategories separately: Autistic Disorder, Asperger's Disorder, Pervasive Developmental Disorder, Not Otherwise Specified (PDD_NOS), Rett's Disorder, and Childhood Disintegrative Disorder (CDD). The first three are no longer separately identified and are considered as ASD. The last two are no longer included in the ASD diagnosis. While national prevalence numbers have been increasing dramatically, ASD is not a high-incidence disabilities, but rather in the medium range.
Intellectual disability	Cognitive disabilities; developmental disabilities	Ranges from mild to severe but often overlaps with low-incidence disabilities.
Emotional disturbance	Emotional and behavioral disorders	Includes schizophrenia. Does not include children who are socially maladjusted unless it is determined they have an emotional disturbance.
Developmental delay		Allows for noncategorical identification from birth to age 9.
Multiple disabilities	Multiple-severe disabilities	Does not include all students with more than one disability. Criteria vary by state.
Hearing impairment	Hard of hearing and d/Deafness	Includes full range of hearing losses. Deafness is a hearing impairment so severe that processing linguistic information through hearing, with or without amplification, is impaired and adversely affects a child's educational performance. The term *Deaf* is used to signify those who consider themselves part of the Deaf community.
Orthopedic impairment	Physical impairments; physical disabilities; developmental disabilities	Is often combined with health impairments because there are many overlapping conditions.
Visual impairment [includes blindness]	Visual disabilities; low vision and blind	Includes full range of vision loss.
Deaf-blindness	Deafblind	Causes severe communication and other developmental and educational needs.
Traumatic brain injury		Must be acquired after birth.

FIGURE 1.2 ■ Number of Children Ages 3–21 Served Through IDEA by Special Education Category

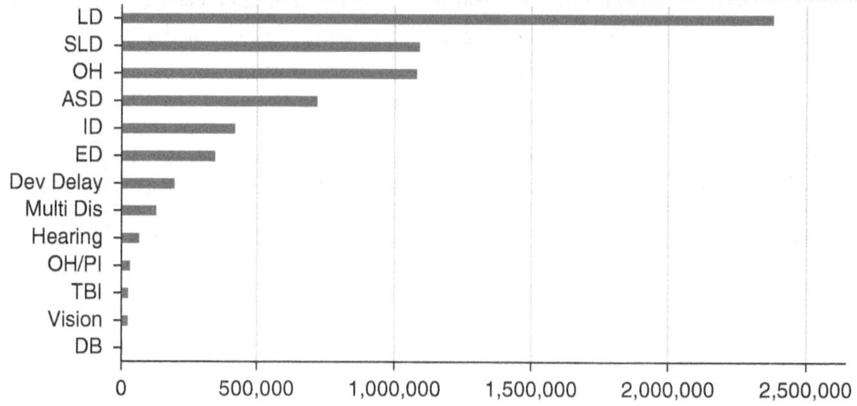

Source: OSEP fast facts: School aged children 5 through 21 served under Part B, of the IDEA (2021 May 26). https://sites.ed.gov/idea/osep-fast-facts-school-aged-children-5-21-served-under-idea-part-b-21/.

SUMMARY

You have now embarked on what we believe is an exciting course of study. You have begun to learn about the challenges that exceptionalities and unique learning needs present to the individuals involved and to their families, teachers, and friends. You have already learned that many of these challenges can be overcome when the educational system is responsive to the individual needs of these students. You also know that responses to such challenges must be rich with validated practices that are supported by teams of professionals working together in collaborative partnerships. For students with disabilities, the education system should be inclusive but also flexible enough to strike an intelligent balance between FAPE and LRE—types of education, services, and placement—for each individual. As you are learning, many provisions, requirements, and legal mandates guide your role as an inclusive educator. Sometimes, these principles can seem overwhelming and confusing, but when all of the hard work pays off, and students soar, their accomplishments are everyone's to share. As you read this text, the puzzle of inclusive education will come together as you reach an understanding about how to teach and accommodate every academic and social area where students with disabilities and unique learning needs require intervention.

REVIEW THE LEARNING OBJECTIVES

Let's review the learning objectives for this chapter. If you are uncertain about and cannot talk through the answers provided for any of these questions, reread those sections of the text.

1.1 Explain the five steps outlined in the ADAPT Framework.

The five steps of the ADAPT Framework are (1) Ask, (2) Determine, (3) Analyze, (4) Propose, and (5) Test. In the first step, I am figuring out what I am requiring the student to do. In the second, I am determining the prerequisites of the skills needed to execute the task. In the third, I am analyzing the student's strengths and weaknesses. In the fourth, I am proposing and implementing the adaptions needed in the instructional activity, the instructional content, the instructional delivery, and the instructional materials. Finally, in the fifth step I am assessing whether the adaptions helped the student accomplish the task.

1.2 Describe four guidelines that should be applied to determine an inclusive education for each student with a disability.

For education to be both inclusive and responsive, a delicate balance must be maintained between an appropriate education and placement in the least restrictive environment possible.

Therefore first, special education placement decisions must be individually determined because services should be tailored to the needs of each student with disabilities. Second, no single answer is possible for all students with disabilities. Third, students with disabilities need an array of services (and placements) available to them for the delivery of individualized education programs that range in intensity and duration. Fourth, the guiding principle must be based not on placement alone but also on how students can best access the general education curriculum, master academic targets, and develop life skills they need to succeed when they are adults.

1.3 Identify the nine foundational tenets of special education.
Nine fundamental tenets provide the foundation for special education: (1) a free (at no cost to the parents) appropriate public education, (2) delivered in the least restrictive environment possible, (3) provided as a response to systematic identification procedures, (4) guided by specified individualized education programs (IEPs), (5) involving the family, (6) comprehensively involving related service professionals who provide expertise related to the impact of the disability, (7) with maximum access to the general education curriculum, (8) reliant on the implementation of evidence-based practices, and (9) frequently monitored for progress.

1.4 Explain the history and development of special education.
Many people believe U.S. special education began in 1975 with the passage of the national law we now call IDEA, but it actually began more than 200 years ago. In 1799, farmers in southern France found a young boy living in the woods, and they took this "wild child" to a doctor in Paris. Jean-Marc-Gaspard Itard, the doctor who now is recognized as the father of special education, used many of the principles and procedures of explicit instruction still implemented today to teach this boy, who they named Victor and who probably had intellectual disabilities. In the early 1800s Edouard Seguin, one of Itard's students, came to the United States and began efforts to educate students with disabilities. It was another 75 years before education became a right in the United States, something all students with disabilities were entitled to receive.

1.5 Discuss the four different perspectives of disability.
Different lenses can be used to understand or conceptualize disabilities. The perspective used influences the response to the disability. If one applies a deficit perspective, then individuals with disabilities are "less than average," deficient, or somehow less than their peers without disabilities. One result can be low expectations. Another way to think about disabilities is to consider culture and acknowledge that the same individual might be considered different or as having a disability in one culture but not in another. It is important for educators to understand that families from various cultures bring their values and understandings to school. The third perspective about disabilities is sociological and holds that a person is considered to have disabilities not because of the traits the individual exhibits, but because of society's treatment of that individual, their background, and life situation. Finally, some believe that people with disabilities belong to a historically underrepresented group, like other historically underrepresented groups in America. Therefore, people with disabilities are denied full participation as a consequence of their status, and the appropriate response is to end discriminatory practices through civil rights protections.

1.6 Identify the 14 special education (disability) categories outlined by the federal government.
The federal government and most states group students with disabilities into 14 special education categories (13 exceptionalities but 14 categories): specific learning disability, speech or language impairments, intellectual disability, emotional disturbance, multiple disabilities, hearing impairment (hard of hearing), deafness, orthopedic impairment, other health impaired, visual impairment, autism, deaf-blindness, traumatic brain injury, and developmental delay.

REVISIT THE OPENING CHALLENGE

Check your answers to the Reflection Questions from the Opening Challenge and revise them on the basis of what you have learned.

1. Do you think Ms. Thomas and Mr. Salazar are overly concerned about their students' varied needs? Do you think they are just having first-year-teacher jitters? Why or why not?
2. What advice would you give them about planning for their students with disabilities and for those with other unique learning needs?
3. How can they learn more about the special education services their students should be receiving this year?
4. In what ways can Ms. Thomas and Mr. Salazar be responsive to all their students' needs?

KEY TERMS

accommodations
Americans with Disabilities Act (ADA)
array of services
assistive technology (AT)
Assistive Technology Act of 2004 (ATA, or Tech Act)
assistive technology device
bell-shaped curve
community-based instruction
congenital
continuum of services
coteaching
curb cuts
curriculum-based measurement (CBM)
data-based individualization
de minimis
disabilities
due process hearings
early intervening
Education for All Handicapped Children Act (EHA)
efficacy
evidence-based practices
free appropriate public education (FAPE)
full inclusion
functional skills
handicap
high-incidence disabilities
high-leverage practice
inclusive education
individualized education program (IEP)
individualized family service plan (IFSP)
Individuals with Disabilities Education Act (IDEA)
intensive intervention
itinerants
least restrictive environment (LRE)
life skills
low-incidence disabilities
mainstreamed
multidisciplinary teams
No Child Left Behind Act (NCLB)
normal curve
paraprofessional
perinatal
postnatal
prenatal
prevalence
progress monitoring
Public Law (PL) 94-142
pull-in programs
pull-out programs
related services
Section 504 of the Rehabilitation Act of 1973
special education
special education categories
typical learners
Universal Design for Learning (UDL)

PROFESSIONAL STANDARDS AND LICENSURE

For a complete description of Professional Standards and Licensure, please see the appendix.

CEC Initial Preparation Standards

Standard 1: Learner Development and Individual Learning Differences

INTASC Core Principles

Standard 1: Learner Development

Standard 2: Learning Differences

Praxis II: Education of Exceptional Students: Core Content Knowledge

I. Understanding Exceptionalities: Basic concepts in special education

II. Legal and Societal Issues: Federal laws and legal issues

III. Delivery of Services to Students with Disabilities: Background knowledge

NOTES

1. In this text, we refer to students who are part of the Deaf community and use ASL as their primary means of communication as *Deaf.* We refer to students who have profound hearing loss as *deaf; d/Deaf* refers to both groups.
2. Although regional and personal preferences about specific terms used to identify ethnic and racial groups vary, these terms are the ones used by the federal government. Throughout this text, we use a variety of terms in an attempt to achieve balance.

iStock.com/FatCamera

2 DELIVERY OF INDIVIDUALIZED SERVICES TO STUDENTS WITH DIFFERENT LEARNING NEEDS

LEARNING OBJECTIVES

After studying this chapter, you will be able to meet the following learning objectives:

2.1 Describe how the five components of the ADAPT Framework are put into action.

2.2 Discuss the purpose of the three tiers used in the multi-tiered systems of support (MTSS) framework.

2.3 Explain the seven steps of the evaluation and identification process.

2.4 Summarize situations that can put children at risk for poor school and life outcomes.

2.5 List the required members of individualized education program teams.

2.6 Identify the individualized plans for students with unique learning needs: the four individualized education plans for students with disabilities and the additional statement for transition and the one for students who do not qualify for special education services.

2.7 Name four related services and the professionals who provide those services.

Opening Challenge

How All These Special Education Services Come Together

Elementary Grades. Mr. Taylor has been teaching fourth grade for several years, but he had not taught a student with severe and complex disabilities in his general education classroom. Until now, all his students with disabilities have had mild to moderate learning challenges, and he has always worked well with the special education teacher to meet those students' needs. It is November, and the school year is well under way. He has assigned his students the right instructional groups, has a good understanding of each student's strengths and struggles based on district assessments, and has arranged for the necessary accommodations for each student. The new student, Emma, is joining his class in a few days. She just moved to River City from another state, and her individualized education program (IEP) came with her. Because her previous IEP indicates multiple learning needs, the school's support team decided to immediately implement the River City's IEP process so that all services were in place for Emma when she starts her new school. As Mr. Taylor prepares materials for the upcoming IEP meeting, he begins to wonder, *"How many education professionals will be assigned to Emma? Who will be at Emma's IEP meeting? How can I possibly meet all of her needs and still be sure that the rest of the students get the instruction they need?"*

Secondary Grades. Ms. Rymes is a 10th-grade history teacher at Independence High School. She has been teaching for 7 years and has worked with students with learning disabilities (LDs), and attention deficit hyperactivity disorder (ADHD). This year, Ms. Rymes has several students with learning disabilities who have reading disabilities and one student who has a mild intellectual disability in the two history classes she teaches each day. Two students' IEPs are up for reevaluation, so Ms. Rymes has to attend those students' IEP meetings. She has not attended a reevaluation before, so she is unsure what to expect. She knows that the students' assistive technology (AT) needs must be considered in the meeting, but she is confused about what "considering" actually means. She is also concerned about the services her students might require and how providing those services works in high school classes. As she plans her lessons for the first month of school, she thinks about her inclusion of other students with disabilities. She plans to make an appointment with the special education teacher to discuss her students' needs and how their IEPs can be implemented in her classes. She also needs guidance to prepare for the upcoming IEP reevaluation meetings. Ms. Rymes wonders, *"What is in each student's IEP that I have to be mindful of for my instruction? What does an IEP reevaluation meeting entail? How is AT 'considered'? What services might be added to the IEPs and how will I be able to work with various professionals and teach my history classes? How is the special education teacher going to help me?"*

Reflection Questions

In your journal, write down your answers to the following questions. After completing this chapter, check your answers and revise them on the basis of what you have learned.

1. Are Mr. Taylor and Ms. Rymes overly concerned about being able to meet their students' needs? Why or why not?
2. What advice would you give them about working with special education teachers regarding any supports and services specified in their students' IEPs?
3. What kind of assistance should these teachers expect from the IEP team members?
4. Is Mr. Taylor justified in expressing concerns about the educational progress of Emma's classmates? Why or why not?
5. How can special education and related service professionals help Mr. Taylor and Ms. Rymes support their students' needs and enable them to teach the rest of their class?
6. How does the multi-tiered systems of support model affect instruction in these teachers' classes?
7. How can the ADAPT Framework be utilized to address the needs of students with IEPs in these teachers' classes as they provide an inclusive education for all their students?

For an education program to be appropriate for each infant, toddler, and student with a disability, it must be individualized. When education is appropriate, the results can be astounding. It is clear to us that there is no single answer to the individual educational needs of every student with a disability: no standard program, no single service delivery option, no single place where education is received, and no single curriculum. The idea of an appropriate and individualized education program has been verified and validated time and time again as the process enacted to develop IEPs for each student with a disability is applied. With this in mind, in this chapter we continue our presentation of the ADAPT Framework, which educators can use to make appropriate adaptations for individualizing their instruction for students with disabilities. As noted in Chapter 1, the Individuals with Disabilities Education Act (IDEA) indicates that students with disabilities must have access to the general education curriculum; adapting instruction can promote success in helping students not only access the curriculum but also benefit from appropriate instruction. Also, in this chapter you will be introduced to multi-tiered systems of support (MTSS)—including response to intervention (RTI) and Positive Behavioral Interventions and Supports (PBIS)—individualized plans, and students with special learning needs who do not fall under an IDEA disability category.

ADAPT IN ACTION

We introduced you to the ADAPT Framework in Chapter 1. Its five steps were highlighted in Table 1.1 and are fleshed out here in Chapter 2 in Table 2.1, where we provide examples of how the process works. Refer back to this chapter's Opening Challenge where Ms. Rymes has students with reading and learning disabilities. In the following scenario, she is seeking information from the special education teacher about how to work with these students in her history class.

Ms. Rymes Seeks Information

A: Ask, "What am I requiring the student to do?" Students must be able to read class materials, including the textbook and handouts.

D: Determine the prerequisite skills of the task. Students must be able to read text and comprehend the material.

A: Analyze the student's strengths and struggles. Ms. Rymes's students with learning disabilities do attend class every day and are able to work in small groups; they are able to read the materials but have difficulties comprehending the vocabulary and text content provided each day in class.

TABLE 2.1 ■ Using the ADAPT Framework

A	D	A		P	T
ASK "What am I requiring the student to do?"	**DETERMINE** the prerequisite skills of the task.	**ANALYZE** the student's strengths and struggles.		**PROPOSE** and implement adaptations from among the four categories.	**TEST** to determine whether the adaptations help the student accomplish the task.
		Strengths	Struggles		
Students must be able to read class materials, including the textbook and handouts.	1. Read text.	x			
	2. Comprehend the material.		x	*Instructional delivery and instructional activity:* The special education teacher will teach the student a comprehension strategy. *Instructional materials:* The special education teacher will provide vocabulary study materials.	Weekly chapter tests will be assessed to determine whether the adaptations are promoting comprehension.

Her student with ADHD has difficulty focusing on the assignments, and her student with intellectual disabilities cannot read the grade-level textbook or supplementary reading materials.

P: Propose and implement adaptations from among the four categories. The special education teacher proposes that she teach the students with learning disabilities a comprehension strategy and provide vocabulary study materials to help them comprehend the textbook and handouts. The special education teacher suggests that she implement a study skills strategy for the student with ADHD and find a comparable text and supplemental reading materials with lower readability levels for the student with intellectual disabilities.

T: Test to determine whether the adaptations helped the student accomplish the task. Ms. Rymes gives chapter tests weekly and through progress monitoring directly assesses each student's reading abilities. Their responses to these assessments will be reviewed together to determine whether the adaptations are promoting comprehension.

You now have your first example of putting the ADAPT Framework into action. You will find many such examples across the text. Next, we discuss MTSS as a means for providing appropriate services to students with learning and behavior problems and also identifying students who require individualized instruction.

MULTI-TIERED SYSTEMS OF SUPPORT

Multi-tiered systems of support (MTSS) is the broad framework for tiered instruction and includes **response to intervention (RTI)** for academics and **Positive Behavioral Interventions and Supports (PBIS)** for behavior expectations and social behavior. See Figure 2.1 for a diagram of the framework. MTSS is a prevention and intervention model with the goal of identifying, providing necessary

FIGURE 2.1 ■ The MTSS Schematic

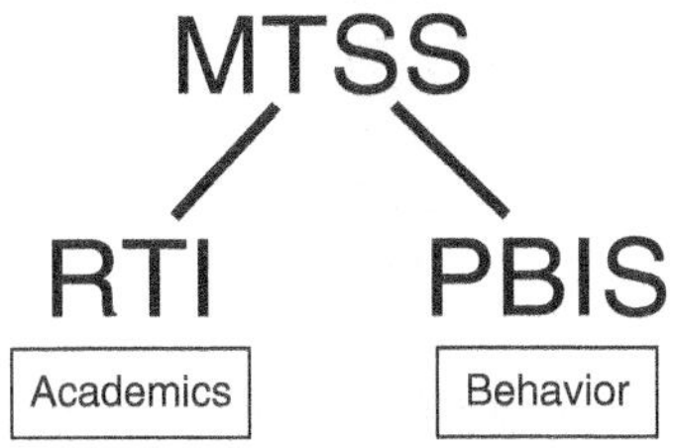

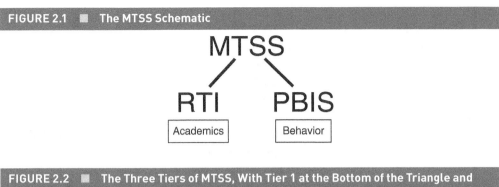

FIGURE 2.2 ■ The Three Tiers of MTSS, With Tier 1 at the Bottom of the Triangle and Tier 3 at the Top

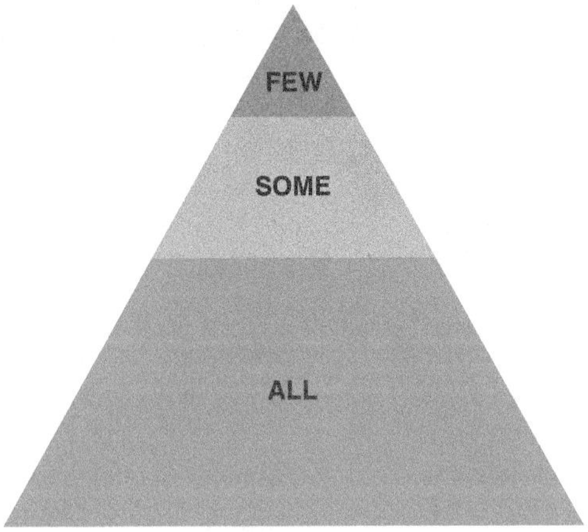

Source: Courtesy of The Center for Positive Behavior Intervention and Supports.

supports, and improving each student's academic performance or reducing or eliminating inappropriate behavior. MTSS is considered a prevention model because the approach aims to bring assistance to students long before the path to school failure is set or they qualify for special education services. Figure 2.2 illustrates this three-tiered system: All students are supported in the first tier, Tier 1, with validated instructional procedures, whether for behavioral or academic issues or both. Tier 2 uses data-based individualization for those who cannot achieve the learning expectations in the general education class without additional supports. The most intensive tier, Tier 3, is reserved for the few students who need the most intensive, individualized instruction or intervention.

Figure 2.2 shows the three instruction levels of the MTSS model: Tier 1, Tier 2, and Tier 3. Many school districts employ a three-tiered level of instructional support, although some districts offer four or more levels of instructional intensity. In this text, we use the more common three-tiered approach. Multitiered instructional support involves tiered levels of increasingly intensive intervention at the primary, secondary, and tertiary levels. Tier 1, the primary level, consists of high-quality, evidence-based core instruction for *all* students; approximately 75–90% of all students can benefit from this typical, core instruction. Tier 2, or secondary intervention, involves about 10–25% of students who have been identified through **universal screening** as being **at risk** and in need of intensified instructional support. Tier 3, the tertiary level, is more intense intervention and is appropriate for approximately 5–10% of students. This group of students continues to demonstrate poor performance in spite of receiving evidence-based instructional practices in Tiers 1 and 2; as a result, these students qualify for more intense intervention in Tier 3. However, for some students who perform very poorly during universal screening, the Tier 3 level of support may be immediately necessary.

RTI is a system of providing evidence-based instruction to all students and successively more intensive intervention to those students who demonstrate sustained academic problems. The RTI framework is used to intervene with struggling learners in the early grades with the intention of preventing referrals to special education because of inadequate instruction. Typically, a special education teacher consults with the general education teacher to help determine what screening procedures to use, how to collect data on the student's performance in the area of concern, and what instruction or accommodations to provide. In Chapter 9, we explain how RTI is also used for early identification of specific learning disabilities, rather than relying on psychoeducational assessments to determine whether a discrepancy between intellectual ability and achievement exists. Chapter 9 provides details about how students with learning disabilities are identified and how learning disabilities influence academic learning.

PBIS is a schoolwide approach to reduce discipline problems, prevent behavior problems, deal with social and emotional problems, and provide intensive interventions for the small group or individual students who require that level of support. We provide more detailed information about Tier 3 services for behavior and social issues and the entire PBIS process in Chapter 10.

Whether to address behavior or academics, MTSS has some common features. As shown in Table 2.2, six essential components are included in the MTSS model. These combined components contribute to improved student outcomes.

Universal Screening

For academic areas, RTI universal screening includes measures that are brief and administered by teachers to all students in their respective grade level. Those students whose scores fall below a designated percentile, such as the 25th percentile (i.e., below average performance), receive further progress-monitoring measures to confirm that they have low performance compared to their typically achieving peers and to confirm that, without intervention, they will likely continue to show poor academic performance (Oates et al., 2021).

Progress monitoring involves systematically assessing student performance in relation to the delivery of intensive interventions. Progress-monitoring measures for academic areas, such as reading and mathematics, are brief assessments that teachers administer weekly or bi-weekly. The results from these measures are used to make instructional decisions about each student's progress in relation to intensive interventions; this is known as **data-based decision making**. Data are used to determine movement within the multitiered system and whether students are benefiting from intensive interventions.

The implementation of PBIS is schoolwide, involving everyone at a school, including the principal, school staff, teachers, paraprofessionals, and all related services personnel. The Center on Positive Behavior Interventions and Support (2021) provides many tools to assist schools implement all tiers for behavior and social skills, even a screening tool for universal screening. For this to occur requires substantial professional development and support. It also requires considerable communication. Often

TABLE 2.2 ■ Components of MTSS

Essential Components	Descriptions
1. Universal screening	Schoolwide process of identifying students who are at risk for poor performance in learning or behavior
2. Tiered instruction	Tiered levels of increasingly intensive instruction at the primary (Tier 1 or core), secondary (Tier 2), and tertiary (Tier 3) levels
3. Effective interventions, both evidence-based practices and high-leverage practices	Use of interventions that have been identified through methodologically sound research procedures or proven effective over years of use that result in positive outcomes
4. Progress monitoring	Ongoing and systematic assessment of students' performance
5. Schoolwide approach	For both behavior and academic skills, the entire school is committed to its implementation
6. Parent involvement	For communication and follow through parents should be involved and committed to the process

schoolwide "buy-in" is more difficult at the high school level. High school educators typically give priority to academics, and these schools are much larger than the enrollment at elementary and middle schools. In addition, adolescents are seeking more independence and less adult authority. These challenges can be overcome by specific strategies for high school environments, such as sharing data that demonstrates the need for a schoolwide approach and including all school staff in the development of the PBIS plan to develop expectations and approaches for solutions to behavioral issues at the school (Martinez et al., 2019).

In Chapter 1, we stressed the importance of family involvement and engagement and do so again in this chapter and throughout this text. In fact, recall that parent participation is a requirement set forth by the Supreme Court in *Endrew F. v. Douglas County School District* (2017). When it comes to their child's behavior, often parents need assistance to prepare for the IEP meeting so the goals are better understood and families can participate in ways to improve behavior at both school and home (Kern et al., 2021). Also, educators need to pay special attention to their attitudes and practices to overcome barriers to the development of trust and effective home-school collaboration and foster equitable and positive home-school communication and shared decision making. Such relationship building is particularly critical for families of color (Witte et al., 2021).

Tier 1 (All)

Effective general education core instruction using evidence-based, validated practices is the foundation for *all* students and is typically aligned with state or national standards. High-quality core instruction for students with disabilities incorporates individualized plans and interventions, which increase access to the general education curriculum. As you learned in Chapter 1, the majority of students with disabilities receive a substantial proportion of their education in general education classrooms. Therefore, high-quality core instruction must be responsive to the needs of these students, but Tier 1 must also be responsive to the needs of struggling students, some of whom have not yet been identified as students with disabilities and others who will never qualify for special education services but have difficulties meeting the expectations of the general education curriculum.

Evidence-based practices, when integrated into the general education curriculum and teaching process, can and do make real differences for every student—those with and those without disabilities. We introduced many of these practices in Chapter 1, and we discuss them in more detail throughout this book as we talk about specific curricular areas such as reading, writing, and mathematics.

Tier 2 (Some)

Students who are identified as being at risk for having low academic performance during universal screening or through progress monitoring in the general education class require more-intensive intervention support. For these students, instructional features such as longer durations of instruction (anywhere from 10–20 weeks), smaller group size, adapted instruction (review the ADAPT Framework), and frequent progress monitoring are essential. The same is true for students who cannot meet the behavioral expectations of typical classroom settings. Because their inappropriate or disruptive behavior breaks the opportunities for academic learning, many of these students require Tier 2 support for both academic and social behavior. Special attention and intervention seek to prevent behavioral infractions. Those techniques you will learn more about in Chapter 10.

Tier 3 (Few)

In some but not all states, Tier 3 means special education services. Whether or not Tier 3 is reserved for students with identified disabilities, students who qualify for Tier 3 intervention did not make adequate progress during Tier 2 and demonstrate persistently low performance and require sustained and intensive services and instructional support. Students facing academic challenges typically perform below the 10th percentile on academic curriculum-based measures (see Chapter 9), which suggests that their ability to respond proficiently is limited. Those students who exhibit complex social, emotional, or behavioral problems typically have a **behavior intervention plan (BIP)** as part of their

IEP and receive services from highly prepared behavior analysts or teachers. Adjusting instructional features and individualizing as needs dictate are critical for students in Tier 2 and particularly for those in Tier 3. It is important to know that states and school districts leaders may have different guidelines and approaches for the implementation of MTSS. Therefore, you should review the guidelines and approaches for the state and school district in which you take a teaching position, whether in general education or special education. Although specific procedures for implementing RTI or PBIS are not stipulated in IDEA, a multi-tiered system must be used and is operationalized in different ways across states. For example, a problem-solving process and a standard protocol approach are common practices for operationalizing the MTSS framework.

In the problem-solving process, the RTI team uses the procedures shown in Figure 2.3 for each of the tiers. The problem-solving approach involves team decision making and the use of intervention options to meet the individual needs of students with learning or behavior problems.

In Figure 2.4, the standard treatment protocol approach is illustrated. For Tier 2, this approach may involve scripted lessons or standard intervention procedures for behavior, for instance, to ensure that regardless of who is teaching the students, the instruction or interventions remain consistent and are implemented with fidelity. In Tier 3, although a standard treatment protocol approach may still be used, given the severe and sustained needs of Tier 3 students this approach includes adaptations for

FIGURE 2.3 ■ Problem-Solving Approach for MTSS

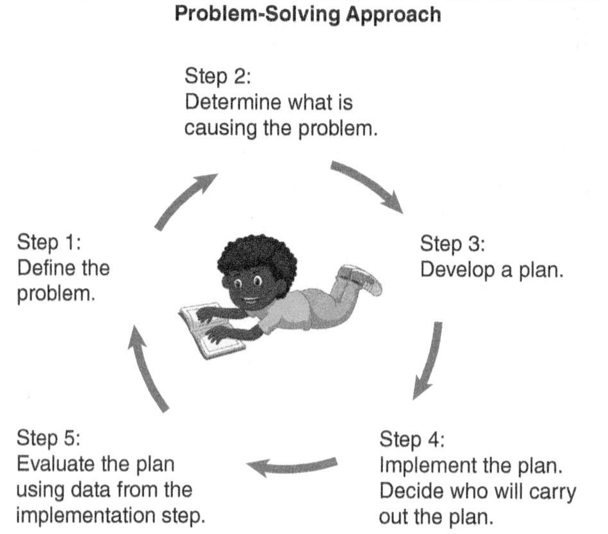
Problem-Solving Approach
Step 2:
Determine what is causing the problem.
Step 1:
Define the problem.
Step 3:
Develop a plan.
Step 5:
Evaluate the plan using data from the implementation step.
Step 4:
Implement the plan. Decide who will carry out the plan.

FIGURE 2.4 ■ Standard Treatment Protocol Approach

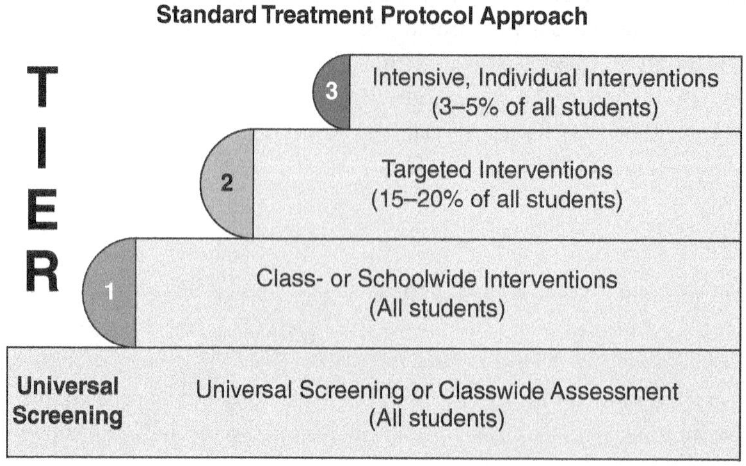
Standard Treatment Protocol Approach
TIER
3
Intensive, Individual Interventions (3–5% of all students)
2
Targeted Interventions (15–20% of all students)
1
Class- or Schoolwide Interventions (All students)
Universal Screening
Universal Screening or Classwide Assessment (All students)

Source: The IRIS Center (2018) https://iris.peabody.vanderbilt.edu/module/rti01.

individualizing the intervention, as needed. Regardless of which approach is used, practices identified in Table 2.2 are still employed.

Now we turn our focus to a discussion about the procedures for evaluating and identifying students for special education services.

THE EVALUATION AND IDENTIFICATION PROCESS

IDEA mandates that an individualized program be delivered to every infant, toddler, and student who is identified as having a disability and needing special education. The purposes of these individualized programs are to ensure that each individual

- receives a free appropriate public education;
- is provided an education in the least restrictive environment;
- receives education specific to the student; and
- is provided services with the expectation of outstanding results.

Students' IEPs are the plans or road maps created to guide instruction and the delivery of services that are the foundation for an appropriate education. Although some students with unique learning needs or disabilities receive accommodations for their special conditions through Section 504 of the Rehabilitation Act, only those with disabilities defined by IDEA are required to have IEPs. Thus, some students with a disability (e.g., a limb deficiency that does not affect educational performance) who do not require special education services do not have an IEP, though in some states they might have what is often referred to as a 504 plan. Conversely, sometimes students without disabilities do have an IEP. For example, in some states, students who are gifted or talented are included in special education. Although education of these students is not included in the federal special education law, those states often take their lead from IDEA and develop IEPs for students who are gifted or talented.

IEPs focus on students' strengths and on their individual needs. Parents and school districts' education professionals must agree on these plans for the delivery of special services. IDEA is very specific about the requirements of IEPs and the process to be used in their development and implementation (71 Fed. Reg. 46539 [2006]). The law spells out the minimum processes or steps that are to be used when developing individualized programs offered under the auspices of special education. States often impose further requirements in addition to those that are outlined in IDEA and monitored by the federal government. Because there are many local variations on the rules surrounding IEPs, we present here what the national law requires and do not address specific regulations that various states expect school districts and teachers to follow.

The formation of an individualized program can be organized into seven steps (see Figure 2.5), beginning with prereferral and ending with evaluation and reviews of a student's program:

1. Prereferral
2. Referral
3. Identification
4. Eligibility
5. Development of the IEP
6. Implementation of the IEP
7. Evaluation and reviews

Now let's look at these seven steps in more detail to get a better understanding of what each means and how they form the IEP process.

FIGURE 2.5 ■ The Seven Steps in the Individualized Education Program Process

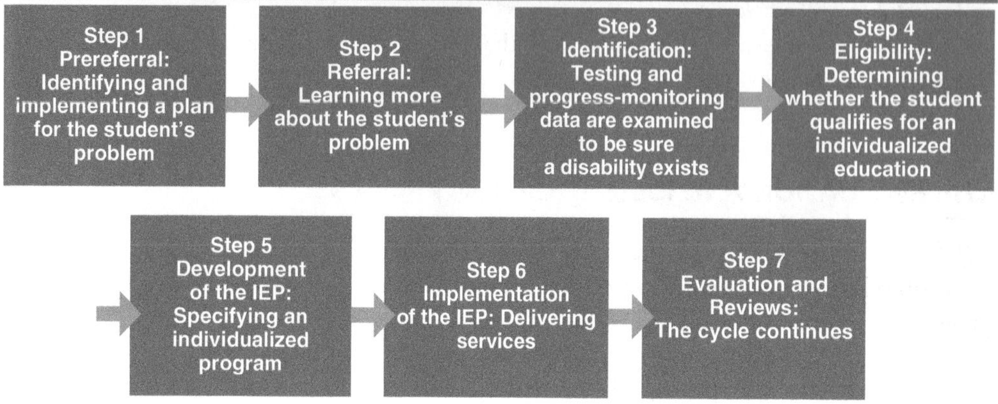
Step 1 Prereferral: Identifying and implementing a plan for the student's problem
Step 2 Referral: Learning more about the student's problem
Step 3 Identification: Testing and progress-monitoring data are examined to be sure a disability exists
Step 4 Eligibility: Determining whether the student qualifies for an individualized education
Step 5 Development of the IEP: Specifying an individualized program
Step 6 Implementation of the IEP: Delivering services
Step 7 Evaluation and Reviews: The cycle continues

Step 1: Prereferral

At this first step, the general education teacher and the school's support team ensure that the target student has received high-quality instruction and additional instructional assistance, if necessary. During this step and as required by IDEA, the school's support team must become confident that neither poor teaching (the application of practices that are not evidence based) nor a need to learn the English language explains the student's inadequate performance. The team may be called a prereferral team, a multidisciplinary team, or an RTI team if the RTI model is utilized. The purpose of the team is to

- document and explain how and when the student is struggling;
- determine the effectiveness of classroom adaptations and additional assistance;
- monitor the student's progress during the application of high-quality instruction; and
- prevent inappropriate referrals

For schools that are implementing an RTI framework of assessment and interventions, activities include screening students for learning or behavioral difficulties, implementing evidence-based practices, and documenting student responses to these practices. In general, before any formal referral for special education services is made, teachers, school-based education professionals, and family members work together to determine whether the general education teacher alone can resolve a student's educational or behavioral difficulties. The assessments used during this step are intervention based and conducted in the student's general education class using the direct measures of performance outlined in data-based individualization (Morris-Mathews et al., 2020). Teachers implement evidence-based, effective teaching practices and use assessment measures to document how students respond to this instruction. They also systematically differentiate instruction more intensively to address individual learning or behavioral needs.

Prereferral activities are intended to address individual students' learning or behavioral needs through the use of effective practices to prevent unnecessary referrals to special education, which are costly in time, money, and resources for formal assessments. You as a teacher may receive both assistance and consultation from specialists during this phase of the IEP process. Students whose learning remains challenged—those who continue to struggle—are referred to special education and the next step of the IEP process.

Step 2: Referral

There are different reasons for referring students to special education. For example, typically, the referral process begins sooner for children with very severe disabilities because their disabilities are obvious at birth or during infancy or in early childhood, as is often the case with students with autism (see

Teachers and families may be involved in the prereferral step. Prereferral activities are intended to address individual students' learning or behavior needs to prevent unnecessary referrals to special education.

iStock/peepo

Chapter 5 for a discussion about autism and Chapter 6 for a discussion about less frequent disabilities). Children with visible indications of a disability (e.g., facial differences resulting from Down syndrome or use of hearing aids due to a hearing impairment) or other signals of significant developmental delay (e.g., an 18-month-old child not walking independently or a 3-year-old not talking) are usually identified early and receive early intervention services during infancy and their preschool years.

Other signs involving young children often trigger referrals. For instance, young children who are at risk of having disabilities because of improper prenatal care, low birth weight, accident or trauma during infancy, or child abuse can be referred for possible special services. A toddler who does not respond to loud sounds and is not walking by age 2 and a preschooler who has excessive tantrums are both candidates for early referrals. These students likely have received special education services for years. Why is this so? For infants, toddlers, and preschoolers, IDEA stresses the importance of an activity called **child find**, wherein those with disabilities are actively sought (71 Fed. Reg. 46539 [2006]). In these cases, referrals can come from parents, a social service agency, public health nurses, daycare professionals, or a medical doctor. Such children and their families usually come to school expecting an individualized education because they have received multidisciplinary services during the preschool years.

Other reasons for referral during the elementary or secondary school years focus more on academic difficulties and behavior problems. For example, students whose academic performance is significantly behind that of their classmates despite having received RTI Tier 2 or Tier 3 interventions are prime candidates for special education referrals. Also, those students who continually misbehave and disrupt the learning environment despite PBIS often draw the attention of their teachers and are targeted for intervention and (ultimately) referral for special education services. Documentation of academic and behavioral interventions already conducted and data from progress-monitoring procedures are part of the information that is used during the referral and identification steps.

It is important to know that cultural and linguistic diversity (CLD) alone (students who speak languages other than English) is not a reason for a referral to special education. As you will learn in Chapter 4's section about the RTI framework and CLD learners, it is important for educators to distinguish the difference, for example, between limited English proficiency and a learning disability.

Step 3: Identification

Once a referral has been made, the student's formal evaluation must be initiated within 60 days. The purpose of the evaluation or identification step in the IEP process is to determine whether a student has a disability, whether special education services are required, and what types of services are needed.

Multidisciplinary teams consisting of professionals who have expertise in each area of concern conduct evaluations and assessment. Each member helps to evaluate the student's unique strengths and struggles. For example, if a student is suspected of having a language impairment, a **speech/language pathologist** is a member of the team. If there may be a hearing problem, an **audiologist** participates, and so on. For students who are 16 years old or older, evaluation includes assessments related to the need for transition services for moving either from school to work or from secondary to postsecondary education (Office of Special Education Programs [OSEP], 2017).

Evaluation and assessment information can come from a broad range of sources, including the student's parents and family members. The professional who actually coordinates the identification process varies by state and district. In some states the assessment team leader is a school psychologist, an educational diagnostician, or a psychometrician. In other states, a teacher from the student's school leads the team's efforts.

During the identification step, many different types of data are used to inform the team about the student's abilities and possible issues. Medical history, information about social interactions at school and at home, adaptive behavior in the community, and educational performance are considered. Tests of intelligence, of academic achievement, and of acuity (vision and hearing) are usually part of the data used to make identification decisions about students and their potential special education status. Other information such as AT evaluations, school observations of classroom and social behavior, examples of academic assignments, curriculum-based measurements of reading and mathematics skills obtained as part of the RTI approach, and portfolio samples of classroom performance also are important pieces of evidence used in this step of the IEP process.

Together, data from these sources are used to develop a profile of the student. One result of the identification step of the IEP process can be a determination that the individual does not have a disability. In these instances, the IEP process is discontinued. For those individuals who do have identified disabilities, this phase of the process results in a baseline of performance data to guide the development of the IEP and, later, to help judge the program's effectiveness.

Step 4: Eligibility

The information from the identification step is used to determine eligibility for special education services. To receive services through IDEA, the student must have one of more the disabilities we outlined in Chapter 1. In addition, the disability *must adversely affect the individual's educational performance.* The education of those students who do not meet the eligibility requirements remains the sole responsibility of general educators. However, if collectively the information from Step 3 indicates a disability for those students, then the IEP team determines what components of the full range of special education and related services are needed so that an appropriate education can be planned and ultimately delivered. In some cases, students do not require services from a special education teacher, but rather a related services provider. For example, a student with a physical disability whose academic performance is relatively on par with classmates may only require services from a physical therapist. The education of those students with disabilities who are eligible for special education services becomes the shared responsibility of general education teachers and administrators, special education teachers and administrators, and the appropriate related service professionals.

Step 5: Development of the Individualized Education Program

After thorough completion of the prereferral, referral, identification, and eligibility steps of the IEP process, it is time to develop the actual individualized plan—the roadmap to FAPE. As you learned in Chapter 1, the U.S. Supreme Court, in its 2017 ruling *Endrew F. v. Douglas County School District*, requires that the educational program outlined must be of high quality and include goals that are more than de minimus and have high expectations. To ensure challenging, ambitious, and attainable educational programs, the foundations for the IEP are laid out in **present levels of academic achievement and functional performance (PLAAFP)** statements (The IRIS Center, 2019a). This relatively new component of every IEP must include descriptions of the following:

- the student's current needs in academic and/or functional skill areas, such as social skills, communication, independent living, and/or mobility;
- how the disability affects inclusion in the general education curriculum;
- current levels of performance in terms of providing baseline data against which progress will be measured and evaluated;
- the appropriate special education services that aim to meet the student's annual goals. (IDEAs That Work, 2018)

Different plans are designed for different age groups (e.g., infants and toddlers, school-age students) and different needs of students (e.g., behavior intervention plans, 504 plans). We describe each of these plans in the next section in some detail, but regardless of the specific plan, their development follows the general guidelines used in the IEP process. For now, it is important for you to know that parents and the education professionals who are all part of the student's IEP team make important decisions about what services and placements constitute an appropriate education for this individual at this step of the IEP process. The assessment results are used to help make these decisions. It is at this point that the IEP team begins its work to outline the individualized education needed for each student. Collectively, the team members, who include parents and the student (if appropriate), now use the knowledge they have gained to identify resources needed for that student to access the general education curriculum, determine the appropriate goals for improvement, and then craft a high-quality education program for the student. Of course, goals must include greater success with the general education curriculum or independence and a community presence later in life. It is at this point that the services and supports that become part of the student's appropriate education are specified.

Step 6: Implementation of the Individualized Education Program

Once the IEP is developed, the student's services and individualized program begin. The IEP contains components that stipulate what constitutes an appropriate education for the student, the extent to which the student participates in the standards-based general education curriculum, the accommodations or adaptations the student receives both for instruction and for assessment, and the array of multidisciplinary services from related service providers that supports the student's educational program. For students with severe disabilities, such as significant cognitive disabilities, who may be participating in a different curriculum or whose goals differ from those of the general education age-appropriate standards-based curriculum, alternative academic achievement standards and alternative assessments should be aligned and noted on the IEP.

Minor adjustments in students' goals or in the benchmarks that indicate attainment of those goals do not signal a need for a new IEP or another IEP meeting; services continue. However, major changes in goals, services, or placement do require parents to be notified in writing. Some changes, particularly if they involve a more restrictive placement, may necessitate a meeting of the IEP team and the parent or guardian. Most often, this situation arises when issues surrounding discipline are the reason for the change in placement or services. Later in this chapter, you will learn more about behavior intervention plans (BIPs), which must be developed as part of students' IEPs when serious behavioral infractions (e.g., bringing guns or drugs to school, fighting, or being out of control) occur. Also, in Chapter 10 you will learn about effective interventions that should help resolve behavior issues, which affect both the individual and their classmates when rules are violated.

Step 7: Evaluation and Reviews

IDEA requires accountability for each IEP developed. IEPs must be reviewed annually. Concerns about the paperwork and administrative burdens on educators and administrators have been voiced since the initial enactment of IDEA. However, in a detailed study, the U.S. Government Accountability Office (GAO, 2016) determined that consensus among educators, school district officials, and state education agency administrators was that the benefits of the IEP process outweigh such concerns. The purpose of the IEP and ensuing review meetings is to ensure that students are meeting their goals and making educational progress. Because accountability measures determine whether the student is making progress, educators are careful to describe expectations for tasks and skills the student needs to learn in terms that can be evaluated. Whether the IEP process is for an infant or toddler (an IFSP) or for a schoolchild (an IEP and possibly a transition component), the expectation is that frequent assessments of the individual's performance will occur and annual IEP reviews ensure collaboration among all educators, related service providers, and families.

RISKS FOR DISABILITIES AND SPECIAL EDUCATION IDENTIFICATION

Many reasons explain why so many children and youth find themselves at risk for being identified as having disabilities or unfortunate life circumstances. We strongly believe that all educators, in fact the public at large, need to understand the possible results of conditions that too many find themselves confronted with and what actions might resolve or lessen the impact of these unfortunate situations. For these reasons, we discuss risk situations in many places in the text.

Students are at risk for school failure or underachievement if their family situations, personal conditions, and life events negatively affect their school lives. Although educators may not be able to influence some of the many factors that place students at risk, they can make a difference in these students' education by carefully identifying academic, behavioral, and social problems that can result from these factors and then implementing and monitoring plans to address them. Here we discuss who is at risk, possible conditions that contribute to risk, and ways to tackle the problems.

iStock.com/SDI Productions

Definition of *At Risk*

Students who are at risk of being identified as having a disability or struggling at school may have experiences, living conditions, or characteristics that contribute to school failure. Informal experiences such as interactions with other children, interactions with adults, and activities contribute to language and cognitive development in the early years of a child's life. Students who have limited life experiences, lower expectations, and fewer academic opportunities because of family situations, family income, and even geography lag behind their peers right from the start before entering school. Living conditions such as poverty, neglect, homelessness, recent immigration, physically and/or verbally abusive situations (including bullying), and drug or alcohol abuse contribute significantly to the risk. In addition, students who struggle with depression, exhibit suicidal tendencies, are coping with the death of a loved one, or are experiencing a divorce in their family may also have limited capacity to cope with the demands of the educational setting and are also at risk for poor school outcomes. Careful coordination and collaboration between the family and a team of professionals (e.g., social workers, school counselors, medical professionals, psychologists, and educators) are needed to tackle the challenges caused by these conditions. All students at risk benefit from academic and social support services and often respond to the same instructional practices that help students with disabilities learn the general education curriculum.

Educational and life challenges often contribute to students' giving up and dropping out of school. Although the dropout rates for all students improved from 2010 to 2019 from 8.3% to 5.1%, the rates are still disproportionate across students from different backgrounds (National Center for Education Statistics, 2021). The highest dropout rates were among American Indian/Alaska Natives (9.6%), Pacific Islanders (8%), Hispanics (7.7%), and Blacks (5.6%). Unfortunately, the economic and employment picture is bleak for students who drop out of high school because they lack the education and experience employers seek in more competitive high-salary positions.

Conditions That Contribute to Risk

Many conditions that contribute to risk affect students' performance in schools. In this section, we discuss several of these risk factors to help you better understand them as you work with children in inclusive settings. Here are just a few examples:

- poverty,
- homelessness,
- migrant or immigration status, and
- the conditions of some schools.

As you will see from the data presented, it is likely that as a teacher you will have students who face challenges from at least one of these circumstances.

Poverty

The link among childhood poverty, poor school outcomes, and disabilities is clear and well documented (Taylor, 2017). The most important predictor of student success in school is readiness to learn to read. Unfortunately, many children from high-poverty homes enter school with limited readiness skills. The percentage of students who are eligible for free or reduced-price lunch is the common indicator used for the percentage of students who experience childhood poverty. The percentages are most alarming! Students who attend high-poverty schools are Hispanic (38%), Black (37%), American Indian/Alaska Native (30%), and Pacific Islanders (23%); only 7% of White students attended such schools (NCES, 2023).

The COVID-19 pandemic revealed to educators another great disparity between students of poverty and those from more affluent homes. It is clear that access to the Internet has become increasingly important in the lives of most Americans. In fact, many of us can't imagine a world without access to social media, e-mail, television shows, online shopping, and so much more. Many administrators in large urban school districts had not considered the impact and challenges of remote learning, distance education, and schooling of many of their students. Parent levels of education and income were directly related to better Internet access for their children. Although in 2020 only 6% of U.S. students had no access to the Internet at home (Hussar et al., 2020), only 16% of all households had consistent access to the Internet and a computer available for educational purposes (Annie E. Casey Foundation, 2021). Most of the students affected attended high-poverty schools in both urban and rural areas. The long-term impact of a lost school year because of no or limited access to the Internet will not be known for years, but the short-term consequences for these children with and without disabilities was devastating (Colvin, 2021).

Homelessness

Homeless is not equally distributed across the nation and is more concentrated in large cities and among those served by the Bureau of Indian Affairs (National Center for Homeless Education, 2021). In the 2019–20 school year, almost 1.3 million (2.5%) of all students enrolled in public schools experienced homelessness. Students with disabilities (19%), English learners (17%), and migratory students (1%) represented a large proportion of homeless students. However, students of color were disproportionately represented. Although White students accounted for 46% of all students enrolled in the public schools, 26% of them were homeless. However, although Black students represent 15% of all students, this group represented 27% of all homeless students. Hispanic students accounted for 28% of all students but 38% of students experiencing homelessness. Though students with disabilities attending public schools represent almost 14% of the overall student population, 19% of homeless students have an identified disability. Additionally, 31 states report that at least 20% of their homeless students have a disability (National Center for Homelessness, 2020, 2021).

Migrant and Immigrant Status

Along with homeless children, children of immigrants and migrant workers often experience disruption and dislocation—circumstances that can be challenging as they try to cope with frequent transitions from school to school. Children who live in shelters may be embarrassed or afraid they will be judged or stigmatized because of where they live. These students often change schools every few months, breaking the continuity of their education and leaving gaps in their knowledge that result in reduced academic achievement. Educators must understand that their low academic performance occurs because of many factors, including fragmented education, absenteeism, and high risk for health problems.

Conditions of Some Schools

Many school environments contribute to risk for students for a number of reasons, including low performance. Although many of the risk issues that we highlight next are not within teachers' control, they are issues everyone must be aware of and seek the support of policy makers and school officials at the state and local levels to resolve. As you have just learned, a very high proportion of diverse and poor students attend urban public schools, and the conditions of these schools contribute to learning challenges (Bassetti, 2018). Here are some examples. Urban school districts tend to receive less funding than their suburban counterparts, in part because all districts are funded, at least in part, through local property taxes. Urban districts also require more funding because the school buildings are old, out of date, and in need of repair. They also tend to be larger, with greater student enrollments and crowded classrooms, making individualization more challenging.

School environments can be rated as at risk for a number of reasons, including low performance. Resources such as technology and instructional materials are typically limited, which means students do not have the same learning opportunities and experiences as their peers in better-resourced schools.

Students who are identified as "at risk" need teacher support for issues both academic and personal to help them thrive in school.

iStock.com/Juanmonino

Teacher turnover is exceptionally high, resulting in fewer experienced teachers and more first-year teachers to work with these students (Bassetti, 2018; Carver-Thomas & Darling-Hammond, 2017).

Once again, we emphasize that well-prepared teachers and high-quality instruction are critical components in student learning (Lee, 2018; Opper, 2019; Terada, 2019). Research shows that activities such as providing explicit and systematic instruction with multiple opportunities for practice, differentiating instruction based on assessment results, adapting instruction to meet students' needs, and monitoring student progress will improve students' academic outcomes. Unfortunately, unprepared teachers often do not have these skills. Throughout this text you will be learning more about specific effective, evidence-based practices that do make a real difference in the educational outcomes of students.

MEMBERS OF THE INDIVIDUALIZED EDUCATION PROGRAM TEAM

IDEA is very clear about membership on IEP teams (OSEP, 2006a). The exact language of the regulations is found in Table 2.3, but it is important for you as a teacher to remember that each IEP team is individually determined according to the specific needs of students and their disabilities.

As a teacher attending an IEP meeting for one of your students, you can be most helpful in ensuring that the right people are participating and contributing to the development of a meaningful IEP for your student. Review Table 2.3 and consider a student who faces motor challenges resulting from cerebral palsy. Emily is a very bright fourth grader, but she has difficulty engaging in class discussions because her speech is slow, deliberate, and difficult to understand. She uses a walker and finds it challenging to hold a pencil, but she can use a computer keyboard. IDEA is specific about the minimum representation of those members who make up IEP teams for students with disabilities. Who are those essential members? For Emily, IDEA allows for the inclusion of more multidisciplinary professionals. What additional members would be appropriate for Emily's IEP team? To answer these two important questions, it might be helpful to know more about the roles of IEP team members. Some of those roles and responsibilities are highlighted next.

TABLE 2.3 ■ Members of IEP Teams

According to the IDEA regulations, the public agency must ensure that the IEP Team for each child with a disability includes

- The parents of the child;
- A general education teacher who is or will be the student's teacher (if the child is, or may be, participating in the general education environment);
- Not less than one special education teacher who is an expert about the disability and its impact on school performance;
- A representative of the school district, often a special education director or coordinator or school principal;
- An individual who can interpret the instructional implications of evaluation results (this person may also be one of the other listed members, except for the parent);
- At the discretion of the parent or the agency, other individuals who have knowledge or special expertise regarding the child, including related service personnel as appropriate; and
- Whenever appropriate, the child with a disability.

Sources: OSEP (2006a, pp. 2–3); The IRIS Center (2019b).

Roles of Education Professionals

All education professionals working at every school are crucial to positive experiences for students with disabilities. It is surprising to us that after more than 30 years of including more and more students with disabilities in general education classes, the majority of teachers, most principals, and other education professionals still report that they feel ill-prepared to accept responsibilities associated with the education of these students (Johnston & Young, 2019; Mitchell, 2019). When teachers believe that are well-prepared and supported, they are more likely to believe that they will be successful with students with challenging educational needs (Galiatsos et al., 2019). Well-prepared educators can and do make a real difference in the lives and the educational achievements of their students (Cardichon et al., 2020). Teachers who use effective practices and monitor the effectiveness of the instruction they implement ensure that the IEP has outlined the right educational program for each student with a disability. We are confident that you, as a teacher thoroughly prepared with knowledge about effective interventions and the ADAPT Framework, will positively influence the lives of your students with disabilities, as well as others who struggle to meet the demands of the general education classroom.

The school principal has a key role in the IEP process (The IRIS Center, 2019c). Mistakes made can be very expensive to the child and family involved in terms of educational progress, but also to the school district in terms of financial costs and disruption of litigation. Principals who can create strong inclusive environments matter for teachers and students alike (Levin, 2021). Because principals often coordinate management efforts at their site, they help ensure the delivery of special education services, including monitoring the array of services indicated on every student's IEP, and facilitate the coordination of all services from professionals on each student's multidisciplinary team. For example, Emily receives services from a speech/language pathologist, a physical therapist, an expert in AT, and an **occupational therapist**. However, these members of Emily's multidisciplinary team are not permanent or full-time members of the school staff. Their schedules are complicated and often hard to coordinate because each is itinerant, having to travel from school to school, sometimes long distances, to work with individual students and their teachers who need their services across the school district. Also, these professionals often find themselves in crowded schools where they do not have sufficient space or appropriate places to work with individual students or to store their equipment. Principals can lead their school's staff to solve complex coordination issues that itinerant multidisciplinary team members often present, smoothing the way for efficient delivery of related services. Unfortunately, principals feel the least prepared in the area of supporting students with disabilities than all other aspects of their responsibilities (Johnston & Young, 2019).

The IEP process involves a number of important components:

- Prereferral and referral
- Evaluation
- Determination of eligibility
- Development of the IEP
- Implementation
- Annual review
- Re-evaluation to occur every 3 years

Although some students come to school already identified as having a disability and have received special services during their early childhood years, most do not. At the prereferral stage, general and special education teachers often work together to decide whether a formal referral for evaluation should be made. The general education teacher conducts in-class assessments using tactics of various intensities with and without accommodations. Often a special education teacher will consult and assist the general education teacher through this process. Although an actual referral can be made by the parents, it is most often made by school personnel. The parents *must* provide informed consent before an evaluation to determine whether their child has a disability that impacts educational performance. Also, the evaluation must begin within 60 days of the parents' formal consent or sooner if the state's regulations have a shorter timeframe.

The foundation of the development of the IEP rests with the student's evaluation and assessment in all areas of concern, whether it be academic or functional performance. During the next step, eligibility for special education services is determined by asking questions such as, Does the child have a disability? Does that disability affect educational performance? If the answer to either question is no, the process is terminated. If the answers to both questions are "yes," then the actual development of the IEP begins within 30 days. The IEP team, which is individually determined for each student reflecting the results of the evaluation, come together to set meaningful and measurable annual goals and identify the services the student will receive. The educational professionals who will collaborate and work together to achieve these important goals, the frequency and duration of services provided, the settings where the services will be delivered, how they will be evaluated, and most important, the methods and frequency of communicating with the child's parents, will be set.

Once the IEP is developed, its implementation is to be initiated as soon as possible. The student's progress should be monitored systematically and often. If adjustments need to be made to the IEP, the IEP team works together to address the reasons why adequate progress is not being made. The IEP and individual students' progress must be evaluated every 12 months and the IEP is updated accordingly. Every 3 years, the students are to be reevaluated to determine whether they are still eligible and require special education services.

Roles of Families

In Chapter 1 and here in Chapter 2, we discuss the 2017 Supreme Court case about Drew and his family's right to be involved in decisions about his educational program (*Endrew F. v. Douglas County School District,* 2017). Both IDEA and the Supreme Court stress the importance of involving families of students with disabilities in the IEP process and as members of their child's IEP team (Couvillon et al., 2018; 71 Fed. Reg. 46539 [2006]). The IEP process can help develop partnerships among parents and extended family members, schools, and professionals (Witte et al., 2021). This purpose should be actively fostered because the importance of these partnerships cannot be overestimated. When parent involvement is high, student alienation is lower and student achievement is increased. Educators need to recognize, however, that many parents believe schools control the special education process. As a result, many families feel disenfranchised or confused about rules, regulations, and the purpose of special education. Most parents want to participate in their children's education, but sometimes they do not understand the educational system, particularly immigrant families.

Often, families need help to participate effectively in IEP meetings and in the resulting individualized programs (Kern et al., 2021). Here are some tips that teachers can give parents to help them better prepare to participate in IEP meetings (PACER Center, 2020):

- Plan ahead!
- Know when and where the meeting is being held.
- Make a list of important questions to ask IEP team members. Examples: What is my child's daily schedule? How is my child doing in school? Does my child have friends? How well does my child behave? What problems is my child having?
- Outline points to make about your child's strengths.
- Bring records regarding your child's needs, as well as concerns you might have.
- Ask for clarification.
- Be assertive and proactive but not aggressive or reactive.
- Listen and compromise.
- Remain involved with the professionals on the IEP team.
- Know about placement and service options and explore each with the team.

For families who do not speak English well enough to understand the complicated language used to talk about special education issues, participation may seem impossible (Witte et al., 2021). In such instances, schools must welcome family members and people from the community who are fluent in the family's native language and also knowledgeable about the special education process and procedural safeguards guaranteed to families through IDEA. The law encourages the family's maximal participation, so it requires schools to find interpreters to the fullest extent possible. Remember, it is the obligation of educators to include and inform parents and students about the efforts that will be made on their behalf.

Roles of Students

Review Table 2.3 and remember the importance that IDEA places on students participating in their own IEP teams, particularly when adolescents are about to transition out of high school. The law stresses student involvement because it has found that many students are unfamiliar with their IEPs and do not know the goals established for them. One result is a lack of ownership in the school program especially designed for them. Involving students has many benefits (Center for Parent Information and Resources [CPIR], 2017). Particularly if students are active participants, they can learn important skills needed in life. Here are two examples: **Self-determination** is the ability to identify and achieve goals for oneself. **Self-advocacy** consists of the skills necessary to stand up and advocate for what one needs to achieve those goals. These two skills are interrelated and can be fostered during the IEP process when students are involved (OSEP, 2017). Here are some ways in which older students can contribute to their IEP meetings:

- Describe personal strengths, weaknesses, and needs.
- Evaluate personal progress toward accomplishing their goals.
- Bring a list of adaptations and explain how each is helpful.
- Communicate their preferences and interests.
- Articulate their long-term goals and desires for life, work, and postsecondary schooling.

IDEA law stresses the importance of student involvement in their IEPs because, surprisingly, many students are unfamiliar with the content and the goals established for them within their IEPs. Involving students in the process has many benefits.

iStock.com/TerryJ

Now, we will discuss individualized plans more specifically. Think about what you have learned in Chapter 1 and in Chapter 2 so far that could help you write an IEP with members from the multidisciplinary team.

INDIVIDUALIZED EDUCATION PLANS AND PROGRAMS

Five plans for individualized programs serve to coordinate and document what constitutes the appropriate education for each infant, toddler, and student with disabilities. The plans that guarantee an appropriate education to those with disabilities are as follows:

1. The IFSP—for infants and toddlers
2. The IEP—for preschoolers through high school students
3. An additional statement of transitional services—initiated at least by age 16 to help those students who require special education services to make successful transitions to independence, community living, and work
4. A BIP—for those students with disabilities who commit serious behavioral infractions
5. 504 plan—for students who do not qualify for special education services

Let's examine each of these plans in turn.

Individualized Family Service Plans (IFSPs)

Infants or toddlers (birth through age 2) who have disabilities or who are at great risk for disabilities were originally guaranteed the right to early intervention programs through the Education for All Handicapped Children Act (EHA), which was passed in 1986. That right continues today through IDEA. (For a review of IDEA legislation, see Chapter 1.) IFSPs are written documents that ensure that special services are delivered to these young children and their families. The IFSP is the management tool that guides professionals as they design and deliver these children's special education programs. **Service managers** are the professionals who provide oversight and coordination of the services outlined in IFSPs. The key components of these early education management plans are as follows:

- The child's current functioning levels in all relevant areas (physical development, cognitive development, language and speech development, psychosocial development, and self-help skills)
- The family's strengths and needs in regard to the development of their child
- The major outcomes expected, expressed in terms of procedures, evaluation criteria, and a timeline
- The services necessary and a schedule for their delivery
- Projected dates for initiation of services
- The name of the service coordinator
- A biannual (every 6 months) review, with the child's family, of progress made and of any need for modifications in the IFSP
- Indication of methods for transitioning the child to services available for children aged 3 to 5

To many service coordinators and early childhood specialists, the IFSP is a working document for an ongoing process in which parents and specialists work together, continually modifying, expanding, and developing a child's educational program. Children and families who participate in early intervention programs often find these years to be an intense period, with many professionals offering advice, training, guidance, and personalized services, as well as care and concern. Also, the transition to preschool at the age of 3 can be particularly difficult and frightening. One reason for the difficulty is that services that had been delivered primarily at the family's home will now be delivered at a preschool. Therefore, IFSPs include plans for these youngsters and their families to transition from very intensive and individually delivered interventions to more traditional classrooms. IDEA allows states to give families the option of delaying entrance into school-based preschool programs by keeping their child in an early intervention program, but making this decision sometimes results in the family having to pay for some or all of the services (71 Fed. Reg. 46539 [2006]).

Individualized Education Programs (IEPs)

IEPs are the documents that describe the special education and related services appropriate to the needs of students with disabilities who are 3 to 21 years of age. These plans are the cornerstones of every educational program planned for preschoolers (ages 3 to 5) and students (ages 6 to 21) with disabilities (71 Fed. Reg. 46539 [2006]). IDEA delineated what the IEP must contain at the very least, and it is important that every educator know these key components:

- Current performance: The student's present levels of academic achievement and functional performance related to how the student's disability influences participation and progress in the general education curriculum
- Goals: Statement of measurable goals related to participation in the general education curriculum or to meeting other educational needs resulting from the disability
- Special education and related services: Specific educational services to be provided, including accommodations, program modifications, or supports that allow participation in the general education curriculum and in extracurricular activities
- Participation with students without disabilities: Explanation about the extent to which the student will not participate in general education classes and in extracurricular activities alongside peers without disabilities

- Participation in state- and districtwide testing: Description of assessment accommodations needed for these assessments or, if the student will not be participating, a statement listing reasons for nonparticipation and explaining how the student will be alternatively assessed
- Dates and places: Projected dates for initiation of services, where services will be delivered, and the expected duration of those services
- Transition service needs: A transition component for those students (beginning at age 16) whose goals are related to community presence and independence that is included in the IEP to identify postschool goals and to describe transitional assessments and service needs
- Age of majority: A requirement to inform students, beginning at least 1 year before they reach the age of majority, of those rights that transfer to them
- Measuring progress: Statement of how the student's progress toward achieving IEP goals will be measured and how parents will be informed about this progress

To stress the importance of including all of these components in each student's IEP, IDEA Part B regulations specify the procedures that school districts must follow to develop, review, and revise the IEP for each child. Remember that students with disabilities must have age-appropriate standards-based IEPs, which allow for access to the general education curriculum. Students with significant cognitive disabilities may qualify for alternative curriculum and assessments.

IEPs must be written for each student with a disability, so each IEP will be different. Remember Emily, who was described earlier in this chapter? She needs services from several related service professionals, such as a speech/language pathologist, a **physical therapist**, and an **assistive technologist**. Some students, such as in Ms. Cohen's classes, may need help only from a special education teacher or a paraprofessional. Other students may require assistance from many more members of a multidisciplinary team. Academic areas might be reflected, but so might areas not typically part of educational programs for students without disabilities (e.g., fine and gross motor skills and life skills). Services indicated on the IEP must be provided, and they cannot be traded for other services, such as more time in the general education classroom. Services not being readily available (including AT devices and services) is no reason for omitting them from an IEP: If the student needs the service, it must be delivered. In other words, if a student needs the services of an assistive technologist and requires some special equipment, those services and devices must be made available at no cost to parents. In addition, any changes in placement, related services specified in the IEP, or annual goals necessitate another IEP meeting and mutual approval by the family and the school district.

The contents of a student's IEP must be available to all educators who work with the student (71 Fed. Reg. 46539 [2006]). IEPs are meant to be a communication tool. Surprisingly, it is not uncommon for teachers to be unaware of the goals and services required by their students' IEPs. This situation leads one to ask how an appropriate education can be delivered when the educators who interact with students with disabilities do not understand what should comprise the students' education. The answer is obvious: An appropriate education cannot be delivered under these circumstances.

Transition Components of Individualized Education Programs

When IDEA was reauthorized in 1997, plans to help students transition from school to postsecondary experiences became a special education requirement. At that time, such a plan was a separate document—a mini-IEP of its own—for students age 14 and older that was called an individualized transition plan. Since the 1997 reauthorization of IDEA, these plans for assessments and services to prepare for postschool life, or statements of transitional services, are a part of the students' IEPs; they are not stand-alone documents. IDEA increased to 16 the age for initiation of the **transition component of IEPs**. Transitional planning is very important for high school students with disabilities and their families because these individuals' postschool outcomes have much room for improvement. Table 2.4 provides a template for an IEP and transition services.

TABLE 2.4 ■ IEPs and Transition Services

Statements

A statement of the child's present levels of academic achievement and functional performance including

- how the child's disability affects the child's involvement and progress in the general education curriculum (i.e., the same curriculum as for nondisabled children) or for preschool children, as appropriate, how the disability affects the child's participation in appropriate activities.

A statement of measurable annual goals, including academic and functional goals designed to

- meet the child's needs that result from the child's disability to enable the child to be involved in and make progress in the general education curriculum; and
- meet each of the child's other educational needs that result from the child's disability.

For children with disabilities who take alternative assessments aligned to alternative achievement standards (in addition to the annual goals), a description of benchmarks or short-term objectives.
A description of

- how the child's progress toward meeting the annual goals will be measured; and
- when periodic reports on the child's progress toward meeting the annual goals will be provided, such as through the use of quarterly or other periodic reports, concurrent with the issuance of report cards.

A statement of the special education and related services and supplementary aids and services, based on peer-reviewed research to the extent practicable, to be provided to the child, or on behalf of the child and a statement of the program modifications or supports for school personnel that will be provided to enable the child

- to advance appropriately toward attaining the annual goals;
- to be involved in and make progress in the general education curriculum and to participate in extracurricular and other nonacademic activities; and
- to be educated and participate with other children with disabilities and nondisabled children in extracurricular and other nonacademic activities.

A statement of any individual appropriate accommodations that are necessary to measure the academic achievement and functional performance of the child on state- and district-wide assessments.

If the IEP team determines that the child must take an alternative assessment instead of a particular regular state- or district-wide assessment of student achievement, a statement of why

- the child cannot participate in the regular assessment; and
- the particular alternative assessment selected is appropriate for the child.

An explanation of the extent, if any, to which the child will not participate with children who do not have disabilities in the regular classroom and in extracurricular and other nonacademic activities.

The projected date for the beginning of the services and the anticipated frequency, location, and duration of special education and related services and supplementary aids and services and modifications and supports.

Transition Services

Beginning not later than the first IEP to be in effect when the child turns 16, or younger if determined appropriate by the IEP team, and updated annually thereafter, the IEP must include

- appropriate measurable postsecondary goals based on age-appropriate transition assessments related to training, education, employment, and, where appropriate, independent living skills; and
- the transition services (including courses of study) needed to assist the child in reaching those goals.

Rights That Transfer at Age of Majority

- Beginning not later than one year before the child reaches the age of majority (which is 18 years of age in most states) under state law, the IEP must include a statement that the child has been informed of the child's rights under Part B of the IDEA, if any, that will, consistent with 34 CFR §300.520, transfer to the child on reaching the age of majority.

Source: 71 Fed. Reg. 46539 (2006).

In 2018–2019, more students with disabilities graduated from high school with a standard diploma (about 72.6%) than in previous years, but too many still drop out of school (16.6%; OSEP, 2022). Completion rates vary greatly by type of disability. For example, 85.3% of students with speech or language impairments, 82.4% of students with hearing impairments, 82.1% of students with visual disabilities, 71.4% of those with autism, and 63.3% of students with physical disabilities complete high school. However, only 60.1% of students identified as having emotional or behavioral disorders, and 47.3% of those with intellectual disabilities, finish high school with a standard diploma.

Of course, high school completion rates influence participation rates in postsecondary opportunities. One reason why postsecondary education is important is that it is related to long-term life outcomes (e.g., greater annual earnings; Hussar et al., 2020). About 20% of enrolled undergraduates report having a disability. Although in 2017 more youth with disabilities enrolled in a 4-year college or university (48%); a smaller proportion (26%) enrolled in a community college, and only 1% enrolled in a technical school (Harvey et al., 2019). It is important to note the 4-year college undergraduates with disabilities had much lower graduation rates than those without a disability: some 40% as compared to 57% (Postsecondary National Policy Institute [PNPI], 2022). This in part may explain why in 2022 the U.S. Bureau of Labor Statistics reported that 19.1% of individuals with disabilities were unemployed but 63.7% of their counterparts without disabilities were employed. For both groups, employment rates were higher for those with higher levels of education. Workers with a disability were more likely to have part-time employment and work in service occupations.

It is also important for teachers who participate in transition planning to understand that, as adults, these individuals tend to engage in leisure activities less than individuals without disabilities. They participate in organized community groups at a rate much lower than would be expected, and they also get in trouble with the law more often than their typical peers (Harvey et al., 2019). Helping students set goals for themselves, gain work experience, and develop skills needed for independent living can be critical to the life satisfaction experienced by adults with disabilities (CPIR, 2017).

The transition component supplements and complements the IEP, and as you can tell, it has the potential to be very important to the long-term results of your students. Whereas the IEP describes the educational goals that a student should achieve during a school year, the transitional services part of the IEP focuses on the academic and functional achievement of the individual to prepare for adult living (OSEP, 2017). Transition components are designed to facilitate the process of going from high school to any of several postschool options: postsecondary education including vocational education, integrated employment (including supported employment), adult services, or community participation. The last years of school can be critical to the achievement of special education outcomes and to these learners' smooth and successful transition to adulthood.

Behavior Intervention Plans (BIPs)

When any student with a disability commits serious behavioral infractions, IDEA requires that a BIP, which is like an IEP but addresses the behavioral infraction, be developed (71 Fed. Reg. 46539 [2006]). Because inappropriate behavior is so often at the root of special education referrals, of teachers' dissatisfaction with working with students who have disabilities, and of lifelong challenges, we devote an entire chapter to behavior management, development of good social skills, and interventions for serious and persistent behavior issues (see Chapter 10).

Why did BIPs for students who have major behavioral issues become part of students' IEPs? One reason reflects concerns of Congress and the public about violence, discipline, and special education students. Although students without disabilities can be expelled for breaking school rules (e.g., for bringing guns to school or engaging in serious fighting), some students with disabilities cannot. These students can, however, be removed from their current placement and receive their education away from their assigned classroom(s) in what is called an interim alternative educational setting for up to 45 school days. Continued progress toward the attainment of IEP goals must be one intention of the **interim alternative educational setting (IAES)** placement. Students who cannot be expelled are those whose disruptive behavior was caused by their disability. Under the older versions of IDEA, this protection was called the stay-put provision. Through a process called **manifestation determination**, educators figure out whether the disability caused the infraction. All students with disabilities who are violent or said to be out of control must have BIPs developed for them. These plans focus not only on the control or elimination of future serious behavioral infractions but also on the development of positive social skills. In Chapter 10, we provide information about how to write a BIP.

504 Plans

Section 504 of the Rehabilitation Act of 1973, which is being considered for re-authorization, is a civil rights law that prohibits discrimination against individuals with disabilities. It requires federal, state, and local governments to provide access to buildings and other public spaces to people with disabilities through such accommodations as alternatives to stairs (ramps and elevators) and barrier-free sidewalks (via curb cuts that allow wheelchairs to roll from sidewalk to street).

Section 504 also requires that teachers in publicly funded schools make accommodations and modifications for students with disabilities to ensure that they have equal access to an education. Because some students who receive services under Section 504 may not receive special education services, it is the general education teacher's responsibility to make those accommodations and modifications for the nonspecial education students. Let's review how students qualify for services under Section 504 and the educational accommodations that are available to them.

Qualifying for Services Under Section 504

There are students with special learning needs who are not covered under IDEA. However, they may qualify for services under Section 504 because the definition of disability is broader under Section 504 and extends beyond school age. To be eligible for protections under Section 504, the child must have a physical or mental condition that substantially limits at least one major life activity. Major life activities include walking, seeing, hearing, speaking, breathing, learning, reading, writing, performing math calculations, working, self-care, and performing manual tasks. The key is whether a person "has a physical or mental impairment which substantially limits one or more of such person's major life activities" (Yell, 2012, p. 96).

IDEA vs 504

If the student has a disability that adversely affects educational performance, the student is eligible for special education services under IDEA and would also be automatically protected from discrimination under Section 504. However, the opposite is not true: If a student has a disability that does not adversely affect educational performance, the student will not be eligible for special education services under IDEA, but the student will usually be entitled to protections under Section 504. For example, a student with AIDS, a student with attention deficit hyperactivity disorder (ADHD), and a student with chronic asthma are all protected from discrimination under Section 504. Each of these students may also be eligible for special education services under IDEA (under the category "Other Health Impairments" described in Chapter 5), but those decisions must be based on the specific educational needs of each student (Wrightslaw, 2015). Remember, to qualify for services offered through IDEA, the condition or disability *must* substantially impact educational performance. Students with conditions such as drug or alcohol addiction, temporary disabilities resulting from accidents, attention problems, or chronic health issues can qualify as having a disability under Section 504. Although no funding is attached to this legislation, school districts and general education professionals are expected to implement measures to address any special conditions they believe would jeopardize a student's ability to learn.

Providing Educational Services Under Section 504

Under Section 504, students who qualify as having a disability are assessed, and a 504 plan is developed and monitored (see Figure 2.6 for an example). The plan includes accommodations and adaptations, identifies the person(s) responsible for implementation, and lists the procedures for monitoring

FIGURE 2.6 ■ Section 504 Sample Plan

Sample Components of a 504 Plan for a Student with Diabetes

Student's Name: ______________________________

Birth Date: ______________Grade: ______________Type of Diabetes: ______________

Homeroom Teacher: ______________ Bus Number: ______________ Date: ______________

Objectives/Goals of this Plan

The goal of this plan is to provide the special education and/or related aids and services needed to maintain blood glucose within this student's target range of _______ and to respond appropriately to levels outside of this range in accordance with the instructions provided by the student's personal health care team.

1. **Provision of Diabetes Care:** Designated individuals will receive training to be Trained Diabetes Personnel (TDP).
2. **Student Level of Self-Care and Location of Supplies and Equipment:** The student can perform the following diabetes care tasks without help at any time of the day and in any location _____________. The student needs assistance or supervision with the following diabetes health care tasks _____________. The student needs a TDP to perform the following diabetes care tasks _____________.
3. **Snacks and Meals:** The school nurse, or TDP if the school nurse is not available, will work with the student and his/her parents/guardians to coordinate a meal and snack schedule in accordance with the attached Diabetes Medical Management Plan (DMMP) that will coincide with the schedule of classmates to the closest extent possible. The student shall eat lunch at the same time each day, or earlier if experiencing hypoglycemia. The student shall have enough time to finish lunch. A snack and quick-acting source of glucose must always be immediately available to the student.
4. **Exercise and Physical Activity:** The student shall be permitted to participate fully in physical education classes and team sports except as set out in the student's DMMP.
5. **Water and Bathroom Access:** The student shall be permitted to have immediate access to water and be permitted to use the bathroom without restriction.
6. **Checking Blood Glucose Levels, Insulin, and Medication Administration, and Treating High or Low Blood Glucose Levels:** Blood glucose monitoring will be done at the times designated in the student's DMMP, whenever the student feels her blood glucose level may be high or low, or when symptoms of high or low blood glucose levels are observed. Insulin and/or other diabetes medication will be administered at the times and through the means (e.g., syringe, pen, or pump) designated in the student's DMMP.
7. **Tests and Classroom Work:** If the student is affected by high or low blood glucose levels at the time of regular testing, the student will be permitted to take the test at another time without penalty. If the student needs to take breaks to use the water fountain or bathroom, check blood glucose, or treat hypoglycemia during a test or other activity, the student will be given extra time to finish the test or other activity without penalty.

Emergency Contact:

______________________	______________________	______________________
Parent's/Guardian's Name	Home Phone Number	Emergency Phone Number

Approved and received:

______________________	______________________
Parent/Guardian	Date
______________________	______________________
School Representative and Title	Date

Source: Adapted from American Diabetes Association (2012).

the effectiveness of the plan. Accommodations and adaptations might include changes to the physical environment (specialized lighting, a quiet study place), adaptations to curriculum and instruction, accommodations in testing, and assistance with organizing time and activities. In addition to instructional programs, the plan can cover other academically related programs such as field trips and summer programs.

Some students with disabilities who qualify for Section 504 accommodations and adaptations may not be receiving special education services. For these nonspecial education students, the general education teacher is responsible for providing needed accommodations and adaptations.

RELATED SERVICES AND PROVIDERS

Many students with disabilities need help beyond that given through the partnership of general and special education. As you learned in Chapter 1, related services are typically beyond what general and special education teachers can provide and are outlined in IDEA (71 Fed. Reg. 46539 [2006]). Related services are definitely a unique feature of special education, offering a wide range of services and expertise to students and their families. These experts facilitate the attainment of least restrictive environment (LRE) and FAPE.

The three most commonly used related services are speech therapy, physical therapy, and AT. IDEA does not provide a precise list of related services because its authors did not want to be too prescriptive; these services are to be determined by the exact needs of the individual. As Table 2.5 shows, related service professionals may include those who provide AT, audiology, occupational therapy, physical

TABLE 2.5 ■ Explanation of Frequently Provided Related Services Specified in the Individuals with Disabilities Education Act

Related Service	Explanation	Provider
Adaptive physical education (therapeutic recreation)	Assesses leisure function; provides therapeutic recreation and leisure education	Recreational therapist
Assistive technology (AT)	Assists with the selection, acquisition, or use of any item, piece of equipment, or product system used to enhance functional capabilities (assistive technology device)	Assistive technologist
Audiology services	Identifies and diagnoses hearing loss; determines proper amplification and fitting of hearing aids and other listening devices	Audiologist
Counseling services/ rehabilitative counseling	Provides psychological and guidance services, including career development and parent counseling; develops positive behavior intervention strategies	School counselor, social worker, psychologist, guidance counselor, vocational rehabilitation counselor
Diagnostic and evaluation services	Identifies disabilities	School psychologist, diagnostician, psychometrician
Occupational therapy	Improves, develops, or restores the ability to perform tasks or function independently	Occupational therapist
Orientation and mobility training	Enables students who are blind or have low vision to move safely and independently at school and in the community	Orientation specialist, mobility specialist
Physical therapy	Works to improve individuals' motor functioning, movement, and fitness	Physical therapist (PT)

Related Service	Explanation	Provider
School health services	Provides health services designed to enable a student with a disability to participate in FAPE	School nurse
Social work	Mobilizes school and community resources and works in partnership with family members to resolve problems in a child's living situation that affect school adjustment	Social worker
Speech/language therapy	Provides services for the prevention and treatment of communicative disorders	Speech/language pathologist (SLP)
Transportation	Assists with travel to, from, between, and within school buildings, typically using specialized equipment (e.g., special or adapted buses, lifts, ramps)	Orientation specialist, mobility specialist

Source: Adapted from 71 Fed. Reg. 46539 (2006), pp. 1257–1258, 1284–1294.

Many students with disabilities need help beyond that given through the partnership of general and special education. This student requires physical therapy from a related services provider.

iStock.com/FatCamera

therapy, school health services, speech/language therapy, or other services needed by the student. Unfortunately, particularly for students with disabilities with higher prevalence rates (e.g., learning disabilities), some school districts fail to fully consider students' needs for related services. It is important for all teachers to understand that IDEA guarantees all students, regardless of their disabilities, needed related services (Wrightslaw, 2016).

With exceptions for very young children in some states, related services are provided at no cost to the student's family. However, in some cases costs for related services are paid for by agencies other than schools (e.g., Medicare or private insurance companies). Some medical services are considered related services. Here's a guideline to whether a medical service is also a related service: If a school nurse can provide the medical services the student needs, they are likely to be related services. If, however, the services need to be performed by a physician, they are not. The regulations to the IDEA law are clear on this issue. For example, the costs of surgically implanting devices (e.g., cochlear implants, breathing or other such devices), their maintenance, and their replacement are not to be considered a related service. However, related services that assist a child benefiting from special education services shall be provided (IDEA regulations, 34 C.F.R. §300.34 [2022]).

You have learned that at the heart of special education are the professionals who join with families to collaborate and provide multidisciplinary services and supports to students with disabilities. These teams are unique because they are individually determined and their membership reflects the individual needs of the student. These multidisciplinary teams of experts not only deliver critical services to students with disabilities and their families but also are valuable resources to teachers as they strive to meet the needs of each student. You as a teacher should always remember that these professionals are available to help you as well as your student. When everyone works together, IEP teams ensure more than the protection of basic rights guaranteed by IDEA: They orchestrate the best education possible. When each individually arranged IEP team develops partnerships, so that students' programs are coordinated, the results are remarkable, allowing individuals to overcome challenges caused by disabilities.

SUMMARY

The ADAPT Framework and MTSS (RTI and PBIS) are important ways academic and behavioral outcomes can be improved for students with disabilities and students who are at risk for learning problems. Students who are gifted and talented do not typically demonstrate issues with low performance, but many have learning characteristics that warrant specialized instructional approaches. A cornerstone of the federal laws ensuring all infants, toddlers, preschoolers, and students with disabilities a FAPE in the LRE is the individualized education created through the special education process. IDEA guarantees these individuals and their families a tailor-made education program, which is guided by uniquely created planning documents: the IFSP and the IEP. The IEP is further supported, when necessary, by BIPs and the statement of transitional services. These plans bring together multidisciplinary teams of parents, general educators, special educators, and related service providers for the purpose of helping young children and students with disabilities reach their full potential and achieve community presence and independence as adults.

REVIEW THE LEARNING OBJECTIVES

Let's review the learning objectives for this chapter. If you are uncertain and cannot talk through the answers provided for any of these questions, reread those sections of the text.

2.1 Describe how the five components of the ADAPT Framework are put into action.
Putting the ADAPT Framework into action requires the teacher to A—analyze the expectations of the task or assignment, D—determine the requirements or prerequisites of the task or assignment, A—pinpoint where the student has challenges with the assignment, P—select the instructional intervention, implement it, and T—assess its effectiveness.

2.2 Discuss the purpose of the three tiers used in the multi-tiered systems of support (MTSS) framework.
The MTSS framework combines evidence-based interventions and progress-monitoring measures for the purposes of identifying and providing necessary supports to students who have learning (i.e., RTI) or behavior difficulties (i.e., PBIS). The goal is to improve each student's academic performance or reduce or eliminate inappropriate behavior at the least intrusive level necessary before moving on to implement more successively intensive interventions. The MTSS framework targets academic, emotional, behavioral, and social outcomes for students. MTSS is a tiered approach used for both the identification of students with learning difficulties and the implementation of interventions for these students.

2.3 Explain the seven steps of the evaluation and identification process.
IDEA mandates that an individualized program be delivered to every infant, toddler, and student who is identified as having a disability and is in need of special education. The purposes of these individualized programs are to ensure that each of these individuals receives FAPE, is provided an education in the LRE, is specific to the student, and is provided services with the expectation of outstanding results. IDEA requires that these steps, at a minimum, be included in the IEP process: (1) Prereferral, (2) Referral, (3) Identification, (4) Eligibility, (5) Development of the IEP, (6) Implementation of the IEP, and (7) Evaluation and reviews.

2.4 Summarize situations that can put children at risk for poor school and life outcomes.
Many factors contribute to poor school outcomes, particularly for those attending urban schools. Disproportionately, students attending urban schools are diverse and poor (receiving free or reduced lunches), and the schools they attend are often large, old, underfunded, and lacking in modern technology, curriculum materials, and other basics that their counterparts in suburbia take for granted. Compounding these challenges is high teacher turnover rates, leaving these students with the least experienced teachers to meet their complex learning and social needs.

2.5 List the required members of individualized education program teams.
IDEA is very clear about membership in IEP teams (OSEP, 2006a). The parents, general education and special education teacher of the child, and a representative from the public agency are members of the team, along with a person who can interpret the instructional implications of evaluation results. In addition, the team can include, at the discretion of the parent or the agency, other individuals who have knowledge or expertise, such as related services professionals and, whenever possible, the child with a disability.

2.6 Identify the individualized plans for students with special learning needs: the four individualized education plans for students with disabilities and the additional statement for transition and the one for students who do not qualify for special education services.
The plan that guarantees an appropriate education to infants and toddlers (i.e., individuals from birth to age 3) is called the IFSP; the plan for preschoolers and schoolchildren is called the IEP. IEPs may have additional components, such as a transition component for students age 16 or older and a BIP for students with disabilities who violate schools' conduct codes.

Once an IEP is developed, there are three primary purposes of evaluating the student's performance:

- Evaluate the student's progress toward IEP goals.
- Evaluate the effectiveness of services or supports.
- Monitor progress.

Related services are a unique feature of special education, offering a wide range of services and expertise to students and their families. These experts facilitate the attainment of LRE and FAPE. The definition of disability is broader under Section 504 and extends beyond school age. For instance, any condition that greatly limits a major life activity, including the ability to learn in school, is defined as a disability. Students who qualify as having a disability under Section 504 but do not require special education through IDEA are assessed, and a Section 504 plan is developed and monitored. The plan includes the accommodations and adaptations chosen, the person(s) responsible for implementing the plan, and the procedures for monitoring its implementation.

2.7 Name four related services and the professionals who provides these services.
The three most commonly used related services are speech therapy (speech/language pathologist), physical therapy (physical therapist), and AT (assistive technology specialist). However, related services also include school nurses, occupational therapy, and many others.

REVISIT THE OPENING CHALLENGE

Check your answers to the Reflection Questions from the Opening Challenge and revise them on the basis of what you have learned.

1. Are Mr. Taylor and Ms. Rymes overly concerned about being able to meet their students' needs? Why or why not?
2. What advice would you give them about working with special education teachers regarding any supports and services specified in their students' individualized education programs?
3. What kind of assistance should Mr. Taylor and Ms. Rymes expect from the individualized education program team members?
4. Is Mr. Taylor justified in expressing concerns about the educational progress of Emma's classmates? Why or why not?
5. How can special education and related service professionals help Mr. Taylor and Ms. Rymes support their students' needs and enable them to teach the rest of their class?
6. How does the multi-tiered systems of support model affect instruction in these teachers' classes?
7. How can the ADAPT Framework be utilized to address the needs of students with individualized education programs in both teachers' classes as they provide an inclusive education for all their students?

KEY TERMS

504 plan
assistive technologist
at risk
audiologist
behavior intervention plan (BIP)
child find
data-based decision making
fidelity
interim alternative educational setting (IAES)
manifestation determination
multi-tiered systems of support (MTSS)
occupational therapist
physical therapist (PT)
prereferral
Positive Behavioral Interventions and Supports (PBIS)
present levels of academic achievement and functional performance (PLAAFP)
response to intervention (RTI)
self-advocacy
self-determination
service manager
speech/language pathologist (SLP)
transition component of IEPs
universal screening

PROFESSIONAL STANDARDS AND LICENSURE

CEC Initial Preparation Standards

Standard 1: Learner Development and Individual Learning Differences

Standard 2: Learning Environments

Standard 3: Curricular Content Knowledge

Standard 4: Assessment

Standard 6: Professional Learning and Ethical Practice

Standard 7: Collaboration

INTASC Core Principles

Standard 1: Learner Development

Standard 2: Learning Differences

Standard 3: Learning Environments

Standard 4: Content Knowledge

Standard 6: Assessment

Standard 7: Planning for Instruction

Standard 9: Professional Learning and Ethical Practice

Standard 10: Leadership and Collaboration

Praxis II: Education of Exceptional Students: Core Content Knowledge

I. Understanding Exceptionalities: Basic Concepts in Special Education

II. Legal and Societal Issues: Federal Laws and Legal Issues

III. Delivery of Services to Students With Disabilities: Background Knowledge

iStock.com/SDI Productions

3 DEVELOPING COLLABORATIVE PARTNERSHIPS IN SCHOOLS AND WITH FAMILIES

LEARNING OBJECTIVES

After studying this chapter, you will be able to meet the following learning objectives:

3.1 Describe the characteristics of collaboration.

3.2 Explain the critical prerequisite skills for effective collaboration.

3.3 Tell how professionals can work together collaboratively.

3.4 Describe how professionals can collaborate with paraprofessionals.

3.5 Discuss how professionals can collaborate with families.

Opening Challenge

Collaborative Partnerships to Meet the Needs of All Students

Elementary Grades. Mrs. Rojo's inclusive third-grade classroom has students with various strengths and unique learning needs or disabilities. She addresses her students' strengths and needs collaboratively with assistance from professionals, her paraprofessional, and connections to the families of her students. Mrs. Rojo is committed to providing all her students with an appropriate education that takes into consideration their needs. In her classroom she is working with several students who are struggling with reading and mathematics. These students require practices that support typical classroom instruction. She also has several students with emotional disturbance who need structured routines and management procedures so they will be ready to learn. Mrs. Rojo has several students who are English learners (ELs) and need extra instructional support in vocabulary development. (English language learners, or ELLs, are often now referred to as English learners, or ELs. For consistency we will use EL throughout.) One of her students receives services from the speech/language pathologist to correct articulation problems. Mrs. Rojo thinks about the related services providers and other individuals who work in the school community to help all students. *"How can I work collaboratively with all the people who are engaged with my students? I want to build strong partnerships with my colleagues and my students' families."* Mrs. Rojo is not alone. She finds herself in a situation that is very common. Developing and nurturing collaborative partnerships with many individuals, both families and service providers in inclusive classrooms, requires certain skills and practice. These partnerships enhance the learning of all students and build helpful connections between students' home and school environments.

Secondary Grades. Mr. Bower teaches 11th-grade English in a suburban high school. He has six classes each day with one prep period. Mr. Bower has been teaching for 19 years and has seen many changes in the services for students with disabilities. This year he has a student who uses a wheelchair because of the effects of cerebral palsy and has a tablet for accessing the literature texts required for class online. The student also has a paraprofessional who assists him with assignments so that he can keep up with the rest of the class. Mr. Bower collaborates with the paraprofessional by providing lesson plans each week; together they work with the special education teacher who visits the English class to ensure that the student is successful in the class. Mr. Bower wonders about how to work effectively with the paraprofessional besides providing lesson plans. *"I think there must be more that I can do to support the paraprofessional when she is working with my student. I don't have much time during instruction to talk to the paraprofessional. I need to talk with the special education teacher about having a three-way meeting to be sure we are all together."*

Reflection Questions

In your journal, write down your answers to the following questions. After completing the chapter, check your answers and revise them on the basis of what you have learned.

1. What professional collaborative practices can Mrs. Rojo use to help her students with special learning, behavior, and language needs succeed in the general education classroom?
2. How can Mrs. Rojo and Mr. Bower collaborate effectively with their paraprofessional?
3. How can Mrs. Rojo effectively structure parent–teacher conferences and develop home-school communication effectively?
4. What should be the focus of the three-way meeting between Mr. Bower, the special education teacher, and the paraprofessional?

We know that many students with unique learning needs or disabilities receive most, if not all, of their education in the general education classroom (see Chapter 1). Therefore, it is important to establish collaborative partnerships among professionals, paraprofessionals, and families to ensure that all students are receiving appropriate educational services in inclusive settings. (We use the term *families* to denote various family structures, such as extended families, children with guardians, single-parent families, and blended families.) **Collaborative consultation** occurs when the special education teacher or psychologist provides guidance to the inclusive teacher (Hallahan et al., 2019). It can be informal as, for example, when two professionals meet to develop a plan together to help a student with unique learning needs or disabilities, or it can be formalized through a team approach and include related service providers. Collaboration also occurs when teachers work with paraprofessionals who are important members of the educational team. Finally, educators must utilize effective practices to collaborate with families because they are the ones who know the most about the students we serve.

In this chapter, we provide information about the characteristics of collaboration and the foundation skills that are critical for establishing effective, collaborative partnerships. We also discuss models of professional collaboration and ways to develop collaborative partnerships with paraprofessionals and families. We include multicultural considerations when establishing collaborative partnerships and demonstrate how the ADAPT Framework can be used during collaborative activities.

CHARACTERISTICS OF COLLABORATION

Collaboration is a key ingredient of the efforts of inclusive schools to meet the needs of all students in different settings and activities. It is an interactive process that enables teachers with diverse expertise to provide quality services to students with a range of academic and social needs, including students with disabilities, in the general education classroom (Idol et al., 2000). For example, collaboration can occur when (a) a teacher works with parents on ways to improve their child's academic skills, (b) teachers conduct prereferral or RTI interventions to prevent inappropriate referrals to special education, (c) service providers deliver related services, (d) a bilingual instructor and a special education teacher develop a lesson plan together, (e) secondary school teachers coteach a science lesson, (f) the speech/language pathologist and general education teacher team-teach an instructional unit, or (g) general and special educators consult about a student with behavior problems. The purpose of the collaborative process is to successfully include all students in general education activities, to identify ways to adapt the content and materials, and to develop and implement specialized instruction as needed. The following characteristics of collaboration ensure that the process will be successful.

Shared Problem Solving

Shared problem solving consists of identifying, implementing, and evaluating a plan to solve a chosen problem by making decisions together. Shared problem solving can be complex because different perspectives on how to address and resolve issues often arise and must be included (Friend & Cook, 2010). The collaborative process is best accomplished when participants (a) examine the current circumstances using specific criteria (e.g., behavior, time, situational factors, achievement information, nonverbal signals, or verbal comments); (b) identify together any behaviors that are of concern (e.g., homework completion, computation problems, personnel lateness to collaboration meetings, or following through on collaboration plans); (c) specify objectives for problem solving; (d) develop an action plan, including tasks, persons responsible, and time lines; and (e) re-evaluate the plan on an ongoing basis.

Shared Responsibility

Each member of the collaborative team is equally responsible for ensuring that tasks are accomplished during the process. This usually entails dividing up the work in ways that promote parity among team members (Friend et al., 2010). For instance, one person might be responsible for observing a student who is misbehaving in class, and another team member might contact the family to talk about how the student is performing in school. During coteaching, teachers assume shared responsibility for teaching and promoting positive behavior in the classroom. Teachers also share the function of grading assignments and planning instruction.

Voluntary Involvement

Collaboration is a process that individuals should volunteer to engage in, rather than being assigned by school or district-level administration. Research findings support the idea of voluntary participation. According to Scruggs, Mastropieri, and McDuffie (2007), who integrated qualitative research on coteaching, educators believed coteaching should only be voluntary, not an assignment. However, collaboration will not naturally occur merely because someone is assigned to a team to address a situation, issue, or lesson. Ideally, individuals should be collaborating because they want to work together; however, in reality, situations will arise that warrant collaborative partnerships among people who would rather not collaborate for a variety of reasons (e.g., a team member is difficult to work with, an individual would rather "go it alone"). We can learn how to be more effective collaborators by developing important prerequisite skills to ensure effective collaborative partnerships.

CRITICAL PREREQUISITE SKILLS FOR EFFECTIVE COLLABORATION

Establishing collaborative partnerships with families, professionals, and paraprofessionals is a necessary component of effective schools. Partnership means working with people, and to do this well teachers must be prepared in those critical prerequisite skills that foster collaboration. In this section, we discuss communication skills, conflict resolution skills, and multicultural and linguistic diversity considerations that can develop a foundation on which effective collaborative relationships can be built.

Communication Skills

About 20 years ago, Heron and Harris (2000) conceptualized the communication process as consisting of a message that is encoded and transmitted and a received message that is decoded and comprehended. For this process to occur successfully, the speaker and listener must possess effective listening skills, the ability to decode (or figure out) a message, and verbal encoding skills to convey their thoughts. Communication partners have to be aware of and interpret nonverbal signals in messages they send and receive.

Listening is an important skill to develop for decoding and improving communication. It calls for more than just politely hearing what someone else is saying before you speak (Vaughn et al., 2013); it requires maintaining appropriate eye contact, acknowledging the speaker's message with verbal feedback, and maintaining appropriate nonverbal signals. Deterrents to effective listening include being preoccupied and not listening, talking more than listening, second-guessing what the speaker will say and responding inappropriately, making judgments, being distrustful, using language not appropriate to the situation (too technical, for instance, or unmindful of cultural and ethnic values and perceptions), and giving way to fatigue or strong emotions (Friend et al., 2010).

Decades ago, one of the most effective types of listening, **active listening** (Gordon, 1980) was developed as an important part of communication. Active listening is designed to engage the listener in the message being sent, to demonstrate to the speaker that the listener is interested in the message, to enable the speaker to convey specific concerns, and to provide feedback to the speaker to ensure that the message was correctly received and perceived. Active listening can be used effectively in many types of interactions and, particularly, during conversations that may be emotionally charged. Active listening it a key prerequisite communication skill to foster effective collaboration. There are six types of active listening:

1. *Acknowledging* tells the speaker you are listening and may include appropriate nonverbal signals and verbal comments.
2. *Paraphrasing* provides feedback to the speaker about the received, perceived message. The listener repeats to the speaker, in their own words, the message that was conveyed.
3. *Reflecting* tells the speaker the feelings they are verbalizing.

4. *Clarifying* asks for more specific information to help the listener better understand the message.

5. *Elaboration* asks the speaker to provide more information about an idea or about the whole message to broaden the content conveyed to the listener.

6. *Summarizing* requires the listener to reiterate the main ideas of the conversation and the actions that will be taken, if any. Summarizing gives closure to a conversation and provides feedback for all members about the key points discussed.

Communication partners also must be able to convey their message verbally or in writing so it is correctly understood. We can analyze messages conveyed verbally in terms of the way the message is being received, what nonverbal language the listener is conveying, and how the listener is signaling accurate interpretation via feedback. Video technology and social media have added another element to verbal communications with families, professionals, and paraprofessionals instead of relying on just phone calls or face-to-face meetings. Through careful self-analysis and feedback from speakers, listeners can improve their skills so that more effective communication occurs. To facilitate effective verbal communication, Idol and her colleagues (2000) recommended the following procedures:

- Before speaking, organize your thoughts to be sure that they are relevant to the conversation and can be stated succinctly.
- Demonstrate good listening behaviors (discussed earlier) to show that you are indeed interested in the speaker's message.
- Use feedback to show that you are listening and understanding the speaker's message.
- Avoid being judgmental and evaluative.
- Be aware of extraneous factors (e.g., a receiver who doesn't feel well or who has a personal crisis, a parent who may be very angry at another professional yet unconsciously projects the anger onto you, or a paraprofessional who believes that the tasks she or he is assigned are demeaning) that could interfere with the communication process.
- Avoid technical jargon that educators may use as convenient shorthand among themselves. Be specific without using acronyms that the speaker may not know.

Professionals communicate via social media such as Twitter, Instagram, e-mails, texts, blogs, newsletters, and notes. In these cases, participants must be sure that written messages are conveyed appropriately to ensure accurate interpretation. For example, written messages containing spelling or syntactical errors make it clear the writer lacks some basic skills or has not proofread their work. The auto-correct feature of some electronic communications can be helpful or harmful and does not reduce the need to proofread carefully. Jargon should be limited, and brevity is best. Long, detailed messages lose their effectiveness simply because of their complexity and because recipients lack time to read them thoroughly.

Finally, written communication should include a signature, date, and request for a response. Reserve face-to-face or video technology for messages that could be misinterpreted or require opportunities for discussion and questions. Following are a few etiquette tips for various types of written communication:

- Respond to e-mails received during business days within 24 hours, if possible.
- Answer e-mails using the original thread. Avoid using "reply all" unless the response really needs to go back to everyone in the message.
- Even in a private text or e-mail, write only what is appropriate for multiple readers, given that electronic communication can be forwarded to others.

- Be concise.
- Edit for grammar and spelling errors.
- Avoid educational jargon and acronyms when communicating with families.
- Use punctuation and capitalization correctly.

Nonverbal communication is another aspect of communication that requires careful analysis to ensure that the speaker sends appropriate signals and that the listener understands the intended message. Nonverbal communication includes facial expressions, body posturing and movement, use of space, and touch. Nonverbal messages are a powerful form of communication because they tend to be genuine, and they may be more easily conveyed than verbal messages that are emotionally laden.

There are several types of nonverbal communication. For example, facial expressions can be very informative about feelings, trust, and level of disdain or interest. Elevated eyebrows, lack of or regular eye contact, smiles, and frowns convey specific messages to speakers. Facing the speaker, crossing your arms, and sitting in a relaxed position all convey subliminal messages. Touch is a form of communication that needs to be monitored carefully. Some people prefer that speakers or listeners not touch their arms or hug them, for instance (Eaves & Leathers, 2017).

The way we communicate with each other can enhance or impede successful collaborative partnerships. When working in diverse settings, individuals should take into consideration cultural and linguistic factors that are part of the communication process. For example, an interpreter should be available if family members do not speak or understand English. In some cultures, body posture such as nodding your head, smiling, and leaning forward convey openness, interest, and attentive listening. Teachers should learn about the values, perceptions, and culture of communication partners; this is especially true when working with families from diverse cultures. This information can go a long way in enhancing communication and establishing trust on which to build a collaborative partnership. Regardless of how hard we might try to be good communicators, conflict may arise. Thus, conflict resolution skills are another important prerequisite for collaboration. We now turn our attention to this critical area.

Conflict Resolution Skills

Professionals, paraprofessionals, and families are often faced with complex problems—such as the student's need for a paraprofessional or assistive technology—that require careful consideration to help children. Sometimes, issues arise that can lead to conflict. This conflict must be resolved so the partners can move forward with their plans.

Conflict is defined as a disagreement of interests or ideas. In a collaborative relationship, conflict may stem from differences in opinions about strategies, facts, perspectives, or values. Conflict may arise from any of the following situations:

- People perceive that they are forced into situations (e.g., working together, having students with disabilities in their classrooms full time, or implementing a strategy for which no training occurred).
- Roles (e.g., special education teacher as consultant) are not clearly defined.
- Philosophies (e.g., humanistic, disciplinarian) clash.
- Levels of expertise and professional development do not match the demands of the situation (e.g., first-year teacher asked to chair a committee).
- Interpersonal styles (e.g., introvert, extrovert, direct, indirect) vary significantly.
- People are resistant to change (e.g., issues of territory, power, and interest arise in trying new research-based ideas). (Heron & Harris, 2000)

For example, two professionals may be working on a plan they jointly developed for a student; however, one member falls short in completing their agreed-on tasks. Conflict could easily arise because the plan for the student is not being fully implemented. This issue would need to be addressed in a constructive manner that would aid progress toward implementing the plan. Because conflict is inevitable even in the best of circumstances, conflict resolution skills are helpful. Following are helpful guidelines for conflict resolution:

- Do not expect the conflict to go away; it may diminish, but if problems and feelings are not discussed, they will emerge again at another time.
- Confront conflict when it occurs by stating your feelings using an "I-message" (refer to Chapter 10 for more information about I-messages). For example, "I'm feeling uncomfortable with this situation," or "I'm sensing that maybe we're not on the same wavelength." In essence, this is a reality check—an effort to determine whether your perceptions are accurate. If not, then promptly discussing the situation as you perceive it could prevent further misperceptions and possible problems.
- Avoid being judgmental or accusatory: "You're not listening," "You're late again," "That idea didn't work the last time and won't work this time."
- Use self-disclosure if appropriate: "I'm feeling really unsure about how to handle this problem and could use some assistance."
- Maintain open, ongoing communication even if it is just notes to other members. A major source of conflict is lack of communication between partners and the perception (or observation) that one person is moving ahead without talking the plan through with others.
- Use active listening: send I-messages, paraphrase, summarize, and clarify. These techniques can go a long way in developing a better understanding of how members feel and how they perceive situations.
- Discuss conflict at a time when members are not pressed to return to their classroom and are not in the midst of a situation that might interfere with the process of conflict resolution. Timing is an important consideration.
- Use problem-solving steps to reach consensus and identify a plan of action. This helps members to focus on a procedure that promotes communication, discussion, and resolution.
- Recognize that sometimes conflict might not be resolved and that partnerships could be terminated temporarily. Many reasons (including lack of interest, power, insecurity, bad timing, mistrust, and inability to establish congruent objectives) account for the inability of members to resolve conflict. Focus on letting go and finding an alternative, productive way to handle the situation if further action is required.

TECH NOTES

STUDENT RESPONSE SYSTEMS

Student response systems are educational tools that allow teachers to monitor their students' learning in real time using interactive software to promote communication regarding students' understanding of instruction. Teachers can ask questions to check for student understanding and determine possible difficulties with the material. Using PowerPoint presentations, teachers generate questions about the content and students respond to interactive questions with devices such as "classroom clickers." The students' responses are displayed in the PowerPoint presentation in a graphical form for discussion; some students may need to rethink their answers. Teachers can monitor students' understanding about the content and adjust their instruction accordingly based on the students' responses.

Multicultural and Linguistic Diversity Considerations

Culture permeates all of society and all interactions. Each of us belongs to a cultural group that is distinguishable by its customs, traditions, beliefs, foods, and dress, as well as by a specific ethnicity, religious affiliation, or racial background. Thus, educators must be aware of their own cultural values, the way they have been socialized professionally, and the cultural values of their collaborative partners. Cultural awareness can help promote collaboration among professionals.

HOW PROFESSIONALS CAN WORK TOGETHER COLLABORATIVELY

Many professionals, such as general and special education teachers; school psychologists; counselors; social workers; administrators; and speech/language, physical, or occupational therapists, are part of the school community that is responsible for working together to provide a quality education for all students. In Chapter 2 you read about related services and the professionals who provide them. For example, speech/language pathologists provide services for the prevention and treatment of communication disorders. In this section, we talk about the need for collaborative professional partnerships and models of collaboration that promote inclusive practices.

The Need for Collaborative Partnerships With Professionals

As you know from Chapter 1, the Individuals with Disabilities Education Improvement Act of 2004 (IDEA) requires that students with disabilities be educated to the greatest extent possible in the general education setting. Moreover, general education teachers are required to be part of the IEP team and are responsible for implementing the adaptations identified on the IEP to help students access and master the curriculum. Professionals must work together when educating all students in inclusive classrooms. Collaborative models are used in classrooms across the nation where educators are

Collaborative consultation is an interactive process that enables groups of people with diverse expertise to generate creative solutions to mutually defined problems.

JOHN BIRDSALL SOCIAL ISSUES PHOTO LIBRARY / Science Source

working together to ensure that all students can access the general education curriculum. Next, we will discuss collaboration models.

Models of Collaborative Partnerships With Professionals

There are several models of collaborative partnerships with professionals to help students with unique learning needs or disabilities function more successfully in the general education classroom. We provide an overview of two models: collaboration–consultation and coteaching.

Collaboration–Consultation

The collaboration–consultation model focuses on the partnership between the general education and special education teachers, tapping the expertise of both to provide appropriate services to students. In the collaboration–consultation model, collaboration includes planning, implementing, and evaluating student programs wherein teachers work together to meet the needs of all students. The teachers develop plans that are typically implemented by general education teachers with ongoing support from the special education teacher. The expertise of both professionals, then, is applied in creating and evaluating plans. The plans could be part of prereferral activities to prevent academic problems or could be developed to address the academic, behavioral, or social skills of students in inclusive classrooms.

Idol and colleagues (2000) identified six stages of the collaboration–consultation process.

Stage 1: Gaining Entry and Establishing Team Goals. This stage consists of establishing rapport between or among participants and identifying specifically each member's goals, agenda, and outcomes for the collaborative process. Here it is important to ensure that each participant is clear about what they would like to see occur during the collaborative process and to identify what each member is capable of contributing to the partnership in terms of time, expertise, and commitment.

Stage 2: Problem Identification. In this stage, participants engage in assessment practices (see Chapter 9 for information about assessment techniques) to identify the student's current level of academic performance, behavioral considerations, and affective/emotional status. Assessment data might be obtained from previously administered measures and behavioral rating scales, teacher observation, or current informal assessment measures. On the basis of available data, the participants develop a profile of the student's strengths and weaknesses and identify specific problems that could account for academic and/or behavior problems.

Stage 3: Intervention Recommendations. Specific interventions are recommended for the problem(s) identified in Stage 2. An important aspect of this stage is identifying interventions that teachers can implement easily and that accommodate the unique learning needs of the student. Other students for whom the intervention(s) may be appropriate and effective could be identified during this stage as well.

Stage 4: Implementation of Recommendations. At this point, the intervention is implemented for the targeted problem. The special education teacher might be asked to model the intervention or provide feedback to the classroom teacher about the implementation process. The general education teacher could model an intervention for the special education teacher to learn, or both teachers might work together to implement a behavior management plan. There is room for flexibility in the way interventions are implemented and the way participants in the collaborative process work together to facilitate the plan's success.

Stage 5: Evaluation. Monitoring student progress to determine the effectiveness of the intervention(s) is extremely important. Classroom teachers can administer evaluation measures that help participants in the collaborative process determine whether the intervention is effective.

WORKING TOGETHER

AN EXAMPLE OF THE COLLABORATION-CONSULTATION PROCESS

Mrs. Rojo is concerned about how Jorge is progressing in developing oral reading fluency compared with the other students in her general education class. She has tried working individually with Jorge to practice reading, but she doesn't have enough time during the school day to meet his needs. Mrs. Rojo has collected and graphed data on Jorge's oral reading weekly for six weeks, and it is clear that he is not benefiting from instruction. She decides to initiate the collaboration–consultation process with Mr. Santos, the special education teacher, to identify the next steps to take. Chapter 8 offers suggestions for data-based decision making, which is what Mrs. Rojo and Mr. Santos are incorporating into the collaboration–consultation process.

Stage 1: The teachers agree to develop a plan for Mrs. Rojo to implement in the general education classroom to improve Jorge's oral reading performance. Mrs. Rojo says she needs an intervention that won't take too much more of her time because she is already working with Jorge and a few other students in a small group to improve their reading.

Stage 2: Mrs. Rojo shares Jorge's reading data. She and Mr. Santos agree that Jorge is not responding sufficiently to small-group reading instruction and that he needs an additional intervention to improve his reading fluency. The graphed data show the number of words Jorge correctly read each week, but his improvement is too slow for him to catch up to his classmates by the end of the school year. Mrs. Rojo also decides to share the reading data with Jorge's parents so they are aware of his progress and the need for an intervention.

Stage 3: Mr. Santos and Mrs. Rojo discuss the possibility of taped assisted reading for Jorge. This intervention consists of taping reading passages and having Jorge practice the reading passages several times each day before he works in a small group with the teacher. Mrs. Rojo agrees to have her paraprofessional tape-record the passages, while she continues to collect weekly data on Jorge's reading performance. The taped reading practice along with the small group instruction are noted as a means of differentiating instruction in Tier 1 or core instruction for all students.

Stage 4: Mr. Santos models for Mrs. Rojo and Jorge how to implement the tape-assisted reading practice. Mrs. Rojo continues the implementation process each day for four weeks. She has her paraprofessional oversee the process.

Stage 5: Data collection occurs, which in this case means recording the number of words read correctly during a one-minute timing each week. Mrs. Rojo collects the data to share at the follow-up meeting with Mr. Santos.

Stage 6: Mrs. Rojo, her paraprofessional, and Mr. Santos meet four weeks after the intervention began to review the data. At this time, they decide that Jorge's reading performance is much stronger with the tape-assisted intervention. They agree to continue the intervention and meet again in another four weeks. If the data do not continue to show adequate improvement, they agree they will reconvene sooner.

Follow-up: Essential to an effective collaborative partnership for promoting student success are regularly scheduled meetings of participants to determine whether the intervention is effective and to identify additional potential problem areas that could be addressed during the collaborative process. During Stage 1 participants should commit to meeting times that are convenient to all for discussing student progress. For the collaboration–consultation model to be successful, professionals should work together to identify solutions for students who are having academic, social, and emotional difficulties.

Questions

1. What is the purpose of each stage?
2. What planning is necessary for this partnership to work effectively to support Jorge?
3. Why is data collection an integral part of the process?

Coteaching Model

Marilyn Friend (2006), one of the leading authorities on educational collaboration, defined coteaching as follows:

> A service delivery model in which two educators, one typically a general education teacher and one a special education teacher or another specialist, combine their expertise to jointly teach a heterogeneous group of students, some of whom have disabilities or other special needs, in a single classroom for part or all of the school day. (p. 140)

Both professionals take part in planning, teaching, and evaluating student performance. For instance, a coteaching situation could consist of a speech/language pathologist and a special education teacher where the language expertise of the speech/language pathologist could be combined with the special education teacher's expertise in instructional content to produce a lesson rich in language and content development. Or the special education and general education teachers could work collaboratively to plan, coteach, and evaluate a lesson presented in the general education classroom.

In a coteaching classroom, both teachers take part in planning, teaching, and evaluating student performance.

© Jessica Miller/SAGE

INSTRUCTIONAL STRATEGY 3.1

COTEACHING APPROACHES

The following coteaching approaches can be found in general education classrooms:

One Teaches, One Observes. One teacher leads the class in a lesson, and the other professional (e.g., school psychologist, special education teacher, or counselor) collects academic, behavioral, or social data for a student or the class. The coteachers should change roles periodically so that students recognize the important contributions made by both teachers.

Station Teaching. Three stations are created for small group student rotation. Two teachers teach parts of a lesson in their respective stations. The third station is for students to work independently. Students rotate among the three stations during a designated instructional block of time. Because students are moving from station to station during class, teachers must be able to manage this activity.

Parallel Teaching. Two teachers each instruct half the class on the same material. Student composition of each half is carefully considered. Instruction is differentiated depending on the needs of students in each group. A smaller group increases student participation opportunities. A challenge teachers face with parallel teaching involves space. As you can imagine, when two people are talking at the same time, in this case delivering instruction, students can get distracted or confused. A way to work through this is to have one teacher work with their students while the other teacher has the students work independently; thus, only one teacher is speaking at a time.

Alternative Teaching. One teacher is responsible for teaching the whole class. The other teacher takes a small group for enrichment, remediation, or assessment. In some instances, students who work in small groups could feel like they are being singled out by working with the special education teacher. A way to deal with this is to have teachers alternate between working with the larger group and the smaller group.

Teaming. Two teachers lead whole class instruction by lecturing, debating, or individualizing for specific students' needs. A challenge presented with teaming, and perhaps with all of the approaches, is that both teachers must be content experts, with a thorough understanding not only of the material to be presented, but also of the special vocabulary that accompanies the content. A way to help with this issue is to have both teachers attend content professional development sessions and compare notes during and after the sessions.

One Teaches, One Assists. One teacher leads the lesson and the other teacher circulates to work with individual students as needed. To help with this process, have the students use sticky notes to write their questions and place the notes on the corner of the desk. In this way, the teacher assisting can know right away what the problem is.

For more information about coteaching groups, examine the approaches described by Andrea Honigsfield and Maria Dove (2010). These experts in coteaching describe and provide examples of their seven models of coteaching (see the References section for a link to their work).

Tech Notes illustrates how teachers in a coteaching model of "One Teaches, One Observes" can use real time to monitor students' understanding of the class material.

Coteaching is based on specific underlying assumptions about teaching and professionals' expertise. One assumption is that the coteaching team can bring to the classroom combined knowledge and expertise, which will greatly enhance instruction. Another is that team members can meet individual students' needs more effectively than one teacher.

There are many variations of coteaching partnerships, including teaming for one instructional period or block of time, teaming for the entire day, and assigning a special education and general education team to one class all year long (Villa et al., 2008). Coteaching for one instructional period, especially at the middle and high school levels, is most common. Also, coteachers may involve general education teachers, special education teachers, counselors, bilingual/EL teachers, and speech/language pathologists. The IEP team determines the coteaching members, the instructional content to be taught, and the student's academic, behavioral, and social needs the coteaching members will address.

We provide two examples for applying the use of coteaching models. An example of how some of these coteaching approaches might work is presented in the ADAPT Framework feature below. Refer to Mrs. Rojo's opening challenge to see how she could use station and alternative teaching to provide additional support in her classroom. In ADAPT in Action, Mrs. Rojo uses the ADAPT Framework for planning station and alternative teaching time.

ADAPT IN ACTION

MRS. ROJO USES STATION AND ALTERNATIVE TEACHING TECHNIQUES

A: Ask, "What am I requiring the student to do?" Students must be able to complete mathematics assignments independently in stations.

D: Determine the prerequisite skills of the task. Students must be able to perform the work independently. They need to be able to read word problems and complete them correctly using the steps for word problem solving.

A: Analyze the student's strengths and struggles. The student can attend to the task and work well with others in small groups during station time. The student has difficulty with reading the word problems and does not know the steps for solving the problems.

P: Propose and implement adaptations from among the four categories. During station time, pair the student with a stronger reader who can help read the word problems. Use alternative teaching where the special education teacher can teach the problem-solving steps for word problems.

T: Test to determine whether the adaptations helped the student accomplish the task. The student's work will be assessed for accuracy and completion of the task.

Teachers must explain what they hope to gain from a team effort instructionally and for students. Such disclosure can promote effective communication right from the start of a teaming relationship. Fourth, team members should convey to students the teachers' roles and explain how instruction and discipline will be handled in the classroom. Both teachers should maintain a similar level of authority when working with students. Finally, teachers need to meet regularly to work through problems, evaluate student progress, communicate with families, and plan further instruction. The Working Together feature provides examples for building and implementing the coteaching partnership.

ADAPT Framework: Station and Alternative Teaching

A ASK "What am I requiring the student to do?"	D DETERMINE the prerequisite skills of the task.	A ANALYZE the student's strengths and struggles. Strengths	Struggles	P PROPOSE and implement adaptations from among the four categories.	T TEST to determine if the adaptations helped the student accomplish the task.
Students must possess mathematics skills to work independently and successfully in stations.	**1.** Attend to and perform activities in the independent station.	1			
	2. Read word problems in the station to complete the tasks independently.		2	**2.** Instructional delivery: During station teaching, pair the student with a stronger reader to help read the word problems without teacher help.	**2.** Examine the finished product to determine student performance.

(Continued)

ADAPT Framework: Station and Alternative Teaching (*Continued*)

A ASK "What am I requiring the student to do?"	D DETERMINE the prerequisite skills of the task.	A ANALYZE the student's strengths and struggles. Strengths	 Struggles	P PROPOSE and implement adaptations from among the four categories.	T TEST to determine if the adaptations helped the student accomplish the task.
	3. Know the steps for solving word problems.		3	**3.** Instructional delivery: Use alternative teaching by having the special education teacher provide small group instruction on word problem solving strategies. Ms. Warren will work with the rest of the group to provide additional problem-solving activities.	**3.** Provide word problems for small group instruction. Assess accuracy.
	4. Work well with other students in the independent small group.	4			

Research on collaborative models suggests that teachers note many positive effects of working together. For example, in a 3-year study of effective coteaching teams, Chriss Walther-Thomas (1997) found that general education and special education teachers reported increases in the following:

1. Academic and social gains for students with disabilities
2. Opportunities for professional growth
3. Professional satisfaction
4. Personal support

WORKING TOGETHER

COTEACHING

Mr. Sanchez and Mrs. Voress will use coteaching as a way to provide more support for students with unique learning needs or disabilities in Mr. Sanchez's class. Teaming can help them address the academic needs of students with learning disabilities and of other students who have similar academic difficulties. They decide to proceed by working through the following steps:

1. Establish a coteaching partnership.
   - Identify goals and expectations of the partnership.
   - Share beliefs and values about teaching, discipline, and expectations of students for learning.

- Identify how the partnership will be communicated to parents and the principal.
- Designate a workspace within the classroom for each teacher.
- Identify roles and responsibilities. Here are possible questions to consider:
  - How will discipline be handled?
  - Whose materials will we use to teach lessons?
  - How will we manage progress monitoring and grading?
  - How will we coordinate team instruction?

2. Identify students' needs.
   - Identify each student's strengths and weaknesses.
   - Discuss IEPs for any students that have one.
   - Consider adaptations needed for each student to benefit from instruction.
3. Develop an instructional plan.
   - Find time to plan. Try to set aside at least 45 minutes a week to coplan. Inadequate time for planning is the most frequently cited issue in coteaching. Work with your principal to establish time.
   - Identify a classroom and behavior management system together.
   - Identify student groupings. Group students on the basis of the specific goals and purpose of a lesson and/or the needs of the students. Balance homogeneous grouping with other grouping formats to implement flexible grouping.
   - Select a coteaching model to suit the instructional purpose and students' needs.
   - Develop a plan.
4. Monitor student performance together.
   - Become familiar with standards and accountability for all students.
   - Measure student progress regularly.
   - Develop a record-keeping system.
   - Make instructional-based decisions.
   - Discuss and assign grades together.
   - Conduct teacher–parent conferences together whenever possible.

Questions

1. How can teachers plan for coteaching to occur in inclusive classrooms?
2. What concerns might each of the teachers have about coteaching?
3. How can students benefit from coteaching?

Other studies have shown that special education teachers have felt subordinate to the general education teacher and that time for planning was an issue (Murray, 2004). Careful planning, communication about roles and philosophies, and regular meetings are important. Years ago, Weiss and Lloyd (2002) conducted one of the earliest studies to examine coteaching at the secondary level. These researchers wanted to determine whether it is possible for students with disabilities to receive the specialized education they need with coteaching. They noted that building principals are responsible for ensuring that enough resources, time, and training are provided for coteaching to be successful. Finally, Scruggs and colleagues (2007) conducted a review of literature on coteaching research and concluded that teachers and administrators across the studies strongly supported coteaching, but few of them observed practices that reflected collaborative models advocated by coteaching experts. Scruggs et al. also noted that more research is needed to assess the effects of coteaching on achievement outcomes of students with disabilities.

Collaboration Considerations for English Learners

Early intervention should occur for students who are ELs experiencing learning problems in the general education classroom. Once learning problems are identified, teachers can implement strategies to address special learning needs. Classroom teachers should collaborate with bilingual specialists who can provide assistance on effective instructional practices for ELs (see Table 3.1). Practices can build on the idea of prereferral interventions. These practices include the clinical teaching cycle, peer or expert consultation, the teacher assistance team process, and alternative programs and services for early

TABLE 3.1 ■ Intervention Strategies and Collaborative Partnerships for English Learners

Issue	Strategy
Student experiences difficulty: Implement clinical teaching cycle.	Clinical teaching cycle • Teach skill or content. • Reteach using different strategies if student experiences difficulty. • Conduct informal assessments to identify difficulties. • Adapt instruction based on assessment results. • Monitor student response to instruction regularly.
Problem persists: Request assistance from teacher assistance team.	Teacher assistance team process • The teacher requests assistance from the team. • The team leader reviews the request and obtains additional information if necessary. • The leader arranges a classroom observation. • A team meeting is held. • The team designs an intervention plan. • The teacher implements the plan with assistance as appropriate. • A follow-up team meeting is held to determine student progress. • If the problem continues, the process is repeated.
Problem persists: Refer student to alternative general education programs and services.	Alternative general education programs and services • Use one-to-one tutoring. • Use cross-age tutoring. • Use remedial programs. • Use student and family support groups. • Use family counseling.

Source: Garcia (2002).

intervention for struggling students. For example, the **clinical teaching cycle** entails sequenced instruction, reteaching if necessary, and informal assessment procedures, including assessment of academic and conversational language proficiency. **Peer or expert consultation** can include teachers observing their peers and providing interventions to ELs who need supplemental instruction. Support can also be provided in consultation with an ESL teacher who can furnish information on how to integrate ESL strategies into academic instruction. The **teacher assistance team process** is another option to assist teachers in providing appropriate instruction for ELs. In this model, Ortiz (2002) described a collaborative team approach that discusses the problem, identifies possible interventions, and assists the teacher as needed in implementing strategies.

Next, we discuss developing collaborative partnerships with paraprofessionals. These individuals are critical players in addressing the needs of students with unique learning needs or disabilities, especially students with severe disabilities.

HOW PROFESSIONALS CAN COLLABORATE WITH PARAPROFESSIONALS

Paraprofessionals, or paraeducators, are individuals who work with teachers in a supportive role under the supervision of licensed professionals (IDEA, 2004). Their titles vary across schools and districts; paraprofessionals may be called paraeducators, nonteaching assistants, classroom assistants, teaching assistants, or special support assistants, among other titles. Whatever their title, they are members of the instructional team in classrooms and other educational settings, and they often provide direct services to students and their families.

At one time paraprofessionals spent most of their time performing clerical duties; monitoring the halls, playground, and cafeteria; and supervising students who were being disciplined for behavior problems. However, their role has evolved with increased awareness of the valuable contributions they can make in diverse and inclusive educational settings. Paraeducators are increasingly being relied on to provide special education services to students with more severe disabilities. For example, paraeducators might be responsible for the daily needs, care, mobility support, and behavior support for students with severe disabilities (Gerlach, 2014). In many cases, paraprofessionals can bridge linguistic and cultural connections between the school and the community (Chopra et al., 2004). Thus, they can make connections between their schools and the families and community affiliated with their schools. Preparation for paraprofessional includes the following:

- complete two years of study at an institution of higher education;
- obtain an associate's (or higher) degree; or
- demonstrate, through a formal state or local assessment, knowledge of, and ability to assist in, reading, writing, and mathematics instruction.

These criteria aside, researchers have noted that paraeducators' role has become one of serving a more diverse student population and supporting the inclusion of students with significant disabilities in the general education classroom (Bernal & Aragon, 2004).

Paraprofessionals account for more than half of the nonteaching staff who provide services to students with unique learning needs or disabilities (White, 2004). Today, the demand for paraprofessionals continues as an increasing number of students with disabilities receive their instruction in general education settings and sometimes require services beyond those that general educators can reasonably provide. Additionally, paraprofessionals are needed to help implement community-based instruction for students with more severe disabilities. They may accompany students on public

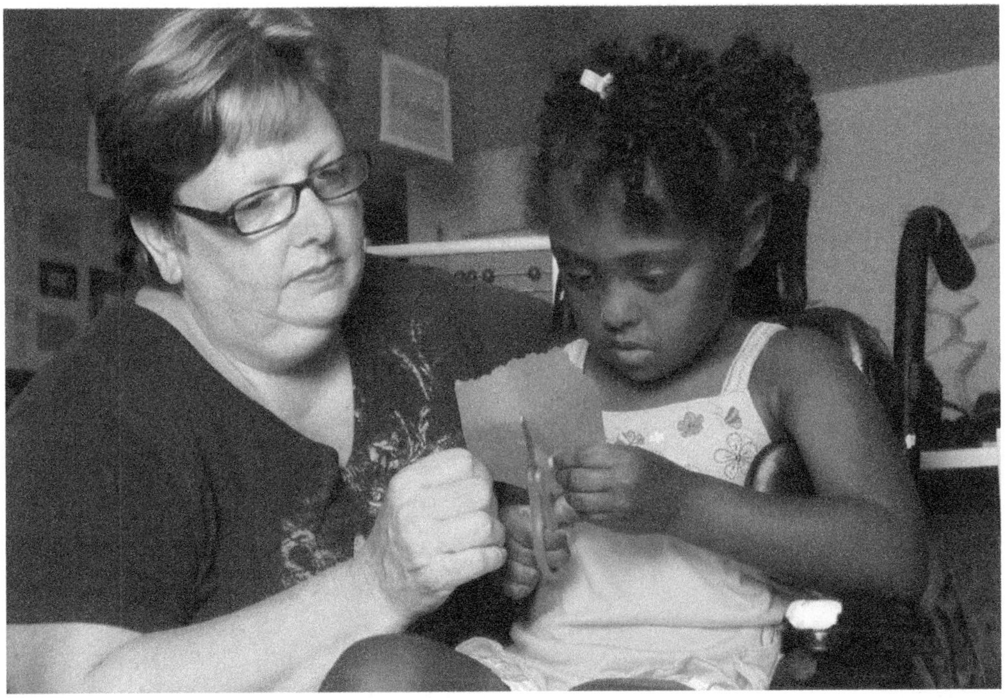

Paraprofessionals account for more than half of the nonteaching staff that provide services to students with unique learning needs or disabilities.

iStock/ktaylorg

transportation to get to the students' job sites, assist students with disabilities in their job-site tasks, and participate with students and teachers in community activities designed to promote recreational and social skills.

Yet Giangreco and Doyle (2007) noted, "At present, there is no international consensus about the extent to which teacher assistants [paraeducators] should be utilized, circumstances that warrant their involvement, the duties they should appropriately perform, or what constitutes adequate training and supervision" (p. 437). Thus, as options expand for providing services and effective instruction to students with unique learning needs or disabilities, the need remains to establish roles and responsibilities for paraprofessionals. Educators must also provide supervision and training. The next two sections address these areas.

Roles and Responsibilities of Paraprofessionals in Collaborative Partnerships

According to IDEA (2004), teachers are responsible for ensuring the delivery of services specified in the IEP. However, paraprofessionals have an important role to play in supporting the delivery of these services. Communication about roles and responsibilities helps everyone understand the expectations when providing services to students and their families. Clear job descriptions that specify roles and responsibilities can facilitate communication between teachers and paraprofessionals. Typically, job descriptions include a definition of the job, general responsibilities, and specific hiring requirements (e.g., amount of education, contractual duty day, and length of school year). The job description usually provides information that school district administrative personnel believe is important for particular roles; teachers and paraprofessionals must abide by the established job guidelines (Gerlach, 2014).

Once job descriptions have been reviewed, teachers and paraprofessionals can work together to delineate specific roles and responsibilities. For example, roles might include instruction, administration, behavior management, assessment, and communication with families and other professionals. Together, teachers and paraprofessionals can develop a responsibilities list for each role and identify areas for training, philosophical discussion, and further explanation. Teachers have the responsibility for developing, implementing, and evaluating their students' IEPs and for protecting the safety and well-being of the students. However, paraprofessionals can greatly assist in a collaborative way to support these responsibilities (Gerlach, 2014). The following include examples of effective practices and responsibilities for working with paraprofessionals that tap their expertise when working with students:

1. Assessment
   - Conducting curriculum-based assessments
   - Scoring curriculum-based assessments
2. Behavior Management
   - Implementing behavior management programs designed with the classroom teacher
   - Awarding points to students for appropriate behavior
   - Monitoring of behavior in small or whole groups
3. Instruction
   - Providing instructional adaptations for lessons taught by teachers
   - Monitoring student work in learning centers
   - Providing small group instruction to students who require more assistance
4. Communication
   - Serving as a link between special education and general education teachers
   - Meeting regularly with the classroom teacher to discuss specific student needs, instructional programs, successes, and concerns
   - Facilitating communication with parents for whom English is not their primary language
5. Clerical Support
   - Conducting tasks to maintain classroom organization and management
   - Developing instructional materials

TABLE 3.2 ■ Barriers and Solutions for Collaborative Partnerships with Paraeducators

Barriers	Solutions
Lack of time	Set aside 30 minutes before or after school several days a week to discuss students' progress.
Differing roles and responsibilities	Discuss roles and responsibilities clearly so each person knows his or her duties.
Differing years of experience	Tap the expertise of paraeducators who have been working at the school longer than the teacher, and help build the self-confidence of new paraeducators.

6. Student Support
   - Working with students in community job–related settings
   - Escorting students during hallway, recess, and lunch activities
7. Professionalism
   - Attending professional meetings with teachers or with other paraprofessionals

Often the paraprofessional is older than the teacher and has been at the school longer; they might also have strong community connections with families, businesses, and children. These dynamics in the relationship between them must be respected; however, they should not undermine the role of the teacher as supervisor and as the person contractually responsible for the education of the students. Teachers must be knowledgeable about and responsive to the cultural differences of their paraprofessionals to ensure effective communication and respect. Through effective communication techniques, teachers can tap the valuable knowledge paraprofessionals possess through their connections with the school and community. Teachers should also be sensitive to the needs of younger paraprofessionals who may lack experience and educational expertise. Table 3.2 provides examples of possible barriers to the development of collaborative partnerships with paraeducators and solutions for removing the barriers.

Supervision and Training of Paraprofessionals

Teachers are typically responsible for supervising and evaluating paraprofessionals with whom they work. In some cases, principals share in the supervisory and evaluative process, but usually teachers assume the greater part of this responsibility.

Ongoing communication is vital to any supervisory situation. Paraprofessionals, like any employee, should be given opportunities to work with their supervisors in choosing how they will be supervised and evaluated. At a minimum, weekly meetings are recommended to review the paraprofessionals' tasks and job performance. Paraprofessionals should be given feedback about their performance, both positive and negative, on a regular basis.

Teachers should examine their supervisory style to ensure they implement practices that foster collegial relationships. An authoritarian style will not promote a spirit of collaboration, but a sharing, direct approach, in which the teacher and paraprofessional have an equal opportunity to reflect on situations, can facilitate a collaborative partnership. Teachers can ask the following questions to promote communication and build a collaborative partnership:

- How do you think we are doing working together as a team?
- What can we do to make our team stronger, to help students more, or to work better with each other?
- What would you like to discuss with me about how our teaming is working?
- What is important to you to make our teaming work well?
- How would you describe our team to others?
- What advice would you offer to another teacher–paraprofessional team just beginning together?

Experienced paraprofessionals contribute important information to relationships between themselves and teachers. For example, Riggs (2005) presented a list of what paraprofessionals identified as important tasks for beginning teachers:

- Know the paraprofessional's name, background, and interests.
- Know about district policies for paraprofessionals.
- View the paraprofessional as a member of the professional team.
- Define roles and responsibilities.
- Supervise the paraprofessional.
- Communicate with the paraprofessional.
- Acknowledge the paraprofessional's experience and knowledge.
- Be respectful of paraprofessionals.
- Assume "ownership" of all students.

Teacher training in effective supervisory practices and evaluation criteria makes it easier to serve in the role of supervisor and evaluator. If training is not available, teachers should seek assistance from their building principal and special education coordinators to identify ways to become an effective supervisor and to conduct employee evaluations. Often, school districts have career ladders for paraprofessionals in which promotion depends on positive evaluations. Therefore, it is in everyone's best interest for teachers to learn about (a) evaluation criteria, (b) ways to conduct an evaluation (e.g., providing feedback, stating strengths and weaknesses, encouraging problem solving and conflict resolution), and (c) techniques to foster professional development in areas where improvement is needed.

Training for paraprofessionals is a critical element of effective supervisory practices. School district human resources offices could team with teachers to identify specific areas in which paraprofessionals might benefit from in-service training. Paraprofessionals may have effective interpersonal skills and a caring attitude but need to acquire skills specific to the students with whom they are working. Many paraprofessionals may be working for the first time with children who have disabilities. These paraprofessionals may not possess the skills necessary to meet individual students' educational, health, medical, and/or language needs. Training options should be available where teachers can instruct paraprofessionals in their classrooms as they work with children. In-service training opportunities should be offered for paraprofessionals. We now turn to collaborative partnerships with families.

HOW PROFESSIONALS CAN COLLABORATE WITH FAMILIES

Families are an integral part of the school community and have been significant contributors to the establishment of special education as a field. Parents know their children better than anyone and can provide critical information that can help teachers understand the students' individual needs. For years, families have been critical to the establishment of special education services by forming organizations, initiating litigation, pushing for legislation, and demanding a free appropriate public education in the least restrictive environment for all students with disabilities. They have clout, and they know their children. Collaboration with them is indispensable. Parental influence continues to this day as educational reform at the elementary and secondary level (e.g., the Every Student Succeeds Act [ESSA] of 2015 and the IDEA of 2004) influences the modification and/or creation of service delivery options for students with unique learning needs or disabilities. In this section, we talk about the importance of developing collaborative partnerships with families and about circumstances in which this collaboration can be promoted. Table 3.3 identifies potential barriers and solutions for collaborative partnerships with families.

TABLE 3.3 ■ Potential Barriers and Solutions for Collaborative Partnerships with Families

Barriers	Solutions
Lack of time	Meet with parents at times that are mutually agreeable. This might necessitate early morning, late afternoon, or evening meetings to accommodate busy work schedules.
Language differences	Have an interpreter present during meetings for parents who do not speak English. Be sure written communication is in the parents' primary language.
Professional jargon	Avoid technical terms and acronyms that might be unfamiliar and confusing to parents.

The Need for Collaborative Partnerships With Families

Collaboration with families should be a major goal of all schools. However, for collaboration to be achieved educators must better understand families. As Pugach and Johnson (1995) noted, we must acknowledge the powerful effect families have on the students with whom we work. Nurturing a collaborative relationship with families and family members is imperative. Like all students, students with unique learning needs or disabilities cannot be viewed in isolation; therefore, we must come to know our students' families; only then can we develop effective collaborative partnerships using the collaboration models discussed below.

Models of Collaborative Partnerships With Families

Teachers can foster successful partnerships with families by employing the prerequisite skills discussed earlier in this chapter. The **family systems approach** is a technique for focusing on school–home relationships within a framework that is responsive to families' needs. We offer tips for working with families from diverse backgrounds, and we suggest ways to encourage successful collaborative parent–teacher conferences and home–school communication.

Family Systems Approach

Collaborative efforts with students' families can be developed through A family systems approach can be utilized to define resources, interactions, and the life cycle (Turnbull et al., 2016). Families may have specific issues such as reactions to a family member with a disability, economic needs, and future planning. Collaborative efforts can be greatly enhanced between home and school if teachers are aware of the (a) family unit (e.g., one- or two-parent family, extended family); (b) resources families need to function with a child with disabilities; (c) family interactions that could affect the children's mental health and school success; and (d) economic, vocational, and educational needs of families.

As part of the family systems approach, educators must understand that families of children with disabilities will probably need support systems that change as the children mature. For example, children with learning problems may manage during the preschool years, but when they enter school issues related to learning can surface for families. Teachers should be prepared to explain instructional programs and services.

For families of children with behavior problems, school can be an arena in which problems arise, misconduct occurs, and negative encounters with authorities result. Unfortunately, families may not be viewed as partners in their child's education if situations focus on what the child is doing wrong rather than on how we can help the child.

For families of children with severe disabilities, an array of services involving various professionals likely will be offered across the grade levels. However, parents will want to know how their child's specific needs will continue to be addressed after high school. Aging parents especially will want to be assured that their child with severe disabilities will be served.

Professionals must ensure that communication with families is seamless across services and grade levels. By viewing collaborative partnerships through a family systems approach, educators can tailor their interactions with families to each family's unique needs. For example, families might have

Families are important members of the school community. Home–school communication can be greatly enhanced by making families part of a positive communication network.

iStock.com/andresr

difficulty finding transportation or child-care services so that they can attend school meetings. They may be dealing with their own health or social issues that preclude their participation in school activities. It is important that school staff identify the needs of their school community and provide necessary support that promotes family participation in school activities. The Considering Diversity feature below offers suggestions for collaborating with families and the community.

Values and perceptions are other areas of the family systems approach that professionals and paraprofessionals must address as they work with students and family members. A person's value system and ways of perceiving information are important factors that can prevent or foster effective home–school communication and collaboration. Values and perceptions are learned from significant adults, home environments, peers, cultural and ethnic groups, and religious and social affiliations. Unfortunately, a person's value system can be influenced by misconceptions, stereotypes, miscommunication, and our own values and perceptions.

Collaborative partnerships can be developed with parents and other family members through parent conferences and home–school communication. Table 3.4 provides the stages and steps of parent–teacher conferences. There are three stages of an effective parent–teacher conference: preconference, conference, and postconference. Specific tasks can occur during each stage to facilitate collaboration and communication. Parent–teacher conferences and home–school communication are important components of building collaborative relationships.

Considering Diversity: Ways to Involve the Family and the Community

Smith, Tyler, Skow, and Smith (2018, p. 100) provided a helpful list of suggestions for family and community involvement:

- Develop an atmosphere of trust and respect.
- Be sure families and communities feel welcome.
- Select and involve community leaders to serve as representatives of both school and home.
- Identify families' preferred means of communication and use it effectively.
- Communicate on a regular, ongoing basis (not just when there is a problem).

TABLE 3.4 ■ Stages and Steps of Parent–Teacher Conferences

Stages	Steps
Preconference Stage	1. Notify families of the time, day, and purpose of the conference. Notification should be written in the primary language spoken at home. Provide options for conference times and days that are mutually convenient for parents as well as for teachers (and other professionals, such as counselors, who might be attending the conference). In many families both parents work, and in single-parent homes the parent is usually employed full time. Flexibility in conference times and days is important to increase the likelihood of parental participation. 2. Review assessment data that describe how the child is progressing academically, socially, and behaviorally. Prepare a summary of important data and information that will help families understand their child's progress. Samples of work can be gathered as evidence of progress or of the need for remediation. Share with families the plans for promoting academic success and addressing instructional problems. 3. Develop an agenda for the meeting, including the starting and stopping times, questions that will be asked, a statement of purpose for the meeting, and time to develop a plan if necessary. Ask family members what topics they would like to discuss as part of the agenda. 4. Arrange the environment to foster a collaborative spirit, including chairs that are designed for adults (a problem at the primary level), the removal of barriers (e.g., tables with large spaces between families and teachers or teacher desks), and the elimination of distractions (e.g., intercom interruptions). 5. Identify key professionals and paraprofessionals who can contribute important information to the conference. This is especially important if the child works with a speech/language pathologist or counselor. The challenge is to ensure that there are not too many professionals present, which might be intimidating to families. In some cases, an initial parent–teacher conference might be a good approach, followed by a second meeting with other professionals, as needed. The key is to create an initial meeting in which rapport and trust can be built. 6. Make arrangements for an interpreter if English is not the primary language or if sign language is needed. In some school communities, a home–school liaison delivers the conference information so families can communicate with school staff right from the start.
Conference Stage	1. Provide a warm welcome; greet family members at the door and guide them to the conference meeting table. A warm greeting and comfortable environment pave the way for a positive start. 2. Present the agenda and be sure that parents' questions and concerns are readily noted for discussion. Specify the time limits, which are important to help keep the conversation on track. 3. Begin with an explanation and display of the child's strengths. Showing work samples and describing positive situations can begin the establishment of rapport and trust. 4. Apprise family members of their child's progress and of the instructional plan for the child. Talk to families about ways to support instruction at home and tips for developing effective study and homework habits. 5. Provide opportunities for family members to discuss their concerns throughout the conference. Don't leave only the last few minutes for them to ask questions. 6. Watch for nonverbal and verbal communication cues that might be signaling discomfort, anger, joy, and so forth. If feelings begin to escalate, acknowledge points and use the communication techniques discussed in this chapter. 7. Jot down important points during the conference; however, check with families about this practice to be sure it does not hinder communication. Writing on carbonless paper provides copies of the notes for each participant and makes the process transparent for all. Taking notes is especially critical if a plan of action must be developed in which families and teachers agree on responsibilities for solving a problem. 8. End on a positive note, summarizing issues, successes, and plans for improvement. This can foster trust and boost the likelihood of other successful conferences occurring.
Postconference Stage	1. Review any notes that were taken during the conference to see whether specific activities must be planned for the following school day. If an agreement is made that certain activities (e.g., moving the child's desk or talking to the child privately more often) will occur, be sure this action is taken the following school day. 2. Discuss concerns about the child and a follow-up plan to address those concerns with other professionals as needed. This may require scheduling an additional conference or establishing stronger home–school communication.

Source: Adapted from Rivera and Smith (1997).

- Use interpreters who are knowledgeable about schools and their programs for effective communication and participation.
- Incorporate materials that reflect the diversity of the community.
- Seek meaningful ways (e.g., actively sharing culture, art, music, and recreational activities) to involve families and communities (as they feel comfortable).
- Treat families with individual respect, and avoid stereotyping on any basis (race, ethnicity, language, or socioeconomic class).
- Hold meetings with families at times and places that are manageable for them.

Parent–Teacher Conference

The parent–teacher conference is a good forum for families and teachers to develop collaborative, communicative partnerships (Pugach & Johnson, 1995). It can serve as a time to establish rapport with family members, to explain information about class activities, to discuss individual students' strengths and weaknesses for educational planning, and to discover family values and perceptions that can promote collaboration and communication. According to Turnbull and colleagues (2016), there are four purposes for the parent–teacher conference:

1. To jointly share information about the child's educational progress
2. To work together in finding solutions to problems
3. To establish rapport and joint responsibility for the child's educational program
4. To exchange information that might contribute to a better understanding of the child's progress and individual needs

Home–School Communication

Home–school communication can be greatly enhanced by making families part of a positive communication network (Lavoie, 2008). It is important for teachers to try, at the beginning and throughout the school year, to focus on the positive behavior of students rather than problems occurring at school. Teachers can send good news about class activities, student progress, and behavior home to families. Then, in the event a contact must be made regarding concerns, a positive foundation already exists on which teachers can discuss current issues.

Lavoie (2008) and Turnbull et al. (2016) offered several suggestions for promoting communication. For example, teachers can send home newsletters describing events, giving special student recognition, mentioning important dates, and so forth to foster communication. Students can participate in the design, layout, and production of the newsletter as a language arts activity, especially with the many desktop publishing software programs now available for students of all ages.

Notes recognizing a child's accomplishments can be sent home periodically. This should be done quietly with the student to reduce public display, which is especially important at the secondary level. Experience has shown that many secondary school students do like special recognition. However, elementary school students usually can deal with public recognition.

Teachers can make positive telephone calls periodically to let families know of their child's progress. Calling families to say, "I just wanted to tell you the good news . . ." can help tremendously in building communication and trust.

Additionally, students can take home samples of good work, along with work that needs improvement and work that shows improvement. Family members can learn about how their children are progressing with the skills that were designated for the semester or school year.

Teachers may start a parent group to discuss topics of concern for many families (e.g., finishing homework, promoting reading at home). Teachers can consider providing childcare for after-hours events so that more family members can take advantage of the parent group.

Other activities that teachers can consider is having families attend class to read with students during reading time. Families can share a special skill. Also, families can serve as tutors to help students who need additional support. At holiday time families can bring cultural and ethnic traditions and customs to share. Finally, families can help teachers make bulletin board displays and learning materials.

Weekly progress reports are yet another way to keep families informed to show areas of growth, achievement, and concerns.

In the long run, the benefits are usually good and promote the type of home–school communication that contributes to the children's progress.

SUMMARY

Developing collaborative partnerships with professionals, paraprofessionals, and families is a foundation of the educational system. Collaborative partnerships pave the way for establishing positive relationships. In this chapter, we discussed types of collaboration characteristics and critical skills such as conflict resolution and communication We also discussed models for collaborating with professionals and families. Finally, given that you might work with paraprofessionals to meet the needs of students with severe disabilities, the roles and responsibilities for you and your paraprofessional should be carefully considered.

REVIEW THE LEARNING OBJECTIVES

Let's review the learning objectives for this chapter. If you are uncertain and cannot talk through the answers provided for any of these questions, reread those sections of the text.

3.1 Describe the characteristics of collaboration.
Successful collaboration includes shared problem solving, shared responsibility, and voluntary involvement. These characteristics imply that the individuals choose to share expertise, decision making, and involvement to promote effective inclusive practices for all students.

3.2 Explain the critical prerequisite skills for effective collaboration.
Communication and conflict resolution skills are important for promoting effective collaborative partnerships. Professionals must also be aware of the cultural, linguistic, and socioeconomic backgrounds of their students and must accommodate differences in values and perceptions.

3.3 Tell how professionals can work together collaboratively.
Effective practices include collaboration, consultation, coteaching, and strategies for English learners (ELs), such as the clinical teaching cycle, peer or expert consultation, the teacher assistance team process, and alternative programs and services.

3.4 Describe how teachers can collaborate with paraprofessionals.
The establishment of roles, supervision and training, and teaming are some approaches that promote effective partnerships between professionals and paraprofessionals. Paraprofessionals should be given opportunities to express their issues and concerns.

3.5 Discuss how professionals can collaborate with families.
Professionals should use a family systems approach when working with families. This approach takes into consideration the range of needs that families have regarding their child's education and well-being. Professionals can also use parent–teacher conferences and home–school communication as opportunities to develop partnerships. Professionals should be mindful of cultural considerations as they work with families.

REVISIT THE OPENING CHALLENGE

Check your answers to the Reflection Questions in the Opening Challenge and revise them on the basis of what you have learned.

1. What professional collaborative practices can Mrs. Rojo use to help her students with special learning, behavior, and language needs succeed in the general education classroom?
2. How can Mrs. Rojo and Mr. Bower collaborate effectively with their paraprofessionals?
3. How can Mrs. Rojo effectively structure parent–teacher conferences and develop home–school communication effectively?
4. What should be the focus of the three-way meeting with Mr. Bower, the special education teacher, and the paraprofessional?

KEY TERMS

active listening
clinical teaching cycle
collaboration
collaborative consultation
conflict
family systems approach
nonverbal communication
paraprofessionals, or paraeducators
peer or expert consultation
student response systems
teacher assistance team process

PROFESSIONAL STANDARDS AND LICENSURE

For a complete description of Professional Standards and Licensure, please see the appendix.

CEC Initial Preparation Standards

Standard 2: Learning Environments

Standard 6: Professional Learning and Ethical Practice

Standard 7: Collaboration

INTASC Core Principles

Standard 3: Learning Environments

Standard 7: Planning for Instruction

Standard 9: Professional Learning and Ethical Practice

Standard 10: Leadership and Collaboration

Praxis II: Education of Exceptional Students: Core Content Knowledge

II. Legal and Societal Issues: Federal Laws and Legal Issues

III. Delivery of Services to Students with Disabilities: Background Knowledge

iStock.com/skynesher

4 CULTURALLY AND LINGUISTICALLY DIVERSE LEARNERS AND FAMILIES AND GIFTED AND TALENTED LEARNERS

LEARNING OBJECTIVES

After studying this chapter, you will be able to meet the following learning objectives:

4.1 Describe how to best meet the needs of students in our culturally and linguistically diverse classrooms.

4.2 Describe culturally and linguistically diverse gifted students.

4.3 Explain how we can apply the response to intervention (RTI) framework for culturally and linguistically diverse learners.

4.4 Identify what constitutes effective multicultural special education programs.

4.5 Describe bilingual special education.

Opening Challenge

Helping Students With Other Special Learning Needs Access the Curriculum

Elementary Grades. Ms. Grelak has been teaching in the primary grades at Tyler Elementary School for 20 years, during which the school's population has changed a great deal, from mostly White and middle class to a more culturally and linguistically diverse (CLD) mix. This year she has 11 Black students and 19 Latinx students, 9 of whom are English learners (ELs) at various levels of proficiency. She also has a student who recently arrived from Korea who knows very little English. Most of her students qualify for free or reduced-price lunch. A resource teacher provides pull-out English as a second language (ESL) support for Ms. Grelak's ELs for 50 minutes a day, but it doesn't seem to be enough. Ms. Grelak feels frustrated about how best to meet her students' needs. Many seem to be struggling to keep up with grade-level material. She is especially concerned about Gabriel and Allen.

Gabriel's family moved to the United States from Mexico about a year and a half ago when he was 10 years old, and he was placed in a fourth-grade class. He knew very little English when he started school and is still at a beginning proficiency level. Last year, he missed almost a month of school, some when he was ill and some when he and his family went to Mexico to visit relatives for Christmas. Now, in fifth grade, despite being very curious and interested in his schoolwork, he seems to have made little progress and is reading only at a beginning first-grade level. He has trouble concentrating and appears to lack motivation. Ms. Grelak is unsure whether to recommend that he be retained; she suspects he might have a learning disability.

Allen has attended Tyler since kindergarten. He was retained after first grade and is now in the fifth grade. He is well-mannered, good-natured, and popular among his peers. Yet he struggles academically, and he is about 2 years behind in reading and mathematics. Allen's mother is concerned about his lack of progress and works with him at home on practice activities that Ms. Grelak sends home for this purpose. She told Ms. Grelak that Allen is having much more difficulty than either of his older sisters, and Ms. Grelak has decided to refer him for evaluation for possible placement in special education. She suspects he might have developmental delays.

Ms. Grelak thinks, *"I have so many students from diverse backgrounds and many with special learning needs. I want to meet all their needs while trying to teach the curriculum for my grade level and also meet the needs of the other students in my class. I need to better understand how to help them all."*

Secondary Grades. Mrs. O'Malley is in her first year of teaching, having recently gone through the alternative certification program through her state's education agency. After her recent marriage, she and her husband moved from Maine to Arizona. She has a degree in chemistry but decided that, like her mother and father before her, she wanted to be a high school teacher. She was assigned to teach the general education science class. As she looked at her student roster, she noticed that a high percentage of her students had Spanish surnames and many of the students were EL. Even though her certification coursework included some information about ELs, she was concerned that she might have difficulties meeting the needs of her Latinx students. She called her mother, who suggested that she make an appointment with the district's EL specialist to identify resources and receive advice on teaching techniques.

During the meeting, the EL specialist directed Mrs. O'Malley to Arizona's Office of English Language Acquisition Services; she also stated that there would be a session titled "Meeting the Needs of ELs in Content Classes" during the district's professional development training before the start of school. Mrs. O'Malley went home and immediately contacted Arizona's Office of English Language Acquisition Services to obtain information that could help her teach her EL students. She also contacted the district's professional development coordinator to be sure her name was on the list for EL training. By the first day of school, Mrs. O'Malley believed that she had acquired enough information to feel reasonably comfortable working with her students.

Reflection Questions

In your journal, write down your answers to the following questions. After completing the chapter, check your answers and revise them on the basis of what you have learned.

1. What should Ms. Grelak's next steps be with Gabriel?
2. Do you agree that Ms. Grelak should refer Allen for a special education evaluation? Why or why not?
3. In what ways does Allen's level of English proficiency and life circumstances seem to be affecting Gabriel?
4. What characteristics does Gabriel have that seem consistent with those of a gifted student? What characteristics does Gabriel have that seem consistent with those of English learners?
5. What advice would you give Ms. Grelak about instruction for English learners with learning problems?
6. Where might you go to look for information about teaching English learners in your state? What specific questions might you like to have answered?
7. Do you share some of the same concerns as Mrs. O'Malley? Find the website of your home city's school system. Is there information pertaining to culturally and linguistically diverse student populations? What information is provided for parents and teachers?

As you learned in Chapter 1, special education services are available for students with identified disabilities according to criteria established in the Individuals with Disabilities Education Improvement Act of 2004 (IDEA). Students are entitled to supports and services they need to gain from instruction and participate with their peers in the least restrictive environment (LRE). However, it is likely that you will have other students with specific learning needs in your classroom who may not be eligible for special education services under IDEA yet who require special attention to fully attain their potential in school. Additionally, students from CLD backgrounds might need academic and other supports to ensure that they can benefit from instruction in the general education classroom. Supports might be temporary until these students learn enough English or become familiar with school practices. Students with disabilities likely will require long-term supports. Inclusive education is a way to meet the full range of student needs in the classroom as teachers implement validated practices and provide support systems to reach all students. In this chapter, we discuss factors that can affect the educational outcomes of students. Understanding that the types of needs and life situations students bring with them are numerous, we discuss some of the more critical and common needs and circumstances—health-related, cultural, linguistic, economic, social, and academic—and hope you understand that the CLD students, too, require and deserve special attention in your instructional planning and implementation. It is also important to note that within this group of CLD students are students who have exceptionalities that must be recognized. We discuss CLD students who are underrepresented in programs for students who are gifted and talented: those from historically underrepresented groups and those with two exceptionalities (giftedness and disabilities).

MEETING THE NEEDS OF STUDENTS IN CULTURALLY AND LINGUISTICALLY DIVERSE CLASSROOMS

We all have a culture (or cultures), just as we all speak a language (or languages). So, what do we mean when we say *culturally and linguistically diverse (CLD) students?* In the United States, this term has come to mean students with cultural, ethnic, or linguistic backgrounds different from the macroculture and language (Standard English) of the U.S. White majority. Any individual belongs not to just one culture or macroculture but to many microcultures (Gollnick & Chinn, 2012). We can think of a macroculture as a society that encompasses overarching cultural factors. For example, democracy is one

Dual language programs are increasingly popular models that strive to help native English speakers develop proficiency in a second language, while helping students who speak a language other than English develop English proficiency.

AP Photo/Charlie Riedel

of those factors valued as part of the U.S. macroculture. On the other hand, a microculture is a group whose members share a trait such as age, class, geographic region, disability, ethnicity, occupation, and so forth (Neuliep, 2015).

Thus, students in our classrooms represent a variety of microcultures, each with its own identity and perspectives.

Our schools must be responsive to and respectful of the richness of diversity as the CLD population continues to increase (U.S. Census Bureau, 2010). This increasing diversity in the general population means more CLD students in schools. Figure 4.1 shows population percentages for racial and ethnic groups in the United States, beginning in 1980 with projected growth to 2060. The U.S. Census Bureau projects that by 2060, the White population will increase by only 7% and at a lower rate than other ethnic groups and will thus constitute an estimated 50.1% of the population, as opposed to the 72.4% reported in 2010 (Nieto & Bode, 2008; U.S. Census Bureau, 2011). The African American population is expected to increase from 12.3% in 2010 to 14.6% in 2050 (Nieto & Bode, 2008; U.S. Census Bureau, 2011). The Hispanic population is expected to increase by a third, from 16.3% in 2010 to 24.4% in 2050 (Nieto & Bode, 2008; U.S. Census Bureau, 2011). Finally, the Asian population is expected to almost double from 4.8% in 2010 to 8% in 2050 (Nieto & Bode, 2008; U.S. Census Bureau, 2011). Certainly, the rise in legal immigration and in the numbers of first-generation U.S. residents has contributed significantly to these figures. More than half of these residents are from Latin America and one-quarter are from Asia (Nieto & Bode, 2008).

The changes in U.S. demographics are also reflected in our schools (Brown & Ortiz, 2014). There are now more than 4.4 million children who are ELs in U.S. schools, meaning they are learning English as a second or even third language (National Center for Education Statistics [NCES], 2014; Nieto & Bode, 2008). Among the more than 300 non-English languages spoken in the United States by individuals aged 5 years and older, Spanish is the first language (L1; also known as home language, natural language, native language, or primary language) of a little over 60% (Ryan, 2013).

We use numerous terms when discussing students whose L1 is other than English. To understand the differences among the terms, see Table 4.1.

Title VII of the Elementary and Secondary Education Amendments of 1967 (PL 90-247) was the first federal policy to recognize the need for specialized instruction for students who do not speak English as their L1. Subsequent amendments in 1974 and 1978 defined bilingual education programs and expanded eligibility to students who had limited English proficiency (Stewner-Manzanares, 1988).

Think back to the Opening Challenge. How are these changing demographic numbers exhibited in Ms. Grelak's classroom? Given the increasing diversity in our society and schools, educators are challenged to learn more about culture and how it influences our thinking, belief systems, values, and interactions. In other words, culture matters. We will now examine the definition of culture and then discuss several programs for CLD students.

Definition of Culture

Culture is a way of viewing the world and interacting within it. Gollnick and Chinn (2012) noted that cultural norms influence our thinking, language, and behavior. Culture is shared; it includes the customs and values that bind us together. These customs developed over centuries in response to environmental conditions. Our cultural identities evolve throughout our lives in response to political, economic, educational, and social experiences. Culture is not static; rather, it is dynamic, complex, and ever-changing.

FIGURE 4.1. ■ Percentage of the Resident U.S. Population, by Minority Race/Ethnicity: 1980 to 2010 and Projections to 2060

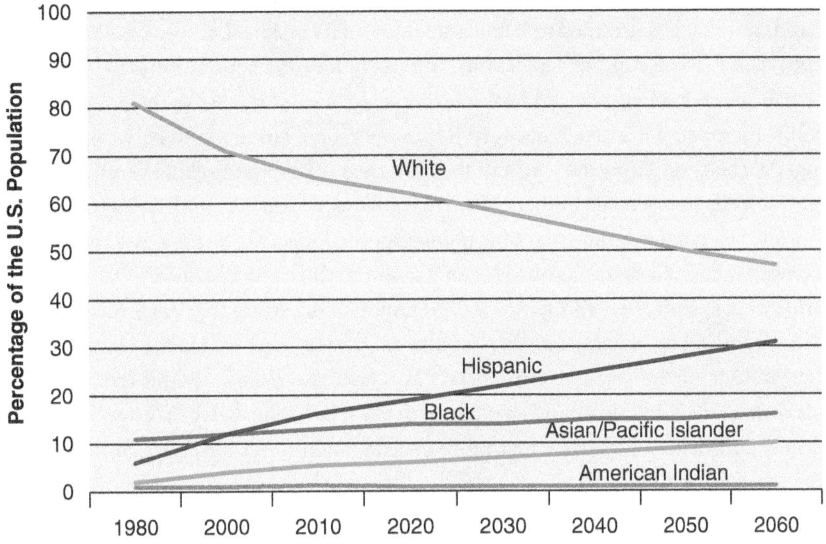

Source: U.S. Census Bureau (2012).

TABLE 4.1 ■ Terms Commonly Associated With Students Whose Primary Language Is Not English

Term	Definition
Bilingual	A bilingual is an individual who is able to communicate successfully in two languages, with the same relative degree of proficiency. It is important to note that bilinguals are rarely perfectly balanced in their use of two languages; one language is usually dominant.
English learner (EL)	An individual who is in the process of actively acquiring English and whose primary language is one other than English. This student benefits from language support programs to improve academic performance in English in reading, comprehension, speaking, and/or writing skills. Other terms that are commonly used to refer to ELs are *language minority students, dual language learner, emergent bilingual, and CLD students.*
Limited English Proficient (LEP)	A term used by the U.S. Department of Education to refer to ELs who are enrolled or are getting ready to enroll in elementary or secondary school and who have an insufficient level of English to meet a state's English expertise requirements. However, the expression *English learner* (*EL*) has started to replace *limited English proficient*, to avoid the implication that non-native-English-speaking students are deficient (National Council of Teachers of English, 2008). The former term for limited English proficient was *limited English speaker* (*LES*) and was used in the first authorization of the Bilingual Education Act (Title VII of ESEA, prior to NCLB) in 1968.
English as a Second Language (ESL)	English as a second language refers to an educational approach designed to support ELs. It is rarely used to refer to individuals.
Non-English Proficient	An EL who has minimal or no proficiency in English.

Source: Bardack (2010).

Cultural identity is learned as part of our ethnic group, but it is also developed as part of our religion, socioeconomic status, geographic region, place of residence (urban or rural), and gender, to name just a few microcultures. Our participation in some microcultural groups may take on more importance at different times in our lives. Schools and classrooms themselves develop their own patterns of behavior and are said to have a culture.

Culture is involved in all learning (Klingner et al., 2014). From the time we are quite young, we are socialized to learn in different ways. For example, in her classic study of children in three different communities, Shirley Brice Heath (1983) noted that only the middle-class White children started school accustomed to the ways of teaching and learning they encountered in their classrooms. They were not surprised when they were asked questions to which their teachers already knew the answers. They knew how to narrate stories in just the style expected by their teachers. Children from different backgrounds, on the other hand, were not accustomed to being asked questions designed to test their knowledge, such as "What shape is this?" Some children had learned in their homes and communities to tell elaborate, complex stories that their schoolteachers did not value because they did not get to the point quickly enough. In other words, there was a mismatch between home and school cultures and between ways of teaching and learning. All the children in the communities Heath studied began school ready to learn, but their schools were not ready to teach all children. When Heath helped teachers understand differences in ways of learning of all their students, they were able to instruct their students in ways that better capitalized on students' strengths and built on the knowledge and skills they brought to school.

In another classic study, Au and Blake (2003) conducted a study that examined the influence of cultural identity (ethnicity, social class, and community membership) on the learning of three preservice teachers. One of the preservice teachers was a Japanese American and the other two were of Hawaiian ancestry. Au and Blake found that preservice teachers who differ in terms of cultural identity may gain important benefits by participating in an education program designed to prepare them to teach in a diverse community.

Teachers who are culturally responsive focus on matching their instruction to the teaching and cultural learning style of their students; teachers understand that there are many sociocultural influences on learning. What can teachers do to help CLD students learn and achieve to their potential? What lessons can Ms. Grelak in our Opening Challenge learn from the research we've discussed? Multicultural education is one approach to working with CLD students, including ELs.

Multicultural Education

We sometimes think of multicultural education as something added on to the curriculum, focusing on the holidays, traditions, and historical contributions of diverse ethnic groups. But multicultural education is much more than that. It is about making sure that schools are a place where all students feel welcomed, valued, and supported. Nieto and Bode (2008) define **multicultural education** as

> a process of comprehensive school reform and basic education for all students. It challenges and rejects racism and other forms of discrimination in schools and society and accepts and affirms the pluralism (ethnic, racial, linguistic, religious, economic, and gender, among others) that students, their communities, and teachers reflect. Multicultural education permeates the schools' curriculum and instructional strategies, as well as the interactions among teachers, students, and families, and the very way that schools conceptualize the nature of teaching and learning. Because it uses critical pedagogy as its underlying philosophy and focuses on knowledge, reflections, and action as the basis for social change, multicultural education promotes democratic principles of social justice. (p. 44)

Nieto and Bode (2008) emphasized that multicultural education should be a central part of comprehensive school reform movements designed to improve schooling for all students and to better prepare them for an increasingly diverse society.

Multicultural education is good for all students. All children benefit from "mirrors and windows"—that is, from seeing themselves reflected in the curriculum as well as from learning about others (Naidoo, 2014). All students benefit from learning that there are multiple perspectives on any issue and from learning how to think critically about these issues. Instruction should build on students' experiences as a basis for further learning and should help them make connections with their own lives. In classrooms that are a place of acceptance and mutual respect and where no one is devalued, teachers recognize that students bring different ways of talking to school, and that linking episodes loosely or using a circular narrative structure is as valid as relating a story in a more linear style. And when a student looks down rather than makes eye contact while the teacher is talking to her, the teacher considers that this might be a cultural norm and not a sign of disrespect. These are examples of culturally responsive instruction. When teachers employ these practices, students are secure and comfortable risk-takers

iStock.com/FatCamera

(Klingner et al., 2014). However, teachers also have the responsibility of teaching students how to act and interact in the mainstream. Teachers can accomplish this by accepting and validating students' home culture and also by teaching them the mainstream cultural norms as another way to interact. Through this process, students learn to be bicultural and how to move seamlessly between their home culture and school culture.

Bilingual Education

Students who are not yet fully proficient in English were previously called **English language learners (ELLs)** but are now typically referred to as **English learners (ELs)**, to emphasize that they are in the process of acquiring English. *Limited English proficient* (LEP) is another term used to mean the same thing and is the label preferred by the government. ELs are a very diverse group (Brown & Ortiz, 2014). Although Spanish is the L1 of the majority of ELs, other languages (including Vietnamese, Hmong, Cantonese, Korean, Haitian Creole, Arabic, Russian, Tagalog, and Navajo) are also well represented in U.S. classrooms. ELs can be refugees or immigrants or long-term ELs. Due to the challenges associated with their moves to the U.S., many immigrants or refugees are students with interrupted formal education. Long-term ELs are students who have been educated in U.S. schools for at least 6 years yet have not developed English proficiency and struggle academically. These groups of students have their own sets of academic needs (NCES, 2014). ELs also vary in other ways, such as their socioeconomic status, nationality, generation in the United States, status (e.g., citizens, legal residents, or undocumented immigrants), and level of education in their home country, as well as the educational attainment of their parents (Hernández & Napierala, 2012). Some ELs are already proficient readers in their L1, while others are not. Thus, even though in some ways ELs have the same needs, such as the need to have their L1 and culture valued and respected by their teachers, in other ways they have varying needs. Each child is an individual.

As noted previously, ELs are entitled to specialized education programs that not only provide content but also ensure that they develop English proficiency. Bilingual education programs vary in the timing of the introduction of English and how long they continue to teach students in their L1. The goal of two-way dual language programs is bilingualism for both English learners and English monolingual students enrolled in the program. Both groups of students receive instruction in English and Spanish. Transitional bilingual programs, on the other hand, provide ELs instruction in their

L1 initially and then reduce the use of the L1 for instruction as they increase the amount of English used. The goal of transitional programs is to use the student's L1 to support the acquisition of English. Finally, English as a second language programs use English for instruction but support student learning with the use of English as a second language strategy to support second language acquisition. These programs are often implemented when the students in the class speak different L1s.

WORKING TOGETHER

In the Opening Challenge, you met Mrs. O'Malley, a first-year teacher who was concerned that she may not have had sufficient preservice training and experiences with ELs to meet their needs in her science class. She met with a consultant from her school district, who offered state resources and identified an upcoming professional development session that might also provide useful information. Today, with increasingly complex standards being developed and implemented with the Common Core State Standards across the curriculum, it can be overwhelming for teachers to understand the standards and integrate them within their daily lessons. Consulting teachers who specialize in students whose L1 is other than English are excellent resources who can assist teachers in areas such as (a) setting up the classroom, (b) being ready to teach ELs from the first day of class, and (c) dealing with classroom management (Celic, 2009). In addition, the consulting teacher can help teachers with their lesson plans, model how to administer lessons, and provide feedback after observing their teaching.

Questions

1. Consider each of Celic's (2009) three areas listed above and identify ways in which your current or future classroom can be designed to facilitate learning for ELs.
2. Consider a lesson plan you have developed, either for a class in your program or to teach if you are a practicing teacher. Highlight sections of the lesson plan that are "EL friendly," and underline sections that might need to be altered to meet the needs of students who struggle with English. What percentage of the lesson components were EL friendly compared with those that were not?
3. How can Mrs. O'Malley apply the three areas (Celic, 2009) to getting ready for the first day of class?

Disproportionate Representation of Culturally and Linguistically Diverse Students in Special Education

It is true that CLD students are not any more likely than their peers to have true disabilities. Yet, despite the best intentions of their teachers and other school staff, CLD students are disproportionately **overrepresented** in special education programs relative to their percentages in the overall school-age population (Sullivan & Bal, 2013). CLD students are overrepresented only in the high-incidence disability categories (e.g., learning disabilities, intellectual and developmental disabilities, and emotional or behavioral disorders), not in the low-incidence disability categories (e.g., visual, auditory, or orthopedic impairment; Office of Special Education Programs [OSEP], 2014). Medical doctors are able to diagnose these latter disabilities, usually before a child starts school. However, school staff usually identify high-incidence disabilities after the child has started school. Therefore, these are referred to as the judgmental categories because the diagnosis relies so heavily on professional judgment (Sullivan & Bal, 2013).

When we examine nationally aggregated data, we can see an overrepresentation or disproportionate representation among Black students (see Table 4.2), and there are stark differences across states (NCES, 2014). The federal government reports two ways of calculating students' representation in special education categories: by risk indices and by risk ratios. We calculate the risk index by dividing the number of students in a given racial or ethnic group who are placed in a particular disability category by the total enrollment for that racial or ethnic group in the school population. The risk ratio is the risk index of one racial or ethnic group divided by the risk index of another racial or ethnic group. The risk ratio provides a comparative index of the risk of being placed in a particular disability category and is the indicator of disproportionate representation preferred by the U.S. Department of Education's Office of Special Education Programs (OSEP).

Unfortunately, disability labels, such as learning disabilities (LD), emotional disturbance (ED), and intellectual disabilities (ID), stigmatize students and may result in lowered expectations from their teachers, families, and even themselves. Labels can lead to diminished educational and life outcomes for these students (Shobo et al., 2012). Now, think back to the Opening Challenge. How does this information about overrepresentation influence your thinking about what Ms. Grelak should do about Allen and how Mrs. O'Malley should get ready for the first day of class?

What can we do to address disproportionate representation and overrepresentation? We can examine our own assumptions about how students learn and why they struggle and then consider what we each can do to improve learning opportunities for students. Regrettably, explanations for students' under-achievement and inappropriate placement in special education have focused on perspectives about students' homes and communities. Ethnically diverse learners can and do excel in schools when culturally responsive and relevant teaching is in place (Shealey et al., 2011) Culturally responsive and appropriate teaching occurs when teachers capitalize on their students' culture, prior experiences, and performances to provide instruction that engages students intellectually, emotionally, socially, and politically.

TABLE 4.2 ■ Ethnic Representation in U.S. Special Education, 2012 (National Aggregates in Percentages)

Special Education Disability	American Indian or Alaska Native	Asian	Black or African American	Hispanic/ Latino	Native Hawai'ian or Other Pacific Islander	White	Two or more races
Autism	4.2	18.0	5.5	5.8	5.1	8.9	8.6
Deaf-blindness	#	#	#	#	0.1	#	#
Developmental delay[a]	4.9	2.0	2.5	1.4	3.3	2.2	3.0
Emotional disturbance	6.3	2.5	8.8	3.9	4.8	6.4	8.5
Hearing impairments	0.9	2.9	0.9	1.4	2.3	1.1	1.0
Intellectual disabilities	6.8	7.6	10.5	6.8	5.9	6.4	60
Multiple disabilities	2.4	2.8	2.2	1.6	2.8	2.4	#
Orthopedic impairments	0.5	1.5	0.6	1.0	0.9	1.0	0.8
Other health impairments	11.1	7.9	12.8	8.9	10.1	15.6	149
Specific learning disabilities	46.4	26.7	41.8	49.0	52.9	36.0	35.6
Speech or language impairments	15.8	26.7	13.7	19.4	10.6	19.1	18.9
Traumatic brain injury	0.4	0.5	0.4	0.3	0.3	0.5	0.5
Visual impairments	0.4	0.8	0.4	0.4	0.9	0.5	0.4

#Percentage was nonzero but less than 0.05 or 5/100 of 1%.

[a]States' use of the *developmental delay* category is optional for children ages 3 through 9 and is not applicable to children 10 and older.

Note: National aggregates are in percentages. Percentage was calculated by dividing the number of students ages 6 through 21 served under *IDEA*, Part B, in the racial/ethnic group and disability category by the total number of students ages 6 through 21 served under *IDEA*, Part B, in the racial/ethnic group and all disability categories, then multiplying the result by 100. The sum of column percentages may not total 100 because of rounding.

Sources: U.S. Department of Education, National Center for Education Statistics, Common Core of Data (2017). These data are for the 50 states; Washington, DC; Bureau of Indian Education schools; the four outlying areas (Puerto Rico, the Northern Mariana Islands, American Samoa, Guam); and the three freely associated states (Federated States of Micronesia, the Republic of the Marshall Islands, and the Republic of Palau). For actual data used, go to the OSEP website at http://www.ed.gov/about/reports/annual/osep.

CULTURALLY AND LINGUISTICALLY DIVERSE GIFTED STUDENTS

Gifted and talented students can be found in every racial, ethnic, socioeconomic, and linguistic group. Although slightly more than half of states mandate services for gifted students, relatively few have laws or regulations that offer educational protections for gifted students like those found in IDEA for students with disabilities, and definitions of giftedness vary from state to state (Davidson Institute, 2021b). No national standards for educational services for these students exist (Rinn et al., 2022). Regardless, these students tend to have the following characteristics, which are reflected in many states' definitions (Davidson, 2021b):

- Advanced thinking and comprehension
- Emotional intensity
- Extreme self-awareness
- Intensive curiosity
- Excellent memory

The Jacob K. Javits Gifted and Talented Students Education Act, which was first enacted in 1988 (PL 100-297) and continues today, does not provide funding for school services except for special projects, particularly those that address students from traditionally underrepresented groups (U.S. Department of Education, 2022). Although gifted and talented students do not necessarily face the same kind of challenges as most children who receive special education services because of their unique needs, they confront other obstacles. In fact, many gifted and talented learners are frequently stifled by educational approaches that do not challenge their cognitive abilities or help them achieve their full potential. For these reasons, many researchers, parents, policymakers, and education professionals believe these students need and benefit from special programs and services (Gentry et al., 2019; Lubinski & Benbow, 2021). First, we must describe the prevalence of gifted and talented learners and consider what over- and underrepresentation means.

Prevalence

Using tests of intelligence (IQ) alone and no measures of other aspects of giftedness or talents, the expectation is that some 6% of the student population should qualify for gifted education (Davidson Institute, n.d.). However, across the United States, the participation rate in programs for gifted and talented students, at 6.6%, is far less than expected if all students with outstanding intellectual abilities and talents were included, and participation rates vary greatly, particularly when race and ethnicity are disaggregated from the total numbers. Additionally, the most consistent predictors of identification of risk for disability include students' gender, race, socioeconomic status, and number of suspensions. As you can see, Table 4.3 provides percentages for all American students who participate in programs for gifted and talented students. For example, what the federal government considers "Asian students" includes students who are Cambodian, Hmong, and from other Asian communities that are not well-represented among students identified as gifted and talented. Regardless, these data are revealing and lead many educators to believe that the definitions and concepts of giftedness need to be broadened (Gentry et al, 2019; National Society for the Gifted & Talented, 2018; Sgueglia & Paul, 2022).

Twice Exceptional Students Are a Special Case

Twice exceptional students—those with outstanding intellectual abilities but who also have at least one disability—are the most under-identified and underserved group of students in schools today (Davidson Institute, 2021a). For example, these students may have, in addition to giftedness, learning disabilities, autism spectrum disorders, emotional and behavioral disorders, or attention deficit hyperactivity disorders. In less frequent cases, they may be deaf-blind, be d/Deaf, or have visual

TABLE 4.3 ■ Participation Rates in the General School Population and in Programs for Gifted and Talented

Race/Ethnicity	Percentage of School Population	Percentage in Programs for Gifted and Talented
White	47.0	8.1
Black	15.1	3.6
Hispanic	27.2	4.5
Asian	5.3	12.1
Pacific Islander	.04	3.7
American Indian/Alaskan Native	1.0	4.9
2 or more races	4.1	7.2

Sources: National Center for Education Statistics. (2023). *Enrollment and percentage distribution of enrollment in public elementary and secondary schools, by race/ethnicity and region: Selected years, fall 1995 through fall 2030*, https://nces.ed.gov/programs/digest/d21/tables/dt21_203.50.asp

National Center for Education Statistics. (2021). *Percentage of public school students enrolled in gifted and talented programs, by sex, race/ethnicity, and state: Selected years, 2004 through 2017-18*, https://nces.ed.gov/programs/digest/d21/tables/dt21_204.90.asp

disabilities. These disabilities are uniquely described in Chapters 5 and 6. It is important to understand that disabilities often mask their intellectual prowess (Josephson et al., 2018). These students present many of the characteristics of gifted students that we discussed previously, but they tend to express the following characteristics (Davidson Institute, 2021a, 2022):

- Outstanding critical thinking skills
- High levels of curiosity
- Low self-esteem due to perfectionism
- Poor social skills
- Strong ability to concentrate in areas of interest
- Poor reading and writing skills
- Behavior problems due to stress, boredom, and lack of motivation
- High levels of anxiety

Despite their many strengths, these students tend to underperform. Clearly, these students need special supportive services to achieve to their potential, which they are unlikely to receive. Their educational programs typically focus on their identified disabilities exclusively.

However, experts reasonable assume that 6% of these students, despite their disabilities, should receive services for their giftedness as well. Although the number of these students who actually receive support for their unique abilities and talents is unknown, it clearly is far less than 6% (Davidson Institute, 2021a).

Over- and Underrepresentation for Gifted Education

The big take-away from the data in Table 4.3 is that White and Asian students are overrepresented in programs for gifted and talented students, and Black and Hispanic students are underrepresented. What reasons might explain these data? What are the implications for these students? Finally, what are the solutions for resolving these inequities?

Reasons for Disproportionate Representation

Although giftedness exists across all groups of learners regardless of their economic status, membership in a historically underrepresented group, or where they attend school, students in the U.S. do not have sufficient access to and participation rates in programs for gifted and talented youth (National Association for Gifted Children, 2019). One reason often stated is testing bias, but that is an oversimplification of the problem (Calvan, 2021). Many of these students do test lower—not because of their abilities, but rather due to their opportunities.

Despite efforts to desegregate America's schools, which began in the 1960s, today's schools are racially and economically segregated (Reardon et al., 2022). Racial segregation and the magnitude of achievement gaps are strongly associated. Racial segregation is also highly related to economic segregation, which contributes to how well students perform academically or what is referred to as "achievement gaps."

Students from historically underrepresented groups are more likely to attend urban and rural schools where resources are more limited and teachers' expectations for their students are lower than those in more affluent school districts (Szymanski, 2021). Options for advanced placement and programs for gifted and talented students are also greatly reduced. These environmental facts contribute to lower participation rates and also the underachievement often noted for these learners.

Part of the problem is access. Overall, schools with higher enrollments of students who are from families experiencing poverty have substantially fewer programs available for their gifted and talented students (Yaluyma & Tyner, 2018). This fact is particularly true for schools with higher enrollments of Black and Latinx students. These students' disadvantages begin early in life with less access to high quality early childhood programs, homes filled with books and educational toys, and fewer opportunities for extracurricular activities (Reardon et al., 2022). As a result, the precursors to ultimate achievement gaps start long before a child comes to school.

Further, the problem of underrepresentation is exacerbated for students who are not proficient in the English language. Despite the fact that being able to speak two (or more) languages requires keen cognitive ability, bilingualism is frequently treated as a disadvantage in need of remedial efforts rather than as a strength that requires **enrichment**.

To better understand this group of students, several researchers and school systems have identified the characteristics that some CLD students exhibit. Many of the characteristics are shown in Table 4.4.

Teachers can help their CLD gifted learners to be successful in many ways. First, they should value students' cultures, languages, and experiences. Teachers can build a connection among home, school, and community (e.g., inviting families to share their history). Teachers can maintain high standards for all students by focusing on content that incorporates multicultural education and instructional strategies that focus on students' strengths, such as problem solving and creativity (Shealey et al., 2011).

Finally, they can implement evaluation procedures that utilize multiple criteria and measures such as assessments of nonverbal ability, behavior checklists, student portfolios, and teacher observation. When possible, students should be assessed in their L1 (National Center for Research on Gifted Education, 2015). Additional information about effective practices for including ELs in gifted education can be found at the National Center for Research on Gifted Education, Washington, DC.

Implications

To address many of the challenges we just discussed will take major efforts by states, school districts, educators, the public, and policy makers (Barshay, 2019). Ways to resolve the basic funding disparities of urban, rural, and suburban school districts must be addressed (Gentry et al., 2019). High quality educational programs, including those for gifted students, need to be equally available. Teachers must be better prepared to meet the individual needs of all their students. Everyone must become part of the solution or the result will be continued lower achievement of a large portion of the school population, along with dissatisfaction with public education.

Solutions

Many ideas have been proposed about how to solve the problems associated with disproportionate representation of some groups of students. One suggestion is to change the way students are identified or qualify for gifted education. Instead of using national norms, such as selecting students who score

TABLE 4.4 ■ Possible Characteristics of Culturally and Linguistically Diverse Gifted Students

Characteristic	Dominant Culture	Nondominant Cultures
Curiosity	May raise hand to ask questions. May stay on task. May express self well. May expect shared experiences and common understandings. May be more curious about how things work than about people.	May think questioning is rude. May be frustrated by not having the language necessary to ask questions. May not have foundation of shared experiences. May be curious about different experiences. May experience lack of understanding by teachers, peers, and others. May enjoy questions with shock value. May be more curious about people than about how things work.
Task Commitment	May stick with task. May be confident in ability.	May have own priorities. May not see relevance in schoolwork.
Sense of Humor	May begin with shared experiences and understandings. May use dominant language with others. May use subtleties with language.	May have difficulty showing humor in dominant culture's language. May use put-downs. May be class clown. May demonstrate humor, tell jokes in one language and not the other.
Keen Interests	May be good at many things. May enjoy learning new things. May enjoy collections. May enjoy book series.	May make decisions without regard for consequences. May appear random. May have trouble finding closure.
Use of Language	May express self well in formal register. May be able to elaborate well on others' ideas. May have fairly even language profile.	May be very expressive in casual register. May have trouble listening and staying attentive to others. May be uneven in ability to speak, listen, read, write. May make clever, silly, or inappropriate responses. May be opinionated, good talker but unable to support ideas or provide substance to ideas. May tell stories, enjoys listening to stories in L1, own culture. May acquire new language quickly.
Self-Efficacy	May feel safe. May feel in control.	May feel unsafe, insecure. May feel like a victim.
Problem Solving	May be good at solving teacher problems. May apply learned rules to problem solving.	May be good at solving street problems. May be creative in fending for self. May not be interested in following rules.
Asynchronous maturity	May be taken care of by adults. May be often protected from adult concerns.	May be responsible for younger siblings. May act as translator and interpreter for adults. May be needed, used in adult situations.

Source: Adapted from the Boulder Valley School District Office of Advanced Academic Services (2010).

in the highest 5% nationwide, the idea is to select students who score in the top 5% at the school they attend. This method would increase the number of Black and Latinx students from schools where they attend in high numbers; however, researchers question the merits of such concepts (Barshay, 2019). First, White and Asian students who meet the national criterion might no longer qualify in some school districts. Second, data seem to indicate that the Black and Latinx students who have participated in such programs do not excel at expected levels.

Another method includes a variety of forms of acceleration, ranging from grade skipping to moving up to another grade's math or social studies class but then returning to join their age-peers for the rest of the school day. For middle school and high school students, acceleration might mean taking honors classes or advanced placement courses. And, for high school students, it could take the form of attending a college course for academic credit (Bernstein et al., 2021; Lubinski & Benbow, 2021). The advantages of acceleration opportunities are many. For example, no additional instructors need to be hired, no special programs need to be developed and implemented, and the outcomes are proven. The number of students participating in advanced placement courses has doubled since 2014, including many students from historically underrepresented groups (College Board, 2019). They are passing the AP exam at incredible rates, which has many benefits including an increased likelihood of attending college, staying in college, graduating, and having less tuition to pay.

Some experts believe that home and school communication and partnerships need to be improved (Lockhar & Mun, 2020). Families that do not have experience with higher education or even with the culture of American schools often do not come to their children's educational experience with the trust or understanding of how they can help their children succeed in school. Building partnerships with families can be a critical variable in the support needed to encourage their children to participate in gifted education opportunities, take advanced placement courses, and remain involved in their own schooling.

Another solution is more drastic, but it is a response to the inequities we have discussed. Some school districts are phasing out their gifted education programs for elementary school students (Calvan, 2021). One such district is in New York City, but other districts like Boston and Seattle are considering similar options. However, at least in New York, the parent pushback was so great that the new mayor decided on another option: to expand the gifted and talented program so that every student in the system would have opportunities for acceleration programs (Sgueglia & Paul, 2022). Clearly, there is no consensus about the best solution to solving the inequalities resulting from gifted education programs in the public schools.

Possibly, one solution might rest with identifying gifted and talented students in different ways and not predominately based on the scores from tests of intelligence. For example, schools and teachers might look for students who possess at least some of the common characteristics associated with giftedness and exceptional talents. Although some students can be considered globally gifted, most gifted students excel in some areas and not others. Students who are gifted are a heterogeneous group who differ from each other in abilities, interests, motivation, behavior, and needs. And yet they do share some characteristics. The National Society for the Gifted and Talented identified these characteristics across six areas: creative thinking, general intellectual ability, specific academic ability, leadership, psychomotor ability, and visual/performing arts abilities (see Table 4.5).

TABLE 4.5 ■ Common Characteristics of Gifted and Talented Children in Six Areas

Area	Characteristics	
Creative Thinking	• Is an independent thinker • Exhibits original thinking in oral and written expression • Comes up with several solutions to a given problem	• Possesses a sense of humor • Creates and invents • Is challenged by creative tasks • Improvises often • Does not mind being different from the crowd
General Intellectual Ability	• Formulates abstractions • Processes information in complex ways • Is observant • Is excited about new ideas • Enjoys hypothesizing	• Learns rapidly • Uses a large vocabulary • Is inquisitive • Is a self-starter
Specific Academic Ability	• Has good memorization ability • Has advanced comprehension • Acquires basic skill knowledge quickly	• Is widely read in special interest area • Has high academic success in special interest area • Pursues special interest with enthusiasm and vigor
Leadership	• Assumes responsibility • Has high expectations for self and others • Has fluent, concise self-expression • Foresees consequences and implications of decisions	• Has good judgment in decision making • Likes structure • Is well-liked by peers • Is self-confident • Is organized

Area	Characteristics	
Psychomotor Ability	● Is challenged by difficult athletic activities ● Exhibits precision in movement ● Enjoys participation in various athletic opportunities	● Excels in motor skills ● Is well coordinated ● Has good manipulative skills ● Has high energy level
Visual/Performing Arts Abilities	● Is outstanding in sense of spatial relationships ● Has unusual ability in expressing self, feeling, moods, etc., through dance, drama, music, etc.	● Has good motor coordination ● Exhibits creative expression ● Has a desire for producing own product (not content with mere copying) ● Is observant

Source: National Society for the Gifted & Talented (2018).

APPLYING THE RESPONSE TO INTERVENTION FRAMEWORK FOR CULTURALLY AND LINGUISTICALLY DIVERSE LEARNERS

Some CLD students do have disabilities and can gain from appropriate services in special education programs. RTI integrates assessment and instruction to foster student performance and reduce the overrepresentation of CLD students in special education. (Review your understanding of RTI from Chapter 2.) Within a RTI framework, instructional procedures address students' learning needs. Student performance and ways to identify students who need Tier 2 and Tier 3 support are important within this framework. There are several advantages of RTI, such as an emphasis on the prevention of problems rather than on remediation, the use of measures that assess the skills needed in each area, and systematic implementation of interventions to mitigate learning problems. A culturally and linguistically responsive RTI framework is responsive to the needs of CLD students. This framework guarantees that cultural and linguistic factors specific to diverse learners are considered and addressed, which means that when a student is identified as having a learning disability, the learning disability is a result of difficulty and *not* only cultural and linguistic differences.

Because placement in Tiers 2 and 3 is based on student performance on screening and progress-monitoring measures, students from CLD backgrounds are often overidentified as in need of these services. Furthermore, the most consistent predictors of risk for disability include students' gender, race, socioeconomic status, and number of suspensions. Table 4.6 provides assessment recommendations for making data-based decisions.

The support needed by each of these students is different. It is critical to ensure that assessments include procedures that take into consideration the time needed to develop language skills and the learning context and environmental factors that could be impacting learning. We present questions for instruction, assessment, and the learning environment in the Considering Diversity feature as a way to determine whether children have had ample opportunities to learn before being considered for special education referral. In Table 4.7, we compare and contrast the characteristics associated with learning disabilities, the process of acquiring a second language (L2), and cultural influences.

Evidence-based instruction is an essential component of RTI. There is agreement among researchers that explicit instruction in phonics, fluency, vocabulary, and comprehension strategies is associated with improved reading outcomes. Teachers can make certain that core instruction is effective by including teaching methods and strategies that have been validated with students from CLD backgrounds. Teachers also can use culturally and linguistically relevant material. Teachers should make adaptations to curricular and instructional practices designed to address the language and literacy needs of CLD students. A well-implemented RTI framework can reduce the number of CLD students inappropriately referred to special education. However, students who require special education should attend programs that address the specific needs of each CLD student through multicultural special education instruction.

TABLE 4.6 ■ Assessment Recommendations

Recommendations
Develop procedures to make data-informed decisions about students' movement within and across tiered instruction and determine eligibility for referral to remedial or special education that include information on the quality of core and supplemental instruction, students' language proficiency and past educational placement, and home and community factors.
Identify assessments that are technically adequate and have been normed on student populations that are similar to the population in your school.
For bilingual programs, identify parallel assessments in English and the students' L1 to ensure that students' growth is adequately tracked. For example, alternate the language of progress-monitoring measures to track literacy growth in both languages.
Ensure that assessment procedures generate valid and reliable data for determining instructional placement for individual students and for informing instructional programming decisions.
Ensure that procedures facilitate appropriate and timely decision-making.
Use data in students' L1 and/or calculate their rate of growth by using data from previous years.
Promote collaboration between grade level and the school-wide RTI team and use students' data to identify school-level and grade level trends or issues.
Work toward an **objective referral process** by using both confirming and disconfirming perspectives.

TABLE 4.7 ■ Some Similarities Between Learning Disabilities and Language Acquisition

Behaviors Associated With Learning Disabilities	Behaviors Associated With Acquiring a Second Language
Difficulty following directions	Difficulty following directions because the directions were not well understood. Following directions can be more difficult to remember in a second language.
Difficulty with phonological awareness	Difficulty auditorily distinguishing between sounds not in one's L1, or sounds that are presented in a different order.
Slow to learn sound-symbol correspondence	Confusion with sound-symbol correspondence when L1 uses a different script, or has letters or sounds that do not exist in English.
Difficulty remembering sight words	Difficulty remembering sight words when word meanings are not understood.
Difficulty retelling a story in sequence	Difficulty retelling a story in English without the expressive skills to do so. The student might understand more than he or she can convey (i.e., receptive skills in English might be stronger than expressive skills).
Confusion with figurative language	Confusion with figurative language, idioms, pronouns, conjunctions, and words with multiple meanings.
Slow to process a challenging language	Slow to process a challenging language because it is not well understood.
May have poor auditory memory	May seem to have poor auditory memory if sounds or words are unfamiliar or not well understood.
May have difficulty concentrating	Learning in a second language is mentally exhausting; therefore, ELs may seem to have difficulty concentrating at times.
May seem easily frustrated	Learning in a second language can be frustrating.

Source: Adapted from Klingner (2014).

EFFECTIVE MULTICULTURAL SPECIAL EDUCATION PROGRAMS

The field of multicultural special education focuses on research and expertise to guide educators in making knowledgeable decisions (Shealey et al., 2011). The goals of multicultural special education are to reduce inappropriate referrals, improve assessment procedures, and increase instructional and support services. Validated instructional practices designed for CLD students with unique learning needs or disabilities should be emphasized and taught in culturally responsive, supportive learning environments (Shealey et al., 2011). Validated practices is a theme throughout the chapters in this book, where you will read about how to teach instructional content that supports the learning needs of CLD students.

A common definition of culturally responsive teaching is "using the cultural knowledge, prior experiences, frames of reference, and performance styles of ethnically diverse students to make learning . . . more relevant and effective for them" (Gay, 2010, p. 31). After conducting a systematic review of the literature, Piazza, Rao, and Protacio (2015) identified practices in five areas that are effective for student with learning disabilities, ELs, and students from culturally diverse backgrounds. Table 4.8 shows the areas and the roles each area plays, including examples of practices.

TABLE 4.8 ■ Five Areas of Effective Practices

Area	Role	Practices
Dialogue	Dialogue provides students opportunities to use language as a tool. Dialogues provide students opportunities to use new language and vocabulary, connect new to known concepts, and expand their worldview (Comber, 2013; Medina, 2010).	• Dialogic interactions among teachers and students • Dialogic interactions among peers
Collaboration	Collaboration refers to practices that provide students opportunities to construct meaning through social interactions with more experienced or able peers providing scaffolding and practice.	• Peer-assisted learning strategies (PALS) • Classwide peer tutoring • Group discussions
Visual representation	The use of visual representations (e.g., charts, graphs, maps, or photographs that are culturally relevant when appropriate) is helpful in developing students' conceptual knowledge when their linguistic skills are limited.	• Models, drawings, diagrams, tables, realia, online visual tools, etc.
Explicit instruction	Modeling includes explicit discussion of expectations with examples drawn from students' culture and language. Instructional scaffolding refers to teacher support that uses students' contributions and their background to extend and deepen their understanding. Responsive feedback provides students with individualized support regarding performance that is sensitive to the students' cultural background and experiences.	• Clear and concise instructions • Modeling • Instructional scaffolding • Responsive feedback • Gradual release of responsibility
Inquiry	Inquiry provides students' opportunities to generate questions in an area of interest or a specific content area, to record information, or to make sense of their learning.	• Opportunities to seek out information, to write, and reflect on what is learned

Source: Adapted from Piazza et al. (2015).

BILINGUAL SPECIAL EDUCATION

The goal of bilingual special education is to help students develop English proficiency, as well as proficiency in their home language. Bilingual students with unique learning needs or disabilities, like other students with unique learning needs, may benefit from instructional support in a variety of settings where the language of instruction is the most important consideration and should be consistent across settings. For instance, if a student receives reading instruction in their L1 in the general education classroom, then other reading instruction should also be in the L1.

The majority of ELs with disabilities have learning disabilities, primarily reading difficulties. Yet compared with ELs without disabilities, ELs with disabilities likely receive fewer language support services, and the supports are only in English. Furthermore, these students may face many misconceptions (and realities); teachers should be aware of the associated implications (see Table 4.9).

For example, Orosco and Klingner (2010) observed in RTI classrooms and noted the value of aligning assessment and interventions. They also noted that one of the more successful teachers "provided direct and explicit native-language instruction that was socially and linguistically meaningful by connecting it to students' cultural and linguistic experiences" (p. 278). The most advantageous programs incorporate students' home cultures and include L1 instruction as well as a focus on English language development. This deliberate and intensive focus on language makes bilingual special education distinct from generic special education (Klingner, 2014).

TABLE 4.9 ■ Misconceptions and Realities About the Language Acquisition Process

Misconception	Reality	Implications
Bilingualism means equal proficiency in both languages.	Someone who is bilingual is proficient in two languages. However, this does not mean they are equally proficient in both languages; they are usually dominant in one language.	1. ELs are students with a wide range of proficiencies in their home language and English. 2. Bilingual students may be stronger in some areas in their home language and stronger in other areas in English.
Semi-lingualism is a valid concept and "non-non" classifications indicate that children have limited proficiency in their home language and English (based on test results). However, in most cases, one language is dominant.	Semi-lingualism and "non-non" categories are the results of tests that do not measure the full range and depth of language knowledge among ELs acquiring two languages simultaneously.	1. The vast majority of children begin school having acquired the syntactic and morphological rules of the language of their community. However, when they are placed in programs that limit their opportunity to keep developing their home language, there is often a decline in their proficiency. 2. Current language assessment measures rarely capture the full range of skills that bilingual children bring to the classroom. 3. Limited-limited classifications are not useful in making program placement decisions. In such cases determining which language is dominant is necessary. 4. Other forms of authentic assessment can be used to determine language proficiency levels of ELs, including natural language samples.
The more time students spend receiving English literacy instruction (being immersed in it), the faster they will learn to read in English.	Students who receive some home language literacy instruction achieve at higher levels in English reading than students who do not receive it.	1. Instruction in English and interactions with English speakers are important but not enough to provide the optimal support for ELs to be able to fully participate in classroom learning and achieve to their potential. 2. Some skills developed in students' native language transfer to English, particularly when teachers help students make connections across languages. 3. Students acquire English when they receive input that is understandable (i.e., by using language in context, providing background knowledge, using visual and context cues, clarifying vocabulary).
Errors are problematic and should be avoided.	"Errors" are a positive sign that the student is making progress, and are a necessary aspect of second language acquisition.	1. Overgeneralizing grammatical rules from one language to another is a natural, normal aspect of second language acquisition; this is referred to as *interlanguage*. 2. Errors such as confusion with verb tenses, plurals, possessives, word order, subject/verb agreement, and the use of articles are common among ELs and should not be interpreted as signifying that a student has a disability. 3. Code-switching is common among bilingual individuals around the world and should not be considered a sign of confusion.

Misconception	Reality	Implications
ELs are not ready to engage in higher level thinking until they learn basic skills.	ELs are equally capable of engaging in higher level thinking as their fully proficient peers.	**1.** Instruction and practice at every grade level must provide frequent opportunities for ELs to engage in higher level thinking. **2.** Instruction should ensure that ELs of all proficiency levels have multiple entry points to access content.
All ELs learn English in the same way at about the same rate; a slow rate of acquisition indicates a possible disability.	The length of time it takes students to acquire academic language in English varies a great deal, from four to seven years or more.	**1.** Many different variables affect the language acquisition process. **2.** Even when ELs appear to be quite proficient in English, they may not yet have acquired full academic proficiency. **3.** The reasons for an EL's struggles when learning to read are more likely to relate to the language acquisition process than to a disability.

Source: Klingner (2014, pp. 6–7).

Considering Diversity: Equal Opportunity to Learn

Federal law stipulates that before children can be considered to have a disability, they must have received an adequate opportunity to learn. Thus, if students have missed too much schooling, they have consequently not received sufficient instruction. Moreover, if students have attended school but the instruction has not been coherent or appropriate for their needs, then these students have not received an adequate opportunity to learn. The following questions can help make this determination:

Instruction

- Is the instruction at the appropriate level for the student—not too difficult or too easy?
- Is the instruction comprehensible—either provided in the student's L1 or taught with sufficient supports to be understood?
- Is the instruction meaningful, motivating, and interesting for the student?
- Does the instruction explicitly help the student make connections between what he or she already knows and new learning?
- Are culturally relevant materials and culturally appropriate instructional practices used?
- When the student does not make progress, is he or she taught in different ways in a more intensive manner?
- Has the instructional model been validated with students who are similar to the student?
- Is the teacher implementing the instructional model with fidelity? If the teacher is making adaptations, are they consistent with research?
- Is the student's language acquisition supported?

Assessment

- Is the student's learning of what he or she has been taught assessed?
- Is the student allowed to demonstrate learning in multiple ways, including in their L1 if appropriate?
- Does the assessment process inform instructional decisions?
- How does the student's rate of progress compare with the learning rates of their peers?
- Is the student reaching benchmarks?

Learning Environment

- Is the classroom learning environment a warm, supportive, and collaborative one, where students help each other and all students' contributions are valued?
- Does the teacher build positive, supportive relationships with students?
- Does the teacher work well with students' families and the community?
- Does the teacher help most CLD students succeed to high levels?

This last point deserves elaboration. In other words, if most of a student's peers are doing well but they are not, that is quite a different scenario from one in which most students in the class are struggling. If just one or two children are struggling, this reaffirms that they need additional support. If almost everyone is making little progress, the teacher should reexamine their instruction. Referring to the Opening Challenge, how can Ms. Grelak use the answers these questions yield to think about Gabriel's learning problems?

Linguistic Support

Language development should be a necessary goal of instruction, whether in students' L1, in English, or in both. Students profit from explicit instruction in vocabulary that is conducted through preteaching and ongoing reinforcement. Visuals and graphic organizers can bring words to life and make the words meaningful for students. Students can also benefit from instruction that develops their higher-order thinking and problem-solving skills. Opportunities to practice and apply learning also should be part of daily instruction (Bryant et al., 2014). The information found in Table 4.10 might be helpful as you develop linguistic supports for EL students.

TABLE 4.10 ■ Language Proficiency Continuum

Level	English learners' characteristics	How do English learners gain language?	What do English learners understand?	What can English learners do?
1	Can be silent for an initial period Recognizes basic vocabulary and high-frequency words May begin to speak with few words or imitate others	Multiple repetitions of language Simple sentences Practice with partners Use visuals and realia Model, model, model Check for understanding Build on cultural and linguistic history	Instructions such as "listen," "line up," "point to," "repeat color," "tell," "touch," "circle," "draw," "match," "label"	Use gestures Use other native speakers Use high-frequency phrases Use common nouns Communicate basic needs Use survival language (i.e., words and phrases needed for basic daily tasks and routines, e.g., *bathroom, no, yes*)
2	Understands phrases and short sentences Begins to use general vocabulary and everyday expressions Grammatical forms may include present, present progressive, and imperative	Multiple repetitions of language Visual supports for vocabulary Preteach content vocabulary Link to prior knowledge	Present and past tense School-related topics Comparatives/superlatives Routine questions Imperative tense Simple sequence words	Routine expressions Simple phrases Subject–verb agreement Ask for help
3	Increased comprehension in context May sound proficient but has social, *not* academic, language Inconsistent use of standard grammatical structures	Multiple repetitions of language Use synonyms and antonyms Use word banks Demonstrate simple sentences Link to prior knowledge	Past progressive tense Contractions Auxiliary verbs/verb phrases Basic idioms General meaning Relationship between words	Formulate questions Compound sentences Use precise adjectives Use synonyms Expanded responses

Level	English learners' characteristics	How do English learners gain language?	What do English learners understand?	What can English learners do?
4	Very good comprehension More complex speech and with fewer errors Engages in conversation on a variety of topics and skills Can manipulate language to represent his or her thinking but may have difficulty with abstract academic concepts Continues to need academic language development	Multiple repetitions of language Authentic practice opportunities to develop fluency and automaticity in communication Explicit instruction in the use of language Specific feedback Continued vocabulary development in all content areas	Present/perfect continuous General and implied meaning Varied sentences Figurative language Connecting ideas	Range of purposes Increased cultural competence Standard U.S. grammar Solicit information
5	Communicates effectively on a wide range of topics Participates fully in all content areas at grade level but may still require curricular adjustments Comprehends concrete and abstract concepts Produces extended interactions to a variety of audiences	May not be fully English proficient in all domains (i.e., reading, writing, speaking, listening) Has mastered formal and informal language conventions Multiple opportunities to practice complex grammatical forms Meaningful opportunities to engage in conversations Explicit instruction in the smaller details of English usage Focus on gaps or areas still needing instruction in English Focus on comprehension instruction in all language domains	Analyze Defend Debate Predict Evaluate Justify Hypothesize and synthesize Restate Critique	May not yet be fully proficient across all domains Comprehends concrete and abstract topics Communicates effectively on a wide range of topics and purposes Produces extended interactions to a variety of audiences Participates fully in all content areas at grade level but may still require curricular modifications Increasing understanding of meaning, including figurative language Read grade-level text with academic language support Support their own point of view Use humor in native-like way

Source: Adapted from Brown and Ortiz (2014).

Validated Instructional Practices

There are a variety of instructional practices that show promise when teaching ELs with disabilities. For example, Vaughn and colleagues (2006) provided ELs with reading support in their L1. Validated practices in English have focused reading interventions paired with language development activities, such as modeling, gesturing, visuals, and explicit instruction in English usage (Vaughn et al., 2005).

Reading comprehension and/or content learning are enhanced through the use of graphic organizers (Goldenberg, 2008) and collaborative strategic reading (CSR; Klingner et al., 2012), which includes collaboration as a major instructional component through peer tutoring and cooperative learning. You will learn more about these approaches in later chapters.

Curricular Modifications

Goldenberg (2008) noted the importance of providing CLD students with curricular modifications.

Modifications might include the following:

- Providing taped textbooks.
- Highlighting textbooks and study guides.
- Using supplementary materials.
- Giving directions in small, distinct steps.
- Using written backup for oral directions.
- Using bilingual dictionaries.

CLD students with and without disabilities benefit from culturally responsive instruction in learning environments that are positive and supportive. Students do well when they are valued and cared about, when their strengths are recognized and used in their learning, when their achievement is carefully monitored, and when they are provided with appropriate instruction and effective, timely support when needed. A strong oral language component must be included in ELs' instruction. Now think back to the Opening Challenge; how can Ms. Grelak improve instruction to meet Gabriel's needs and how can Mrs. O'Malley think about incorporating some of the practices listed above to get ready for the first day of class?

SUMMARY

*Sections of this chapter were written originally by Sylvia Linan-Thompson, University of Oregon, with contributions from the late Janette K. Klingner, University of Colorado at Boulder, and Margarita Bianco, University of Colorado at Denver and Health Sciences Center, Denver.

Students from CLD backgrounds have specific learning needs. The rapid demographic changes occurring in our nation are reflected in our CLD student population. With the numbers of ethnically and racially diverse students expected to grow significantly over the coming years, and with their strong current representation, educators must ensure that the educational system is responsive to the needs of all students. We must aim to understand linguistic and cultural differences so that no students are misdiagnosed as having a disability. Multicultural programs, bilingual programs, multicultural special education, and bilingual special education programs provide ways that diverse students' needs are addressed. RTI is a means for attending to the learning needs of CLD students and CLD students who may require special education services. Additionally, students who are gifted and talented are a unique group of students who have a variety of special learning needs. Teachers should understand the characteristics of these students and ensure that students from all groups are considered for gifted and talented identification. Specialized programs must be in place for these students to guarantee that they receive a strong educational experience to prepare them to reach their potential.

REVIEW THE LEARNING OBJECTIVES

Let's review the learning objectives for this chapter. If you are uncertain and cannot talk through the answers provided for any of these questions, reread those sections of the text.

4.1 Describe how to best meet the needs of students in our culturally and linguistically diverse classrooms.

There are many ways that we can meet the needs of CLD students. First, teachers who are culturally responsive strive to match their instruction to the teaching and learning style of their students. Second, multicultural education is about making sure that schools are a place where all students feel welcomed, valued, and supported. Teachers can accomplish this by accepting and validating students' home culture and by teaching them the mainstream cultural norms as another way to interact. Third, ethnically diverse learners can and do excel in schools when culturally responsive and relevant teaching is in place; such teaching occurs when teachers utilize learners' culture, prior experiences, and performance styles to provide instruction that engages students intellectually, emotionally, socially, and politically. Fourth, teachers can help their CLD gifted learners to be successful in many ways. Teachers should value students' cultures, languages, and experiences.

4.2 Explain how we can apply the Response to Intervention (RTI) framework for culturally and linguistically diverse learners.

A culturally and linguistically responsive RTI framework that responds to the needs of CLD students includes all of the major components of RTI. This ensures that teachers consider and address cultural and linguistic factors unique to diverse learners. Teachers can ensure that core instruction is effective by incorporating teaching methods and strategies validated with students from CLD backgrounds.

4.3 Identify what constitutes effective multicultural special education programs.
The goals of multicultural special education are to reduce inappropriate referrals, improve assessment procedures, and enhance instructional and support services. CLD students with unique learning needs or disabilities should be taught with validated instructional practices in culturally responsive, supportive learning environments.

4.4 Describe bilingual special education.
Bilingual special education has as a goal helping students develop English proficiency while attending to their learning needs. Bilingual students with unique learning needs or disabilities, like other students with unique learning needs, may receive additional instructional support in a variety of settings. The most important consideration is the language of instruction. The language of instruction should be consistent across settings. Other important components are integrating the four language domains, including providing oral language instruction in English and the L1, using explicit and interactive instructional approaches, allowing flexible language use, and bridging skills from students' L1 to English.

4.5 Describe culturally and linguistically diverse gifted students.
Culturally and linguistically diverse gifted students can be described as historically underrepresented groups having one or more exceptionalities (e.g., giftedness and disabilities). They demonstrate characteristics across six areas that are associated with being gifted and talented: creative thinking, general intellectual ability, specific academic ability, leadership, psychomotor ability, and visual/performing arts abilities. However, students likely will excel in some of these areas rather than all of the areas.

REVISIT THE OPENING CHALLENGE

Check your answers to the Reflection Questions from the Opening Challenge and revise them on the basis of what you have learned.

1. What should Ms. Grelak's next steps be with Gabriel?
2. Do you agree that Ms. Grelak should refer Allen for a special education evaluation? Why or why not?
3. In what ways does Allen's level of English language proficiency and life circumstances seem to be affecting Gabriel?
4. What characteristics does Gabriel have that seem consistent with those of a gifted student? What characteristics does Gabriel have that seem consistent with those of English learners?
5. What advice would you give Ms. Grelak about instruction for English learners with learning problems?
6. Where might you go to look for information about teaching English learners in your state? What specific questions might you like to have answered?
7. Do you share some of the same concerns as Mrs. O'Malley? Find the website of your home city's school system. Is there information pertaining to culturally and linguistically diverse student populations? What information is provided for parents and teachers?

KEY TERMS

culture
English language learners (ELLs)
English learners (ELs)
enrichment
gifted and talented
multicultural education
objective referral process
overrepresented

PROFESSIONAL STANDARDS AND LICENSURE

For a complete description of Professional Standards and Licensure, please see the appendix.

CEC Initial Preparation Standards

Standard 1: Learner Development and Individual Learning Differences

INTASC Core Principles

Standard 1: Learner Development

Standard 2: Learning Differences

Praxis II: Education of Exceptional Students: Core Content Knowledge

I. Understanding Exceptionalities: Human Development and Behavior

II. Legal and Societal Issues: Federal Laws and Legal Issues

III. Delivery of Services to Students With Disabilities: Background Knowledge

iStock.com/Phynart Studio

5 UNDERSTANDING LEARNERS WITH THE MOST COMMON DISABILITIES OR CONDITIONS

LEARNING OBJECTIVES

After studying this chapter, you will be able to meet the following learning objectives:

5.1 Explain how students from different ethnic and racial groups are overrepresented and underrepresented in IDEA categories of special education.

5.2 Name the 14 special education categories for students with disabilities.

5.3 Compare and contrast the three schemes or ways disabilities are grouped to organize special education.

5.4 Discuss the attributes of students with learning disabilities.

5.5 Identify the attributes of students with speech or language impairments.

5.6 Discuss the attributes of students with attention deficit hyperactivity disorder.

5.7 Examine the attributes of students with autism spectrum disorders.

5.8 Recognize the attributes of students with intellectual and developmental disabilities.

5.9 Discuss the attributes of students with emotional or behavioral disorders.

Opening Challenge

Working in Inclusive Classrooms

Elementary Grades. Mr. Samora is several months into his third year of teaching and is so glad that he was assigned to second grade all 3 years. He loves working at Jackson Elementary School, and he has great students. The more experienced teachers are always there for him. They answer questions and help him navigate the bureaucracy, figure out how to get paperwork through the system, and think through issues related to his students' programs and how to respond well to their learning challenges. The teachers and administrators all work together as a team. When Mr. Samora received a note from the central office asking him to come to a meeting because the individualized education program (IEP) team was considering a change of diagnosis for one of his students, he first went to some of the senior teachers at his school for information about this process to help him prepare for the meeting.

The IEP team was concerned about his student Sonia, who has received special education services since kindergarten. Mr. Samora knows Sonia's history well and has met with her parents on several occasions. Sonia did not begin talking until she was about 3 years old. As a kindergartner, she was unable to rhyme words, could not identify sound–letter relationships as well as her peers, was behind in language development, and seemed to have difficulty keeping up with her classmates. In kindergarten, Ms. Dowdy, Sonia's teacher, referred her for speech and language services. Sonia qualified for special education and was identified as having language impairments. Now, however, the speech and language therapist thinks it's important to reclassify Sonia as having learning disabilities. Mr. Samora cannot understand the concern. Sonia is receiving special education help, and she is improving. He wonders, *"Why are we going to spend so much time on changing a special education label for Sonia? Do all these different special education categories make a difference in the way we teach? Will all the professional time spent on reclassification actually benefit Sonia?"*

Secondary Grades. Mrs. Lupino teaches ninth-grade history at Martin Luther King Jr. High School. She is getting ready for her fifth year of teaching and is reviewing student record folders to learn about students in her class and their individual needs. The special education teacher, Mr. Patton, is meeting with her to review the IEPs of three students she will have in her classes. One student has a learning disability (LD), another has attention deficit hyperactivity disorder (ADHD), and a third student has a mild emotional and behavioral disorder (EBD). The students all will be in her fifth-period class, and the special education teacher will work with her and the students in the class during that period. Reading is an issue for her student with the learning disability; the student with ADHD needs assistance with paying attention and staying on task; and the student with an emotional and behavioral disorder is on a behavior plan. Mrs. Lupino starts to think about questions for Mr. Patton. *"What are the learning characteristics of these three students? How severe are their disabilities? How can Mr. Patton help me meet my special education students' needs while I continue to be responsible for all of the other students in my class?"*

Reflection Questions

In your journal, write down your answers to the following questions. After completing the chapter, check your answers and revise them on the basis of what you have learned.

1. Do you think identifying students by specific disability is useful?
2. Why do you think Sonia's special education label is being reconsidered at this point in her schooling?
3. Is Sonia's situation unusual? Why or why not?
4. Will a change in category influence the way Mr. Samora teaches Sonia?
5. Will it change the services Sonia receives?
6. What do you think are some learning characteristics of the three students in Mrs. Lupino's class?
7. What help might she be looking for from Mr. Patton (the special education teacher) for these three students?

Before students with the most common disabilities are discussed, it is important to note overall prevalence figures for students in special education as a context for the information in this chapter and in Chapter 6. To begin, about 7.2 million, or 15%, of U.S. public schoolchildren aged 3 to 21 have a disability that affects their educational performance to such a degree that they require special education services (National Center for Education Statistics [NCES], 2022). The largest group of students qualifying for special education services through IDEA is those with learning disabilities (33%), followed by students with speech or language disorders (19%). Together, the students with multiple disabilities, hearing impairments, physical disabilities, visual impairments, traumatic brain injuries, and deaf-blindness account for only 2% of all students with disabilities. We talk about those disabilities in Chapter 6. Figure 5.1 illustrates the number of students aged 5 to 21 with disabilities across the special education categories identified in Chapter 1.

Disabilities create very special needs for individuals, their families, and the education system. Teachers and other educators can help students achieve their potential by addressing their special needs, by providing them with many opportunities for learning and for success, and by ensuring they receive a high-quality education. Teachers who are well-prepared, use evidence-based practices and instructional procedures, and provide students with additional assistance or accommodations can make real differences in the educational lives of these students (Cardichon et al., 2020; Lambert, 2022; West, 2022). In this text, we provide you with tools that improve the results of all students. Before you learn about how to teach these students effectively, let's think more about students with disabilities and specifically about the most common special education categories. More information about prevalence figures for students from diverse backgrounds is provided in the Considering Diversity feature.

FIGURE 5.1 ■ Distribution of Children Aged 5 to 21 Served Under IDEA, Part B, by Disability Type

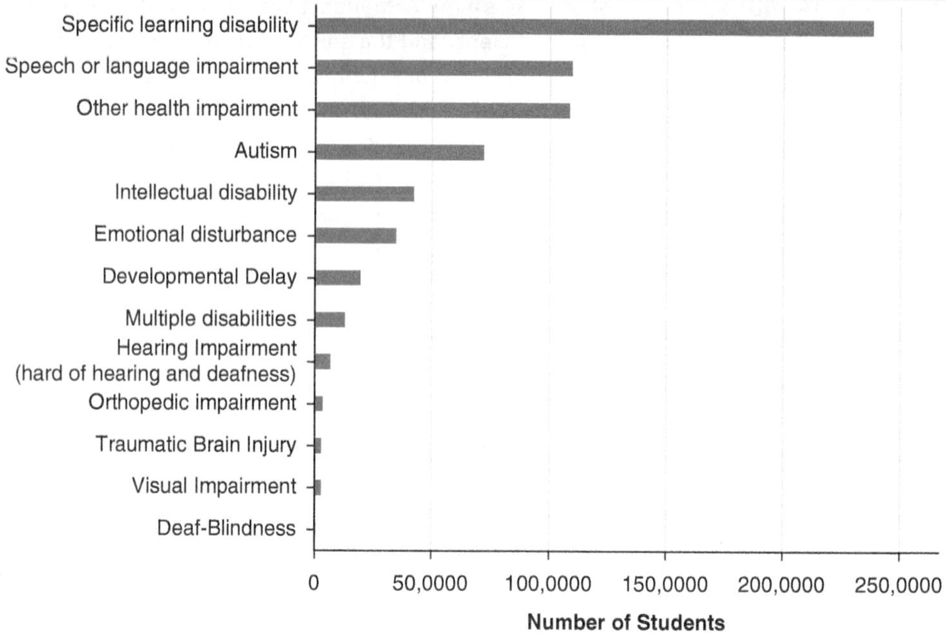

Source: Office of Special Education Programs (2020).

CONSIDERING DIVERSITY: OVERREPRESENTATION AND UNDERREPRESENTATION OF STUDENTS IN SPECIAL EDUCATION CATEGORIES

As we discuss in other chapters, the overrepresentation of schoolchildren from some racial and ethnic groups has been an issue in the field of special education for many years (Barrio, 2017). The underrepresentation of schoolchildren from other racial and ethnic groups—for example, those of Asian heritage—also has been an issue for different reasons. As you review the statistics that follow, think about why children and youths from various racial and ethnic groups are identified as needing special education services while others require services to a lesser degree. The following provides information about special education services delivered through IDEA by ethnic and racial group for infants and toddlers aged birth through 2 and children aged 3 to 21.

- Infants and toddlers served under IDEA, Part C, in 2020:
  - White and Native Hawai'ian or Other Pacific Islander children were somewhat more likely to be served than children of other racial and ethnic groups combined.
  - Black children were as likely as children of all other racial and ethnic groups combined to be served.
  - American Indian or Alaska Native, Hispanic/Latino, Asian, and mixed-race children were by group somewhat less likely to be served than all other racial/ethnic groups combined.
- Students aged 3 through 21 served under IDEA were represented in special education in the following ways (NCES, 2022):
  - White students comprise 15% of those students identified as having a disability in the general population of children attending public schools.
  - Black children, who have a much smaller representation in the general population, comprise 17%.
  - Hispanic or Latinx students comprise 14%.

- American Indian/Alaska Native students constitute 19%.
- Pacific Islander students made up 12%.
- Students from two or more races comprised 15%.

CATEGORIES FOR STUDENTS WITH DISABILITIES

In Chapter 1 and also in Figure 5.1, we list the 14 special education categories served through IDEA. Remember, not all students with disabilities receive special education services. Those whose educational performance is not adversely affected by their disabilities receive services and assistance through Section 504. For example, many students with physical disabilities do fine academically and do not need special education services. They do well learning the content of the general curriculum alongside their peers who do not experience physical challenges. Some of these students may need assistance or accommodations, such as special floor mats so their wheelchairs can glide easily into the school building or the classroom, or services provided by physical therapists or an assistive technologist to reduce the impact of the disability on learning. Other students may have special needs and are entitled to accommodations as well as extra help, as is the case for many students with ADHD. Throughout this book, you are learning about students who have learning and behavioral challenges that general education teachers can address to help them achieve their potential.

WAYS DISABILITIES ARE ORGANIZED FOR SPECIAL EDUCATION

Three major schemes are used to group disabilities for the purposes of meeting educational needs. One scheme uses disability types or special education categories (learning disabilities, intellectual disabilities). Another scheme groups students by the severity of the disability (mild, moderate, severe). And the third considers disabilities in terms of prevalence (most and least common). Another way to organize disabilities relates to how school districts are reimbursed from their respective states for providing services to students with disabilities. For example, some states provide different reimbursement amounts for various special education categories. Students with learning disabilities might be funded at a lower level than students with autism spectrum disorder. Other states differentially fund according to the level of students' severity or complexity of services required because of additional costs for related service providers who are part of multidisciplinary teams. The same system works for students with more common (higher levels of prevalence) or less common disabilities (those that are less prevalent). If you are wondering, like Mr. Samora, whether labeling students in different ways will benefit the students, these funding issues might be one explanation. Let's look at each organizational system in turn.

Special Education Categories

In the previous section, we discussed the special education categories used by IDEA and many parent organizations (e.g., the Learning Disabilities Association of America and the Autism Society of America). When it comes to schoolchildren, the government has decided to define disabilities using a categorical approach, and states are required each year to use these federal categories to report the numbers of students with disabilities being served (NCES, 2022). Although many states use slightly different terms than those used by the federal government, the similarities are obvious. With the inclusion of developmental delay, 14 categories or groups are used in this system. Notice that giftedness is not included in the prevalence figures because it is not part of IDEA, although many states include gifted and talented students within their special education services umbrella. The prevalence rate for gifted and talented learners is estimated to be a bit more than 6% (National Association for Gifted Children, n.d.) and includes students who benefit from services to address their intellectual levels, talents, and creativity. We discussed them in Chapter 4.

Perspectives on Disability

Possibly because it is so difficult to change federal and state laws, the names some government agencies use for disabilities might not always be what parents and professionals consider modern or up to date. In this text, we try to use terms preferred by individuals who have each specific disability, parents of children with each disability, and the respective professional organizations. Here are a few examples of how terms and thinking about specific disabilities vary: Ideas and research about autism have been developing rapidly, particularly as its prevalence rate continues to increase. IDEA still uses the term *autism*, but the more current conceptualization of this disability is much broader, as reflected by the name *autism spectrum disorder* (ASD). Other examples of differences among terminology used in IDEA and by professional organizations and parents exist. For example, IDEA calls it *emotional disturbance*, but most professionals and parents use the term *emotional or behavioral disorders, emotional and behavior disorders*, or just *behavior disorders*. IDEA uses the term *specific learning disabilities*, but parents, professionals, and individuals with the condition usually use the term *learning disabilities* instead. Also, IDEA includes students with ADHD in the "Other Health Impairments" category, grouping them with students with significant health issues. You might be wondering the utility of this categorical approach, but as you will learn from later discussions about each category, it does have some benefits, like bringing special assistance to students who are blind, d/Deaf, or have specific health problems.

However, it is important to understand some reasons why the categorical approach is often criticized. For example, not all instructional methods are uniformly effective for all students labeled with a specific disability. Knowing that a student has learning disabilities does not help a teacher know which reading method to use. Educational interventions must be matched to the individual learner's performance, not to a special education category (Morris-Mathews et al., 2020). Many interventions effective with one student with a disability are also powerful for classmates without disabilities who have learning difficulties. Thus, although special education categories have proved not to offer precision in guiding instructional decision making, they do remain the primary way students are identified, labeled, and qualified for special education services.

Although not found in a separate disability category, asthma is a common chronic illness among children and is classified in the "Other Health Impairments" category. Most children with asthma do not qualify for special education services through IDEA because their educational performance is not affected, but rather they are served through a 504 plan. ADHD, another common condition, is also found in this category.

AP Photo/The Daily Times, James B. Hale

Severity of Disability

As we have just noted, many educators believe that special education categories and the resulting labelling of individuals have little or no educational function. Some professionals prefer a noncategorical approach that groups students by the severity of their problems, not by the type of disability they have. How does this system work?

Instead of thinking about the specific disability, educators consider how the condition affects an individual's performance. Typically, four groupings are used: mild, moderate, severe, and profound. This system reflects the types of supports the individual needs in life and at school (Schalock et al., 2021a, 2021b). Individuals with mild disabilities require some accommodations, and those with severe disabilities require intensive supports and assistance for a sustained period of time. We must be very cautious, however, when thinking about disabilities by level of severity. First, it is a mistake to assume that one disability, such as intellectual disability, is more severe than another, such as stuttering. All disabilities are serious, and the effects on the individuals and their families can never be minimized. Second, each disability grouping takes in a continuum of severity from mild to severe. It is incorrect, for instance, to think all learning disabilities are mild.

Today, both the categorical and noncategorical approaches are used in classrooms. Students are identified and reported to the federal government by disability, but fewer and fewer separate schools or classes are available for students with a specific disability (Office of Special Education Programs [OSEP], 2022). Some professionals and advocacy organizations (e.g., TASH, an organization representing individuals with severe and profound disabilities) have advocated for the closure of all segregated programs for students with disabilities (TASH, 2018). Thus, although IDEA requires that students qualify for special education by being identified as having a specific disability, schools typically serve these students according to their needs and educational performance. In both general education classes and special education classes, students with disabilities are classmates but do not always share the same disabilities.

Neither of these first two organizing systems—by category or severity—is related to the number of individuals affected. Another way to organize our thinking about disabilities is thus to group them by how often they occur. For example, some disabilities (e.g., learning disabilities) occur more frequently than others; more students have mild disabilities than have severe disabilities. Let's consider organizing by prevalence.

Prevalence of Disability

Remember, in Figures 1.2 and 5.1, you learned that disabilities are not equally distributed across special education students. Almost half of all students with disabilities are identified as having learning disabilities, and many of the other disabilities are very rare. Clearly, the response to an individual's disability varies, not because of the size of that group, but because the nature of each disabilities differs. For example, students with severe visual loss often require specialized services from a multidisciplinary team of professionals, such as orientation and mobility specialists, assistive technology specialists, or vision teachers who know braille instruction. On the other hand, general education teachers work with many students who have low vision and in some cases work with specialists to make needed adjustments (e.g., special seating closer to the blackboard and out of the glare of light from windows) and accommodations (e.g., access to enlarged print) so these students can access the general education curriculum.

We have organized our discussions about students with disabilities by the prevalence of the entire group. In this chapter, you will learn about students with disabilities that are more frequent than those we discuss in Chapter 6. Figure 5.1 reminds you of the order of prevalence for each special education category. In each separate section about a special education category, you will find an overview, commonly adopted definitions, an explanation of the types of conditions found with in that group, and learning characteristics. We begin examining by thinking about the most common disability among school children: learning disabilities. Clearly, teachers encounter students with this disability every school day in almost every classroom. Therefore, it is important that educators and specialists work together to ensure that all students receive an appropriate education. The following Working Together feature illustrates how educators and specialists can collaborate for educational planning and instruction.

WORKING TOGETHER

UNDERSTANDING STUDENTS WITH UNIQUE LEARNING NEEDS

Think back to the Opening Challenge where Mr. Samora and Mrs. Lupino are preparing for their classes. Both teachers understand that they will be teaching students with disabilities alongside students without disabilities. They are encountering two situations that are important to recognize; Mr. Samora is learning about the importance of assigning the correct disability label to a student, and Mrs. Lupino wonders how the special education teacher, Mr. Patton, can help her. Whether working in a team, as in Mr. Samora's situation, or consulting with the special education teacher, as in Mrs. Lupino's situation, classroom teachers must be informed about special education and collaborative practices to promote student success. It is important for Mr. Samora to understand why reclassifying a label (e.g., language impairment to learning disability) promotes appropriate services, such as providing more academic support, for the student with a disability. Mrs. Lupino needs to work with Mr. Patton to ensure that when they are teaching together, the needs of her three students with disabilities are addressed according to their IEP requirements. Both situations necessitate conveying of information to the classroom teachers to benefit their students with disabilities.

Questions

1. What questions might Mr. Samora ask at the IEP team meeting?
2. How can the speech and language therapist help Mr. Samora understand why the label is being changed?
3. What information should Mr. Patton provide to Mrs. Lupino?
4. How can the special education teacher work with the three students with disabilities in Mrs. Lupino's class?

ATTRIBUTES OF STUDENTS WITH LEARNING DISABILITIES

As you learned in Chapter 1 and in the Overall Prevalence section of this chapter, learning disabilities is the largest special education category (review Figure 5.1); it represents 3.4% of the total public school enrollment and 34% of all students identified as having a disability (OSEP, 2022). Two-thirds of students identified with learning disabilities are male, although public school enrollment is almost evenly split by sex. Often incorrectly considered a mild condition, learning disabilities are serious. A learning disability is a severe, pervasive, and chronic condition that requires intensive intervention (Lerner & Johns, 2015). It is important for educators to recognize that learning disability is a complex and lifelong condition (Eunice Kennedy Shriver National Institute of Child Health and Human Development, 2018) and, for most of these students, requires very specialized data-based instruction (Fuchs et al., 2017).

Unfortunately, in the past and too often today, learning disabilities are not identified until students are well into their school years. Up until 2004, a learning disability was diagnosed largely by identifying an aptitude-achievement discrepancy analysis (i.e., academic underachievement is identified by low achievement test scores and at least average cognitive [IQ] measure scores and determining that the underachievement is not caused by receiving inadequate instruction or learning English as a second language). However, to get a significant gap between aptitude and achievement requires a student to be about 2 to 3 years behind in academic learning. You can now see why under this system, students are not typically identified until third grade, even though teachers recognize the problems as early as kindergarten. This is why the aptitude-achievement discrepancy model is often been called the "wait to fail" problem. Today, MTSS and RTI methods that you learned about in Chapter 2 help to bring effective practices to students early, often referred to as early intervening. In many cases, intervening early prevents school failure and the ultimate diagnosis of learning disabilities. For others, it brings services to students once problems are recognized, not after waiting for years of failure to qualify for services, thereby reducing the impact of academic and social problems associated with this disability.

Definition

Although definitions of learning disabilities differ across the states, the federal government's definition, the one included in IDEA 2004, is the basis for all used by states and school districts. The IDEA definition, along with that of the National Institutes of Health (NIH), are found in Table 5.1. Notice that the NIH definition reflects a more modern approach that has less of a medical orientation and acknowledges that *learning disabilities* is a general term referring to a heterogeneous group of disorders.

Types

To better understand the diversity—the heterogeneity—of students with learning disabilities, let's examine these common profiles or types of learning disabilities:

- Overall unexpected underachievement
- Reading disabilities (dyslexia)
- Mathematics disabilities (dyscalculia)
- Written expression disabilities (dysgraphia)

Despite having normal intelligence, students with learning disabilities do not achieve academically on a par with their classmates without disabilities. Some face challenges in almost every academic area or **unexpected underachievement** (Fuchs et al., 2017). Reading and writing, obviously, are important skills; in school, students must be able to read information from a variety of texts (e.g., social studies, science, literature) and write using varying formats (e.g., essays, reports, creative writing, notes). As the complexity of academic tasks increases, students not proficient in reading and writing find it difficult to keep pace with higher academic expectations (Gilmour et al., 2019). As they progress through school, reading disabilities compound and make it very difficult to perform well on other academic tasks, which contributes to overall underachievement.

The most common type of learning disability is reading disability, which is sometimes referred to as dyslexia (National Institute of Neurological Disorders and Stroke [NINDS], 2023). Early signs include difficulties with phonological processing or the manipulation of sounds or being able to rhyme words. Fortunately, early identification and direct instruction can eliminate or reduce the ultimate difficulties with reading skills. It is important for teachers to understand that often a reading disability is not isolated and that these children often have problems with written language, solving arithmetic

TABLE 5.1 ■ Definitions of Learning Disabilities

Source	Definition
IDEA 2004[1]	*Specific learning disability* means a disorder in one or more of the basic psychological processes involved in understanding or in using language, spoken or written, that may manifest itself in an imperfect ability to listen, think, speak, read, write, spell, or do mathematical calculations, including such conditions as perceptual disabilities, brain injury, minimal brain dysfunction, dyslexia, and developmental aphasia. Specific learning disability does not include learning problems that are primarily the result of visual, hearing, or motor disabilities; mental retardation, now known as intellectual disabilities; emotional disturbance; or environmental, cultural, or economic disadvantage.
NIH[2]	Learning disabilities are disorders that affect the ability to understand or use spoken or written language, do mathematical calculations, coordinate movements, or direct attention. Although learning disabilities occur in very young children, the disorders are usually not recognized until the child reaches school age.

Sources: [1]U.S. Department of Education (2006); [2]*"Learning disabilities: Definition."* NINDS Learning Disabilities Information Page by National Institute of Neurological Disorders and Stroke (NINDS), National Institutes of Health, 2022.

word problems, and many other academic tasks. Some estimates indicate that 60% of students with reading disabilities also have mathematics disabilities (Dyslexic Advantage Team, 2021).

Some experts have long thought learning disabilities reflect deficits in the ability to process or remember information; some refer to this as problems with working memory (Torgesen, 2002). Teaching memory skills is not a substitute for directly teaching reading comprehension or arithmetic word problem solving for mathematics (Fuchs et al., 2022; Fuchs et al., 2021). What appears quite certain is that students with learning disabilities do not learn at the same rate or in the same ways as their classmates (Gilmour et al., 2019). The instruction or intervention typically used in general education programs is not sufficient and does not help them improve; more intensive individualized intervention is necessary (Morris-Mathews et al., 2020). Despite these seemingly overwhelming challenges, as you will learn later in this text, many of these problems associated with academic learning can be overcome with explicit instruction, data-based decision making, and sustained as well as intensive efforts. We have devoted separate chapters to each of these important instructional areas (see Chapter 9 for assessment and data-based decision making, Chapter 10 for social skills, Chapter 11 for reading, Chapter 12 for writing, Chapter 13 for mathematics, and Chapter 14 for content area instruction).

Although reading problems are the most common reason for referral, more than 50% of students with learning disabilities also have mathematics learning disabilities (Compton et al., 2012). Some seem to have difficulties with mathematics alone, but for most, this difficulty is part of an overwhelming and pervasive underachievement.

Characteristics

Unexpected underachievement has long been considered the defining characteristic of learning disabilities (Bryant et al., 2000), meaning affected students perform significantly below their peers and below levels that teachers and parents would expect from children of their ability. Although some students have problems in only one academic area, most have pervasive problems that affect the entire range of academic and social domains. Teachers often cite this group's heterogeneity as challenging because it

Problems associated with academic learning can be overcome with explicit instruction and intensive efforts. What benefits might this student receive from individualized instruction?

iStock.com/FatCamera

seems that each student requires a unique response, an important reason why data-based instructional decision making is so important (Fuchs et al., 2017; Morris-Mathews et al., 2020).

Finally, most individuals with learning disabilities have problems with social skills, and the results are negative self-concepts, an inability to make friends, ineffective approaches to schoolwork, and poor interactions with others (Vaughn & Bos, 2020). For example, many students with learning disabilities are naive and unable to judge other people's intentions accurately. They cannot understand nonverbal behaviors, such as facial expressions, and therefore they do not comprehend other people's emotional messages. This inability puts them at a great disadvantage and may result in low acceptance by their peers and teachers. Difficulty with social skills, coupled with low achievement and distracting classroom behaviors, in turn influences the social status of students with learning disabilities. Peers may consider them overly dependent, less cooperative, and less socially adept. Consequently, they are less likely to become leaders—or even to be included in groups. Teachers can play an instrumental role in reducing peer rejection. One approach was suggested about 25 years ago and remains popular today: pair these students with classmates without disabilities in areas of mutual interest (Harris & Graham, 1999). For example, teachers might assign students with common interests like sports, music, or a hobby to work together on an academic task such as a science report.

Table 5.2 list common characteristics found among this group of learners, but remember each individual is different from others and these characteristics do not universally occur in all students with learning disabilities.

Many students with learning disabilities need to use alternative means or assistive technology to do their schoolwork. For example, a student with severely impaired writing abilities may find that the speech recognition system, a standard feature of personal computers, is helpful when writing term papers. Another student who cannot read well enough to keep up with classmates as they read their sixth-grade social studies textbook might profit from using the digital version of the text and the speech output option. This chapter's Tech Notes feature provides information about the use of computer tablets as an example of how technology can promote access to the curriculum and independence.

TABLE 5.2 ■ Characteristics of Students With Learning Disabilities

Academic	Social	Behavioral Style
• Prone to unexpected underachievement • Resistant to treatment • Difficult to teach • Unable to solve problems • Demonstrates uneven academic abilities • Weak in basic language skills • Possess poor reading skills in word reading, fluency, and/or comprehension • Possess poor written language skills in spelling, grammar, and written expression • Possess poor mathematics skills in numbers sense, calculations, math reasoning, and problem solving • Have difficulties with metacognitive and cognitive abilities • Have memory deficits • Unable to generalize	• Immature • Capable of socially unacceptable behavior • Prone to misinterpret social and nonverbal cues • Poor decision-making skills • Victimized • Unable to follow social conventions (manners) • Rejected • Naive • Shy, withdrawn, insecure • Unable to predict social consequences	• Inattentive • Distractible • Hyperactive • Impulsive • Poorly coordinated • Unmotivated • Dependent • Disorganized

TECH NOTES

MOBILE DEVICES

The use of mobile devices rather than desktops or laptops has been gaining in popularity as a means for delivering instruction and helping students to access the curriculum. Mobile devices (e.g., mobile phones, tablets), typically have a touch-screen display and allow for Internet access. These devices have the potential to be useful tools for students with disabilities for the following reasons: (a) the availability of downloadable, inexpensive apps; (b) the touch-screen feature that allows students with disabilities to use the device without having to operate a mouse or a touchpad; (c) instant turn on/off ability; and (d) Internet access and built-in video, a camera, and audio hardware features. Instructional applications, commonly called apps, have gained in popularity for use with mobile technologies to help students acquire skills in various academic areas. A computer can read the content for students who have difficulties reading textbooks written at grade level. Students who cannot prepare reports without many formatting and spelling errors benefit from word processing software with spell and grammar checkers and sequential heading structures. For those with basic computational difficulties, basic and commonly available software can perform those tasks. Time management can also be a challenge for students with learning disabilities, and again, commonly available time management software is built into everyday systems we all use.

ATTRIBUTES OF STUDENTS WITH SPEECH OR LANGUAGE IMPAIRMENTS

Learning disabilities form the largest special education category, but the federal government allows students with disabilities to be reported in only one special education category. Thus, a fourth-grade student with reading/learning disabilities and also a speech problem might well be included in the learning disabilities category but also receive services from a speech/language pathologist as a related service. Although 33% of children and youth aged 3 to 21 served through IDEA have learning disabilities, 19% have speech or language disorders (OSEP, 2022). However, they have the highest rate (88%) of being included in general education classes for at least 80% of the school day, followed by students with learning disabilities (75%). Because of the relationship between having language problems as a preschooler and having later problems with reading and writing, during the early school years speech and language impairment is clearly the larger special education category. For children between the ages of 3 to 5, speech or language impairments is the largest category with almost 40% of all children served in that age group (OSEP, 2022); but that percentage drops to 16% for students aged 6 to 21, when the percentage of those with learning disabilities increases to 37% of all students served through IDEA. When we consider both primary and secondary disabilities, speech or language impairments are clearly the most common disability among schoolchildren, especially when they are young. Speech and language are the foundations for many things we do as humans.

As you will learn from our discussion about the types of speech or language disorders, these areas are really quite separate. Students with speech disorders such as stuttering, articulation problems, and voice issues typically do not have a language disorder, but both do affect one's ability to communicate effectively and with ease. Communication requires the receiver to use eyes, ears, and even tactile (touch) senses (as do those who use braille) to take messages to the brain where they are understood and to interpret the sender's code so it has meaning. If either the sender or the receiver has a defective mechanism for sending or receiving the information, the communication process is ineffective. We distinguish among three related terms: *communication, language*, and *speech*.

- Communication: The process of exchanging knowledge, ideas, opinions, and feelings through the use of verbal or nonverbal language
- Language: The rule-based method of communication relying on the comprehension and use of the signs and symbols by which ideas are represented
- Speech: The vocal production of language

Next, let's turn our attention to the definitions or explanations of speech or language disorders.

Definition

Although they make up a single special education category and are defined together as one disability, speech impairments and language impairments are really two separate but related disabilities. Table 5.3 provides both the IDEA definition as well as the definition adopted many years ago by the American Speech-Language-Hearing Association (ASHA, 1993), the nation's largest organization representing professionals in the areas of speech, language, and audiology.

Types

Both types of communication disorders—speech impairments and language impairments—can be further subdivided. The three types of speech impairments follow:

1. Articulation problems: The process of producing speech sounds is flawed, and resulting speech sounds are incorrect. Table 5.4 describes each of the four articulation problems.
2. Fluency problems: Hesitations or repetitions interrupt the flow of speech. Stuttering is one type of fluency problem.
3. Voice problems: The voice is unusual in pitch or loudness given the age and gender of the individual.

Some young children between 3 and 5 years of age demonstrate misarticulations and dysfluencies (nonfluencies) in the course of normal speech development. These misarticulations are not usually indicative of a problem in need of therapy (Ramig & Shames, 2006).

Many people recall the types of articulation errors by using the acronym SODA: Substitution, Omission, Distortion, and Addition.

TABLE 5.3 ■ Definitions of Speech or Language Impairment

Source	Definition
IDEA 2004[1]	Speech or language impairment means a communication disorder, such as stuttering, impaired articulation, a language impairment, or a voice impairment, that adversely affects a child's educational performance.
ASHA[2]	A speech and language disorder may be present when a person's speech or language is different from that of others of the same age, sex, or ethnic group; when a person's speech and/or language is hard to understand; when a person is overly concerned about his or her speech; or when a person often avoids communicating with others.

Sources: [1]USDE (2006, p. 1265); [2]American Speech-Language-Hearing Association Ad Hoc Committee on Service Delivery in the Schools (1993, pp. 40–41).

TABLE 5.4 ■ Types of Articulation Errors

Error Type	Definition	Example
Substitution	One sound is used for another. This is a common misarticulation among small children.	Intended: I see the rabbit. Substitution: I tee the wabbit.
Omission	A sound or group of sounds is left out of a word.	Intended: I want a banana. Omission: I wanna nana.
Distortion	A variation of the intended sound is produced in an unfamiliar manner.	Intended: Give the pencil to Sally. Distortion: Give the pencil to Sally. (the /p/ is nasalized).
Addition	An extra sound is inserted or added to one already correctly produced.	Intended: I miss her. Addition: I missid her.

Language impairments are not typically broken down into types, but we often discuss problems with language in terms of the aspect of language where the problem exists.

- Syntax: The rule system used for all language (oral, written, and sign)
- Semantics: The intent and meaning of spoken and written statements
- Pragmatics: The application of language based on the social content

Rules in each language govern the way vowels, consonants, their combinations, and words are used. The relationship between development of an awareness of sounds in words (phonological awareness) during the preschool years and later ease of learning how to read has been discussed for years (Bishop, 2006). To prevent reading failure later during the school years, teachers should refer preschoolers who have problems mastering phonology to specialists for early intervention.

Characteristics

The ability to distinguish among three language-related situations helps general education teachers make prompt and correct referrals and avoid misidentifying students:

1. Language impairments
2. Language delays
3. Language differences

A typical 3-year-old can use some fairly sophisticated language. At the same age, a child with language impairments might speak in only two-word utterances. We look not just at how quickly or slowly a child develops language but also at how the child's language development is different from that of typical peers.

Children with language delays generally acquire language in the same sequence as their peers but more slowly. Many do not have a disability and catch up with their peers. However, some children who acquire language in the correct sequence do so very slowly and never complete the acquisition of complex language structures. For example, most children with intellectual disability have language delays, and their language development is below the norm for their age, but most do not develop a language impairment (Marrus & Hall, 2017).

What about children who are learning English as a second language? Many teachers have difficulty determining whether a child who is not a native speaker of English is merely language different or has a language impairment (Prezas & Jo, 2017). Truly mastering a second language takes a long time. Many English learners (ELs) may appear to be fluent because they converse with their classmates on the playground and express their basic needs in the classroom, but even so they may not yet have developed sufficient English fluency to participate fully in academic instruction. Speaking English as a second language does not result in a disability, but some ELs may be slow in mastering their second language, particularly if poverty is present, and some do have language impairments.

Dialects of American English are not impairments, either. They result from historical, social, regional, and cultural influences on speech, but children who speak them are sometimes perceived by educators as inferior or misidentified as having language impairments. Teachers need to understand and be sensitive to the differences between dialects and language impairments, but when in doubt, they should seek the advice of specialists. Speech/language pathologists who can distinguish between language differences and language impairments are proficient in the rules of the particular child's dialect and in the use of nondiscriminatory testing procedures. It is equally a mistake to assume students have disabilities simply because of their cultural or linguistic backgrounds and to fail to qualify students for services they need for fear of being discriminatory.

ATTRIBUTES OF STUDENTS WITH ATTENTION DEFICIT HYPERACTIVITY DISORDER

Whether a student's ADHD is considered a primary or a secondary condition and whether it negatively influences educational performance, ADHD does result in special needs that can be met by perceptive and effective teachers. These students often have a difficult time at school and also in later life (APA, 2013). They tend to experience social rejection, poor school performance, and display antisocial behaviors. They are more frequently than peers without ADHD injured because of risky behavior. They are often the targets of teasing or bullying. Despite these negative outcomes, positive features are present as well. Many of these students exhibit intense creativity, exuberance, and excitement. They apply unique approaches to learning and solving problems, which may be why many artists, innovators, and entrepreneurs self-report having ADHD.

It is impossible to give you exact information about how many children and youth have ADHD, but a considerable number of students are affected. Remember, as we discussed in Chapter 1, ADHD is one condition identified by IDEA in the "Other Health Impairments" category. Other conditions that are included in this overarching special education category are reviewed in Chapter 6, along with other less frequent disabilities. States are not required to report the number of students served through IDEA who specifically have ADHD; however, estimates are that some 9.8% of all schoolchildren are affected (Centers for Disease Control [CDC], 2022b). Some of the reasons that there are problems in determining the prevalence of ADHD follow:

1. ADHD is not a separate category called out in IDEA 2004, so states do not report ADHD students separately to the federal government.
2. Not all students with ADHD are eligible for special education services. If the condition does not adversely influence their academic performance, they receive accommodations, but *not* special education services, for their unique learning needs through Section 504 of the Rehabilitation Act of 1973 (see Chapter 1).
3. Because many ADHD symptoms overlap with those of other disabilities, many students with ADHD or who have ADHD symptoms are served through other special education categories, such as learning disabilities or emotional or behavior disorders.
4. Students who have ADHD and another disability—**coexisting disabilities**—are reported in their primary disability category and their ADHD goes unreported.
5. ADHD may be underidentified, with some organizations reporting that 40% of youth with diagnosable (but not necessarily diagnosed) ADHD symptoms don't get treatment. (ADDITUDE, 2018)

Whether a student's ADHD is considered a primary or a secondary condition and whether it negatively influences educational performance, ADHD does result in special needs that can be met by perceptive and effective teachers.

Definition

Table 5.5 gives the IDEA 2004 definition of Other Health Impairments, where ADHD is mentioned, and the DSM-5 (APA, 2013) definition of ADHD. As you review this table, think about what ADHD is and what it is not.

Types

ADHD is a complicated condition. Students with ADHD tend to fall into three main groups:

1. Those who do not qualify for special education
2. Those who qualify for special education
3. Those who have coexisting disabilities

TABLE 5.5 ■ Definitions of Attention Deficit Hyperactivity Disorder

Source	Definition
IDEA 2004[1]	ADHD is listed as one condition within the "Other Health Impairments" category. *Other health impairments* means having limited strength, vitality, or alertness, including heightened alertness to environmental stimuli that results in limited alertness with respect to the educational environment, that **i.** Is due to chronic or acute health problems such as asthma, attention-deficit disorder (ADD) or ADHD, diabetes, epilepsy, a heart condition, hemophilia, lead poisoning, leukemia, nephritis, rheumatic fever, sickle cell anemia, and Tourette syndrome; and **ii.** Adversely affects a child's educational performance.
DSM-5[2]	In its DSM-5 manual, APA calls ADHD "a persistent pattern of inattention and/or hyperactivity-impulsivity that interferes with functioning or development" (APA, 2013, p. 59). **A.** Several inattentive or hyperactive-impulsive symptoms were present prior to age 12 years. **B.** Several inattentive or hyperactive-impulsive symptoms are present in two or more settings (e.g., at school, work, or home). **C.** There is clear evidence that the symptoms interfere with, or reduce the quality of, social, academic, or occupational functioning. **D.** The symptoms do not occur exclusively during the course of schizophrenia or another psychotic disorder and are not better explained by another mental disorder (e.g., mood disorder, anxiety disorder, dissociative disorder, a personality disorder, or substance intoxication or withdrawal).

Sources: [1]34 CFR Parts 300 and 303, *Assistance to States for the Education of Children with Disabilities and the Early Intervention Program for Infants and Toddlers with Disabilities;* Final Regulations (p. 46757), U.S. Department of Education, 2006, *Federal Register*, Washington, DC; [2]*"Attention-Deficit-Hyperactivity Disorder: Definition."*; American Psychiatric Association, *Diagnostic and Statistical Manual of Mental Disorders*, 5th ed., 2013, pp. 59–66.

Most students with ADHD approach learning differently from typical learners. Some have difficulty focusing attention to learn tasks, and many have organizational challenges. They also have difficulty paying close attention to details and/or make careless errors. Teachers can make a real difference in the educational experience for students with ADHD:

- Provide structure to the classroom routine;
- Implement a classroom management system where rules, expectations, and consequences are clear;
- Teach academic content directly;
- Hold high expectations;
- Encourage appropriate academic and social performance;
- Teach students strategies for study skills and self-management;
- Make instructional decisions through an individualized data-based approach.

Students with ADHD whose educational functioning is seriously affected by the condition do qualify for special education services. Many experience problems in both academic achievement and social skills. These students' poor academic performance is often due to their distractibility and their inability to focus on assignments for long periods of time. According to Ros and Graziano (2018), "The social functioning profiles of children with ADHD are marked by impairments across diverse domains as they tend to experience greater rates of peer rejection, have lower levels of social skills, and have impaired social cognitions" (p. 213). They also come to judge themselves as social failures and tend to engage in solitary activities such as playing computer games and watching television. This situation can contribute to alienation and withdrawal.

Characteristics

The three main characteristics associated with ADHD follow:

1. Hyperactivity
2. Impulsivity
3. Inattention

The judgment about whether a certain level of a specific activity is too much, or "hyper," is often subjective, and this makes **hyperactivity** difficult to define. If, for example, we admire the behavior, we might describe the child as energetic or enthusiastic rather than hyperactive. Nevertheless, the DSM-5 gives some good examples about which there is considerable consensus (APA, 2013). Hyperactivity and impulsivity can be manifested by

- fidgeting or squirming in a seat;
- not remaining seated when expected to do so;
- running or climbing excessively in situations where it is inappropriate;
- having difficulty playing or engaging quietly in leisure activities;
- appearing to be often "on the go" or as if "driven by a motor"; and
- talking excessively.

Students with ADHD, and many with learning disabilities, are said to be impulsive (APA, 2013). **Impulsivity** may explain why they are unable to focus on the relevant components of problems to be solved or tasks to be learned and why they often disrupt the learning environment for an entire class. The third characteristic teachers and researchers commonly observe is **inattention** (Vaughn & Boss, 2020). Children who do not focus on the task to be learned or who pay attention to the wrong features of the task are said to be distractible. Table 5.6 provides specific examples of characteristics of ADHD.

The most common approach to treatment of ADHD is medication, either alone or in combination with behavior treatment (CDC, 2022b). The FDA has approved more than 31 different medications for the treatment of ADHD. Some medications are stimulants, while others are not. Arriving at the correct dosage and specific medication is more of a trial and error process than one might assume. Parents, teachers, and medical professionals often work together to find the "right" drug to use with the best outcomes and fewest side effects. ADHD medications need to be monitored carefully because children grow quickly and the effective dosage will need to change often. Behavioral techniques, direct and systematic instruction, and good home/school partnerships are essential components to effective programs for these students.

ATTRIBUTES OF STUDENTS WITH AUTISM SPECTRUM DISORDER

Autism, or autism spectrum disorder (ASD), has received considerable attention in the media and the public in recent years. The reasons for all this public attention are understandable: The prevalence of the condition is on the rise, the causes remain unknown, and some cases can be very severe. Part of the confusion is because ASD has gone through many changes in how the disability is conceptualized. ASD has also been at the center of considerable controversy, particularly regarding the misconceptions about the role of vaccines in the condition's causes. Educators also need to understand how and why this disability area has evolved because many older notions of this condition linger and result in many misperceptions about the individuals involved. Before providing you with current information about its prevalence, definitions, types, and characteristics, let's consider this disability's origins and evolution.

TABLE 5.6 ■ Characteristics of Attention Deficit Hyperactivity Disorder

Either inattention or hyperactivity-impulsivity must have persisted for at least 6 months. Either condition must be at a level that is both maladaptive and inconsistent with development and must include six (or more) of the following symptoms.

Inattention	Hyperactivity-Impulsivity
• Often fails to give close attention to details or makes careless mistakes in schoolwork, work, or other activities • Often has difficulty sustaining attention in tasks or play activities • Often does not seem to listen when spoken to directly • Often does not follow through on instructions and fails to finish schoolwork, chores, or duties in the workplace (not due to oppositional behavior or failure to understand instructions) • Often has difficulty organizing tasks and activities • Often avoids, dislikes, or is reluctant to engage in tasks that require sustained mental effort (e.g., schoolwork or homework) • Often loses things necessary for tasks or activities (e.g., toys, school assignments, pencils, books, or tools) • Is often easily distracted by extraneous stimuli • Is often forgetful in daily activities	• Often fidgets with hands or feet or squirms in seat • Often leaves seat in classroom or in other situations in which remaining seated is expected • Often runs about or climbs excessively in situations in which it is inappropriate (in adolescents or adults, may be limited to subjective feelings of restlessness) • Often has difficulty playing or engaging in leisure activities quietly • Is often "on the go" or often acts as if "driven by a motor" • Often talks excessively • Often blurts out answers before questions have been completed • Often has difficulty awaiting turn • Often interrupts or intrudes on others (e.g., butts into conversations or games)

Source: Adapted from *Diagnostic and Statistical Manual of Mental Disorders*, Fifth Edition, Text Revision (Copyright 2013) (pp. 59–66). American Psychiatric Association.

ASD has always been part of the human condition, but it was first identified by a Swiss psychiatrist, Eugen Bleuler, in 1911 to describe patients with schizophrenia who withdrew into their own worlds. Bleuler coined the term *autism.* In 1943, an American psychiatrist, Leo Kanner, further described autism that only included individuals with severe problems in language, cognition, and social behavior (Blacher & Christensen, 2011; Kanner 1943). At about the same time, Hans Asperger, a psychiatrist working in Austria, described a group of individuals who were high functioning and often had extreme talents and unique abilities to talk about their favorite subjects in great detail, but had little empathy for others and were unable to make friends (Asperger, 1944/1991). This condition became called *Asperger's syndrome.* In 1994, the American Psychological Association (APA) added Asperger's syndrome to its list of pervasive developmental disorders (APA, 2000), which explains the now outdated view that ASD consisted of five conditions often thought of as an umbrella of disorders. However, in 2013, APA reconceptualized ASD and described one condition, ranging from mild to severe problems with cognition, communication, and socialization (APA, 2013). This is how ASD is understood today and in part explains why the prevalence rates used today are far greater than those reported in earlier years.

Let's look at those changes in prevalence rates across time and across different federal agencies. According to the CDC (2022a), in 1985, only about 1 in 2500 children was diagnosed with ASD, but by 1995, that rate jumped to 1 in 500. According to the CDC's Autism and Developmental Disabilities Monitoring (ADDM) Network (CDC, 2023a), in 2002 about 1 in 150 children was identified as having ASD; in 2018, it reported that 1 in 44, or 2.3% of the general population of children, had ASD; and in 2023, it reported that as many as 1 in 36 children in the United States has ASD, a prevalence rate of almost 2.8%. This is more than a 6,800% increase in the last 30 years! The CDC (2023a) also estimates that 1 in every 23 boys has now been diagnosed with ASD, which is 4 times higher than the prevalence for girls.

In the school year 2021–2022, IDEA served 1.1% of the resident school-age population for ASD, while it served 3.4% of the resident school-age population through the learning disabilities category (OSEP, 2022). Although the rates are much lower than CDC's, both rates have shown increases. OSEP (2018), which collects the IDEA statistics, reported that about 0.8% of schoolchildren between the ages of 6 and 21 received special education services in 2015 because of autism—up from about 0.3% in 2005. The differences are probably due to the IDEA requirement that educational performance must be adversely affected; regardless, the alarming growth is of great concern to parents, policymakers, and professionals, and it is also confusing. Has there truly been a dramatic increase in ASD? Or does the increase reflect a more inclusive and broader definition or better diagnostic methods (CDC, 2022c)? These questions are difficult to answer.

Individuals with autism and their families have been the victims of many fads and faulty information. First and foremost, autism is *not* caused by vaccines (Autism Speaks, 2022). Nor is it caused by mercury or metal poisoning (Autism Science Foundation, 2022). Second, many treatments are not effective (e.g., gluten free diets, bleach therapy, horseback riding, dolphin therapy, prism glasses). ASD is also not caused by poor parenting or calling mothers "refrigerator mothers," a terribly harmful, erroneous thought proffered by Bruno Bettelheim in 1967. It is important for educators and families to be good consumers of research and be critical of claims that are testimonials or descriptive "studies" that are not founded in well-designed experimental research.

We close this opening section with one more indication of how this disability area is changing. At the beginning of this text, we stressed the importance of how people are referred to; specifically, person-first or disability-first language. It is a very important that educators be sensitive to these issues. In recent years, the preference has been changing among parents and individuals themselves to the use of disability-first language. Although people-first language (e.g., an individual with autism, a person with ASD) is still used, more often terms like *autistic person* are preferred by many. As with other disabilities and conditions, it is advisable to ask the individuals involved for their preference.

Definition

Two different definitions of autism or ASD are used today: the IDEA definition is used by educators and the APA or DSM-5 definition is used by psychologists, psychiatrists, and the medical profession. Each is found in Table 5.7.

TABLE 5.7 ■ Definitions of Autism and ASD

Term	Definition	Source
Autism	*Autism* means a developmental disability significantly affecting verbal and nonverbal communication and social interaction, generally evident before age three, that adversely affects a child's educational performance. Other characteristics often associated with autism are engagement in repetitive activities and stereotyped movements, resistance to environmental change or change in daily routines, and unusual responses to sensory experiences. **(i)** Autism does not apply if a child's educational performance is adversely affected primarily because the child has an emotional disturbance [as defined by IDEA]. **(ii)** A child who manifests the characteristics of autism after age three could be identified as having autism if the criteria [above] are satisfied.	IDEA '04, U.S. Department of Education

(Continued)

TABLE 5.7 ■ Definitions of Autism and ASD (*Continued*)

Term	Definition	Source
Autism spectrum disorder	**A.** Persistent deficits in social communication and social interaction across multiple contexts, as manifested by the following, currently or by history. **1.** Deficits in social-emotional reciprocity **2.** Deficits in nonverbal communicative behaviors used for social interaction **3.** Deficits in developing, maintaining, and understanding relationships **B.** Restricted, repetitive patterns of behavior, interests, or activities, as manifested by at least two of the following, currently or by history. **1.** Stereotyped or repetitive motor movements, use of objects, or speech **2.** Insistence on sameness, inflexible adherence to routines, or ritualized patterns of verbal or nonverbal behavior **3.** Highly restricted, fixated interests that are abnormal in intensity or focus **4.** Hyper- or hyporeactivity to sensory input or unusual interest in sensory aspects of the environment **C.** Symptoms must be present in the early developmental period (but may not become fully manifest until social demands exceed limited capacities, or may be masked by learned strategies in later life). **D.** Symptoms cause clinically significant impairment in social, occupational, or other important areas of current functioning. **E.** These disturbances are not better explained by intellectual disability (intellectual developmental disorder) or global developmental delay. Intellectual disability and autism spectrum disorder frequently co-occur; to make comorbid diagnoses of autism spectrum disorder and intellectual disability, social communication should be below that expected for general developmental level.	American Psychiatric Association, DSM-5 (partial definition)

Sources: From 34 CFR Parts 300 and 301, *Assistance to States for the Education of Children with Disabilities and Preschool Grants for Children with Disabilities*; Final Rule (pp. 1260–1261), U.S. Department of Education, August 14, 2006, *Federal Register*, Washington, DC; *"Autism Spectrum Disorder Definition."* American Psychiatric Association, *Diagnostic and Statistical Manual of Mental Disorders*, 5th ed., 2013, pp. 50–59.

Types

Although the American Psychiatric Association (2013) describes ASD as one condition, it does provide specifics that help us understand the range of impact from mild to severe. For example, while ASD is described as "persistent deficits" in social communication and interactions, some individuals are totally nonverbal and use pictures, whether on simple picture boards or computer systems, to communicate (Bondy & Frost, 2002; Hart & Banda 2010; Pyramid Educational Consultants, 2012, 2022), but others communicate verbally and interact with other people, albeit in atypical ways. Similar examples can be provided for the other parts of the APA definition. Restricted and repetitive behaviors cross all levels of severity; however, for some it could manifest as having to line all the toys up in a specific order or eating one type of food on a plate first and then the next, and so on. For others, it may mean repeating activities in isolation over and over again. Many of these individuals have an intellectual disability, sometimes so severe that it affects all of life's functioning. However, others display gifted skills and knowledge. Think of Elon Musk, who acknowledges having autism, and who owns companies that make one of the most popular electric cars, take satellites into space, and make other incredible scientific contributions. The point here is to make no assumptions about ASD and those involved for the manifestations are as unique as the individuals.

Characteristics

According to the CDC (2022g, 2022 h), most children with ASD exhibit the following characteristics:

- Avoids or does not maintain eye contact
- Does not respond to their names until 9 months of age
- Does not use facial expressions to show feelings such as happy, sad, and angry by 9 months
- By age 1, does not play interactive games, uses few or no gestures
- Repeats words or phrases over and over again, which is called echolalia
- Does not change activities easily, which can result in tantrums
- Obsessively focuses on parts of objects, like the wheels of a toy car
- Flaps hands, rocks body, or spins in circles and sometimes is self-injurious
- Displays anxiety, stress, excessive worry, and can have either extreme fear or none at all

The above listing are just a few examples of frequently observed characteristics of ASD. Remember, severe cases are rare and they require the sustained and intensive services of highly trained professionals, delivered in separate educational settings. It is unlikely that those with the most severe cases access the general education curriculum; however, those with mild to moderate ASD profit well in inclusive classes with the proper supports.

All children with ASD have impairments in communication, impairments in social skills, and restricted and repetitive behavioral patterns or range of interests. The skills of children diagnosed with ASD vary greatly, from being nonverbal and withdrawn into their own worlds of unusual behaviors to being highly creative and gifted.

iStock/WallyBird

ATTRIBUTES OF STUDENTS WITH INTELLECTUAL AND DEVELOPMENTAL DISABILITIES

According to the federal government, almost 0.6% of U.S. students ages 3 to 21 are identified as having intellectual and developmental disabilities (OSEP, 2022). Recent data show that some 409,619 children with intellectual and developmental disabilities were served across the country. Far fewer students with intellectual and developmental disabilities attend inclusive educational settings for most of their school days than their counterparts with other disabilities: 16.5% attend general education classrooms 80% of their school day; 28% participate between 40% to 79%; and almost 49% are educated less than 40% of the school day in general education classrooms (OSEP, 2022).

How a special education category is named should not determine how and where students with specific disabilities are educated and what they are taught. For example, years ago the category called *mental retardation* brought to mind separate classrooms, separate schools, even separate living and schooling in institutions and strict adherence to a curriculum of life skills and self-help skills and training for low-level jobs. Rosa's Law, which you learned about in Chapter 1, banned the term *mental retardation* from all federal and state language. Today, the public, professional organizations, educators, and policymakers embrace the term *intellectual disability* to replace an outdated view of this disability and believe alternative curricula and placements should not be paired to a specific disability. Instead, schools should offer the general education curriculum to all students, and different curricular options should then be extended to students who have demonstrated that they either cannot successfully access the standard curriculum offered in general education or require instruction in areas needed for them to achieve their life goals.

People often make many incorrect assumptions about intellectual and developmental disabilities. First, they assume the disability is infrequent and therefore of low prevalence. Second, they assume it is always severe. This erroneous belief probably stems from this field's origins. Recall the famous story recounted in Chapter 1 about Victor, the young boy found in the forest of southern France by farmers in 1799. That boy became known as the Wild Boy of Aveyron, and the Parisian doctor who cared for Victor, Jean Marc Gaspard Itard, is acknowledged as the father of the field of special education. Clearly, the first special education child had severe disabilities and challenges. Here's what is true: Like all disabilities, intellectual and developmental disabilities occur along a continuum ranging from mild to very severe conditions.

Definition

Today, two different definitions of intellectual disability are used: one by the states and one by professionals. The IDEA definition, shown in Table 5.8, is used or adapted by most states. The other definition, which most professionals prefer, was originally developed in 2010 and revised in 2021 by the American Association of Intellectual and Developmental Disabilities (AAIDD), the oldest professional organization in the United States working on behalf of these individuals. The AAIDD definition (Schalock et al., 2021a) is considerably more detailed than the IDEA definition, but notice that both definitions call out limitations in intelligence and **adaptive behavior**, conceptual, social, and practical skills needed in everyday life. The AAIDD definition also calls out the need for supports, which we discuss in the Characteristics section a bit later.

One of the two defining features of intellectual and developmental disabilities is problems with cognition or intellectual functioning. Despite long-term and continuing concerns about the use of standardized tests of intelligence (IQ tests) and attempts to move away from the use of such potentially discriminatory tests, the 2021 definition encourages the use of well-standardized and nationally normed IQ tests (Schalock et al., 2021b). Although the use of IQ scores can lead to many mistakes and erroneous assumptions about individuals' abilities, other means of assessing cognitive abilities can be judgmental, inconsistent, and even inaccurate. Also, having a nonstandardized approach complicates the diagnostic process. The concept of using IQ scores is based on the normal or bell-shaped curve

TABLE 5.8 ■ Definitions of Intellectual and Developmental Disabilities

Source	Definition
IDEA 2004[1]	*Mental retardation* (as it is called in this legislation) means significant subaverage general intellectual functioning, existing concurrently with deficits in adaptive behavior and manifested during the developmental period, that adversely affects a child's educational performance.
AAIDD[2]	Intellectual disability is characterized by significant limitations both in intellectual functioning and in adaptive behavior as expressed in conceptual, social, and practical adaptive skills. This disability originates before age 22. The following five assumptions are essential to the application of this definition: **1.** Limitations in present functioning must be considered within the context of community environments typical of the individual's age peers and culture. **2.** Valid assessment considers cultural and linguistic diversity as well as differences in communication, sensory, motor, and behavioral factors. **3.** Within an individual, limitations often coexist with strengths. **4.** An important purpose of describing limitations is to develop a profile of needed supports. **5.** With appropriate personalized supports over a sustained period, the life functioning of the person with intellectual disability generally will improve.

Sources: [1]USDE (2006, p. 1263); [2]*Intellectual Disability: Definition, Diagnosis, Classification, and Systems of Supports* (pp. 13-15), by R. L. Schalock, R. Luckasson, and M. J. Tassé, J. R. (2021a), Silver Spring, MD

that we discussed in Chapter 1, where an intelligence quotient (IQ) score of 100 represents the mean or average of the general population, with one-half falling above 100 and the other half below. For a diagnosis of intellectual disabilities, the individual must score at least two standard deviations below the mean for that standardized test (below a score of 75). As you look again at Figure 1.1 in Chapter 1, notice that more scores occur closer to the mean or top of the bell-shaped curve and fewer scores the further away from the mean. In other words, more individuals fall within the higher range and fewer and fewer in the lower bands of scores. Table 5.9 explains how IQ test scores are interpreted for intellectual disabilities.

The second defining characteristic of intellectual and developmental disabilities is adaptive behavior: skills everyone uses to function in daily life, such as eating, dressing, using the toilet, having mobility, preparing meals, using the telephone, managing money, taking care of the home, and taking medication. People with intellectual and developmental disabilities, as well as many people without disabilities, can have difficulties with such skills that can impair their ability to function independently.

As with intelligence, AAIDD (Schalock et al., 2021a) recommends that standardized tests be used to assess abilities in adaptive behavior. Like IQ scores, the adaptive behavior score must be at least two standard deviations below the mean. That score might be overall or in at least one of the following areas:

- Conceptual Skills (e.g., expressive and receptive language, reading and writing, money concepts, self-directions)
- Social Skills (e.g., social interactions with others, self-esteem, being easily manipulated or naïve, following rules, being responsible)
- Practical Skills (e.g., eating, dressing, preparing meals, housekeeping, taking care of oneself, skills relating to employment)

Results indicating limitations in any of the following areas demand supports or assistance, which we discuss in the Characteristics section.

1. Home Living: Activities pertain to an individual's personal care
2. Community and Neighborhood: Activities relate to participating in community activities
3. School Participation: Activities involve being an active member of class and school activities
4. School Learning: Activities focus on being successful with school tasks and assignments
5. Health and Safety: Activities pertain to maintaining healthy habits and keeping oneself safe
6. Social: Activities involve skills associated with interacting with others in various settings
7. Advocacy: Activities focus on self-advocacy

TABLE 5.9 ■ Classifications of Intellectual Disability by Severity of Cognitive Abilities

Levels of Severity	Range of IQ Scores	Outcomes
Mild	50 to 74	Learning difficulties, inability to work, can maintain social relationships, contributes to society
Moderate	35 to 49	Marked developmental delays during childhood, limited degree of independence in self-care, has adequate communication and academic skills, requires varying degrees of support to live and work in the community
Severe	20 to 34	Continuous need for supports in all aspects of life
Profound	Under 20	Severe limitations in self-care, continence, communication, and mobility; requires continuous and intensive supports

The primary goal of supports is to help the person meet the demands of life's various contexts. Because support needs have only recently found their way into the special education field, there are few support programs that have been proven effective by research. However, there is a growing body of research that has demonstrated that a combination of assistive technology devices and **assistive technology services** can help bridge the gaps between functional limitations and independent functioning (e.g., Bryant et al., 2012; Bryant et al., 2010; Fisher & Shogren, 2012; Wehmeyer et al., 2012).

Types

One way to consider the types of this disability is to think about causes. Some of these conditions are genetic in origin, others are environmental, still others are caused by an interaction of biology and the environment, some are diseases, and, unfortunately, some are caused by child abuse and neglect. Of the three most common causes, two are genetic in origin and one is due to toxins. First identified in 1991, the most common inherited cause of intellectual and developmental disabilities is **fragile X syndrome (FXS)**, which affects about 1 in 7,000 males and 1 in 11,000 females (CDC, 2022 f). Boys with FXS have an average IQ of 55. Girls have less significant cognitive limitations but are still affected cognitively. These individuals also have many other problems including seizures, sleep disorders, attention problems, irritability and aggression, along with self-injury.

The other common genetic cause, **Down syndrome**, is due to a chromosomal abnormality; the individual is born with 47 instead of 46 chromosomes (CDC, 2023b). About 6,000 babies (1 in 700 births) are born each year with Down syndrome. Certain physical characteristics, such as a flattened face; small ears, hands, and feet; eyes shaped like almonds; and small ears, are typical of people with Down syndrome. The degree of cognitive difficulty varies, usually ranging from mild to moderate. As a group, they are prone to other problems, including hearing impairments, ear infections, sleep disorders, and heart defects. Individuals with Down syndrome tend to have reduced opportunities for satisfying friendships, social outlets, and recreation. Teachers can help by encouraging them to be more active and to play sports with their peers during recess.

The third common cause of intellectual disabilities is toxins in the environment. Lead poisoning lurks in the environment despite the fact that lead-based paints and lead in gasoline have been banned for years. Poor children and families are at the greatest risk because their neighborhoods, where lead remains in the dirt, are often close to freeways and near closed factories that produced high levels of lead by-products. One well-known example is the pollution of the drinking water in Flint, Michigan (World Population Review, 2022a). In a study of the children exposed in Flint, only 55% of them had IQ scores in the normal or above normal range (Zheng et al., 2021). Unfortunately, Flint is not an isolated case of pollution in the drinking water. In a recent study, it was found that 25% of all licensed day care centers in California have dangerously high levels of this metal in the drinking water (Pineda, 2023). The majority of these settings are in low-income areas. The culprits seem to be drinking fountains that were not used during the COVID-19 pandemic, resulting in toxins building up. Another such example is the Excide battery recycling plant in Vernon, near downtown Los Angeles (World Population Review, 2022b). The plant has been closed for many years but its legacy will live on. It emitted toxic metal dust that affected some 10,000 properties within 1.7 miles of the plant, impacting neighboring towns of Boyle Heights and Maywood, both poor communities with a predominately Latinx population (Ylanan et al., 2023). Most of these areas have not been cleaned up adequately, leaving many at continuing risk of lead poisoning. Although about 4,600 properties have been cleaned, the state and city have not yet cleaned the strips of land surrounding these properties, risking exposure of children and pets to dangerous toxins. That effort will now be addressed at a cost of $67 million, years and years after the plant closed and filed bankruptcy (Briscoe, 2023). Stories like this exist across rural and urban American today.

Besides these three most common reasons for intellectual disabilities, other causes exist. Here's another example of a hereditary condition that is a cause of intellectual disabilities. Persons with phenylketonuria (PKU) are unable to metabolize phenylalanine, an amino acid that then builds up in the body to toxic levels that damage the brain. If untreated, this condition eventually causes intellectual disability. Changes in diet, including strictly eliminating certain foods that contain phenylalanine, such as milk, can control phenylketonuria and reduce its devastating impact. Here, then, is a condition rooted in genetics but brought on by the environment—by ingesting milk. Prompt diagnosis and parental vigilance are crucial to minimizing the associated problems. Teachers can help by monitoring these students' diets and ensuring that snacks and treats provided by classmates' parents for sharing do not include milk products that might be harmful.

Now let's look at some disabilities that do not have a hereditary link. One well-recognized nonhereditary type of birth defect is the most common and preventable cause of intellectual and developmental disabilities: fetal alcohol spectrum disorder (FASD; CDC, 2022d, 2022e). This condition results from the mother drinking alcohol during pregnancy. A person with FASD might have abnormal facial features, such as a smooth ridge between the nose and upper lip (this ridge is called the philtrum), a small-sized head, poor coordination, hyperactivity, attention problems, poor memory, difficulties with academics, learning disabilities, speech and language delays, intellectual disabilities, and poor reasoning and judgement. The tragedy with FASD is that it is preventable if pregnant women refrain from drinking alcohol. These are only a few examples of causes of intellectual disabilities.

Characteristics

According to AAIDD, the two defining characteristics of intellectual and developmental disabilities are

1. Problems with cognition; and
2. Problems with adaptive behavior

Resulting in

3. Need for systems of support to sustain independence (Schalock et al., 2021a, 2021b).

Impaired cognitive ability can have pervasive effects, whether the disability is mild or severe. Learning new skills, storing and retrieving information from memory, and transferring knowledge to either new or slightly different situations are challenges for these individuals. Short- and long-term memory are often impaired, making it hard for them to remember events or the proper sequence of events, particularly when the events are not clearly identified as important. Even when something is remembered, it may be remembered incorrectly, inefficiently, too slowly, or in inadequate detail. Teachers can help students with memory problems develop memory strategies and learn to compensate by having them create picture notebooks that lay out the sequence of steps in a task that needs to be performed, the elements of a job that needs to be done, or a checklist of things to do before leaving the house.

Through **explicit systematic instruction** and the delivery of supports, adaptive behavior can improve. However, for these gains to happen, it is sometimes necessary for students to receive a separate curriculum that targets life skills, which are skills used to manage a home and job and to engage in activities in the community. When goals for independent living become the target of instruction, students may then have reduced access to the general education curriculum and to their typically learning classmates, but important skills needed in later life (e.g., job skills, independent living, money management, transportation, recreation) become the targets of instruction and all contribute to improved adaptive behavior.

All of us also use **systems of support**. We ask our friends for advice. We form study teams before a difficult test. We expect help from city services when there is a crime or a fire. We join together in a neighborhood crime watch group to help each other be safe. And we share the excitement and joys of accomplishments with family, friends, and colleagues. For individuals with intellectual and developmental disabilities, systems of support are a means for promoting independence and bridging the gap between classroom expectations and the student's current levels of functioning. Supports can be offered at different intensity levels—intermittent, limited, extensive, pervasive—and can be of different types (Schalock et al., 2021a):

- Natural supports: The individual's own resources, family, friends, and neighbors, as well as coworkers on the job or peers at school

- Nonpaid supports: Neighborhood and community groups, such as clubs, recreational leagues, and private organizations
- Generic supports: Public transportation, states' human services systems, and other agencies and services to which everyone has access
- Specialized supports: Disability-specific services such as special education, special early intervention services, and vocational rehabilitation

Supports are meant to enhance an individual's functioning and personal well-being. However, it is important they are "person-centered," reflecting the individual's interests and desires. For example, if the person with intellectual disabilities wants to go to a movie or amusement park, they should participate in the decision about what to see or where to go. Friends are natural supports, but often it is difficult for people with disabilities to make friendships, which can be fostered in many ways. Teachers can help by pairing students with similar interests. Organizations also play an important role. For example, Best Buddies International was developed with this purpose in mind. In one well-known program, the organization pairs middle and high school students with intellectual disabilities with student volunteers to help increase participation at school and in the community. The intent is to form friendships that assist with schoolwork, attend high school sports activities, or enjoy a leisure-time event. With chapters in every state, its impact has been far-reaching.

ATTRIBUTES OF STUDENTS WITH EMOTIONAL OR BEHAVIORAL DISORDERS

Emotional or behavioral disorders, like all disabilities, range from mild to severe, but for all impacted the problems are chronic, pervasive, and serious. Unfortunately for many, their problems, like depression or withdrawal, are under-identified and treatment is not delivered at all or in a timely fashion. On the other hand, students with aggressive behavior or who continually act out are more immediately identified by teachers, family members, and friends. The federal government reports that fewer than 5% of all students with disabilities served through IDEA have emotional or behavioral disorders (NCES, 2022). Well over half of these students attend general education classes for 80% or more of the school day (OSEP, 2022). However, it is likely that these figures substantially underestimate the prevalence of these problems. Why might this be so? First, the definition is unclear and subjective. Second, because the label is so stigmatizing, many educators and school districts are reluctant to identify many children, which may be why the percentage of students identified as having emotional or behavior disorders has been on the decline over the past decade (OSEP, 2020). Another way to interpret the decline might also rest with new intervention procedures (i.e., PBIS), which we discuss later in this section and also in Chapter 10, being implemented across the nation. The third reason we just mentioned: Many students are not identified or identified long after they should be.

Students with emotional or behavior disorders, aged 14 to 21, have the highest dropout rate and are less likely to graduate than all other students with disabilities (OSEP, 2020). These students are also less likely to participate in general education classes at least 80% of the school day and more likely to be educated in separate schools than all students with disabilities. They are removed from their educational placement (in- and out-of-school suspensions, expulsions, and interim alternative educational settings) because of disciplinary reasons at substantially high rates than another other group of students with disabilities.

Important factors in prevalence for this group of learners are sex and race and ethnicity (Ryberg et al., 2021). Black students have the highest out-of-school expulsion rate and also receive harsher punishment than any other group of students (Del Toro & Wang, 2021). The vast majority (73%) of children identified as having emotional or behavioral disorders are males (OSEP, 2020). When compared to other groups, this category has the highest ratio of boys to girls of all special education categories. The reason for this difference is not clear, but it is probably linked to boys' higher propensity to be troublesome and violate school rules, coupled with girls' tendency toward less-disruptive, internalizing behavioral issues that are less likely to result in referral but are clearly serious.

Definition

IDEA uses the term *emotional disturbance* to describe the characteristic of children to whom we refer as having behavioral or emotional disorders. Remember that this condition is expressed over a long period of time, is obvious to many observers, and adversely affects educational performance. Table 5.10 gives the IDEA and National Mental Health and Special Education Coalition (NMHSEC) definitions of emotional or behavioral disorders (Forness & Knitzer, 1992). Look carefully at the differences between these two definitions. Notice that IDEA uses the term *emotional disturbance*, while the NMHSEC definition uses the term we use in this text, *emotional or behavioral disorders*. Professionals and parents prefer that latter term because they believe that it is less stigmatizing and more positive, while the term *emotional disturbance* sends a message of deep psychological problems that are not in the realm of educators. The nation's professional organization of special education (the Council for Exceptional Children's Division for Emotional and Behavioral Disorders) uses the term *behavior disorders*. However, remember that school personnel have to use the IDEA term because that law funds school programs for these children.

Types

Several ways can be used to frame the types of emotional or behavioral disorders. One way is to divide emotional or behavioral disorders into three groups:

1. Externalizing
2. Internalizing
3. Low incidence

TABLE 5.10 ■ Definitions of Emotional or Behavioral Disorders

Source	Definition
IDEA[1]	*Emotional disturbance* means a condition exhibiting one or more of the following characteristics over a long period of time and to a marked degree that adversely affects a child's educational performance: • An inability to learn that cannot be explained by intellectual, sensory, or health factors • An inability to build or maintain satisfactory interpersonal relationships with peers and teachers • Inappropriate types of behavior or feelings under normal circumstances • A general pervasive mood of unhappiness or depression • A tendency to develop physical symptoms related to fears associated with personal or school problems Emotional disturbance includes schizophrenia. The term does not apply to children who are socially maladjusted, unless it is determined that they have an emotional disturbance.
NMHSEC[2]	The term *emotional or behavioral disorder* means a disability characterized by behavioral or emotional responses in school so different from appropriate age, cultural, or ethnic norms that they adversely affect educational performance. Educational performance includes academic, social, vocational, and personal skills. Such a disability • is more than a temporary, expected response to stressful events in the environment; • is consistently exhibited in two different settings, at least one of which is school related; and • is unresponsive to direct intervention in general education, or the child's condition is such that general education interventions would be insufficient. Emotional or behavioral disorders can coexist with other disabilities. This category may include children or youths with schizophrenic disorders, affective disorders, anxiety disorder, or other sustained disorders of conduct or adjustment when they adversely affect educational performance.

Sources: [1]USDE (2006, p. 1262); [2]Forness and Knitzer (1992, p. 13).

Students who exhibit externalizing and internalizing behaviors are the two main groups of students with emotional or behavioral disorders, but they do not account for all the conditions that result in placement in this special education category.

Externalizing behaviors are characterized by an undercontrolled, acting-out style that includes behaviors we could describe as aggressive, argumentative, impulsive, coercive, and noncompliant. These behaviors are expressed outwardly, usually toward other persons, and generally include some form of hyperactivity, including persistent aggression and a high level of irritating behavior that is impulsive and distractible. Some examples of externalizing behavior problems follow:

- Does not follow classroom or schoolwide rules
- Violates basic rights of others
- Has tantrums
- Is hostile or defiant, argues
- Ignores teachers' reprimands
- Causes or threatens physical harm to people or animals
- Intimidates, threatens
- Violates societal norms or rules
- Steals, causes property loss or damage
- Uses lewd or obscene gestures
- Is physically aggressive
- Demonstrates obsessive compulsive behavior
- Is hyperactive

As you learned in previous chapters and also later in this chapter, research about the effectiveness of PBIS over the last several decades has demonstrated that externalizing behaviors can be improved through systematic interventions delivered by teachers. Although it is clear these children are hard to teach and can disrupt the learning environment for all members of the class, procedures developed to be implemented within a MTSS framework have demonstrated that classroom rules, structure, praise and systematic feedback, and systematically increasing the intensity of interventions through a three-tiered system can both prevent and reduce a considerable amount of disruptive behavior.

Internalizing behaviors are characterized by an overcontrolled and inhibited style that includes behaviors we would describe as withdrawn, lonely, depressed, and anxious (Kauffman & Landrum, 2018). Students with internalizing patterns tend to exhibit behaviors that reflect the following:

- Depression
- Withdrawal
- Anxiety

Anorexia, bulimia, depression, and anxiety are examples of internalizing behaviors. **Anorexia** and **bulimia** are serious eating disorders that usually occur during students' adolescent years, but they have been increasingly found in younger children, typically among girls and often because of their preoccupation with weight and body image, their drive for thinness, and their fear of becoming overweight. With anxiety, individuals seem to worry obsessively about almost everything, paralyzing them from any productive learning (Flannery et al., 2023). Typically, these concerns are about everyday events, which seem to others as irrational:

- "What if we run out of gas before getting to school?"
- "What if I get a bad grade?"

- "What if our house floods?"
- "Is my puppy going to get sick?

Often hard to recognize in children, **depression** includes components such as feelings of guilt, self-blame, feelings of rejection, lethargy, low self-esteem, and negative self-image. Children's behaviors when they are depressed may appear so different from the depressed behaviors of adults that teachers and parents may have difficulty recognizing them. Even so, a child who is severely depressed might engage in self-injurious behaviors. Anxiety disorders may be demonstrated as intense response upon separation from family, friends, or a familiar environment; as excessive shrinking from contact with strangers; or as unfocused, excessive worry and fear.

Within this way of organizing emotional or behavior disorders, the final group to consider is an additional group of very infrequent conditions. Each is very rare but is quite serious when it does occur. For example, schizophrenia is extremely rare in children, although approximately 1% of the general population over the age of 18 have been diagnosed as having the disorder. It usually includes bizarre delusions (e.g., the belief that your thoughts are controlled by the police), hallucinations (e.g., voices telling you what to think), the loosening of associations (e.g., disconnected thoughts), and incoherence. Schizophrenia places great demands on service systems. Children with the disorder have serious difficulties with schoolwork and often must live in special hospital and educational settings during part of their childhood. Keep in mind that emotional or behavioral disorders are more common disabilities, but the category includes many different specific conditions, including many that are themselves considered fairly rare conditions.

The other framework for organizing the types of emotional or behavioral disorders is by subgrouping these students by their conditions. Table 5.11 highlights some of the conditions of emotional or behavioral disorders more frequently identified in children.

TABLE 5.11 ■ Types of Emotional or Behavioral Disorders

Type	Explanation	Treatment Options
Anxiety Disorder	Irrational fear of everyday situations; most common type of disorder in children	Although it is highly treatable, only about 37% receive treatment
Bipolar Disorder	A serious medical condition that causes mood swings from highs to feelings of sad and hopelessness	Treatment involves a combination of medication and psychosocial treatment
Eating Disorders (anorexia and bulimia)	Extremes in eating, ranging from too much to not enough; females are much more likely to develop these conditions	Many aspects of life contribute to eating disorders and each much be addressed with a combination of psychological and nutritional counseling along with medical and psychiatric monitoring
Obsessive-Compulsive Disorder (OCD)	An anxiety disorder, characterized by recurrent and unwanted thoughts and repetitive behaviors such as handwashing, counting, checking, or cleaning	Children with OCD should be treated by a licensed mental health care professional; psychiatric medication may be prescribed
Psychotic Disorders	An umbrella term used to describe severe mental disorders; the main symptoms are delusions and hallucinations	Treatment needs to be individualized but typically involves a combination of medications and psychotherapy/counseling
Depression	Recurrent and extended periods of negative thoughts and hopelessness	Most successful treatments typically include a combination of psychotherapy and medication
Posttraumatic Stress Disorder (PTSD)	Includes both physiological and psychological responses, experienced by people who have experienced a traumatic event	Medication alone does not solve the problem, which often requires medication and psychotherapy

Sources: Adapted from Center for Parent Information and Resources (2021), National Alliance on Mental Illness (2023), and International OCD Foundation (2023).

Characteristics

Social skills are the foundation for practically all human activities in all contexts—academic, personal, vocational, and community—and we use them to interact with others and to perform most daily tasks. Possibly more than any other group of children with disabilities, students with emotional or behavioral disorders present problems with social skills to themselves, their families, their peers, and their teachers (Kauffman & Landrum, 2018). One related characteristic, antisocial behavior, seems to be a prime reason for these students' referrals to special education. Antisocial behavior includes impulsivity and poor interpersonal skills with both peers and adults. These students' behavior patterns can be self-defeating, impairing their interactions with others in many negative ways. Most students with externalizing behavioral disorders exhibit at least some of the following behaviors in excess:

- Tantrums
- Aggression
- Noncompliance
- Coercion
- Poor academic performance

Fortunately, intervention can make a difference and improve the outcomes for students with externalizing or internalizing behaviors. Almost 30 years ago, the application of the MTSS framework for behavior intervention, Positive Behavioral Interventions and Supports (PBIS) began developing and interventions were being validated that prevent and improve social and emotional behavior of schoolchildren (Center on Positive Behavioral Interventions and Supports [Center on PBIS], 2022, 2023a). In Tier 1, all students are provided with a positive, predictable learning environment, structure, and support to learn and follow classroom and schoolwide rules. For those who cannot meet those expectations, Tier 2 supports are provided (Ikhnana, 2022). At this stage, a behavior intervention plan (BIP), which you learned about in Chapter 2, is developed and becomes part of the students' IEP if they are already receiving services through IDEA, or the student is referred to the school's special services team to determine whether the student has a disability and is eligible for special education services. Tier 2 provides students with a number of data-based interventions. For example, some students and families might be guided by daily behavioral data–based report cards. Interventions (e.g., rewards, consequences, supportive feedback) are directed at remediating the specific behaviors of concern (PBIS World, 2023). Some students skip Tier 2 because their behavior is either too severe or dangerous to others and enter Tier 3 services, which begin with a **functional behavior assessment**. This assessment determines what events trigger the undesirable behavior, carefully defines the behavior, and determines the consequences that maintain the behavior. Most students who receive services through Tier 3 have been identified as having a disability and are receiving services through IDEA. Remember, Tier 3 services are designed for a few students (1–5% of all students). Here, students receive services delivered by highly trained specialists (e.g., ABA analysts, mental health experts; Center on PBIS, n.d.). The interventions are intensive, individualized, and data-driven. Multidisciplinary teams of mental health professionals join educators and administrators to plan and deliver services to students and their families (Center on PBIS, 2023b).

Emotional or behavioral disorders are difficult to define. Important features of the condition are that it is expressed over a long period of time, is obvious to many observers, and adversely affects educational performance.

iStock/BartCo

At the beginning of this chapter, we noted that all students identified through IDEA as having a disability have problems with their educational performance. Here, too, even though emotional or behavioral disorders have their roots in social behaviors, the condition negatively affects academic performance. Regardless of intellectual potential, students with emotional or behavioral disorders typically experience academic problems (Council for Exceptional Children, 2018). Clearly, being in personal turmoil affects our ability to attend to school tasks and to learn in general. Failure at academic tasks compounds the difficulties these children face not only in school but also in life. We already mentioned their exceptionally high dropout and poor graduation rates, which impact employment opportunities. There is also evidence that when students are engaged in academic work, their disruptive behaviors decrease. Thus, in addition to helping these students with their behavior, it is constructive for teachers to address their academic skills. Participating in inclusive educational settings teaches them to interact with others appropriately and to learn social rules and expectations.

SUMMARY

The vast majority of the nation's students are typical learners. The special instructional needs that many students present to their teachers and schools are considerable and varied. Students with disabilities are guaranteed an appropriate and individualized education, tailored to each of their exceptional learning needs, through IDEA. Other students who do not qualify for special education but have a disability are entitled to accommodations through Section 504. And many others require a special response to their unique learning challenges so that they can reach their potential and profit maximally from school.

Certainly, unique instructional interventions arise from disabilities, but they come from a variety of other sources as well. Some students have learning and behavioral challenges that result from conditions that are not disabilities but that still put students at risk for school failure, dropping out, or underachievement. What you should now understand is that the majority of America's students present an exciting mixture of learning strengths to each classroom situation.

REVIEW THE LEARNING OBJECTIVES

Let's review the learning objectives for this chapter. If you are uncertain and cannot talk through the answers provided for any of these questions, reread those sections of the text.

5.1 Explain how students from different ethnic and racial groups are overrepresented and underrepresented in IDEA categories of special education.

The data make it clear that students from different racial and ethnic backgrounds are identified at different rates, showing definite over- and underrepresentation in special education categories. When considering their representation in the general school population, Black, American Indian/Alaskan Native, and Pacific Islander students, along with those from mixed races, have a much greater representation than one would or should expect. The other groups are somewhat underrepresented.

5.2 Name the 14 special education categories for students with disabilities.

Some students with disabilities are not special education students because their disability does not negatively affect their educational performance and, therefore, they do not meet the requirements of IDEA for special education services. IDEA specifies 13 special education categories plus one more for students for a total of 14: learning disabilities, speech and language impairments, other health impairments, autism spectrum disorders, intellectual disabilities, emotional disturbance, developmental delay, multiple disabilities, hearing impairments (hard of hearing and deafness), deafness, orthopedic and physical disabilities, traumatic brain injury, visual disabilities, and deaf-blindness. ADHD is not a separate special education category.

5.3 Compare and contrast the three schemes or ways disabilities are grouped to organize special education.

Three major schemes are used to group disabilities for the purposes of meeting educational needs. One classification system uses disability types or special education categories (e.g., learning disabilities, intellectual disabilities). Another groups students by the severity of the disability (mild, moderate, severe). And the third considers disabilities in terms of how often they occur (frequent incidence, less frequent incidence).

5.4 Discuss the attributes of students with learning disabilities.
The largest special education category is learning disabilities, which can be severe, complex, pervasive, and lifelong. Learning disabilities are characterized as unexpected underachievement and as resistant to treatment. Learning disabilities are disorders that affect the ability to understand or use spoken or written expression, perform mathematical calculations, coordinate movements, or direct attention. Problems with reading and writing are the most common, yet a significant number of students with learning disabilities may also have mathematics learning disabilities.

5.5 Identify the attributes of students with speech or language impairments.
Although they make up a single special education category, speech impairments and language impairments are really two separate but related disabilities. Speech or language impairments result in problems with communication, language, and/or speech. Speech impairments include articulation, fluency (stuttering), and voice problems. Many students with disabilities receive services from both special education teachers and speech/language pathologists. Language impairments are not the same as language differences, and their prevalence changes by age (i.e., the number lessens across the school years). Speaking English as a second language does not result in a disability, but some ELs may be slow in mastering their second language. Dialects of American English are also not impairments.

5.6 Discuss the attributes of students with attention deficit hyperactivity disorder.
ADHD is a condition included in the IDEA 2004 category of "other health impairments." Behaviors associated with ADHD (e.g., distractibility and hyperactivity) are also symptomatic of other disabilities, such as learning disabilities and emotional or behavioral disorders. Most students with ADHD approach learning differently from typical learners. About half of the individuals with this condition are eligible for special education because their educational performance is adversely affected by the condition; most of the other students with ADHD receive supports and accommodations through Section 504. It is estimated that more than half of all students with ADHD do not qualify for special education services because their condition does not seriously affect their educational performance.

5.7 Examine the attributes of students with autism spectrum disorders.
The key features of ASD are that it is one condition that ranges from mild to severe and that it has unique characteristics that affect social interactions. All children with ASD have impairments in communication, impairments in social skills, and restricted and repetitive behavioral patterns or range of interests. The skills of children diagnosed with ASD vary greatly from being nonverbal and withdrawn into their own worlds of unusual behaviors to being highly creative and gifted.

5.8 Recognize the attributes of students with intellectual and developmental disabilities.
Intellectual and developmental disabilities result in problems with cognitive functioning, adaptive behavior, and independence. Individuals with intellectual disabilities have problems with cognition or intellectual functioning and demonstrate difficulties with adaptive behavior. Responses to intellectual disabilities include different intensities of supports (intermittent, limited, extensive, pervasive) and different types of supports (natural supports, nonpaid supports, generic supports, specialized supports). Also, teachers and administrators should promote success by providing these students opportunities to access the general education curriculum, develop friendships, and participate in sports and extracurricular activities.

5.9 Discuss the attributes of students with emotional or behavioral disorders.
Emotional or behavioral disorders can be externalizing (e.g., aggressive, argumentative, impulsive, coercive, noncompliant), internalizing (e.g., overcontrolled, inhibited, withdrawn, lonely, depressed, anxious), or low incidence (e.g., schizophrenia). Internalizing behaviors (e.g., anorexia, bulimia, depression, anxiety) are less frequently identified early, and externalizing

behavior disorders are highly associated with delinquency. Problems with social skills cause issues for the students themselves, their families, their peers, and their teachers. Evidence indicates that early intervention can make a difference in the lives of these individuals.

REVISIT THE OPENING CHALLENGE

Check your answers to the Reflection Questions from the Opening Challenge and revise them on the basis of what you have learned.

1. Do you think identifying students by specific disability is useful?
2. Why do you think Sonia's special education label is being reconsidered at this point in her schooling?
3. Is Sonia's situation unusual? Why or why not?
4. Will a change in category influence the way Mr. Samora teaches Sonia?
5. Will it change the services Sonia receives?
6. What do you think are some learning characteristics of the three students in Mrs. Lupino's class?
7. What help might she be looking for from Mr. Patton (the special education teacher) for these three students?

KEY TERMS

adaptive behavior
anorexia
assistive technology services
bulimia
coexisting disabilities
depression
Down syndrome
echolalia
explicit systematic instruction
externalizing behaviors
fragile X syndrome (FXS)
functional behavior assessment
hyperactivity
impulsivity
inattention
intelligence quotient (IQ)
internalizing behaviors
language delays
language different
language impairments
loudness
pitch
pragmatics
resistant to treatment
semantics
stuttering
syntax
systems of support
unexpected underachievement

PROFESSIONAL STANDARDS AND LICENSURE

For a complete description of Professional Standards and Licensure, please see the appendix.

CEC Initial Preparation Standards

Standard 1: Learner Development and Individual Learning Differences

INTASC Core Principles

Standard 1: Learner Development

Standard 2: Learning Differences

Praxis II: Education of Exceptional Students: Core Content Knowledge

I. Understanding Exceptionalities: Human Development and Behavior

Juan Silva/Getty Images

6 UNDERSTANDING LEARNERS WITH LESS COMMON DISABILITIES OR CONDITIONS

LEARNING OBJECTIVES

After studying this chapter, you will be able to meet the following learning objectives:

6.1 Explain the attributes of students with less common disabilities.

6.2 Identify the attributes of students with health impairments.

6.3 Describe the attributes of students with multiple disabilities.

6.4 Explain the attributes of students with developmental delay.

6.5 List the attributes of students with physical disabilities.

6.6 Distinguish among the attributes of students who are d/Deaf and hard of hearing.

6.7 Discuss the attributes of students with visual disabilities.

6.8 Summarize the attributes of students with traumatic brain injury.

6.9 Describe the attributes of students with deaf-blindness.

Opening Challenge

Preparing for Students With Less Common Disabilities

Elementary Grades. Ms. Traun has been teaching general education classes for 10 years. She has successfully included many students with disabilities in her classes and has had great experience working with many special education teachers and related service experts, and she has team-taught with special education teachers. Ms. Traun has had related service specialists work with students in her classroom so they can better demonstrate effective techniques and to promote generalization.

She has just received a letter from the district office informing her that she is to receive a new student next week. The letter described her new student, Josh, as having multiple and complex disabilities. Her principal has scheduled a meeting with her tomorrow afternoon to discuss this new student. Ms. Traun wants to make sure she plans for Josh's learning and behavioral needs, so she makes a list of questions to ask the principal about Josh. She is wondering what complex disabilities means. She is thinking that all of her students with disabilities have complex learning and behavioral needs. What could this mean for how she teaches? She wonders, *"What services and supports will Josh need? Am I prepared to work with Josh to address his needs? How can I help my other students accept Josh? What can I do to help my other students in the class provide the respect and support Josh's needs, both within the classroom and on the playground? Does Josh use assistive technology, and, if so, what do I need to know about any devices he uses?"*

Secondary Grades. Mr. Dehiya has been teaching high school for 9 years. Two months into the school year, one of his students, Abooksigun, was severely injured in an automobile accident. After months of rehabilitation, Abooksigun, who now uses a wheelchair, is ready to return to class. Mr. Dehiya is concerned that his classroom may not be sufficiently accessible to allow Abooksigun the freedom to move about like his other students. He decided to go online to see what information might be available. After several entries into his search engine, the information he found proved practically worthless. He was sure that most of what he found was just plain common sense, but he was also sure that he had not thought of everything he needed to consider before Abooksigun rejoined the class. He decided to restructure and rearrange his classroom with the help of his students, many of whom had been friends with Abooksigun for years. He also reached out the special education coordinator to seek assistance from a related services provider working with his district. Mr. Dehiya knew there would be challenges ahead and so many things to consider, like seating arrangements for individual and group work, access to the hallway but also to the teacher's desk, and safety concerns for Abooksigun and his classmates. He felt confident that he, Abooksigun's fellow students, and the special education team could come up with a plan and would deal with unforeseen issues as they arose.

Reflection Questions

In your journal, write down your answers to the following questions. After completing the chapter, check your answers and revise them on the basis of what you have learned.

1. Do you think Ms. Traun will need to plan for her new student differently than she has for other students with disabilities? If so, in what ways? If not, why not?
2. What learning characteristics might she have to consider as she makes initial plans for Josh?
3. How might her plans change after she learns what disabilities Josh has?
4. Provide Ms. Traun with five questions or issues she should discuss with her principal.
5. What do you think Mr. Dehiya, the related services provider assigned to help, and the entire class figured out to accommodate his student and his wheelchair and also improve classroom accessibility?
6. Why do you think Mr. Dehiya decided to have his students help restructure the classroom? Do you think this was a good idea?
7. What should be included in his classroom layout?

In Chapter 5, you learned about disabilities that are the most prevalent. In fact, the four most common—learning disabilities, speech or language impairments, other health impairments (which includes ADHD), and ASD—comprise more than 80% of all students receiving special education services! The remaining 10 special education categories when added together comprise less than 20% (U.S. Department of Education, 2023). Less common disabilities, by contrast, are just that: disabilities that don't occur as often. In 2020–2021, although disabilities affected about 15% or 7.2 million children and youth aged 3 to 21 (National Center for Education Statistics [NCES], 2002), when the four most common are removed from the calculation, the remaining disabilities affected slightly less than 1% of the general population of schoolchildren (OSEP, 2021). Figures 6.1 and 6.2 show the dramatic differences in size of the special education categories served through IDEA.

ATTRIBUTES OF STUDENTS WITH LESS COMMON DISABILITIES

As we just explained, the most obvious attribute is prevalence. A second common feature is people's typical, but inaccurate, perceptions about them. Too many people assume that if a condition or disability is not common, it must automatically lead to severe problems. In fact, most of these disabilities range in severity from mild to severe. For example, physical disabilities are not common when compared to other disabilities, but most of the individuals affected do not even qualify for special education because their disability does not negatively affect their performance. Of course, some less frequent disabilities, by their nature, can result in very serious challenges. The conditions classified as multiple severe disabilities are obvious examples.

No disability should be minimized—they are all serious—but many of the least common disabilities do tend to require an intensive response. When negative assumptions about disabilities are not permitted but high expectations and effective interventions are the norm, the outcomes can be remarkable. Let's think about a few examples. Possibly the most famous person to have struggled with deaf-blindness[1] is Helen Keller. Keller was a woman of many accomplishments, but none of her achievements, which included graduating from Radcliffe with honors in 1904, would have occurred without the intensive, pervasive, and sustained supports and interventions she received from her teacher, Anne Sullivan, and her family (Keller, 1988).

FIGURE 6.1 AND 6.2 ■ **Number of Students With Disabilities Aged 5 (in Kindergarten) to 21, by Disability Category, Served Under IDEA, Part B, in the U.S., Outlying Areas, and Freely Associated States: SY 2019–20**

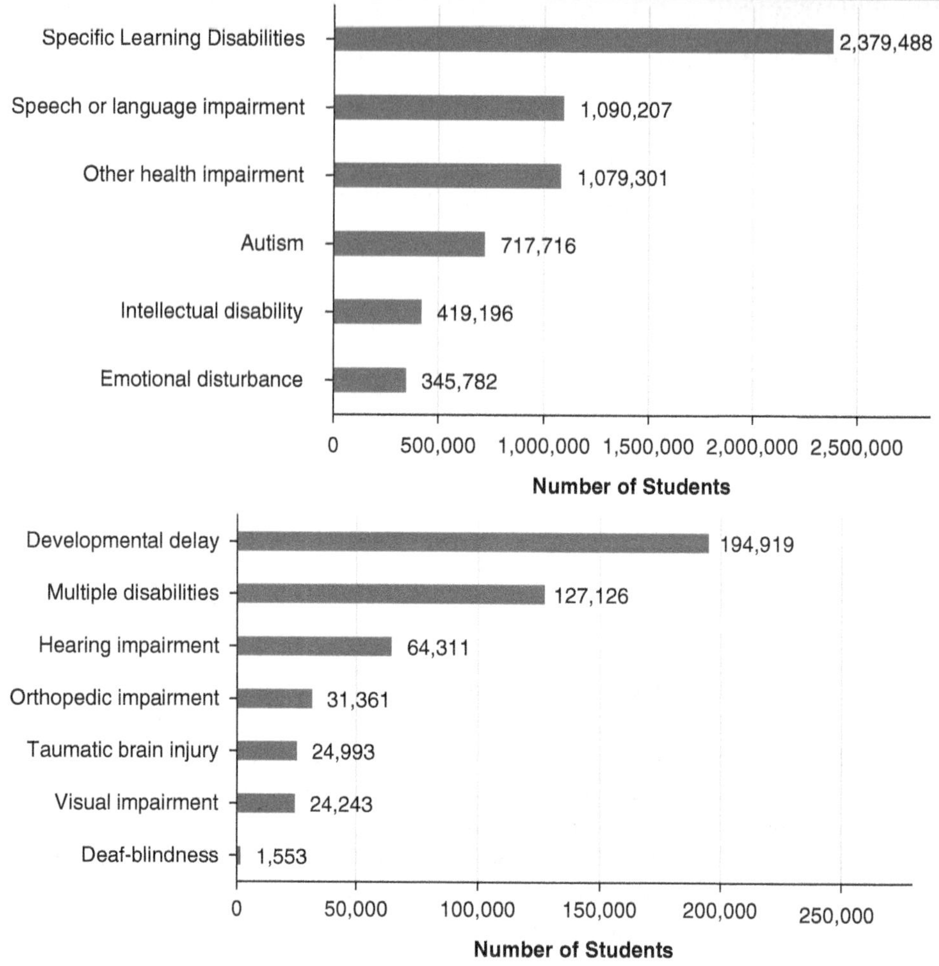

Source: OSEP (2021).

Today, stories like Helen Keller's are more commonplace. For example, Haben Girma, a product of an inclusive elementary and secondary education, is the first deaf-blind person to graduate from Harvard Law School (Girma, 2019). After her graduation in 2013, she became an attorney for a disability rights advocacy group and currently is a disability advocate. Erik Weihenmayer, a person who is blind and is a cycling enthusiast, scaled Mount Everest in 2001 and since then has become one of 150 climbers who have scaled all seven of the highest summits in the world (see https://erikweihenmayer.com/). Troy Kotsur, who uses American Sign Language (ASL) to communicate, is the first Deaf male actor, and the second Deaf actor, to receive a best supporting actor Oscar award for his breakthrough role in the 2021 film, *CODA*. The first Deaf actor to receive an Oscar was Marlee Matlin for her 1987 role in *Children of a Lesser God;* she also appeared in *CODA*. Kotsur is the first Deaf actor to win a Screen Actors Guild Award in an individual acting category (see https://www.imdb.com/name/nm1319274/). These individuals aren't heroes: They are people striving, like most of us, to do the best they possibly can. The clear message from these and so many people with less common disabilities is that we must never make assumptions about what any individual can accomplish, even if their aspirations seem unrealistic.

With the most recent reauthorization of the Elementary and Secondary Education Act of 2015, all but 1% of students will be taking high-stakes exams to demonstrate they are functioning academically at grade level. Now that the vast majority of states have adopted the Common Core State Standards, instructional content has become more challenging for all students, including those with more severe disabilities. Teachers such as Ms. Traun might be nervous when they find that a student with "complex and multiple" disabilities will be on their roster. Information provided in this and later chapters will help address their concerns.

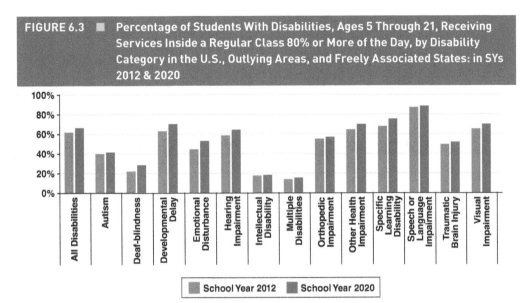

FIGURE 6.3 ■ Percentage of Students With Disabilities, Ages 5 Through 21, Receiving Services Inside a Regular Class 80% or More of the Day, by Disability Category in the U.S., Outlying Areas, and Freely Associated States: in SYs 2012 & 2020

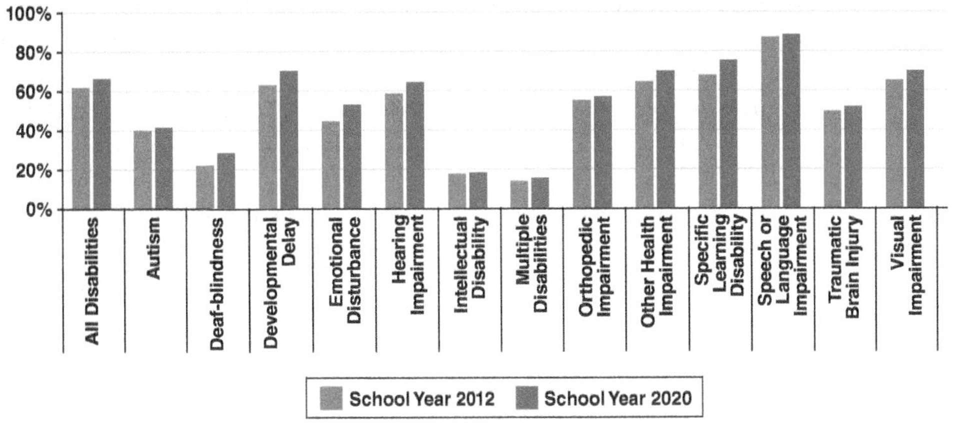

Source: OSEP (2022b); U.S. Department of Education (2021).

The third attribute of these disabilities collectively is that they tend to be more visible or readily observed. Nonexperts can usually identify a middle school student who is blind, and classmates know which of them has a physical disability almost immediately; however, they might not know that a classmate is dealing with depression.

The fourth common characteristic is that you will probably not teach many students with these conditions during your career because of their nature and their relatively low prevalence. Many children with these disabilities require substantial and intensive special education services and supports outside the general education classroom. Although they tend to be included in general education classes less frequently, they and all students with disabilities are increasingly attending classes in general education. Figure 6.3 shows the different rates of inclusion for each special education category, and it also allows you to see how those rates changed between 2012 and 2020. It is important to note that in 2020, more than 66% of all students with disabilities spent more than 80% of their school day in inclusive settings (OSEP, 2022b). What this fact does not tell you is that an additional 16% of all students with disabilities spent between 40% and 79% of their entire school day in inclusive settings. A relatively small percentage (less than 13%) attended inclusive settings less than 40% of the school day. Although the rates of inclusion do vary by disability, general education teachers need to know that the likelihood is that they will teach students with a wide range of disabilities at some point during their teaching careers.

Each of the less common disabilities we discuss here in Chapter 6 is unique and presents an array of special needs. Teachers who understand these conditions make important differences in the lives of affected students and their families. Let's think about these disabilities in their order of prevalence.

ATTRIBUTES OF STUDENTS WITH HEALTH IMPAIRMENTS

As we mentioned in Chapter 1, about 25 years ago the federal government, during one of its reauthorizations of IDEA (typically done every 5 years), identified ADHD as one condition in the "Other Health Impairments" category. Before then, this category was very small, representing some 2% of students with disabilities and fewer than 0.1% of all students (OSEP, 1996). Now the category of Other Health Impairments accounts for 16.8% of all students identified as having a disability (OSEP, 2022a). We are confident that the disproportionately larger size of this formerly low-incidence category is due to the inclusion of students with ADHD. We have already discussed those students' special needs in the previous chapter; in this section, we talk about students with other conditions in the "Other Health Impairments" category. Because the **other health impairments** or special health-care needs category does not call out all the conditions included, states do not keep specific prevalence information for all of the different health problems experienced by students served through IDEA. Regardless, data collected by other federal agencies and private organizations confirm that the number of children affected with other health impairments is relatively low.

Although it is estimated that 5.8% of children in the U.S. have asthma, which is the leading cause of school absences (Asthma and Allergy Foundation of America, 2022), most of them do not receive special education services because except in extreme cases, their educational performance is not affected. Epilepsy, a neuromotor condition, is often thought of as a physical disability, but it is called out by IDEA as a health impairment. It affects 0.6% of schoolchildren, and 70% of the cases in which children have two or more seizures are controlled by medication (Centers for Disease Control [CDC], 2020a). Type 1 diabetes occurs in children at a rate of 0.35% (CDC, 2021a), and sickle cell disease occurs in 0.02% of all children, but 0.2% of Black children (CDC, 2020b). You should see from these statistics that children with less common health conditions represent a small proportion of the school population.

IDEA 2004 places health problems and physical problems into separate categories. We discuss physical disabilities separately later in this chapter; however, these two disabilities often overlap and often occur in combination. For example, some individuals with cerebral palsy also have other health problems. Also, like their counterparts with physical disabilities, many students with other health impairments or special health-care needs do not need or qualify for special education services, yet they do require accommodations because of their fragile situations.

Definition

The federal government uses the term *other health impairments* to describe, collectively, conditions and diseases that create special health-care needs for children. In the IDEA definition (71 Fed. Reg. 46539 [2006]), some conditions are called out. It says that health impairments are due to chronic or acute health problems such as asthma, ADHD, diabetes, epilepsy, a heart condition, hemophilia, lead poisoning, leukemia, sickle cell anemia, and Tourette syndrome. However, to be served through IDEA, these conditions must adversely affect the child's educational performance. Note that many specific health conditions are called out in this federal definition, but many other conditions—such as blood conditions, cancer, cystic fibrosis, tuberculosis, and the so-called STORCH infections (syphilis, toxoplasmosis, rubella, cytomegalovirus, herpes)—are also included though not called out.

For a number of years, the term ***medically fragile*** was used to describe all children with special health-care needs, but it is now applied more selectively. Medically fragile is a status that is not assigned to any specific condition but rather describes the individual's health situation noted in the previously mentioned conditions. Because of numerous advances in medical technology, students can survive health crises and move in and out of fragile status. Sadly, years ago many children would have been too ill or not have lived long enough to go to school. Even though they are now stable enough to attend school, medically fragile students require ongoing medical management. Thus, teachers must be familiar with emergency procedures for them; the "if, then" (i.e., "if this occurs, then do this") must be carefully planned in collaboration with doctors and the school's medical professional. Although steps for worst-case scenarios must be arranged, in most cases the accommodations required for these children are not terribly dramatic. (However, not having backup power for a child's ventilator could have disastrous results.) Years ago, when medically fragile students entered their classroom, teachers would panic and complain that they were not equipped or trained to work with these students. Now, teacher preparation programs devote some, though probably not enough, time preparing teachers for the contingency, which often includes collaborating with the school nurse or other health-care professional in the school.

Types

In general, there are two major groups of students with health impairments:

1. Those with a chronic illness
2. Those with an infectious disease

As you will recall from our initial discussion about health impairments, many of these conditions are very rarely seen in children. All children have episodes of illness during childhood, but most are brief and not very serious. For a small number of children, however, illnesses are chronic, lasting years or even a lifetime. Children with **chronic illnesses** often do not feel well enough to focus their attention on instruction. They are also absent often, causing them to miss a substantial part of their education.

Asthma is the most common chronic disorder of children. This pulmonary disease has for years been the leading cause of school absences among all the chronic diseases (Asthma and Allergy Foundation of America, 2022). A person with asthma usually has difficulty breathing (often called labored breathing or labored respiration) that is sometimes exhibited by shortness of breath, wheezing, and coughing. Years ago, many people believed asthma was a psychological disorder. It is not and never was: It is physical in origin. Many allergen-related factors, such as classroom pets, chalk dust, dirt in the environment, dust mites, and pollen, can trigger an asthma attack, as can non-allergen-related physical activity or exertion. Triggers vary for each individual with asthma. Many students who have asthma are unable to participate in sports or even in physical education activities. Those who are able to participate often use inhalers to assist them in their breathing. Few actually need special education, but they do need special accommodations so their illness does not hinder their learning.

Human immunodeficiency virus (HIV) is a potentially fatal viral infection transmitted primarily through exchange of bodily fluids during unprotected sex or by the use of contaminated hypodermic needles. It is the virus responsible for the deadly acquired immunodeficiency syndrome (AIDS) and can be communicated to a child by an infected mother. Before blood-screening procedures were instituted, the virus was also transmitted through blood transfusions. The effects of the infection in children include central nervous system damage, additional infections, developmental delay, motor problems, psychosocial stresses, and death. HIV/AIDS is an infectious disease, but unlike most others such as flu and the common cold, it is serious and can be life threatening. The disease is very uncommon in young children, but unfortunately it is more common in teenagers because of dangerous life choices such as using drugs and/or engaging in unprotected sex. For many years, parents and educators were concerned that noninfected children could catch the disease from a classmate. It is now clear that this is highly unlikely. With proper precautions (e.g., using latex gloves when treating a child's scrape and following normal sanitary procedures), everyone at school is safe and will not catch this disease. There have been numerous medical advances and public awareness programs in the past decades that have changed dramatically the fears associated with HIV/AIDS. Still, teachers need to be aware of potential hazards and respond accordingly if, for example, children or colleagues get bloody noses or cut themselves.

Characteristics

The health-care needs of some children are so consuming, requiring special accommodations and considerations, that everything else becomes secondary. The treatment goals for these youngsters are to stay strong, healthy, and active, and to lead as normal a life as possible. Although education is a major part of their childhood, many face barriers to efficient learning, such as the following:

- Fatigue
- Absences
- Inconsistent ability to pay attention
- Muscle weakness
- Loss of physical coordination

Some symptoms are directly related to medications and treatment, and others are a function of the disease, illness, or condition. For example, children who are receiving cancer treatment go through periods of feeling too sick to profit from much of the instruction that occurs during the school day; during this time, they might have frequent absences or even some long periods when they are unable to attend school. Instead, they receive a special education option outlined in IDEA 2004, **home-bound/hospital instruction**, in which an itinerant teacher helps them maintain progress in the curriculum by coming to their home or to a hospital (OSEP, 2018). Sometimes, technology helps students stay connected with their classmates. For example, simple video options (e.g., Zoom, FaceTime) are now

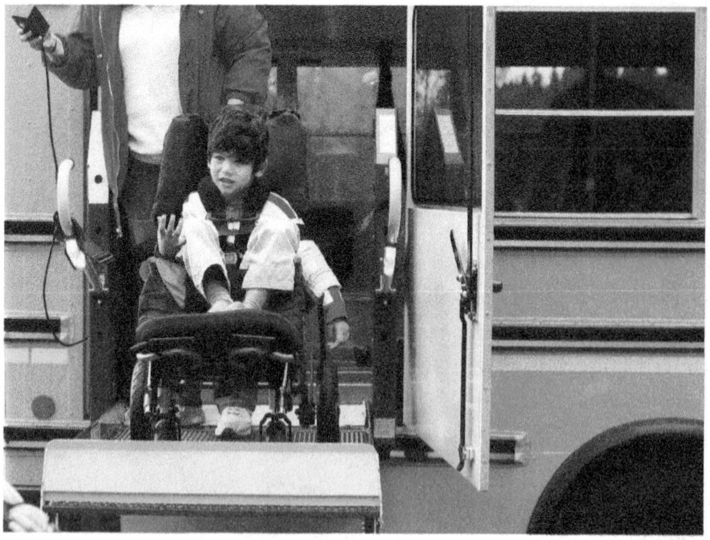

Some students' health situations require special accommodations and considerations. Their treatment goals are to stay strong, healthy, and active and to lead as normal a life as possible.

iStock.com/jarenwicklund

widely used through computers, tablets, or smartphones to allow a student who cannot come to school to join class discussions during a social studies class or watch a demonstration of a science experiment online. Clearly, opportunities for students with health challenges are much greater today than they were only a few years ago. Possibilities for participating in and accessing the general education curriculum from a distance are available, and all students who face such challenges now have opportunities to learn, if they have a dedicated computer and a reliable Wi-Fi connection, a difficulty found among many American children during the COVID-19 pandemic.

Most students with health impairments are served through 504 and not IDEA. Regardless, the American Pediatrics Association (2008) has long recommended that children with special health-care needs have a separate **Emergency Care Plan**, which is readily available to school personnel and provides detailed contact information for the child's doctor, family, and what procedures to follow in cases of emergencies. (A free copy of the information form can be downloaded from https://www.acep.org/by-medical-focus/pediatrics/medical-forms/emergency-information-form-for-children-with-special-health-care-needs/.)

The IDEA definition calls out epilepsy as a health impairment, though people think of it as a physical disability because it is a neuromotor condition. Although it can be chronic in some cases, most of these children attend general education classes, access the general education curriculum, and participate in inclusive classes. However, all teachers must know about seizure disorders or epilepsy because they are more prevalent than some other health conditions and seizures can happen at any time. Although only 0.6% of children aged 0 to 17 years have epilepsy, that means in a school of 1,000 students one would expect six to have epilepsy (CDC, 2020a). A person with epilepsy often has recurrent seizures resulting from the sudden, excessive, spontaneous, and abnormal discharge of neurons in the brain. The result can be loss of consciousness or changes in the person's motor or sensory functioning. The frequency of seizures may vary from a single isolated incident to hundreds in a day. Some children actually anticipate their seizures because they experience a **preictal stage**, or an **aura**, and they have heightened sensory signals of an impending seizure, such as a peculiar smell, taste, vision, sound, or action. Others might experience a change in their behavior. Knowing about an aura pattern is helpful because it allows an individual to assume a safe position or warn teachers and classmates before a seizure begins.

Some seizures are characterized by short lapses in consciousness, and it can be difficult to recognize that a student is experiencing anything out of the ordinary. Because some types of seizures are not very dramatic, a teacher might wrongly assume that the child is merely daydreaming or not paying attention. In other types of seizures, the child may think the environment has become distorted and strange and that inexplicable events and feelings are occurring. Teachers might incorrectly believe the child is acting out, clowning around, or exhibiting bizarre behavior patterns. Of course, the most serious type of seizure, the one most of us think of first, is characterized by convulsions and loss of consciousness. The behaviors associated with these seizures may at first be frightening to teachers and to other students in the class, but knowing what to expect and what to do in the event of a seizure reduces stress (and the danger to the individual student). The school nurse, the student's parents, or the special education teacher can be great resources when planning for the special needs of such students.

Teachers need to know what to do if a seizure happens to one of their students. Figure 6.4 provides a quick guide. Teachers also need to dispel the fears of classmates who may have been frightened by their classmate's behavior and be sure to welcome the student who has had a seizure back to the classroom much as they would a student with any other health impairment.

FIGURE 6.4 ■ Seizure Tips

Seizure First Aid
How to help someone having a seizure
1
STAY with the person until they are awake and alert after the seizure.
✓ Time the seizure ✓ Remain Calm
✓ Check for medical ID
2
Keep the person SAFE.
✓ Move or guide away from harm
3
Turn the person onto their SIDE if they are not awake and aware.
✓ Keep airway clear
✓ Loosen tight clothes around neck
✓ Put something small and soft under the head
Call 911 if...
Seizure lasts longer than 5 minutes
Person does not return to their usual state
Person is injured, pregnant, or sick
Repeated seizures
First time seizure
Difficulty breathing
Seizure occurs in water
Do NOT
✕ Do NOT restrain.
✕ Do NOT put any objects in their mouth.
Rescue medicines can be given if prescribed by a health care professional
Learn more: epilepsy.com/firstaid

Source: From *Seizure First Aid* by the Epilepsy Foundation (2020). Retrieved from https://www.epilepsy.com/sites/default/files/upload/image/SFA%20Lockscreen.jpg

Now, let's turn our attention to another rare health condition that we mentioned earlier. Although the prevalence of sickle cell anemia is low in the general school population, it is much higher among Black and Hispanic children. For this reason, teachers in urban schools and in schools with a high percentage of these children should be aware of this condition and how it affects the individuals involved. The Considering Diversity section of this chapter provides descriptive information about sickle-cell disease (or sickle-cell anemia) and prevalence rates, which are highest among Black and Hispanic individuals in the U.S.

Considering Diversity: Sickle-Cell Disease

One health condition in particular disproportionately affects Black people: sickle-cell disease (sometimes called sickle-cell anemia), which affects approximately 1 out of every 500 Black births. Among Hispanics, sickle-cell disease affects approximately 1 in every 16,300 births (National Center on Birth Defects and Developmental Disabilities, 2022). Sickle-cell disease or **sickle-cell anemia** is a hereditary, life-threatening blood disorder that causes the red blood cells to become rigid and take on a crescent, or sickle, shape, which is how the disease got its name. During what is called a sickling crisis, this rigidity and the crescent shape of the cells do not allow blood to flow through the vessels, depriving some tissues of oxygen and resulting in extreme pain, swollen joints, high fever, and even strokes. The pain can occur in a person's back, knees, arms, chest, or stomach. Educators need to know that many children who have this condition could miss a considerable amount of school. To reduce the students' stress resulting from missed assignments and instruction, teachers should develop strategies with the students and their families to compensate for missed school days. For example, a child who lives close to the affected student could serve as a peer tutor who brings assignments home to the student and explains important instructions provided during the school day.

ATTRIBUTES OF STUDENTS WITH MULTIPLE DISABILITIES

Students with multiple disabilities represent only 0.17% of the entire school population (U.S. Department of Education, 2023). As a group, they are also the least likely (15% of all special education students) to attend a general education class for 80% or more of their school day (OSEP, 2022b). In other words, few general education teachers have a student with multiple disabilities as one of their full-time students.

Teachers need to avoid the temptation of describing these students in terms of deficits, instead thinking in terms of what the students can do with a variety of supports across many of life's dimensions. The emphasis for students with multiple disabilities is on developing skills that promote independence and community presence (Brown et al., 2016). Ironically, in some cases that means teaching individuals how to depend on others to access the system of supports—the network of people who provide assistance (see the section about students with intellectual disabilities in Chapter 5)—required to achieve maximal independence.

The current outlook for individuals with multiple severe disabilities is very different from what it was only a few decades ago. Not long ago, adults with severe disabilities spent their lives in large residential institutions with no access to the community and no chance to participate in mainstream society. Their educational opportunities have also increased. Before the original IDEA (the Education for All Handicapped Children Act) was passed in 1975, many were excluded from school and had no opportunity to benefit from a special education complete with the related services they needed. It was not until the 1960s and 1970s that researchers began to turn their attention to developing and validating instructional procedures and services that are especially effective for these learners. In addition to access to the general education curriculum, their education now includes the following:

- Expressions of choice
- Self-determination
- Functional skills training
- Social skills training
- Community-based instruction
- Supports and planning for the transition to adult life

Many individuals with multiple disabilities also face other challenges, including medical problems such as seizure disorders, vision or hearing problems, heart disease, and cerebral palsy. Consequently, they and their families deal with many professionals and disciplines, including many that have different styles of interaction, specialized terms and jargon, and approaches. Such multiple interactions can complicate an already difficult situation. It is often the classroom teacher who helps families balance schooling, family life, and the series of professionals who interface with them and their children.

Definition

The IDEA definition of multiple disabilities explains that students who are identified with this disability have concomitant impairments (such as intellectual disabilities along with blindness and/or an orthopedic impairment). Most of these students have intellectual disabilities that are *not* in the mild range. The combination of these conditions results in severe educational needs that cannot be accommodated in special education programs designed for solely one of the impairments. Also, multiple disabilities *does not include* those with deaf-blindness (71 Fed. Reg. 46539 [2006]). These combinations of disabilities and conditions lead to unique learning needs. For example, individuals with a cognitive disability might need supports to pay bills and manage a budget. If they also have a moderate hearing loss, they might need assistance to facilitate communication at the doctor's office, yet they might function at work with only natural supports from coworkers.

Types

Each individual with multiple severe disabilities is unique. The possible combinations of conditions are so numerous, and the ways in which the symptoms associated with these conditions can manifest so different, it makes little sense to group these students by type. Instead, we will spend a little time thinking about common characteristics they present to themselves, their families, and their teachers.

Characteristics

Individuals with multiple disabilities display a wide range of skills and abilities, as well as a wide range of problem areas in need of intensive instruction. According to the Child Advocacy Network of Disability Organizations (2023), this group of individuals shares some common characteristics:

- Limited speech or communication
- Difficulty in basic physical mobility
- Tendency to forget skills that are rarely used
- Trouble generalizing skills from one situation to another
- A need for support in major life activities (e.g., home care, leisure, community use, vocational)

Another common characteristic of those who have multiple severe disabilities is the response to the challenges to gain independence and participation in the community. Typically, in order for someone to accomplish these goals, they need intensive and pervasive supports from a wide range of individuals and systems, but they also tend not to access the general education curriculum. Rather, their instruction is more focused on functional skills needed in daily life. The ITPs, which are part of their IEPs, often reflect goals related to employment, community participation, recreation and leisure, continuing education, independent living, and self-determination. Achieving such goals usually involves instruction in the community, in the natural settings where skills of transportation, time management, work, and leisure time happen later in life. However, that does not mean that they should be excluded from typical schools and school activities. Through those opportunities, they and their classmates can develop friendships, learn important social skills, and learn from each other.

Also, technology can help people with disabilities and their families address and compensate for their disabilities (Bryant et al., 2012). The federal government continues to invest a considerable amount of money and interest in technology because it is clear that assistive technology (AT) has improved outcomes for students with multiple severe conditions (Bryant et al., 2012). The data on which the government bases these conclusions indicate that technology helps these individuals

- communicate more effectively;
- increase their levels of independence;
- control their environments;
- have greater mobility; and
- gain access to information.

Technology has opened up avenues of communication for many students who are unable to communicate with others through oral speech. What forms of alternative and augmentative communication are available for students with disabilities?

The Washington Post / Contributor/Getty Images

Technology allows many students who are unable to communicate with others through oral speech to interact with others and participate in school and in life (Bryant & Bryant, 2011). Let's look at one example. **Augmentative and alternative communication devices (AAC)**, which include software and hardware devices for communicating, can be very beneficial to individuals with these disabilities (National Institute on Deafness and Other Communication Disorders, 2019). Whether in the form of simple devices, such as communication boards, or complicated speech synthesizers that actually speak for the individual, technology now allows individuals to make their needs known, express their feelings, and interact with others (Bryant & Bryant, 2011). In the most straightforward systems, words and/or pictures are placed on a flat surface or in books. Students communicate by pointing to the appropriate symbols. Symbols are customized to the individual; the words or symbols on the board reflect the individuals and important features of the environments in which they operate. Some boards are simple homemade projects, while others use quite sophisticated technology readily available on mobile devices, iPads, tablets, and laptops. Many of these only require the individual to touch a picture or series of pictures to communicate their needs and desires. Your job as a teacher is to encourage the use of these techniques and to help shape them into a reliable system of communication for the student. When your students have these communication tools, learning and social interaction can take place.

ATTRIBUTES OF STUDENTS WITH DEVELOPMENTAL DELAY

A child who is not speaking by the age of 3 is likely to have a problem that could be a significant disability. But which disability? It could be an intellectual disability, ASD, a learning disability, or a speech or language impairment. Rather than forcing a diagnosis that might be incorrect or a problem that may be resolved, IDEA 2004 allows preschoolers ages 3 to 5 and children up to age 9 who show a general delay in development to receive special education services under the nonspecific category **developmental delay**, created in 1991. This label is not to be confused with developmental disabilities, which we discussed in the intellectual disabilities section of Chapter 5. The special education label *developmental delay* is most often applied to children between the ages of 3 and 5. About 0.03% of the resident population served in the United States (well over 250,000) were identified as having developmental delays (U.S Department of Education, 2023). In 2019, developmental delay was the largest category used for children of this age group, comprising 40% of all young children receiving services through IDEA (320,107 of 798,488; OSEP, 2022a). Creating this label was actually the federal government's first move toward supporting a noncategorical approach to special education. It means that, unlike their counterparts without disabilities, some youngsters are entitled to a free appropriate public education during the preschool and early elementary years without being identified with a specific disability. The main purpose of this special education category has been to reduce the chances of misidentifying children as having one disability when in fact they have another, but more important, this option brings early intervention services to these preschoolers and their families.

Definition

So as not to mislabel, or incorrectly identify, children with disabilities between the ages of 3 and 9, IDEA 2004 has allowed states to provide special services to those who exhibit general developmental delays without also identifying them as having a specific disability. Not all states use this option, though most do provide services through IDEA by using this unique category.

Types

Preschoolers with developmental delays have a wide range of disabilities or simple delayed development, not disabilities that are specifically identified during their early years. Many states, therefore, use the developmental delay option for qualifying these children for special education services between the ages of 3 and 5. Other states, though, choose to identify children as being "at risk" for developmental delays when they are infants or toddlers (Center for Parent Information and Resources, 2016), and some states include children younger than 3 and older than 5 years. For example, although preschoolers with severe visual disabilities can be readily identified, children with general delays in language and motor skills might receive services but not be assigned a categorical identification. Eligibility for receiving services under developmental delay varies from state to state.

Characteristics

The main characteristic of youngsters with developmental delays is that they have general delays in their development. Professionals use this designation for one of two main reasons: (1) they are hesitant to assign a potentially incorrect disability label to the child, or (2) they believe the child might just be developing slowly and with early intervention services will catch up to peers on critical developmental markers such as speech, motor skills, and social skills. Although the federal government allows noncategorical identification of students up to the age of 9, as children get older the percentage in this category decreases dramatically (U.S. Department of Education, 2023).

ATTRIBUTES OF STUDENTS WITH PHYSICAL DISABILITIES

Physical disabilities are clearly an infrequent condition experienced by children in today's schools. They represent only 0.04% of the entire school population nationwide (U.S. Department of Education, 2023). Many adults with physical disabilities received a very different education than today's students who face physical challenges. In years past, they were not allowed to join their brothers, sisters, and friends at their neighborhood schools. They were bused to special schools equipped with state-of-the-art equipment like therapy pools and staffed with related services professionals such as physical and occupational therapists. But these facilities were segregated, and only students with disabilities attended. When these individuals grew up, many became disability advocates. They have fought hard to enlarge the educational options available to students with disabilities, and specifically, they have sought the closure of separate, sometimes also called center schools, for schoolchildren with physical disabilities. The result of their efforts is that students with physical disabilities attend school alongside typical learners in inclusive school settings. Many receive therapy from related services professionals. For some, their only teachers are general educators who provide accommodations guided by special education professionals.

The present and future for individuals with physical disabilities is changing rapidly. Advances in prosthetics and robotics are enabling people with missing arms and legs to move independently, Although prosthetics—artificial limbs—have been available for centuries, today's versions are more cosmetically appealing and more functional. Compare Captain Hook in the story of Peter Pan to the prosthetic running blades used today by athletes who compete in major running events and to hands and limbs that almost look like real hands and legs. The future holds considerable promise.

WORKING TOGETHER

PROMOTING ACCESSIBILITY

Earlier you met Mr. Dehiya, a high school teacher whose students helped restructure his classroom to make it accessible for one of his students who had been injured in a car accident and who now uses a wheelchair to move about. Remember, Mr. Dehiya chose to go online to learn more about wheelchair accessibility, but he found little useful besides what he thought was just plain common sense. He decided to have every one of his students, including Abooksigun, help solve problems associated with a bulky wheelchair in the classroom. But, Mr. Dehiya was delighted that the district assigned Ms. Espinoza, a trained and licensed occupational therapist, to work with him and the entire class to help make the classroom and the entire school environment more welcoming and safe for everyone. Ms. Espinoza is an expert in AT assessments designed to create a student–technology match that would allow students to access the general education curriculum, but she also has extensive experience and training in helping businesses develop accessible workplaces or help clients who have sustained injuries access daily living activities. She is very familiar with the needs of wheelchair users and has developed a keen eye for identifying what might or might not be the effective and efficient change in a room to allow for maximum accessibility and safety. They all thought through how to set up the room for small-group activities, independent work, and full class discussions. It was amazing to everyone what they hadn't thought of, like how in case of emergencies everyone could safely exit the class! They made good use of Ms. Espinoza's time, for she is one of only two occupational therapists working with the district, having to travel long distances to work with a few students across many school settings. They all decided that they would try out the new classroom "seating" arrangement for a few weeks and make a list of what works well and what does not. She will then come back and meet with Abooksigun individually and also the whole class to reassess the learning environment and modify as necessary.

Questions

1. What considerations would you think about when designing your classroom's seating arrangements for students with a variety of different disabilities?
2. Who would you seek out to help you organize your classroom?

Definition

IDEA 2004 uses the term ***orthopedic impairments*** to refer to conditions that we call physical disabilities and others call physical impairments. The definition calls out that the impairments are caused by a congenital anomaly, a disease, or other reasons, such as cerebral palsy, amputation, fractures, or burns causing contractions (71 Fed. Reg. 46539 [2006]). In order for students with physical disabilities to receive special education services, their physical disability must adversely affect their educational performance. However, if their disability does not adversely affect their educational performance, they still might be able to receive necessary related services through 504.

Types

The two major groups of physical disabilities are

1. neuromotor impairments, and
2. muscular/skeletal conditions.

Neuromotor conditions include cerebral palsy, spinal cord disorders, muscular dystrophy, polio, and multiple sclerosis (MS). Remember our earlier discussion about epilepsy. Although it is neuromotor condition, IDEA calls it out as a health impairment, which is where epilepsy is discussed. When the central nervous system, which consists of the brain and the spinal cord, is damaged, the result is a neuromotor impairment that limits muscular control and movement. Muscular/skeletal conditions include juvenile arthritis, limb deficiencies, and skeletal disorders. Individuals with muscular/skeletal conditions usually have difficulty controlling their movements, but the cause is not neurological. Regardless of the type of physical disability, some individuals need special devices and technology even to do simple tasks—walking, eating, or writing—that most of us take for granted. Let's think about each of these types of physical disabilities in turn.

The two most common neuromotor impairments are cerebral palsy and spina bifida. Cerebral palsy is a result of damage either before (prenatally), during (perinatally), or immediately after (postnatally) the child's birth, usually because of insufficient oxygen flow to the brain (National Center on Birth Defects and Developmental Disabilities, 2023). The condition can also be acquired during the first 3 years of life. In these cases, it is usually caused by brain damage resulting from accidents, brain infections, or child abuse. Cerebral palsy is not a disease but rather a nonprogressive and noninfectious condition that results in severe motor impairments. Regrettably, once it has been acquired it cannot be cured (at least as of now). Spina bifida, a very rare condition, is a type of neural tube defect that is apparent at birth. It can happen anywhere along the spine when the neural tube does not close all the way. The size and location of the opening affects the severity of the condition and can result in mild to severe physical and intellectual disabilities (CDC, 2023). Fortunately, today, early treatment, usually surgery, and a balance of folic acid in the expectant mother can reduce the impact of this condition, though it often remain remains serious.

One of the most common muscular/skeletal conditions seen in children, **limb loss**, results from a missing arm or leg. Regardless of whether the impairment occurred before or after birth, it is a major impediment to normal physical activity and functioning. Emerging technology, particularly **robotics** (or the use of robot technology), now provides much assistance to those with missing limbs. Artificial limbs make possible movements that only a few decades ago were thought to be impossible.

Juvenile arthritis is a relatively common muscular/skeletal condition affecting joints and the function of muscles. Although there are many different forms of this disease, it is usually chronic and painful. Juvenile arthritis usually develops in early childhood and often causes significant school absences. Children often need help keeping up with their classmates because they miss so much class instruction. Teachers must understand that their students with this condition may be able to move about in the classroom inconsistently (better or worse at different times of the day) and that sitting for extended periods of time can cause them to become stiff and experience considerable pain. Children with juvenile arthritis need to be allowed to move around a lot. Those who have a high rate of absences probably need tutoring and extra help in order to keep up with their peers.

Characteristics

Physical disabilities range from mild to severe and in many cases are only one of multiple conditions an individual may face. However, remember that physical disability and cognitive disability do not go hand in hand. Let's consider the characteristics of a few physical disabilities.

Some students with disabilities need to use special devices and technology to do basic physical tasks such as walking, playing, eating, or writing.

Iparraguirre Recio/Getty Images

Individuals with cerebral palsy whose motor functioning is affected show the following characteristics, alone or in combination: jerky movements, spasms, involuntary movements, and lack of muscle tone. Many have impaired mobility and poor muscle development. They sometimes also need braces to help support the affected limbs and make them more functional or to prevent more problems and limitations on mobility. Proper positioning of the body also must be considered. Many children need wedges, pillows, and individually designed chairs and worktables so they can be comfortable, breathe more easily, avoid more problems, and participate in group activities. Although some degree of intellectual and developmental disabilities may be present in about half of these children, others may be intellectually gifted. It is a tragic mistake to assume that cerebral palsy and intellectual and developmental disabilities always occur together.

Students with physical limitations and their teachers face significant challenges during the school day. All schools must meet the special architectural codes required by the Americans with Disabilities Act of 1990 and must be barrier-free. Regardless, these students' worlds are often filled with physical barriers that must be overcome before they can achieve independence and a normal life. Surprisingly, students who use wheelchairs still face physical barriers at some schools. For example, classes are scheduled on the second floor although no elevator is available, bathrooms are not accessible, or passageways are too narrow for a wheelchair to pass through. These facts could explain why many individuals with a limb deficiency have difficulties adjusting to their situation. Eliminating barriers, even obvious physical ones, can be more difficult than you might think. Often, it is the student's teacher who must advocate for improvements to the bathroom, the lunchroom, the playground, the gymnasium, the music room, the library, and the bus. Remember, too, that barriers are not only physical: Integration might necessitate accommodations beyond the curb cuts (those breaks in sidewalk curbs that allow wheelchairs, roller bags, and even skateboards to move freely to the street), ramps, elevators, and bathroom alterations required by law. Most children will respond warmly and proudly to your subtle reminders that everyone enjoys being included in all aspects of school.

ATTRIBUTES OF STUDENTS WHO ARE DEAF AND HARD OF HEARING

The words *deaf* and *Deaf*[2] both refer to individuals with severe and profound hearing losses, but they have very different implications. Possibly more than any other group of people with disabilities, Deaf individuals unite as a community. Their separate language and culture bind them together, and they feel much as people who live in different countries feel about each other and about those who do not share the same language, history, literature, and art. Deaf culture originated in the U.S. during the 1800s on Martha's Vineyard (Groce, 1985; Rinze & Tange, 2021) because the settlers of this island came from Kent, England and carried a recessive gene for deafness. More than 25% of the islanders were Deaf and they, along with all the hearing residents, used ASL. It is an example of the most inclusive community imaginable. Because the Deaf citizens attended the School for the Deaf in Connecticut, they were literate, while many of the hearing residents were not. Everyone relied on each other. The island was relatively isolated for more than 200 years and everyone lived and worked together. The Deaf earned average or above average wages and were full members of society.

Perspectives on deafness and inclusion differ. Some people with average hearing consider deafness a disability, a sad condition that isolates those affected from family and society. Members of the Deaf community believe that the traditional way of thinking of inclusive is restrictive, isolating them from each other. To those in the Deaf community, however, deafness is one aspect that binds them together as a historically underrepresented group rich in culture, history, and language. The language of the Deaf community is ASL, a language that uses signs, has all the elements of other languages (grammar, syntax, idioms), and is not parallel to English in either structure or word order. ASL is not a mere translation of oral speech or the English language (as is signed English); it is a fully developed language. In fact, many states allow ASL as an option to meet the high school foreign language requirement, and the same is true at many colleges and universities. As the language of the Deaf community, ASL is used in all aspects of Deaf culture. For example, plays are written in ASL and performed by Deaf theater groups around the world, and a base of folk literature has developed over the years. This community unites in many ways by coming together socially and by advocating against discrimination and for justice. Clearly, this disability is different from other disabilities in so many ways. However, not all people who cannot hear consider themselves Deaf and members of the Deaf community. The best indicator of how people think about themselves in this regard is whether they capitalize the "D" in *deaf*.

Educators need to understand that not all people with hearing impairments are d/Deaf. Although many people have hearing problems, almost half are older than 65. The rate for children is much lower, affecting about 0.09% of the general school population (U.S. Department of Education, 2023). Approximately 2 to 3 in every 1,000 babies are born with a hearing problem (National Institute on Deafness and Other Communication Disorders, 2021). We do not know what percentage of children with hearing impairments have profound hearing loss, although some estimates are that they represent about 25% of the total group. These calculations do include students who do not need special education because hearing aids or assistive devices allow them to hear well enough to participate in typical classroom activities. Of those served through IDEA, almost 64% receive their education in general education classes for more than 80% of the school day, while about 12% attend separate schools for the Deaf (OSEP, 2022a).

Definition

There are two types of hearing problems that result in disabilities. These are identified in Table 6.1. Deaf students have a hearing loss so severe that, with or without help from a hearing aid or an assistive hearing device, it seriously affects their ability to process spoken or auditory information by hearing. Clearly, these students' educational performance, their interactions with others, and their participation in the community are influenced by their hearing problems.

TABLE 6.1 ■ Categories of Hearing Impairments by Severity of Loss

Severity of Loss	Explanation
Mild hearing loss	An inability to hear or understand speech that is soft or at a distance
Moderate hearing loss	Typical speech is hard to understand
Severe hearing loss	Even loud speech is hard to understand
Profound hearing loss	Only assistive listening devices (e.g., hearing aids, cochlear implants) enable the individual to understand information presented orally

Students with hearing problems that are less severe—those whose hearing falls into the range considered "hard of hearing"—are also eligible for special education services. Most states do not specify a specific level of hearing loss that serves as a guideline for which students qualify for special education and which do not. Such states simply indicate that a student's hearing problems (whether permanent or fluctuating) must adversely affect educational performance. Experts vary in their definitions of hearing loss and in the point at which they believe it has educational significance. Although many states provide a cutoff score, usually including at least a 20-decibel loss in the speech range in the better ear, even a precise score on an **audiogram** cannot guide educators in assessing the significance of a hearing loss because individuals respond differently. Whether a student qualifies in the d/Deaf or the hard-of-hearing group, teachers should remember that all hearing losses are serious. Of course, at some point, the level of severity substantially influences the way in which students need to be taught and the degree to which they understand oral communication.

Types

The dimensions used to describe hearing problems follow:

- Type of loss
- Age of onset
- Degree of loss

The two general types of hearing loss are conductive and sensorineural. Conductive hearing loss is due to blockage or damage to the outer or middle ear that prevents sound waves from traveling (being conducted) to the inner ear. Generally, someone with a conductive hearing loss has a mild to moderate disability. Some conductive hearing losses are temporary; in fact, we have all probably experienced a conductive hearing loss at some point in our lives, for example, as a consequence of the change in air pressure when flying in an airplane or driving through the mountains. Children often experience head colds and ear infections that result in a temporary loss of conductive hearing. By the time they are 3 years old, five out of six children have experienced some kind of ear infection that results in a temporary hearing loss (National Institute on Deafness and Other Communication Disorders, 2021). If the hearing loss was caused by a head cold, once the infection clears up the hearing difficulties also disappear.

Other causes of conductive hearing losses can usually be corrected through surgery or other medical techniques. Damage to the inner ear or the auditory nerve results in a sensorineural hearing loss and is more difficult to improve through technology or medicine. Some people refer to this type of hearing loss as *nerve deafness*. Individuals affected by a sensorineural loss are able to hear different frequencies at different intensity levels; their hearing losses are not flat or even. Sensorineural losses are less common in young children than the conductive types, but teachers need to understand that hearing aids can have mixed results with sensorineural losses.

The age of onset—that is, the age when the hearing loss occurs—is important. Individuals who are born d/Deaf or become d/Deaf before they learn to speak and understand language are referred to as *prelingually deaf.* Congenital hearing loss is found in 1.7 per 1,000 infants screened at hospitals today (CDC, 2021b); genetic factors are the most likely causes. Their inability to hear language seriously affects their ability to communicate with others and to learn academic subjects taught later in school. Adventitious hearing loss occurs later after birth, and **prelingual deafness** occurs before the child learns to speak and understand speech. One in 10 of those who are prelingually deaf has at least one Deaf parent; they are referred to as CODA (child of Deaf adults), as in the movie of the same name. Children in this group typically learn to communicate during the normal developmental period. However, instead of learning oral communication skills, many learn through a combination of manual communication (sign language) and oral language. These young Deaf children are taught ASL as their native language, develop communication at the normal developmental periods, as infants sign with their hands, and learn English as their second language through reading and writing.

Those whose severe hearing loss occurs after they have learned to speak and understand language are called **postlingually deaf**. Many are able to retain their abilities to use speech and communicate with others orally.

The degree of loss is measured in decibels (dB) and Hertz (Hz). Softer, quieter sounds have lower decibel measurements; louder sounds have higher decibel numbers. Decibel levels range from 0 to 120 dB and are used to test how well an individual can hear different frequencies; a child with normal hearing should be able to perceive sounds at 0 dB. In the United States (other countries might not use the same terms), we associate hearing loss with different decibels levels. A mild hearing loss occurs at 26 to 45 dB. People with a mild hearing loss may have some difficulty hearing speech, and even what might be considered a mild hearing loss can be serious for children who are still learning to talk. A moderate hearing loss occurs at 46 to 65 dB, which results in greater difficulty hearing speech. A severe loss (66–85 dB) results in considerable difficulty hearing speech; a person with this level of hearing loss is usually considered d/Deaf rather than hard of hearing. At 85 dB or more, a profound loss is evident, and even the most effective hearing aids might not help a person hear speech. At the profound level of loss, cochlear implants become an option for some.

For examples of what different decibel levels sound like, see Figure 6.5. Common sources of loud sounds or noise in our environment are shown in this figure. Many are considered dangerous because, with continued exposure, they can cause noise-induced hearing loss. As a teacher, you can help your students to understand the importance of being careful with sound. For example, students should know that listening to mobile devices with the volume turned up high will eventually result in hearing problems.

The pitch, or frequency, of sounds is measured in a unit called the hertz (Hz). The normal ear hears sounds that range from approximately 20 Hz to 20,000 Hz; speech sounds fall about in the middle of the human hearing range (between 250 Hz and 4,000 Hz). An audiogram is used to plot how well an individual hears at various combinations of hertz and decibels and also at various bands of pitch and loudness. Typically, the accommodations for and communication styles of students who are hard of hearing or d/Deaf differ. For example, students who are hard of hearing might need to sit closer to the

FIGURE 6.5 ■ Decibel Levels of Noise in American Environments

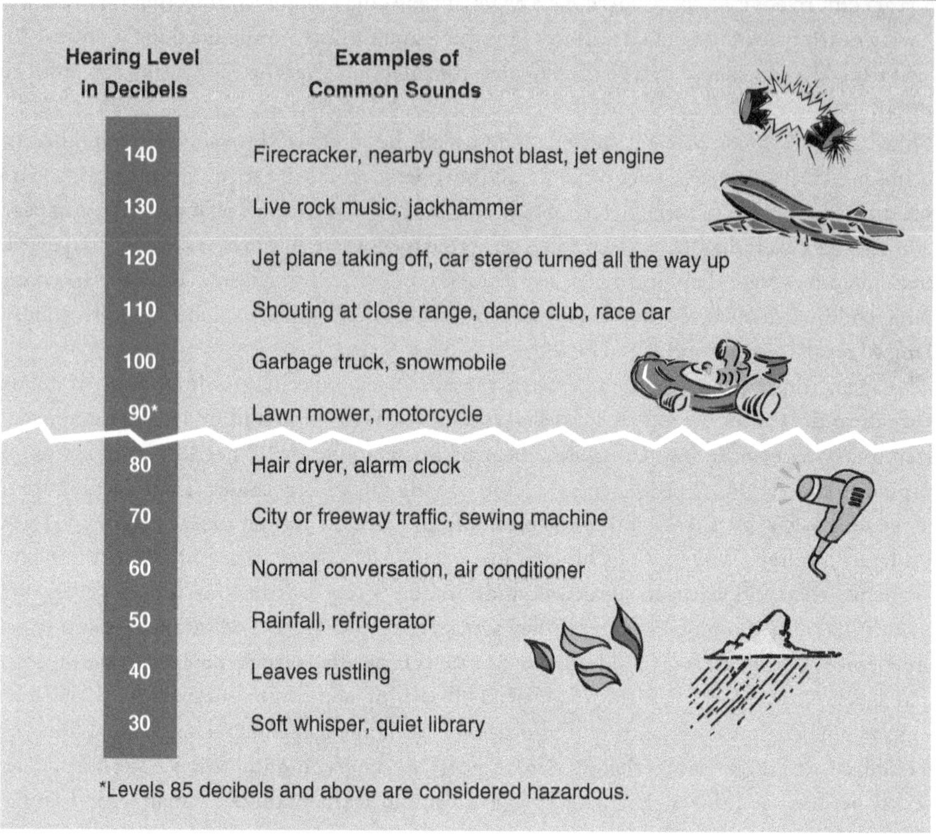
Hearing Level in Decibels
Examples of Common Sounds
140 Firecracker, nearby gunshot blast, jet engine
130 Live rock music, jackhammer
120 Jet plane taking off, car stereo turned all the way up
110 Shouting at close range, dance club, race car
100 Garbage truck, snowmobile
90* Lawn mower, motorcycle
80 Hair dryer, alarm clock
70 City or freeway traffic, sewing machine
60 Normal conversation, air conditioner
50 Rainfall, refrigerator
40 Leaves rustling
30 Soft whisper, quiet library
*Levels 85 decibels and above are considered hazardous.

teacher or have a classmate assist with note taking, whereas a student who is d/Deaf might need an interpreter to profit from lectures.

Throughout this text, we have included notes about technology that can be used to help individuals in the classroom. In many instances, the technology is referred to as an AT device. The Tech Notes feature that follows provides information about the importance of identifying the proper student–technology match.

TECH NOTES

FINDING THE RIGHT ASSISTIVE TECHNOLOGY DEVICE

Making a student–technology match is usually the responsibility of an AT evaluation team, whose members could include the student's special education teacher, general education teacher, speech-language pathologist, physical therapist, occupational therapist, the student's family, the student, and/or whoever is involved in the student's learning. In the case of students who are d/Deaf or hard of hearing, the team convenes to identify any AT device that may be needed to help provide the students with access to the general education curriculum. As part of the process, a series of questions can be asked to better understand the students and their needs:

- How do the students utilize their residual hearing?
- What types of hearing technology are the students using or have they used in the past?
- Do they use sign language and/or an interpreter?
- Can they access what the teacher says at the front of the room, while the teacher walks around, or with the teacher's back turned to the class while writing on the board?
- Can they access what their peers say during class discussions or group activities or while in challenging environments?
- Do they have access to fire/tornado alarms? Announcements?
- Do they have a way to contact home in an emergency? Community supports?

- Are movies/videos shown in class? Do the students, families, and staff know how to access captioning?
- How do they communicate with others—family, peers, and community?
- Are the students able to take notes and watch the teacher/interpreter effectively?
- How do they access information during group activities—lectures, programs, or events?

Once these questions have been answered, the AT evaluation team can then consider the students and their learning context to identify AT devices and services that may help enhance learning. As a teacher, you will likely be a member of an AT evaluation team; it is best to attend the meeting knowing that your input is essential in helping make a student-technology match.

Characteristics

Deaf and hard-of-hearing students are individuals with different learning needs and abilities, and teachers cannot make uniform judgments about the accommodations and services they require based on information about an individual student's amount or type of hearing loss. One student with a moderate loss might not profit from typical instructional methods such as lectures and oral directions alone, whereas another student with the same profile might function well without supports.

Another factor to consider is whether the individual has cognitive impairments along with hearing loss. In some conditions, these disabilities go hand in hand. These may include visual disabilities, intellectual and developmental disabilities, learning disabilities, behavior disorders, and cerebral palsy, which often are caused by the same disease or accident that caused the hearing loss. Many individuals with Down syndrome have hearing losses, but certainly not all. Students whose deafness is inherited, however, tend not to have multiple disabilities. And, often those with more than one disability, including hearing impairment, are counted and served through other special education categories.

Two areas are of great concern to educators working with d/Deaf students: academic achievement and speech ability. A long-term problem for individuals who are d/Deaf is their academic achievement, particularly in the area of reading; however, great gains are being made (Cawthon et al., 2023). Although they are still somewhat behind their hearing peers, advances in the use of evidence-based practices, as well as technologies, are making real differences in academic achievement.

Technology has changed the lives of many individuals with hearing problems. Whereas only 50 years ago students with mild to moderate hearing deficiencies could not hear teachers' instructions or classmates' discussions, improvements in surgery and in hearing aids and listening devices allow today's students to profit from education alongside their classmates without disabilities. Some do not even qualify for special education. More improvements are on the horizon. Medical technology holds the promise of both preventing and curing deafness at some point in the future. In 2000, d/Deaf children as young as 1 year old were allowed to receive cochlear implants, which are surgically implanted assistive hearing devices designed to help those with sensorineural hearing loss gain useful hearing. By the end of 2019, about 65,000 children had received the implants (National Institute on Deafness and Other Communication Disorders, 2021). Although not a cure for deafness, implants hold great promise for many individuals with profound hearing loss. Contrary to popular belief, cochlear implants are not universally successful and do not automatically allow children to hear and communicate. Many of these individuals use both their implants and ASL together. However, implants remain controversial in the Deaf community, where deafness is accepted and celebrated and ASL remains the preferred communication mode for some. For deaf children born of hearing parents, it is a more popular choice because their hope is that their children will learn oral speech and use it with family and friends.

ATTRIBUTES OF STUDENTS WITH VISUAL DISABILITIES

According to the World Health Organization (2022), approximately 2.2 billion people worldwide have visual disabilities, and about 1.1 billion of them are blind. However, it is estimated that more than 80% of these individuals are age 50 or older, and the prevalence is much higher in developing countries. The

NCES (2022) reports that 26,000 students in the U.S. receive services for visual disabilities through IDEA. They represent only 0.03% of the general population of American students (U.S. Department of Education, 2023) and only 0.3% of children served through IDEA (OSEP, 2022a). Today, about 69% of students with visual disabilities spend more than 80% of their school day in general education classrooms, most likely at their neighborhood school, and receive support from a resource specialist or itinerant teacher (OSEP, 2022a). These students participate in the general education curriculum with their sighted classmates and, if they do not also have multiple disabilities, tend to perform well academically. They also have the highest high school graduation rates of all students with disabilities. Most use aids, such as glasses or technology, that enlarge type to enhance their vision for accessing information and moving independently at school and in the community. Devices such as personal digital assistants and audio books allow people who are blind or visually impaired to access print, appointment calendars, and other management tools (American Foundation for the Blind, 2018). Most people who have blindness or low vision prefer the term *visual disabilities*, which we use in this text. Some prefer identity-first language (blind children and adults) while others prefer people-first language (children and adults with visual disabilities).

Definition

The IDEA definition of visual impairment means that even with correction the visual loss affects the child's educational performance (IDEA, 2004). Although they represent a very small proportion of the general school population (0.03%), with most having low vision that can be accommodated in the general education class, all teachers must be ready to make adjustments to their classroom environments for these students. Help to make these adjustments comes from many related services providers and specialized teachers.

When people see normally, two important aspects of their vision are working well: acuity and peripheral vision. Problems can occur in one or both of these aspects of vision, resulting in a disability. **Visual acuity** measures how well a person can see at various distances. We measure normal visual acuity by testing how accurately a person can see an object or image 20 feet away. Normal vision is thus said to be 20/20. A person whose vision is measured at 20/40 can see at 20 feet what people who do not need visual correction (glasses or contact lenses) can see at 40 feet away. The width of a person's field of vision, or the ability to perceive objects outside the direct line of vision, is called **peripheral vision**. This aspect of vision helps people move freely through their environment.

Today, most states have adopted eligibility criteria that reflect a functional definition of visual disabilities. The basic premise is that a student has a visual disability when, even with correction, educational performance is adversely affected. In other words, the issue is how much **residual vision** a person has or can use to do well in school. States and school districts vary in the criteria they use to determine eligibility for special services.

Types

Many professionals talk about visual disabilities in four very different ways:

1. By identifying the reason for the visual loss
2. By considering the severity of the problem
3. By taking into account when the loss occurred
4. By determining whether the criteria for being considered legally blind are met

Numerous conditions can lead to visual loss that results in a disability. The conditions with which most of us are familiar are myopia (nearsightedness), hyperopia (farsightedness), and **astigmatism** (inability to focus), but many other conditions, only some of which can be prevented or corrected, can damage the eye, compromise its structure, and undermine its functioning.

Typically, persons with visual disabilities are divided into two subgroups:

1. Those with low vision
2. Those who are blind

Parents and professionals tend to employ functional definitions for these two subgroups. In other words, children with low vision use their sight for many school activities, including reading. Children who are blind do not have functional use of their vision and may perceive only shadows or some movement. These youngsters must be educated through tactile and other sensory channels.

Blindness can occur at any age, but its impact varies with age and with age of onset. Individuals can be

- congenitally blind, with onset at birth or during infancy; or
- adventitiously blind, with onset after the age of 2.

This distinction is important because people who lose their sight after age 2, and hence are adventitiously blind, remember what some objects look like. Those who are congenitally blind were too young when the loss occurred to remember what things look like. The later the disability occurs, the more they remember. Visual memory is an important factor in learning because it can influence our development of concepts and other aspects important to learning.

Although it is not related to how well people can use their vision, another way to categorize people with visual problems is in terms of whether they meet the definition of being legally blind: central vision of 20/200 in the better eye with correction and a visual field no greater than 20 degrees. The designation of legally blind allows individuals to receive special tax benefits and materials from the federal government and private agencies. It is not used by schools. Because the definition does not exclude people who have some functional use of sight, many individuals who are legally blind use print, not **braille**, to read.

Characteristics

The way individuals with visual disabilities access information sets them apart as a group, but the use of aids and technologies helps provide positive information outcomes (American Foundation for the Blind, 2018). Contrary to popular belief, the vast majority use vision as their primary method of learning and means of participating in the community. For many students, the amount of vision they have left—their residual vision—can be further developed through training and practice. The vision of some is static, remaining the same from day to day, whereas others find that their ability to see varies with the day, time of day, or setting. For some, higher or lower levels of illumination, or changes in distance and contrast, affect how well they can see, but for others, these variations make little difference. This fact is important for teachers to understand because where a child sits in a classroom, the amount of glare or light on reading materials or the white board, or even the time of day can make great differences in how well a child can use residual vision for learning, For most, optical aids such as glasses have a positive effect.

A common characteristic of young blind children is difficulties with play and social skills. They tend to seek out adults rather than classmates. They avoid spontaneous play and prefer to play with concrete objects. Blind children also experience social isolation, an area where teachers can be of great assistance by fostering situations where everyone is included in classroom activities, makes friends, and joins in games. However, some characteristics of many of these children can be off-putting to classmates. For example, they tend to stand too close (invade personal space), ask irrelevant questions, don't understand how to take turns, and engage in inappropriate affection. Again, teachers can help provide direct instruction, feedback, and also work with classmates to be more accepting.

Literacy development has long been a major objective for students with visual impairments who need direct instruction in reading. Most read print, usually via enlarged type. Others read via braille, and many others access printed materials by listening to books through a computer or a personal reader (i.e., someone who reads for others). Because it is so important to be able to read, IDEA 2004 insists that instruction in the use of braille be considered for every student who has severe visual loss (Jackson, 2014).

Although students with visual disabilities participate in inclusive classrooms at a very high rate, they must also learn skills related to being independent, such as accessing transportation, moving freely in their environment, and acquiring life skills such as cooking, doing laundry, cleaning the home, and so on. Therefore, **orientation and mobility** are major curriculum targets. Orientation is the mental map people have of their surroundings. Most of us learn landmarks and other cues to get from one place to another. As a teacher, you can assist students with severe visual loss by helping them understand emergency evacuation procedures, recognize exit paths from the school buildings, and learn how to move safely through the school environment, which he or she should learn to know well, both during normal school hours and in times of stress. Many schools and districts have designed emergency preparedness plans for students with disabilities. You can also make sure students know landmarks in the classroom environment so they are free to move around independently.

Because of the importance of literacy and the ability to read, IDEA 2004 insists that instruction in the use of braille be considered for every student who has severe visual loss.

BSIP SA / Alamy Stock Photo

The ability to travel safely and efficiently from one place to another is called mobility. Most adults who are blind use the long cane, also called the Hoover cane, which is named after its developer, Richard Hoover. However, tapping the cane along a sidewalk or pavement of the street does not always help the individual avoid the many obstacles in modern society. For example, silent traffic signals, escalators, elevators, and public transportation, to say nothing of protruding and overhanging objects that are undetectable with mobility canes, can be very dangerous. Nor do canes tell users where they are or how to get to their next location. Guide dogs or service animals are another option. Although there are no definitive statistics available, the number of individuals who use guide dogs is relatively small. It has been estimated that only about 2% of people who are blind or who have low vision work with guide dogs (Cosgrove, 2023). As a teacher, you can help students who are assisted by a service animal by helping classmates understand that the animal is not a pet and should be left to do the important job that took years of training for it to master.

Apps and other smart technologies are gaining in popularity and use for everyone, but for people with severe visual loss they can provide incredible freedom. Global positioning system (GPS) technology provides new orientation and mobility system advances for people with severe visual loss and may well be "the" mobility system of this century. For example, built-in smart phone mapping available from Google and Apple, along with locations of Wi-Fi hot spots, not only include street names and locations, but also millions of points of interest (American Foundation for the Blind, 2020). They can answer questions such as "Where am I?" "Where am I going?" and "How do I get there?" They can also be used with long canes, and in some cases, with guide dogs as well. Many more advances in technology are also available and being developed that can warn blind individuals of hazards, like sidewalk construction, to avoid. What the future holds is beyond what we can imagine possible.

ATTRIBUTES OF STUDENTS WITH TRAUMATIC BRAIN INJURY

Traumatic brain injury (TBI) became a separate disability category in the 1990 reauthorization of IDEA. Educators need to know that TBI *is not* a condition present at birth, nor is it due to a stroke, a brain tumor, or other internally caused brain damage. However, it is also important for educators to understand that TBI

- Can be due to a concussion or head injury, possibly from an accident, injury on the playground, or child abuse;
- Is not always apparent or visible;
- May or may not result in loss of consciousness.

Teachers can be very helpful to children with TBI and their families by being alert to signs of TBI that might not be noticeable when the incident originally occurs. Often, students do not want to acknowledge that they were engaged in risky behaviors, like not wearing a helmet when riding a bicycle or skateboarding. They might not want to admit to themselves or their coaches that they had a head injury when playing football, basketball, or some other sport because they want to keep playing.

In 2021, students with TBI who required special education services only represented .038% of the entire school population (OSEP, 2023). The majority of those students were male (62.49%) and more likely to be White. This probably reflects the sports and risky behaviors of boys over girls. Students between the ages of 5–11 are less likely to be served than those in the 12–17 age range. Among children and youth, 20% of all cases are due to playing contact sports, such as on the field playing football (72%), basketball (42%), and soccer (36%; CDC, 2022a). The most common cause among children and adults is bicycle accidents. Sadly, for children under the age of four, the leading cause is abuse. Many cases of TBI are preventable. Wearing the proper head gear when playing sports or riding bicycles and getting assistance to caretakers of young children who are stressed or overwhelmed can save lives or prevent life-long disabilities (CDC, 2022b).

Fortunately, most individuals who experience TBI overcome their injuries with proper medical treatment and the application of various classroom accommodations during their recovery periods. These students were more likely to graduate from high school and less likely to drop out than all other students with disabilities. They were also more likely to receive their education in inclusive, general education classes 80% of the school day than other groups of students with disabilities (OSEP, 2023). These facts do not mean that TBI should be minimized; attentive teachers should look for warning signs like abrupt changes in attention and quality of schoolwork.

Definition

TBI is *not a* condition present at birth, nor is it caused by stroke, a brain tumor, or other internal cause. The condition is acquired by an external force and can be either an open or closed head injury (71 Fed. Reg. 46539 [2006]).

Types

Like other disabilities, TBI ranges from mild to severe (CDC, 2022a). Those with more severe head injuries receive home instruction, often for a year, before returning to school part time. In many cases the effects eventually disappear, but in some cases they are lifelong.

Characteristics

Children with TBI and their families face great emotional turmoil during the time shortly after the injury. Educators must be alert to student conditions associated with concussions and TBI (e.g., appears dazed or stunned, is confused about events, answers questions slowly) and also be prepared to talk with students about their conditions (e.g., difficulty thinking clearly, difficulty concentrating or remembering, feeling more slowed down; CDC, 2022a).

Alert teachers can be very helpful in early diagnosis and treatment of TBI. Many head injuries are the result of activities in which children commonly engage: riding a bicycle, using playground equipment, or even tussling in the schoolyard. Often, youngsters do not want to admit they fell or forgot to wear a protective helmet or were fighting on the playground. But when a student acts differently, becomes unable to pay attention, or seems unusually tired, seek help from the school nurse to be certain the child has not experienced a head injury. Symptoms may include blurred vision, loss of vision, change in hearing acuity, ringing in the ears, slurred speech, difficulty understanding spoken language, difficulty processing sensory input (via touch, smell, hearing), personality changes, loss of taste and/or smell, paralysis, lethargy, loss of bowel/bladder control, dizziness, inappropriate emotional responses (e.g., irritability, frustration, crying, or laughing), and seizures. Many of these conditions persist and can be mitigated somewhat by medications, but occasionally a condition (e.g., lethargy, inattention) may be demonstrated in the classroom.

ATTRIBUTES OF STUDENTS WITH DEAF-BLINDNESS

We discussed earlier two great examples, Helen Keller and Haben Girma, to illustrate why we should not make assumptions about any person with a disability, even those with the most severe and complex problems, like deaf-blindness. Of course, there are others. Deaf-blindness is exceptionally rare, affecting a fraction of 1% of all schoolchildren (U.S. Department of Education, 2023). The number of children and youth affected varies by the source used. In 2021, the National Deaf-Blind Count (National Center on Deaf-Blindness, 2022a) reported 9,809 children, but the U.S. Department of Education reported that only 1,770 students were served through IDEA under the deaf-blind special education category. Although both numbers are relatively small, why might there be such a discrepancy? The answer rests with definition. Let's look at that next.

Definition

When most people think about deaf-blindness, they think that the individuals involved are both blind and deaf. In other words, they have no functional use of their hearing or vision. In fact, 99% of these children and youth have some residual hearing or vision. The majority of students with deaf-blindness have some functional vision that can be utilized for learning and in everyday activities. Similarly, nearly half of all deaf-blind individuals have adequate residual hearing. In addition to vision and hearing losses, it is estimated that some 85% of these individuals have additional disabilities (e.g., intellectual disability), making certain aspects of their educational programs similar to those of students with multiple disabilities. However, it is important to note that only 0.1% of students with deaf-blindness have severe cognitive disabilities (National Center on Deaf-Blindness, 2022a).

The reason for differences in the prevalence rates may now becoming apparent. It is not that these students are not receiving services, but rather they are served through different IDEA categories. Those with additional disabilities beyond their visual and hearing disabilities are probably served through the multiple disabilities category. The National Deaf-Blind Child Count found that

20% have severe to profound hearing loss while 10% have only light perception or are totally blind (National Center on Deaf-Blindness, 2022a). So the amount of residual hearing or functional vision influences how they are counted. Remember that under IDEA, individuals are identified within only one special education category; therefore, some may be identified as having a visual loss, others as having a hearing impairment, others as having deaf-blindness, and yet others as belonging in the multiple disabilities category.

Types

Some forms of deaf-blindness are progressive, and get worse over time. In all cases, early detection is critical and with infant screening for hearing loss, which is typically done in every state immediately after birth, families and medical teams can make important decisions early in children's lives. Some may decide to seek out hearing aids while others may decide to give their children cochlear implants. Often the families learn ASL so their children learn to communicate using sign language during the normal language development periods. In the families where deaf-blindness exists in older family members, they may decide on genetic counseling. One type of hereditary deaf-blindness is Usher syndrome Type 1, which is found more in certain parts of Louisiana where Cajuns carry the gene (Usher Syndrome Coalition, 2022). Usher syndrome begins with congenital deafness, but as individuals get older their vision abilities decrease (Lenz, 2020). Although at this time medical advances cannot totally resolve these vision and hearing issues, they can help families, individuals, and intervention teams prepare.

Characteristics

Almost half of students with deaf-blindness have sufficient residual vision to read print, use sign language, recognize family and friends, and move about their environments freely. Some deaf-blind individuals can understand speech sounds, hear loud noises, and profit from hearing aids. However, some have such limited vision and hearing that they profit little from either sense. The world for children with deaf-blindness can be exceptionally restricted. For those whose hearing and vision losses are severe or profound, the immediate world may well end at their fingertips. They, their family members, and their teachers must address problems of isolation, communication, and mobility.

Many adults with this disability develop outstanding communication skills, but this achievement does not typically come without considerable effort. Others communicate by using various forms of manual communication—sign language, body language, gestures—to express their needs and "talk" to others (American Association of the Deaf-Blind, 2009). Some use a special kind of sign language called **hand over hand**, in which two people use the palms of each other's hands to sign through touches. Helen Keller and her teacher, Anne Sullivan, used this communication technique.

SUMMARY

Although fewer than 1% of all students have disabilities that are less common, these disabilities include hundreds of discrete conditions. The federal government has designated eight disabilities, plus the flexible, noncategorical grouping "developmental delay" for children between the ages of 3 and 9, as being low incidence. In this chapter, you learned that students with low-incidence disabilities exhibit complex and unique learning characteristics that challenge themselves, their families, and their schools. Their conditions and disabilities influence what they are taught and how they are taught to a greater degree than is true for many of their peers with and without disabilities. These students often require unique responses so that they can access the curriculum, participate fully in the school community, and be successful students. The types of supports, accommodations, and instruction must reflect the evidence-based practices you will learn about throughout this academic term. Despite the challenges and barriers many of these students face, they hold great promise of attaining remarkable accomplishments.

REVIEW THE LEARNING OBJECTIVES

Let's review the learning objectives for this chapter. If you are uncertain and cannot talk through the answers provided for any of these questions, reread those sections of the text.

6.1 Explain the attributes of students with less frequent disabilities.
Infrequent disabilities have a low prevalence, so relatively few individuals and families are affected, but they often require intensive and unique responses to their very special needs. Combined, they include many fewer students than each of the four most common disabilities. These unique responses include many, and sometimes complex, accommodations, as well as long-term interventions, instruction not typically included in the general education curriculum (e.g., braille), and the inclusion of many different related services professionals (e.g., assistive technologists, physical therapists, and speech/language pathologists).

6.2 Identify the attributes of students with health impairments.
The key features of most health impairments are fatigue, absences from school, inconsistent ability to pay attention, muscle weakness, and problems with physical coordination. Examples of health impairments include chronic illnesses (e.g., asthma, epilepsy, sickle-cell disease) and infectious diseases.

6.3 Describe the attributes of students with multiple disabilities.
The key features of multiple disabilities include the presence of more than one disability; goals that include independence and community presence; provision of supports that are ongoing and intensive; and problems with generalization, communication, memory, and life skills. Most of these students have intellectual disabilities along with at least one other disability; the multiple disabilities category does not include deaf-blindness.

6.4 Explain the attributes of students with developmental delay.
The key feature of developmental delay is that disability is noncategorically described (no disability label required). This means qualifying students for special education services is typically used for preschoolers between ages 3 and 5 but could include children up to the age of 9.

6.5 List the attributes of students with physical disabilities.
The key features of physical disabilities vary with the condition that caused the physical disability. For example, orthopedic impairments, limb deficiencies, and juvenile arthritis result in problems with structure and functioning of the body; cerebral palsy can have multiple outcomes. Many students with physical disabilities do not receive special education services through IDEA because their disability does not adversely affect their educational performance, but rather they receive related services through 504.

6.6 Distinguish among the attributes of students who are deaf and hard of hearing.
The key features of the category deaf and hard of hearing vary by type (conductive or sensorineural), age of onset (prelingually or postlingually deaf), and degree of loss (hard of hearing or deafness). All these conditions usually result in problems with communication, academic achievement, and speech ability. Those who are Deaf consider themselves as part of the Deaf community that is bound by the use of ASL, arts, history, and culture.

6.7 Discuss the attributes of students with visual disabilities.
Low vision and blindness are typically categorized in terms of functional use of sight, age of onset (e.g., congenitally blind, adventitiously blind), and degree of loss (e.g., low vision, legally blind). Key issues for these individuals are attaining literacy (e.g., braille or print), developing orientation and mobility skills, and developing maximal use of residual vision and sight for daily functioning. Those with blindness use touch and hearing as their primary means of accessing

information; those with low vision use their sight to access information. This group has the highest high school graduation rate of all disability groups served through IDEA.

6.8 Summarize the attributes of students with traumatic brain injury.
Traumatic brain injury (TBI) can be temporary, lasting about a year. In these cases, the symptoms are mild and are similar to those of learning disabilities. But in other cases, the conditions are severe, and many individuals experience hospital or home instruction for some period of time. For these people, the results can be long-lasting and require medications to help alleviate the conditions. In some instances, conditions associated with TBI, such as inattention and lethargy, can be challenging to the student and teachers.

6.9 Describe the attributes of students with deaf-blindness.
Deaf-blindness is the occurrence of coexisting hearing and visual impairments; neither disability has to be severe or profound in nature. This exceptionally infrequent disability can result in problems with isolation, communication, and mobility.

REVISIT THE OPENING CHALLENGE

Check your answers to the Reflection Questions from the Opening Challenge and revise them on the basis of what you have learned.

1. Do you think Ms. Traun will need to plan for her new student differently than she has for other students with disabilities? If so, in what ways? If not, why not?
2. What learning characteristics might she have to consider as she makes initial plans for Josh?
3. How might her plans change after she learns what disabilities Josh has?
4. Provide Ms. Traun with five questions or issues she should discuss with her principal.
5. What do you think Mr. Dehiya, his class, and a related service provider decided to consider when reorganizing seating arrangements and classroom organization?
6. What issues did they need to address?
7. Why do you think Mr. Dehiya decided to have his students help restructure the classroom? Do you think this was a good idea? Why or why not?

KEY TERMS

asthma
astigmatism
audiogram
augmentative and alternative communication devices (AAC)
aura
braille
chronic illnesses
developmental delay
Emergency Care Plan
hand over hand
home-bound/hospital instruction
limb loss
medically fragile
orientation and mobility
orthopedic impairments
other health impairments
peripheral vision
preictal stage
prelingual deafness
postlingually deaf
residual vision
robotics
sickle-cell anemia
traumatic brain injury (TBI)
visual acuity

PROFESSIONAL STANDARDS AND LICENSURE

For a complete description of Professional Standards and Licensure, please see the appendix.

CEC Initial Preparation Standards

Standard 1: Learner Development and Individual Learning Differences

INTASC Core Principles

Standard 1: Learner Development

Standard 2: Learning Differences

Praxis II: Education of Exceptional Students: Core Content Knowledge

1. Understanding Exceptionalities: Human Development and Behavior

NOTES

1. Although many people with deaf-blindness prefer people-first language, others prefer disability-first language and use terms like *deaf-blind individuals.* Also some organizations and agencies hyphenate deaf-blindness, while others do not and use the term *deafblindness.*
2. In this text we use d/Deaf when the terms *deaf* and *Deaf* are combined.

Tetra Images/Jamie Gill/Brand x Pictures/Getty Images

7 DESIGNING AND DELIVERING DIFFERENTIATED INSTRUCTION

LEARNING OBJECTIVES

After studying this chapter, you will be able to meet the following learning objectives:

7.1 Explain differentiated instruction.

7.2 Describe the ADAPT Framework.

7.3 Identify effective instructional practices for designing and delivering instruction.

7.4 Explain how instructional grouping practices can promote effective, differentiated instruction.

Opening Challenge

Designing and Delivering Instruction

Elementary Grades. Mrs. Santiago is an experienced fourth-grade teacher with 24 students in an urban, public school district. In Mrs. Santiago's school, more than half of the students qualify for free or reduced-cost lunch, and about one third of the students are English learners (Els). Mrs. Santiago's fourth-grade class includes one student with a learning disability (LD) in reading and writing, and one student with LDs in mathematics, both of whom are performing about 2 years below grade level in each subject area. Mrs. Santiago has three EL students who speak Spanish or Mandarin; they attended bilingual classes in the early grades. The language support team in Mrs. Santiago's school had agreed that the three students were ready to move into English instruction classes; however, one student continues to require pull-out services from an EL specialist to strengthen academic vocabulary for the content subjects (e.g., science, social studies). Mrs. Santiago reflects about her class: *"I have students with different disabilities and language needs. In reviewing the fall universal screening results, about one fourth of my class has academic challenges, which means they likely will need differentiated instruction for reading, writing, or mathematics. I also need to address the needs of my students who are ELs and students with LDs. The individualized education program provides goals and ideas for adapting instruction for my students with disabilities."*

Secondary Grades. Ms. Benz is a 10th-grade social studies teacher at a high school in the same school district as Mrs. Santiago, with similar demographics in her classes. She has four inclusion classes out of a total of eight class periods daily. Her inclusion classes include students with LDs in reading who have IEPs. The special education teacher, Ms. Cordova, participates in the weekly 10th-grade social studies teachers' planning meetings to discuss how the students with LDs are doing and how she can help with meeting individual students' needs during her time in the inclusion classes. As Ms. Benz prepares for an upcoming 10th-grade social studies teacher meeting, she reflects on her instructional practices and how the students with LDs are doing: *"I have students this year with a range of reading and writing difficulties, which is challenging when students read text or topical information packets in class and for homework. Some students with disabilities also struggle when writing reports on topics I teach each semester. Ms. Cordova supports these students while she coteaches with me and provides additional support to the students on types of writing and content area reading in the resource setting. I know I should differentiate instruction to meet all student needs, but my preparation is in social studies and not in differentiating instruction for students with academic difficulties. I will have to depend on the special education teacher, Ms. Cordova, to help me in my inclusion classes with the students with LDs."*

Reflection Questions

In your journal, write down your answers to the following questions. After completing the chapter, check your answers and revise them on the basis of what you have learned.

1. What ways can Mrs. Santiago and Ms. Benz differentiate instruction for all of their students who require academic assistance?
2. How can Mrs. Santiago and Ms. Benz differentiate instruction for their EL students?
3. How can Mrs. Santiago and Ms. Benz use the ADAPT Framework to differentiate instruction for their students?
4. What effective instructional practices can Mrs. Santiago and Ms. Benz use to differentiate instruction for their students with disabilities to foster success with the curriculum?
5. What instructional grouping practices can help Mrs. Santiago and Ms. Benz provide effective, differentiated instruction for their students?

Educators who teach in inclusive classrooms have responsibilities for their typically achieving students as well as for students with disabilities and other unique learning needs, such as students who are at risk for academic failure and those who speak English as a second language. Educators must differentiate instruction so that all of their students benefit from instruction. Teachers can adapt instruction to specifically meet the needs of students with disabilities. In this chapter, we discuss ways to differentiate instruction, including using the ADAPT Framework. We also explain effective instructional practices and grouping practices to help students with learning challenges and students with disabilities access and master the curriculum.

DIFFERENTIATED INSTRUCTION

Differentiated instruction is instruction that is responsive to the diverse needs of all students. We use the term *differentiated instruction* broadly with a focus on curriculum, instruction, services, and instructional intensity. Keep in mind that most students benefit from some differentiation in instruction over the course of the school year. In this chapter, we examine what differentiated instruction means and then we present examples of ways educators can differentiate their instruction to address the diverse learning needs present in their classrooms. Examine Figure 7.1 to see a continuum for differentiating instruction. Notice how differentiation is less intensive for more students in terms of curriculum, adaptations, services, and instruction and becomes increasingly more intensive for fewer students. As you read the description of the continuum, think about the students' needs presented in the Opening Challenge, keeping in mind that some students have disabilities, some students are ELs, and other students might be at risk for learning difficulties.

In Figure 7.1, the base level of the triangle reveals the core or general education curriculum and instruction, which is provided to all students. Instruction provided to all students is known as Tier 1 in a Response to Intervention (RTI) model, as you learned in Chapter 2. Instructional intensity increases for some students to address their individual learning needs; this is known as Tier 2. Students who qualify for Tier 2 exhibit academic or behavioral challenges. These students could benefit from adaptations and interventions to supplement core instruction. Finally, at the top level of the differentiation continuum we see how the needs of students with more severe disabilities must have sustained, intensified, adapted, or modified instruction and curriculum that is aligned with their individual needs as identified on their IEP.

FIGURE 7.1 ■ A Differentiating Instruction Curriculum

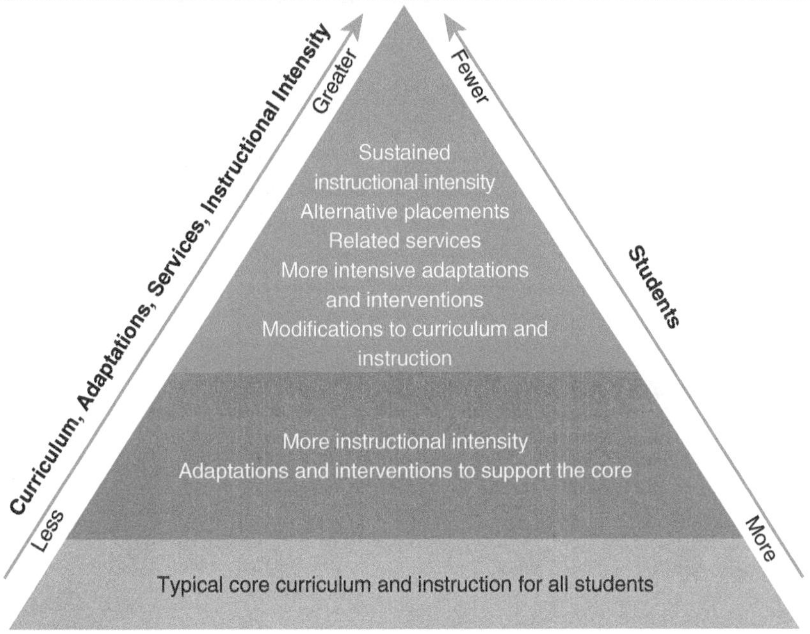

There are many ways to differentiate instruction. For example, one way is to use flexible grouping practices. Students with same-ability or mixed-ability skills can work on a topic to complete an in-class activity. Another way to use flexible grouping practices is to assign students to different groups as an ongoing practice based on your knowledge of the instructional needs of students. In core instruction, flexible groupings are common; however, as we move up on the continuum, small, same-ability groups will be necessary in order to intensify interventions. A second way to differentiate instruction is to use time that is designated for small group or individualized instruction. For example in core instruction (Tier 1), additional instruction in a skill may be needed for a small group of students. Small group instruction can serve as an additional boost to help students be more successful. The students who need additional small group, intensified instruction should receive frequent work on specific skills until their accomplishments are not only substantially improved but maintained, as well. However, fewer students will need sustained instructional intensity. These students will require instruction for a longer period of time, which may mean an entire academic year.

A third way to differentiate instruction is through the use of certain staff, who provide support in different settings. Staff may include special education teachers and speech/language pathologists. Usually specialized teachers provide more intensive, adapted instruction in academics and language skills in general education inclusive classes or pull-out settings such as a resource or language therapy setting. These teachers and pathologists work with students with identified disabilities.

A fourth way to differentiate instruction is to change or modify the curriculum. This type of change applies to fewer special education students and may involve a life skills curriculum for students with intellectual or developmental disabilities. These students receive some of this curriculum with a special education teacher in an inclusive classroom or in a life skills class, particularly at the middle and high school levels.

Now, think back to Chapter 2 regarding the RTI model. You can see how the three levels and the continuum in Figure 7.1 relate to a multi-tiered approach to instruction and intensified intervention for students with mild to severe disabilities. Now that you have learned about the differentiation continuum, consider the needs of students in Mrs. Santiago's and Ms. Benz's classes. Where might some of their students' learning needs fall on the differentiation continuum? What evidence is presented in the Opening Challenge to support your perspective about the students?

In the Considering Diversity feature, we present strategies that teachers can implement for differentiating instruction for ELs. We then turn our attention to the ADAPT Framework.

Considering Diversity: Strategies for Differentiated Instruction for English Learners

There are many strategies that teachers can use for differentiating instruction to address the needs of ELs. Here we present examples of strategies that consider the amount of time some ELs need to process and understand instruction, grouping strategies, presentation strategies, and response strategies. After you read about universal design for learning (UDL) principles and guidelines in Chapter 8, return to this chapter and apply what you have learned to the content in this chapter. Identify examples in the following strategies of the UDL principles and guidelines. Consider how some of the strategies for ELs also can be applied to students who are struggling with instruction, such as those in the Opening Challenge.

Consideration of Time Strategies

- Chunk instruction into shorter segments to allow time to check work.
- Expand assignments over a longer period of time.
- Extend wait time for oral responses.
- Plan challenging tasks and subjects earlier in the day or period, or at different, better times for the student.

Grouping Strategies

- Provide small-group instruction.
- Pair or group ELs with buddies who will assist with explaining tasks.
- Work one-to-one with students.

Presentation Strategies

- Assign support staff to work with ELs in addition to the classroom teacher.
- Provide substantial repetition of language: repeat, restate, rephrase, reread.
- Keep language consistent when describing or explaining; synonyms, idioms, and metaphors may be confusing at first. Gradually introduce figurative language to expand language development.
- Introduce and develop new vocabulary using a picture dictionary and other visual aids.
- Use bilingual dictionaries during reading and writing assignments to clarify meanings when possible.
- Keep explanations and directions brief and concise: Focus on key concepts and vocabulary.
- Highlight and explicitly teach key vocabulary needed to accomplish the assigned task.
- Enhance oral presentations with visual and written support, graphic organizers, and modeling.
- Present material through multiple modes, using media and other technology.

Response Strategies

- Encourage and allow for nonverbal responses such as pointing, nodding, drawing pictures, using manipulatives, and completing graphic organizers.
- Adjust expectations for language output (e.g., student speaks in words and phrases, simple present-tense statements).
- Allow shortened responses.
- Pair ELs with strong English speakers and writers (called buddies).
- Encourage buddies to take a dictated response during pair work where ELs explain concepts.
- Allow ELs to dictate responses into a recorder for their written work.

Source: Adapted from Price and Nelson (2003).

THE ADAPT FRAMEWORK

The **ADAPT Framework** is a device that educators can use to individualize instruction to meet the learning and behavioral needs of struggling students, including students with disabilities. The framework is an example of a device that can be used for differentiating instruction and be applicable to those students who require greater curriculum adaptations and intensified instruction. Instruction is differentiated and intensified in the sense that it is individualized to meet a student's specific needs. In Chapter 2, we introduced the ADAPT Framework. In this section, we provide further information about adaptations and the framework. We know that adaptations have three characteristics in common. First, they are individualized, focusing on the strengths of the individual. Second, they are relevant to the lesson's objective. Third, they must be effective to help a student learn the content. If at first an adaptation does not help the student benefit from instruction, then we make additional adaptations until student performance improves and is maintained. Examining student performance on tasks provides a good indicator of the effectiveness of the identified adaptations.

The ADAPT Framework has five steps to guide your decision making about selecting and evaluating adaptations:

1. **A**sk, "What am I requiring the student to do?"
2. **D**etermine the prerequisite skills of the task.
3. **A**nalyze the student's strengths and struggles.
4. **P**ropose and implement adaptations from among the four instructional categories (content, materials, delivery, and activity).
5. **T**est to determine whether the adaptations helped the student accomplish the task.

Let's take a look at each step to see how to apply the ADAPT Framework in your class with students who have unique learning needs, whether these are disabilities, second language learners, or students who are at risk for poor academic performance. Throughout the remaining chapters, you will read about specific ways to use the ADAPT Framework in academic, social, and behavioral areas.

ADAPT Steps

The first step is **A**sk, "What am I requiring the student to do?" For example, second-grade students are expected to learn basic academic concepts and skills, demonstrate the ability to get along with others, and listen to the teacher. In high school, students are required to take notes in class, complete their homework, learn from textbooks, conduct and write about research, and pass end-of-semester exams. These setting-specific demands are typical of the **core curriculum**—content that is taught to all students in the general education setting (Lenz & Deshler, 2004).

The second step is **D**etermine the prerequisite skills of the task. This step means identifying what students must be able to do to meet the teacher's instructional requirements. Teachers can break down the task to identify specific prerequisite skills. For example, at the elementary level, to add two numbers ($? = 9 + 3$), students must be able to (a) understand the value of the numerals 9 and 3, (b) know the meaning of the + and = symbols, (c) use an effective strategy to obtain the solution, (d) know that equations can be written in different ways ($? = 3 + 9$, in this case), and (e) write the numeral 12 correctly.

At the secondary level, students are typically required to take notes in class. What prerequisite skills related to taking notes are necessary for a student to be successful? You understand the second ADAPT step if you replied with any of the following: listening, identifying important information, writing, summarizing the notes, and studying the notes for a test. Identifying prerequisite skills is an important step in the ADAPT Framework because it forms the basis for addressing the remaining steps and is a step that teachers often overlook.

The third step, **A**nalyze the student's strengths and struggles, means identifying each prerequisite skill of a task (from Step 2) as a strength or struggle for an individual student. You can use assessment practices to ascertain areas of strengths and struggles. For example, regarding our addition problem ($? = 9 + 3$), a teacher can ask the student to perform the computational steps out loud to determine whether the steps for arriving at the answer demonstrate strengths or struggles (see Chapter 9 for assessment practices). If a student identifies the numerals and symbols correctly, then these prerequisite skills can be listed as strengths. If a student uses the strategy of starting with 1 and counting up to 12 rather than starting with 9 and counting on 3 to get 12, then the teacher suspects the strategy called "count on" might be lacking and thus is a struggle. Of course, the student should be given several similar problems to "think aloud" to confirm that an effective strategy is lacking.

The teacher can observe whether numerals are written correctly; in this case, the student wrote "12," which is a strength. If 12 was written as 21, then writing numerals correctly is a struggle. Referring to our note-taking task, teachers can ask for a copy of a student's notes to analyze them for the prerequisite skills of identifying and recording the important information and summarizing the information.

In the fourth step, **P**ropose and implement adaptations from among the four instructional categories (content, materials, delivery, and activity), the teacher considers the student's strengths and struggles to identify appropriate instructional adaptations. Bryant and Bryant (1998) originally identified adaptation categories for the ADAPT Framework from which educators can choose when identifying adaptations that should be individualized for the student and important to the task. You will see that there are four adaptation categories in the framework: (1) instructional activity, (2) instructional content, (3) instructional delivery, and (4) instructional materials:

- **Instructional activity** is the actual lesson used to teach and reinforce skills and concepts. Sometimes a different instructional activity is needed if students do not benefit from the original lesson.
- **Instructional content** consists of the skills and concepts that are the focus of teaching and learning, that is, the standards and curriculum that local school districts require educators to teach. For example, the Common Core State Standards (National Governors Association Center for Best Practices and Council of Chief State School Officers, 2010) provide information about mathematics domains and related standards that should be part of each school district's curriculum where the Common Core State Standards have been adopted.
- **Instructional delivery** is the way the activity is taught, including grouping practices, instructional steps, presentation techniques, practice techniques, and student activities.
- **Instructional materials** are aids such as textbooks, kits, hardware, software, and manipulatives. In any subject area, there are multiple types of instructional materials that teachers can use to address various learning needs. You will read about many examples in later chapters.

Let's see how the adaptation categories can be utilized. Returning to our addition problem (? = 9 + 3) and Mrs. Santiago, she realizes the need to reteach the "count on" strategy. She decides to teach a small group of students (instructional delivery) who need to be retaught the "count on" strategy; included in this small group is her student with a mathematics LD. She uses easier facts (instructional content), such as 3 + 2 = 5, and then increases to more difficult facts, such as 8 + 2 = 10 and 9 + 3 = 12. Mrs. Santiago reviews the idea of greater than (instructional content) to be sure the students know the addend that is the larger of the two. She has chips (instructional material) for students to use to keep track of the number of the second addend when counting on from the larger number. For instance, for 8 + 2, there are two chips to move as the students starts with 8, the larger number, and orally counts on 2 more while moving each chip for each count to equal 10.

In our note-taking example, several adaptations are important. The student can record the lecture (instructional material) and then identify key ideas. Or a note-taking strategy (instructional activity) such as Note Shrink, discussed in Chapter 14, can be explained to a small group of students (instructional delivery).

The fifth step, **T**est to determine whether the adaptations helped the student accomplish the task, focuses on assessing student progress. For example, returning to our addition problem (? = 9 + 3), during a progress-monitoring task, Mrs. Santiago can check to see whether problems that can be solved with the "count on" strategy are solved correctly. In the note-taking example, a final copy of the student's notes can be graded and the test on which the notes are based can be examined to see whether information from the notes is included in the answers.

We have provided an ADAPT Framework example for Mrs. Santiago's students. Now think about Ms. Benz and determine how she can apply the ADAPT Framework with her struggling students. What are your ideas? In the remaining chapters, you will encounter many examples of the ADAPT Framework in action and you will see applications that illustrate quickly and simply how the ADAPT Framework can be implemented. Look for these features as you read.

EFFECTIVE PRACTICES FOR DESIGNING AND DELIVERING INSTRUCTION

In this section, we discuss practices that educators can use when designing and delivering instruction to ensure that all students—including students with disabilities—learn the content. To begin, we provide findings from research studies that should be included when designing and delivering instruction.

Translating Research Findings Into Instructional Practices

Over the course of decades, research findings have shown specific practices that produce positive learning outcomes for students with special learning needs, including explicit instruction and **cognitive strategy instruction** (CSI; Swanson & Deshler, 2003). **Explicit instruction** focuses on designing and delivering instruction for academic concepts and skills through the use of specific, evidence-based practices. These practices include stating the lesson's objective, reviewing related skills, and activating background knowledge. Additional practices include demonstrating how to do the task with modeling and thinking the steps aloud, providing examples and non-examples of how and how not to do the task, ensuring multiple opportunities for practice, giving immediate corrective feedback as needed, telling students how they are doing, and monitoring student progress (Archer & Hughes, 2011; Brophy & Good, 1986; Coyne et al., 2011; Rosenshine, 1987). CSI is the process of teaching cognitive strategies (steps or a routine) and metacognitive strategies (self-regulation strategies; Montague & Dietz, 2009). Explicit instruction procedures are demonstrated in the CSI routines as well as **verbal rehearsal** (i.e., students practicing the strategy steps to mastery) and self-monitoring. The goal of CSI is for students to incorporate the routine and self-monitor the use of the routine when related to academic tasks. For example, cognitive strategies for understanding material from a textbook include activating background knowledge, predicting, and paraphrasing; metacognitive strategies include asking, "Can I make connections between my background knowledge and what I am reading?" "Were my predictions accurate?" and "Does my paraphrase contain the most important information and is it in my own words?" CSI can be used to teach students with and without disabilities.

In a classic research study on the effectiveness of interventions to teach students with LDs, Swanson, Hoskyn, and Lee (1999) found the following practices from explicit and cognitive strategy instruction to be very effective; they called these practices the combined model for designing and delivering instruction:

- Sequencing: Breaking down the task, providing step-by-step prompts
- Drill-repetition-practice: Daily testing of skills, repeated practice
- Segmentation: Breaking down skills into parts and then synthesizing the parts into a whole
- Directed questioning and responses: Asking process or content questions of students
- Control of task difficulty: Sequencing tasks from easy to difficult, teaching prerequisite skills
- Technology: Delivering instruction via multimedia
- Teacher-modeled problem solving: Demonstrating processes or steps to solve a problem or explaining how to do a task
- Small group instruction: Delivering instruction to a small group
- Strategy cues: Reminding students to use strategies, modeling the think aloud technique.

As you read about teaching practices in later chapters, remember the practices described above for learning and notice how they are integrated into instructional practices.

Designing Instruction

We discuss several areas that teachers consider when designing their lessons for all students, including those with special learning needs.

Types of Knowledge

Different types of knowledge for different content areas are applicable across the grade levels. They include discrimination, factual knowledge, procedural knowledge, conceptual knowledge, and metacognitive knowledge (Mastropieri & Scruggs, 2014).

Discrimination. Discrimination is the ability to distinguish one item (e.g., a letter, number, letter sound, math sign, state, or piece of lab equipment) from another. Discrimination occurs when students are first learning new information and requires the student to identify and pay attention to the important features of an item. Students with learning difficulties can have difficulties discriminating among items. Teachers should teach the relevant features of items and then present similar items among which discrimination is necessary. For example, to distinguish between the numbers 12 and 21, students can learn that 12 has a 1 and 2 where the 1 can be color-coded or made larger to emphasize the relevant feature that 1 is first in 12. The same can be done for 21. Once students can identify each number separately, teachers can present the numbers together for them to name. Students should practice discriminating among items such as similar letters (b, d, m, w, p, q) and numbers (6, 9, 21, 20, 102, 120), words with similar sounds (pet, pit, pig, big), symbols (+, –, ×), and concepts that are similar (e.g., types of plants). For older students, discrimination learning occurs when they are required to name pieces of lab equipment before instruction begins or mathematics items such as a compass or protractor before a geometry lesson.

Factual Knowledge. The ability to memorize, retain, and recall information is factual knowledge. Examples include number combinations (e.g., 3 + 4 = 7), vocabulary definitions, historical events and dates, parts of speech in English or a foreign language, and parts of a plant. Students with unique learning needs may have problems learning factual information because of problems with deciphering, remembering, and recalling the information. These students can benefit from strategies that teach them how to memorize and recall information (Schumaker & Deshler, 2006). Students must learn many facts across the content areas so that they can apply information to their learning. Chapter 14 contains additional information on ways to help students retain and recall content information.

Procedural Knowledge. Learning a set of steps that are followed to complete a task involves procedural knowledge. Examples include the steps to solve an arithmetic problem, conduct a lab experiment, develop a historical timeline, and follow a strategy to read difficult words or to comprehend text. Students with unique learning needs may have problems with procedural knowledge because it requires memorizing a series of steps in the correct sequence and the ability to conduct each step. It may also be necessary to teach prerequisite knowledge. For example, if students are following a series of steps to multiply 32 × 64, they must know the steps and the prerequisite knowledge of 4 × 2, 4 × 3, 6 × 2, regrouping, and 6 × 3. Modeling, lots of practice, and error correction are examples of ways to teach procedural knowledge. Cue cards containing the steps of the procedure also can be useful for students to refer to until they learn the steps.

Conceptual Knowledge. Knowledge about principles, models, and classifications entails conceptual knowledge. In essence, **concepts** are categories of knowledge. Concepts range in level of abstractness. For instance, the concept of a table is concrete and easy for most students to understand, and it can be easily represented. The concept of democracy, however, is very abstract and requires multiple examples.

Visual displays can help students understand concepts. For example, the concept that the word *table* represents can be described using the categories dimensions, function, and types of construction. Students can create collections of words and pictures that represent a concept. For instance, pictures of different types of tables can be collected, and descriptive words can be selected to describe the concept (e.g., claw-legged table). Price and Nelson (2003) recommended that teachers conduct a concept analysis of content to be taught prior to instruction. The concept analysis should include the following:

- Identification of the critical concepts to be taught as part of a unit or chapter
- Definitions of the concepts
- List of attributes or characteristics of the concepts
- List of noncritical attributes that are not essential for understanding the concept

- List of examples
- List of nonexamples
- List of related concepts

Metacognitive Knowledge. Metacognition is often described as thinking about the strategies we use to tackle tasks. It is knowledge about how people learn and process information or tasks. Students need to understand how they learn and process information. Teachers can model how to develop self-regulation questions for given tasks. For example, teachers can model questions for developing a plan for accomplishing a given learning task, monitoring comprehension when reading text, and evaluating progress toward the completion of a task (Pintrich, 2002). Examples of self-regulation questions for metacognitive knowledge were discussed previously in this chapter. Additional examples include developing a plan for accomplishing a given learning task: "What do I need to do to accomplish the task?" "What is my plan for accomplishing the task?" "What are the steps?" and "What questions will I ask myself to be sure I can accomplish each step?"

All students can benefit from self-regulation strategies, especially students with unique learning needs who may have difficulties with knowing how to take a more active role in their own learning. Table 7.1 provides information about types of knowledge and instructional techniques for teaching them. See if you can think of other examples for each type of knowledge.

TABLE 7.1 ■ Types of Knowledge and Instructional Techniques

Types of Knowledge	Instructional Techniques
Discrimination	Model how to identify the relevant features. For example, point out the lower part of the "b" and say that by adding a similar part to the top you make a "B." Small "b" is in big "B." Present a "d." Point out the lower part of the "d" and say that by adding a similar part to the top you do not make a big "B." So, "d" is not "b." Provide practice and error correction on discrimination activities. Prompt students if they require additional help making discriminations. For example, "Can you put a similar part on the top of 'b'?" "What letter did you make?" "What letter is this 'b'?" Initially, teach letters, numbers, and sounds that are dissimilar; then introduce items that are similar and focus on the relevant distinguishing features. For example, a 3 only has one side compared to an 8. Put a line under 6 and 9 to help students distinguish where the circle part of the number appears.
Factual knowledge	Present information in categories rather than in long lists. Have students use visual displays to organize the factual knowledge. Reduce the amount of information to be learned. For instance, focus on multiplication facts ×7 then ×8, and finally ×9 before mixing the facts. Teach strategies to aid in remembering, such as counting strategies for math facts. Starting big and counting on is a good strategy for specific facts (see Chapter 13). Provide concrete and pictorial examples of content-area factual knowledge. Show videos that depict the factual knowledge. Take field trips that focus on the information to be learned. Provide multiple opportunities for students to engage with content actively and in ways that aid memory associations (e.g., categorization, visual displays, and mnemonics; see Chapter 14).
Rules	Teach content knowledge and behavior rules. Have students repeat the rules. Provide examples of how the rules look in use and what happens when the rules are broken. Provide practice opportunities to help students recall the rules, especially at the beginning of the school year or after a winter break or spring break.
Procedural knowledge	Model using "think aloud" to demonstrate how to use a series of steps to solve a problem. Provide repetition and opportunities to practice each step. Chunk some of the steps to be taught so that students learn a small number of steps of the total number of steps each time. Coach students through the use of the steps. Allow students to watch a peer use the steps.
Conceptual knowledge	Name and define the concept. Teach the critical and noncritical attributes of the concept. Have students find examples that illustrate the concept. Provide multiple examples of concepts. Provide nonexamples for students to discriminate from examples. Use concrete and pictorial examples. Have students explain in their own words the meaning of the concept. Have students keep a concepts dictionary.
Metacognitive knowledge	Provide examples of questions students can ask themselves to foster self-regulation of their metacognitive knowledge for tasks. Ensure that students learn the self-regulation, metacognitive strategies for different tasks. Remind them to implement these strategies to promote independent, active, responsible learning.

Source: Adapted from Mastropieri and Scruggs (2014).

Instructional Techniques

Instructional techniques that promote meaningful associations of knowledge include clustering, elaboration, and mnemonic devices (Mastropieri & Scruggs, 2014; Schumaker & Deshler, 2006).

Clustering. Clustering requires categorizing information in an important way. For example, when teaching about states, they can be clustered according to the category of geographic region (e.g., New England states, West Coast states). Students have a better chance of learning the information when you (or they) reduce the amount of information to learn all at once and organize it in a meaningful way. Information can also be organized and presented in visual displays such as semantic maps and relationship displays (Vaughn & Bos, 2011). Examples of semantic maps and relationship displays are provided in Chapter 14.

Elaboration. Adding more details to facts to aid in memorization, retention, and recall constitutes elaboration. According to Mastropieri and Scruggs (2009), elaboration helps students remember information. Students can identify what they know about a topic to help them make elaborative sentences. Take the following list of animals: giraffe, elephant, lion, and leopard. Students might create the elaborative sentence "The giraffe and elephant fear the lion and leopard" to help them remember it.

Mnemonic Devices. These devices are techniques for aiding memory by forming meaningful associations and linkages across information that appears to be unrelated (Mastropieri & Scruggs, 2014). Mnemonic devices help students learn content-area vocabulary, memorize lists of factual information, and read multisyllabic words (Bryant & Bryant, 2003; Schumaker & Deshler, 2006).

Examples of mnemonic devices include acronyms and acrostics, which help students recall lists of information. An acronym is a word made from the first letters of the words to be learned. For example, the acronym HOMES refers to the Great Lakes (Heron, Ontario, Michigan, Erie, and Superior). Students have to learn and remember the acronym, HOMES, and also what each letter represents. An acrostic is a sentence where the first letters of the words stand for the items to be remembered as well as their correct order. For example, the first letters in "Every Good Boy Deserves Fudge" stand for the notes on a musical staff: E, G, B, D, F.

Mnemonic devices are procedures for helping students remember information by forming valid associations and connections across information that seems to be unrelated. Think about how mnemonic devices could help students memorize the planets in the solar system.

Critical Thinking

Critical thinking involves reasoning to learn new concepts, ideas, or problem solutions (Mastropieri & Scruggs, 2014). Students of all ages are able to think critically with guidance and perhaps with the teacher modeling how to think critically. Examples of critical thinking include reasoning about how to solve a problem with a peer, predicting the ending of a novel, and determining how to solve a problem. Students with unique learning needs might experience problems with critical thinking if they have not been taught how to think critically because they lack the prior knowledge and background that would help them understand issues, or because their earlier instruction focused more on factual and procedural knowledge. Students with unique learning needs are able to learn to think critically and should not have experiences only with factual and procedural knowledge.

One way to help students think critically is to include activities that focus on the domains that promote critical thinking (Krathwohl, 2002). Table 7.2 provides useful information about how to do so. In Table 7.2, cognitive domains are identified and described in Column 1 (remembering, understanding, applying) and examples of verbs relevant to each domain are located in Column 2. The content from Column 2 can be translated into class assignments (Column 3) and activities (Column 4). It is easier to develop critical thinking skills by drawing from the higher-order domains (numbers 3–6) on the list. However, these domains encompass knowledge taught through the lower-level domains, thus there is a place in instruction for each domain.

TABLE 7.2 ■ Critical Thinking

Critical Thinking Domain	Relevant Sample Verbs	Sample Assignments	Sample Sources or Activities
1. **Remembering** Retrieving, recognizing, and recalling relevant knowledge for a content topic such as reading a science text. Identify content that should be remembered such as definitions for content vocabulary. Use verbal rehearsal to practice naming steps for a cognitive strategy.	Acquire, Define, Distinguish, Draw, Find, Label, List, Match, Read, Record	1. Define each of these terms: *encomienda, conquistador, gaucho* 2. What was the *Amistad?*	Written records, films, videos, models, events, media, diagrams, books
2. **Understanding** Constructing meaning from oral, written, and graphic messages through interpreting, exemplifying, classifying, summarizing, inferring, comparing, and explaining. Understand uses and implications of terms, facts, methods, procedures, concepts.	Compare, Demonstrate, Differentiate, Fill in, Find, Group, Outline, Predict, Represent, Trace	1. Compare an invertebrate with a vertebrate. 2. Use a set of symbols and graphics to draw the water cycle.	Trends, consequences, tables, cartoons
3. **Applying** Carrying out or using a procedure through executing or implementing. Make use of, apply practice theory, solve problems, use information in new situations.	Convert, Demonstrate, Differentiate between, Discover, Discuss, Examine, Experiment, Prepare, Produce, Record	1. Convert the following into a real-world problem: velocity = dist./time. 2. Experiment with batteries and bulbs to create circuits.	Collection of items, diary, photographs, sculpture, illustration
4. **Analyzing** Breaking material into constituent parts, determining how the parts relate to one another and to an overall structure or purpose through differentiating, organizing, and attributing. Take concepts apart, break them down, analyze structure, recognize assumptions and poor logic, evaluate relevancy.	Classify, Determine, Discriminate, Form generalizations, Put into categories, Illustrate, Select, Survey, Take apart, Transform	1. Illustrate examples of two earthquake types. 2. Dissect a crayfish and examine the body parts.	Graph, survey, diagram, chart, questionnaire, report
5. **Evaluating** Making judgments based on criteria and standards through checking and critiquing. Set standards; judge using standards, evidence, rubrics; accept or reject on basis of criteria.	Argue, Award, Critique, Defend, Interpret, Judge, Measure, Select, Test, Verify	1. Defend or negate the statement: "Nature takes care of itself." 2. Judge the value of requiring students to take earth social studies.	Letters, group with discussion panel, court trial, survey, self-evaluation, value, allusions
6. **Creating** Putting elements together to form a coherent or functional whole; reorganizing elements into a new pattern or structure through generating, planning, or producing. Put things together, bring together various parts, write theme, present speech, plan experiment, put information together in a new and creative way.	Synthesize, Arrange, Blend, Create, Deduce, Devise, Organize, Plan, Present, Rearrange, Rewrite	1. Create a demonstration to show various chemical properties. 2. Devise a method to teach others about magnetism.	Article, radio show, video, puppet show, inventions, poetry, short story

Source: Krathwohl (2002).

Now consider how you could design a lesson by including activities addressing the cognitive domains that foster critical thinking. If you are not yet familiar with lesson writing, then identify existing lessons from curriculum guides or that are on education websites to determine the degree to which critical thinking tasks are incorporated. Now, think about how information from the types of knowledge and critical thinking domains can be combined for instruction.

Delivering Instruction

There are instructional steps and techniques designed to help all students learn and master the curriculum. The instructional steps include an advance organizer, presentation of subject matter, guided practice, independent practice, and closure. You will see "I do," "We do," "You do" for presentation of subject matter, guided practice, and independent practice, respectively. This is student-friendly language because you can say, "I do the first problem to show you how to find a solution, then we do more problems together. I will find out how much you have learned when you do the independent practice."

We also include types of questions to focus on lower- and higher-order thinking (critical thinking) and a questioning strategy that can be used during instruction. Finally, refer back to the content in this chapter under "Translating Research Findings Into Instructional Practices" to review information about explicit instruction and cognitive strategy instruction. Also, review the list of practices from the Swanson et al. (1999) study. All of these practices can be implemented as part of delivering instruction.

Advance Organizer

An **advance organizer** is a set of activities to prepare students for the lesson's content (Lenz & Deshler, 2004; Schumaker & Deshler, 2006). Advance organizers tell students the purpose of the lesson (objectives), motivate students by sparking their interest, and activate background knowledge by reviewing related information. Such a review helps students warm up for the lesson, promotes active engagement, and provides teachers with information about students' current levels of understanding before new material is introduced. In planning and implementing advance organizers, teachers should consider their students' background knowledge, experience, and ability with prerequisite skills for the new task, the vocabulary to be learned, and the level of abstraction of the new learning (Price & Nelson, 2003). Think ADAPT!

Examples of items to include in an advance organizer include the following:

- Writing the objective on the board and explaining how it will be taught
- Explaining the importance of learning the objective and asking students to provide examples of how they can use the new information
- Providing an active technique such as role playing, seeing a video clip, or taking a field trip before instruction to build background knowledge about a topic
- Having students create a concept map or specifically tell what they already know about the topic to be studied
- Providing a review of related information for students to make connections

Presentation of Subject Matter (I Do)

In this step, teachers present instructional content related to the **instructional objective**, which states the skill to be taught, the action, and the criterion for success. For example, "Given five spelling words (condition), the student (audience) will write definitions and use the words in sentences (behavior) with 90% accuracy for two days (degree: criterion for success)." Although the wording for instructional objectives might vary slightly across school districts, the key idea is that the instructional objective sets the focus for the lesson for the steps of instructional delivery. We think about the A-B-C-Ds of writing instructional objectives: A is the audience, B is the behavior or action, C is the condition for instruction, and D means the degree to which performance is expected.

Instruction can focus on facts (e.g., number of U.S. states, state capitals), rules (e.g., spelling, mathematics), cognitive and metacognitive strategies (e.g., reading strategy, paragraph-writing strategy), and concepts (e.g., place value, social studies vocabulary, health). When presenting facts, rules, and procedures,

An advance organizer consists of activities to prepare students for the lesson's content. Here, students prepare for a lesson by watching an overview of the topic on a video.

iStock.com/FatCamera

for example, teachers should model, or demonstrate, how to do problems to arrive at the correct responses, and the appropriate thinking processes, by using the think aloud procedure. Students can imitate the teacher's modeling orally, in written form, or motorically (e.g., by manipulating objects). Examples should be provided to illustrate new information, and nonexamples can help, too. For instance, an example of democracy is the right to vote; a nonexample of democracy is one person controls the government.

Teachers can ask questions to foster discussion and engage students in the lesson. They should ask different types of questions (what, why, how) and provide sufficient wait time (3 or 4 seconds) between asking a question and calling on a student to answer it. Asking a question and then calling on a student by name maintains a moderate level of concern, which means students need to pay attention because they won't know when or if they will be expected to answer questions. A good example of how to maintain a moderate level of concern is the popsicle stick routine. The teacher has a jar with students' names on the sticks (one name per stick). The teacher asks a question and then pulls a stick and calls on that student to answer the question. Maintaining a moderate level of concern also can promote on-task behavior, which means students are listening and engaged in instruction. Calling on a student by name first and then asking a question allows other students to tune out (low level of concern). Finally, teachers should use appropriate pacing when delivering instruction to keep students engaged and demonstrating on-task behavior. Appropriate pacing is shown when students can learn the content without being overwhelmed and frustrated. If pacing is too slow students can become bored and exhibit off-task behavior (Coyne et al., 2011). For struggling students, teachers can provide extra practice on smaller segments of information. For example, math facts can be grouped into segments (e.g., the ×6 facts, the ×7 facts), vocabulary word lists can be reduced to fewer words in a list, and the number of questions to answer can be minimized (e.g., tell students to just do the even-numbered problems).

Guided Practice (We Do)

Guided practice involves practices that teachers and students either do together or that students do individually or in small groups with the teacher's guidance. The practices are intended to involve students in practicing what they have learned. When students are learning a new skill, they must have many chances to practice the skill with the teacher's guidance. Distributed practice involves practice opportunities conducted over a period of time. Cumulative practice consists of practice of previously taught related skills (Archer & Hughes, 2011). For example, if students learned multiplication facts with 5 as one factor to criterion (e.g., 90% accurate) and are now learning multiplication facts with 2 as one factor to criterion, they would practice these facts together (mixed up). Both types of practice, distributed and cumulative, are efficient practices to promote the maintenance of skills.

There are several instructional practices that are part of good teaching and that can be included in the presentation of subject matter and guided practice steps. First, teachers can **check for understanding**. When teachers check for understanding they are asking questions associated with the instructed or practiced content to determine those students who are struggling and require more instruction. For example, check for understanding can be done after content is presented or during guided practice. All students should be given opportunities to respond during check for understanding so that teachers can identify those students who may need additional support. Teachers can use the following techniques to check for student understanding (Price & Nelson, 2003):

- Present information that was taught (e.g., fact, rule, procedure) and ask students to show, by signaling thumbs up or thumbs down, whether the information is correct.
- Use response cards for students to indicate their response to the teacher's statement or question.
- Have students show their responses using materials such as manipulatives in math.
- Have students write their responses to be turned in for checking.
- Have students write their responses on white boards.

Second, **error-correction procedures** or feedback should be given to correct errors and to provide feedback so that students do not practice errors or learn incorrect information. Error-correction procedures include stopping the student if an error is made, modeling the correct response, and having the student repeat the correct response.

Third, **scaffolding** (i.e., providing extra support and guidance) is important as students learn and practice new concepts and skills. Think of a scaffold on a building that is put up to help workers with a task and is gradually removed over time when less scaffolding is needed. The same is true for academic scaffolding; scaffolds are implemented to help support students and then gradually removed when the support is no longer needed. To review examples of scaffolds, return to the "Translating Research Findings into Instructional Practices" section and review the list of practices that Swanson et al. (1999) found. Think about which of these practices can be used to provide more support for struggling learners initially and then gradually lessened and removed when students become more proficient.

Fourth, **active participation** improves engaged time and on-task behavior. **Engaged time** is the amount of time students are involved in learning. Ways to promote engagement include having students make some type of response (e.g., oral, written, constructing) or exhibit behavior (e.g., demonstrating eye contact, paying attention) to indicate that they are paying attention, listening, and remaining engaged. Relatedly, **academic learning time** focuses on the quantity of time students are actively engaged in appropriate learning tasks and are being successful. Active-participation activities can improve student engagement and increase academic learning time (Archer & Hughes, 2011). Figure 7.2 provides examples of active-participation activities.

Independent Practice (You Do)

Independent practice is the "you do" part of the lesson. "You do" means that students are given a task to finish on their own. Often, this task leads to a product of some kind The purpose of independent practice is to determine whether students mastered the instructional objective for that lesson and whether they met the criterion, such as 90% accuracy. Independent practice happens in the classroom or as homework and suggests that students have demonstrated a good understanding of the skill and no longer require teacher supervision or guidance. Students with unique learning needs can benefit from cues from the teacher such as, "Remember to apply the strategy you learned today" or "Work carefully" or "Show your work."

FIGURE 7.2 ■ Examples of Active-Participation Activities

1. Use Jigsaw (Slavin, 1991) as a technique to engage all students in learning and sharing information (see the section on cooperative learning on page 289).
2. Use Think-Pair-Share-Write (students work with a partner to share their response to a question; students turn in their own written responses).
3. Use "Numbered Heads Together" (Kagan, 1990) (students in groups discuss the response to an answer; each student has a number; the teacher calls on one number to provide the answer). This works really well to review the meanings of concepts and terms.
4. Have students brainstorm responses to questions; call on students randomly to provide answers.
5. Require students to take notes.
6. Use peer pairs for practice (see the discussion of small groups in the section on grouping structures).
7. Have students find pictorial representations for content being learned (students can make time lines with significant events pictured or drawn along the time line).
8. Use response cards. Card 1 can be used when questions require a yes/no or true/false response. Words can be color-coded so that teachers can quickly scan the students to be sure the correct color (word) is displayed. Cards 2 and 3 are pinch cards. The teacher can present a definition and the student "pinches" the answer (puts thumb and forefinger next to the answer). Students should be told, "Hold your response card at chest level. I will give you a question (or definition). I will say 'think,' and then you show me. Hold up your card with the correct answer or pinch the correct answer."

Card 1
Yes/No or
True/False Card

Yes
True

No
False

Card 2
Pinch Card
Rectangle

- Pyramid
- Cylinder
- Isosceles trapezoid
- Parallelogram
- Triangle

Card 3
Pinch Card

- Length
- Area
- Volume
- Perimeter

If there are students who have not met the learning objective criterion, then teachers must reteach the skill or concept targeted for that lesson. Think ADAPT! This is the Test part of the framework. If a group of students needs reteaching, then it behooves the teacher to try a different adaptation.

Closure

Closure happens at the end of a lesson and usually takes only a few minutes. During closure, teachers and students review the instructional objective, review what has been learned, and discuss follow-up plans. Closure activities can be brief, but they are an important part of the lesson and need to be considered when time is designated for instructional planning.

Table 7.3 offers questions to help teachers reflect on their instructional practices during the steps.

Types of Questions and Questioning Strategy

Teachers can monitor student comprehension of an instructional objective by asking specific questions. Presenting different types of questions can help students think about what they are learning. Students can show their knowledge about a topic by answering convergent questions. Convergent, lower-order

TABLE 7.3 ■ Reflective Questions to Guide Instructional Decision Making

Instructional Step	Reflective Questions
Advance Organizer	• Do I have the students' attention? • Is the instructional objective stated specifically? • Do students appear to be interested in the lesson? • Is there sufficient review of background or related content? • Is there vocabulary that needs to be reviewed? • Are students making connections across skills?
Presentation of Subject Matter	• Are students comprehending the lesson? • Is modeling effective? • Do I need to provide more examples? • Do students understand after error correction?
Guided Practice	• Are all students engaged actively in learning? Do I need to provide more examples? • Are more practice opportunities necessary? Do I need to give more prompts? • Do students understand after error correction? Is the grouping practice effective for instruction? • Are there vocabulary words that require further instruction? • Are the practice opportunities appropriate?
Independent Practice (can also be homework)	• Are students ready for independent practice? • Are students capable of completing activities independently? • Are students achieving high levels of accuracy on independent practice activities? • Am I providing feedback for activities?
Closure	• Do I allow enough time for closure? • Do all or most of the students have opportunities to engage in closure activities? • Do I still have students who do not understand the instructional objective? • Are students able to relate the lesson's objective to other learning?

questions usually have one answer and start with who, what, or when. Answers to these questions are essential to indicate student understanding about a topic. **Divergent, higher-order questions** tap critical thinking skills because they require students to make inferences, to analyze or synthesize information, and to evaluate content. These questions start with, "What could happen . . .?" "What if . . .?" "What do you think caused . . .?" "Why do you think . . .?" "How were the characters alike and different?" and "How could events be changed to affect the outcome?" Critical thinking must be developed through divergent questioning strategies and coaching. Revisit the critical thinking domains and think about how these types of questions relate to the cognitive domains.

The response-dependent questioning strategy can help students who are struggling with specific content to reach the correct answer to a question. The questioning strategy has remained viable for years and is shown in Table 7.4.

In the next section, we discuss practices for instructional groups. Think about how different grouping practices can be used with the whole class and with students with unique learning needs. Consider how Mrs. Santiago and Ms. Benz can use grouping practices to meet the needs of their diverse learners.

TABLE 7.4 ■ Response-Dependent Questioning Strategy

Steps	Questioning Strategy	Example	Response
Step 1: Opening Question	Teacher asks question about subject being presented.	*Example:* Asks student to make the sound of the digraph EE.	*Response:* Student makes correct sound; if incorrect, proceed to Step 2.
Step 2: Constructed Response	Teacher seeks correct response by prompting student to focus on specific knowledge or information from which a correct response can be constructed.	*Example:* Think about the rule we have learned for two vowels together.	Response: Student makes correct sound; if incorrect, proceed to Step 3.
Step 3: Multiple Choice	Teacher provides choice of two responses; one of the responses is correct.	*Example:* Is the sound "ee" (makes long "e" sound) or "e" (makes short "e" sound)?	*Response:* Student selects correct sound; if incorrect, proceed to Step 4.
Step 4: Restricted Alternative	Teacher eliminates the incorrect response from Step 3 but does not provide the answer.	*Example:* EE (points to letters on chalkboard) does not make the "e" (makes short "e" sound) sound. What is the correct sound of EE?	*Response:* Student provides correct response; if incorrect, proceed to Step 5.
Step 5: Complete Model	Teacher provides correct response.	*Example:* Teacher points to EE on chalkboard and makes "ee" sound.	*Response:* Student imitates correct response.

Source: Adapted from Stowitschek, Stowitschek, Hendrickson, and Day (1984).

HOW INSTRUCTIONAL GROUPING PRACTICES CAN PROMOTE EFFECTIVE INSTRUCTION

Instructional grouping practices can include whole group instruction, flexible small groups, and one-to-one teaching. Peer tutoring is another grouping practice that can help students who need more opportunities to practice their skills. Finally, teachers have used cooperative learning structures for years to enrich practice in student-centered instruction. Consider how to use these practices when designing and delivering instruction.

Instructional Grouping Practices

Whole Group

In whole group instruction, the teacher presents a lesson to the entire class. Whole group instruction is often selected to teach content-area subjects, such as science, social studies, and health, and is common at the secondary level. Activities for whole groups include direct, explicit instruction on new information (e.g., vocabulary, rules, concepts), read-alouds, and presentations.

Researchers have demonstrated that whole group instruction can be effective for students of different abilities (Gersten et al., 1987). Whole group instruction permits all students to hear responses from peers. Teachers can pace instruction to maintain student engagement and work individually with students following instruction. However, there are disadvantages to whole group instruction such as limited error correction, pacing that may be too fast for some, and the use of instructional objectives that may not be appropriate for everyone. Teachers must be sure the instructional objectives are applicable for most of the students. Teachers also should allocate time for those students in need of further individualized, differentiated instruction.

Flexible Small Groups

Flexible small groups comprise three to five students including those students with the same or different abilities. The purpose of flexible small groups varies according to students' individual needs.

The grouping composition is flexible in the sense that a student who is in a group for reteaching a mathematics concept might not need to be in a group for additional reading support.

Same-Ability Groups

All of the students in same-ability groups are usually performing similarly on a specific skill and require extra instruction. For struggling students, extra practice on instructional objectives is often necessary. For students who are high achieving, gifted, or talented, same-ability groups can provide enrichment activities.

Research findings demonstrate the efficacy of this grouping practice. Small group instruction produces better academic outcomes for students with disabilities than whole group instruction (Schumm et al., 2000; Vaughn et al., 2001). The major advantage of small group instruction is that students can receive more modeling, prompting, error correction, and pacing that is better suited to their individual needs than in whole group instruction. The challenge is to ensure that the remainder of the class is actively engaged in purposeful tasks. Having backup tasks ready for those students who require teacher assistance when it is not available, and for those who finish their tasks before small group instruction ends, can help ensure that all students are actively learning.

Mixed-Ability Groups

This instructional grouping practice consists of students who are achieving at different levels on skills. This grouping practice can help students to work on projects and to make presentations. The advantage is that the students can learn from each other. Importantly, there is little evidence that mixed-ability groups adversely affect the learning of students who are gifted and talented (Tieso, 2005).

One-to-One Groups

In one-to-one teaching, teachers provide instruction to students on the basis of their specific learning and behavioral needs. For example, a student might need prompts, feedback, or directions to begin working on or learning an instructional objective. A student's behavior may warrant individualized instruction away from other students in the classroom.

One-to-one instruction has been shown to minimize student frustration and be more responsive to instructional demands. The advantage of this grouping practice is that individual students receive

Students performing at varying levels both academically and socially can learn from one another in mixed-ability groups.

iStock.com/FatCamera

support for their learning. Teachers must plan activities so other students are busy as well. Furthermore, one-to-one instruction may be problematic to achieve in general education classrooms because of the number of students in these classrooms and time constraints. In this case, students with disabilities who are in inclusion settings will likely need support from their special education teacher. If the general and special education teachers team teach, then assistance can be given to students with disabilities and other students with unique learning needs. If the special education teacher spends the day going in and out of some classrooms to work with her students, then support will be limited. Peer tutoring and cooperative learning are two possible ways to provide more support for struggling students.

Peer Tutoring

Peer tutoring is an instructional grouping practice where pairs of students work on assigned tasks for extra practice. Several peer tutoring models are noteworthy, such as classwide peer tutoring (Delquadri et al., 1986) and peer-assisted learning strategies (PALS; Fuchs et al., 1997). Research findings on peer tutoring models have indicated that peer tutoring can improve the academic achievement of students (Heron et al., 2006). Years of research have shown that peer tutoring increases student involvement and opportunities to respond, review, and practice skills and concepts.

The peer tutoring relationship consists of a tutor–tutee pairing. Instruction and feedback can be provided to teach students with disabilities and students who are at risk for academic difficulties (Heron et al., 2006). For instance, in reading a higher-performing peer can be paired with a student who is reading at a lower level and who requires additional instructional support. The peers take turns serving as reading coach and reader. The reading coach reads the designated reading passage for a short time period; the reader then reads the same passage for the same time period. The partners provide error correction as needed and praise for good reading. This passage reading should be followed by comprehension questions. These same procedures can be applied in mathematics, vocabulary development, and spelling.

With this grouping practice, students develop academic skills, form relationships, and gain the instructional support they need to address learning and behavioral problems. Among the challenges are allocating time to teach tutors their role responsibilities, matching students appropriately, monitoring the pairs, and assessing progress. However, it should be noted that there is a group of students with disabilities who may not benefit from the peer tutoring model in reading (McMaster et al., 2006). Importantly, students whose reading skills are significantly lower than the rest of the class likely will require explicit instruction.

Cooperative Learning

In **cooperative learning**, mixed-ability, small groups can focus on academic and social skills. The purpose of cooperative learning is for students to learn to work collaboratively to achieve similar academic and social goals; however, students must be accountable to the team for their individual efforts (Johnson et al., 1994).

Numerous research findings on cooperative learning have been obtained in different academic areas (e.g., mathematics, reading, social studies) with students who have disabilities, students who are typically achieving, and students who come from diverse backgrounds. A classic review of the research literature showed that in most cases, students tend to obtain academic and social skills benefits from this instructional arrangement (Slavin, 1991).

Several models of cooperative learning are suitable for many classrooms. The models share similar characteristics such as group academic and social goals, heterogeneous student groups, task structure, cooperation, and individual and group accountability. Table 7.5 provides information about cooperative learning models.

Preparation for cooperative learning should involve considering the following questions:

- What are the academic and social skills instructional objectives?
- What task or activity can be used to teach the instructional objectives?

- How can the elements of cooperative learning be promoted?
- How will student groups be formed?
- What environmental factors must be considered?
- What management techniques will be used?
- What is the teacher's role during group activities?
- How will individual and group progress with instructional objectives be monitored?
- What difficulties might students with unique learning needs or disabilities encounter in cooperative learning groups?

TABLE 7.5 ■ Selected Models of Cooperative Learning

	Teams–Games–Tournaments	Learning Together	Jigsaw
Steps	1. Teacher presents material to be studied. 2. Students work in teams to learn material. 3. Students compete in tournament games with peers of similar ability, answering questions about the material practiced in teams. 4. Points are awarded on the basis of performance in tournaments. 5. Team (original cooperative learning team) scores are obtained from points that members accrue in tournament games. 6. Team standings are announced weekly.	1. Teacher explains academic task, cooperative goal structure, and criteria for success to group teams. 2. Students are responsible for learning material and making sure group members learn material as well. 3. Students provide encouragement and assistance to team members. 4. Teacher monitors group work and intervenes to provide task assistance or teach collaborative skills. 5. Student work and group functioning are evaluated. 6. Students are arranged to promote face-to-face interaction. 7. Teams construct one group product.	1. Teaching material is divided into parts and assigned to group members. 2. Students learn how to communicate with and tutor other students. 3. Subgroups of students with the same material meet, learn, and then share their material with the original team members. 4. All members of the team must learn all parts of the material. 5. Teachers monitor groups, providing assistance, encouragement, and direction.
Goals	1. Students learn academic material. 2. Students help team members learn material.	1. There is an academic task goal. 2. There is a cooperative/collaborative/social goal.	1. Students learn a part of the material and then teach this to other team members.
Student Groups	1. They are heterogeneous, diverse groups. 2. There are four to five students per team. 3. Everyone must learn concepts.	1. They are heterogeneous, diverse groups. 2. There are two to six students per team.	1. They are heterogeneous, diverse groups. 2. There are four to seven students per team.
Task Structure	1. There is group-paced instruction. 2. Teams work together to study material.	1. There is group-paced instruction. 2. Teams work together to study topic/concept/material/problem—"We all sink or swim together." 3. Everyone must learn concepts and participate. 4. Student roles may be assigned. 5. Only limited materials are provided, thus necessitating interdependence.	1. The structure is cooperative/interdependent. 2. Students learn a section of material pertaining to a topic and then teach that material to group members.

(Continued)

TABLE 7.5 ■ Selected Models of Cooperative Learning (*Continued*)

	Teams-Games-Tournaments	Learning Together	Jigsaw
Cooperation	1. Students help each other to learn material so members will do well in tournaments.	1. Students help each other learn material. 2. Students demonstrate collaborative/ social group skills (e.g., providing feedback, elaborating, sharing, staying on task, doing one's share of the work).	1. All students must work together to learn all the material on a topic.
Accountability/ Evaluation	1. Everyone is responsible for his or her own learning. 2. Everyone is responsible for ensuring that other team members learn concepts. 3. Each member's tournament contributes to a group score.	1. Everyone is responsible for his or her own learning. 2. Everyone is responsible for ensuring that other team members learn concepts. 3. Members may be asked to explain group answers, take a test, or edit another person's work.	1. All students are accountable for learning all the material.
Group Processing		1. Group members evaluate their ability to work as a team according to set criteria at the conclusion of their work. 2. Group members determine group skills that should be worked on to promote better collaboration.	

There are several advantages of cooperative learning, as shown in Slavin's (1991) review of the research literature. First, because students must work together toward common goals, there is a need for some amount of collaborative behavior. Second, group work entails verbal interactions, which can create opportunities to develop language skills. Third, cooperative learning means students are responsible for solving problems. Fourth, cooperative learning work fosters social interactions and peer acceptance (Slavin, 1991).

Cooperative learning activities depend upon considerable planning and preparation. For instance, teachers must ensure that all students participate fully because the bulk of the work should not fall on the shoulders of only a few students. Finally, teachers must be sure students are able to perform the instructional objectives successfully both with group members and individually. The Working Together feature shows how professionals can collaborate to determine how to differentiate content, instructional approach, grouping, and materials for students who are having difficulties—in this case, during a mathematics lesson.

WORKING TOGETHER

COLLABORATING TO DIFFERENTIATE INSTRUCTION

Mrs. Bell is teaching her fifth-grade students different ways to represent fractions and wants them to compare and order fractions according to fractional parts. She provides a review of different fractions and key vocabulary. Mr. Rivera, the math specialist, has encouraged the classroom teachers to provide students with number lines and fraction strips to represent fractional parts, so Mrs. Bell has incorporated these into her instructional practice. She has the students work in small, mixed-ability groups to compare and order fractions before they apply this factual knowledge to problem solving. Ms. Chavez, the special education inclusion teacher, works with the students with mathematics LDs to provide more specialized instruction on fractions. As Mrs. Bell circulates among the small groups, she listens to group discussions and notices that several students seem confused. She sits with them and asks questions to check their understanding of the assignment, the vocabulary, and the use of the number lines and fractions strips for comparing and ordering fractions. She decides to model the procedure once more and watches students complete the next example; she also provides error correction as needed. She instructs the students to complete the next few problems as she circulates among the other groups and makes notes about student progress in her assessment notebook. During the fifth-grade teachers' planning period, Mrs. Bell and the other two fifth-grade teachers (Mr. Rivera and Ms. Chavez) discuss the progress-monitoring data from the fractions lessons. They discuss how Mr. Rivera and Ms. Chavez can help students who are struggling during mathematics instruction. Having Ms. Chavez working with struggling students in small groups and Mr. Rivera providing tips for effective instruction on fractions are viewed by the fifth-grade teachers as effective collaborative practices for now. The teachers have agreed to stagger their math instruction time so that Ms. Chavez can work in all of the classes.

Questions

1. How can Mr. Rivera help Mrs. Bell better understand the difficulties struggling students are having learning fractions?
2. What cooperative learning model can Mrs. Bell and Ms. Chavez use to maximize Ms. Chavez's support of struggling students?
3. How can Mr. Rivera and Mrs. Bell team teach a lesson on fractions?

SUMMARY

Access to the general education curriculum is critical for each and every student. Designing and delivering differentiated instruction to meet the needs of all students, including those with unique learning needs, ensures that students can benefit from instruction and learn the curriculum. The ADAPT Framework is a tool that can help teachers differentiate instruction that is responsive to the individual needs of students. Special education teachers have a role in inclusive settings to ensure that students with disabilities are accessing the curriculum and that their IEP goals are being addressed and monitored. As teachers design, deliver, and evaluate instruction, they can identify effective practices from the adaptations categories (e.g., instructional activity, instructional content, instructional delivery, and instructional materials) to address specific student learning needs. We know that adaptations should be individualized to the learner, relevant to the curriculum, and effective to improve learning outcomes. We know a great deal about what constitutes effective instructional practices for students with unique learning needs or disabilities. These practices focus on designing and delivering instruction, teaching different types of knowledge, and employing questioning techniques. Grouping practices such as whole group and small group instruction are a critical component of effective instruction. Finally, cooperative learning structures offer opportunities for mixed ability grouping and students learning from their peers.

REVIEW THE LEARNING OBJECTIVES

Let's review the learning objectives for this chapter. If you are uncertain and cannot talk through the answers provided for any of these questions, reread those sections of the text.

7.1 Explain differentiated instruction.

Differentiated instruction is instruction that takes into consideration the diverse needs of every student. The term *differentiated instruction* involves a focus on curriculum, instruction, services, and instructional intensity. There are several ways to differentiate instruction. One way is to use flexible grouping practices where some students may need additional assistance in a skill (same ability) or groups are composed of different abilities (mixed ability) on a topic to complete an in-class activity. A second way is through the amount of time designated for small group or individualized instruction. A third way is through the use of specialized staff, such as special education teachers and language therapists who work in different settings. A fourth way is to change or modify the curriculum.

7.2 Describe the ADAPT Framework.

The ADAPT Framework consists of questions that relate to the ADAPT mnemonic:

- **A**sk, "What am I requiring the student to do?"
- **D**etermine the prerequisite skills of the task.
- **A**nalyze the student's strengths and struggles.
- **P**ropose and implement adaptations from among the four categories (e.g., instructional activity, instructional content, instructional delivery, and instructional materials).
- **T**est to determine whether the adaptations helped the student accomplish the task.

7.3 Identify effective instructional practices for designing and delivering instruction.

Effective instructional practices include designing for and delivering instruction. When designing instruction, teachers consider types of knowledge (e.g., discrimination, factual, rules, procedural, conceptual, or metacognitive), instructional techniques, and the critical thinking domains. When delivering instruction, teachers should include the following instructional steps: an advance organizer, presentation of subject matter, guided practice, independent practice, and closure. Teachers should also incorporate different types of questions and the questioning strategy.

7.4 Explain how instructional grouping practices can promote effective, differentiated instruction.

Grouping practices include whole group instruction, flexible small group, and one-to-one teaching. Other effective grouping practices include peer tutoring and cooperative learning. The whole group format works well where common instructional objectives are identified, the teacher delivers the lesson, and students respond orally or in writing. Flexible, small groups include same-ability groups and mixed-ability groups. Teachers use same-ability groups to provide extra instruction and support to those students who are most in need of additional assistance. Mixed-ability groups can be used for students to work on projects and to make presentations. One-to-one instruction enables teachers to tailor instruction to individual students and their specific learning and behavioral needs. In tutoring, pairs of students can work on assigned skills, usually for extra practice. Cooperative learning structures can be effective with mixed ability grouping where students learn from one another.

REVISIT THE OPENING CHALLENGE

Check your answers to the Reflection Questions from the Opening Challenge and revise them on the basis of what you have learned.

1. What ways can Mrs. Santiago and Ms. Benz differentiate instruction for all of their students who require academic assistance?
2. How can Mrs. Santiago and Ms. Benz differentiate instruction for their English learner students?
3. How can Mrs. Santiago and Ms. Benz use the ADAPT Framework to differentiate instruction for their students?
4. What effective instructional practices can Mrs. Santiago and Ms. Benz use to differentiate instruction for their students with disabilities to foster success with the curriculum?
5. What instructional grouping practices can help Mrs. Santiago and Ms. Benz provide effective, differentiated instruction for their students?

KEY TERMS

academic learning time
acronym
acrostic
active participation
ADAPT Framework
advance organizer
check for understanding
cognitive strategy instruction
concepts
convergent, lower-order questions
cooperative learning
core curriculum
cumulative practice
differentiated instruction
distributed practice
divergent, higher-order questions
engaged time
error-correction procedures
explicit instruction
guided practice
independent practice
instructional objective
level of concern
mixed-ability groups
on-task behavior
peer tutoring
same-ability groups
scaffolding
verbal rehearsal
wait time

PROFESSIONAL STANDARDS AND LICENSURE

For a complete description of Professional Standards and Licensure, please see the appendix.

CEC Initial Preparation Standards

Standard 1: Learner Development and Individual Learning Differences

Standard 2: Learning Environments

Standard 3: Curricular Content Knowledge

Standard 5: Instructional Planning and Strategies

Standard 6: Professional Learning and Ethical Practice

Standard 7: Collaboration

INTASC Core Principles

Standard 4: Content Knowledge

Standard 7: Planning for Instruction

Standard 8: Instructional Strategies

Praxis II: Education of Exceptional Students: Core Content Knowledge

II. Legal and Societal Issues: Historical Movements/Trends

III. Delivery of Services to Students with Disabilities: Background Knowledge

iStock.com/zoranm

8 PROMOTING ACCESS TO THE GENERAL EDUCATION CURRICULUM

LEARNING OBJECTIVES

After studying this chapter, you will be able to meet the following learning objectives:

8.1. Explain Universal Design for Learning.

8.2. Describe the guidelines that should be followed for textbooks and instructional materials to promote student access to the general education curriculum.

8.3. Explain assistive technology devices and services for promoting access to the general education curriculum.

Opening Challenge

Planning and Delivering Instruction

Elementary Grades. Mrs. Bell is an experienced and effective fifth-grade teacher with 26 students in a large, urban, public school district. In Mrs. Bell's school, 72% of the students qualify for free or reduced-cost lunch, and 12% are English learners (ELs). Mrs. Bell's inclusion classroom includes two students with reading, writing, and mathematics learning disabilities (LDs), who are performing about 2 years below grade level in each subject area. Her three EL students speak Spanish or Vietnamese and attended bilingual classes in the primary grades. The language support team in Mrs. Bell's school agreed that the three students were ready to move into English instruction classes; however, one student requires pull-out services from an EL specialist. Mrs. Bell also has her first student, Paul, who has cerebral palsy. Paul uses a wheelchair and has good communication skills but struggles with fine motor tasks such as writing with a pencil and using a keyboard. Mrs. Bell reflects about her class: *"I have a range of abilities and needs this year. In reviewing the fall academic assessment scores, I see that about one third of my class requires extra help with reading, writing, and mathematics. I also have to be sure that I am addressing the needs of my students who are ELs and students with LDs and cerebral palsy. Differentiating instruction is critical for the success of all my students."*

Secondary Grades. Ms. Mendez is a ninth-grade biology teacher at a high school in the same school district as Mrs. Bell, with similar demographics. Of her eight class periods, three are inclusion classes, with a larger proportion of students with disabilities, including some students with LDs and one student who was diagnosed with high-functioning autism spectrum disorder. The special education teacher now joins the weekly science teachers' meetings to identify how best to meet individual students' needs. As she prepares for an upcoming team meeting, Ms. Mendez reflects on her instructional practices: *"The range of reading, writing, and mathematics abilities is challenging, particularly when students read text in class and for homework. Judging from performance on science tests, some students have not mastered the mathematical concepts and skills required for science instruction, and the writing skills of some are also weak. When planning lessons, I know I should include practices that help all students access the curriculum but I am not sure where to begin. My training is in the sciences, not in basic academics, so I will have to rely on the special education teacher, Ms. Patterson, to support the inclusion students and me."*

Reflection Questions

In your journal, write down your answers to the following questions. After completing the chapter, check your answers and revise them on the basis of what you have learned.

1. How can Mrs. Bell and Ms. Mendez implement the principles of Universal Design for Learning into their instructional practices to promote access to the general education curriculum?
2. How can Universal Design for Learning principles benefit students who are English learners?
3. How can Mrs. Bell and Ms. Mendez ensure that the textbooks and instructional materials they use are appropriate for all of their students to access the general education curriculum?
4. How can assistive technology help Mrs. Bell's students with disabilities access the general education curriculum?

A variety of practices was used in inclusive schools to ensure that all students have opportunities to learn in a supportive school environment and to have access to the general education curriculum. Having **access to the general education curriculum** means being able to (a) learn the knowledge and skills we expect all students to learn; (b) benefit from evidence-based instruction that is designed, delivered, and evaluated for effectiveness; and (c) use materials, facilities, and labs that facilitate learning.

For many at-risk students and students with disabilities, learning the critical academic knowledge and skills is challenging because of learning difficulties such as sensory, memory, communication, motor, behavioral, and cognitive problems. Therefore, educators must identify practices that help students with difficulties to access the general education curriculum so that they can have opportunities to learn much like their peers. In this chapter, we address accessing the curriculum through the use of Universal Design for Learning principles, an examination of curricular materials with struggling students in mind, and assistive technology (AT).

UNIVERSAL DESIGN FOR LEARNING

Universal Design for Learning (UDL) is a technique for providing instruction for all students, including learners with disabilities. UDL is a framework that provides ways to minimize barriers to learning and promote accessibility to curricula and **pedagogy**, or teaching practices, for all learners, including students with and without disabilities as well as ELs (CAST, 2011). The goal is to promote students' ability to master the curricula within a flexible environment that features ways content can be explained to account for individual differences (CAST, 2011). According to the Higher Education Opportunity Act of 2008, UDL

(a) provides flexibility in the ways information is presented, in the ways students respond or demonstrate knowledge and skills, and in the ways students are engaged; and

(b) reduces barriers in instruction, provides appropriate accommodations, supports, and challenges, and maintains high achievement expectations for all students, including students with disabilities and students who are limited English proficient.

Table 8.1 shows the guidelines essential to UDL (see CAST, n.d. for additional information). We will refer to UDL throughout this chapter section.

Universally designed curricula and pedagogy consists of three principles (Rose et al., 2006). The first principle is **multiple means of representation**, in which information is presented in various formats to reduce sensory and cognitive barriers. For example, text can be accompanied by audio for students who are blind, and graphics can enhance the content for students who are deaf or who have LDs. Closed captions on video are another option.

The second principle, **multiple means of action and expression**, refers to the ability of students to respond in different ways. For example, voice recognition software, scanning devices, and switches help

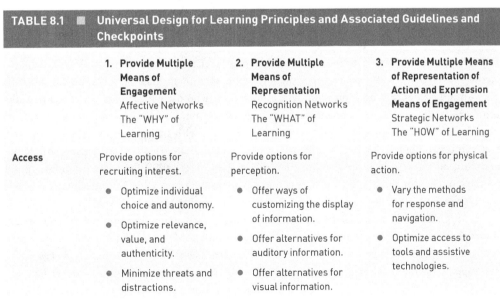

TABLE 8.1 ■ Universal Design for Learning Principles and Associated Guidelines and Checkpoints

	1. Provide Multiple Means of Engagement Affective Networks The "WHY" of Learning	**2. Provide Multiple Means of Representation** Recognition Networks The "WHAT" of Learning	**3. Provide Multiple Means of Representation of Action and Expression Means of Engagement** Strategic Networks The "HOW" of Learning
Access	Provide options for recruiting interest. ● Optimize individual choice and autonomy. ● Optimize relevance, value, and authenticity. ● Minimize threats and distractions.	Provide options for perception. ● Offer ways of customizing the display of information. ● Offer alternatives for auditory information. ● Offer alternatives for visual information.	Provide options for physical action. ● Vary the methods for response and navigation. ● Optimize access to tools and assistive technologies.

(Continued)

TABLE 8.1 ■ Universal Design for Learning Principles and Associated Guidelines and Checkpoints (*Continued*)

Build	Provide options for sustaining effort and persistence. • Heighten salience of goals and objectives. • Vary demands and resources to optimize challenge. • Foster collaboration and community. • Increase mastery-oriented feedback.	Provide options for language and symbols. • Clarify vocabulary and symbols. • Clarify syntax and structure. • Support decoding of text, mathematical notation, and symbols. • Promote understanding across languages. • Illustrate through multiple media.	Provide options for expression and communication. • Use multiple media for communication. • Use multiple tools for construction and composition. • Build fluencies with graduated levels of support for practice and performance.
Internalize	Provide options for self-regulation. • Promote expectations and beliefs that optimize motivation. • Facilitate personal coping skills and strategies. • Develop self-assessment and reflection.	Provide options for comprehension. • Activate or supply background knowledge. • Highlight patterns, critical features, big ideas, and relationships. • Guide information processing and visualization. • Maximize transfer and generalization.	Provide options for executive functions. • Guide appropriate goal-setting. • Support planning and strategy development. • Facilitate managing information and resources. • Enhance capacity for monitoring progress.
Goal Expert learners who are...:	Purposeful and motivated	Resourceful and knowledgeable	Strategic and Goal-Directed

Source: © CAST (2018). Universal design for learning guidelines version 2.2 (graphic organizer), Wakefield, MA: Author.

principle, **multiple means of engagement**, consists of actively engaging students in activities and making available more than just a single mode of representation and expression to address their needs and interests. Using the computer is an example of providing different ways to engage students in the learning process.

UDL stems from the concept of **universal design**, which began in the field of architecture (King-Sears, 2009). Let's examine universal design as it relates to the Americans With Disabilities Act of 1990 (ADA). ADA requires that the physical environment must be accessible for individuals with disabilities. For example, curb cuts allow people who use wheelchairs to access sidewalks, cross streets, and move independently as they shop or go from a parking lot to a restaurant. Curb cuts also help cyclists, people pushing strollers, and people with shopping carts as they walk from stores into parking lots. By removing barriers, people with disabilities can participate in daily life, and curb cuts also help people without disabilities (see Mace, 1998 for an inspirational speech by the late Dr. Ronald L. Mace, who was one of the people responsible for introducing the term *universal design*).

UDL guidelines are also beneficial when teaching students from culturally and linguistically diverse backgrounds. For example, for the "Provide Multiple Means of Representation" principle, teachers can adjust their English vocabulary to the student's level of understanding (*Checkpoint 2.1*) and support instructional language by repeating, rephrasing, and extending the student's language (*Checkpoint 2.4*). Teachers can use nonverbal **cues** such as gestures, pictures, objects, and other instructional materials to facilitate comprehension (*Checkpoint 2.5*). Teachers can preview new content by teaching key vocabulary, asking questions to stimulate thinking about the new content, and making linkages among students' experiences (*Checkpoint 3.1*).

Universal Design for Learning and Its Applications

Each UDL principle consists of three guidelines and several checkpoints. For example, refer to Table 8.1, the principle "Provide Multiple Means of Representation" that consists of "Provide options for perceptions," a guideline, and "Offer ways of customizing the display of information," a checkpoint for that guideline and principle.

The principles of UDL are featured within the UDL guidelines (CAST, 2011). Applying the principles of UDL to curricula and pedagogy provides opportunities for teachers to adapt goals, strategies, materials, and tests, which will allow for access to all students and to remove or minimize barriers to students' learning. The intent is to make the curriculum and instruction flexible enough to address the diverse learning needs pervasive in general education classrooms (CAST, 2011; Rao et al., 2014).

UDL is endorsed in education and included in the Individuals with Disabilities Education Act 2004 (IDEA)as a way to foster access to the curriculum and instruction for all learners. But it's important to understand the evidence that supports these practices (Edyburn, 2010). Fortunately, findings from research studies on the effects of using the principles of UDL on student performance are promising (Hall et al., 2015; Kennedy et al., 2014; King-Sears et al., 2014). In fact, in their review of the research on UDL, Ok, Rao, Bryant, and McDougal (2017) indicated, "Findings of our review suggest that UDL-based practices hold promise for diverse students in grades PreK–12. UDL-based instructional practices provide flexibility and scaffolds that promote access to the general education curriculum and support achievement on academic outcomes" (p. 136).

Now that you have read about UDL, return to Chapter 7 and the Considering Diversity feature. Recall that the feature dealt with strategies for differentiated instruction for ELs. Consider how Mrs. Bell can use the strategies with the ELs in her classroom, particularly relating to the UDL guidelines and principles discussed in this chapter. Also, read the Working Together feature below to identify how Mrs. Bell collaborated with the EL specialist to help her better meet the needs of the EL students in her classroom. How might this information be useful to you as you work to meet the needs of any EL students you teach?

GUIDELINES FOR TEXTBOOKS AND INSTRUCTIONAL MATERIALS TO USE WITH STUDENTS WHO HAVE UNIQUE LEARNING NEEDS

Textbooks

Textbooks are a primary source for subject-area content. Textbooks are used to teach science, social studies, and other content. Textbooks are a good source of instructional content, but they often present challenges for students who have disabilities:

- The reading level of the textbook probably is more advanced than the ability of the student who has reading difficulties or disabilities. For students to benefit from reading a textbook, the material should be at their **instructional reading level**, the level at which they can read at least 90% of the words on the page and comprehend the same amount of content.
- The organization or structure of the text content can be hard for students with reading problems to follow. The text might lack, or the student might not be familiar with, key words that signal different types of text organization (e.g., cause/effect, compare/contrast). Recognizing how text content is organized helps readers comprehend the material. In addition, many of the words in content area textbooks have more than one meaning. For example, the word *current* can have one meaning in a history text (e.g., current events) and another in a geography text (e.g., the river's current; see Chapter 14 for more information).

- Textbooks usually do not include enough **direct instruction** or explicit instruction to help struggling students learn content. For example, there might not be sufficient practice opportunities or examples.

In Chapter 11, we provide additional information about textbooks for students with reading difficulties. In Chapter 14, we offer suggestions for selecting and using content-area textbooks with struggling readers, especially at the secondary level.

Instructional Materials

Guidelines for selecting and using instructional materials should be responsive to (a) the student with the disability and (b) the content and methodology.

Student Considerations

- What are the student's present levels of academic achievement and functional performance?
- Concerning students' IEPs, are the instructional materials appropriate for meeting those goals?
- Does the student seem to be motivated to accomplish tasks? If so, under what conditions?
- Does the student remain focused and persist with tasks? When does the student appear to lose focus and persistence?
- Are the students' prerequisite skills sufficient for using the instructional materials? For example, if a mathematics lesson involves the use of manipulatives, are they appropriate for the student who has cerebral palsy and associated fine motor problems?
- Can the student benefit from the teacher using audiovisual materials to support teacher lectures?

Teachers can consult the IEP to identify a student's current levels of functioning as teachers make decisions about whether or how to adapt instructional materials. Finally, it's important to determine a student's interest in content and materials and identify where in the learning process the student stops

iStock.com/SolStock

trying or struggles. Motivation is a key component of successful learning, and knowing students' level of endurance helps teachers understand learners' needs more fully.

Instructional Content and Methodology Considerations

- Is the content age appropriate?
- Does the content address state standards and the core curriculum?
- Does the instructional material specify a sequence of skills?
- Is information about teaching strategies included?
- Are there sufficient opportunities to practice new skills?
- Are generalization and maintenance activities included?
- Are there supplemental activities to keep more advanced students interested and motivated?

Age appropriateness of instructional materials should be taken into consideration as part of the selection process. For example, high-interest or controlled vocabulary materials can be used with older students who have limited reading abilities. These materials focus on topics that appeal to older students, such as current events, sports, and entertainment personalities, yet are written with grade-specific vocabulary to take into account limited word recognition and reading abilities. Equally important is the relationship between the materials and the curricular expectations from the school district and state. Teachers are held highly accountable through high-stakes state assessments to teach the content on which students will be assessed, so materials selected for instruction must reflect this content.

Teachers can use a sequence for teaching skills and then be sure the instructional materials match this sequence. For example, when math instruction focuses on addition facts (e.g., 6 + 9, 7 + 3), then the instructional material should include problems that align with this skill. Subtraction math facts should not be included. However, the next skill in the sequence could include subtraction math facts and materials that focus on these types of problems.

Instructional materials might include review activities (for maintenance), teaching strategies, practice opportunities, and enrichment activities (for generalization purposes). Teachers must carefully examine the materials to figure out how the instructional material can best be used in a lesson and what adaptations might be needed.

Often, teachers have to adapt instructional materials to meet an individual learner's needs. Extension exercises or alternative methodologies might be offered as part of the instructional materials. Other adaptations might include providing more practice opportunities, using only portions of the material, rewording multistep directions, and breaking instructional components down into smaller activities. Also, scaffolds provide instructional opportunities for students who struggle with the lesson as written. Although some instructional materials might offer a list of potential scaffolds, teachers are responsible for determining when scaffolds are needed and which scaffolds are appropriate given the content being taught.

Adaptations for Curricular Materials

Textbooks and instructional materials are important components of instruction and must be selected wisely. Textbooks sometimes are assigned to teachers, but those teachers must still analyze them critically to see what difficulties students might encounter when accessing the material. Instructional materials are used when concepts are first presented, during guided practice, and as part of independent practice activities. For example, students can use math manipulatives as part of place value instruction, complete **graphic organizers** during independent seatwork, or use a scale as part of a cooperative learning activity on measurement. These materials must also be chosen carefully to augment instruction. Table 8.2 provides examples of ways to adapt instructional materials.

TABLE 8.2 ■ Examples of Adaptations for Instructional Materials

Task/Instructional Materials	Student Struggles or Challenges	Material Adaptation
Reading directions or instructions/ workbooks, worksheets	Reading or understanding written directions or instructions	Have students underline important words (circle, underline, draw). Rewrite directions or instructions using easier words. Explain the directions or instructions to the student. Say, "Tell me what you need to do first." "What do you need to do next?" Reduce the number of directions or instructions.
Reading books, word lists, textbooks, literature	Reading words	Record for the student to listen to the reading or use audio books (electronic books). Use high-interest and low- vocabulary materials.
Comprehending text	Comprehending material	Provide graphic organizers (see Chapters 11 and 14). Provide questions for students to answer after they read a few paragraphs.
Completing worksheets	Completing items of worksheets	Reduce the number of items. Reformat using borders to separate important information. Use color to highlight important information.
Reading text or worksheets	Seeing the material	Enlarge font size. Use a font that has simple lettering. Provide a magnifier. Use screen magnification software. Use color. Contrast the foreground with the background.
Computing mathematical problems using workbooks or worksheets	Identifying symbols (=, +, ×)	Have students circle the symbol and state its meaning. Have students highlight the symbol with color before proceeding. Provide a cue sheet with the symbols and their meaning. Enlarge the font size of symbols to make them more readily visible.

WORKING TOGETHER

Although Mrs. Bell is an experienced teacher, she has found it helpful to collaborate with the EL specialist who works with one of Mrs. Bell's EL students in a pull-out program. When they first met, Mrs. Bell shared that she knew little about working with students who were not English proficient, and she was concerned that, as she was having more and more EL students in her classroom, her teaching would be insufficient for those students.

In their first meeting, the EL specialist, Mr. Garcia, shared with Mrs. Bell some information from an Education Northwest document by Deussen and colleagues (2008) titled "What Teachers Should Know About Instruction for English Language Learners" (i.e., English learners). The document lists important considerations for all teachers, and also for those who teach language arts, mathematics, social studies, and science. Because Mrs. Bell teaches all of these subjects in her fifth-grade classroom, she listened as Mr. Garcia read from the document.

What All Teachers Should Know

Principle 1: ELLs move through different stages as they acquire English proficiency and, at all stages, need comprehensible input.

Principle 2: There is a difference between conversational and academic language; fluency in everyday conversation is not sufficient to ensure access to academic texts and tasks.

Principle 3: ELLs need instruction that will allow them to meet state content standards.

Principle 4: ELLs have background knowledge and home cultures that sometimes differ from the U.S. mainstream.

Principle 5: Assessments measure language proficiency as well as actual content knowledge.

What Language Arts Teachers Should Know

Principle 6: The same basic approach to learning to read and write applies to ELLs and non-ELLs, but ELLs need additional instructional supports.

Principle 7: Many literacy skills transfer across languages.

What Mathematics Teachers Should Know

Principle 8: Mathematics has its own language and representational system, and ELLs struggle to understand math concepts in this language.

Principle 9: Mathematic word problems are particularly challenging for ELLs.

What Social Studies Teachers Should Know

Principle 10: The density and complexity of social science textbooks and other texts can be particularly challenging for ELLs.

Principle 11: Some ELLs bring background knowledge that differs from what is assumed in textbooks.

Principle 12: Social studies courses require sophisticated and subject-specific uses of language.

What Science Teachers Should Know

Principle 13: Science inquiry poses particular linguistic challenges for ELLs.

Principle 14: The norms and practices of science may or may not align with the cultural norms of ELLs.

After going over the principles together, Mrs. Bell and Mr. Garcia decided to meet every two weeks to further discuss the information in the document and to brainstorm how Mrs. Bell could use the knowledge to enhance her teaching. Before their second meeting, Mrs. Bell read the entire document, which further explained the principles and provided a springboard for later discussions.

From Education Northwest's (2008), What Teachers Should Know About Instruction for English Language Learners. Used with permission.

ASSISTIVE TECHNOLOGY DEVICES AND SERVICES FOR PROMOTING ACCESS TO THE GENERAL EDUCATION CURRICULUM

In 1991, a training session conducted by International Business Machines, better known as IBM, included the following classic quote: "For people without disabilities, technology makes things easier. For people with disabilities, technology makes things possible" (p. 2). This quote remains relevant in today's classrooms and other environments.

AT helps students gain access to the curriculum in general education settings and environments in and out of school. By focusing on a student's functional capabilities, AT fosters independence for students with disabilities. Independence is evident in helping them to communicate and socialize with their peers; participate across settings such as the playground, classroom, cafeteria, and library; and demonstrate their learning of the curriculum. **Functional capabilities** refer to those capabilities—such as vision, hearing, communication, mobility, cognition, and motor control—that individuals use to compensate for struggles that are disability-related. For example, an individual who has good hearing but is blind might want to read a chapter in a textbook. Listening to the chapter in an electronic book format provides access to that material. When selecting AT devices, it is essential to focus on strengths when deciding on devices that can help individuals access their environments.

iStock.com/zeljkosantrac

Assistive Technology Devices

IDEA 2004 defines an AT device as "Any item, piece of equipment or product system, whether acquired commercially off the shelf, modified, or customized, that is used to increase, maintain, or improve the functional capabilities of children with disabilities" (20 U.S.C. 1401[1]). Let's take a look at the definition's first component, which includes the unit itself and can be an item (e.g., a Hoover cane to help a person who is blind with mobility), a piece of equipment (e.g., a motorized wheelchair to help an individual with physical disabilities move about), or a product system (e.g., a computer with speech output software that reads the text on the screen). The intent is to foster access and independence for individuals with disabilities by increasing their functioning. Therefore, an AT device is anything bought or made that helps a person who has a disability accomplish tasks that would otherwise be difficult or impossible to perform (Bryant & Bryant, 2011).

AT devices can be viewed along a continuum from low-tech to high-tech devices. High-tech devices are usually electronic such as computers. Computers with their various capabilities, talking calculators, electronic books, screen reader and voice recognition software, and powered wheelchairs fall in the high-tech end of the continuum. Pencil grips, different types of fonts and sizes for text, a grab bar in the shower, and a magnifier are at the low-tech end. For example, for a student who has a mathematics LD, a calculator may be identified in the IEP as an AT device to help the student solve basic facts for word problems. A calculator provides a perfect example: For individuals who do not have a mathematics LD and who use calculators to help balance their checkbook, the calculator would be a helpful device; for individuals with a mathematics LD who need the calculator to balance their checkbook, the calculator is an AT device.

Assistive Technology Services

An assistive technology service was defined by the Assistive Technology Act of 2004 (ATA, or Tech Act) as, "Any service that directly assists a child with a disability in the selection, acquisition, and use of an assistive technology device." The term includes

(A) the evaluation of the needs of a child with a disability, including a functional evaluation of the child in the child's customary environment;

(B) purchasing, leasing, or otherwise providing for the acquisition of assistive technology devices by such child;

(C) selecting, designing, fitting, customizing, adapting, applying, maintaining, repairing, or replacing assistive technology devices;

(D) coordinating and using other therapies, interventions, or services with assistive technology devices, such as those associated with existing education and rehabilitation plans and programs;

(E) training or technical assistance for such child, or, where appropriate, the family of such child; and

(F) training or technical assistance for professionals (including individuals providing education and rehabilitation services), employers, or other individuals who provide services to, employ, or are otherwise substantially involved in the major life functions of such child. (20 U.S.C. 1401[2])

How are the terms *assistive technology device* and *assistive technology service* related? The answer is simply that they go together. A device of some sort (e.g., a wheelchair, a computer, Braille text, or an FM listening system) may be necessary for a person with a disability to meet challenges related to impaired mobility, cognitive function, or sensory function. But the services associated with such AT devices must also be available. How will the device be purchased? Who will assess whether the device and the person are a good match? Who will train the student to utilize the device properly? How will teachers, other professionals, family members, and others with whom the AT user interacts learn how to provide personal and educational supports, in and out of the classroom? And how will these people and their services be coordinated? These questions must be answered for devices and services to be effective. In too many classrooms, AT devices sit on shelves because the teacher or student (or both) don't understand how to use them. For more information about AT devices and services to support students' unique learning needs, refer to http://www.closingthegap.com.

Importance of Assistive Technology

Tech Notes, below, details information about Dragon Anywhere and Dragon Professional Individual, which is voice recognition software that Mrs. Bell can use to help Paul write in his electronic reading journal.

AT devices can be grouped into categories that share their purpose and function. These categories include seating and positioning, mobility, communication, adaptive toys and games, adaptive environments, computer use, and instructional aids (Bryant & Bryant, 2011).

Seating and positioning devices promote the best posture and seating arrangement. For instance, students might move from one location to another using a wheelchair, sit during conversation and instruction, and have help while eating. Key professionals who work with seating and positioning issues are called physical and occupational therapists.

Mobility refers to the act of movement. Mobility devices include scooter boards, vehicular modifications, wheelchairs, and white canes. Mobility issues can be discussed with rehabilitation engineers, physical and occupational therapists, and orientation and mobility specialists. Communication devices help people make up for expressive language (speaking) problems by focusing on their abilities to understand language and to express their thoughts, ideas, and needs. This category consists of augmentative and alternative communication (AAC) devices. AAC devices can support vocalizations when speech is not understood by a communication partner and can provide a way for an individual to speak. Aided AAC systems could be electronic (e.g., a speech generation device) or nonelectronic (e.g., a communication book or eye gaze communication board). Unaided AAC systems range from body language and facial expressions to American Sign Language and Signed Exact English. The speech/language pathologist or a specialist who work with individuals who are d/Deaf or hard of hearing are key members of the IEP team when AAC system decisions are to be made.

TECH NOTES

DRAGON ANYWHERE AND DRAGON PROFESSIONAL INDIVIDUAL

Dragon Anywhere, from Nuance Communications, is a voice input and voice output application that is available for the iPhone or iPad. Individuals with upper extremity or vision disabilities, LDs, or spinal cord injury are the target groups for this product. According to its app page on the App Store, Dragon Anywhere is "professional-grade mobile dictation. Easily dictate documents of any length, edit, format, and share them directly from your iPhone or iPad—whether visiting clients, a job site, or your local coffee shop." Again, from the Dragon Anywhere App Store page, new features (at the time of this writing) include

- New correction menu similar to Dragon desktop solutions.
- Train Words feature teaches Dragon exactly how you pronounce words and eliminates spelling errors.
- General usability improvements and performance enhancements.

Dragon Professional Individual, also from Nuance (https://www.nuance.com/dragon.html), is the desktop version and is available for Mac and PC. Dragon has a hands-free procedure, so individuals can speak freely and control applications with voice commands to move the cursor or click on the screen. The software was designed to help with writing, editing, and proofreading tasks. The software includes recognition training so that it can learn how the user speaks. Also, the software comes with a USB headset microphone and Bluetooth wireless capabilities.

Adaptive toys and games can be considered recreational. They provide children with disabilities an opportunity to play with toys and games to help them develop cognitive skills and to socialize with their peers. The toys and games might include devices with a sound so children who are blind can discern among them. Game board markers might have large tops so children with motor problems can grasp and hold them. Electronic toys can be modified so that children with fine motor problems, such as having trouble with an on–off toggle switch, can activate the toy by using a button switch. Early childhood professionals work with assistive technologists and occupational therapists to design attributes that help all students to interact with toys and games.

Adaptive environments (control of the environment) are devices and ways that help a person to control the environment for daily living, working, schooling, playing, and so forth. For example, remote control units are useful for turning lights on and off, responding to the doorbell, opening doors, or turning a computer on and off in the home, school, or workplace. In the classroom, widening aisles can promote mobility for a student who uses a wheelchair. Other adaptive environment devices include curb cuts; Braille words for restrooms, elevators, and hotel room numbers; grab bars in showers; and automatic door openers.

Computer access devices include keyboard overlays (templates that lie on the keyboard to define the key space for responding), pointers, and screen reader and voice recognition software. For example, by using voice recognition software, a student whose upper body control is limited but whose speech is a strength can speak into a microphone and tell the computer what functions to employ. For people who are blind and whose hearing is a struggle, alternative output devices for computer use, such as screen reader software, are necessary. Screen reader software reads the text displayed on the computer screen. Educators, occupational therapists, and rehabilitation specialists typically assist with computer access.

Finally, instructional aids provide access to the curriculum, instruction, and instructional materials. Access to information can come via a screen reader program that allows access to the Internet for research for a student who is blind, and remediation can come from math or reading instructional software. Instructional software can provide students with additional opportunities to practice on academic and problem-solving skills as they continue to receive instruction from the classroom teacher.

Figure 8.1 provides guidelines for evaluating and selecting instructional apps and software.

Examples of Smart Phones and Apps for People With Disability

Sesame Phone smart phone: Operating the smartphone using only one's head

Sesame Phone is a touch-free mobile phone based on the Google Nexus 5, which already includes accessibility features. People with mobility disabilities could use and benefit from this smart phone to access apps.

Text-To-Speech apps: Including apps that read aloud whatever is inputted

Individuals with reading disabilities or who have visual impairments could benefit from these types of apps.

iPad apps: Using a variety of apps to aid in everyday living skills and classroom learning

Given the increased popularity of iPads in classrooms, identifying various apps should be incorporated into instructional planning for students with disabilities.

Rosenberg (2017) has a list of apps for students with various types of disabilities.

Classroom teachers can work with assistive technologists and special education teachers to decide which instructional aids, apps, and smart phones are most suitable to help students with disabilities access the curriculum (Bryant & Bryant, 2011). Table 8.3 provides examples of AT devices students with disabilities can use, in accordance with their IEPs, to access and benefit from instruction and function successfully in various environments.

AT devices will be necessary to help Paul access instruction; Paul is Mrs. Bell's student who has cerebral palsy. She decides to use the ADAPT Framework (see Chapter 7) to make adjustments to a reading comprehension activity, which involves writing, for Paul.

According to IDEA (2004), several AT services can be used to ensure that devices are accurately identified and used. For example, the selection of appropriate AT devices based on an evaluation of individuals in their natural environments is an important service. Assistive technologists, diagnosticians, audiologists, occupational therapists, speech/language pathologists, and special and general education classroom teachers can participate as members of the AT evaluation team, depending on the student's needs. Each professional contributes information about how the student is performing in relation to academics, communication, motor development, vision, or hearing. One evaluation example is the *Functional Evaluation for Assistive Technology* (Raskind & Bryant, 2002), which enables professionals to rate the performance of a student on listening, speaking, academics, memory, organization, motor tasks, and behavior. Professionals such as occupational therapists, speech/language therapists, and audiologists have their own criteria for evaluating student performance.

FIGURE 8.1 ■ Guidelines for Software and Apps Evaluation and Selection

A. Basic Information

Name of software or app ______________________________

Publisher ______________________________ Cost ______________

Hardware/mobile device requirements ______________________________

B. Description

Grade level(s) ______________ Reading level of text (if applicable) ______________

Instructional area(s) ______________________________

Purpose ______________________________

Type: _____ Tutorial _____ Drill and practice _____ Simulation _____ Game

Instructional Objectives _____ yes _____ no

List objectives if stated ______________________________

How is information presented? (check all that apply) _____ Speech _____ Music

_____ Graphics (pictures) _____ Text (words) _____ Animation

How do the visuals look? (check all that apply) _____ Screen is too busy

_____ Graphics enhance, rather than distract from, purpose _____ Print is legible

_____ Print size age-appropriate

What is the quality of the sound? (check all that apply)

_______ Sound is clear/audible _______ Speech is audible _______ Sound is distracting

_______ Rate of speech is appropriate

C. Instructional Design

Directions are clear, easy to read, and short _____ yes _____ no

Examples or models are provided _____ yes _____ no

Pacing is appropriate _____ yes _____ no

Practice opportunities are provided _____ yes _____ no

Error correction is provided _____ yes _____ no

Difficulty level can be individualized_____yes_____no

Reinforcement (visual and/or auditory) is present _____ yes _____ no

A recordkeeping/evaluation option is available _____ yes _____ no

D. Content

Appropriate to stated objectives _____ yes _____ no

Factual and accurate _____ yes _____ no

Free of gender, cultural, or racial bias _____ yes _____ no

Relates to school's curriculum _____ yes _____ no

Relates to student's IEP _____ yes _____ no

E. Technical Considerations

User Demands (respond to any that apply) Academic ______________________

Physical/motor ______________________

Computer or mobile device knowledge ______________________

Technical vocabulary ______________________

Functions (check all that apply) _____ Save work in progress _____ Print in progress _____ Alter sound _______ Return to main menu at any point in program _____ Change pace

Teacher Demands (respond to any that apply)

Amount of instruction to students for using software ______________________

Installation procedures ______________________

Level of student monitoring ______________________

Preparation needed before using software ______________________

Source: Adapted from Ok et al. (2016).

TABLE 8.3 ■ Examples of Assistive Technology Devices

Use of Device	Assistive Technology Device
For Students to Access Reading	
To enlarge text, screen magnifier software, screen magnifier	Large-print books, larger font size, hand-held magnifier, closed-circuit television
To enhance text and graphics	Eyeglasses, color contrast, pictures, Braille text
To convert text to speech	Screen reader software, talking dictionaries, electronic books
For Students to Access Writing	
To increase use of writing tools	Pencil grips, writing paper with colored lines, writing templates
To enhance writing productivity	Electronic/talking spell checker/dictionary, voice recognition software, talking word processor software (e.g., WriteOutloud, CoWriter), voice dictation input
To use alternative writing tools	Computer, keyboard enhancements (keyguard, repeat rate adjustments [e.g., stickie keys that remain depressed for longer time]), electronic notetakers (with Braille), pointing device to access keyboard, alternative keyboards (e.g., Intellitools, on-screen keyboard), switches and scanning devices
For Students to Access Mathematics	
To support calculation	Calculator with print output, talking calculator, calculator with large keypad, on-screen calculator, graph paper for problems with writing and aligning
To support measurement	Measuring devices with tactile output, measuring devices with speech output, talking thermometers
To support time telling	Talking watches, watches with large faces, watches with tactile output
For Students to Access Study Skills	
To help with time management	Talking watches, calendars as planners with pictures if necessary, speech output devices to remind about dates
To support memory and organization	Hand-held recorders (e.g., mobile devices) to input important times, dates, and things to do; visual organizers (e.g., color-coded folders)

(Continued)

TABLE 8.3 ■ Examples of Assistive Technology Devices (*Continued*)

Use of Device	Assistive Technology Device
For Students to Be Able to Listen/Communicate	
To listen in class	Hearing aids, AT systems (e.g., FM)
To communicate	Communication boards (electronic and nonelectronic), speech amplifier, TTY/TTD (teletype devices), mobile devices (e.g., smartphones, tablets)
To listen to multimedia	Closed captions on videotapes and TV, computer-generated speech output
To promote safety	Signaling systems (telephone ring signal, door knock signal, smoke alarm with strobe light)
For Students Who Require Mobility Support	
To enhance orientation and mobility	Eyeglasses, grab bars, white cane, tactile signage, power or manual wheelchairs, motorized scooter

Source: Adapted from Technology and Media (n.d.).

For example, when AT is being considered during an IEP meeting for a student with a reading disability, the AT specialist works with classroom teachers to determine reading strengths and areas of difficulty. The specialist might ask classroom teachers specific questions about reading requirements in the classroom and about the student's performance on these tasks. The AT specialist seeks the opinions of a speech/language pathologist if language problems are also observed. Together, professionals can make decisions about devices that can help the student with reading tasks. The evaluation process is ongoing; changes could occur in a student's environment or setting, strengths and struggles, and maturity (Bryant & Bryant, 2011; Raskind & Bryant, 2002).

ADAPT IN ACTION

READING, WRITING, AND ASSISTIVE TECHNOLOGY

Mrs. Bell has students read sections from a chapter and answer comprehension questions in their reading journal for part of the class period. She then has students share their responses to the questions to check their understanding and to promote class discussion. Paul has good reading and comprehension abilities and can readily participate in discussions. Paul is adept at using a computer to do his work and is familiar with its word processing and spell-check features. He has an electronic reading journal to ease difficulties associated with holding a pencil and writing. A laptop computer has been customized to fit on the tray of his motorized wheelchair. The computer keyboard has been equipped with a keyguard, which is an overlap placed on top of the keys to minimize him accidentally hitting the wrong keys as he types. However, Mrs. Bell notices that Paul seems to tire when working on his reading journal and falls behind the other students in answering all of the questions. She decides to consult the assistive technologist, Ms. Parette, to identify further AT adaptations to address Paul's needs.

A: Ask, "What am I requiring the student to do?" "I want my students to be able to read text and answer comprehension questions and share their answers."

D: Determine the prerequisite skills of the task. "I want my students to answer comprehension questions in their journal about a section of the chapter from a social studies textbook. They need to be able to discuss their answers with the whole class."

A: Analyze the student's strengths and struggles. Paul's reading comprehension skills are good and he is able to engage in discussions about the material. However, he has motor problems that make turning pages in a textbook and writing difficult. Although he is using a computer for writing, he seems to have problems when doing multiple typing assignments and turning pages in his textbook. He is not keeping up with his peers.

P: Propose and implement adaptations from among the four categories. After conducting several observations of Paul engaging in the reading and writing tasks, Ms. Parette recommends an electronic page turner and Dragon Dictate voice recognition software for writing assignments, and she will teach Paul and Mrs. Bell how to use them.

T: Test to determine whether the adaptations helped the student accomplish the task. Mrs. Bell will monitor whether Paul is completing all of the reading comprehension questions in his electronic journal and how well the page turner seems to be helping him read his section of the textbook. Ms. Parette will conduct observations as well and compare notes with Mrs. Bell.

Training is another example of an AT service (Rieth et al., 2004). Training on AT devices is imperative for students or users of the devices, their families, and professionals such as classroom teachers, speech/language pathologists, and occupational therapists. Professionals must be trained on how devices work, how to integrate them into instruction when working with students, how to troubleshoot if a device fails and how to assess students to make an appropriate match between device and needs. Training should be an ongoing priority to ensure that both users and professionals remain informed. Training is part of teacher preparation programs and a part of ongoing in-service training (Rieth et al., 2004). Paraprofessionals too must become qualified in the use of AT devices to work effectively with their students who depend on them. Once training is completed and the device is used, follow-up examinations should be conducted to ensure that the device is producing the expected outcome.

Finally, because devices can often go home with students, family members must know how to use them accurately. If electronic devices prove overwhelming, more training may be needed for successful implementation (Lemons, 2000).

It is crucial to include families in selecting AT devices and to listen to their viewpoints (Bryant & Bryant, 1998). Team members must consider family viewpoints about disability and how services that are intended to be helpful may be interpreted. The family's experience and comfort level with technology are very important, especially if they are helping their child use the technology at home. Finally, family members should know what outcomes educators wish to achieve by having the student use a particular AT device. These outcomes should show the family's interest and values in fostering their child's independence.

Assistive Technology Integration

As teachers create instruction, they should think about the curriculum and learning objectives students will be taught. Teachers should also consider the way instruction will be delivered (using grouping, modeling, guided practice). They must also consider the strengths and needs of their students with IEPs and how AT devices can foster their active participation in lessons (Bryant & Bryant, 2011; Rieth et al., 2004). Finally, teachers should consider the environmental requirements for the devices, such as whether the devices produce distracting sounds or require electricity. Students can use headphones with devices such as talking calculators, speech output, and tape recorders. It is important to know that the location of electrical outlets will dictate where devices, which require electricity, can be set up. Other devices may require batteries, which are often preferable when mobile environments are part of the setting.

During instruction, teachers should monitor how easy it is for the student to use the device and whether further training is necessary. Teachers should monitor their students' ability to keep pace with their peers in completing the tasks. Practice with the nuances of the device may be necessary so students can accomplish the maximum benefits from using it.

Finally, teachers should take into consideration the fatigue factor when using the device. Some devices, such as keyboarding with computers, may be tiring and interfere with productivity. Evaluating the effectiveness of integrating AT requires the input of professionals, family members, and students. We now consider using the principles, guidelines, and checkpoints of UDL in a lesson as another example of how teachers can make the curriculum accessible for all learners in an RTI model.

UNIVERSAL DESIGN FOR LEARNING IN ACTION

UNIVERSAL DESIGN FOR LEARNING LESSON

Note: This UDL-based lesson was developed, in part, using an adapted version of the CAST UDL Lesson Builder (http://udlexchange.cast.org/home).

Title: World War I

Subject: Social Studies: American History

Unit Description: This lesson is part of a group of lessons that focus on World War I.

Unit Goals: The purpose of this unit is to understand the sociopolitical issues and causes of World War I.

Lesson Goals: The purpose of this lesson is to provide background about the events that led to World War I through the perspective of the U.S. presidents in power at the time.

Methods: Advance organizer: Tell the student(s) that the purpose of the day's lesson is to help them become familiar with events that led to World War I. A video from a special series about the Roosevelts will be used to address perspectives about the war from U.S. presidents in power before and during the war (http://www.pbs.org/kenburns/the-roosevelts).

Introduce and Model New Knowledge:

1. Show a clip of President Theodore Roosevelt that portrays his perspectives surrounding world events that eventually caused the United States to enter World War I (*Checkpoint 5.1: Use multiple media for communication*). Give students questions to answer following the clip to check their understanding of the video's content. Have students share their responses with a partner (*Checkpoint 8.3: Foster collaboration and community*).
2. Give each pair of students an opportunity to share one idea from the video. Return to sections of the video that support these ideas (*Checkpoint 3.3: Guide information processing, visualization, and manipulation*).

Guided Practice:

1. Have students work in cooperative learning groups to read information from their social studies text on the causes of World War I by relating this content to the video clip.
2. Have student groups create a graphic organizer of the causes of World War I (Checkpoint 3.2: Highlight patterns, critical features, big ideas, and relationships; Checkpoints 3.3 and 8.3).
3. Have a representative from each group display their graphic organizer to the whole class and explain the group's thinking (*Checkpoint 5.1: Use multiple media for communication*).

Independent Practice:

1. At the end of the lesson, have students answer a set of questions about the causes of World War I.

SUMMARY

Access to the general education curriculum is critical for each and every student. Research has demonstrated the potential of UDL to help provide access to instruction. As part of quality instruction, teachers select materials that match their students' abilities and adapt instructional materials to accommodate individual learner's needs. Finally, AT devices and services hold great promise in helping students with disabilities be active and independent participants in the educational setting.

REVIEW THE LEARNING OBJECTIVES

Let's review the learning objectives for this chapter. If you are uncertain and cannot talk through the answers provided for any of these questions, reread those sections of the text.

8.1 Explain Universal Design for Learning.
UDL is a means for differentiating instruction for all students, including learners with disabilities. The principles, guidelines, and checkpoints of UDL provide ways to remove or minimize barriers to learning and promoting accessibility to curricula and pedagogy, or teaching practices, for all learners, including students with and without disabilities and ELs. The goal is to foster the development of learners to achieve mastery of the curricula within a flexible environment that features various ways content can be conveyed to account for individual differences.

8.2 Describe the guidelines should be followed for textbooks and instructional materials to promote student access to the general education curriculum.
For textbooks and instructional materials, consider the student and the instructional content and methodology. Regarding the student, identify the student's present levels of academic achievement and functional performance when selecting materials, and consider whether the material can be used to meet IEP goals. Regarding content and methodology, decide whether the material is age appropriate. Determine whether it includes a sequence of skills and teaching strategies. Ensure that there are sufficient opportunities to practice new skills and that generalization and maintenance activities are included.

8.3 Explain assistive technology devices and services for promoting access to the general education curriculum.
An AT device is anything that is bought or made that helps a person with a disability accomplish tasks that would otherwise be difficult or impossible. AT devices can be grouped into categories, including positioning and seating, mobility, communication, adaptive toys and games, adaptive environments, computer use, and instructional aids.

AT services are those activities that ensure adoption and maintenance of appropriate devices. One such service is evaluating the functional capabilities and struggles of individuals with disabilities to aid in the selection of appropriate devices to promote access and independence. Another service is the training of professionals, paraprofessionals, families, and users. Training should include how devices work, how to integrate devices into settings, how to troubleshoot if a device malfunctions, and how to evaluate students to determine an appropriate match between device and needs.

REVISIT THE OPENING CHALLENGE

Check your answers to the Reflection Questions from the Opening Challenge and revise them on the basis of what you have learned.

1. How can Mrs. Bell and Ms. Mendez implement the principles of Universal Design for Learning into their instructional practices to promote access to the general education curriculum?
2. How can Universal Design for Learning principles benefit students who are English learners?
3. How can Mrs. Bell and Ms. Mendez ensure that the textbooks and instructional materials they use are appropriate for all of their students to access the general education curriculum?
4. How can assistive technology help Mrs. Bell's students with disabilities access the general education curriculum?

KEY TERMS

access to the general education curriculum
cues
direct instruction
functional capabilities
graphic organizers
instructional reading level
multiple means of action and expression
multiple means of engagement
multiple means of representation
pedagogy
universal design

PROFESSIONAL STANDARDS AND LICENSURE

For a complete description of Professional Standards and Licensure, please see the appendix.

CEC Initial Preparation Standards

Standard 1: Learner Development and Individual Learning Differences

Standard 2: Learning Environments

Standard 3: Curricular Content Knowledge

Standard 5: Instructional Planning and Strategies

Standard 6: Professional Learning and Ethical Practice

Standard 7: Collaboration

INTASC Core Principles

Standard 4: Content Knowledge

Standard 7: Planning for Instruction Standard 8: Instructional Strategies

Praxis II: Education of Exceptional Students: Core Content Knowledge

II. Legal and Societal Issues: Historical Movements/Trends

III. Delivery of Services to Students With Disabilities: Background Knowledge

iStock.com/FatCamera

9 ASSESSMENT AND DATA-BASED DECISION MAKING

LEARNING OBJECTIVES

After studying this chapter, you will be able to meet the following learning objectives:

9.1 Describe how data can be used to make instructional decisions.

9.2 Explain why we assess students.

9.3 Describe how we assess students with unique learning needs.

9.4 Explain how we adapt and modify assessments for students with unique learning needs.

Opening Challenge

Determining What Students Know

Elementary Grades. Mr. Watson is in his 25th year as a fourth-grade teacher. One of his students, Angel, excels as a reader but struggles with mathematics. Angel barely passed his third-grade high-stakes mathematics test, but in the fourth grade he is experiencing difficulty with more advanced mathematics skills and concepts. He has always been a hard worker but has difficulty with basic computation and struggles with mathematics vocabulary and solving word problems. Now that he is working on fractions and algebra readiness skills and concepts, he gets easily confused and frustrated and shuts down. Mr. Watson met with the school's multi-tiered systems of support (MTSS) coordinator and interventionist, Ms. Reid, to discuss Angel's progress. At the start of the school year, Angel fell below the district's benchmark for mathematics on the beginning-of-year universal screener. As a result, Ms. Reid provided supplemental, Tier 2 instruction, while Mr. Watson continued to provide Angel with core mathematics instruction from the district-adopted **basal textbook**.

After 10 weeks of supplemental instruction, Angel continued to struggle with core instruction's skills and concepts and again failed to meet the benchmark to exit the MTSS program. Angel's score on the middle-of-year benchmark test did not surprise Ms. Reid because Angel was also struggling with the skills and concepts she was teaching during Tier 2 intervention. Under ordinary circumstances, Angel would continue with another round of supplemental instruction, but, because of the severity of Angel's problems, Ms. Reid and Mr. Watson decided to refer Angel for a special education evaluation to determine whether he might have a mathematics learning disability (LD). A variety of tests were administered, as dictated by district policy. His standardized mathematics tests showed that Angel was performing very poorly compared to his peers; other test scores in reading and writing were above average when compared to those in the tests' national normative sample. Based on the accumulated evidence, it was determined that Angel did have a mathematics LD, and he is now receiving special education support in his inclusion classroom with Mr. Watson.

Secondary Grades. Ms. Rodriguez has been teaching for 12 years, the past 6 years at the sixth grade; she has twice won her district's Teacher of the Year Award. Her state has recently revamped its standards and high-stakes tests. Ms. Rodriguez's students will be taking the test in the spring to determine whether they will move on to Grade 7. Ms. Rodriguez has a diverse classroom, and the achievement levels range from very low to very high. She is confident that some of her students could take the test now and do quite well. Others in her classroom are so low-achieving that she wonders whether she will be able teach them the skills they need to pass. She has decided to implement progress monitoring for her entire class. She will collect data on her students' progress in reading, math, and science, the three areas being assessed in the spring. She will tailor her instruction to their needs and monitor their achievement throughout the school year.

Two students in particular concern Ms. Rodriguez. She shared her concerns with a respected colleague. *"Marilou is new to the school and has serious reading problems. She is unable to decode words and has very little comprehension of the written science material she is assigned. Juanita, my other challenging student, has attention issues. She is very bright and capable but has difficulty paying attention and sitting still. She is also easily distracted; Juanita is very social and often stops working to chat with her friends."*

Although Ms. Rodriguez has worked with students who have attention problems, she indicated the following: *"None of my former students compare to Juanita. Her condition is exacerbated by muscle control issues. She has fine motor problems that cause her to struggle when she has to grasp, pick up, or use small objects. Her friends help her write answers when they are in working in small groups, but I want Juanita to be able to do the work independently. I am at a loss."*

Reflection Questions

In your journal, write down your answers to the following questions. After completing the chapter, check your answers and revise them on the basis of what you have learned.

1. How can Mr. Watson set up a progress-monitoring procedure?
2. How can Mr. Watson set goals and chart his students' progress?
3. How can Ms. Rodriguez teach Marilou science and test her abilities when she cannot read?
4. What measures are available to identify Juanita's attentional difficulties and Angel's mathematics struggles?
5. How can assessments be used to identify specific student strengths and struggles and inform instruction?

Assessment is a term that refers to any technique by which teachers and other professionals gain information about students. Students can be assessed to measure academic performance, intelligence level, behavior tendencies, emotional stability, and attention challenges. Often, people equate assessment with testing. However, tests are one form of assessment but not the only one (McMillan, 2018). When working with students who have unique learning needs, teachers use various techniques, including testing, to understand their work and abilities.

Teachers can collect assessment information every time they watch their students play together or complete an assignment. In assessment terminology, this watching is called conducting observations. Observation includes the observer watching students do something and thinking about what they are doing and why they are doing it. Teachers' observations are ongoing, which makes observation a valuable tool for measuring student engagement or behavioral or academic changes (Bryant et al., 2015; Flower et al., 2013). Furthermore, teachers can gain information by questioning the student, the student's other teacher(s), and the student's parents or classmates. Information can be obtained through interviews or through a questionnaire or survey. The key to assessment information is that the results must be valid; that is, the results must truly represent the abilities and needs of the students being assessed. In this chapter, we examine educational assessment by addressing how we use data to make instructional decisions, why we assess students, how we assess students with unique learning needs, and how we can adapt and modify assessments to ensure that when we collect information from students, we do so in a way that produces valid results. To begin, however, we discuss the importance of data-based decision making and how we can use our assessment results to facilitate effective instruction.

DATA-BASED INSTRUCTIONAL DECISIONS

More than four decades ago, Stan Deno and Phyllis Mirkin (1977) published a text titled *Data-Based Program Modification*. This book provided teachers and other professionals with a systematic way to collect data and use the information to plan instruction and determine whether the intervention is working. Simply put, this data-based intervention (DBI) test-teach-test procedure compared a student's current level of performance with that of his or her peers, decided how much progress the student needed to make to catch up with his or her peers, selected an intervention best suited to close the gap, and tested students periodically to determine whether adequate progress was being made to continue the intervention or make changes. In the past two decades, DBI has been used in many MTSS and special education classrooms, as educators have realized the importance of using data to inform instruction and monitor progress.

In its description of DBI, the National Center on Intensive Intervention (2013) noted key points to remember about DBI:

- DBI is a validated process, and not a single intervention program or strategy.
- DBI is an ongoing process in which intervention and assessment are linked and used to adjust a student's academic or behavior program over time. DBI is not a one-time fix. It is not a single static intervention program.

- DBI is often domain specific, meaning that a student may receive DBI in one domain (e.g., reading, behavior), or even on one component of that domain (e.g., reading comprehension, social interactions), while receiving core or supplemental instruction in other domains (e.g., word-level reading, schoolwide expectations). DBI can be implemented in multiple domains at the same time, responding to the learning and behavioral needs of the student.
- Students with the most intensive needs likely will require DBI over a sustained period of time. Decisions about if and when to reduce the intensity and individualization of the intervention must take into account the student's responsiveness, as well as the breadth and nature of skill deficits to be addressed (National Center on Intensive Intervention, 2013, p. 4).

One may ask, "Why are we discussing intervention in an assessment chapter?" We do so because we see assessment and intervention as two sides of the same coin. That is, assessment and intervention are inseparable, except when it comes to describing them. As you will read about in this chapter, we assess frequently as we teach because we need to know whether the student is learning what we are teaching. When we assess students using traditional tests or observations, we are doing so in relation to what has been and what is being taught. In other words, we use data to make decisions and to determine what we do next. Keep this in mind as you read this chapter.

WHY WE ASSESS STUDENTS

There are several reasons why we assess students with unique learning needs. Here we discuss a few key purposes.

Identifying Strengths and Weaknesses

A major purpose of assessment across various areas such as reading, writing, mathematics, and classroom behavior is to gather information about what students with unique learning needs can do well (strengths) and what they struggle with (weaknesses). For example, Marilou, in Ms. Rodriguez's class, has difficulty reading, and Juanita has attentional issues. Often, teachers use assessments called **diagnostic measures** because these measures assess a student across a variety of skill areas. The areas can be within a construct (e.g., assess several different reading skills) or they can be more global (e.g., measure reading, writing, and mathematics).

When teachers make comparisons among an individual student's abilities, they are performing an **intra-individual difference** comparison. These comparisons are important because they allow us to identify what students need to work on to help improve any problem areas that might be discovered.

Determining Relative Standing

In contrast to making intra-individual comparisons (comparing performance across different skill areas), teachers can compare one student's performance to that of other students. In this case, the teachers are making **inter-individual** comparisons. Many school districts administer an achievement test in the spring of each year. This test—perhaps the Iowa Tests (Seton Testing Services, 2016), the Stanford Achievement Test (Pearson Assessments, 2018), or some similar test—measures students' skills, such as reading, mathematics, and writing, and provides an index of relative standing, that is, how well a student's test performance compares with their peers', either nationally or locally. Professionals provide normative scores that show each student's performance compared to that of other students across the country (i.e., a national average) and/or to those within the school district (i.e., a district average). These types of tests are called **norm-referenced tests** and compare student performance to the norm, or typical performance. About a month or two after testing, the school is sent the test results by the test publisher. Results can be shared with parents and placed in each student's cumulative folder, the school's record of each student's academic activity. District superintendents and principals also use the test scores to identify how the schools within the district compare with one another and how a particular district compares with others across the country.

Other tests can also provide results that compare student performance to a normative sample. When students are referred for possible disabilities that can qualify them for special services, individual achievement tests and cognitive assessments can be administered. A student's scores on these tests can also be compared to scores obtained by those in the norm group, indicating how a student is scoring compared to peers: average, above average, below average, very poor, or very superior.

Informing Instruction

An important question a teacher should ask when reviewing assessment results is, "How can assessment results help me know (inform me) what I should be teaching my student?" This is an example of using assessment data to inform instruction or guide instructional efforts.

For example, when administering a reading test to Marilou, whether it is a standardized test or an informal reading inventory, Ms. Rodriguez can observe how Marilou reads aloud. She may conduct a miscue or error analysis to see what words she missed as she read and to make judgments about her word identification skills. If Marilou continuously left off suffixes or inflectional endings, those skills could be targeted for instruction. If she correctly responded to literal comprehension questions but missed a sizable proportion of inferential or evaluative questions, Ms. Rodriguez may decide to focus reading instruction on making inferences or evaluations.

Determining Program Eligibility

In some cases, assessment data are used to identify exceptionalities, such as intellectual and developmental disabilities, LDs, emotional or behavioral disorders, or giftedness, and to determine whether students are eligible to receive special program services. These programs might be related to special education, Section 504 of the Rehabilitation Act of 1973, or dyslexia, to name but a few. There is no test for exceptionalities, per se. Instead, assessment professionals (usually psychologists or educational diagnosticians) administer a battery of tests, make observations, and conduct interviews (in other words, perform a number of assessments), and they examine the results with certain criteria in mind. There are established procedures for diagnosing exceptional conditions, and a team of people (including classroom teachers and parents) talk about the results of the assessments and decide whether the student qualifies as having a particular disability or exceptionality.

In today's schools, program eligibility can include decisions pertaining to MTSS. Specifically, test results are used to identify struggling students who can benefit from response to intervention (RTI) programs. In this case, students who meet eligibility requirements (in the elementary grades, scoring below an established cut-off on a universal screener; in middle and high school grades, perhaps failing a portion of a high-stakes exam) to receive supplemental instruction or intensive intervention, depending on the severity of the problem.

The role of the classroom teacher when determining program eligibility cannot be overemphasized. Teachers are the educational professionals who know the student best, and theirs is an important voice that lends credibility to the assessment findings that shape the decision-making process. For instance, Mr. Watson referred Angel to the IEP team for having potential LDs in mathematics. After conducting the initial assessments, the school psychologist recommended that Angel be identified as having a reading LD but not a mathematics LD. The assessment data did not indicate a mathematics LD, but they did show a reading problem. Mr. Watson, having worked with Angel for months, had never noticed a reading problem. In fact, he had always been impressed with the student's abilities as a strategic reader. If Mr. Watson does not speak out during the meeting and provide contrasting evidence, there is a good chance that the student may be misdiagnosed as having a reading LD. Test data alone should not be used to make eligibility decisions. Data should come from a variety of sources, including daily work samples, which in this case would show that Angel is an accomplished reader in class. A follow-up assessment requested by Mr. Watson and Ms. Reid identified Angel as having a mathematics LD.

Grading

Perhaps the most common form of assessment that teachers use involves assessing students for grading purposes—that is, assigning a numeric or letter index based on a student's performance within a specified academic calendar period (e.g., an 8-week period or semester). To see whether students learned their spelling words, teachers might administer a spelling test at the end of the week and record the percentage correct in their grade book. An end-of-chapter test might be administered after completing a science unit. In many instances, these tests have been prepared by the publisher of the textbook being used in class, but just as often teachers create their own tests. Whichever approach is used, test grades are assigned and constitute a portion of each student's final grade for the course.

Leniency errors occur when teachers score all papers positively and assign high scores. Conversely, severity ratings occur when teachers score all papers negatively and assign consistently low scores. Central tendency errors occur when teachers tend to score all papers in the average range, limiting high scores and/or low scores.

Personal bias errors can occur when teachers tend to let stereotypes influence student ratings. A teacher could score a paper higher because "Jimmy has a disability, and he tries hard." Conversely, a teacher might score a paper lower because of a preconceived notion that a student with a disability cannot be successful in the classroom.

Finally, logical errors might occur when teachers tend to associate one characteristic with another. For example, teachers may grade papers higher for students who demonstrate high academic aptitude and give lower scores when the opposite is true.

This is not to say that all teachers make these types of errors. But these errors do occur, and teachers should be on the lookout for them.

Determining Adequate Yearly Progress

According to the Every Student Succeeds Act of 2015, educators must ensure that all students make **adequate yearly progress** (AYP), so it is important for teachers to collect assessment data to determine whether students are making progress toward their end-of-year goals (Smith et al., 2018). Teachers want students to be performing at a certain level by the end of the school year. These end-of-year assessments are sometimes called **high-stakes assessments** because districts and schools use the results to monitor the effectiveness of their teaching efforts. Test results also can determine whether students advance to the next grade or graduate from high school; in other words, the stakes for some students are really high.

Many states differ in the way they determine AYP and what tests are used to measure it. We urge you to visit your local district's or state education agency's website to look up the expectations for your area schools and state. If you are currently teaching or if you soon will be, you may already have attended meetings about your school and district requirements.

Documenting Progress

Progress monitoring is particularly important in MTSS programs. In fact, progress monitoring is considered one of MTSS's nonnegotiables, meaning that no MTSS program should be without it. In our MTSS work, we typically use four types of progress monitoring that cut across some of the areas we have already discussed. As you can see in Table 9.1, progress-monitoring measures are designed to answer specific questions relating to measurement. **Benchmark** checks are used as a universal screener and designed to answer these questions: "Where does the student stand in comparison to his or her peers?" and "Does the student qualify for intervention?"

Universal screeners in MTSS are usually administered three times each year: at the beginning, in the middle, and at the end of the school year. A benchmark (that's why we use the term *benchmark check*) is the score on the test that determines qualification for intervention (earlier we used the term *determining program eligibility*). Students who score at or above the benchmark are seen as doing well

TABLE 9.1 ■ Description of Progress-Monitoring Tools

Progress-Monitoring Tool	Purpose	Administration	Examples
Benchmark check	To answer these questions: "Where does the student fall in comparison to his or her peers," and "Does the student qualify for intervention?"	Benchmark checks are given to all students in the fall, winter, and spring of the year.	Four 2-minute timed tests assessing number and operation skills (e.g., magnitude comparisons, number sequences, place value, addition/subtraction combinations), which are summed to form a total score.
Daily check	To answer the question "Did the student meet the objective of the day?"	Daily checks are administered only to students receiving intervention at the end of each day's lesson.	Several items that assess the content of the lesson. Administered as part of independent practice, the daily check total score should allow for one mistake yet still achieve mastery (e.g., for a five-item daily check, mastery is set at 80% correct).
Unit check	To answer these questions: "Has the student mastered the content of the unit/chapter as presented across a two-week (or so) period?" and "Has the student maintained daily learning across an elongated time	Unit checks are administered only to students receiving intervention at the end of the 2-week intervention unit or chapter.	Ten to twenty items that assess the content taught during the unit/chapter. Tests can be a pregenerated component of the commercial or research intervention, or unit checks can be created using items from the daily checks. With at least 10 items, mastery can be set at 90%.
Aim check	To answer the question "Is the student making progress toward his or her intervention goal?"—which is usually the next benchmark.	Aim checks are administered twice per week to students receiving intervention. Some teachers choose to administer aim checks to all students once every week or two weeks.	Aim checks should be alternative forms of benchmark checks. It is best to create four or five forms of the aim check to ensure that students do not remember answers from a single form.

Source: Cuillos et al. (2011).

in the subject matter being tested and therefore do not qualify for the RTI intervention. Students who score below the benchmark are seen as needing the intervention.

We look at benchmark check scores as falling within three categories: A, B, and C (these stand for levels of performance on the benchmark check, not letter grades). We call those who score above the 35th percentile A students; the A stands for "All ahead full," which means teachers should continue to do what they are doing with these students because it is working—the students are learning what is being taught. Students who score between the 25th percentile (our benchmark) and the 35th percentile are B students, meaning "Be alert." Students who score at the B level percentile have met the benchmark, but not by much. Teachers should be alert while teaching these students because they are potential candidates for falling below the benchmark during the next round of testing. Do they struggle with new skills and concepts? Do they require additional help when they struggle? Do scaffolds need to be introduced to help them learn these new skills and concepts?

Finally, those who score below the benchmark—that is, below the 25th percentile—are C students, and C stands for "Change." These students qualify for the RTI program, so their teachers change what they are doing by providing supplemental instruction (referred to as Tier 2 instruction in Chapter 1) in addition to their core instruction (Tier 1).

When the next round of testing occurs, students receiving supplemental instruction may reach the benchmark, leave Tier 2, and remain in Tier 1 full time. Some students who met the benchmark in the previous round of testing may now miss it. These students (very often the B students from Round 1) now qualify for Tier 2 intervention, which supplements their Tier 1 instruction.

The next type of progress-monitoring measure is the daily check, which is given only to students who are receiving Tier 2 or Tier 3 instruction (see Chapter 2 for information about MTSS). The question being asked with the daily check is, "Did the students meet the objective of the day's lesson?" Daily checks are given at the end of each lesson, often in the form of independent practice items. They are important because if students fail to meet the lesson's objective and continue to fail to meet other lessons' objectives, the odds they will do well on the next benchmark check are slim—they probably will not have learned enough during the period between benchmark checks to show improvement. If a student does poorly on two or three daily checks, the intervention teacher should consider making some kind of change in the student's teaching. For example, the student might have to be moved to a different group that is functioning at a lower level than the current group. Or perhaps the student will be part of a smaller group, one that allows the interventionist to check for understanding more often, add additional scaffolds, or adapt instruction more often or in different ways.

The third measure in progress monitoring is called a unit check, which is similar to the end-of-chapter test found in many textbooks. Unit checks, like daily checks, are administered only to intervention students. The questions being asked here are, "Has the student mastered the content taught of the unit/chapter as presented across a 2-week (or so) period?" and "Has the student maintained daily learning across an elongated time frame?"

Many RTI interventions consist of lessons that are combined into a unit or module. The unit check consists of representative items across the lessons that comprise the unit or module. Often, these items are selected from daily checks; so, for example, if a unit is composed of 20 lessons, a unit check might be composed of 20 items, one item from each lesson. Experienced teachers often note that students seem to be learning just fine, as might be the case when the student meets the objective by scoring well on all daily checks. But when a unit check is given, for some reason a student might perform poorly—they have forgotten what was taught earlier and have not maintained learning across the time spent on the unit. One can only imagine how frustrating that must be for the teacher—and the student.

The final check in this progress-monitoring system, the aim check, is designed to answer the question, "Is the student making progress toward his or her intervention goal?" Most often the intervention goal is to score at or above the benchmark on the next benchmark check (the next administration of the universal screener). The aim check should be four or five measures that are alternative forms of the benchmark check. Often the aim check is administered every 2 weeks during intervention, but sometimes it can be administered more often; aim check performance is graphed or charted to show growth and movement toward the benchmark.

See Figure 9.1 for an example. Here, Andre's initial benchmark check score is plotted on the graph (he answered 16 items correctly). The next benchmark check will be given 10 weeks later, and to meet it Andre must score 42 points, so that score is plotted on the chart. A line is drawn from his first score to the goal; this line is called an aim line, which is where the term aim check comes from. Andre scored 20 points on his first aim check 2 weeks later, which is plotted on his graph. (By the way, students often do their own charting, which gives them ownership of the process while allowing them to see their own growth; this is often called **self-regulation**.) Two weeks later, Andre scored 22 points, and 2 weeks after that, he again scored 22 points.

To conclude, it is important for teachers to use assessment data to document progress, a process often called progress monitoring. In some cases—in MTSS, for example— progress- monitoring measures can vary in type and purpose.

Tech Notes provides an overview of creating graphs to measure student performance.

FIGURE 9.1 ■ Sample Charted Performance for Andre: Comparison of Standard Scores to One Another and Percentile Ranks and Descriptors

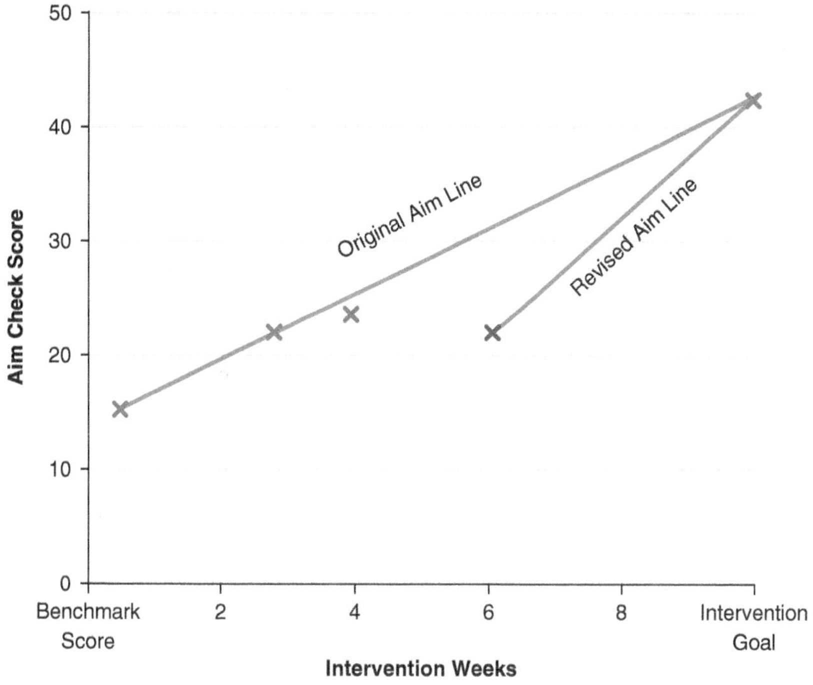

TECH NOTES

GRADING CHARTS

When monitoring progress, it is typical to create a graph of student performance that includes the results of an initial assessment, usually in the form of a pretest, and a goal, a point total that the student is supposed to score at the end of the intervention (usually a benchmark of some kind). A line is drawn from the initial test score to the goal, and that line presents a path to success—the results of periodic testing should continue to improve and mirror the aim line (or that is the hope). As each periodic test is given, the score is plotted on the graph to present a visual depiction of progress.

Although graphs and charts can be drawn by hand, Microsoft Excel provides a means to do so electronically. To create a graph, open Excel and save the document as something like "Progress-Monitoring Chart for Juan." On the first line, write Date, Session, Score, and Aim in the first four columns. Under date, enter the dates in each row that you will be collecting data (for example, Jan 4, Jan 6, Jan 11, Jan 13 for data collected twice a week beginning on January 4). Under Session, write 1 to 20 (for 20 data collection sessions over a 10-week period). Under Score and Aim, write the pretest score (for example, 22). Now enter the next benchmark under Aim on the same line as the last session. In our case, the benchmark is 56, so write 56 in the Aim column in the same row as Session 20. Then subtract the pretest score from the benchmark score (56 – 22), giving the difference of 34 points—the student must increase his pretest score 34 points to reach the benchmark at the end of the intervention. Next, divide 34 by the number of sessions minus 1 (20-1), or 34/19. The quotient is 1.7895. Click on line 3 in the Aim column. Then, in the formula box (next to *fx*), enter = D2+1.7895 and press the "Enter" or "Return" key. The number 21.7895 will appear. Copy that box and paste it into the remaining boxes down to the last Aim number entered (56). You will then see numbers fill in the previously empty boxes. Now, highlight the Score and Aim boxes from the first to the last, and go to the Chart icon at the top of the Excel sheet. Click on Chart and several options will appear. Click on Line, then Marked Line. A chart will then appear on the Excel sheet, with an Aim Line created. As you enter each subsequent Score after progress-monitoring testing, performance will be added to the graph. Save the document and you are good to go! Note: If you get stuck, simply type the following into your search engine: "Create an aim line in Excel YouTube"—several demonstration video options should appear. Enjoy!

Legislative Protection Related to Assessment

Over the years, assessment has been used inappropriately to identify people as having disabilities they do not really have or to exclude children from programs for which they would otherwise be eligible. Students from racial or ethnic groups that are not part of the dominant U.S. culture are often at a disadvantage when taking standardized tests. Also, students who have not yet truly mastered English may not adequately demonstrate their abilities in such testing situations. Differences in culture and in language contribute to some students being misidentified as having a disability or being excluded from education programs for students who are gifted (Boulder Valley School District Office of Advanced Academic Services, 2010).

For example, some children who spoke no English or had limited English proficiency were administered intelligence tests in English and diagnosed as having intellectual and developmental disability because of their low test scores (Smith et al., 2018). Clearly, the results of such tests are not valid because they do not reflect the test takers' intelligence. Instead, they simply reflect students' inability to respond to questions they do not understand.

To stress the importance of nonbiased evaluations, IDEA 2004 has required that nondiscriminatory testing be established in each state. Assessment authorities have provided numerous procedures that test authors can undertake to reduce bias and therefore create measurement instruments that are nondiscriminatory (Salvia et al., 2017; Taylor, 2003). Before selecting tests for use with students who are culturally and/or linguistically different, teachers, school psychologists, educational diagnosticians, and other assessment professionals should consult the tests' technical manuals to see whether procedures were undertaken to reduce test bias. The manuals should provide empirical evidence, in the form of research studies and statistical analyses, supporting the tests' use in nondiscriminatory assessment.

Perhaps the most common form of assessment teachers encounter is assessing students for grading purposes.

iStock/Steve Debenport

ASSESSING STUDENTS WITH UNIQUE LEARNING NEEDS

Over the years, many terms have been used to describe the types of assessments used to measure student knowledge. For example, tests have been considered to be standardized or nonstandardized, formal or informal, or summative or formative, depending in large part on how the results of the tests were used. Earlier we discussed the purposes of assessment. Here we discuss three types of assessments that are given and how they differ from one another.

Norm-Referenced Tests

Norm-referenced tests interpret a person's performance by comparing it to that of their peers. We discussed this earlier when we talked about benchmark checks. In school, **norm-referenced interpretations** answer the question, "How does my student compare to others of the same age or grade?" This comparison can be made by comparing students with others in their classroom, with others in their school or district, or, most commonly in nationally standardized tests, with others across the country.

When interpreting students' results on a norm-referenced test, we need to know what the reported test scores mean. Most tests report results using raw scores, standard scores, **percentiles**, **age equivalents**, or **grade equivalents**.

Before we discuss the scores, we need to spend a little time talking about normative samples. A normative sample consists of the people who were given the test to develop an average score against which to compare the scores we are to report. If the test reports national norms, the test has been administered to many students across the country. Many tests have normative samples wherein thousands of people were tested at each age. Whatever the numbers, these scores are used to create the national average that serves as a comparison score for a particular student.

Raw scores are simply the total number of points a person is awarded. In a test where the student has to spell 30 words and gets 20 correct, a raw score of 20 is recorded. On a rating scale that has a Likert-style rating system (e.g., a behavioral rating scale with behaviors listed, in which the rater is asked how often a student exhibits that behavior and selects 1 for *never*, 2 for *sometimes*, 3 for *frequently*, or 4 for *always*), the raw score is the total number of points for the ratings. By themselves, raw scores mean little. Think about one test that contains 30 items and another that contains 70 items. Raw scores of 25 on these tests mean different levels of understanding, even though the numbers are the same. Raw scores are best translated into one or more of the **derived scores** described in Table 9.2.

TABLE 9.2 ■ Comparison of Standard Scores to One Another and Percentile Ranks and Descriptors

Standard Score	Percentile Rank	Scale Score	T-Score	Z-Score	Description
145	99.9	19	80	+3.0	Very Superior
140	99.6	18	77	+2.67	Very Superior
135	99	17	73	+2.33	Very Superior
130	98	16	70	+2.00	Superior
125	95	15	67	+1.67	Superior
120	91	14	63	+1.33	Above Average
115	84	13	60	+1.00	Above Average
110	75	12	57	+0.67	Average
105	63	11	53	+0.33	Average
100	50	10	50	0.00	Average
95	37	9	47	−0.33	Average

(Continued)

TABLE 9.2 ■ Comparison of Standard Scores to One Another and Percentile Ranks and Descriptors (*Continued*)

Standard Score	Percentile Rank	Scale Score	T-Score	Z-Score	Description
90	25	8	43	−0.67	Average
85	16	7	40	−1.00	Below Average
80	9	6	37	−1.33	Below Average
75	5	5	33	−1.67	Poor
70	2	4	30	−2.00	Poor
65	1	3	27	−2.33	Very Poor
60	0.4	2	23	−2.67	Very Poor
55	0.1	1	20	−3.00	Very Poor

Source: Adapted from Dumont-Williams (n.d.).

Norms for many tests are presented in terms of standard scores, derived scores that have an average score, or mean score, and a set statistical standard deviation. Table 9.2 depicts the relationship of several standard scores typically reported in tests. Standard scores are valuable because they allow teachers both to make inter-individual comparisons (i.e., to determine how a student compares with the national or local average) and to assess intra-individual differences (e.g., strengths and weaknesses a person exhibits across test scores).

Percentiles are also provided for most norm-referenced tests. Percentiles, or percentile ranks, as they are often called, are convenient and popular because they are so easy to understand. Percentiles range from 1 to 99, and they represent where the person would rank when compared with 99 of their peers. If a student achieves a percentile of 59 on a math test, it means that only 40 people scored as well as or better than they did on the test.

A percentile rank of 59 does not mean a student got 59% of the items correct on a particular test. This is a common misconception. A percentile indicates a person's standing relative to that of their peers based on test performance, not the percentage of items they got right on a test.

Age equivalents are provided for many test scores. These values indicate the age level from the normative sample that corresponds to the student's raw score on each of the tests. For instance, for a fifth-grade student who was administered an intelligence test, an age equivalent of 3 years, 4 months simply means that students of that age in the normative sample scored the same raw score as the fifth grader. Be cautious: This result does not mean the older student has the same intelligence (or mental age, as it is sometimes inappropriately called) as a 3-year-old.

Grade equivalents also may be assigned to test scores, especially achievement tests. Similar to age equivalents, these values indicate the normative grade level that corresponds to a raw score made by a student on each of the tests or subtests administered.

Grade equivalents are reported frequently in achievement testing, but they are often misinterpreted. When a reading test reports a grade equivalent of 3–2 (third year, second month of school), it does not necessarily mean the student reads like a third grader. It means simply that the student achieved the same raw score as children in the third grade, second month of the school year when they took the test.

Informal reading inventories are unique tests that report scores in terms of grade equivalents (Kritikos et al., 2018). They typically consist of a graded word list that students are given to read as members of the normative sample (a list of first-grade words, a list of second-grade words, and so forth). The highest level of word list read at 90% or 95% provides a grade equivalent index. For instance, if an 11th grader reads a graded word list and can successfully read only words on the sixth-grade list, reading the seventh- and eighth-grade lists at less than 90% accuracy, they have a grade equivalent index, based on that specific inventory, of the sixth grade. That does not mean the student reads like a sixth grader; it simply means they couldn't read words at a higher level on that particular list. The inventory might stop there, or it might have the student then read graded passages, usually from the kindergarten level up to the Grade 12 level. When the student can no longer read 90% to 95% of the words correctly, the examiner stops and assigns a grade-equivalent reader level index for the student.

Progress-Monitoring Measures

Schools today place a particular emphasis on monitoring students' progress. This is due jointly to the AYP requirement of the Every Student Succeeds Act and to the progress-monitoring requirements of RTI. Curriculum-based measures (CBM) are ideally suited for monitoring progress because they are closely aligned with what is being taught in the classroom. We present more on CBM in a later section of this chapter.

Criterion-Referenced Tests

Unlike norm-referenced tests that compare performance against that of peers, **criterion- referenced tests** compare performance to mastery of the content being tested (Taylor, 2003). The most common reason for evaluating students is to determine whether they have learned what has been specifically taught. For example, imagine a teacher has given a daily lesson on adding two-digit numerals to three-digit numerals and then follows up by giving a quiz. If the students get most of the quiz items correct, the assumption is that they have mastered the subject matter. If a student answers only half the items correctly, there is little doubt they have not mastered the content and reteaching is needed.

Mastery can be determined only when the student has had a sufficient number of opportunities to demonstrate competence. Response to a single item is not sufficient because it is no guarantee the student who fails to answer correctly would not answer the next 99 items correctly if given the opportunity. Likewise, answering the item correctly is no guarantee that the student wouldn't miss the next 99 opportunities. As a rule of thumb, only when a student can correctly answer 80% to 90% (or better) of the items can we assume mastery has been achieved. It is uncommon to base mastery on fewer than five items; a student with at least five items can slip up on one yet still demonstrate mastery by answering the others correctly. Assessing for mastery should include the opportunity to make a careless mistake without making a misleading interpretation inevitable. Table 9.3 and Figure 9.2 show sample math scope-and-sequence charts with skills that students should master.

Once the items have been selected, administer and score the test and check for mastery. For each row of items, did the student get at least four correct? If so, we can assume the student has mastered the skill. If not, assume that the student has not mastered the skill and continue teaching the skill. Teachers should review each skill periodically to ensure students have maintained their mastery. Students need ongoing practice to maintain their skill sets.

TABLE 9.3 ■ Sample Math Scope-and-Sequence Chart

This scope-and-sequence chart for addition is representative of what can be found in elementary mathematics teacher's edition textbooks. We provide it as an example of content criterion reference measures.
Addition of two 1-digit numbers to 10, horizonal alignment
Addition of two 1-digit numbers to 10, vertical alignment
Addition of two 2-digit numbers (no renaming)
Addition of two 3-digit numbers (no renaming)
Addition of two 2-digit numbers, zero in addend (no renaming)
Addition of two 3-digit numbers, zero in addend (no renaming)

FIGURE 9.2 ■ Sample Items Based on the Math Scope-and-Sequence Chart in Table 9.3

2 + 3 =	5 + 1 =	4 + 4 =	2 + 8 =	0 + 9 =
3 +6	0 +4	2 +5	8 +1	2 +3
13 +25	43 +52	28 +50	57 +21	64 +33
183 +215	637 +121	843 +126	241 +530	389 +410
25 +50	61 +20	48 +30	27 +60	85 +10
243 +305	727 +102	631 +250	814 +105	174 +620

Testing for Students' Strategies

Teachers often ask themselves, "How did José come up with that answer?" or "What was Lizzy thinking?" Some assessments are intended to identify strategies students use when they are problem solving. Students rarely arrive at a solution haphazardly; there is almost always a reasonable explanation of how they derived it. One of the most challenging yet interesting purposes for assessing math performance, for example, is to target the strategies a student employs during computation or problem solving. It is intriguing to find out why a student generates a correct or incorrect response.

We believe no mathematics assessment, for instance, is complete without what we term **process assessment**. Simply put, the goal of process assessment in mathematics is to identify the manner in which students derive a particular answer when solving a problem. More often than not, students solve math problems conventionally by utilizing standard school methods (algorithms). At times, however, they are unable to grasp the taught algorithm, so they design alternative means to derive the answer.

By way of illustration, consider the problem $43 - 27 = x$. The correct difference, 16, can be derived by (a) understanding the conceptual nature of place value and applying proper regrouping techniques, (b) failing to grasp the nature of place value conceptually yet knowing how to apply regrouping techniques, or (c) knowing nothing about either place value or regrouping but using an invented procedure (e.g., counting on from 27 to 43 and writing down the number of counts made along the way).

The second procedure, **active process assessment**, generally employs some form of flexible interviewing, whereby the student discusses aloud what they are thinking during computation. For instance, the teacher might ask a student to think out loud while doing a math problem. By listening to the student's explanation, the teacher can identify the strategies employed. The teacher generally asks follow-up questions to further probe the student's strategies. To illustrate, consider a student who calculates 43 – 27 and states, "We can't do 3 minus 7, so I borrow 1 from here (10's place) and put 3, then I put 1 next to 3 (1's place), and 13 minus 7 is 6, 3 take away 2 is 1 . . . 16." A follow-up question might be "Okay. Tell me why you crossed out the 4 and put 3 above it." Based on the student's response, the teacher can gain insight into the student's knowledge of place-value concepts.

Screening Tests

Sometimes teachers wish to identify quickly and efficiently who is struggling in a particular area and who is not. Usually, teachers can identify their students who are having problems just by working with them, but administering a screening measure helps validate those impressions. Although the most efficient screeners are group administered because good group tests provide valid scores in a short time, individual tests can be given. The screening process often leads to more diagnostic, comprehensive testing, but as is the case with RTI and its universal screening component, it qualifies students for supplemental instruction. (Note: See our earlier description of Benchmark Checks in Table 9.1.)

Various types of screening instruments are available, some highly standardized and others less so. Torgesen and Bryant's (2005) *Test of Phonological Awareness* is an example of a highly standardized instrument for screening students for phonological awareness and phonics skills. The test is group administered to kindergarten, first-grade students, or second-grade children, and those who score below a set benchmark need more comprehensive testing.

But not all screening needs to be highly standardized. For example, teachers know their students well enough to complete rating scales about their abilities and provide valid and reliable information for screening purposes. Teachers who have had a month or two to observe and work with their students can be asked simply to rate each student's performance along a five-point continuum from poor to superior, or they can use a more detailed rating scale that spans academic and behavioral areas.

Diagnostic Assessments

Diagnostic measures are like survey batteries in that they survey, or assess, numerous different areas. They provide more in-depth assessment than screening measures and take longer to administer. For that reason, screening measures are used to limit the number of students who need to be administered diagnostic measures. For example, students who do not meet benchmarks might then be administered the second edition of the Comprehensive Test of Phonological Processes (Wagner et al., 2013) to identify strengths and weaknesses across phonological awareness abilities. Or they might be given the most recent edition of the Test of Word Reading Efficiency (Rashotte et al., 2012) to assess in-depth phonics skills.

Schools typically use two types of diagnostic measures. The first is a global achievement measure that examines a variety of areas. The Woodcock-Johnson IV Test of Achievement (Schrank et al., 2014), for example, contains more than a dozen subtests that examine reading, writing, mathematics, and other areas of achievement. By administering all Woodcock-Johnson IV subtests, examiners obtain a comprehensive overview of a student's skills across subject matter.

The Woodcock Reading Mastery Test, third edition (Woodcock, 2011), is a second type of diagnostic measure. This test examines only reading, but it does so by studying many subcomponents of reading, such as comprehension and basic skills. Comparing and contrasting scores within the measure provides for an intra-individual analysis of reading strengths and weaknesses. Many such tests provide detailed analyses of strengths and weakness across mathematics, writing, and other academic skills.

Diagnostic measures also exist for assessing behavior, attention, anxiety, adaptive behavior skills, and other areas related to school success. With these scales, the term *diagnostic measure* takes on a subtly different meaning. Not only are the measures broad-based in their content, but they may actually be used to diagnose a condition. One of the most popular scales used for assessing attention problems is the Conners Rating Scale (3rd edition; Conners, 2008). Because attention deficit hyperactivity disorder (ADHD) must be observed across several settings, this rating scale is completed by parents and teachers, who report on the child's behaviors at home and in the classroom. Such a procedure allows for an ecological assessment because it looks at behavior across settings and locations and collects data from multiple sources—in this case, the parents and one or more teachers. With the Conners Rating Scale, the teacher (or parent) reads a list of student behaviors and rates the extent to which each behavior is present for a particular child. The more behaviors the student exhibits that correspond to those who have ADHD, the greater the likelihood the student has ADHD.

Before we continue, recall that diagnostic tests are not so named because they diagnose conditions. Although usually true, this statement requires clarification. The results of diagnostic tests can lead to a diagnosis of a disability by special education team members. The team typically consists of the student's parents, psychologists, diagnosticians, teachers, a representative from special education, and the principal and other professionals. Team members examine the data provided by diagnostic tests, observations, work samples, and so on and come to a decision about a person's eligibility for special education services. Although test scores are key contributors to the process, it is important to remember this oft-cited dictum: "Tests don't diagnose; people diagnose" (Wiederholt & Bryant, 2012).

Observations

Yogi Berra, one of baseball's greats, once said, "You can observe a whole lot just by watching." On the surface, this statement seems redundant; watching and observing are seemingly the same. But this is not necessarily true. Rather, people watch so they can observe. Watching is seeing. Observing is seeing as well as learning as well as making decisions about what you are seeing.

Teacher observations thus provide valuable data that should be combined with the data from other assessments to make educational decisions. Teachers can observe students and make performance judgments in many ways (see Chapter 10 on behavior). In Figure 9.3, we provide an example that yields objective data on students as they work by examining a target student (the student you are concerned about) and their peers. The observation tool is a chart for recording behaviors over a 20-minute time span. Each slash represents an occurrence of the behavior of interest—in this simple case, object noise and out of place.

Peer performance is important because it serves as a basis for comparison. To arrive at an assessment of performance, simply divide the target student's total number of slashes by the number of slashes for the peers. The resulting quotient provides an index of observed behavior. In our example, the target student was observed making object noise twice as much as the peers (2.0). But for out of place, the target student was actually in place more often that the peers (0.8). By comparing the student with peers, we can identify whether the behavior is student specific or is actually being done by other students in the class as well.

Teacher observations made during instruction can yield considerable worthwhile information. Effective instruction calls for checking for understanding throughout a lesson, which means more than simply asking, "Any questions?" or "Do you understand?" Most students, especially struggling students, will not ask questions or admit to not understanding. So they remain silent, having little or no idea what was taught. Teachers should question students directly to check for understanding and observe student responses to determine whether their students get it or not. For example, if the topic pertains to a story being read, ask, "Why?" or "What of it?" questions, or questions such as, "What is the author trying to say here?" to gauge student understanding. Students' answers provide a wealth of information about their level of understanding, and such questions can be asked across content areas.

Interviews

Teachers can obtain a great deal of important information about the children they teach from the students' parents or guardians. When developing a diagnostic profile of a student, evaluators ask parents or guardians questions about their child's birth, developmental milestones, illnesses, social skills, and interests. This case history can provide basic information that helps the teacher or educational

FIGURE 9.3 ■ Sample Observation Form

Behavior (Target Student)	1	2	3	4	5	6	7	8	9	10	11	12	13	14	15	16	17	18	19	20	Total
Object Noise	/		/			/				/	/			/		/		/	/	/	10
Out of Place	/						/		/						/						4
Behavior (Peers)	**1**	**2**	**3**	**4**	**5**	**6**	**7**	**8**	**9**	**10**	**11**	**12**	**13**	**14**	**15**	**16**	**17**	**18**	**19**	**20**	**Total**
Object Noise	/		/			/						/						/			5
Out of Place		/	/						/		/									/	5

Object Noise 10/5 = 2.0
Out of Place 4/5 = 0.8

Teachers can obtain a great deal of important information about the development of a child from their students' family members.

iStock.com/SDI Productions

diagnostician better understand the child's overall development. However, because recall of developmental history may be sketchy or not totally accurate, try not to rely too heavily on this information. Rather, interpret it, along with information obtained from other teachers and from the students themselves, within the total context of assessment data.

Teachers and students can also be interviewed. Overton (2011) suggested that teachers are in a unique position to consider several important characteristics of their students. For example, how prepared is the student each day? How does the student begin assignments during class? If distracted, how does the student perform? Does the student complete their homework assignments? Does the student respond in class? Such questions provide the interviewer with a sense of the student's behaviors that may not be noted during a particular observation.

Think-aloud interviews are a type of process assessment aimed at identifying the cognitive strategies students use to solve mathematics problems, comprehend reading material, explore a social studies scenario, conduct a science experiment, and so forth (Kritikos et al., 2018). In the think-aloud interview, the teacher asks a student to think out loud as they perform a task. Interview questions might include the following: (a) "What are you thinking?" (b) "How will you solve this task or problem?" (c) "What is another way to solve the problem?" (d) "What do you think the answer might be and why do you think that?" and (e) "How would you explain this problem to another student?"

Several factors must be present for the think-aloud interview to be used appropriately. First, the interviewer must be a good observer of student performance. Second, the person must be knowledgeable about the scope and sequence of the curriculum being used. Third, the interviewer must be familiar with cognitive strategies the student may be employing (Kritikos et al., 2018). For example, if a student is asked to explain (think out loud about) how to add a group of four blocks to a group of five blocks, and the student puts the two groups together and then starts counting from one to arrive at the answer, further questions are needed to determine the extent of her or his knowledge of numbers and groups and of her or his ability to use the count on addition strategy. These questions might include, "What is an easier way to count all the blocks besides starting with one?" and (given five blocks), "What different arrangements can you make with the blocks to show five?"

Through the think-aloud interview, it is possible to gain an understanding of how a student approaches the problem or task and an understanding of what strategies are being used.

This information might lead to the development of new instructional objectives or to a change in the intervention. The interview information, along with other data, can help teachers better understand the processes their students use to solve problems or tasks and the effectiveness of these processes.

Although thinking out loud can be effective, many children with learning problems have difficulty expressing their thoughts aloud and require a different interviewing method. We have found that role-playing can be very effective in identifying what students are thinking as they work, similar to what was described earlier as process assessment. In this instance, the student plays the role of teacher and the teacher assumes the student's role. As an example, you might tell your student, "I have an idea. You be the teacher and show me how to subtract 17 from 35." The following dialog may take place (T is the Teacher; S is the student):

S. First write down 35 on your wipe board.
T. (writes 35) Like this?
S. Yes, very good. Now below the 35, write 17, and make a line under it and put a minus sign in front of the 17.
T. (writes 17, but the alignment is off) Okay, what's next?
S. That's close, but you have to make sure the 1 is in the 10's place below the 3 and the 7 is in the units place below the 5. You sort of have it mixed up. Watch me (models correct placement).
T. (erases the incorrect alignment and writes the proper way) Oh yeah, I forgot.
S. It's very important that the numbers line up. Now the next thing is to subtract the numbers in the unit column. You can't go 5 minus 7 because you always have to subtract the smaller number from the bigger number. So I can't do 5 minus 7, I have to do 7 minus 5, and 7 minus 5 is 2, so write the 2 below the line in the units column.

The process continues, but you already have found that the student has a subtract misconception. Simply by looking at the student's work (what we called passive process assessment earlier), the teacher might be able to draw this conclusion, but this approach confirms the misconception.

Both interviewing methods serve the same purpose. Teachers may choose one to use consistently or may alternate the methods for the sake of variety. The key is to use some form of interview to identify efficient and inefficient strategies students are employing.

Rating Scales and Checklists

Rating scales and checklists are valuable sources of information that can be used as part of the assessment process (Reynolds et al., 2009). Typically, rating scales and checklists provide a listing of skills or abilities, and the rater provides responses indicating how well a person performs each skill. Sometimes the responses are dichotomous—that is, the skills are either present or absent. Dichotomously scored rating scales are really checklists. Other scales offer a range of responses and use a Likert-type response format. Tables 9.4, 9.5, and 9.6 provide examples of these types of scoring options.

Table 9.4 demonstrates the use of a dichotomous checklist to examine early childhood behaviors. Tables 9.5 and 9.6 are rating scales that examine writing. Table 9.5 provides a **holistic evaluation** of writing and Table 9.6 provides an analytic approach.

Rubrics

Rubrics are increasingly being used to evaluate writing samples (see Table 9.7). Here we see another way to evaluate a writing sample. Rubrics are very similar to rating scales; they are important to understand because they are often used in tests that measure state standards in writing. Our sample rubric is one similarly used when assessing the Common Core State Standards (CCSS) writing standards for ninth and tenth graders writing a narrative text. As you can see, it examines five areas: exposition, narrative techniques and development, organization and cohesion, style and conventions, and conclusion. Criteria are provided for five scores, ranging from exceptional (worth five points) to inadequate (one point). Scorers usually read and reread each student passage several times with these areas and scoring criteria in mind.

TABLE 9.4 ■ Example of a Checklist Used with Preschool Children

Self-help skills		
Yes	No	Attempts to wash face and hands
Yes	No	Helps put toys away
Yes	No	Drinks from a standard cup
Yes	No	Eats using utensils
Yes	No	Attempts to use the toilet
Yes	No	Attempts to dress self
Language development		
Yes	No	Follows simple directions
Yes	No	Verbalizes needs and feelings
Yes	No	Speech can be understood most of the time
Yes	No	Speaks in sentences of three or more words
Basic skills development		
Yes	No	Can count to 10
Yes	No	Recognizes numbers to 10
Can name the following shapes		
Yes	No	Circle
Yes	No	Square
Yes	No	Triangle
Yes	No	Star
Can identify the following colors		
Yes	No	Red
Yes	No	Blue
Yes	No	Green
Understands the following concepts		
Yes	No	Up and down
Yes	No	Big and little
Yes	No	Open and closed
Yes	No	On and off
Yes	No	In and out
Social development		
Yes	No	Plays independently
Yes	No	Plays parallel to other students
Yes	No	Plays cooperatively with other students
Yes	No	Participates in group activities

Directions: Circle Yes or No to indicate whether each skill has been demonstrated.

TABLE 9.5 ■ Example of a Holistic Scoring Rubric

Classification	Description	Rating
Excellent	The student demonstrated a thorough understanding of both concepts and could accurately describe in detail similarities and differences and give examples. This is an exemplary response.	5
Good	The student demonstrated a good understanding of the concepts and could describe similarities and differences and give examples.	4
Average	The student demonstrated an adequate understanding of the concepts and could describe some similarities and differences. Depth of understanding was limited and there were gaps in knowledge.	3
Marginal	The student showed limited understanding of the concepts and could provide no more than vague references to similarities and differences. Some information was clearly inaccurate. Examples were either vague, irrelevant, or nor applicable.	2
Poor	The student showed very little understanding of the concepts and was not able to describe any similarities or differences.	1
Very poor	The student showed no understanding of the concepts.	0

Source: Reynolds et al. (2009, p. 235).

Essay item: Compare and contrast communism and fascism. Give examples of the ways they are similar and the way they differ.

TABLE 9.6 ■ Example of an Analytic Scoring Rubric

Area	Poor (0 points)	Average (1 point)	Above Average (2 points)	Excellent (3 points)
The student demonstrated an understanding of communism.				
The student demonstrated an understanding of fascism.				
The student was able to compare and contrast the concepts.				
The student was able to present relevant and clear examples highlighting similarities and differences.				
The response was clear, well organized, and showed a thorough understanding of the material.				

Source: Reynolds et al. (2009, p. 235).

Unlike many rating scales, rubrics have lengthy descriptions of the scoring criteria, making scoring decisions somewhat less subjective. However, it takes considerable time and practice to learn to use rubrics to score writing passages. Teachers often attend lengthy workshops where they learn how to score passages using rubrics, and they practice scoring passages with other teachers and compare their scores. It is not uncommon to find considerable differences of opinion early on during the training, but as discussion and further practice sessions are conducted, closer agreement is reached. It is critical that whoever scores a rubric arrives at a similar score. In assessment language, this is called interscorer reliability, which we discussed below in the "Technical Adequacy" section.

TABLE 9.7 ■ Narrative Scoring Rubric

Description	5 Exceptional	4 Skilled	3 Proficient	2 Developing	1 Inadequate
Exposition: The text sets up a story by introducing the event/conflict, characters, and setting.	The text creatively engages the reader by setting out a well-developed conflict, situation, or observation. The text establishes one or multiple points of view and introduces a narrator and/or complex characters.	The text engages and orients the reader by setting out a conflict, situation, or observation. It establishes one or multiple points of view and introduces a narrator and/or well-developed characters.	The text orients the reader by setting out a conflict, situation, or observation. It establishes one point of view and introduces a narrator and/or developed characters.	The text provides a setting with a vague conflict, situation, or observation with an unclear point of view. It introduces a narrator and/or underdeveloped characters.	The text provides a setting that is unclear with a vague conflict, situation, or observation. It has an unclear point of view and underdeveloped narrator and/or characters.
Narrative Techniques and Development: The story is developed using dialogue, pacing, description, reflection, and multiple plot lines.	The text demonstrates sophisticated narrative techniques such as engaging dialogue, artistic pacing, vivid description, complex reflection, and multiple plot lines to develop experiences, events, and/or characters.	The text demonstrates deliberate use of narrative techniques such as dialogue, pacing, description, reflection, and multiple plot lines to develop experiences, events, and/or characters.	The text uses narrative techniques such as dialogue, description, and reflection that illustrate events and/or characters.	The text uses some narrative techniques such as dialogue or description and merely retells events and/or experiences.	The text lacks narrative techniques and merely retells events and/or experiences.
Organization and Cohesion: The text follows a logical sequence of events.	The text creates a seamless progression of experiences or events using multiple techniques (e.g., chronology, flashback, foreshadowing, suspense, etc.) to sequence events so that they build on one another to create a coherent whole.	The text creates a smooth progression of experiences or events using a variety of techniques (e.g., chronology, flashback, foreshadowing, suspense, etc.) to sequence events so that they build on one another to create a coherent whole.	The text creates a logical progression of experiences or events using some techniques (e.g., chronology, flashback, foreshadowing, suspense, etc.) to sequence events so that they build on one another to create a coherent whole.	The text creates a sequence or progression of experiences or events.	The text lacks a sequence or progression of experiences or events or presents an illogical sequence of events.

(Continued)

TABLE 9.7 ■ Narrative Scoring Rubric (*Continued*)

Description	5 Exceptional	4 Skilled	3 Proficient	2 Developing	1 Inadequate
Style and Conventions: The text uses sensory language and details to create a vivid picture of the events, setting, and characters.	The text uses eloquent words and phrases, showing details and rich sensory language and mood to convey a realistic picture of the experiences, events, setting, and/or characters.	The text uses precise words and phrases, showing details and controlled sensory language and mood to convey a realistic picture of the experiences, events, setting, and/or characters.	The text uses words and phrases, telling details and sensory language to convey a vivid picture of the experiences, events, setting, and/or characters.	The text uses words and phrases and telling details to convey experiences, events, settings, and/or characters.	The text merely tells about experiences, events, settings, and/or characters.
Conclusion: The text provides a conclusion that follows from the course of the narrative. The conclusion provides a reflection on or resolution of the events.	The text moves to a conclusion that artfully follows from and thoughtfully reflects on what is experienced, observed, or resolved over the course of the narrative.	The text builds to a conclusion that logically follows from and reflects on what is experienced, observed, or resolved over the course of the narrative.	The text provides a conclusion that follows from and reflects on what is experienced, observed, or resolved over the course of the narrative.	The text provides a conclusion that follows from what is experienced, observed, or resolved over the course of the narrative.	The text might provide a conclusion to the events of the narrative.

Source: iParadigms, LLC (2012, p. 5).

Work Samples

Work sample analysis is a procedure that helps teachers assess academic skills by looking at students' permanent products (Kritikos et al., 2018) to identify types and frequencies of errors. This information can help teachers establish instructional objectives or select a new intervention.

The most common type of work sample analysis is error analysis, which is fairly easy to conduct. The teacher (a) identifies the objective of the assignment, (b) spells out the mastery criteria for the work, (c) examines work sample products, (d) documents error types, (e) asks students to explain how they arrived at an erroneous solution, and (f) makes instructional recommendations. For instance, in mathematics the teacher could (a) establish that students are expected to complete 10 word problems at 90% accuracy, (b) examine the story problems completed by students, (c) record the percentage correct, (d) examine each problem to identify the types of errors made (e.g., erroneous computation, incorrect diagram to depict information, incorrect use of key word technique), (e) ask students to explain how they solved the problems, and (f) identify additional instructional objectives, based on the error types and student explanations, to rectify the problems. In oral reading, the teacher could record error types (e.g., substitutions, omissions, additions) and the number of errors. If the number of incorrect responses is significant, the teacher can institute a remedial plan.

The error analysis procedure can yield good information for designing the instructional program. It is important to ask students to explain their answers. Through careful analysis of work samples coupled with student explanations, teachers can pinpoint faulty conceptual or procedural knowledge that they can then remediate.

School Records

Teachers glean information about their children from a variety of sources, such as the measures we described earlier. But they can also find information in students' cumulative folders (or cumulative records or files, as they are also called), which contain academic and behavioral history data.

School records can be a valuable source of information about student academic and social progress. Records of attendance, achievement test scores, curricular materials used during instruction, anecdotal notes, and student work provide a composite overview of the student's progression through the grades. Teachers can use this information to document particular problems that might have been evident in earlier grades, attendance patterns, techniques that were implemented earlier, classroom and behavioral interactions, and teacher concerns. Again, although this is important information, teachers might need to interpret some pieces (e.g., anecdotal notes) cautiously because of reliability concerns. That is, people can inconsistently interpret information found in the records.

Portfolio Assessments

Portfolio assessment is a means of monitoring student learning and evaluating the effectiveness of instructional programs and decision making. Portfolios contain student-selected work samples and sometimes student notes about how the samples were created and edited or improved. Portfolio assessment can compare student progress to curricular objectives and instructional methods, focus our evaluation on process rather than just on product, measure student academic achievement and classroom learning more directly, and assist in evaluating the effectiveness of instruction.

Reynolds et al. (2009) noted that portfolios are typically scored using evaluation rubrics. These rubrics should specify all evaluation criteria that needs to be considered when evaluating the students' work products, provide explicit qualifications for performance levels for all criteria, and indicate whether the criteria are applied holistically or analytically.

For students with learning and behavior problems, portfolio information should be related to curricular goals included in the IEP. Obviously, such information typically would include academic and social skills, but can also include behavior and adaptive functioning, academic and literacy growth, strategic learning and self-regulation, and language and cultural aspects that can be linked to the IEP.

Students with learning and behavior problems typically lack specific academic skills and effective cognitive strategies that promote efficient learning. Therefore, portfolio assessment should include examples of completed products (e.g., math problems or writing samples), with analyses that document the types of strategies employed during problem solving or drafting/editing. Notes taken during writing conferences can accompany writing samples.

Frequent measures of student progress can help teachers monitor learning and implement decision-making criteria. For example, it is possible to measure fluency in oral reading twice a week to determine the effect of the instructional intervention: Collect rate data and analyze student growth, implement decision rules regarding rate of student progress, and store graphs in the portfolio until the next timing. The important point about the timeline used for collecting and assessing portfolio items is frequency. For students with learning and behavior difficulties, teachers should monitor progress regularly to determine whether instructional techniques are indeed promoting student academic growth.

Behavioral Assessments

Most students go through periods in their lives that affect their behavior and personality. Events at home or with their peers can cause children to act out or to become depressed or anxious. Typically, these periods do not last long, and the students bounce back. For some students, however, behavior problems occur for a long time and are systematic. For these students, assessments can help identify emotional problems that are symptomatic of disabilities.

Earlier we mentioned that the third edition of the Conners Rating Scale (Conners, 2008) has a parent and teacher rating component. This allows for an ecological evaluation—that is, one that considers multiple ways to collect information, such as across people or settings. Across the scales, the responses to one or two items may not be indicative of a serious behavior problem. But students whose ratings are consistently problematic across settings when observed by different people could well have serious behavioral or emotional conditions. The advantage of using ecological assessments, whether gathered in one scale or several measures, is that they allow teachers and others to determine whether the problems occur in just one setting or are pervasive across multiple settings and people. We provide several examples of less-standardized assessment procedures for behavior concerns. All the techniques contribute to identifying problem behaviors and ameliorating them.

Functional Behavior Assessment

According to Stephanie M. Hadaway and Alan W. Brue in their 2016 text titled *Practitioner's Guide to Functional Behavioral Assessment*, functional behavior assessment (FBA) was introduced into special education law with its inclusion of the 1997 version of IDEA (Public Law 105-17). FBAs are used to identify information that will be needed to complete a behavior intervention plan (BIP), discussed in Chapter 10.

The IDEA Partnership (http://www.ideapartnership.org/) is composed of more than 50 groups interested in special education, and they have provided a handy description of how to create and conduct an FBA, use the information obtained in the FBA to create a BIP, and how to monitor the BIP to ensure that the plan is meeting the student's needs. Figure 9.4 provides a handy reference to steps that can be used in the FBA/BIP process. Here, we'll discuss the first four steps because they are the ones that deal with assessment.

Define the problem behavior. The first step in any FBA is to define any problem behaviors that the student exhibits. When identifying the behavior, it is important to ensure that the behavior is (a) easily observed, (b) can be counted, (c) has a beginning and an ending, and (d) occurs more than once. By ensuring that behaviors meet these four criteria, educators can be certain that the behaviors can be seen and measured. It is also important to note that the behaviors identified must be specific. For example, a behavior such as "Andre is mean to classmates," is vague. A better behavior would be "While lining up to leave the classroom, Andre hits and/or kicks his classmates."

Devise a plan to collect data. The IDEA Partnership identifies two ways to collect data, either directly or indirectly. Direct methods involve observing the student and recording the behaviors seen and what factors are involved with the behavior. In Andre's case, it would be useful to note whether Andre initiates the hitting or kicking or perhaps does so only after another student initiates the contact either physically or verbally. Indirect methods may include things such as looking at the student's records, interviewing the teacher or others, and/or having the teacher or others complete a questionnaire or checklist. Such information is valuable in obtaining an ecological perspective of how others perceive the problem behavior(s) and could indicate what might motivate or cause the student to engage in the behavior. In other sections of this chapter, we discuss many of the tools that can be used to both directly and indirectly collect important information.

Compare and analyze the data. Once the data are gathered, it is important to use the information to paint the big picture by summarizing the information gained in the previous steps. An FBA summary could include information divided into four categories,

1. Target behavior: What is the problem behavior that the student engages in?

   In Andre's case, he hits or kicks his classmates.

2. Setting: Where do the behaviors occur: in class, in the hallway, on the playground, elsewhere?

   Andre's behavior occurs in the classroom as students line up to go outside.

FIGURE 9.4 ■ How to Create and Conduct a Functional Behavior Assessment and a Behavior Intervention Plan

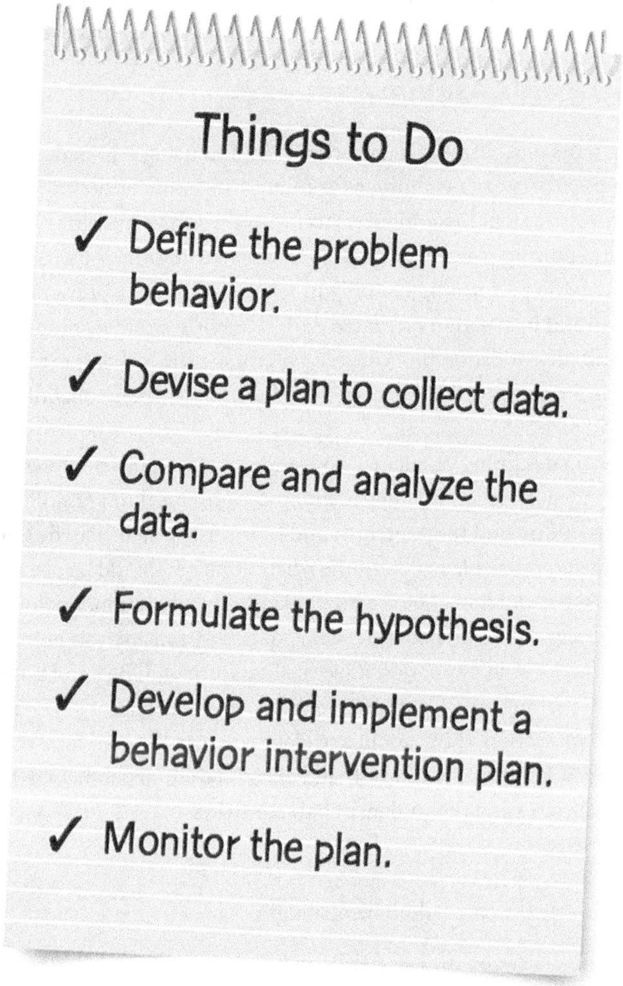

Things to Do
✓ Define the problem behavior.
✓ Devise a plan to collect data.
✓ Compare and analyze the data.
✓ Formulate the hypothesis.
✓ Develop and implement a behavior intervention plan.
✓ Monitor the plan.

Source: Idea Partnership (n.d.). Used with permission.

3. Antecedents: What triggers the event?

   Andre initiates the contact most of the time, perhaps because he has difficulty standing in line and waiting for the line to move. However, on occasion, the behavior occurs because a classmate (either accidentally or intentionally) bumps into him.

4. Maintenance behavior: What consequences exist that cause the behavior to continue?

   According to the information obtained during direct and indirect observations, Andre appears to receive an intrinsic reward from being physically dominant, even though the behavior gets him into trouble.

Formulate the hypothesis. According to the IDEA Partnership, "Based on the data you collect, give your best, educated guess to explain the function or reason for the behavior. Generally speaking, problem behaviors serve two basic functions: To get something, and/or to avoid and escape something." In Andre's case, he enjoys recess, so he does not appear to get physical with his classmates to avoid recess; thus, the hypothesis probably involves the intrinsic pleasure he receives through intimidation.

The IDEA Partnership provided a second type of FBA summary. This one involves the four W's: Who, What, When, and Where. This one may be more useful, depending on the behavior presented.

Remaining steps of the FBA shown in Figure 9.4 deal with how the information is used to write a BIP and monitor its effectiveness. How the FBA information will be used varies depending on the purpose and goals of the BIP, but, generally, the BIP will take information obtained during the FBA to identify potential strategies to reduce or eliminate problem behaviors, whatever they may be.

Curriculum-Based Measures (CBM)

Progress monitoring relies on collecting data periodically and using it to make instructional decisions. CBM has gained in popularity as a technique for monitoring student performance while considering curricular goals and instructional techniques. Accordingly, CBM measures are typically the assessments of choice for monitoring student progress over time. Professionals use assessment measures that determine how students are performing not only in relationship to the peer group but also in relationship to the curriculum and instruction presented daily. Recently, progress monitoring has also become a critical feature of LD identification procedures that employ the MTSS procedure. See the Working Together feature for information about how general education teachers collaborate with special educators to establish an MTSS implementation.

To assist educators in designing, implementing, and evaluating instruction to meet the needs of an increasingly diverse student population, assessment procedures must be versatile yet valid. With CBM, the content of the curriculum and the content found in the assessment are the same. The teacher uses material from the students' curricula to determine where students should be placed, what their instructional objectives should be, and how they are progressing. In this section, we describe (a) the purposes of CBM, (b) ways to design CBM measures, (c) data collection and analysis procedures, and (d) procedures for pairing instruction and evaluation. (See the literature on CBM and precision teaching, both use graphing, decision-making rules, and intervention recommendations to guide the instructional process.) As you read each section, think about a student you may know or have observed who struggles in an academic subject. What considerations should occur at each step to help reduce the need for later adaptations based on the test's and the student's characteristics?

CBM has several purposes:

- To measure directly the curriculum being taught
- To establish a link between students' IEPs and classroom instruction
- To provide a means for monitoring student progress and evaluating the effectiveness of an intervention being used to teach the instructional objective
- To obtain data during the prereferral stage about students' progress in the general education setting without special education services
- To provide a more culturally fair or culture neutral means of assessing the progress of youngsters from culturally and linguistically diverse backgrounds
- To determine initial placement in a task analysis of skills

Thus, CBM offers an alternative to other standardized testing procedures as a means for teachers to place students in an intervention program, monitor progress during an intervention, and evaluate instructional programs being implemented.

Designing Curriculum-Based Measures

CBM can help identify the initial instructional placement and measure students' progress across the identified instructional objectives. Before identifying instructional placement within the designated curriculum, teachers should refer to the IEP and identify the goals designated for instruction. By examining these goals, teachers can begin to develop an idea of the content and skill areas that require instruction. The next step is to design the placement CBM. Taylor (2003) listed five steps to follow when constructing CBMs for instructional purposes.

STEP 1: Analyze the curriculum.

Examine the curriculum and match to student's goals on the IEP. An example of a goal might be, "The student will compute whole numbers."

STEP 2: Prepare items to match curriculum objectives (task analysis).

Break down Step 1 into smaller steps that can become instructional objectives. Instructional objectives for the goal identified in Step 1 might include the following: two-digit + one-digit numbers with no regrouping, two-digit + two-digit with no regrouping, three-digit + two-digit with no regrouping, three-digit + three-digit with no regrouping, two-digit + one-digit with regrouping, two-digit + two-digit with regrouping, three-digit + two-digit with regrouping, and three-digit + three-digit with regrouping to the tens and hundreds place. Select items that match each objective (e.g., 12 + 7; 34 + 15; 596 + 78).

STEP 3: Probe frequently.

Develop sufficient items (four or five) for each objective to ensure the student has enough opportunities to respond frequently in the time frame allowed. Develop several versions of the measure for testing across several days. Administer the test once a week or once every 2 weeks throughout the intervention.

STEP 4: Load data into a graphing format.

Once data are obtained, have students graph (i.e., chart) the data so they can self-monitor their progress.

STEP 5: Yield to results

Determine whether students are making progress toward their goals. If they are, continue the intervention. If a student is not making progress, however, try regrouping or adapting the instruction to better meet individual student needs. The key is to always follow the results of the assessment to make data-based instructional decisions.

A major component of CBM is the collection and evaluation of data for determining placement and progress in an instructional sequence. A data collection system that accurately measures the targeted skill is selected, and teachers implement specific data analysis procedures to determine whether their intervention is, indeed, making a difference with the students.

Teachers can incorporate charting into their progress monitoring using CBM data, similar to what was discussed in the Documenting Progress section above. An example appears in Figure 9.5. Here, a student has been given 40 addition and subtraction facts to calculate in 1 minute. The number of items answered correctly in that time span (calculations correct per minute, CCPM, on the y-axis of the graph) is graphed on a sheet of paper. The students can do this themselves to see their own progress.

FIGURE 9.5 ■ Sample Chart Depicting Correct Calculations per Minute

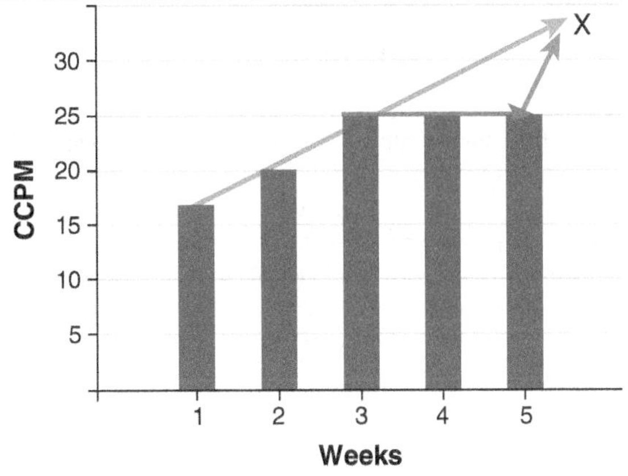

In our sample, the student's scores were graphed weekly, (see the x-axis). Through Week 3, the student was making progress toward his end-of-semester objective (marked with an X). But then, for three consecutive weeks, the student's scores plateaued. We have drawn an arrow to show how much progress is needed in the short time remaining before the end of the semester. The arrow demonstrates that changes must be made in the program to ensure sufficient progress toward the student's goal.

Technical Adequacy

Whatever they are, assessment measures must be technically sound or adequate. Two important aspects of technical adequacy are reliability and validity.

Reliability means the assessment instrument must yield consistent results (Salvia et al., 2017). There are several types of reliability. Internal consistency reliability tells us whether items of a measure consistently assess the same thing (e.g., spelling, addition). Results achieved on a measure one day should match results achieved if the assessment is conducted again a short time later (usually from a day to 2 weeks); this is called test-retest reliability. When measures have multiple forms, such as Form A, Form B, and Form C (this is common in progress monitoring), alternative forms reliability demonstrates that each form provides similar scores. Interscorer agreement or interobserver reliability demonstrates that scorers or observers are all seeing the same thing when they score a measure (e.g., a writing rubric) or when they observe a student in the classroom. The less reliable a measure is, the less confident we can be in the results of a test, observation, or scoring system.

Measures must also yield valid results; in other words, scores must reflect performance on the construct the measure claims to be assessing (Miller et al., 2013). A spelling test that consists of addition and subtraction items is not a spelling test, obviously, and the test's scores would never be considered a valid performance estimate of spelling abilities. But spelling test authors must go farther than simply creating a measure that looks like it is assessing spelling (face validity). They must demonstrate that the items have content validity or come from a legitimate source and meet basic statistical criteria, have criterion-related validity and so produce results similar to those of established spelling tests, and have construct validity, meaning they produce results associated with the construct being measured. Test authors can demonstrate their test's construct validity by showing that the measures produce results related to other written language skills, that students get higher test scores as they get older and become better spellers, and that the test differentiates known poor spellers from known good spellers.

Teachers should be mindful of technical adequacy when they administer measures, when measures are administered by others such as school psychologists or diagnosticians, or when they attend meetings such as IEP meetings. Most publishers of assessment instruments provide evidence of technical adequacy in their accompanying technical manuals, but when attending meetings about measures that are not known to them, teachers can inquire about the technical adequacy of the instruments administered. It is critical that decisions about students based on assessment results should be made only when measures are technically sound.

WORKING TOGETHER

RESPONSE TO INTERVENTION IMPLEMENTATION

With the passage of IDEA 2004, school districts can now use the MTSS procedure to help in the LD identification process. This procedure uses a multitiered approach to identify early those students who may be at risk for having LDs and to intervene in kindergarten, Grade 1, or Grade 2 to help reduce the likelihood that students will be misidentified as having LDs.

General education teachers work closely with special educators to help set up a multitiered system wherein young children are given CBMs in the fall of the school year. Those students who fall below preset benchmarks, often set at the 25th percentile, are targeted for small group supplemental instruction in the second tier. Students receiving the supplemental instruction continue to receive regular class instruction in the core curriculum but also are provided additional, small group instruction using validated practices designed to help them increase their skill levels to those of their peers.

Special educators can help general education teachers identify reliable CBMs that yield valid results and can also help teachers identify research-based supplemental instructional procedures. Every 2 weeks or so, CBMs are readministered and provide an index of growth for each student receiving supplemental instruction. If the students are making progress, no changes are made to the supplemental program. However, instruction for students who are not making sufficient progress is modified to better meet their needs. After 8 to 12 weeks of supplemental instruction, mid-year testing is used to determine whether the students can exit the second tier of intervention or need to continue such instruction for an additional 8 to 12 weeks. After spring testing, students who do not make sufficient progress may be identified as having an LD if they meet additional, federally prescribed criteria.

Clearly, assessment plays a critical role in the MTSS process. Additional testing using highly standardized tests may also be administered in the determination of a LD, but CBM is at the heart of the assessment process.

Questions

1. What types of questions might a general education teacher ask a special educator as they discuss MTSS-related issues?
2. Put yourself in the position of the general education teacher. How might you find information about your school's MTSS program? What questions might you need to have answered?
3. Why are assessments important during the MTSS process?

ADAPTING AND MODIFYING ASSESSMENTS FOR STUDENTS WITH UNIQUE LEARNING NEEDS

Assessment adaptations include any change in administration, scoring, and interpretation procedures made specifically because of a test taker's ability. Their purpose is to level the playing field, meaning each test taker has the same chance as any other student to succeed, whether the assessment is a high-stakes test or Friday's spelling quiz.

The discussion of assessment adaptations begins by exploring universal design as it applies to assessment. We then briefly discuss the role of parents in making test adaptations or accommodations. Then we introduce different adaptation categories. The section concludes with a discussion of assessment adaptations by examining two specific applications where assessment adaptations may or may not be warranted: high-stakes testing and grading. We also briefly discuss alternative assessments. Many of the adaptation procedures described in the section can be generalized to any number of additional scenarios related to assessments.

Universal Design for Assessment

As described in Chapter 8, the term *universal design* refers to barrier-free systems that meet the needs of everyone, including people with disabilities (Smith et al., 2018). Initially used in conjunction with accessible housing for people with and without disabilities, universal design has expanded to teaching and testing. The premise is that curricula and assessments should be made accessible to all students by "remov[ing] barriers to accurate measurement of learner knowledge, skills, and engagement" (CAST, 2011, p. 8).

With regard to universal design for assessment, more than 15 years ago Thompson, Johnstone, and Thurlow (2002) provided some suggestions for making tests more accessible to all students that are still relevant today:

- Select an inclusive assessment population. When developing items, think about all students who will participate in the assessment. Ideally, examiners would afford examinees equal opportunity to prepare for a test.
- Precisely define test content. Define what is to be tested so that irrelevant cognitive, sensory, emotional, and physical barriers can be removed.

- Choose accessible, nonbiased items. Build accessibility into items from the beginning, and use bias review teams to ensure that quality is retained in all items.
- Be amenable to accommodations. Test design must facilitate the use of need accommodations (e.g., all items can be communicated in braille).
- Provide simple, clear, and intuitive instructions and procedures. Make sure students are easily able to follow the directions for taking a test.
- Ensure maximum readability and comprehensibility. For example, use plain language strategies and other approaches that reduce ambiguity and increase understandability.
- Ensure maximum legibility. Apply characteristics that ensure easy decipherability to text, tables, figures and illustrations, and response formats.

Parental Involvement

Parents are (or should be) active participants in all aspects of their children's education, including assessments. They should be aware of, and sign off on, testing accommodations that have been suggested for their child. In addition, parents can request testing accommodations the district should consider. The Partnership for Assessment of Readiness for College and Careers (PARCC, 2013) has written a parental guidebook that outlines roles and responsibilities; see the link in the References to download a copy of the guide.

One section of the guide is titled "What Parents Can Do to Support Their Child." Here is what PARCC offers to parents:

- Familiarize yourself with the Common Core State Standards. Talk to your child's teachers about what they are learning.
- Learn about the PARCC assessments—their purpose, what they measure, and how the results will be used.
- Learn about PARCC accessibility features and accommodations. Identify those that your child may need or find helpful to use at home, in the classroom, and on the PARCC assessments.
- Find out how your child's teachers are preparing for the assessments and how they are helping your child get ready.
- Talk to your child about the accommodations they already use on tests. Discuss whether or not your child thinks they are helping them. Share this information with your child's teachers—or encourage your child to share their ideas with teachers.
- Share information about your child's strengths and needs related to using computers for work assignments with educators. Include information about the types of strategies your child uses routinely to complete homework assignments and other tasks in the home and the community.
- Encourage your child to use the accessibility features and/or accommodations identified in their IEP or Section 504 plan at home, if possible.
- Ask about the technology your child will be using for the PARCC assessments. Ask about how your child can practice using the technology during school.
- Make sure your child is willing to use the accommodation(s) and/or accessibility feature(s). Inform their teacher if your child is having difficulty using an accommodation.
- Research possible state and/or regional technology centers for information on matching student needs with allowable assistive technology. (PARCC, 2013, p. 4)

To make assessments accessible to all students, teachers should give simple, clear, and intuitive instructions and ensure that students are easily able to follow the directions.

iStock.com/aldomurillo

As a teacher, you will likely be the first person that parents contact with questions about their student's testing. Check with your district to see if a parental handbook is available that can provide useful information. If there is one, provide parents with a copy, but at the same time explain its content. If there is no handbook available, create one and have it checked by decision makers in your district assessment office. In any case, remember that not all parents understand education language, and even though these handbooks are typically written with parents in mind, no two parents are alike. Many will need the material presented in a way that they can understand, and they trust you with that task.

Adaptation Categories

Assessment adaptations tend to cluster around four basic areas: (a) **input adaptations**, (b) output adaptations, (c) time and/or schedule adaptations, and (d) location adaptations. We add a fifth area, (e) academic qualifications, which deals more with curriculum issues than with testing adaptations.

Input Adaptations

Input adaptations adjust the way students access test stimuli and questions. More than 25 years ago, Hammill, Brown, and Bryant (1992) identified three testing input formats that remain relevant today for assessment adaptations: listening (the test taker listens to instructions and/or test questions), reading print (words and numbers), and looking at stimuli, such as spatial tests that have the student look at a two-dimensional, unfolded drawing and ask what the object would look like if folded into a three-dimensional object. The input of test items should suit the needs of all students, including those who have a disability. For example, a student with a reading LD is unlikely to do well on a science test if they have to read the question. In this instance, recognizing student needs allows teachers to adapt the test input to allow the student to demonstrate acquisition of science knowledge. Remember, the test is meant to assess what the students know about the science content, not how well they read. Reading is simply a format that allows testing to be done in a group setting.

To illustrate that the key considerations for input adaptations deals with the content that is being assessed by the test, consider Marilou, a student we met earlier in Ms. Rodriguez's class. In two weeks, she is going to take two tests, back to back, that require reading paragraphs and responding to multiple-choice questions. The first test is a measure of reading comprehension, and the second test assesses knowledge of science concepts. Because Marilou has a LD in reading, she struggles with both test formats, so she decides to speak with Ms. Rodriguez about possible input adaptations.

Marilou will probably not be allowed to use an adapted input format for the reading comprehension test, but she is likely to receive adaptations for the science test. Why? The content of the reading test is reading. Adaptations that remove reading from the task defeat the purpose of the test; in other words, changing the input format changes the content being measured. This is one litmus test of any assessment adaptation. If the content being measured by the assessment is altered, the adaptation proposal is likely to be unsound.

Science content, on the other hand, would not be altered if we remove reading as the input format. The test uses reading as an efficient way to test large numbers of students' understanding of science because the assumption is that all (or at least most) test takers can read the paragraphs and questions. But reading ability itself is not being tested. Thus, because the content of the assessment is not being changed, altering the input format to speech would be legitimate.

Output Adaptations

Output adaptations adjust the way a test taker responds to test questions. Output formats include speaking, minor (providing a one- or two-word response); speaking, major (responding with sentences); manipulating objects (e.g., blocks or coins); marking an answer sheet (the familiar "fill in the bubble"); pointing; drawing; and writing print. If a test's output format interferes with its ability to provide valid scores for a student who has a disability, output adaptations can be made.

Consider Juanita from the chapter's opening example, who has a neurological impairment that affects her fine motor skills. As a result of this disability, Juanita has trouble grasping a pencil, and when she finally controls it, she has difficulty using the pencil to write or make identifiable marks. Juanita is studying to take a social studies exam in three days. This exam requires students to read multiple-choice questions and respond by filling in bubbles of a Scantron sheet. Thus, the test's output format will make it nearly impossible for Juanita to mark the answer sheet (completely filling in a bubble without going outside the bubble). Clearly, the test's content has nothing to do with filling in bubbles on an answer sheet; it is measuring social studies skills. Therefore, it is likely that Ms. Rodriguez will alter the test's output format for Juanita to allow her to better respond to the test questions.

Time and/or Schedule Adaptations

When appropriate, teachers may extend testing time and may also change the way the time is organized. Extended time is a common test adaptation. The idea is that people with reading LDs, even if they are able to read the text, do so at a much slower rate than their peers without LDs. Thus, the slow readers will not have the same opportunity to complete the test as their peers without LDs.

Most tests have time limits. Most students are expected to complete all of the test items in the prescribed time allocation. Students with disabilities who are not be able to complete the test in the allotted time will receive time adaptations. In addition, a test could be organized to provide 25 minutes for one test to be taken, give students a 5-minute break, and then call for a second test to be administered after the break. Some students, by the nature of their disability, may be fatigued and require a longer break between test administrations. Depending on the circumstances, the students might be allowed to wait longer before completing the rest of the test. Such an adjustment is a schedule adaptation.

Location Adaptations

Location adaptations change the setting in which a test is administered or the conditions of the test setting. Some students have disabilities that affect their ability to perform when distractions occur around them. For these students, a conventional testing setting, perhaps a classroom with windows overlooking the playground where students are playing, might be inappropriate, and an isolated setting may be an appropriate location adaptation. In addition, some students with behavior issues may need to be tested in a situation that minimizes the effects of their behavior on others.

Academic Qualifications

Although they are not really adaptations in the true sense of the word, academic qualifications are used to identify whether a person should take the test in the first place. Most students with disabilities, by law, participate in the general education curriculum, so they will take the same tests as their nondisabled peers. However, some students with severe disabilities have IEPs that focus on special academic areas such as life skills. In this instance, alternative assessments may be deemed to be more appropriate than a test that measures mastery of content the students haven't been taught.

Adaptations for High-Stakes Testing

Most states have adopted the CCSS (National Governors Association Center for Best Practices & Council of Chief State School Officers, 2010). For the first several years of the CCSS, there was no standard high-stakes assessment that measured performance on the standards. States that had adopted the CCSS were left to either adjust their state's high-stakes tests to conform to the new standards or continue to test the non-CCSS content that had been assessed by the previously administered instruments. To remedy the situation, the Smarter Balanced Assessment Consortium and the PARCC wrote and field-tested a standardized assessment. Non-CCSS states will continue to use their own high-stakes tests.

Curricular Content

Usually, a team of curriculum experts meets and creates, for each subject area, a list of skills they want taught to their state's students. Essentially, they are telling teachers across the state what is important for all students in their classrooms to learn in kindergarten, Grade 1, and so on through high school. Through this process, state departments of education tell their teachers and population, "This is important for all children in [any state]. We care enough about our children's education that we have created a set of skills all children should have before they go on to the next grade. Also, we want to make sure that all students in our state are learning the same content, so if students move within the state, they will be able to transition to the school more easily." Supposedly, when students have learned everything they should know in the third grade, they are ready to learn the material in the fourth grade, and so on until graduation.

Assessment Issues

Once the curriculum skills have been set, a team of experts creates a test to measure those skills, and these state exams form the basis for most states' high-stakes testing. Think about the logic behind the testing. It begins with "These are the skills that all students in the state of [any state] need in order to graduate from high school." Then it moves to, "If students need to know this information by the end of high school, what skills do they need at the end of the ninth grade? What skills and concepts did the curriculum experts decide ninth-grade students should possess? We'll create a test of those skills, which students will take at the end of ninth grade. If they fail the test, they have to repeat the ninth grade until they are ready for the 10th grade." Most states do not test at every grade level; they pick key grades for testing, usually two or three years apart. For most students in states with this policy, high-stakes testing can begin as early as the third grade.

High-stakes testing has a dramatic effect on teachers and students. First, teachers have to teach the skills the state has specified. Fortunately, most publishers of basal textbooks understand this, so they work to ensure a correspondence between these enumerated skills and the skills that are taught in textbooks. If there are gaps, teachers are responsible for filling them.

As we have already noted, not all students have to participate in high-stakes testing. If a student has a disability, the student's IEP might state that they are **exempt** from such testing. However, states are increasingly devising alternative tests for students with disabilities. This approach stems from the belief that all students should be accountable for learning.

Adaptation Issues

If a student with a disability is going to take a high-stakes test, test adaptations may be made to compensate for the student's disability. The decision to do so is not made haphazardly. Usually, states and districts have set policies governing the choice; teachers might wish to consider the following six-step procedure. (Note: Throughout this section, we deal with disability-related adaptations for high-stakes testing.)

STEP 1: As the IEP committee, discuss whether the student should participate in state and district assessment.

This step has three components:

A. Examine a student's IEP goals and the content of the educational program or the state's curriculum.

B. Examine the purpose of the state- and districtwide assessments and the content of the assessments.

C. Measure the match between the student's educational program and the content of the assessment.

If there is no match between the student's educational program and the content of the assessment, the student may be exempted from the testing. If there is a match, the next step in the process is to determine whether adaptations are warranted.

STEP 2: As a committee, discuss the student's need for test adaptations.

IEP committees should examine the input and output formats of the state- and district-wide assessments and the IEP and student work samples to determine whether the formats of the assessment will yield valid results. If the committee agrees that the formats match the student's abilities, there is probably no need for adaptations. If, however, the formats preclude achieving valid results because they do not allow for the student's limitations (e.g., Sonya's inability to read precludes her using reading as an input format that yields valid results), adaptations might be needed.

STEP 3: As a committee, identify test adaptations that respond to the student's needs identified in Step 2.

Earlier, we described several areas where adaptations typically take place. To review, do input concerns preclude obtaining valid results in a typical setting? Does the output format need to be altered to ensure that the student can complete the task? Or, if they read slowly because of the disability, is more time needed to complete the task? If the student is easily distracted, is a different testing location needed?

STEP 4: As a committee, document your decision in the IEP. If the IEP committee decides the student should not participate, members should recommend an appropriate alternative assessment.

STEP 5: As a committee, collect data and develop procedures for monitoring the effectiveness of adaptations.

What type of data should teachers collect? Usually, there are four sources of data. First, collect student scores on two versions of the same test, with and without adaptations. Remember that it is entirely possible the student will fail the test because they do not know the answers to the test items. Adaptations don't guarantee success; they are designed to guarantee only that the results are valid. If the student doesn't know the content and, with adaptations, demonstrates that lack of knowledge, then the results are valid.

Interview the students after testing to gauge their reactions. Did the adaptations work? Are there other issues that arose during testing that you need to know about?

Teachers also must be interviewed. This interview can be conducted at any time to learn about a particular student's academic characteristics, but it is important to know whether test adaptations have been used successfully in class. Ideally, each teacher will be a member of the committee and will provide input during each stage of the process.

STEP 6: Finally, interview the student's parents.

What are their perceptions of the testing process and the way it affects their child? Parents will be dramatically affected by the results of the high-stakes assessment, so they need to have input throughout the process, and their reactions to the committee's findings and the testing process should be documented. Ideally, they too have been members of the committee, but that is not always the case.

Alternative Assessments

Although states differ in the options they make available to students with disabilities in high- stakes testing, all states have some sort of alternative testing plan available. The Every Student Succeeds Act has dictated that no more than 1% of students may be assessed using alternative assessments. As a result, such assessments are usually administered only to students with severe cognitive disabilities or those whose disability requires alternative means for testing.

The National Center on Educational Outcomes (NCEO) suggests three approaches that states may use when conducting alternative assessments. Alternative assessments based on alternative achievement standards are used with students with the most severe cognitive limitations. "These assessments are based on the grade-level content covered by the typical assessment used with all students, but they do so at reduced depth, breadth, and complexity. These assessments describe achievement based on what a state determines is a high expectation for these students" (NCEO, 2013, para. 3).

Alternative assessments based on modified achievement standards can be administered to students with disabilities who are accessing the general education curriculum that is covered by the general assessment but who may need more time to take the test. According to NCEO (2013, para. 4), "These assessments measure a student's mastery of grade-level content but are less difficult than grade-level achievement standards." States that use these alternative assessments are in the process of discontinuing this option.

Alternative assessments based on grade-level achievement standards "include the same grade-level content as the general assessment and describe achievement in the same way as the general assessment" (NCEO, 2013, para. 5). These alternative assessments are for students with disabilities who require alternative testing formats or procedures that typically are not included as part of the general assessment or are not addressed with use of accommodations.

Some organizations, such as the National Center and State Collaborative and the Educational Testing Service, have been working with selected states and groups for years to construct and field-test reliable alternative assessments that yield valid results. Much of this work is aligned with the CCSS. Other states are taking it upon themselves to create their own alternative assessments, particularly those that have chosen not to adopt the CCSS. In these cases, the alternative assessments focus on individual state standards.

ADAPT IN ACTION

MARILOU: ADAPTING TEST INPUT

Earlier we introduced you to Marilou, a student in Ms. Rodriguez's class. Marilou is new to the school and has serious reading problems. She is unable to decode words and has very little comprehension of written science materials she is assigned. Ms. Rodriguez has just completed a science unit and is about to administer a paper-and-pencil, multiple-choice test to her students. Think about Marilou and the problems such a test might present. Use the ADAPT Framework to find a way to test Marilou's knowledge of the science unit that produces valid results.

A: Ask, "What am I requiring the student to do?" Marilou must read test items and select a response from four choices, a typical multiple-choice test.

D: Determine the prerequisite skills of the task. Marilou must be able to listen to instructions, read the test items and each response choice, recall her science knowledge to identify the answer to each question, and circle her answer, A, B, C, or D.

A: Analyze the student's strengths and struggles. Ms. Rodriguez recognizes that Marilou will struggle with reading the test items and each response choice.

P: Propose and implement adaptations from among the four categories. For "reading the test items and each response choice," Ms. Rodriguez can reduce the number of test items by sampling the material and selecting the items that best differentiate between successful and unsuccessful readers (instructional content). She can also give Marilou a digital player to listen to the test questions and response choices (instructional material). Ms. Rodriguez can also choose to read Marilou the items aloud; she can either circle her answers on the scoring sheet or state her answers (delivery of instruction).

T: Test to discover whether the adaptations helped the student accomplish the task. Ms. Rodriguez will examine the test to determine student performance with the adaptations.

SUMMARY

This chapter presents techniques for promoting positive behavior and facilitating social skills. Both of these areas can greatly influence a teacher's success in promoting an atmosphere for learning. Identifying specific behavioral and social tasks will help teachers plan effective adaptations and interventions that can provide students with skills to use not only in the classroom but also schoolwide and in the community.

By utilizing assessment practices, teachers will realize quickly how successful their adaptations and intervention programs are in promoting an environment that is conducive to learning. Implementing practices discussed in this chapter will help students with disabilities become more involved in the classroom and be better accepted by their peers.

REVIEW THE LEARNING OBJECTIVES

Let's review the learning objectives for this chapter. If you are uncertain and cannot talk through the answers provided for any of these questions, reread those sections of the text.

9.1 Explain why we assess students.
There are several reasons for assessing students. One reason is to identify strengths and weaknesses. Another reason is to determine the student's relative standing in class compared with the other students. Informing instruction, documenting progress, and determining program eligibility are yet other reasons. Finally, grading and determining adequate yearly progress are reasons for assessing students.

9.2 Describe how we assess students with unique learning needs.
Norm-referenced tests compare a person's performance with that of their peers. Criterion-referenced tests measure abilities against a mastery standard. And non-referenced tests examine the strategies that a person uses when problem solving. CBMs provide information that is curriculum specific, and performance-based assessments allow for authentic information gathering that cannot be obtained using conventional assessments.

9.3 Explain how we adapt and modify assessments for students with unique learning needs.
Assessment adaptations include any change in administration, scoring, and interpretation procedures we make specifically because of a test taker's ability. Their purpose is to level the playing field, meaning each test taker has the same chance as any other student to succeed, whether the assessment is a high-stakes test or Friday's spelling quiz.

REVISIT THE OPENING CHALLENGE

Check your answers to the Reflection Questions in the Opening Challenge and revise them on the basis of what you have learned.

1. How can Mr. Watson set up a progress-monitoring procedure?
2. How can Mr. Watson set goals and chart his students' progress?
3. How can Ms. Rodriguez teach Marilou science and test her abilities when she cannot read?
4. What measures are available to identify Juanita's attentional difficulties and Angel's mathematics struggles?
5. How can assessments be used to identify specific student strengths and struggles and inform instruction?

KEY TERMS

active process assessment
adequate yearly progress
age equivalents
assessment
basal textbook
benchmark
construct validity
content validity
criterion-referenced tests
criterion-related validity
cumulative folders
derived scores
diagnostic measures
ecological assessment
exempt
grade equivalent
high-stakes assessments
holistic evaluation
informal reading inventory
input adaptations
inter-individual
intra-individual difference
norm-referenced interpretations
norm-referenced tests
observations
percentiles
process assessment
reliability
screening
self-regulation
survey batteries
validity

PROFESSIONAL STANDARDS AND LICENSURE

For a complete description of Professional Standards and Licensure, please see the appendix.

CEC Initial Preparation Standards

Standard 1: Learner Development and Individual Learning Differences

Standard 3: Curricular Content Knowledge

Standard 4: Assessment

INTASC Core Principles

Standard 2: Learning Differences

Standard 4: Content Knowledge

Standard 6: Assessment

Praxis II: Education of Exceptional Students: Core Content Knowledge

III. Delivery of Services to Students with Disabilities: Assessment

iStock.com/evgenyatamanenko

10 PROMOTING POSITIVE BEHAVIOR AND FACILITATING SOCIAL SKILLS

This chapter was written with the assistance of Dr. Andrea Flower.

LEARNING OBJECTIVES

After studying this chapter, you will be able to meet the following learning objectives:

10.1 Describe practices that can be used to foster student relationships and communication.

10.2 Explain ways that can be used to communicate effectively with students.

10.3 Discuss effective classroom arrangement practices.

10.4 Explain the goals of misbehavior.

10.5 Discuss ways that problem behaviors can be assessed.

10.6 Describe instructional strategies that are available for behavior problems.

10.7 Explain how safer schools can be promoted.

Opening Challenge

Addressing Behaviors and Social Problems

Elementary Grades. Mr. Abbar is midway through his 15th year of teaching and in his fifth year of teaching second grade. Three weeks ago, a new student, Miranda, joined his class after moving from another state. Miranda was diagnosed as having autism spectrum disorder (ASD) as a preschooler and has been in inclusive settings throughout her schooling. Mr. Abbar has never had a student diagnosed with ASD and, because Miranda is new to his class, he did not have a chance to attend professional development sessions about Miranda's challenging behaviors. Miranda presents social and behavioral challenges that Mr. Abbar has not confronted before. For example, when Suzanne, a classmate, came to school with a new haircut, Miranda blurted out, "Ewwww, that's ugly," causing Suzanne to start crying and other classmates to yell at Miranda, resulting in a meltdown. Miranda speaks without thinking at times; because of the statements she makes, her classmates sometimes see her as a bully. Miranda also demands to go first in activities, refuses to work in small groups with other students, does not respond well to changes in routine, and screams when she does not get her way or is frustrated.

For 3 days per week for half a day, a special education teacher comes into the classroom to provide support. She works with Miranda as Mr. Abbar teaches lessons. The special education teacher, Ms. Davidson, rephrases Mr. Abbar's instructions at times to make the lessons more accessible and also serves to calm Miranda when she gets frustrated or upset. Once each week, the special education teacher meets with Mr. Abbar during his planning period to provide professional development on how to meet Miranda's unique demands.

Secondary Grades. It is October of Ms. Nguyen's third year of teaching eighth-grade English, and she is planning lessons for the upcoming week. She connects her lessons to the Common Core State Standards and the district's curricula. She makes sure that there are activities that keep her students engaged. Depending on the lesson, she pairs students with disabilities with students who have stronger skills. However, things are not going very well for her students with disabilities. Ms. Nguyen is puzzled about three students who seem to challenge her day in and day out. She has read their school folders, but she believes that she doesn't know them well.

One student, Ingrid, is identified as having attention deficit hyperactivity disorder (ADHD). Ms. Nguyen studied this condition in her teacher-preparation program and even worked with one student with ADHD during student teaching, but having a student with ADHD in her class all day long is wearing her out. Ms. Nguyen begins to question her ability to work effectively with Ingrid: *"How can I get her to pay attention? How can I help her get organized? She forgets what to do and can't remember to return homework. Why does she have so few friends? Am I really prepared to help this child learn?"*

Her second student, Marco, is identified as having a mild emotional or behavioral disorder. He was retained in fifth grade. Ms. Nguyen worries about Marco: *"I don't really understand his disability. Why is he so defiant? He seems to do things on purpose just to be disruptive and get everyone's attention. He calls out—I mean he answers without being called on—frequently. What can I do with him so that he will stop interfering with my teaching? Why does he bully the other children? Shouldn't he be in a special education classroom?"*

Finally, Ms. Nguyen turns her thoughts to Marion, who has a learning disability in reading and writing: *"She seems so lost during group instruction and spends way too much time fiddling with things in her desk, sharpening her pencils, and being off task. Why can't she work with the other students? What's wrong?"*

Ms. Nguyen asks herself, *"How can I help these students behave? What can I do about their social skills? How do I know whether my teaching practices are working?"*

Reflection Questions

In your journal, write down your answers to the following questions. After completing the chapter, check your answers and revise them on the basis of what you have learned.

1. If you were Mr. Abbar, in what areas would you seek professional development help from the special education teacher?
2. How might Mr. Abbar be able to identify specific challenges that Miranda presents?
3. What advice would you offer Ms. Nguyen about getting to know her students better?
4. How can Mr. Abbar and Ms. Nguyen foster student relationships and communication?
5. How can both teachers help their students with their behavior?
6. How can both teachers determine whether student behavior skills are improving?
7. How can Mr. Abbar and Ms. Nguyen use the ADAPT Framework to promote positive behavior?

Teachers must create and manage a classroom environment that fosters student learning and interactions, reduces situations that promote the occurrence of problem behaviors, and addresses those unacceptable behaviors that interfere with teaching and learning. For example, consider Ingrid, Marco, and Marion in the Opening Challenge. Practices are available that teachers can use to help students with their behavior and social problems. Some of these practices are discussed in this chapter. Research findings have shown that teacher focus on creating and managing the classroom, student behavior, and social aspects of learning involving behavior management and applied behavior analysis (ABA) promote an environment that is conducive to teaching and learning (American Psychological Association, 2014; Wolfgang, 2009).

This chapter presents practices that teachers can use to improve student relationships and communication. You will learn about ways to promote appropriate behavior and to facilitate the social skills of all students. You will also learn about treatments that could be necessary for a small number of students so that they can succeed in inclusive settings. Assessment techniques will help you identify behaviors and social skills that require treatment and determine whether these treatments are effective. Finally, you will learn about positive behavioral supports, a process supported by the Individuals with Disabilities Education Improvement Act (IDEA, 2004; Office of Special Education Programs [OSEP], 2004), and also about ways to promote safer schools. The ADAPT Framework will be implemented throughout the chapter so that you can learn how to use the framework to promote positive behavior and to facilitate social skills in your classroom.

PRACTICES THAT CAN BE USED TO FOSTER STUDENT RELATIONSHIPS AND COMMUNICATION

There are a number of practices you can use to cultivate good relationships with—and among—the students you teach.

Know Your Students

Students' attitudes, beliefs, experiences, and backgrounds influence their perspectives about school and learning and how they interact with their teachers. Teachers who get to know their students quickly can design their teaching according to students' interests, background experiences, and attitudes. In this way, teachers demonstrate they care about their students' learning. Teachers should take time to get to know their students by talking with them before school, between classes, during a conference, and in small groups. Taking time to talk to students is one of the most powerful techniques for fostering positive relationships and creating an effective learning community.

To learn more about their students with disabilities, teachers can examine their students' IEPs (for a complete discussion on IEPs, see Chapter 2) to determine their academic and social goals. IEPs can provide beneficial information about those areas in which the students need support. It is possible that these areas might be prerequisite skills for the behavior and social skills tasks that teachers expect from their students. For example, if students are expected to follow classroom directions and the student's IEP indicates that assistance is needed to help the student follow directions, the teacher may need to adapt the delivery of directions for that student by shortening the length of directions and including cues and reminders. With practice, these adaptations can be implemented naturally and with minimal effort. Often, adaptations benefit many students in the classroom, including those who have IEPs.

Student Relationships

Teachers can also get to know their students through a variety of activities. For example, students can complete an **interest inventory** that includes a series of questions good for a particular age group. It can help teachers learn more about their students' backgrounds, interests, and perspectives. Questions that help teachers get to know students better include the following:

- "How many brothers and sisters do you have?"
- "What is your favorite movie and why?"
- "What was the name of the last book you read that you enjoyed?"
- "What is your favorite sport?"
- "What do you like to do after school?"
- "What do you like to do on the weekends?"
- "What is your favorite television show?"
- "Who is your hero and why?"
- "How do you know if someone is your friend?"
- "How can we help people who are mean to other people?"
- "If you could change one thing about school, what would it be and why?"
- "What do you like most about school?"
- "How do you spend time with your family?"
- "If you could change one thing in your life, what would that be?"

Answers to these sample questions, obtained orally or in writing, can provide teachers with information about their students. Information from the interest inventory can be used to begin discussions and help decide which books to select for class literature groups, topics for group work, and ideas for research. Interest inventory answers also can provide important information about students' cultural background and experience (Zakrzewski, 2012).

Motivational Practices

Conducting practices that will motivate students is another way that you can promote positive student interactions. When creating or implementing instruction, it is important to target what motivates students to perform well, whether academically, behaviorally, or socially. For example, at times students may be bored or frustrated with the academic tasks presented to them. Those who have been identified as gifted and talented might not be challenged adequately in inclusive settings with the general education curriculum. Enrichment activities included in instructional materials or in basal textbooks (i.e., those used to teach subject-area content) are good resources for extra tasks needed by those students who are gifted and talented. In contrast, students with learning and behavior difficulties have experienced different degrees of success and failure with academic and social interactions. These successes and failures influence their motivational levels for classroom activities and assignments.

Later in this chapter, information about functional behavior assessment (FBA) is discussed. FBA can help teachers determine reasons why students are not motivated to do their best in class. Using FBA to identify specific reasons can influence how teachers access teaching. For example, if some students are reluctant to work on a research project, giving them more instruction in the steps for doing research or in getting online to locate research materials may increase their motivation to complete a research project.

Older students may exhibit challenging behavior that is often prompted by a lack of motivation for tasks that continue to frustrate them. For example, older students with reading difficulties have spent years struggling with textbook reading. As the challenges of the classroom shift from "learning to read" to "reading to learn," older students could demonstrate problem behavior that is an expression of their frustration. Given that older students are allowed to legally drop out of school, teachers of older students with academic and behavior problems are challenged to conduct effective techniques for motivating them.

When teaching students of all ages, it is important to differentiate between students with a skill deficit (i.e., the student has not mastered specific skills) and those with a performance deficit (i.e., the student does not consistently exhibit the skill or behavior even though it is in the student's repertoire). Teachers should spend time teaching new skills to students who show a skill deficit. Learning new skills can be motivating for some students who have spent years struggling. Empowering students with new knowledge and the understanding that they can really do it can go a long way toward providing motivation and creating a positive learning community. In comparison, students who demonstrate performance deficits require different procedures. These are students who have learned the skill but lack the motivation to perform under certain circumstances or with certain people. For these students, some of the following motivational techniques can be helpful to foster a positive learning community:

1. Know your students' names and use their names as often as possible.
2. Plan for every class; never try to wing it.
3. Pay attention to the strengths and limitations of each of your students. Reward their strengths and strengthen their weaknesses.
4. If possible, set your room in a U-shape to encourage interaction among students.
5. Vary your instructional strategies; use lectures, demonstrations, discussions, case studies, groups, and more.
6. Review the learning objectives with your students. Be sure students know what they are expected to learn, do, know, etc.
7. Move around the room as you teach.
8. Make your classes relevant. Be sure students see how the content relates to them and to the world around them.
9. Be expressive. Smile.
10. Put some excitement into your speech; vary your pitch, volume, and rate.
11. Give lots of examples.
12. Encourage students to share their ideas and comments, even if they are incorrect. You'll never know what students don't understand unless you ask them.
13. Maintain eye contact and move toward your students as you interact with them. Nod your head to show that you are listening to them.
14. Provide opportunities for students to speak to the class.

15. Be available before class starts, during break, and after class to visit with students.

16. Return assignments and tests to students as soon as reasonably possible. Provide constructive feedback.

17. Be consistent in your treatment of students.

18. Make sure that your exams are current, valid, and reliable. Tie your assessment to your course objectives.

19. Plan around 15- or 20-minute cycles. Students have difficulty maintaining attention after a longer period of time.

20. Involve your students in your teaching. Ask for feedback. (University of Nebraska–Lincoln, Office of Graduate Studies, n.d.)

Positive Relationships With Students

Some students are not motivated to tackle the academic activities at hand. They might not see the relevance of the tasks or might not be interested in how activities are presented. To increase motivation, activities must be conducted in a way that is meaningful to students. What are some examples of meaningful activities? Meaningful activities connect learning to students' interests and encourage them to become involved in their learning. **Student-centered learning** is a type of learning that involves students in the learning process through the use of hands-on activities, discussions, and decision making. Student-centered learning is widely supported as an effective way for teaching and learning (Powell, 2013). Offering exciting learning experiences, such as class plays, group assignments, mock TV news productions, and field trips, encourages student involvement. Actively involving students in the learning process and helping them make connections to real-life situations motivates them to participate in and complete activities (Neo et al., 2012).

Responsive to Cultural Differences

Demographic changes within our society mean that today's classrooms include students from diverse linguistic, ethnic, racial, and socioeconomic backgrounds (Diallo & Maizonniaux, 2017). This rich background of diversity, together with a wide range of individual and familial experiences, serves as a substantial foundation for classroom instruction (Lopez, 2017). Teachers should learn about the social and behavior norms of various cultural, ethnic, and racial groups. Teachers should check their curricula and classroom literature to determine whether students can see themselves reflected in the lessons. Promoting positive student relationships means educators have to be sensitive to the diverse norms in their classrooms (Klingner et al., 2014). For example, in some cultures (e.g., Native American, Hawaiian), there is a spirit of cooperation that is contrary to the focus on competitiveness that is found in other cultures and in many of today's classrooms (Smith et al., 2018).

It is important for teachers to understand behavior patterns that are socially acceptable in some cultures so that they can avoid the possibility of misidentifying students as having behavior disorders. For example, students who show behavioral interactions that are opposite of "mainstream" behavior could be mistakenly identified as having emotional or behavioral disabilities. The misdiagnosis of a disability, and consequently inappropriate assignment to special education, can be disastrous for a student. The results can mean reduced expectations from parents and teachers, low self-esteem, and feelings of inferior achievement.

For example, in Chapter 4 you read about the disproportionate representation of African American and Hispanic students in special education. Some parents, educators, and policymakers believe that one reason for these students' disproportionate representation could rest in a conflict between teachers' perceptions and expectations and students' cultural identity. Take a few moments to read the example in the Considering Diversity section below on the potential conflict between a teacher's perceptions and a student's cultural identity.

How can teachers better understand the cultural values and norms in today's diverse classrooms? How can they plan and implement practices that are responsive to cultural and ethnic norms? Teachers can learn more about their students through observation, questionnaires, and student-teacher conferences. They can ask students how they like to work (alone or in a group), how large a group they prefer, how they seek adult feedback, how they feel about being praised publicly and privately, how they respond to rewards, and how they are disciplined. Student input will help teachers create student-centered activities. Teachers can learn how students from diverse backgrounds perceive the rules and expectations imposed by the teaching staff and the school. Additionally, it is important for teachers to understand how families perceive school environments and the discipline of their children. Teachers can strive to integrate these values and norms into a more cohesive learning community.

Considering Diversity: Mixed Messages?

One expression of cultural identity among African American male adolescents is a walking style that many educators consider nonstandard. The stroll, as it is sometimes called, is characterized as a swaggered or bent posture, with the head held slightly tilted to the side, one foot dragging, and an exaggerated knee dip. This raises questions about making assumptions on the basis of behaviors related to cultural identity. For instance,

- How can a student's walk contribute to a teacher's perceptions about individual student achievement, aggression, or need for special education?
- How might a teacher's perceptions about students' behavior influence referrals to special education?

Some answers to these questions come from research. Based on students' styles of walking, teachers made the following decisions about middle school boys:

- Boys who stroll, regardless of race or ethnicity, are more likely to be judged by teachers as having lower achievement than those who use standard walking styles.
- Those who stroll are viewed as being more aggressive and deviant.

Without information about academic achievement, these boys are also thought of as needing special education. In other words, teachers are likely to mistake cultural differences, such as walking style, with cognitive and behavioral disabilities, placing those students at risk for underachievement, inappropriate referrals to special education, and misidentification as students with disabilities (Belgrave & Brevade, 2015).

WORKING TOGETHER

ASSISTANCE WITH BEHAVIOR MANAGEMENT: LEARNING READY

Mr. Abbar does small-group, Tier 2 instruction as part of his response to intervention (RTI) responsibilities. He has been having difficulties with managing the behavior of some of the students in his small groups. He met with the special education teacher, Mr. Asad, to identify a strategy to help the students remain engaged during his reading, writing, and mathematics treatments. Mr. Asad suggested that he use Learning Ready, a strategy that can be applied to whatever content is being taught. During mathematics, he calls it Math Ready; when applied to reading, he calls it Reading Ready. He presented a picture of a hand that shows the components of Math Ready (see Figure 10.1). Each digit represents something that the students should be doing to remain engaged during a lesson. He places the Math Ready graphic on the table where instruction is taking place. On the first instructional day, he goes over each component and provides examples and

FIGURE 10.1 ■ Depiction of Math Ready

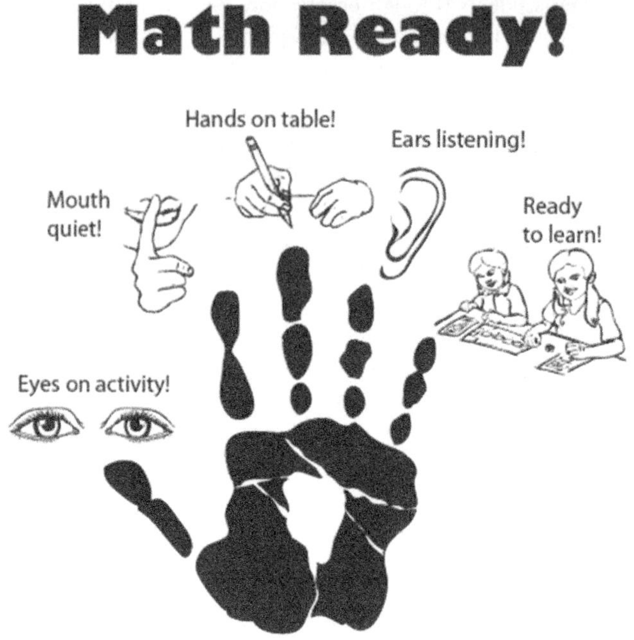

nonexamples of each. Students practice being Math Ready before the lesson begins. Periodically, if he notes a student or two not being Math Ready, he simply states, "Math Ready," and his students usually reengage.

1. Eyes on activity! Students' attention should be on the teacher or on the worksheet/materials being used in the lesson.
2. Mouth quiet! It is difficult to speak and listen at the same time, so the idea is to have students speak when appropriate but be quiet when the teacher or peers are talking.
3. Hands on table! Children often slouch when they are seated, and we want them to be in a position where they can write with proper posture. Having hands on the table also reduces the likelihood that children's hands will be on one another.
4. Ears listening! This is the yang to "Mouth quiet's" yin. During instruction, the teacher often provides and verbally explains multiple examples. Students listen to the instruction and respond to questions designed to check for understanding. Listening is a critical piece of the engagement puzzle.
5. Ready to learn! If the students are engaged by adhering to the previous four guidelines, they are ready to learn.

Mr. Asad added that intermittent checks for Learning Ready are useful. He sets a vibrating timer at different times—30 seconds, 2 minutes, and so forth—for a total of eight checks over the course of a 30-minute lesson. When the timer vibrates, he checks the students for being Math Ready. If they are, he places a token in a jar. At the end of the day, if they accumulate at least seven tokens as a group, they receive a sticker.

Questions

1. Think about your observations of or experiences with teaching small groups. What types of challenging behaviors did you encounter? How might Mr. Asad's suggestions be helpful?
2. In a small group in class, practice Mr. Asad's strategy. How long does it take to feel comfortable observing the students, managing the timer, and employing the token system?

WAYS TO COMMUNICATE EFFECTIVELY WITH STUDENTS

In addition to using techniques that promote a positive learning community, teachers can foster the goal of expected behavioral and social skills tasks by all students.

Clear and Consistent Messages

Communication is an important component of classroom learning communities. Poorly stated behavioral and social expectations and inconsistent ways of managing the results of mixed messages detract from a positive tone in any classroom. Behavioral and social expectations, and the consequences for following (or not following) them, should be communicated to students. Consequences must be consistent if students are to interpret teachers' messages seriously. For example, if being late is an unacceptable behavior, then it should be addressed every time it happens. Ignoring the problem sometimes and reacting to it at other times sends mixed messages to students about expected behavior and social skills.

Sometimes, even though expectations for behavioral and social tasks are clearly communicated, students may continue to struggle. Thomas Gordon's (2003) *Teacher Effectiveness Training* program, which remains widely used, enables teachers to understand how to handle some of these problem situations. Gordon's approach is based on the work of Carl R. Rogers, who did research on emotional and self-concept development. Rogers thought that people react to an emotionally supportive approach that consists of openness and understanding.

According to Gordon (2003), if a problem behavior intrudes on the teacher's or the other students' rights, or if it is a safety issue, the teacher should own the problem (Wolfgang, 2009). Teachers can respond to such problems with an I-message: The teacher tells students their feelings without blaming the students. Let's compare a good I-message and a poor one for the same problem.

Problem: Several students interrupt the teacher when she is explaining assignments.

Good I-message: "When students interrupt (problem behavior) me when I am speaking, I have to repeat what I just said (effect of the behavior), and that frustrates me (feelings)."

This example tells the students the problem, its effect, and the feelings of the person sending the I-message.

Poor I-message: "I want you to stop interrupting me. If you do that again, you'll have to stay after school."

This example orders the students to stop a behavior and uses a threat to curb it. The teacher is in a position of power. According to Gordon (2003), practices such as ordering, threatening, and warning are roadblocks to effective communication (Wolfgang, 2009; see Table 10.1 for examples of Gordan's 12 roadblocks to communication).

Clearly communicated behavioral and social skills tasks, delivery of consequences, and the use of I-messages all contribute to effective communication (Wolfgang, 2009).

Rules and Consequences

Rules are a necessary part of society; this is true for the classroom as well. Rules give parameters, structure, and predictability. Rules let students know the limits! Without rules, students are left to determine the teacher's expectations and guidelines for appropriate behavior and social skills. Sometimes, teachers assume that students know how they are supposed to act in class. Unfortunately the codes of school conduct often are implied and not communicated carefully. In some school situations, students learn about the rules only when they break them and are punished for their errors. How can teachers communicate rules so that students can meet the behavioral and social expectations of the classroom? Teachers can use a class meeting to involve students in establishing classroom rules by asking them, "What rules do we need so that I can teach and you can learn in a safe classroom?" Here are a few tips for selecting rules (Canter, 2010):

- Four to six rules are enough; having too many rules makes it difficult to monitor compliance.
- State rules in a positive manner, such as, "Follow directions."
- Select observable rules that apply throughout the day. "Be respectful" is difficult to observe, is too vague, and could require the teacher to take instructional time to ask, "Is that respectful?" A specific rule such as "Raise your hand to speak in group discussion" is more effective.
- Involve students in setting the rules. This is especially important for older students so that they believe they have a voice in the decision-making process.

TABLE 10.1 ■ Gordon's 12 Roadblocks to Communication

Response	Example
Some typical responses that communicate nonacceptance:	
1. Ordering, directing, commanding	"You must do this."
2. Warning, admonishing, threatening	"You had better get your act together if you expect to pass my class."
3. Moralizing, preaching, using the words *should* and *ought*	"You should leave your personal problems out of the classroom."
4. Advising, offering solutions or suggestions	"I think you need to get a daily planner so you can organize your time better to get your homework finished."
5. Teaching, lecturing, giving logical arguments	"You better remember you only have 4 days to complete that project."
These next responses tend to communicate inadequacies and faults:	
6. Judging, criticizing, disagreeing, blaming	"You are such a lazy kid. You never do what you say you will."
7. Name-calling, stereotyping, labeling	"Act your age. You are not a kindergartner."
8. Interpreting, analyzing, diagnosing	"You are avoiding facing this assignment because you missed the directions due to talking."
Other messages try to make the student feel better or deny there is a problem:	
9. Praising, agreeing, giving positive evaluations	"You are a smart kid. You can figure out a way to finish this assignment."
10. Reassuring, sympathizing, consoling, supporting	"I know exactly how you are feeling. If you just begin, it won't seem so bad."
This response tends to try to solve the problem for the student:	
11. Questioning, probing, interrogating, cross-examining	"Why did you wait so long to ask for assistance? What was so hard about this worksheet?"
This message tends to divert the student or avoid the student altogether:	
12. Withdrawing, distracting, being sarcastic, humoring, diverting	"It seems like you got up on the wrong side of the bed today."

Source: From Gordon, T. (2003). Teacher effectiveness training. First Revised Edition. New York: Three Rivers Press. Adapted with permission. pp. 44–48.

Once rules are selected, they should be shared with the principal and students' families. The rules should also be posted. Rules should come with both positive recognition and consequences. When students follow the rules, then praise, special notices, privileges, and other types of positive recognition provide helpful **reinforcement** (Canter, 2010).

When rules are not followed consequences ensue. Here are some items to consider when deciding on consequences:

- The consequence should match the infraction; that is, the consequence must make sense for the misbehavior or broken rule. For example, the consequence for being late to class once should be different from that for being late 4 days in a row.
- The consequence should be something that the teacher can manage. If the consequence is "stay after school," the teacher might have to give up planning time at the end of the day.

When students exhibit minor problem behavior, teachers can intervene by giving instruction on how to behave appropriately.
iStock.com/jacoblund

- Consequences should be applied consistently and as soon as possible after the infraction. If consequences are applied inconsistently, students get mixed messages about following the rules.
- Consequences need to be communicated clearly to students. They should know what will happen when rules are broken and when they are followed.

Rules must be taught. They must be explained, reinforced, and reviewed regularly. Teachers should work closely with special education colleagues regarding follow through of rules and logical consequences for students with disabilities. For instance, a student with mild emotional or behavioral disabilities may have an IEP with certain standards for rules. Likewise, students who lack the ability to shift among different settings and teachers may need extra support in remembering the rules.

Daily Schedule

Most people like to be informed about the schedule of events so that they know what to expect during the course of the day, week, or even vacation period. Teachers can communicate the schedule to students, to prepare them for what to expect each day. Doing so will help students to know what is going to happen and be prepared for it. A classroom schedule helps students see the routines and activities of each day.

Several routines can be part of one week. For example, one routine can be used on 2 days and a different routine on 3 days. The teacher can help students by reviewing the schedule for the day or for the class period.

For students who struggle with certain academic subjects or tasks, issues might occur during those times of the day associated with those subjects or tasks. For instance, if reading is a challenging activity for a student, the student might get out of their seat, start talking to a friend, or take extra time to go to the reading table for instruction. Think back to Marion in the Opening Challenge. Marion has a learning disability in reading and writing. Her teacher identified problems with her remaining on task and getting her work done.

What can be done about this academic problem? The Premack Principle is a highly effective technique for motivating students to complete tasks (Education Portal, 2015). With the Premack Principle, activities that are more demanding or challenging (e.g., reading and writing for Marion), and thus less preferred are done earlier in the day or class period. Less-demanding and more-preferred activities are scheduled for later in the day or class period so that students have something to work toward. In some cases, earned or free time (i.e., designated time during the school day that is provided for students who have completed their work) can be scheduled later in the day. Some parents use the Premack Principle to get their children to eat: "When you finish your dinner you can have dessert!" Astute teachers have used the Premack Principle for years to help students complete classroom tasks.

Good Directions

What does it mean to provide good directions? The teacher should tell students what they are supposed to do including remembering and following the directions. Here are some tips for providing good directions and communicating them effectively:

- Be concise; too many words may confuse students or be difficult to remember. Two or three single-step actions are sufficient.
- State directions right before the activity.
- Check student understanding of the directions. For example, consider the following directions: "In pairs, I want you to first (use a visual signal showing one finger) read the paragraph together; second (showing two fingers), underline words you don't know; and third (showing three fingers), write two sentences about the paragraph." The teacher does a quick check for understanding by asking students what they are supposed to do.

Transition Procedures

Transition is the time when students are changing activities or classes. Transition may be less structured time, so in this case transition can be a challenging or students who need structure as part of their routine. For instance, students may struggle with moving from one activity to another in the classroom or across settings in the school. In some cases, when students complete small-group work, the teacher would expect them to return to their desks without problems. Unfortunately, this is not always the case.

What difficulties are noted for transitions? Sometimes, teachers do not denote sufficient attention to student movement in the classroom during transitions. At other times, the teacher may not have clearly communicated expectations for student behavior during transitions. How teachers have students make transitions may not be the most effective ways for students to change activities. For example, asking all students to line up for lunch or move into group work at the same time can invite problems.

How can teachers communicate effectively during transition times? Here are several transition suggestions:

- Signal to students that it is time to finish their work because soon they will be moving to the next activity. Providing a verbal reminder such as, "Finish up what you are doing because the bell will ring in 10 minutes," signals how much time students have to complete their work and get ready for the next activity or class.
- Gain student attention prior to the transition to provide directions for the transition. Use **teacher proximity** (e.g., standing at the front of the classroom), a visual signal (e.g., flickering the lights), or a verbal signal (e.g., counting backward from 5 to 1) to gain students' attention. Then, directions for the transition to another activity in the classroom or to another location, such as the next class or the cafeteria, can be provided. One teacher shared her strategy for gaining student attention: "All eyes on me." She taught her students to reply in unison, "All eyes on you." It works!
- Communicate the transition plan and behavioral expectations. For instance, younger students could be told that they need to meet in their spelling groups at the carpet area and that they

should walk to the mat quietly. Older students could be told that they should return to their seats and gather their belongings to get ready for the bell to change classes.

- Praise students who follow the transition plan and meet behavioral expectations. Provide specific praise, thank students for following the directions given, and demonstrate the appropriate behavior if convenient. For example, announcing "The Red group went to the mat quietly with their spelling materials; thank you for following the directions" or "The group working on computers did a nice job of logging off and returning to their desks quietly" tells students specifically what they did appropriately that related to following transition directions.

Specific Praise

Specific praise is complimenting or verbally rewarding students for their work. Providing specific praise is a way to communicate behavior and social expectations. Specific praise is a form of attention and feedback that has been studied for many years; it has been shown to be very powerful in bringing about positive behavior in classrooms (Haydon & Musti-Rao, 2011). Although easy to implement, specific praise is not used very much in many classroom settings. Thus, one of the easiest treatments for managing behavior remains untried in many classrooms. Think back for a moment to Miranda in the Opening Challenge; recall her problems with saying hurtful things without thinking. Mr. Abbar gives her a card with a happy face (instructional material) to remind her to make positive statements and provides specific praise (instructional delivery) when he "catches" her giving a compliment to a classmate. He can also conduct periodic roleplaying with small groups to facilitate positive social communication.

What guidelines are important to consider when using specific praise to promote positive behavior?

- Make the praise specific. For example, a teacher who wants students to raise their hands to speak during group discussions can acknowledge a student who demonstrates this task by saying, "Thank you, Marco, for raising your hand to speak instead of shouting out." This praise is specific to the task of raising a hand, which the teacher expects students to demonstrate during class discussions. This praise also gives Marco positive attention.
- Consider the age of the student or students being praised. For instance, teachers cannot praise 10th-grade students in the same way they do first graders. Older students might not respond favorably to a teacher who praises them publicly, but a private word can mean a great deal.
- Use praise judiciously. This means that teachers should focus on the behavior or social skill that they want students to demonstrate. Excessive praise loses its reinforcing value.

Next, we describe classroom arrangements that can address problem behaviors.

EFFECTIVE CLASSROOM ARRANGEMENT PRACTICES

Teachers in classrooms that have students with behavior challenges or students with ASD typically use applied behavioral analysis (ABA) practices. Many of these practices consist of behavior modification or similar practices. These practices are designed to reduce or eliminate problem behaviors and increase more instances of positive behaviors. We will take a look at some of the main features of ABA.

Most people would attribute the beginnings of ABA to B. F. Skinner (1938). You might have learned about your ABA practices from your psychology coursework. Skinner worked with rats and shaped their behavior by using reinforcers, which are events or objects that increase or decrease the likelihood that a specific behavior will occur.

Praise is one of the best-known examples of a reinforcer: When you do something and someone praises you, it's likely you will repeat the behavior that caused the response. On the other hand, if you do something that results in someone being sad or angry, the response is likely to be negative; in most instances, the negative response will likely mean that you won't do the "something" again. This is the basis of the stimulus-response theory related to ABA: For every stimulus (or action), there is a response (either a personal or environmental reinforcer). One popular technique of ABA for working with students who have behavior challenges or ASD is Antecedent Behavior Consequence (ABC): Antecedent (an event or action that precedes a problem behavior), Behavior (what the student does in response to the antecedent), and Consequence (what happens after the behavior occurs).

Here is a scenario to consider that involves ABC. Think back to Suzanne who had come to school with a new haircut. When Miranda saw the new haircut she stated, "Ewwww, that's ugly." Miranda's reaction caused Suzanne to start crying and other classmates to start yelling at Miranda. In this scenario, the new haircut would be the antecedent, Miranda's comment would be the behavior, and Suzanne's crying and the other classmates' reactions to Miranda would be the consequence. The teacher could work with Miranda about responding in a different way to Suzanne's haircut, which would result in a different behavior. However, Miranda might have enjoyed making Suzanne cry and seeing the response of her classmates. In this case, Miranda got the students' attention, which is often the response that students with behavior challenges seek. To modify Miranda's behavior, Mr. Abbar will need to identify a reinforcer that is more important to Miranda than students' attention, even when negative. He knows that Miranda loves to read stories about animals (she says she wants to be a veterinarian when she grows up). With this in mind, Mr. Abbar tells Miranda that the next time she compliments a person on their appearance, she can take 10 minutes after recess to read an animal story. This behavior modification goal is to change Miranda's behavior from negative to positive and provide an important consequence that makes it beneficial. See Parsonson (2012), *Evidence-Based Classroom Behaviour Management Strategies,* for more information about ABA.

Now we will focus on information about the classroom, which is the setting in which the educational experience occurs.

Physical Arrangements

An important aspect of effective classroom management is the physical arrangement of the classroom. How can you design the environment? Arranging learning centers in less-distracting parts of the room can reduce problems. For example, in elementary classrooms it makes sense to place the reading, writing, and listening centers next to one another, assuming that students are using headphones in the listening center. However, the art center should be situated away from students' seats and quieter centers. At the secondary level, instructional supplies and materials for students could be located away from students' desks and computers or tablets can be placed in another section of the room.

Traffic Patterns

Traffic patterns are the paths students take to move about the classroom. Traffic patterns must be considered as students move about the classroom. How can traffic patterns make a difference? How the furniture is arranged and where the instructional materials (e.g., pencil sharpener, computers, books, lab instruments) are located can alter how students move about the classroom as they go from whole-group to small-group instruction. The following tips can help manage classroom traffic patterns:

- Separate instructional areas.
- Provide adequate movement space.
- Provide access to the most-frequented areas. (Emmer & Evertson, 2017)

Emmer and Evertson (2017) suggested that teachers simulate student movement in the classroom to uncover possible problem areas. For example, a student who uses a wheelchair will need more navigational space in the classroom. To accommodate the student who uses a wheelchair, the room arrangement will likely require wider spaces for the student to move about the room.

Seating Arrangements

Another consider is how students' desks are arranged. Teachers should decide on the types of activities and desired student interactions so that they can arrange the desks into rows and groupings. Yet another thing to consider is specific student behavioral needs. For instance, certain students' desks might need to be situated in proximity to the teacher. Students who are distracted easily or who are likely to socialize probably will need preferential seating (i.e., closer to the teacher). A student who is easily distracted should sit in an area where there is less movement by peers, rather than in an area that is visited regularly during the day (e.g., by the pencil sharpener).

With-It-Ness

With-it-ness (Thompson, n.d.) is the ability of teachers to see all of the students in the classroom all of the time so that they can be aware of student interaction. Why is with-it-ness so important? Teachers must be aware of classroom activities and student behavior that potentially can contribute to misbehavior and social problems. For instance, nooks and crannies may provide students with private space, but they minimize teachers' abilities to be aware of what is going on in the classroom. Thompson provides a list of nine steps that teachers can take to promote with-it-ness. As you read each step, think about the classrooms you have observed. How often have you seen examples of teachers' with-it-ness?

1. Don't ever turn your back on a class.
2. Be alert to signs and signals among your students.
3. Be prepared so that you can focus on students instead of the lesson.
4. Develop your personal multitasking skills.
5. Stay on your feet and monitor.
6. Arrange your class so that you can see and be seen.
7. Don't distract students when they are working.
8. Pace lessons so that they flow in a businesslike manner.
9. Quietly correct off-task behavior and then move on. (Thompson, n.d., p. 1)

Classroom Observation

Taking time to observe the classroom environment, including traffic patterns, seating arrangements, and student interactions, can provide information about changes that may be needed. Observation can help teachers identify behavior problems to decrease and student involvement to increase with those students who tend to be quiet or uninvolved with their peers. Asking students, particularly older ones, about factors such as temperature, noise, furniture, and arrangements also can help to establish a classroom environment that is useful for learning, managing behavior, and facilitating social interactions.

This section presented practices that teachers can use to help all students understand and accomplish behavior and social skills tasks in the classroom. We know there is also a group of students who exhibit difficulty managing their behavior. For these students, it is helpful to understand the goals of misbehavior and to be familiar with treatments that can address problem behavior.

GOALS OF MISBEHAVIOR

Student behavior has been studied for years to better determine why problem behaviors occur and to identify ways to foster positive behavior. Viewpoints about the causes of inappropriate behavior have shaped the development of approaches and systems for managing inappropriate behavior. Inspired by Alfred Adler's work on the connection of behavior to social acceptance, Rudolph Dreikurs (1968) and

TABLE 10.2 ■ Goals and Techniques for Handling Misbehavior

Goal	Description of Misbehavior	Techniques
Attention getting	The student engages in behavior that demands excessive praise or criticism.	Ignore the behavior. Give an I-message. Lower your voice. Change the activity. Praise appropriately behaving students.
Power and control	The student tries to manage situations, get their own way, or force himself or herself on others.	Leave the scene. Have the student repeat the desired behavior. Remove the student from the group. Change the topic.
Revenge	The student engages in hurtful and malicious behavior.	Implement a time-out. Take away a privilege.
Inadequacy	The student does not cooperate or participate and avoids or escapes situations.	Adapt instruction. Break tasks down into smaller steps. Provide more praise. Showcase successes. Teach positive encouraging talk, such as, "I can do it."

Source: Adapted from Wolfgang (2009).

Dreikurs and Cassel (1972) suggested that people's behavior, including misbehavior, is goal driven. Goal-driven behavior is performed to achieve social acceptance. If students are not successful in achieving social acceptance, misbehavior occurs that can be annoying, hostile, destructive, or helpless. Some students believe that inappropriate behavior will glean an adult's positive attention. However, the attention these students get is negative. Unfortunately, these students are desperately seeking positive acceptance but they do not know how to achieve it. They need to learn appropriate **prosocial behaviors**—behaviors that are positive and that build relationships—to achieve the acceptance they are seeking.

Teachers can help students recognize their mistaken goals and can offer alternatives for social acceptance (Wolfgang, 2009). When teachers understand the goals of misbehavior, appropriate techniques can be conducted to increase positive behavior and to decrease or eliminate inappropriate behavior. Table 10.2 provides information about the goals of misbehavior and offers examples of techniques for handling mistaken goals. Additional instructional techniques are provided in the next section.

ASSESSING PROBLEM BEHAVIORS

How can positive behaviors and problem behaviors be described when they occur? What behaviors are acceptable? How can the occurrence of problem behaviors be assessed? Teachers must be able to describe behaviors that are desirable as well as those that are intrusive to teaching so that they can design and assess treatment plans.

Behavior Identification

An identified behavior should be observable, measurable, consistent over time, and of great concern (e.g., interfering with teaching or learning). Teachers must be able to describe the behavior that is identified. For example, calling out can be observed, and it can be counted for a designated period. Calling out is a behavior that, although not serious, interferes with class discussions and can be labeled as rude and relatively disruptive. Returning to the Opening Challenge, "How many times Marco 'calls out' during a 15-minute discussion after viewing the film" tells us that calling out is the behavior that is being observed for 15 minutes. Ms. Nguyen can measure it consistently over time by using a tally system to record how many times Marco calls out. Information on the identified behavior can help Ms. Nguyen describe the problem behavior (calling out during a discussion), determine how often it occurs (measuring the behavior for a time period), and know whether the behavior (calling out) is decreasing and whether a desirable behavior (hand raising) is increasing when a treatment plan is implemented.

Identified behavior can be indicated in the form of behavioral objectives that include a condition, a behavior, and a criterion for improvement. The following examples include these three components and relate to our three students from the Opening Challenge.

- In the reading group (condition), Marion will stay in her seat (behavior) for 20 minutes (criterion).
- During the daily 10-minute whole class morning discussion (condition), Marco will raise his hand (behavior) each time (criterion) he wishes to participate.
- For writing activities (condition), Ingrid will have her pencil (behavior) each day (criterion) to complete the writing assignments.

Observational Techniques

For students who engage in minor transgressions, recording observations of positive behavior and problematic behavior anecdotally in a notebook or on lesson plans might be sufficient to note how students are progressing with behavior intervention plans (BIPs) or to identify possible problems. Often, observational systems can provide information helpful in the design, implementation, and evaluation of behavior programs.

Observational systems can determine how often or how long a problem behavior occurs. Table 10.3 provides observational systems that can be used to gather data about the identified behavior and to assess the effectiveness of the treatment. Think about behaviors you have seen in classrooms and select the observational system you would use to measure that behavior. Remember that the system should be sensitive to the behavior. For example, if a student

TABLE 10.3 ■ Systems for Observing and Assessing Behavior

System	Description and Example Behaviors
Event recording	Number of occurrences of the identified behavior is recorded using a count or tally (e.g., | | | | = 4). Session time period (and hence opportunities to respond) is held constant. Example behaviors: hand raising, talk-outs, tardiness, pencil sharpening, tattling.
Interval recording	Number of intervals in which the identified behavior occurs or does not occur is counted. Session time period is divided into small intervals (e.g., 10-minute group time is divided into 10-second intervals). Occurrence of the identified behavior during any portion of the interval is noted by a plus (+); nonoccurrence is noted by a minus (-). Each interval has only one notation; percentage of occurrence of the identified behavior for the session time period is calculated by dividing the number of intervals in which the behavior occurred by the total number of intervals and multiplying by 100. It can be challenging to record occurrences of behavior and teach at the same time, but this method provides a more accurate picture of the occurrences of a behavior than time sampling. Example behaviors: out of seat, talking with neighbors.
Momentary time sampling	Number of intervals in which the identified behavior occurs is counted. Session time period is divided into larger intervals (e.g., 1-hour group time is divided into 10-minute intervals). Occurrence of the identified behavior at the end of the interval is noted by a plus (+); nonoccurrence is noted by a minus (-). Each interval has only one notation; percentage of occurrences of the identified behavior for the session time period is calculated by dividing the number of intervals in which the behavior occurred by the total number of intervals and multiplying by 100. In momentary time sampling, it is easier to record occurrences of behavior and teach, but it provides a less accurate picture of the occurrences of behavior than interval recording. Example behaviors: out of seat, talking with neighbors, not working on an assignment.
Duration recording	How long a high-rate or continuous behavior occurs is noted. Session time period can be a short period of time, a day or a week; at the onset of the identified behavior, a stopwatch is started to record the cumulative time. Example behaviors: out of seat, temper tantrums, not staying with one's group.

continuously and quickly taps a pencil on the desk, it would be hard to use **event recording** to capture each occurrence of this distracting behavior. Rather, **interval recording** would be a more appropriate system to get a sense of the frequency of the behavior.

Often, it is helpful to display data. Figure 10.2 shows one way to show data collected on an identified behavior. Data displays provide an easy way to see what is happening. In this instance, the teacher was concerned about Patricia's chatting with her neighbors when she was supposed to be writing independently in her journal for 10 minutes each day. The teacher selected the interval recording system to collect data. Prior to implementing a behavior management plan, the teacher collected the first four data points. As shown in the figure, Patricia's percentage of talking was quite high. However, a dramatic decrease in talking (the remaining four data points) is noted with the introduction of a behavioral treatment. What treatment from those discussed in this chapter would you use to reduce the inappropriate talking behavior?

Events that happen before or after the behavior may contribute to its occurrence. Detailed observation of these events can reveal important clues about how to manage the behavior. The ABC log is a good tool for recording observations. "A" stands for events that occur before the behavior of concern (Antecedent), "B" is the behavior of concern (Behavior), and "C" stands for the events that happen after the behavior occurs (Consequence). The ABC log can be used for collecting data about what is going

FIGURE 10.2 ■ Displaying Data Collected with Interval Recording

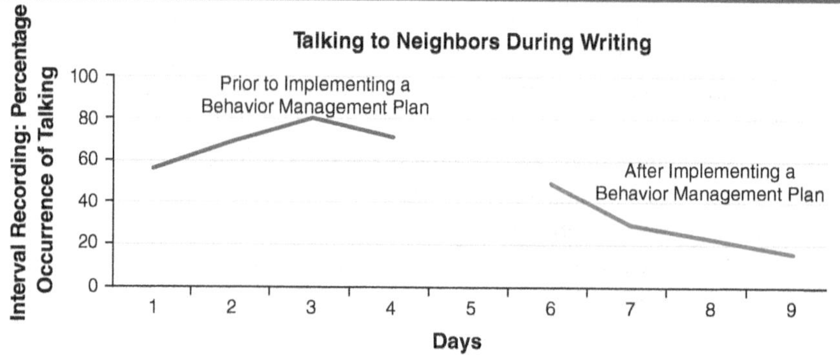

FIGURE 10.3 ■ Antecedent Behavior Consequence Log

Date/Time	Antecedent Events or Situations	Behavior	Consequence
12/01 10:30	1. **Teacher (T):** "Luisa, Sarah, and Ben come for reading."	2. **Luisa:** "I need to sharpen my pencil." Luisa sharpens her pencil. She stops and talks to Ricardo. Luisa pokes Stephanie with her pencil. Stephanie hits Luisa. 4. Luisa wanders around the room.	3. **T:** "Okay, stop that." The teacher goes over to the students and separates them. Stephanie cries. 5. The teacher sends Stephanie to the nurse and has a private conference with Luisa, who loses recess for the day.

Source: Adapted from Lovitt (2000).

The team hypothesized that Marion's pencil sharpening and poking served the purpose of avoiding the reading task because of her difficulties with reading. The incident has attracted the attention of the whole class. And although she was given detention that day, she had the teacher's undivided attention, negative as it was, during the class time.

The ABC log technique can be easily adapted to a format that offers students the opportunity to self-evaluate and self-manage their behavior. Ms. Martinez plans to use the strategy to help Marion be prepared for class.

on with the student and the classroom. These data can help the teacher make informed decisions about why problem behavior is occurring. An example is provided in Figure 10.3. Review the data and try to determine what is generating or maintaining the behaviors. Based on your idea, what would you do next? For example, Marion's reading abilities can be assessed with the possibility of providing more intensive reading treatment to help her learn to read better.

ADAPT IN ACTION

MARION: ANTECEDENT BEHAVIOR CONSEQUENCE

Ms. Nguyen thinks about Marion as she prepares to teach the lesson. Ms. Nguyen decides to implement the ADAPT Framework to identify how Marion can avoid antecedents that cause her negative behavior.

A: Ask, "What am I requiring the student to do?" Ms. Nguyen notes, "The students will learn how to complete and implement an ABC log."

D: Determine the prerequisite skills of the task. Ms. Nguyen realizes that students have to learn what each letter (A, B, and C) means. After she provides examples of antecedents, behaviors, and consequences from real-life experiences, students have to provide their own examples. Students have to think about what causes their actions, both positive and negative, so that they can see the connection between antecedents and consequences. Students have to discriminate between antecedents that cause positive behavior and those that cause negative behavior and what happens to them after positive and negative behaviors occur. Students then have to identify a plan to deal with the antecedents that cause negative behaviors. For example, if the cause is hearing "It's time to work on reading," having pencils already sharpened and avoiding conflict would be positive behaviors rather than having to sharpen the pencil and poke a fellow student, which would cause the student to receive disciplinary action. Finally, students select one of their own behaviors to change. Students can keep a record of the behavior in a journal.

A: Analyze the student's strengths and struggles. Ms. Nguyen reflects on Marion's skill set with regard to the lesson: "She knows what causes the behavior, reading instruction, and she knows what she does and that poking a classmate gets her in trouble, so she can identify that as needing to be worked on. What she struggles with is coming up with a solution and implementing a plan to change her behavior. She'll need help with that. Also, she has trouble writing, so she'll need help completing her ABC log."

P: Propose and implement adaptations from among the four categories. Ms. Nguyen knows that she will have to meet with Marion to help her identify an action plan. They determine together that Marion will begin her day by sharpening five pencils and then going directly to her desk and placing them in a box. This simple step (A Delivery of Instruction adaptation) will ensure that she has a pencil when her small reading group meets. When it is time to meet, she will bring the box of pencils and not open it until seated, which will reduce the likelihood of her poking a classmate on the way to her group. Ms. Nguyen then helped Marion complete her ABC log using the computer.

Marion's teacher had created a table on the computer similar to that found in Figure 10.3 using Don Johnston's Write: OutLoud. Marion simply spoke into a microphone and words appeared onscreen. In this way, she could "write" by speaking to complete the ABC log. Ms. Nguyen and Marion signed a contract stating that (a) if Marion kept her ABC log current and (b) if Marion came to her reading group with sharpened pencils inside the box and refrained from poking others, she would be given 15 minutes at the end of the week to play games on Ms. Nguyen's iPad.

T: Test to determine whether the adaptations helped the student accomplish the task. After the activity was over, Ms. Nguyen kept a running record of the times Marion came to the activity with her pencil box full of sharpened pencils. She also recorded the number of times Marion got through the activity without poking her classmates with the pencil. Finally, at the end of each day, Ms. Nguyen would check the ABC log to make sure it was current and complete.

ADAPT Framework: For Marion

A ASK "What am I requiring the student to do?"	D DETERMINE the prerequisite skills of the task.	A ANALYZE the student's strengths and struggles. Strengths	 Struggles	P PROPOSE and implement adaptations from among the four categories.	T TEST to determine whether the adaptations helped the student to accomplish the task.
The students will learn how to complete and implement an ABC log.	**1.** Provide their own examples of antecedents, behaviors, and consequences.	1			
	2. Think about what causes their actions, both positive and negative, so that they can see the connection between antecedents and consequences.	2			
	3. Discriminate between antecedents that cause positive behavior and those that cause negative behavior and what happens to them.	3			
	4. Select one of their own behaviors to change.	4			
	5. Identify a plan to deal with the antecedents that cause negative behaviors.	5	5	**5.** Instructional delivery: Teacher meets with student to develop a plan.	**5.** Teacher determines whether pencils are sharpened and student refrains from poking fellow students.
	6. Keep a record of the behavior in a journal after positive and negative behaviors occur.	6	6	**6.** Instructional materials: Student uses Write: OutLoud to create and complete the ABC chart.	**6.** Teacher checks the ABC log for accuracy.

Another source of data is reviewing existing records. Records can include office referrals, attendance records, counselor information, and cumulative school folders. Also, interviews with family members and support personnel can provide important clues about the events that cause or maintain problem behavior. We review instructional strategies for positive behavior next.

INSTRUCTIONAL STRATEGIES FOR BEHAVIOR PROBLEMS

Sometimes, specific treatments must be implemented to promote positive behavior in the classroom.

Planned Ignoring

Planned ignoring, sometimes referred to as the ignore strategy, is the planned, systematic withdrawal of attention by the individual from whom the attention is desired. This individual could be the teacher but could also be a classmate.

Planned ignoring is an appropriate treatment if the behavior is a minor infraction that poses no threat of harm to others (Emmer & Evertson, 2017). Behaviors such as threatening others or fighting will probably not be influenced quickly enough by ignoring and should be dealt with quickly and directly. The landmark research that clearly demonstrated the power of adult attention on nursery school children's behavior was conducted more than 60 years ago (Allen et al., 1964). Results showed the connection between behavior and the usage and withdrawal of teacher attention.

What guidelines apply to planned ignoring? First, the person who is doing the ignoring must be the individual whose attention is being desired. It is important to know whose attention a student is seeking. How can a teacher determine this? Adult attention is extremely important to younger children, which is why teachers see immediate and often dramatic changes when they praise or ignore younger students. However, as students get older, the attention of the peer group increases in importance, and the teacher's influence lessens. This is why ignoring older students when they are off task probably will not be effective. Second, planned ignoring must be implemented consistently, even if the behavior of concern increases. It is common for inappropriate behavior to increase when planned ignoring is first introduced. In fact, some students will purposefully exhibit inappropriate behavior to gain the teacher's attention. However, planned ignoring can quickly become an effective treatment when implemented consistently, even during the brief escalation period (Corrol et al., 2009). As experienced teachers have noted for years, when a student's behavior does not achieve the desired effect, the behavior will usually stop. However, teachers should be aware of students who engage in attention-seeking behavior and provide them with positive attention for appropriate behavior.

Problem Behaviors

Redirecting Inappropriate Behavior

Redirection is the process of informing a student that they made an error and asking the student to describe the appropriate behavior. The student is provided an opportunity to show the appropriate behavior with reinforcement. Redirection is an effective way to help a student stop a problem behavior and receive further instruction on appropriate behavior. Much like specific praise and planned ignoring, redirection is a helpful treatment if the behavior is relatively minor and results from the need to remind students about appropriate behavior.

When students exhibit minor problem behaviors, the teacher can intervene by giving instructions on how to behave appropriately. Students should be told the desired behavior and should be provided with support for showing the appropriate behavior. With a focus on the positive, a reprimand—a negative response to problem behavior—is avoided. A reprimand does not provide the student with the opportunity to practice the correct behavior and receive reinforcement. For example, if a student calls out rather than raises his hand during discussion, the teacher can talk privately with the student, telling the student that calling out is inappropriate and asking the student to explain what he should have done during discussion (raise his hand to contribute). Then, in further class discussion, contingent on hand raising, specific praise could be provided for the appropriate behavior. Redirection is a positive treatment to achieve the desired behavior. Think back to the Opening Challenge, and to Marco who calls out and may be desiring Ms. Nguyen's attention; she can redirect his calling out by privately having him explain to her what he can do besides calling out and by praising him with positive attention each time he raises his hand.

Contingent Observation

Sometimes problem behavior occurs during small-group work or during an activity when peers may be reinforcing the student's misbehavior. Peer reinforcement may result in increased levels of the problem behavior. **Contingent observation** is a form of time-out whereby a disruptive student is removed from an activity but is still permitted to observe the activities. Contingent observation can be conducted if it seems that the peer group is contributing to the problem behavior. The advantage of this treatment is that the student can observe other student participating appropriately in the group work, which can limit the loss of instruction. It is important to ensure that the contingent observation period is long enough to make a difference but not so long that the student loses interest in rejoining the group.

Managing Classroom Behavior

Criterion-Specific Rewards

With **criterion-specific rewards**, students earn privileges only as they reach desirable levels of the target behavior. This treatment is used widely in schools. Rewards are given to students who achieve determined levels of improvement (the criterion level) for a specific academic, behavioral, or social skill. Rewards could include the following:

- Tangible items, such as food, trinkets, or prizes
- Token reinforcers, such as smiley faces, stickers, or points toward a payoff
- Social reinforcers, such as praise, positive notes, or positive calls to parents
- Activity reinforcers, such as a one-night no-homework pass, 10 minutes of extra recess time, or earned time to select a desired activity in the classroom (e.g., listening to a tape)

However, a reward for one student might not hold the same interest for another. Consequently, it is necessary to learn from students what rewards are most enticing to them. Also, something that is rewarding in September may not be desirable to students in November. Rewards will probably lose some of their interest to students over time; therefore, rewards must be changed to achieve results. Table 10.4 provides a list of suggested rewards for elementary and secondary students.

Think back to the Opening Challenge; Ms. Nguyen is reflecting about Ingrid. Recall that she has been identified as having ADHD. She has difficulties staying organized and being prepared to work. Ms. Nguyen uses a certificate as a reward when Ingrid achieves the desired goal of an organized desk, which in turn helps her be prepared for class.

Contracting

Contracting consists of setting up a written agreement between two groups that designates a targeted behavior that needs improvement. This technique is sometimes necessary for students whose problem behaviors do not seem to respond to other treatments. Alberto and Troutman (2017) suggested that contracts can be an effective treatment for teachers to implement because the requirements for reinforcement are written down, which can help busy teachers remember how behavior for certain students will be managed.

The following are simple guidelines for implementing contracts:

1. The desired behavior and a reward that is meaningful to the student must be identified.
2. The conditions for earning the reward must be stipulated as part of the contract, including the desired behavior and the time frame.
3. The contract should contain an *If. . . then* statement and include the behavior, condition, criterion, and reinforcer (Alberto & Troutman, 2017).
4. The teacher and the student should sign the contract. A sample contract is shown in Figure 10.4.

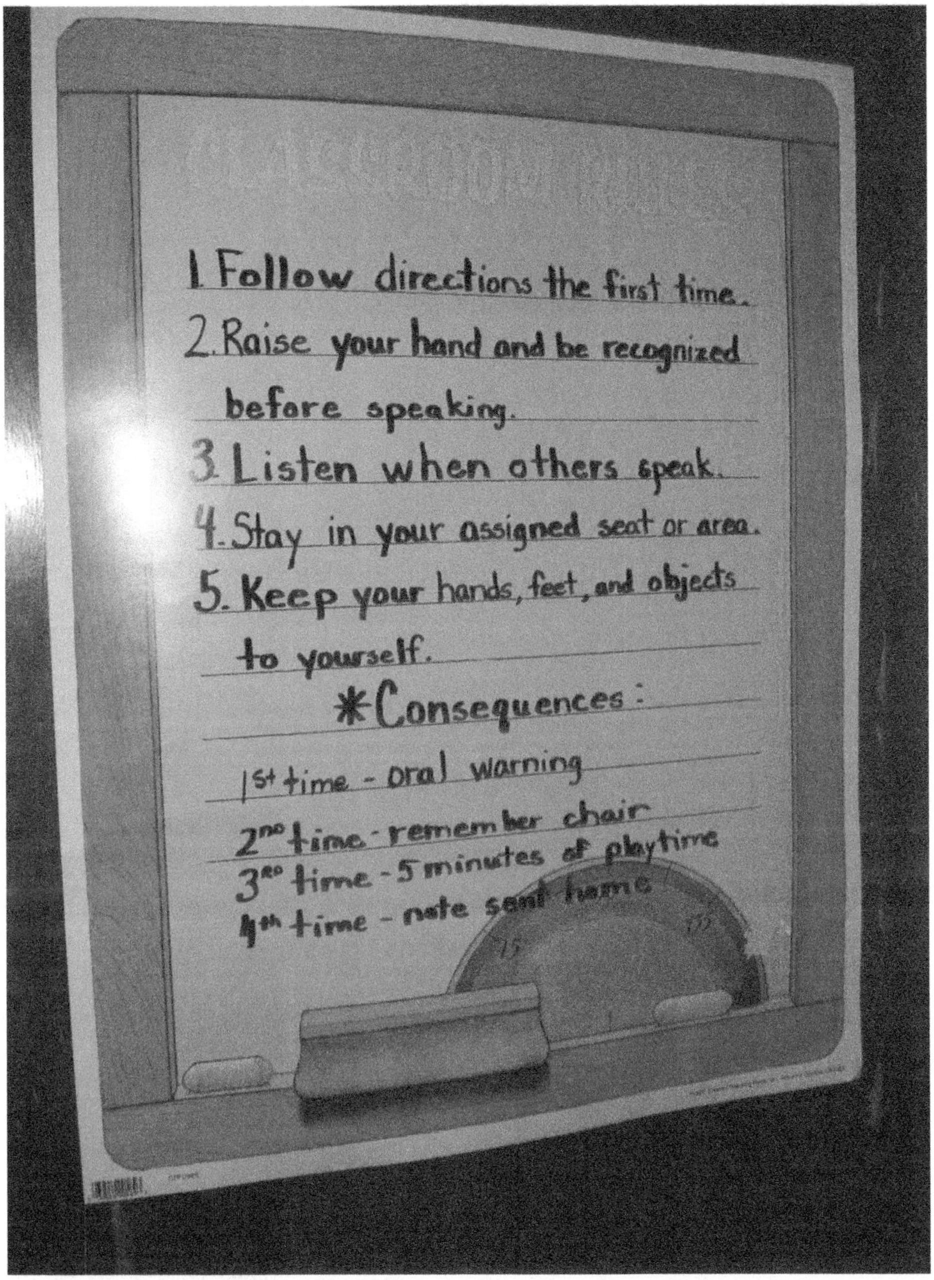

Classroom rules should be posted. Rules should come with both positive recognition and consequences. When students follow the rules, praise, special notices, privileges, and other types of positive rewards may be earned.

Shawn Rossi/ Creative Commons Attribution 2.0 Generic

Here are a few guidelines to remember when using an **interdependent group contingency**. First, be sure that the student involved is able to perform the desired behavior and stop the inappropriate behavior. If not, unnecessary pressure could be placed on a student who causes the group to lose its opportunity for the reward. Second, plan for the possibility that several students might actually enjoy ruining the program for the group. If this occurs, special arrangements must be made for the noncompliant students.

Let's return to Ms. Nguyen. She decides to implement the "Good Behavior Game," which was developed by Barrish, Saunders, and Wolf in 1969 (see also Flower et al., 2013). Ms. Nguyen is concerned that many of her students don't work well independently while she is conducting small-group work. In particular, Marion struggles with this expected task. Ms. Nguyen decides to focus on improving the behavior of working independently. She divides the class into teams. When the timer sounds,

TABLE 10.4 ■ Suggested Rewards for Elementary and Secondary Students

Type of Reward	Examples
Academic Activities	• Go to the library to select a book. • Help a classmate with an academic assignment. • Help the teacher to present a lesson (e.g., by completing sample math problem on blackboard, reading a section of text aloud, assisting cooperative learning groups on an activity). • Invite an adult reading buddy of student's choice to classroom to read with student. • Listen to books on tape. • Play academic computer games. • Read a book of their choice. • Read a story aloud to younger children. • Read aloud to the class. • Select a class learning activity from a list of choices. • Select a friend as a study buddy on an in-class work assignment. • Select friends to sit with to complete a cooperative learning activity.
Praise/Recognition	• Spend time (with appropriate supervision) on the Internet at academic sites. • Be awarded a trophy, medal, or other honor for good behavior/caring attitude. • Be praised on schoolwide announcements for good behavior or caring attitude. • Be praised privately by the teacher or other adult. • Design—or post work on—a class or hall bulletin board. • Get a silent thumbs up or other sign from teacher indicating praise and approval. • Have the teacher call the student's parent/guardian to give positive feedback about the student. • Have the teacher write a positive note to the student's parent/guardian. • Post drawings or other artwork in a public place. • Post writings in a public place. • Receive a "good job" note from the teacher.

Source: Intervention Central (n.d.).

FIGURE 10.4 ■ Sample Behavior Improvement Contract

IF John Evans [the student] is in his seat and prepared to work [the desired behaviors] when

the bell rings [the condition] every class period for a week [the criterion], THEN he will earn a

"no-homework pass" for one assignment for the following week [the reinforcer, or reward].

____________________ ____________________

(Student/date) (Teacher/date)

the team whose members are on task during independent work is given a point. At the end of each day, the team with the most points earns 10 minutes to work on an activity of their choice (something the class values as important). The members of the other team who haven't earned enough points have to continue with their independent work. Eventually, Ms. Nguyen sets a criterion of five points as the goal for earning the reward.

Self-Regulation

Self-regulation occurs when individuals manage their own behavior. Using self-regulatory practices, individuals try to avoid situations that lead to inappropriate behavior or stop problem behavior if it has already started. Self-regulation is a type of self-management (i.e., the implementation of specific treatments by the targeted student to manage their own behavior). Studies have shown that self-management techniques (or self-mediated techniques, as they are sometimes called) are effective for both elementary and secondary students (Ryan et al., 2008). Self-management techniques are desirable because they actively involve the student in the learning process and foster independence and decision making. Examples of self-regulation techniques are counting to 10 before reacting, using self-talk to work through a problem, and walking away from a problematic situation. Obviously, these techniques depend upon the teacher helping the student know how to recognize a problem situation and when to use the appropriate technique.

Let's examine some guidelines for implementing the self-regulation treatment. Modeling and role-playing are effective ways to help students learn self-regulation techniques. Teachers must determine which techniques are more appropriate for younger or older students. The students' use of self-regulatory techniques will increase as they receive reinforcement and see the effects of the techniques. Figure 10.5 is an example of a Countoon. Students can use the Countoon to self-regulate by recording occurrences of a desired behavior, such as "Raises hand to speak," and the problem behavior, such as "Calls out." The technique of self-recording to monitor one's own behavior can lead to increases in the desired behavior and to decreases in the problem behavior. In the following section, we offer instructional strategies for more serious behavior.

Sometimes, students exhibit problem behaviors that require more intensive treatments. We provide examples of treatments that you can use to reduce or eliminate these problem behaviors.

Time-Out and Seclusion Time-Out

Time-out is a treatment that removes the student from a situation that is reinforcing the inappropriate behavior. **Seclusion time-out**, in which the student is placed in an isolated room, is used for severe, out-of-control behavior. With seclusion time-out, the student is removed from a situation that is spurring and maintaining the problem behavior. In this case, the student is placed in a neutral environment, which can be a small room where the student is isolated for a specific period of time (Alberto & Troutman, 2017). Seclusion time-out is popular because it provides the student a chance to calm down, think about what happened, and rejoin the group in a short time period. However, the Council for Children with Behavioral Disorders (2009) cautioned, "Seclusion to control behavior should be used only under the following emergency circumstances and only if all three of these elements exist:

- The student's actions pose a clear, present, and imminent physical danger to them or to others;
- Less restrictive measures have not effectively de-escalated the risk of injury; and

FIGURE 10.5 ■ Countoon

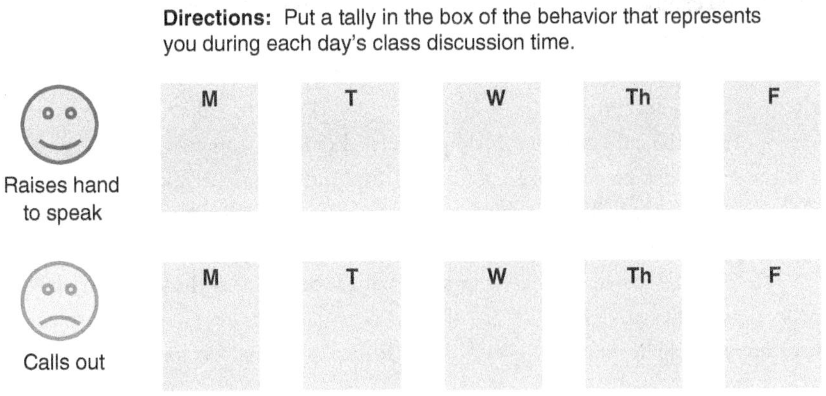

Directions: Put a tally in the box of the behavior that represents you during each day's class discussion time.
M
T
W
Th
F
Raises hand to speak
M
T
W
Th
F
Calls out

Self-management techniques are appealing because they actively involve the individual in the learning process. These techniques require the teacher to help the student know how to recognize a problem situation and when to use the appropriate technique.

iStock.com/katleho Seisa

- The seclusion should last only as long as necessary to resolve the actual risk of danger or harm or while awaiting the arrival of law enforcement or crisis treatment personnel such as when the student has possessed a weapon or committed a crime." (p. 10)

In-School Supervision

In-school supervision is recommended only for severe behavior problems and only after other positive treatments have been tried but didn't succeed over a period of time. Because students miss class, this treatment is usually saved for major disruptive acts, such as fighting (Emmer & Evertson, 2017). In this situation, school privileges are suspended. Students must spend their time completing schoolwork in a quiet environment. Students should not consider in-school supervision a better place to be than in class. The advantage of this treatment for teachers is that they do not have to miss their lunch breaks or planning periods to supervise disruptive students; rather, someone is assigned to supervise the in-school suspension room. The advantage for students is that they are required to complete schoolwork and are in school rather than out on the streets. The in-school supervision treatment serves as a hindrance to future disruptive behavior. Let's see how problem behaviors can be assessed.

IDEA (2004) requires the use of positive behavior treatments and supports and FBA for students with disabilities who exhibit challenging behavior. To meet this federal mandate, many schools now use three-tiered models or multitiered systems of support (MTSS) to prevent and react to challenging behavior. You probably have thought of tiered systems with regard to RTI and academics; tiered systems can also be used to deal with behavior. For example, MTSS for behavior provide classwide and schoolwide supports at the core or general education level (Tier 1); targeted, preventive, small-group treatments at the secondary prevention level (Tier 2); and individualized support at the tertiary level (Tier 3; Sugai & Horner, 2009). The core level fosters appropriate behavior for all students by establishing behavioral expectations and treatments. Students who do not appropriately respond to core supports may require more intensive, frequent supports that are provided at the secondary level. The Tier 2 treatment level addresses students with at-risk behaviors who can benefit from instructional treatments focused on reducing harm (Lane, 2007). As with academic supports for RTI, some students may still need more intensive, frequent, and supportive treatments than provided at the secondary level. Tertiary, or Tier 3, treatments support individual students through individualized treatments such as FBA and function-based treatments (Sugai & Horner, 2009).

Schoolwide positive behavior support (SWPBS) is an example of MTSS through which core, secondary, and tertiary supports can be utilized along a continuum. SWPBS is a framework, not a curriculum, treatment, or program. As such, SWPBS can be developed to meet the needs of the students with whom it is being conducted. As Sugai and Horner (2009) suggested, SWPBS is a technique that should lead to "sustained use of evidence-based practices related to behavior and classroom management" (p. 309).

MTSS for behavior is dynamic because it is continually developing and changing. Recent advances in this field have included SWPBS at the core or general education level. SWPBS addresses schoolwide social cultures and provides behavioral supports for students with challenging behavior, including those with emotional or behavioral disorders (Sugai & Horner, 2009). For students with emotional or behavioral disorders, the prevention elements of MTSS can be crucial for addressing their complex academic and behavioral challenges to intervene early, when student behavior is most easily changed (Lane, 2007).

The continual evolution of MTSS for behavior is an important element of students' education. Researchers and practitioners must understand the current evidence-based practices that promote improved behavioral outcomes and continually find ways to foster improved outcomes for learners who exhibit multiple, challenging risk factors. With more than 18,000 U.S. schools implementing MTSS for behavior (http://www.pbis.org), researchers are needed to study the critical elements of each level of MTSS. Teachers just beginning their careers should become very familiar with using MTSS to help them manage behavior in their classrooms. School and district leaders must be able to support teachers as teachers implement behavior supports.

TECH NOTES

BEHAVIOR MANAGEMENT APPS FOR THE CLASSROOM

One of many challenges for new or less-experienced teachers is behavior management. How do we keep our students engaged, eliminate (or at least reduce) problem behaviors, and praise students when we "catch them being good?" Even experienced teachers may struggle with behavior management if they have one or more students in their class who have emotional disturbance or behavior disorders.

A goal of SWPBS, as we have mentioned in this chapter, is to address school social cultures while providing behavioral supports for all students, including those with behavior disorders. In the past decade, technology has become an important component of SWPBS. Many of these technology components are available as apps that can be used with mobile devices to help teachers and students monitor classroom behaviors such as being on task, arriving to class on time, determining whether students are ready when instruction begins, and so forth. In some instances, teachers can alert students during class activities by sending a message such as, "Are you paying attention?" Students respond, and the teacher records and stores their answers. Now, one may ask, "How do we know when the student is telling the truth?" Teachers can periodically select students to check for response accuracy or have any number of ways to assess the validity of student responses.

In some cases, SWPBS programs (e.g., HERO) are very comprehensive and sophisticated; in other cases (e.g., Class Dojo, Remind), apps are less so and are designed for a particular purpose or a few behavioral purposes. Go online and enter into your search engine, "Best apps for classroom behavior management" or "Apps used for positive behavior supports." Naturally, some of the links will be advertisements for specific apps or programs, and some will be ratings published by certain online resources. By devoting 30 minutes or so to reading the information from the links, you will get a general idea of what kind of apps are available to help you manage behavior in your classroom. As always, if you are considering using apps in your classroom for any purpose, do extensive research to find the best program for you and your students.

Functional Behavior Assessment

We introduced FBA in an earlier chapter on assessment. FBA is "a systematic set of strategies that is used to determine the underlying function or purpose of a behavior, so that an effective intervention plan can be developed" (Florida Association for Behavior Analysis, 2018, para. 2). Students participate in behavior because it gets them something they want (e.g., teacher attention) or helps them avoid something they do not want (e.g., time-out). Thus, the behavior has a function, goal, or purpose. Conditions in the classroom also can cause behaviors. FBA is used to show what the student is doing and under what circumstances.

As noted in the assessment chapter, the goals of the FBA are as follows:

- Identify the problem behavior. Be sure that the behavior can be easily observed, can be counted, has a beginning and an ending, and occurs more than once.
- Create a plan for collecting data about the student's behavior using both direct and indirect methods of data collection.
- Compare and analyze the data. What is the **target behavior**? In what settings does the behavior occur? Does the student exhibit the behavior when dealing with all teachers or just one? What happens that prompts the behavior (the antecedent)? Does the behavior continue for a time or does it end fairly quickly?
- Formulate the hypothesis. Make an educated guess as to why the behavior occurs. The four reasons why students misbehave (see Table 10.2) might be helpful in this regard.

Examples of ways to collect data as part of the FBA to write the BIP include the ABC log, student and parent interviews, and review of school records and documents.

Behavior Intervention Plan

Teachers who can explain the function or purpose of problem behavior can act more effectively with students by planning and implementing appropriate interventions. A BIP provides teachers with a road map for changing inappropriate behavior and teaching new, appropriate skills. Findings from the FBA can contribute to the BIP. Earlier, we introduced you to Miranda, a student in Mr. Abbar's class. With the help of a behavior specialist, a FBA was conducted and a BIP written (see Chapter 9 for information about FBAs). As a result, Mr. Abbar, along with others who taught Miranda, were able to better meet the Miranda's needs while managing her behavior (see Instructional Strategy 10.1).

INSTRUCTIONAL STRATEGY 10.1

CREATING A BEHAVIOR INTERVENTION PLAN

Instructional Objective

Miranda will be provided with a BIP to improve her behavior in school.

Instructional Content

Behavior

Instructional Material

Student's FBA, BIP chart

Instructional Delivery

Grouping: Individual

Teaching Procedures

1. Meet with a behavioral intervention team and with the student and/or parent(s).
2. From the student's FBA, identify antecedent events, problem behaviors, and consequences.
3. Generate a hypothesis as to the cause(s) of the problem behavior that will result from the BIP.
4. Determine the goal of the BIP.
5. Create the BIP, including the intervention, person responsible, and the assessment.

Behavior Intervention Plan

Student: Miranda James

School: Fairview Elementary School, **Grade:** 2

General Education Teacher: Mr. Abbar

Special Education Teacher: Ms. Davidson

Results From the FBA

Problem Behaviors: Student refuses to move to and work with students in a small group.

Data Collection: The behavior specialist observed the student in Mr. Abbar's class and also during lunch and recess to identify patterns of misbehavior. He asked Mr. Abbar and Ms. Davidson to complete a teacher checklist that dealt with Miranda's behavior in and out of the classroom; he also interviewed Miranda and her parents (separately) about Miranda's life in and out of school.

Data Analysis: Miranda exhibits her problem behavior across school settings. She prefers to work, eat, and play alone, and when she is asked to work in small groups (an antecedent), she either acts out or remains silent and ignores her classmates. The behavior continues until the group work time ends.

Hypothesis: Teacher attention (redirection, reprimands) results in instructional time lost because of lack of compliance for working in small groups. Miranda does not seem to exhibit behavioral challenges at home, so it is concluded that she may act out because of self-perceived inadequacies that cause her to balk when asked to work with others. It is also thought that she needs to be in control of any activity she is involved in, which angers her classmates and causes her to feel and be isolated.

Intervention Goal

The intervention goal is to increase compliance for working in small groups on academic tasks; in this example, reading fluency–building in small groups.

TABLE 10.5 ■ Building Reading Fluency in Small Groups

Intervention	Person Responsible	Assessment
● Have the student practice the reading passages that will be used in small groups.	● Special education teacher	● Observation: Student is reading aloud in the group.
● Provide the passages on tape for the student to practice at home.	● Special education teacher ● Parents	● Observation: Student is reading aloud in the group.
● Change the group membership to be more heterogeneous.	● Special education teacher ● General education teacher	● Observation: Student works with group members.
● Give the student a strategy for letting the teacher know when the reading material is too difficult and thus will cause embarrassment.	● School ● counselor	● Conference between counselor and teacher to assess when the student is using the strategy.
● Provide specific praise (in note format) for using the strategy.	● Special education teacher ● General education teacher	● Observation: Student uses the strategy.

Classroom teachers can expect other school personnel, such as the special education teacher, school psychologist, and counselor, to work together to conduct the FBA and to write, implement, and evaluate the BIP. An example of how professionals collaborate to conduct the FBA and to write the BIP is shown in the Working Together feature. Take a moment to read this example.

WORKING TOGETHER

THE FUNCTIONAL BEHAVIOR ASSESSMENT AND BEHAVIOR INTERVENTION PLAN

The process of conducting an FBA and developing a BIP is a team effort that can involve the special education teacher, general education teacher, counselor, speech/language pathologist, and other professionals, as appropriate. Consider the following example to learn about possible roles for each professional and the student.

Mrs. Evans, the eighth-grade social studies teacher, was concerned about the behavior of one of her students with a diagnosed emotional or behavioral disability. She has tried several interventions to address the misbehavior, to no avail. She called together the school support team to work with her on the next step. The team decided that the needs of the student warranted an FBA.

Mrs. Evans indicated that she could use the ABC log to collect data on the situational events prior to and following the behavior of concern. She agreed to do this for a week. The special education teacher agreed to collect quantitative data using an observational system so that the frequency could be identified. The counselor agreed to interview the student's mother, which might help shed light on events at home that could help the team understand the student's behavior. Finally, the counselor agreed to review school records and interview the student.

After the FBA was finished, the data analyzed, and the hypotheses generated, the team wrote the BIP together. Collectively, they identified the interventions that could reasonably be implemented to teach the student more appropriate behavior and to reduce the misbehavior. They agreed to give the plan 2 weeks and then reevaluate.

Questions

1. How can the ABC log be implemented in the classroom during the instructional day?
2. What is important for Mrs. Evans to remember when she observes the "B" part of the ABC log?
3. Pretend you are the counselor. What questions would you ask the student's mother?

PROMOTING SAFER SCHOOLS

It is important to build relationships with children and youth and to recognize possible problems before the problems escalate and become serious. With this in mind, we provide guidelines for safer schools.

Guidelines for Safer Schools

Educators must identify ways to handle violence and aggressive behavior to make schools safer for all. According to Smith et al. (2018), the following guidelines can make for safer schools:

- Consistent rules, expectations, and consequences across the entire school
- Positive school climate
- Schoolwide strategies for conflict resolution and dealing with student alienation
- High level of supervision in all school settings
- Cultural sensitivity

- Strong feelings by students of identification, involvement, and bonding with their school
- High levels of parent and community involvement
- Well-utilized space and lack of overcrowding

Dealing With Bullying

Bullying is a critical issue in schools. Educators need to handle bullying as one means for creating safer schools. As White and Loeber (2008) noted, "Bullying can create a climate of fear and discomfort in schools and communities" (p. 380). The act of bullying is intended to harm the victim and is one of the most significant risks to students (Raskaukas & Scott, 2011). Bullying is becoming more and more prevalent among today's youth in school and online, according to recent bullying statistics. Cyberbullying is on the rise more than any other type of bullying. Many students report seeing bullying in chat rooms, social networking websites, and Facebook.com. Major types of bullying include verbal, social, physical, cyberbullying, and racist, religious, and homophobic bullying, along with bullying of people with disabilities. Bullying is noted at all grade levels. The person doing the bullying tries to exert power and control over the person being bullied. Bullying most often occurs in Grades 6 through 10, with about 3 in every 10 students being involved in bullying, as either the bully or the victim (http://www.bullyingstatistics.org). Limited research on bullying and disabilities suggests that students with disabilities have a greater chance of being bullied than their nondisabled peers (Rose & Gage, 2017). Ways to prevent bullying including providing a bullying policy, consequences for bullies, and educating potential victims of bullying. More tips for preventing bullying can be found at http://www.bullyingstatistics.org/content/prevent-bullying.html. Table 10.6 provides decision-making and problem-solving steps.

Boys commit more physical types of bullying, while girls tend to exhibit more psychological types of bullying, such as excluding and gossiping about the victim. Both boys and girls report being victimized by bullies.

There are several characteristics of students who engage in bullying and victims of bullying. In both cases, students show problems with social and psychological adjustment. Such maladjustment is shown in students having difficulties with friendships and reporting feelings of isolation. According to Rose et al. (2012, p. 4), some students with disabilities who bully others may have social information

Teaching problem-solving and decision-making skills is an important part of the social skills curriculum at all grade levels. What social skills are needed to help these students complete their group assignment?

iStock.com/MachineHeadz

TABLE 10.6 ■ Decision-Making and Problem-Solving Steps

What Is the Step?	What Is Involved?	What Intervention Can I Use?
STEP 1: Gathering information	Identify information needed to make a decision and solve the problem.	Hold a class meeting. Conduct a brainstorming session. Have students collect data. Use the ABC log process. Involve the school counselor.
STEP 2: Problem identification	State the precise nature of the problem in observable, measurable terms.	Have students identify the problem; use the criteria—observable and measurable—to evaluate the wording. Take a vote to obtain consensus about the problem.
STEP 3: Solution generation	Describe specific solutions to the problem.	Brainstorm solutions with students. To help students generate solutions, have them answer the following questions: • What happens when the problem does not occur? • What does our classroom look like when this problem does not occur? • Who needs to help solve this problem? • What would happen if . . .?
STEP 4: Decision-making criteria	Establish criteria for selecting the best solution.	Use data from the ABC log to help guide solution generation. Have students describe the resources needed for each possible solution. Rule out those solutions that require unrealistic resources (e.g., too much time, too many people, too much money). Rank-order possible solutions with 1 = best idea.
STEP 5: Action plan	Develop a specific plan using the solution, including who does what, and by when.	Write the action plan using either a class meeting or a designated team of students. Post the action plan.
STEP 6: Evaluation	Meet to determine whether the action plan is working and whether the problem has been solved.	Conduct a class meeting to assess the action plan. Revise if necessary. Set another timeline for reevaluating.

processing deficits: "A lack of social skills may be related to the lack of assertion, a lack of self-control, or both."

The Office for Civil Rights and the Department of Justice have indicated that bullying may also be considered harassment when it is based on a student's race, color, national origin, sex, disability, religion, or disability.

Bullying behaviors may include

- unwelcome conduct such as verbal abuse, name calling, epithets, or slurs;
- graphic or written statements;
- threats;
- physical assault; and
- other conduct that may be physically threatening, harmful, or humiliating.

Source: From PACER's National Bullying Prevention Center (2018).

Teaching problem-solving and decision-making skills is an important part of the social skills curriculum at all grade levels. What social skills are needed to help students interact more appropriately with their peers?

iStock.com/PeopleImages

What can be done to address this critical problem? Recall that in the Opening Challenge, Mr. Abbar noticed that some students thought that Miranda was a bully because of the mean things she would sometimes say. Remember bullying is a major issue in schools today and any perceived threat should be addressed. Behavioral strategies for all students can be conducted to address the bullying problem:

- Make bullying prevention and treatment part of the curriculum. Students should understand that there are bullies, victims, and bystanders who reinforce the bullying behavior. Provide information about the types of bullying—physical, verbal, and psychological—including examples. Students might want to describe examples of bullying as well.
- Involve school administrators, teachers, families, and the community. School procedures for preventing and responding to bullying should be developed and shared with students and families.
- Work with the school counselor to identify effective strategies to handle and report acts of bullying. Have the school counselor conduct age-appropriate discussions with students about power, aggression, and control. Ask the school counselor to meet privately with students to conduct individual or small-group discussions about feelings related to self-concept, social relationships, and other situations in school or at home that may be problematic.

It is important to understand that students with disabilities are not immune to being bullies themselves. In a 2012 study, Swearer et al. found that students with observable disabilities such as language impairments, hearing impairments, and mild intellectual disabilities not only are bullied but may also bully others because of revenge or frustration. The same study also discussed how students with behavior problems may also bully others as a result of being bullied themselves. The authors conclude their discussion by stating, "A culture of respect, tolerance, and acceptance is our only hope for reducing bullying among all school-aged youth" (p. 518).

SUMMARY

This chapter presents techniques for promoting positive behavior and facilitating social skills.

Both of these areas can greatly influence a teacher's success in promoting an atmosphere for learning. Identifying specific behavioral and social tasks will help teachers plan effective adaptations and treatments that can provide students with skills to use not only in the classroom but also schoolwide and in the community.

By utilizing assessment practices, teachers will realize quickly how successful their adaptations and treatment programs are in promoting an environment that is conducive to learning. Implementing practices discussed in this chapter will help students with disabilities become more involved in the classroom and be better accepted by their peers.

REVIEW THE LEARNING OBJECTIVES

Let's review the learning objectives for this chapter. If you are uncertain and cannot talk through the answers provided for any of these questions, reread those sections of the text.

10.1 Describe practices that can be used to foster student relationships and communication.
There are a number of practices you can adopt to cultivate good relationships with—and among—the students you teach, including getting to know your students, using motivational practices, being responsive to cultural differences, and considering student meetings.

10.2 Explain ways that can be used to communicate effectively with students.
Managing teacher behavior can facilitate the accomplishment of expected behavioral and social skills tasks by all students. Some techniques include communicating clear and consistent messages, explaining the rules and consequences, explaining the daily schedule, providing good directions, describing transition procedures, and using specific praise.

10.3 Discuss effective classroom arrangement practices.
There are several practices. Examine the physical arrangement and observe traffic patterns. Consider seating arrangements and maintain with-it-ness.

10.4 Explain the goals of misbehavior.
Lack of social acceptance contributes to the goal of misbehavior. Other goals are attention getting, power and control, revenge, and alleviating feelings of inadequacy.

10.5 Discuss ways that problem behaviors can be assessed.
Teachers must be able to describe behaviors that are desirable as well as those that are intrusive to teaching so that they can design and assess treatment plans. Observational techniques and the ABC log can be used to assess problem behaviors.

10.6 Describe instructional strategies are available for behavior problems.
For less serious behavior, several strategies are available, including planned ignoring, redirecting inappropriate behavior, providing contingent observations, providing criterion-specific rewards, contracting, planning interdependent group contingencies, and implementing self-regulation techniques. For more serious behavior, there are several strategies, including time-out, seclusion, and in-school supervision.

10.7 Explain how safer schools can be promoted.
A variety of techniques can be used, including the following:

- Consistent rules, expectations, and consequences across the entire school
- Positive school climate
- Schoolwide strategies for conflict resolution and dealing with student alienation
- High level of supervision in all school settings

- Cultural sensitivity
- Strong feelings by students of identification, involvement, and bonding with their school
- High levels of parent and community involvement
- Well-utilized space and lack of overcrowding

REVISIT THE OPENING CHALLENGE

Check your answers to the Reflection Questions from the Opening Challenge and revise them on the basis of what you have learned.

1. If you were Mr. Abbar, in what areas would you seek professional development help from the special education teacher?
2. How might Mr. Abbar be able to identify specific challenges that Miranda presents?
3. What advice would you offer Ms. Nguyen about getting to know her students better?
4. How can Mr. Abbar and Ms. Nguyen foster student relationships and communication?
5. How can both teachers help their students with their behavior?
6. How can both teachers determine whether student behavior skills are improving?
7. How can Mr. Abbar and Ms. Nguyen use the ADAPT Framework to promote positive behavior?

KEY TERMS

behavioral strategies
classroom management
contingent observation
criterion-specific rewards
event recording
I-message
in-school supervision
interdependent group contingency
interest inventory
interval recording
planned ignoring
prosocial behaviors
reinforcement
rewards
seclusion time-out
signals
sociogram
specific praise
student-centered learning
target behavior
teacher proximity
text
time sampling
traffic patterns
with-it-ness

PROFESSIONAL STANDARDS AND LICENSURE

For a complete description of Professional Standards and Licensure, please see the appendix.

CEC Initial Preparation Standards

Standard 1: Learner Development and Individual Learning Differences

Standard 2: Learning Environments

Standard 3: Curricular Content Knowledge

INTASC Core Principles

Standard 1: Learner Development

Standard 2: Learning Differences

Standard 3: Learning Environments

Standard 4: Content Knowledge

Standard 6: Assessment

Standard 8: Instructional Strategies

Standard 9: Professional Learning and Ethical Practice

Praxis II: Education of Exceptional Students: Core Content Knowledge

I. Understanding Exceptionalities: Human Development and Behavior

III. Delivery of Services to Students: Curriculum and Instruction

iStock.com/monkeybusinessimages

11 TEACHING READING

CHAPTER OBJECTIVES

After studying this chapter, you will be able to meet the following learning objectives:

11.1 Explain the issues that are related to reading instruction.

11.2 Describe the five components of reading.

11.3 Explain phonics and word study.

11.4 Describe reading fluency.

11.5 Describe reading vocabulary.

11.6 Explain reading comprehension.

Opening Challenge

Appropriate Reading Instruction

Elementary Grades. Mrs. Johnson is in her sixth year of teaching at the elementary level in a suburban school district. The district's demographics reflect a rich heritage of diversity. The district also serves a large percentage of students who qualify for free or reduced-cost meals. She taught first grade for 3 years and is now in her third year of teaching second grade.

As part of the district's multi-tiered systems of support program, teachers in kindergarten through second grade must assess all of their students in the fall, winter, and spring to identify those who are at risk for reading difficulties and to monitor their progress as they engage in reading instruction throughout the year. In keeping with district policy, Mrs. Johnson recently administered a reading assessment to screen students for reading problems so that she can provide extra reading support. After analyzing students' test scores, she learns that of her 22 students, 6 scored at the "somewhat at risk for reading difficulties" level and two scored at the "high risk for reading difficulties" level. Based on the test results, Mrs. Johnson reflects: *"Many of my struggling students have problems with word identification—they lack ways to identify words in a list or in their continuous reading passage. Decoding results show that some of the students lack basic skills to figure out unknown words. Based on the phonological awareness items on the test, some students have difficulty with identifying individual phonemes and can't seem to blend or segment sounds to form words. I am concerned that this problem may affect their decoding and spelling skills. All of these students exhibit difficulty with oral reading, which is choppy because they don't know the words by sight. Problems with reading fluency affect their ability to understand the text. I will have to provide them with extra reading support in addition to my regular reading instruction for the entire class."*

Secondary Grades. Mr. Davis is in his second year of teaching seventh-grade reading in a large, urban middle school. In his school district, all struggling readers are required to take a reading course in seventh grade to develop and refine their reading skills, with a special emphasis on reading content-area textbooks. Because his school has a large number of low readers, he has, on average, 35 students per class, with five classes daily. Last summer, he attended a 5-day workshop that focused on strategies for students who have difficulty reading content-area textbooks. He took the course because in the previous school year he was overwhelmed with how many of his students lacked basic reading skills or had problems understanding the material. These problems made it difficult for them to succeed in his class, where many of the students required differentiated instruction, which is challenging with large classes. He observed that they were often unable to identify words on the page, let alone comprehend the text.

Mr. Davis spoke with sixth-grade teachers in his school and found that many of his struggling students experienced the same problems the previous year. Mr. Davis worries that if he doesn't provide support for students who are having reading problems, these students will never be able to read content-area text successfully, which will lead to difficulties in several of their courses, such as science and social studies. He asked Mrs. Levy, a more experienced reading specialist, to help him conduct reading assessments with his students. He reflects on the assessment results: *"Most of the students in my classes are reading two to three grades below their current placement. Some of them have problems with word attack, which causes them difficulties with decoding multisyllabic words found in the textbooks. They won't read out loud in class during literature circles, and I suspect that it's because they have problems with the words in the books and that they are embarrassed. Mrs. Levy indicated that most of the students' oral reading fluency is very low for their grade level. Other students scored well on word identification and moderately well on fluency but exhibit serious problems with comprehension and vocabulary skills. Maybe if I help them use the strategies I learned this summer, they can improve their reading abilities."*

Mrs. Johnson and Mr. Davis have something in common: They both have students in their classrooms who have so much trouble reading that differentiation and instructional adaptations are necessary. Both of these teachers need to provide their students with considerable support to ensure their success.

Reflection Questions

In your journal, write down your answers to the following questions. After completing the chapter, check your answers and revise them on the basis of what you have learned.

1. What specific difficulties might students in Mrs. Johnson's and Mr. Davis's classes exhibit in phonological awareness, phonics and word study, reading fluency, reading vocabulary, and reading comprehension?
2. How can Mrs. Johnson and Mr. Davis use practices for effective reading to structure their reading activities?
3. How can these teachers differentiate instruction and provide adapted lessons to students who require intensive instruction, while meeting the needs of the rest of the class?

Most students enjoy learning to read and write, and many young children enter kindergarten with some, and maybe even considerable, reading skills. This reading ability is due in part to a literacy-rich environment that contains books and includes communication. But some children are not so fortunate. Their homes do not have these reading advantages, or some were unable to attend a preschool that emphasized literacy, or because of disability-related conditions they are unable to benefit from their environmental advantages. These students may be challenged by learning to read. Consequently, these students require special attention and instruction to become good readers. This chapter examines key features of reading instruction and provides examples of effective reading instruction that have been proven useful to teachers who work with struggling students.

More than 20 years ago, the National Reading Panel (2000), commissioned by Congress to evaluate the evidence for early reading instruction, published *Teaching Children to Read: An Evidence-Based Assessment of the Scientific Research Literature on Reading and Its Implications for Reading Instruction*. This report indicated the importance of explicit reading instruction, including instruction in phonological awareness, phonics and word study, reading fluency, reading comprehension, and vocabulary. According to the National Reading Panel, reading instruction must occur for each of these components. Good readers use skills from each component efficiently as they read a variety of texts, such as novels, magazines, newspapers, textbooks, and online material.

ISSUES RELATED TO READING INSTRUCTION

Approximately one in four students has difficulty learning to read. Of those students who show problems learning to read by the end of third grade, many will continue to struggle with reading in later grades, especially in the content areas (Wanzek & Roberts, 2012). Results from the National Assessment of Educational Progress (2023) indicate that reading scores for 13-year-old students declined by four points compared to the previous assessment that was administered in the 2019–2020 school year.

The percentages among students from diverse backgrounds and students who live in poverty or have disabilities are even worse.

Research findings have shown that there are specific problems shown to varying degrees by students who are struggling readers. Some students might have trouble mapping sounds to letters and **letter combinations**. Some students show problems with phonological awareness skills and struggle to learn sound-symbol relationships (or **letter-sound correspondences**, as they are sometimes called) and have limited sight vocabularies (i.e., the ability to recognize words as soon as they are seen). Reading fluency, which is a combination of reading accuracy and rate, might be slow and choppy; problems with fluency interfere with the ability to comprehend text because students spend a great deal of mental energy identifying words. In this case, students find it difficult to concentrate on the meaning of what they are reading. Students who find reading difficult often don't read independently for pleasure. However, extensive reading is one of the best ways to increase reading vocabulary. Thus, vocabulary development may be affected because of limited reading exposure. In short, students become better readers by reading more; struggling readers continue to struggle because they read less, if at all.

Reading skills are fundamental for success in school. How can you provide appropriate reading instruction and adaptations for all your students?

iStock.com/monkeybusinessimages

Older students may also exhibit problems with reading that remain uncorrected from the elementary grades. Older students may have limited strategies for figuring out words that contain multiple syllables. These students often lack techniques for breaking words apart, sounding out the parts, and blending the parts together to read the word. Secondary teachers often indicate that their students with reading difficulties have problems understanding text and are hampered by a limited vocabulary (Bryant et al., 2011). In content area classes such as science or social studies, the textbook may be the major source of information for students. Problems with comprehension and vocabulary can greatly affect the student's ability to be successful at the secondary level. Many struggling readers may not attend colleges or universities, but they can continue their education at the postsecondary level thanks to community colleges. If their reading problems persist, they experience many of the same challenges they faced in high school.

Some students with reading problems are identified as having **dyslexia**, a language-based reading disability thought to affect 20% of school-age students. Dyslexia is a lifelong condition found in people from all backgrounds. Although dyslexia tends to run in families, it is not necessarily genetic in origin (Welcome Centre Human Genetics, 2017). Bryant, Bryant, Hammill, and Sorrells (2004) reviewed the literature on dyslexia and identified the following research-based characteristics of the condition:

- Makes sound–letter association errors when reading aloud.
- Has poor memory for letters and words.
- Reads slowly when reading orally.
- Reads slowly when reading silently. Substitutes words of similar meaning while reading aloud (e.g., substitutes *thermos* for *flask*).
- Substitutes phonetically similar words while reading aloud (e.g., substitutes *chair* for *cheer* or *then* for *when*).
- Reads with flat, disjointed, or nonmelodic (dysrhythmic) intonation when reading orally.
- Does not remember letter sequences in printed syllables.

- Interchanges short words, especially articles (e.g., substitutes *a* for *the*) when reading orally.
- Omits inflectional endings (e.g., *-s, -ed, -ing*) when reading aloud.
- Cannot break a word into syllables.
- Cannot combine syllables into words.
- Reverses sounds (e.g., *pan* as *pna*) when reading aloud.
- Reads as though each word is encountered for the first time.
- Cannot call pseudowords (e.g., *nim, klep*).
- Calls words correctly but does not know their meaning.
- Adds words when reading aloud.
- Cannot retell what has been read.
- Cannot comprehend a passage without reading it more than once.

Appropriate instruction and the use of instructional adaptations can help most struggling readers learn to strengthen their reading skills. Teachers must focus on teaching the skills of the five components of reading shown in Figure 11.1 and help students use these skills with various types of text. For some students with dyslexia, technology can help them access the text. It is important to understand, however, that simply listening to text being read does not ensure comprehension. Much of the information in the Tech Notes feature is appropriate for use with text-to-speech technology, which is described below.

FIGURE 11.1 ■ The Five Components of Reading

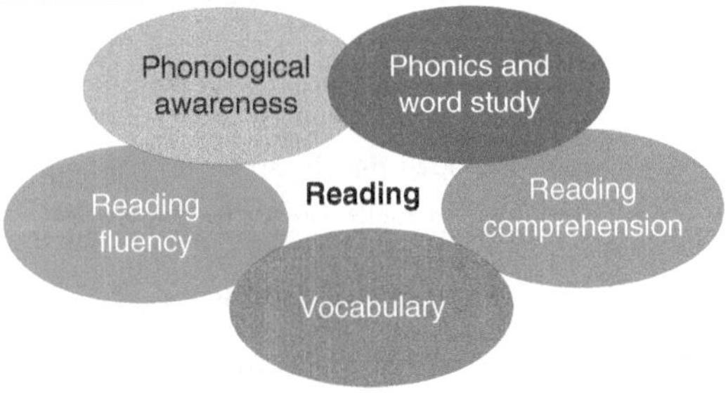

TECH NOTES

USING AUDIO DEVICES TO ACCESS PRINT

Mark, Dan, and Maureen are students who have used recorded books for years to help them access print materials that would have been inaccessible otherwise. Dan has a learning disability in reading, Mark is visually impaired, and Maureen is blind. As Mark states, "Audiobooks have been a godsend to my education. I would definitely recommend audiobooks for all those people that print is not an option for. Audiobooks provide an invaluable resource which brings the printed word to the visually impaired world."

Android and iOS devices, personal computers, and DAISY devices can all be used to access audiobooks. Such devices may help students with reading difficulties bypass their disability by listening to prerecorded text (e.g., books, journals, newspapers). Prerecorded texts (audiobooks) are available from a number of sources, including Learning Ally (formerly Recordings for the Blind and Dyslexic), the Library of Congress, many local libraries, and several private companies. Considerable progress has been made on making available audiobooks to those who need them. For more information, see the website for the Library of Congress's World Digital Library (https://www.loc.gov/collections/world-digital-library/). Also, a variety of apps are available through the Library of Congress's web site.

Audiobooks can help level the playing field for students with print disabilities. As Dan mentions, "There is no reason that a student with a print disability should be at a disadvantage to anyone. They just have to find the way that they learn and work in their own way."

Maureen, discussing how audiobooks can help with pleasure reading, adds, "Books are usually a good companion when there is no one around to talk to. I like to go into the world of characters I'm reading about and get involved with their problems because sometimes it's easier to solve their problems than my own."

According to Learning Ally, research has demonstrated that audiobooks have helped students in areas such as improved comprehension, increased motivation, increased self-confidence, improved attitudes toward reading, and reading accuracy (https://www.learningally.org/Adults/Why-Audiobooks-Work). Users can download the free Learning Ally Link at their favorite app store.

Source: Some of this material was used with permission from M. Raskind and B. R. Bryant, 2002, *Functional evaluation for assistive technology*, Psycho-educational Services.

THE FIVE COMPONENTS OF READING AND PHONOLOGICAL AWARENESS

Researchers and practitioners have identified teaching strategies to help students become better readers. In this section, we present information about the components of reading, including examples of lessons that can be used to teach important reading skills and concepts.

Phonological Awareness

Phonological awareness consists of listening skills, including rhyming, blending, and segmenting.

One type of phonological awareness, phonemic awareness, is the ability to segment, blend, and manipulate individual phonemes, which are the smallest units of sound that influence the meaning in words (Reading Rockets, 2017). The most important type of phonological awareness is phonemic awareness. Phonemic awareness is thought to be the most important type of phonological awareness because it is related to phonics instruction, spelling, the ability to read, and the alphabetic principle—the recognition that letters of the alphabet represent sounds in language.

Characteristics of Students Who Struggle With Phonological Awareness

It is not uncommon for beginning readers to have difficulty with the following tasks (Bryant et al., 2013):

- Recognizing or producing words that rhyme
- Blending or segmenting syllables
- Blending or segmenting onset-rimes
- Recognizing that two words begin or end with the same sound or different sounds
- Recognizing that two words contain the same or different medial, or middle, sounds
- Segmenting or blending a word's individual sounds
- Manipulating sounds to identify a new word when a sound is deleted or substituted in a word

Some students who exhibit phonological awareness problems do well in reading, and some poor readers do well when participating in phonological awareness activities. It stands to reason that students who have difficulty blending sounds together to form spoken words probably will have difficulties blending letter sounds together to recognize written words.

Strategies for Teaching Phonological Awareness

Effective phonological awareness instruction can be done by following the guidelines below (Torgesen & Bryant, 2013; Vaughn & Bos, 2015).

- **Assessment:** Consider students' developmental level when planning instruction. Instruction may need to be focused on syllables or onset-rimes if students are not ready for individual phoneme activities. Through assessment, the type of phonological awareness most appropriate for instruction can be determined.
- **Instructional content:** Take into consideration phonological features when selecting words for instruction. First, words with fewer sounds (e.g., *cat, it*) are easier to blend, segment, and manipulate than words with more sounds (e.g., *thread, splash, flat*). Second, the location of the phoneme (initial, medial, or final) influences the level of difficulty. It is easier to change the word *man* to *ran* than it is to change *man* to *men* or to *map*. Third, the properties of sounds should be considered when words are selected for instruction. Continuous sounds like /ssssss/ are easier to blend than stop sounds like /p/.
- **Instructional materials:** Include concrete objects as part of teaching. Objects such as blank tiles, blocks, and chips offer students opportunities to manipulate physical representations of individual sounds. Students can even use their fingers to show each sound as they segment and blend sounds in words.
- **Connections to letters:** Add letters to phonological awareness activities. Once students are familiar with blending, segmenting, and manipulating onsets and rimes and individual phonemes, include letter-sound correspondence. Connecting phonological awareness with letters helps students develop an understanding of the alphabetic principle. For example, teachers can replace blank tiles with letter tiles to have students blend and segment words.

PHONICS AND WORD STUDY

Phonics is the teaching of letter-sound relationships so that students can distinguish unknown words they happen upon in the text. The ability to read words quickly and effortlessly lets students identify words on sight. Good readers also have effective decoding strategies to figure out unknown words. Word identification instruction involves teaching **sight word recognition** and decoding skills. For example, think about how many words you find in a standard dictionary (about 200,000 words). It would be virtually impossible to teach all of those words by using flash cards to have students identify them in print. That is why phonics and decoding instruction are so important because students need to be able to use letter-sound correspondences to identify decodable words they cannot recognize at sight. But there are a number of words that occur so often in print that they can be taught using sight vocabulary instruction.

Characteristics of Students Who Struggle With Phonics and Word Study

Teaching students to identify sight words and to decode unfamiliar words are important components of word identification instruction. Struggling readers at the elementary and secondary levels often have a limited sight word vocabulary and have difficulty recalling words automatically, even after instruction. For these students, consistent practice and review of sight words, along with reading the words in text, is a critical feature of daily instruction. The guidelines for sight word instruction in the next section provides ways to offer the extra practice struggling readers require.

Phonic analysis difficulties vary among students with reading problems. Many students are able to identify letter-sound correspondences and know how to say letter combinations in isolation. For these students, the problem often lies in blending letter sounds together to read words. This difficulty is especially apparent as they try to decode pseudowords (e.g., *zim*) used to assess phonic analysis skills. Conversely,

These students are listening to a book on a CD-ROM while also reading the book in print. What reading skills are these students practicing? What other activities could reinforce these skills?

iStock.com/richiesd

good readers have developed such automaticity in decoding words that it is impossible to tell whether words are in their sight vocabularies or if they are rapidly and effortlessly applying their phonics skills.

Strategies for Teaching Phonics and Word Study

The following guidelines for sight word instruction offer helpful tips for effective teaching in an area that typically requires consistent practice and review for mastery and retention. The guidelines should be conducted regularly and will help teachers plan their instruction (Honig et al., 2012).

- **Assessment:** Use a sight word list to determine which words should be targeted for intervention. One of the more common sight word lists was compiled originally by Edgar Dolch in 1948, but the list is still widely used today because it contains words that frequently appear in print today. Table 11.1 is a reconfiguration of the Dolch List, according to grade level. As you look at the list, think about how many times you see the words when you read, even as you are reading this book.
- **Instructional content**: Teach targeted words that most commonly occur in informational text, literature, and basal readers that your students encounter during reading. Teach the words before students read text containing these words.
- **Instructional content**: Teach irregular words (those that do not have perfect letter-sound correspondence) with common parts and similar sound patterns as word families, such as *would, could*, and *should;* and *other, mother*, and *brother.*
- **Instructional content**: Teach words that have visually similar patterns separately. Words such as *though, thought*, and *through; was* and *saw;* and *were* and *where* should not be taught together.
- **Instructional content**: Teach a limited number of new words in each lesson.

- **Instructional materials:** Use flash cards for instruction and review. Color-code parts of words that require more attention (e.g., color green the *w* in *was* and the *s* in *saw* to focus student attention on the initial sound of the word).
- **Instructional delivery**: Focus student attention on all the letters and sounds of irregular words, including letters or letter combinations that do not follow common English sounds or spellings.
- **Review/maintenance**: Include a cumulative review of key **high-frequency words** (2 to 3 minutes daily).
- **Fluency**: Build fluency once words have been learned. Have students read groups of sight words on flash cards. Show the flash card and ask, "What word?" Students should respond correctly within 3 seconds. Put unknown words in a separate pile for further instruction.
- **Progress monitoring**: Daily, at the conclusion of the lesson, review the words taught to determine which were learned. Review previously taught words on a weekly basis. Put words not remembered back into the instructional content pool of words.

TABLE 11.1 ■ Dolch Basic Word List Organized by Grade Level

Preprimer	Primer	Grade 1	Grade 2	Grade 3
1. the	**45.** when	**89.** many	**133.** know	**177.** don't
2. of	**46.** who	**90.** before	**134.** while	**178.** does
3. and	**47.** will	**91.** must	**135.** last	**179.** got
4. to	**48.** more	**92.** through	**136.** might	**180.** united
5. a	**49.** no	**93.** back	**137.** us	**181.** left
6. in	**50.** if	**94.** years	**138.** great	**182.** number
7. that	**51.** out	**95.** where	**139.** old	**183.** course
8. is	**52.** so	**96.** much	**140.** year	**184.** war
9. was	**53.** said	**97.** your	**141.** off	**185.** until
10. he	**54.** what	**98.** may	**142.** come	**186.** always
11. for	**55.** up	**99.** well	**143.** since	**187.** away
12. it	**56.** its	**100.** down	**144.** against	**188.** something
13. with	**57.** about	**101.** should	**145.** go	**189.** fact
14. as	**58.** into	**102.** because	**146.** came	**190.** through
15. his	**59.** than	**103.** each	**147.** right	**191.** water
16. on	**60.** them	**104.** just	**148.** used	**192.** less
17. be	**61.** can	**105.** those	**149.** take	**193.** public
18. at	**62.** only	**106.** people	**150.** three	**194.** put
19. by	**63.** other	**107.** Mr.	**151.** states	**195.** thing
20. I	**64.** new	**108.** How	**152.** himself	**196.** almost
21. this	**65.** some	**109.** too	**153.** few	**197.** hand
22. had	**66.** could	**110.** little	**154.** house	**198.** enough
23. not	**67.** time	**111.** state	**155.** use	**199.** far

(Continued)

TABLE 11.1 ■ Dolch Basic Word List Organized by Grade Level (*Continued*)

Preprimer	Primer	Grade 1	Grade 2	Grade 3
24. are	**68.** these	**112.** good	**156.** during	**200.** took
25. but	**69.** two	**113.** very	**157.** without	**201.** head
26. from	**70.** may	**114.** make	**158.** again	**202.** yet
27. or	**71.** then	**115.** would	**159.** place	**203.** government
28. have	**72.** do	**116.** still	**160.** American	**204.** system
29. an	**73.** first	**117.** own	**161.** around	**205.** better
30. they	**74.** any	**118.** see	**162.** however	**206.** set
31. which	**75.** my	**119.** men	**163.** home	**207.** told
32. one	**76.** now	**120.** work	**164.** small	**208.** nothing
33. you	**77.** such	**121.** long	**165.** found	**209.** night
34. were	**78.** like	**122.** get	**166.** Mrs.	**210.** end
35. her	**79.** our	**123.** here	**167.** thought	**211.** why
36. all	**80.** over	**124.** between	**168.** went	**212.** called
37. she	**81.** man	**125.** both	**169.** say	**213.** didn't
38. there	**82.** me	**126.** life	**170.** part	**214.** eyes
39. would	**83.** even	**127.** being	**171.** once	**215.** find
40. their	**84.** most	**128.** under	**172.** general	**216.** going
41. we	**85.** made	**129.** never	**173.** high	**217.** look
42. him	**86.** after	**130.** day	**174.** upon	**218.** asked
43. been	**87.** also	**131.** Same	**175.** school	**219.** later
44. has	**88.** did	**132.** another	**176.** every	**220.** knew

Source: From Dolch Word List Reexamined, by D. D. Johnson, 1971, *The Reading Teacher, 24*, pp. 455–456.

Teaching phonic analysis is an important component of early reading instruction. Students must demonstrate a strong understanding of letter-sound correspondence and combinations. Students must also be able to recognize word parts such as phonograms, or rimes, which are parts of a word to which consonants or blends are added to make a word (*an, ip, un*). The following practices can help struggling readers learn to decode using phonic analysis skills (Cunningham, 2017).

- **Instructional content:** Teach letter-sound correspondence in a logical order. Most useful initially are the consonants *b, c, d, f, g, h, k, l, m, n, p, r, s*, and *t*, and the vowels. Present continuous letter sounds (e.g., *s* and /sss/, *m* and /mmm/, *n* and /nnn/) before stop letter sounds (*p* and /p/, *k* and /k/). Select letters that represent sounds found in decodable text students will read.
- **Instructional content:** Introduce the most common sounds of the letters first. Lowercase letters should be taught before uppercase ones.
- **Instructional content:** Teach the letter combinations that most frequently occur in text.
- **Instructional content:** Avoid teaching letter-sound correspondence and letter combinations that sound similar and could confuse students. For instance, /m/ and /n/ and /sh/ and /ch/

should not be taught together. Letter combinations with the same sound, such as /ir/ and /ur/ and /ee/ and /ea/, can be taught at the same time.

- **Instructional content**: Teach phonograms containing letter-sound correspondences that have been introduced. Phonograms or rimes such as *ap, at, ip, it, un*, and *et* paired with initial consonants or onsets provide opportunities to segment and blend sounds to make words. These words should be featured in the decodable text students will read. Decodable texts contain words with the sounds and patterns you have previously taught and students have mastered.
- **Instructional delivery**: Teach students to blend the letter sounds together in a seamless fashion. For instance, students should be taught to say *mmmaaannn* rather than separating the sounds /m/ /a/ /n/.
- **Instructional materials**: Have students read decodable texts.
- **Connections to spelling**: Have students spell the words so their phonics instruction can be reinforced. Spelling and reading are closely related skills. Here are some examples of ways to make connections to spelling:
  - Introduce letter-sound correspondences for spelling as they are being introduced and taught in reading.
  - Have students sort words into spelling patterns.
  - Have students identify words from their text with patterns that match what they are learning in phonics.

Considering Diversity: Anchoring Reading to Culture

Some students experience a disconnect between the instructional materials assigned at school and their personal backgrounds (Grantham & Ford, 2003). When students cannot relate new learning to what they have experienced or what they know, learning challenges increase. Also, when some students see relationships between curriculum content and others can't make such associations, some students may feel affirmed, whereas others sense that they are not valued. The result is often negative feelings about school, as well as disengagement.

Culturally responsive classrooms include culturally relevant teaching and materials that children with different interests and backgrounds can relate to. Teachers can enhance content by using books that include an array of characters from different backgrounds for students to select for book reviews. They can also provide multiple perspectives about historical events in their lectures and examples. For example, books about both Thomas Jefferson's and Sally Hemings's lives can stimulate interesting discussions about the lives of people of different races and different cultures living in America before the Civil War. Activities that represent many diverse cultures broaden everyone's knowledge and understanding of each other.

1. How can teachers provide more culturally responsive instruction to their students?
2. What instructional materials or instructional content might you add to a unit about American history?

The following are guidelines for English learners:

- Discuss letters that may have pronunciations in English that differ from those in the student's first language (e.g., the letter *h* in Spanish is silent). Correct differences of speech sounds carefully.
- Where appropriate, add pictures of words (e.g., on the back of word cards) to help students associate words and meanings and to learn vocabulary.
- Use charts and word banks to categorize words according to patterns.
- Teach rules for decoding words with letters that do not make their most common sound (e.g., silent-*e* words, double-vowel words).

Elkonin (1973) identified a procedure that has been shown to successfully teach blending and segmenting skills (see Instructional Strategy 11.1). This procedure can also be used to help students relate oral responses with letter correspondences to foster an understanding of the alphabetic principle.

INSTRUCTIONAL STRATEGY 11.1

PHONICS ANALOGIES

Instructional content: Initial, middle, and final phonemes
Instructional materials: Elkonin mat and boxes, Chips

Teaching Procedure

1. Give students a mat with blank boxes and letter chips.
2. Place a picture at the top of the mat (e.g., a picture of a man).
3. Ask students to identify and say the word.
4. Tell them that the three boxes stand for each sound in the word *man*. One letter is used to represent each sound.
5. Say the first sound in *man* (/m/) and have the students repeat the sound. Have them identify the letter that represents the /m/ sound: *m*, as they place the *m* chip in the first box.
6. Say the middle sound in *man* (/a/) and have the students repeat the sound. Have them identify the letter that represents the /a/ sound: *a*, as they place the *a* chip in the second box.
7. Say the final sound in *man* (/n/) and have the students repeat the sound. Have them identify the letter that represents the /n/ sound: *n*, as they place the *n* chip in the third box.
8. Tell them to blend the sounds together to form the word while sliding their pointer finger left to right under the boxes. /m/ /a/ /n/
9. Have them say the word . . . *man*.
10. Tell students that they are going to form a new word by changing the first letter and sound in *man*.
11. Replace the picture of a man with a picture of a fan. Ask students to identify and say the word *fan*.
12. Say the first sound in *fan* (/f/) and have the students repeat the sound. Have them identify the letter that represents the /f/ sound: *f*, as they place the *f* chip in the first box.
13. Tell them to blend the sounds together to form the word while sliding their pointer finger left to right under the boxes. /f/ /a/ /n/

Error Correction: If students make an error, say, "Stop. Listen as I model the procedure." Model another word. Have students repeat. Then continue with guided practice.
Guided Practice: Provide several words for the students to work on in groups of three or four (e.g., *ran, pan, Dan*). As they work, circulate and provide error correction and feedback.
Independent Practice: Give each student several words to do alone. Tell the other students to sound out each letter, blending them and then saying the word quickly.
Progress monitoring: After the lesson, give the students 10 words to identify using their blending skills; check for mastery.

READING FLUENCY

Reading fluency is the ability to read text accurately, quickly, and with expression. The ability to read effortlessly and with speed is what fluency is all about.

There are two types of reading fluency. Oral reading fluency consists of rate, or how fast someone reads, and accuracy, or how many words they correctly identify. Oral reading fluency may also include expression or prosody, which means altering pitch, tone, and so forth. **Silent reading fluency** consists of rate and comprehension.

Unfortunately, most teachers do not spend a lot of instructional time building students' fluency. In fact, some teachers do not spend any time at all. However, time spent on fluency building is time well spent.

It is important for older readers to read fluently because of the large amounts of material they have to read for school assignments. Repeated reading, the process of developing fluency through multiple readings of the same passage, fosters reading accuracy, reading rate, and comprehension (Office of Special Education Programs [OSEP], 2014). Research findings have demonstrated repeated reading is very effective in developing the reading fluency and reading comprehension abilities of students with reading difficulties (Kim et al., 2017).

There are many factors that influence reading fluency, such as content and purpose for reading. Moreover, fluency expectations for oral and silent reading differ. Findings from a study by Jan Hasbrouck and Gerald Tindal in 2017 updated their 2006 oral reading fluency rates for first grade (beginning in winter) through sixth grade and are presented in Table 11.2.

TABLE 11.2 ■ Reading Rates for Oral Reading (in Words per Minute)

Grade	Percentile	Fall WCPM*	Winter WCPM*	Spring WCPM*
1	90		97	116
	75		59	91
	50		29	60
	25		16	34
	10		9	18
2	90	111	131	148
	75	84	109	124
	50	50	84	100
	25	36	59	72
	10	23	35	43
3	90	134	161	166
	75	104	137	139
	50	83	97	112
	25	59	79	91
	10	40	62	63
4	90	153	168	184
	75	125	143	160
	50	94	120	133
	25	75	95	105
	10	60	71	83
5	90	179	183	195
	75	153	160	169
	50	121	133	146
	25	87	109	119
	10	64	84	102

(Continued)

TABLE 11.2 ■ Reading Rates for Oral Reading (in Words per Minute) (*Continued*)

Grade	Percentile	Fall WCPM*	Winter WCPM*	Spring WCPM*
6	90	185	195	204
	75	159	166	173
	50	132	145	146
	25	112	116	122
	10	89	91	91

Note: WCPM = words correct per minute.

Source: From Hasbrouck, J. & Tindal, G. (2017). *An update to compiled ORF norms* (Technical report No. 1702). Eugene, OR. Behavioral Research and Teaching. University of Oregon. Reprinted with permission.

Characteristics of Students Who Struggle With Reading Fluency

Beginning readers typically demonstrate the following characteristics:

- exhibit problems with accuracy and speed;
- present basic word reading difficulties;
- have a small sight vocabulary;
- read word by word;
- rarely self-correct their errors during their reading; and
- have difficulty reading aloud in ways that reflect a misunderstanding of the text and are unable to engage listeners.

Strategies for Teaching Reading Fluency

If students read fluently they can then focus on reading comprehension (Kim et al., 2017). To build reading fluency, students should be given multiple opportunities to practice reading words in isolation (e.g., sight words) and text at their independent level; that is, they practice fluency with words they can read with at least 95% accuracy. The following practices can help develop fluency.

- **Instructional content**: Select appropriate text. Fluency instruction is best accomplished using materials at the students' independent reading level, where they recognize many words at sight and identify unknown words quickly. Students should concentrate on reading with an increased rate and not worry about decoding unknown words. Instructional-level materials (90–94% accuracy) can be used, but avoid frustration-level texts (words recognized with less than 90% accuracy). Beginning readers can practice building their fluency by reading decodable texts. In addition, texts for fluency building should be of interest to the students.
- **Instructional delivery**: Model fluent reading or have a fluent reader do so.
- **Instructional delivery**: Teach students word identification skills to build automaticity and obtain a core sight word vocabulary. Help build fluency with isolated words, phrase reading (e.g., reading three- or four-word phrases, such as "in the tree" and "on the large ball"), and connected text.
- **Progress monitoring**: Assess students' oral reading ability at least biweekly. Graph the number of words per minute that are correct. Compare progress to the benchmark fluency rates presented in Table 11.2. Students must make steady progress on each assessment so they will reach the winter and spring benchmarks.

One important strategy to build reading fluency is Paired Reading (or Partner Reading, as it is also called). Paired Reading is depicted in Instructional Strategy 11.2. Mrs. Johnson has used this strategy successfully to increase oral reading fluency with her second-grade students.

INSTRUCTIONAL STRATEGY 11.2

PAIRED READING

Instructional objective: Students will read passages aloud with increased rate and accuracy.
Instructional content: Fluency; reading instructional-level passages
Instructional materials: Copies of reading materials for students, timer, chart paper
Instructional delivery: Paired reading (Partner 1 is a slightly better reader than Partner 2.)

Paired reading is an effective method for developing the oral reading fluency skills of students who read at about the first-grade level (e.g., know some sight words, can blend consonant-vowel-consonant words). This method works well with students who read haltingly and who make careless errors.

Teaching Procedure

1. Divide students into pairs.
2. Select reading passages that the lower-level reading partner can read at no less than the instructional level.
3. Set the timer for 2 minutes for Partner 1 to read the passage out loud while Partner 2 follows along.
4. Repeat step 3, but have Partner 2 read out loud and Partner 1 follow along, helping with unknown words.
5. Repeat step 3 for 1 minute. Partner 1 charts the number of words read in 1 minute (best read).
6. Repeat step 4 for 1 minute. Partner 2 charts the number of words read in 1 minute (best read).
7. Present a new reading passage each Monday for the weekly practice sessions.

Progress monitoring: Review graphs on a regular basis to determine the trend of the data. An upward trend shows that progress is being made with daily practice. A flat or downward trend shows that the passage may be too hard, that not enough practice time has been allotted, or that students are no longer motivated by the reading passage.

WORKING TOGETHER

SPECIALIZED READING INSTRUCTION IN COLLABORATION WITH CLASSROOM TEACHING BRINGS SUCCESS

Vivian M. LaColla
Special Education Teacher, Grade 2, Noxon Road Elementary School, Poughkeepsie, New York

One of my second-grade students was a 7-year-old boy named Robert who had been classified as speech and language impaired, with delays in auditory processing. He had significant deficits in reading, had difficulty writing the letters of the alphabet, and could not identify the names and sounds of most letters. He could not consistently write his name correctly. Robert had trouble reading words with short vowels or high-frequency sight words. In the beginning of his second-grade year, Robert's reading skills were equivalent to those of a kindergartener. Despite—or perhaps because of—the daily struggles his reading problems caused him, Robert was a motivated learner, and I felt strongly that he had the potential to improve his reading abilities significantly. He was also a very quiet child who showed little or no facial expression and did not have much interaction with his peers or involvement in school activities.

Robert's classroom teacher, Mrs. Taryn, and I met at a scheduled time once a week for 30 minutes, as stipulated on Robert's individualized education program. Mrs. Taryn had had students with disabilities in her classroom before, but never a student with Robert's level of reading difficulty. During this meeting time, we discussed the upcoming week's plans and activities. I explained the verbal and visual cues I use in teaching reading as part of my reading program, gave Mrs. Taryn suggestions for breaking down her oral instruction for Robert into smaller steps, and modified her reading assignments and handouts to Robert's reading level. Through this collaboration, I was able to support Mrs. Taryn's instruction by previewing or re-teaching a classroom lesson to Robert during my time with him.

Robert's individualized education program required me also to provide him with direct instruction for reading and writing outside of his regular classroom for an hour a day. When Mrs. Taryn began her reading groups and the other students were settled working on their independent assignments, I would give Robert a secret signal, such as a nod, and we would go to my reading room. Robert never hesitated to leave; the reading room was his safe haven. He felt confident there to read without the pressures of making a mistake in front of his peers. I tried to make sure Robert always felt a sense of success during reading. He never needed redirection or refocusing during our sessions, and he often completed his assignments. There were times when I had to reschedule our reading sessions because of an assembly or because the class was working on whole-group projects that I did not want to take Robert away from. Because of his lack of peer interaction, I knew it was very important for Robert to feel a part of the classroom and school community, and I was confident that rescheduling a reading session would not interfere with his progress.

I used the practices and strategies from the Orton-Gillingham Reading Method and the Alphabetic Phonics Program. These methods teach spelling simultaneously with reading. I used basic word families for his weekly spelling list (we started with words ending with *-at*, etc.). I used controlled readers that had simple word patterns that reflected the lessons we were learning. Robert read a short story many times until he was able to read it fluently, and I charted the time it took him to read the story the first time and the last. Robert enjoyed seeing his graph get higher.

Robert began to make significant progress toward the end of the school year. In the spring, as part of his annual review, I gave Robert the same informal assessments I had used in the fall. I had been certain I would see some growth, but not to this extent. His instructional reading level had improved to the beginning second-grade level. It had jumped up two grade levels! When Robert finished reading the second-grade passage I was using as an assessment, I told Robert I wanted everyone in the school to hear how wonderfully he had just read. I asked him if he would read for Mrs. Taryn so that she would know how well he had done. Robert agreed. As Robert read for Mrs. Taryn, tears welled up in my eyes. Mrs. Taryn began calling on Robert to read in class. We then decided to have Robert integrated into Mrs. Taryn's lower-level reading group. Another wonderful milestone was when Robert was able to take his Friday morning spelling test with his classroom peers! He had been doing so well with the modified spelling list that we decided he should try taking the test with the rest of the class. Robert was so excited to be a part of the class. The first day he was called to read before his reading group, Robert stood tall and proud. As he looked at me with pride, he fought back a huge grin. So I grinned for him!

READING VOCABULARY

Reading vocabulary is the understanding of word meanings. A person's **reading vocabulary** is their comprehension of words that appear in print, or word comprehension. When readers know individual words, they are better able to understand phrases and sentences. Knowing individual words can help students understand new words. Context clues, or surrounding text, particularly when a word has more than one meaning, can help with understanding. Once readers understand sentences, they can understand paragraphs and passage comprehension, which is the ultimate goal of reading.

There are several types of vocabularies. **General vocabulary** is the words that are used on a regular basis during conversation. **Specialized vocabulary** consists of words that have multiple meanings depending on the context. For instance, the word *range* may be in a person's general vocabulary when it refers to a series of mountains, but it shifts into specialized vocabulary when used in statistics to describe all items from the lowest number to the highest number, inclusive, in a data set. **Technical vocabulary** involves words that are used in a particular content area (i.e., **decoding** when used to describe a reading act).

As readers grow older and continue to read, their vocabularies increase. High school and college students encounter words in their readings that, through the use of context and glossaries, will expand their reading vocabularies.

Understanding words is more than simply having words in one's reading vocabulary. It also involves using many of the skills connected to decoding, which was described earlier. For instance, knowing the meaning of prefixes, suffixes, and inflectional endings helps a person understand a combination of free and bound morphemes (e.g., *mis-manage-ment*). Using context clues to derive meaning is also important. For example, the meaning of the word *magnanimous* in the sentence, "The philanthropist's donation to the Boy Scouts of America was a *magnanimous* gesture" might not be fully understood, yet it is likely that the reader can use the context of the sentence to know that it's probably a good thing to be magnanimous.

Characteristics of Students Who Struggle With Reading Vocabulary

Researchers have attempted to identify the vocabulary differences between struggling and good readers. Good readers have a deep understanding of words. Good readers use their background knowledge to comprehend the meaning of words they don't know. Good readers can choose from multiple meanings the correct definition of a word in context. Good readers understand word origins. They know that many words are based on Greek and Latin words. Good readers know word parts (e.g., base words, prefixes, and suffixes), and they understand both denotative and connotative definitions of words. Good readers are able to use context clues. If good readers still do not know the definition of a word, they can use reference materials such as a dictionary or a thesaurus. Finally, good readers are confident in their ability to identify word meanings by using a variety of strategies.

Struggling readers do not show proficiency in all these skills. These readers typically lack confidence to use context clues, or they don't know the clues to begin with. Struggling readers flounder with using dictionaries and often lack the reading ability to use guide words to identify unknown words in the dictionary. As we have seen in word identification, beginning readers have difficulties with identifying prefixes and suffixes, and they have difficulty understanding word parts. Unfortunately, struggling readers' knowledge of word origins is lacking. All in all, beginning readers not only have difficulty identifying words but also struggle with word meanings.

Strategies for Teaching Reading Vocabulary

It is important for all students to receive vocabulary instruction, which produces in-depth word knowledge and increases reading comprehension. Instructional practices must focus on fostering maintenance of new vocabulary to help students comprehend text. Students must learn strategies to develop an understanding of the meanings of words that comprise vocabulary, which is found in content-area text. The following practices can help improve students' vocabularies. After reading, see Instructional Strategy 11.3 to see one way that context clues can be taught.

- **Instructional content**: Teach students to use context clues to figure out meaning in conjunction with other vocabulary instructional approaches. Like the dictionary approach, context clues alone are insufficient for struggling readers. As we mentioned earlier, they might not fully understand the meaning of the word *magnanimous* in the sentence "The philanthropist's donation to the Girl Scouts of America was a *magnanimous* gesture," but readers can use the context of the sentence to know it's probably a good thing to be magnanimous.
- **Instructional delivery**: Integrate vocabulary instruction in the reading lesson. Have students use graphic organizers to map meanings of words. Teach them to use word parts, such as prefixes and suffixes, to understand word meanings. Identify a few words to preteach before the lesson, especially if they are technical words. When possible, combine the definition and contextual approaches for identifying word meanings. Review word meanings after reading by playing games with words and definitions (e.g., *Jeopardy* and *Concentration*) and by creating or elaborating on semantic maps.

- **Instructional delivery**: Provide students with multiple opportunities to practice using words they know. Research has noted that it takes multiple exposures to words to understand them well enough to incorporate them into our vocabulary (OSEP, 2017).
- **Instructional materials**: To use context clues, students must be able to recognize most of the words in the sentence. Therefore, when teaching context clues, use passages at the student's instructional level (90–94% accuracy).
- **Instructional material**: Teach students to use reference materials. Make this one, but not the only, strategy for finding word meanings. Show students how to choose which meaning to apply in a particular context. Have them make connections between their background knowledge and word meaning.

INSTRUCTIONAL STRATEGY 11.3

CONTEXTUAL SEARCHING: WORD MEANING/PICTURE ASSOCIATIONS

Instructional objective: The students will learn how word associations with synonyms, antonyms, and visuals can facilitate their learning and enhance their retention of word meanings.
Instructional content: Vocabulary
Instructional materials: Word Association Chart (Table 11.3); Context Clues Chart (Table 11.4)
Instructional delivery: Grouping: Whole class or small group

Teaching Procedure

1. Give students a copy of Table 11.3 and a vocabulary word. Have them write it in the top-left-hand box of the chart.
2. Have students draw a picture that depicts the word in the picture box.
3. Tell students to write a synonym (or example) and an antonym (or nonexample; tells what the word does not mean) in the boxes.
4. Have students write a definition of the word using the meaning from the picture and the synonym and/or antonym.
5. Direct the students to write a sentence that uses the word. The sentence should contain a type of context clue, in this case a definition clue, that contributes to the meaning of the word (e.g., The opposition, those senators against the measure, argued against the bill's passage).
6. Have students work in small groups to complete the same activity for the next vocabulary word.
7. The students can make posters of their words, share their charts, or create a *Jeopardy*-type game with the words.

Progress monitoring: Have students define the words in a quiz or group project.

Adaptations

- **Instructional content**: Provide fewer words for students to define.
- **Instructional materials**: Eliminate one or two boxes on the chart initially.
- **Instructional delivery**: Have students make posters of their charts showing variations in pictures, synonyms, and antonyms (nonexamples) for vocabulary words.

TABLE 11.3 ■ Word Association Chart

Vocabulary word:	Picture of word:
Associate: Synonym, or example	Associate: Antonym, or nonexample
Write the definition in your own words:	
Write a sentence using the word and that includes a type of context clue:	

TABLE 11.4 ■ Context Clues

Type of context clue	What to look for	Signal words	Sample sentence
Definition	A definition in the sentence	Is, are, is called, means, or Signal punctuation: Set off by commas	Brick made of sun-dried clay is *called* **adobe**. The Native Americans used **adobe**, *or* bricks made of sun-dried clay, to build their homes.
Synonym	A word with a similar meaning to the unknown word	Also, as, like, same, similarly, too	The Zuni built their homes with bricks made of sun-dried clay. The Hopi *also* used **adobe** to build their homes.
Antonym	A word or phrase with the opposite meaning of the unknown word	But, however, in contrast, on the other hand, though, unlike	The Hopi lived in single-family houses, *but* the Iroquois lived in **longhouses**.
Example	Several examples in a list	Such as, for example, for instance, like, including	The Pueblo people grew many **crops** *such as* corn, beans, and squash.
General	General or inexact clues		After 1700, the Pueblos got sheep from the Spanish, and wool replaced cotton as the most important **textile**.

Source: Used with permission from The Meadows Center: For Preventing Education Risk, The University of Texas at Austin and Taylor & Francis.

READING COMPREHENSION

Reading comprehension requires connecting with text and identifying meaning from stories or passages (Honig et al., 2012). Literal comprehension deals with understanding the material on the printed page; inferential comprehension focuses on understanding what is behind the scenes (i.e., that which is not directly stated). Someone with literal comprehension can read a passage on Mount Vesuvius and remember factual information obtained in it (e.g., the eruption of Mount Vesuvius destroyed the city of Pompeii). **Inferential thinking skills** help the reader go beyond the facts stated in the passage and use their own ideas to imagine the writer's thoughts and feelings or those of the people affected by the volcano.

A variety of questioning strategies are important for checking students' reading comprehension. Comprehension questions that require students to remember facts about what was read often begin with the words *define, identify, label, list, match, name, recall, recognize*, or *repeat*. Students are encouraged to understand or construct meanings from what was written when questions begin with such words as *describe, discuss, classify*, and so forth.

Sometimes comprehension questions ask students to use what they have learned from what they have read. Key words in application questions include *implement, predict, relate*, and *show*. Students might be asked to analyze, or separate and explain, the content in paragraphs. When this happens, key words such as *distinguish, cause and effect, compare and contrast, draw conclusions, infer*, and *point out* are often used.

When students have to evaluate text, they are asked to make judgments or decisions by responding to questions that use words such as *conclude, critique, judge*, or *rate*. Finally, some comprehension questions require students to put the elements together and make connections. These *create* types of questions may contain words such as *generate, rearrange, produce*, or *imagine*.

Characteristics of Students Who Struggle With Reading Comprehension

It is known that beginning readers either have little background knowledge about the topic of the passage or they don't know how to activate the knowledge they have. When their understanding falters, students continue to read without monitoring their reading. They have great difficulty creating mental images of what is going on in the passage. Struggling readers have difficulties identifying the main ideas and the way the main ideas are supported by specific details. When asked to summarize what they read, struggling readers either produce a blank stare or repeat the story verbatim. At best, struggling readers may be able to answer literal questions.

On the other hand, good readers are strategic readers. They show the ability to use effective strategies before, during, and after reading to promote reading comprehension. Good readers have strategies to access and understand text, and they can apply their strategies to all kinds of reading materials.

Strategies for Teaching Reading Comprehension

Reading comprehension strategy instruction is critical in helping students become strategic readers. This instruction focuses on teaching students to construct meaning before, during, and after reading by integrating text information with their background knowledge (Honig et al., 2012). Students who can activate and apply whatever background or **prior knowledge** they have regarding a topic are more likely to comprehend a passage than those who cannot.

Students with reading disabilities benefit from comprehension strategy instruction. Collaborative strategic reading (CSR), which was developed by Janette Klingner, is one type of comprehension strategy instruction.

CSR consists of four reading strategies: preview, click and clunk, get the gist, and wrap up. These four reading strategies are joined with cooperative learning to teach students how to understand what they are reading. Before they read, students preview the text to activate their background knowledge. Students brainstorm what they know about the topic and then predict what they will read about based on the text's features (e.g., illustrations and headings). Making predictions is an important activity for strategic readers because it gets students engaged and gives them a reason for reading ahead.

Next, students read a paragraph or two during click and clunk. Students read along (click) until they come to a word they do not know (clunk). Students are taught to use fix-up strategies, written on clunk cards, and vocabulary strategies, such as context clues, to figure out the meaning of unknown words, concepts, or phrases (the clunks). For each paragraph, getting the gist (or find the main idea) requires students to tell who or what they read about and write the most important information about the "who" or "what" in 10 or fewer words. See Table 11.4 for more information about context clues. Finally, students wrap up by summarizing key concepts and asking questions, like "Who?" "What?" "Why?" and "How?" to reflect on important information in the reading passage. Students record their predictions, clunks, gists, and wrap-up questions on a graphic organizer called a learning log. They complete the four strategies in cooperative learning groups to learn from each other and to resolve questions about vocabulary and concepts. The following is a sample lesson designed to teach Get the Gist and also provide a related ADAPT in Action, that shows why and how Mr. Davis adapts the lesson for one of his struggling students, Andre. We conclude this section showing how the Wrap-Up CSR lesson can be taught with Universal Design for Learning (UDL) principles in mind.

INSTRUCTIONAL STRATEGY 11.4

GET THE GIST

Instructional objective: Students will identify the main idea of paragraphs or short sections of text
Instructional content: Reading comprehension, identifying main idea of text
Instructional materials: Copies of a narrative text (e.g., *To Kill a Mockingbird*), Gist Log
Instructional Delivery: Grouping: Whole class divided into small groups of students

Teaching Procedure

1. Tell students that a gist statement is a summary containing about 10 words or fewer that identifies the most important "who" or "what" of a text and the most important information about that "who" or "what." The gist statement must be in their own words. They will learn how

to develop a gist statement, which represents the main idea of a paragraph or short section of text.

2. Model identifying the "who" or "what" and the most important information about the "who" or "what" using a short section of text. In some cases, it might be best to use as an example content that is very familiar to them, such as a segment of *Star Wars* or a local news or sports story. Then move to the story being read, in this case, *To Kill a Mockingbird.*
3. Assign a short section of text from their book (for example, the Chapter 10 scene where Atticus shoots the rabid dog) and have the students work in small groups to identify the "who" or "what" and the most important information about the "who" or "what."
4. Move around the room and check for understanding. Provide feedback for each group and assist anyone who needs help. Often, when students are first working on identifying the gist, they struggle with limiting their gist statement to 10 words or fewer.
5. After the small groups have completed their work, call on a few students to share their gist statements. Compare and contrast students' gist statements as appropriate.

Progress monitoring: After the lesson, check all of the students' gist statements for accuracy.

Source: Adapted from and with permission from Klingner, Vaughn, Dimino, Schumm, & Bryant (2001).

ADAPT IN ACTION

ANDRE: READING COMPREHENSION

Andre is a student in Mr. Davis's seventh-grade reading class. In addition to having a learning disability, Andre also exhibits behavior problems. The behavior problems are an inability to get along well with classmates (and teachers) and a lack of task completion. However, when involved with something that interests him, Andre can be quiet, attentive, and productive. He is usually able to read words written at a fourth-grade level. His reading is fairly fluent. He is able to understand most spoken instructions. He has some difficulty understanding and summarizing text, and his vocabulary is limited. Reread Instructional Activity 11.4 and think about the challenges that Mr. Davis and Andre would face to meet the instructional objective. Consider the task that is associated with the activity. What must the student be able to do (requisite skills) to complete the task and meet the objective? Which of the skills fall within Andre's strengths, and with which skill(s) does Andre struggle? Then look at the sample adaptations provided below.

Working in cooperative groups can help increase student success in reading comprehension.

iStock.com/mediaphotos

After the Get the Gist lesson, Mr. Davis evaluated Andre's understanding of the main idea. He was not satisfied, based on the progress-monitoring data, that Andre understood the main idea or could locate the relevant information in the text. He decided to make the following adaptations after considering the ADAPT Framework.

- **Instructional content:** Reduce the number of pages to be read. Remove the qualification of 10 words or fewer.
- **Instructional materials:** Provide a controlled vocabulary or audiobook version of the text.
- **Instructional delivery:** Pair the student with a stronger reader or student volunteer (someone Andre gets along with), or work one on one with the student.

USING UNIVERSAL DESIGN FOR LEARNING PRINCIPLES TO DESIGN AND INTEGRATE THE PHONICS ANALOGIES LESSON

UNIVERSAL DESIGN FOR LEARNING LESSON

Note: This UDL-based lesson was developed, in part, using the CAST UDL Lesson Builder: http://lessonbuilder.cast.org/

The UDL framework (version 2.2) consists of three main principles (I. Representation, II. Action and Expression, and III. Engagement; CAST, 2018). Each principle has three guidelines and several checkpoints that define them in greater depth. In this lesson plan, we delineate how various instructional strategies meet the UDL checkpoints.

Lesson Overview

Title: Wrap up

Subject: Comprehension: *To Kill a Mockingbird*

Grade Level(s): 8

Duration: 45 minutes

Unit Description

This activity teaches students how to recall important information from the passage.

Lesson Description for Day

Prerequisite skills: Ability to recall important events in the passage.

Goals:

Unit Goals: Recall events from the *To Kill a Mockingbird* passage

Lesson Goals: This activity teaches students how to summarize previously read text and ask questions about the passage

Methods

Anticipatory Set:

Tell the student(s) that the purpose of the day's lesson is to help them understand how to remember important points from a passage in order to summarize what they read.

Introduce and Model New Knowledge:

1. Introduce Atticus Finch to the class as someone who is going to play an important role in the story. Explain that Atticus is a widowed lawyer raising two children, both of whom see their father mainly as an older man who never does anything exciting.

2. Read the section of *To Kill a Mockingbird* that deals with Atticus having to shoot a rabid dog on his street as his two children, Jem and Scout, watch from inside the house. Project a copy of the passage onto the whiteboard.
3. Play a short clip of the movie *To Kill a Mockingbird* (*Checkpoint 1.3: Offer alternatives for visual information*) that covers the material that was read.
4. Have students work in small groups to talk about the sequence of events that occur in the passage using a sequence graphic organizer (*Checkpoint 3.2: Highlight critical features*).
5. Have them create a sequence of events graphic organizer using paper and pencil or PowerPoint (*Checkpoint 5.1: Use multiple media for communication*).
6. Have students discuss what Jem and Scout might be thinking as each event unfolds. Stress to students that, as a learning community, all of their suggestions are welcome and valued (*Checkpoint 3.1: Foster collaboration and communication*). This may be done by role playing, with one student taking the role of a newspaper reporter interviewing Jem and Scout after the shooting. Recall that Maycomb, Alabama is a small community, and an account of the shooting would likely appear in the town newspaper.
7. Generate and answer questions from text:
   a. Have students brainstorm a number of questions about the incident and write them in their learning logs under Questions about the important ideas in the passage.
   b. Have students arrange their questions in a lower- to higher-order thinking level.
   c. Have students collectively answer the questions and arrive at consensus answers. A question that cannot be answered might not be a good question or might require clarification.
8. Review what was learned:
   a. Have students individually write down the most important ideas gathered from the day's reading and their work and discussion in their Wrap-Up Learning Logs under What I learned. This requires them to mentally organize the information and to focus on comprehending the text as a whole (*Checkpoint 3.3: Guide information processing, visualization, and manipulation*).
   b. Students take turns sharing with the rest of the class what they consider to be their best ideas.
9. Provide scaffolds as needed (*Checkpoint 6.3: Facilitate managing information and resources*)
   a. Provide sentence starters for each label on their graphic organizer (*Checkpoint 5.2: Use multiple tools for construction and composition*).
   b. For struggling students, provide a checklist or project-planning guide for setting up the sequence (*Checkpoint 6.2: Support planning and strategy development*).

Provide Guided Practice: (*Checkpoint 5.3: Build fluencies with graduated levels of support for practice and performance*)

1. Provide print, digital, and video versions of *To Kill a Mockingbird*.
2. Select a chapter that will be the focus of the activity—in this case, Chapter 10.
3. Have students work in small groups to create their graphic organizer (*Checkpoint 8.3: Foster collaboration and community*).
4. Ensure that all students understand the importance of valuing each student's contribution (*Checkpoint 7.3: Minimize threats and distractions*).
5. Be prepared to model, for example, how to create a PowerPoint presentation.
6. Check for understanding and provide corrective feedback as needed.
7. Support self-regulation skills by assisting students in setting and monitoring learning and behavioral goals (*Checkpoint 9.2: Facilitate personal coping skills and strategies*).

Provide Independent Practice:

1. At the end of each day, students answer questions related to the new information learned (e.g., How was Jem's and Scout's perceptions of their father changed by the incident? or What might Jem's and Scout's perceptions of their father have been if he had been unable to shoot the dog or had not tried?)
2. When student projects are completed, they will be evaluated using a scoring rubric designed for the product type. Alternative progress monitoring will be available based on discussions with and requirements for individual students. (*Checkpoint 6.4: Enhance capacity for progress monitoring.*)

UDL Guidelines available at http://www.udlcenter.org/aboutudl/udlguidelines/downloads

SUMMARY

Reading abilities vary across students and reading is particularly problematic for students with disabilities. Students must receive instruction in reading with adaptations to enable them to achieve successful reading experiences. Adapting reading instruction can provide students who struggle with more opportunities to improve their performance so that they can participate in reading activities teachers design.

In particular, CSR is an example of a strategy that teachers can use to foster reading improvement. CSR should be taught in two stages. In Stage 1, the teacher models using think-alouds to introduce the four strategies, followed by having the students practice the strategies for several days. During Stage 2, students learn cooperative learning roles and then are divided into small groups to implement CSR with minimal teacher assistance.

REVIEW THE LEARNING OBJECTIVES

Let's review the learning objectives for this chapter. If you are uncertain and cannot talk through the answers provided for any of these questions, reread those sections of the text.

11.1 Explain the issues that are related to reading instruction.
Students sometimes have trouble discriminating sounds in rhyming activities or identifying sounds in words. Further deficits may be noted in the ability to connect sounds to letters and letter combinations. Some students may show adequate abilities with phonological awareness skills but struggle to learn sound-symbol relationships and have limited sight vocabularies. Reading fluency might be slow and choppy; problems with fluency hamper the ability to comprehend text. Older students may have limited strategies for figuring out words with multiple syllables and lack techniques for breaking words apart, sounding out the parts, and blending the parts together to read the word.

11.2 Describe the five components of reading.
Phonological awareness, phonics and word study, reading fluency, reading vocabulary, and reading comprehension.

11.3 Explain phonics and word study.
Phonics is the teaching of letter-sound relationships so that students can distinguish unknown words they happen upon in the text. Good readers also have effective decoding strategies to figure out unknown words. Word identification instruction involves teaching sight word recognition and decoding skills.

11.4 Describe reading fluency.
Reading fluency is the ability to read text accurately, quickly, and with expression. The ability to read effortlessly and with speed is what fluency is all about. There are two types of reading fluency: oral reading fluency and silent reading fluency.

11.5 Describe reading vocabulary.
Reading vocabulary is the understanding of word meanings. A person's reading vocabulary is his or her comprehension of words that appear in print, or word comprehension. Context clues, or surrounding text, particularly when a word has more than one meaning, can help with understanding.

11.6 Explain reading comprehension.
Reading comprehension requires connecting with text and identifying meaning from stories or passages. There are two types of reading comprehension: literal comprehension and inferential comprehension.

The ADAPT Framework can help make instructional adaptations to ensure that students attain the instructional reading objectives. Teachers can examine the instructional task of the lesson and any prerequisite skills students need and, if students lack one or more prerequisites, make lesson adaptations such as providing an alternative activity, changing the instructional content or materials, or using flexible grouping strategies. Once the adapted lesson has been taught, teachers conduct lesson-related assessments to ensure the student attained the instructional objective—that is, learned what was taught.

REVISIT THE OPENING CHALLENGE

Check your answers to the Reflection Questions from the Opening Challenge and revise them on the basis of what you have learned.

1. What specific difficulties might students in Mrs. Johnson's and Mr. Davis's classes exhibit in phonological awareness, phonics and word study, reading fluency, reading vocabulary, and reading comprehension?
2. How can Mrs. Johnson and Mr. Davis use practices for effective reading to structure their reading activities?
3. How can these teachers differentiate instruction and provide adapted lessons to students who require intensive instruction, while meeting the needs of the rest of the class?

KEY TERMS

automaticity
base word
decodable texts
decoding
dyslexia
frustration-level texts
general vocabulary
high-frequency words
inferential thinking skills
irregular words
letter combinations
letter-sound correspondences
morphemes
phonograms
phonological awareness
prior knowledge
reading comprehension
reading fluency
reading vocabulary
sight word recognition
silent reading fluency
specialized vocabulary
technical vocabulary

PROFESSIONAL STANDARDS AND LICENSURE

For a complete description of Professional Standards and Licensure, please see the appendix.

CEC Initial Preparation Standards

Standard 1: Learner Development and Individual Learning Differences

Standard 3: Curricular Content Knowledge

Standard 4: Assessment

Standard 5: Instructional Planning and Strategies

INTASC Core Principles

Standard 1: Learner Development

Standard 2: Learning Differences

Standard 4: Content Knowledge

Standard 6: Assessment

Standard 7: Planning for Instruction

Standard 8: Instructional Strategies

Standard 9: Professional Learning and Ethical Practice

Praxis II: Education of Exceptional Students: Core Content Knowledge

I. Understanding Exceptionalities: Characteristics of Students With Disabilities

III. Delivery of Services to Students: Curriculum and Instruction

COMMON CORE STATE STANDARDS

Reading

Literacy

Craft and Structure

Integration of Knowledge and Ideas

Range of Reading and Level of Text Complexity

iStock.com/Ridofranz

12 TEACHING WRITING

LEARNING OBJECTIVES

After studying this chapter, you will be able to meet the following learning objectives:

12.1 Describe issues that are related to writing instruction.

12.2 Name the stages of the writing process.

12.3 Discuss ways teachers can provide effective instruction and adaptations for writing.

Opening Challenge

Addressing Writing Difficulties

Elementary Grades. Mrs. Ang is reviewing results of the screening assessment that was administered as part of the response to intervention initiative in place in her urban school district. Although she and Mrs. Johnson (introduced in Chapter 11) work in different districts, her district's policy is similar: It requires teachers in kindergarten through fifth grade to assess all their students in the fall, winter, and spring to identify those at risk for, in this instance, writing difficulties and to monitor their academic progress throughout the school year.

Mrs. Ang taught third grade for 4 years and is now in her 7th year teaching fifth grade. In her class of 21 students, 5 are at risk for writing difficulties. In examining the writing assessment results for her five struggling students, she reflects, *"The students exhibited problems across the board. In the mechanics portion of the test, they spelled poorly and failed to follow capitalization and punctuation rules. In their writing passage, the word counts were very low, they tended to write using simple sentences, and there were numerous verb-tense and noun-pronoun agreement errors. I had a very difficult time reading their passages because of poor handwriting. We have no formal assessment data that deal with the stages of the writing process per se, but we teach the writing process at our school and I have many student writing samples that I can examine informally as part of a writing evaluation. I can see by the results of these writing samples that some of my students have really struggled with some or all of the stages of the writing process."*

In thinking about the results of the assessments, Mrs. Ang realizes that most of her students are doing well, but several aren't. She also knows that the writing responsibilities of fifth graders are much greater than the students have faced in previous years. She will have to spend time teaching writing skills as part of her core curriculum while also providing small-group supplemental instruction to her struggling students. During core instruction, Mrs. Ang will be guided by the Universal Design for Learning (UDL) principles as she creates and delivers her writing lessons.

Secondary Grades. Mr. Santos is in his fourth year of teaching 11th-grade English, literature, and writing in a small, rural high school. In his school district, all students are required to take at least 2 years of English composition. Across his five classes, the number of students ranges from a class size of 11 to a class size of 21. During the summer, Mr. Santos attended several workshops on the writing process. In applying what he learned, he noticed that most of his students were adept at brainstorming and topic selection and could produce a first draft. For the most part, students were able to adjust their writing to the purpose of the assignment and to the hypothetical audience who would be reading their works. Some students, however, had considerable difficulty in this regard. Nearly all students had some level of difficulty in organization, but a few of Mr. Santos's students continued to write disjointed paragraphs even after he provided support. Spelling, capitalization, and punctuation were not problematic for most of his students, but a small group of students produced errors across the board and were ill equipped to edit their work for errors. He reflects on his efforts: *"I have to admit that it was a frustrating experience at first. I divided each class into small groups, and students were to work together to brainstorm about a topic of their choosing. One group decided to write letters to admissions directors at their favorite colleges to inquire about scholarships and academic opportunities. They went online to the website of their school of choice and also visited their guidance counselor's office to get some brochures. Each created a rough draft of their letter. When I met individually with them in a writing conference to discuss the revision, editing, and publishing stages, two students were completely lost. They didn't understand why their letter couldn't just go out 'as is.' For the two reluctant students, each stage presented its own challenge. Their revised letters looked almost identical to their originals, with the same disorganization, simple sentence construction, and immature vocabulary as their initial draft. Editing proved extremely difficult. They simply could not spell and struggled in correcting their errors. Capitalization and punctuation were not problem* *areas because every sentence began with a capital letter and ended with a period or a question mark. There were no other punctuation marks or capital letters because of the simplicity of their sentences. I really struggle with how to help them."*

Although teaching at different ends of the education spectrum, Mrs. Ang and Mr. Santos both have students who "get it" and students who don't. Although Mrs. Ang is teaching early writing skills and Mr. Santos is having his students apply skills they supposedly learned years earlier, they both were faced with the challenge of helping their students put words on paper in a meaningful way.

Reflection Questions

In your journal, write down your answers to the following questions. After completing the chapter, check your answers and revise them on the basis of what you have learned.

1. What specific difficulties might students in both teachers' classes exhibit in the writing stages?
2. How can the teachers effectively work with their students during each stage of the writing process?
3. How can these teachers provide lessons adapted to students who require additional instruction?
4. How can writing assessments (see Chapter 9) be used to identify struggling students and to monitor their response to intervention?

Writing is a very important skill for all students at all grade levels. Students' academic performance is related to their ability to express themselves through writing. For instance, students have to take weekly spelling tests, write letters, and write stories. These tasks require efficient writing abilities. To be efficient in writing, students need to have a variety of writing abilities (e.g., generating content, using correct punctuation and capitalization, and writing with appropriate penmanship). Additionally, writing is important for personal communication, postsecondary education, and adult adjustment.

Over the past years, writing instruction has garnered an important place in all classroom settings. With a renewed emphasis on writing in postsecondary settings and adult life, writing instruction necessitates a teacher's focus across all academic subjects (Graham & Harris, 1988a, 1988b; MacArthur et al., 2016; Shapiro, 2004). Thus, more instructional time has been designated to writing and writing assessments for monitoring student progress (Finn et al., 2006).

It is known that writing is a complex act and can be difficult to master. Thus, teachers are having their students produce written works by using a recursive **writing process** that involves different stages of writing (Graves, 1983; Tompkins, 2011). The word ***recursive*** means that writers move back and forth between stages as they write and refine their work. The **prewriting** stage involves activities such as planning and organizing that the writer uses prior to writing. The **drafting** stage is the author's initial attempt to put words on paper using the planning and organization of information developed during prewriting. The **revising** stage involves making changes to the sequencing and structure of the written work to refine the content. In the **editing** stage, writers focus on the mechanical aspects of writing, such as spelling, capitalization, and punctuation. Finally, in the **publishing** stage, the author's work is completed and is publicly shared in some format.

In this chapter, we first examine writing learning disabilities (LDs), otherwise known as dysgraphia, followed by an introduction to the Self-Regulated Strategy Development (SRSD) approach to writing. We then present each stage of the writing process by describing the stage, showing how students struggle with the tasks it entails, providing instructional guidelines for one particular skill at that stage, and showing how a representative lesson within the stage can be adapted to accommodate struggling students' needs.

DYSGRAPHIA

Dysgraphia is a writing disorder that causes problems with handwriting, spelling, and composition (Berninger & Wolf, 2009). Hammill and Bryant (1998) found that students with writing disabilities are hesitant to write at all. When these students do write, their writing is awkward and slow, resulting in limited output (i.e., their essays are too short, and they write relatively few words and sentences). These students spell poorly, omit or repeat letters, add letters, reverse them (e.g., using *b* for *d*), put them in the wrong sequence (e.g., *htnig* for *thing*), confuse vowels, and either do not attempt to spell phonetically or misspell words by overrelying on phonetic rules. Some students misspell so badly their words are indecipherable (e.g., *camelu, huete*). Some students' pencil grip is unconventional, they write letters backward or upside down (called mirror writing), and they form letters correctly but slant the line upward across the page.

From a syntactic and semantic perspective, students with dysgraphia use too many short words, omit word endings, omit words from sentences, write the wrong words (e.g., *hotel* for *house*), produce sentence fragments, and avoid complex sentences. Some students write wordy but content-limited passages. Students may sequence ideas improperly when writing a paragraph. It is important to understand that not all students with writing disabilities or difficulties show all these characteristics. But if you have had the chance to observe writers, you have probably observed several of these behaviors. In fact, you could form a checklist of these behaviors and use it to screen for students who either may be developing poor writing habits or may already have dysgraphia. For these students, help with the stages of writing is critically important.

Instructional Design Features That Promote Success

Karen Harris and Steve Graham (2013) have spent many years developing strategies for struggling students, including those with LDs, to help students become more effective writers. Findings have shown that the application of the SRSD approach to writing helps struggling students to become better writers. Their six stages of writing instruction provide a framework that teachers can use to guide students through the writing process.

Stage 1: Develop and Activate Background Knowledge

Having prior knowledge of a topic is just as important in writing as it is in reading comprehension. In Harris and Graham's (2013) SRSD approach to writing instruction, background knowledge includes "critical vocabulary and understandings students need to successfully understand, learn, and apply writing and self-regulation strategies" (p. 75). As teachers use the SRSD approach, they should note student aversions to writing and doubts about whether they can do the task successfully. Most experienced teachers know that success breeds success, so it is important that students begin to experience success in writing as early as possible.

Stage 2: Discuss It

In this case, "it" stands for what good writers do. One goal is for teachers to discuss with students how good writers find something to write about, learn more about the topic, create an initial draft, and revise and edit their product. Another goal in this step is to have students recognize that the writing process, although challenging at first, can become enjoyable as they see their works develop into thoughtful pieces. Importantly, teachers introduce strategies that students can use to improve their writing.

Stage 3: Model It

Next, teachers model strategies and how to implement them. Students are active participants in the writing process. This form of modeling has two purposes. First, it keeps the students engaged. Second, it provides the teacher with a way to check for student understanding. By observing students do what the teacher has modeled, teachers can determine whether the students understand the procedures. If a problem occurs, the teacher can introduce a scaffold or provide additional examples.

Stage 4: Memorize It

Many strategies in the SRSD approach use memorization and mnemonics, such as POW-TREE, which is presented later in this chapter. Even if a mnemonic is not presented, students must memorize the strategy so they can use it automatically as needed. You have probably used a mnemonic at some point in your life, such as for learning the colors of the rainbow.

Stage 5: Support It

Teachers can support students' writing by carefully monitoring student progress as they plan, draft, revise, and edit their writing. Through experience, teachers learn to identify tell-tale signs of misunderstanding (e.g., crinkled noses, sighs, hands covering the face, or even tears). Teachers can then introduce scaffolds to get students beyond the difficult spots. Even though scaffolds are withdrawn over time as students become more independent in their writing, students tend to remember the scaffolds and can apply them independently when problems arise. Experienced teachers recognize early that struggling students likely will quit when they experience problems during writing. On the other hand, typical students are challenged by difficulties and persist to work through them on their own or with the help of a peer. In other words, good writers self-monitor throughout the writing process.

Stage 6: Perform Independently

The goal of effective writing instruction is independent writing. Throughout the writing process, teachers encourage students to use what they have learned to novel writing experiences and to their other classes. For example, if writing is taught in the English or language arts class, students are encouraged to use their writing skills in science, social studies, or mathematics classes. As students mature, writing becomes an important part of their coursework, and their ability to generalize their strategies to all their classes becomes very important.

Support from teachers is critical for all students as they work to expand their writing abilities.

iStock.com/monkeybusinessimages

THE STAGES OF WRITING

Prewriting Stage of Writing

Many times, the writer has many ideas but struggles to get them onto the page. The prewriting stage helps the writer do some constructive planning before he or she writes a first draft. During the prewriting stage, the student selects a topic, gathers research or information about the topic, determines who the audience will be (i.e., who will read the paper), and so on. Many consider the prewriting stage (or planning stage, as it is sometimes called) the most important stage in the writing process. Research, planning, and organizing set the stage for what is to come.

Characteristics of Students Who Struggle With Prewriting

Hammill and Bryant's (1998) research findings have significant importance to the prewriting stage. As you read each characteristic, think about how it might affect students as they brainstorm, select a topic, conduct research, organize their paper, and so forth—all key features of the prewriting stage. When they tackle the prewriting stage of a writing task, some struggling students demonstrate the following behaviors:

- Do not move from one idea to another
- Approach complex problems in a concrete way
- Veer from the subject at hand to pursue some minor detail
- Are inconsistent in thinking and make illogical arguments
- Have difficulty learning abstract concepts (e.g., *freedom, pronoun*, and *nation*)
- Have difficulty organizing, grouping, and forming concepts
- Do not see cause/effect relationships
- Organize time poorly
- Are rigid and resistant to changes in thought
- Lack stick-to-it-iveness, or persistence
- Are unable to generate worthwhile ideas
- Cannot organize ideas into a cohesive plan of action
- Jump to premature conclusions
- Show poor judgment

Strategies for Teaching During the Prewriting Stage

Numerous activities can help students through the prewriting stage of the writing process. We present a few here.

Using Self-Writing. *Self-writing* encourages writing about the student's own experiences. Students try to capture five or six incidents from their past as briefly but as realistically as possible. Have them do the following:

- Recall morning activities, remember something that happened, and write it down
- Go back in time one to two weeks, remember an event, and write it down

- Go back in time one to two months, recall an event, and write about it, focusing on as many details as can be recalled
- Go back to when they were a young child, recall a fun activity or event, and write about it

Making Lists. Students can make many different lists to find a topic to write about. Nancie Atwell (2010) suggested that students keep lists of past and potential purposes, audiences, topics, and genres. They can also keep lists of events and subjects that interest them, as well as favorite belongings or accomplishments. The teacher can give a general topic such as accidents, courage, or school, modeling by first listing one or two personal events that have to do with that topic. Students then develop lists of their own experiences and share those lists. Sharing often helps trigger memories for those who are having difficulty. Teachers then need to model how to choose the best topic from the list.

Writing Literature. After reading a story, novel, play, or poem, have students brainstorm the themes of the piece and then plan an original work using one of the themes. Or the student can write a story using one of the characters or a setting from the literature or compare/contrast a character in one story with a character in another. Literature, especially children's books, can also be used to trigger memories and promote personal applications.

Brainstorming. Brainstorming is a way to generate ideas. Johnson (2008) noted that most students do not know how to brainstorm, and brainstorming rules must be explicitly taught and modeled.

1. All ideas must be accepted. No criticizing or evaluation is allowed. At this stage, bad ideas are just as important as good ideas.
2. Freewheeling is celebrated. Creative, bizarre, unusual, and silly ideas are welcomed.
3. The goal of brainstorming is quantity. The more ideas generated, the greater the opportunity to find a solution.
4. Hitchhiking is welcome. Hitchhiking occurs when students add to ideas that have already been stated or combine multiple ideas into a single thought.

Source: Adapted from Johnson (2008, pp. 191–192).

Considering Diversity: Writing Assistance for Culturally and Linguistically Diverse Students With Special Needs

Culturally and linguistically diverse students who have special learning needs, such as writing difficulties, can benefit from the following suggestions:

1. Designate adequate time for writing. We suggest that 30 minutes each day be allotted to writing instruction and opportunities for students to practice under the teacher's guidance and with feedback.
2. Provide a variety of writing topics that include topics with which students are most familiar. Students who are learning to write in a second language and have writing difficulties should be allowed to select topics that are related to their background knowledge and experiences. Allowing students to choose their own topics at first can enhance success because students will probably select topics with which they are most comfortable.
3. Establish a writing environment. Teachers can create positive associations with writing by engaging students in different types of writing (informational, making lists, writing

directions, keeping journals) throughout the school day. Students should view writing as a natural means of expression, with links to academic areas such as reading, mathematics, and social studies. Conferencing with students regularly reinforces their writing efforts by providing enthusiastic feedback about written work, as well as suggestions for improvement.

4. Incorporate culturally diverse materials. Surround students with books and materials that depict various cultural heritages. Teachers can use these materials (e.g., pictures in the books) as story starters. For older students, global and national current events can serve as topics for students to write about.
5. Include technology. Students should learn keyboarding skills and have access to computers with word processing programs, spellcheck tools, and specialized assistive technology (AT; e.g., text-to-speech, voice recognition) to facilitate the writing process.
6. Provide explicit instruction during the writing process. Model and think aloud the steps involved in each stage of the writing process. Provide many opportunities for students to hone their writing skills. Carefully assess their progress, and use the results to inform further instruction.
7. Facilitate vocabulary development. For students who are learning new vocabulary, provide word walls and instruction on vocabulary building. Teachers can use the vocabulary strategies discussed in Chapter 11 to help students develop their written vocabulary.

Source: Adapted from Vaughn and Bos (2015b).

Drafting Stage of Writing

The first draft is a first attempt to put ideas onto the page. During the drafting stage, writers simply translate their ideas into written form. Improving the draft comes later.

Characteristics of Students Who Struggle With Drafting

When preparing students to make initial drafts of their work, consider the characteristics of struggling writers (Hammill & Bryant, 1998). Struggling writers typically

- write without considering the purpose for their work, who will read what they write, or the form their writing should take;
- focus too little attention on meaning, concentrating instead on mechanics and writing "rules";
- have little knowledge about the elements of text structure, such as word order and vocabulary; and
- avoid taking risks.

Strategies for Teaching During the Drafting Stage

During the drafting stage of writing, students put their prewriting ideas into a written draft form. Bryant and Bryant (2011) described how word prediction programs support the writing process by helping students select related words to complete their thoughts (see this chapter's Tech Notes feature).

Instructional delivery: Use examples and nonexamples to demonstrate effective text structure.

Instructional delivery: Provide students with multiple opportunities to practice writing effective sentences.

Instructional delivery: Model how to write a variety of sentences in a paragraph. Check for student understanding, and provide corrective feedback.

Earlier we introduced Karen Harris and Steve Graham's SRSD. One of the instructional strategies that they developed, POW-TREE, involves pre-writing and drafting. Students are taught the strategy and apply it as they consider topics (pre-writing) and write paragraphs (drafting). The strategy is described in Instructional Strategy 12.1. Note that the strategy is from Harris and Graham's SRSD work, so the lesson is designed with their framework in mind.

INSTRUCTIONAL STRATEGY 12.1

IMPLEMENTING A WRITING STRATEGY

Instructional activity: POW-TREE
Instructional objective: Planning and writing paragraphs
Instructional content: Opinion essay
Instructional materials: Writing instruments (pen/paper; computer); sticky notes
Instructional Delivery: Grouping: Whole class

Teaching Procedure

Discuss It

1. Tell the students that you will teach them two strategies that they can use to decide what to write about and then draft a paragraph; the first is POW, which can be used in any writing activity; the second is TREE, which has been proven effective when writing an opinion essay—that is, writing something to share with others that describes your feelings on a particular topic or issue.

Model It

2. Teach POW.

   P stands for "Pick an idea." What does P stand for? (Students respond in unison.) The first thing to do in writing is to pick an idea, which means to select a topic. Why is that important? (You have to have something to write about.)

   O stands for "Organize notes." What does O stand for? (Students respond in unison.) Once you have an idea that you want to write about, you write down what you know about the topic. If you don't know a lot about the topic, where can you find information? (Possibilities include online sources, books, magazines.) Sticky notes are great tools to use when creating notes. You can write down something about the topic on a sticky note and then put the notes together that have something to do with each other. That is what we mean when we say organize notes: We put the notes together that have something in common. For example, if my idea is to write about pets, I can organize my notes by the different animals that people have for pets.

   W stands for, "Write and say more." What does W stand for? (Students respond in unison.) Once you have your notes organized, it's time to write paragraphs. This is where TREE comes in. For now, pair with a neighbor.
3. Use the document projector to show the following list of topics:

   Saturday school days

   Year-round schooling

   4-day school weeks, 8 hours per day

   3-day school weeks, 10 hours a day

   Boys or girls school only

   Homework-free weekends
4. Tell the students that they are to use the P in POW to pick their idea. For example, homework-free weekends: They are to write a paper providing their opinion on whether teachers should assign homework on Friday.

5. Direct the students to use the sticky notes to write individual sentences about why they are for or against homework-free weekends. They are to use the O in POW to organize their ideas. Give them 20 minutes to create and organize their notes; they can use their iPad or computer to go online to help generate their notes. Give them 10 minutes to work, after which they will finish POW and move to TREE. Circulate among the students to ensure on-task behavior and to answer any questions that arise.
6. After 10 minutes, move to finish POW with the W and introduce TREE.

They will use TREE to help them with the W in POW: Write and say more.

T in TREE stands for "Topic sentence." What does T stand for? (Students respond in unison.)

R in TREE stands for "Reasons: three or more." What does R stand for? (Students respond in unison.)

The first E in TREE stands for "Explain reasons, say more about each reason." What does the first E stand for? (Students respond in unison.)

The second E in TREE stands for "Ending: Wrap it tight." What does the second E stand for? (Students respond in unison.)

Now let's go over each one again, this time for your topic.

Memorize It

7. Once POW-TREE has been introduced, have students memorize the mnemonic so they can recall the strategy and apply it on their own.

Support It

8. Go through the steps one at a time, explaining how they can use their organized notes to write three or more sentences supporting the main idea. If need be, discuss what a main idea is and provide examples and nonexamples. Also, model how to ensure that the sentences pertain to the main idea. Then model how to create a good ending sentence that wraps up the paragraph. Finally, have the students use TREE to generate additional paragraphs for their opinion essay.

   Progress monitoring: Meet with the students in a conference after they have created their draft. As you participate in this conference, check that they have followed POW-TREE and created a sound argument using paragraphs containing a topic sentence, at least three sentences that support the main idea in the topic sentence, and a quality wrap-up sentence. Then, with the class, move to the revising stage.

Source: Adapted from Harris et al. (2002).

Revising Stage of Writing

During the revising stage, the focus shifts from the writer to the reader. Students revise what they have written so that it will be easy for the reader to understand. Revising will demonstrate the writers' knowledge of the topic using the most appropriate form and tone.

Characteristics of Students Who Struggle With Revising

Struggling writers have difficulty revising their work because they lack the appropriate skills. Their approach to the revision process is quite different from the approach used by their same-age typical peers (Hammill & Bryant, 1998). Struggling writers

- have little knowledge about how to improve their writing;
- have trouble recognizing errors in word order and vocabulary use that might affect meaning;
- lack strategies and skills for correcting errors in their work; and
- make revisions that do not address the errors they have made, so the overall quality of their draft remains the same.

TECH NOTES

WORD PREDICTION PROGRAMS

Word prediction programs are often used by struggling writers to select words. The student begins to type, and the word prediction program offers alternatives that can be used to help write a sentence; the writer then selects the word and continues typing as new words come into view. Word prediction programs often include speech synthesis to read the text and the various word options that appear on the screen. Bryant and Bryant (2011) described two popular word prediction products that are widely used:

- Co:Writer (Don Johnston Inc.) was designed to add word prediction, grammar, and vocabulary to word processing programs. In addition to word prediction described earlier, Co:Writer helps student with phonetic/invented spelling, and the grammar feature corrects grammatical errors and helps students practice their writing skills. Co:Writer is available at most app stores.
- WordQ for Chrome (Quillsoft) can be used with a text editor or word processing programs as described previously; the writer selects a word with either a mouse click or keystroke. When a word, phrase, or sentence is highlighted, WordQ for Chrome reads the text aloud. An interesting feature of this program involves the use of a temporary disappearing word prediction box that allows the writer to work through the document without distraction. The WordQ for Chrome app, available in English or French to those with a Gmail account, installs locally onto a PC, Mac, iPad, or Chromebook.
- Abilipad (AppyTherapy) is an app that provides customizable notepads and keyboards for the iPad. In addition to word prediction, this app provides text-to-speech options that help students as they attempt to become successful writers. An important component of Abilipad is its spellcheck feature, a valuable tool for struggling writers.

Strategies for Teaching During the Revising Stage

As students look at each section of their paper during the revising stage, have them participate in peer conferencing. Before the peer conferences, writers can review their work for possible improvements.

Instructional content: Have students ask themselves the following questions:

- Has the author written for a specific audience?
- Is the purpose for writing clear?
- Is the information presented in a logical sequence?
- Does the writer stay on topic?
- Are there topic sentences with supporting details?
- Is there a strong conclusion?

As students answer these questions, they should highlight the parts of their text that relate to them.

Instructional activity: Select several sentences from a passage. For each sentence, delete a word and provide three options. The student selects the option that best fits the sentence syntactically and semantically.

Instructional delivery: Model ways to ask the questions and revise a paper on the basis of the answers.

Peer revision is a powerful tool for students to use to improve their initial draft. We provide one example of peer revision in Instructional Strategy 12.2 and follow it with an ADAPT in Action feature to show how Mr. Santos uses the ADAPT Framework to ensure that one of his students, Saul, can employ the strategy effectively.

INSTRUCTIONAL STRATEGY 12.2

PEER REVISION

Instructional activity: Peer revision
Instructional objective: Revising documents
Instructional content: Revising of whole passage
Instructional materials: None
Instructional delivery: Grouping: Students in pairs

Teaching Procedure

1. Have the students divide into pairs.
2. Model how to consider questions before giving the paper to a peer reviewer.

   Does the paper fulfill its intended purpose?

   Will the audience understand what you have written?

   Does the form of the paper fit the purpose and intended audience?

   Is the paper interesting?

   Is there anything that can be done to make the paper more interesting?

   Are there enough details or examples in the content of the paper?

   Does it read right?
3. Teach students explicitly how to make revision symbols during peer revisions. Provide examples and nonexamples, and provide multiple opportunities to practice (Haager & Klingner, 2005).
4. Have peer reviewers also answer the questions in Procedure 2. Model appropriate interactions between peer reviewers and writers, such as providing constructive criticism and avoiding caustic remarks. Give examples and nonexamples of appropriate comments.
5. Give the same passage to all student pairs. Direct each pair to role-play and practice peer revision. Check for student understanding, and provide praise or corrective feedback as warranted.
6. Have students revise their own drafts and then exchange papers with a peer for a peer review. Periodically check for understanding, and provide praise and corrective feedback. Ensure that students are staying on task and taking this revision process seriously. If need be, stop the process and model once again how to provide constructive criticism.

   Progress monitoring: As you check for understanding during guided practice, provide error correction or praise. Meet with the students in a conference after they have revised their papers following peer revision. As you participate in this conference, examine the actual edits and see how the students have revised their papers on the basis of the revision suggestions. After the final paper has been turned in, be sure to grade in terms of what was taught during the revision process. It does little good to teach revising skills if students are not held accountable for errors that slip through.

To add words, insert ^ between the words and write the added word above the ^.	big Tom had a ^ dog.
To take words out, draw a line through the word to be omitted.	Marcy didn't ~~not~~ think she could help.
To change the order of two consecutive words, draw a around the words.	Pedro and sister his went shopping for new school clothes.
As a reminder to add ideas, use this mark:	tell which dog The dog is furry and friendly.
To insert a space between run-on words, use a / and the # sign.	# Marcus enjoyed/playing football with his teammates.
When a lowercase letter needs to be uppercase, use a triple underline:_______	Tom likes mary a lot. (triple underline)

ADAPT IN ACTION

SAUL: PEER REVISION

Saul is a student in Mr. Santos's class. He has several LDs, specifically in reading and writing and thinking and reasoning. He is a concrete thinker, has difficulty problem solving, is easily distracted, makes illogical arguments, has difficulty with abstract concepts, reasons illogically, and exhibits several other problems associated with reasoning LDs. Saul struggles reading text beyond the primary level and has limited comprehension, although his listening comprehension is excellent. He writes short, choppy sentences and goes off on tangents from sentence to sentence. His mechanical skills are poor to nonexistent.

After the lesson, Mr. Santos evaluated Saul's understanding of the revision process. He was pleased with Saul's comments regarding the purpose of his paper. But when they reversed roles, Saul was unable to use his partner's input to revise his paper effectively. He decided to make the following adaptations after considering the ADAPT Framework.

A: Ask, "What am I requiring the student to do?" Mr. Santos wants Saul to be able to interpret his writing partner's input and revise his own paper.

D: Determine the prerequisite skills of the task. Saul needs to be able to focus on a single sentence at a time.

A: Analyze the student's strengths and struggles. Saul understands the objective of the writing exercise and the purpose of peer feedback, but he is unable to internalize his peer's comments and use them to revise his own work.

P: Propose and implement adaptations from among the four categories. Mr. Santos will provide a list of sentence starters to help Saul replace his short, choppy sentences and have Saul choose one and complete the sentence appropriately.

T: Test to determine whether the adaptations helped the student accomplish the task. Mr. Santos will work one-on-one with Saul until Saul demonstrates competence with the strategy.

ADAPT Framework: For Saul

A ASK, "What am I requiring the student to do?"	D DETERMINE the prerequisite skills of the task.	A ANALYZE the student's strengths and struggles.		P PROPOSE and implement adaptations from among the four categories.	T TEST to determine whether the adaptations helped the student accomplish the task.
		Strengths	Struggles		
I want Saul to be able to interpret his writing partner's input and revise his own paper.	1. Needs to be able to focus on a single sentence at a time.			1. Instructional Content: Focus on a single sentence at a time.	1. and 2: Monitor progress as future writing assignments arise
	2. Comprehend feedback and implement it in his paper.			2. Instructional Materials: Provide list of sentence starters to help Saul replace his short, choppy sentences, and have Saul choose one and complete the sentence appropriately.	
				3. Instructional Delivery: Work one on one with Saul. Mr. Santos will replace the peer until Saul demonstrates competence with the strategy.	

During the writing process, teachers can have students collaborate with each other during writing conferences. These conferences allow students to share their work with their peers (or the teacher) to receive important feedback. Even though conferences occur during the revising and editing stages, they can also be held during the prewriting or drafting stages as students share and discuss their ideas and first drafts. Other ideas include having a display area for students' writing, modeling writing, thinking aloud while working through the writing process, establishing a post office, designing activities around students' interests, and having students write, write, write!

Editing Stage of Writing

After students have revised their drafts, they move to the editing stage with a focus on ensuring that the written piece is grammatically and mechanically correct, including examining for inconsistencies in mechanics and grammar choices, such as lack of subject-verb and pronoun-antecedent agreement and the appearance of sentence fragments or run-ons.

Editing requires a variety of strategies that must be explicitly taught to help writers become competent at finding and correcting their mistakes. As writers become better editors, they can correct grammar and mechanical errors during the revising stage.

During the editing stage, students can first edit their own papers and then share their papers with at least one other person. This opportunity to practice makes writers/editors better at finding mistakes in their own writing, thus helping them create drafts with fewer errors.

Characteristics of Students Who Struggle With Editing

We considered the characteristics of students with writing disabilities earlier in this chapter; many are particularly relevant for students who struggle during the editing stage. To review, these students

- spell poorly;
- use too many short words;
- omit words in sentences;
- omit endings of words;

Editing requires a variety of strategies that must be explicitly taught to help writers become competent at finding and correcting their mistakes.

iStock.com/FatCamera

- write the wrong words;
- write sentence fragments;
- avoid writing complex sentences; and
- sequence ideas improperly when writing a paragraph.

Strategies for Teaching During the Editing Stage

A number of instructional strategies can help students when editing.

Instructional materials: Have the writers use checklists while they act as the first editor of their own work. They should ask themselves the following:

- Did I express myself clearly? Will the reader understand what I wrote?
- Did I write any sentence fragments?
- Did I capitalize the first word in each sentence?
- Did I capitalize proper nouns?
- Did I end each sentence with the correct punctuation mark?
- Did I spell all the words correctly?
- Did I use semicolons correctly?
- Did I use proper verb tenses?
- Did I use apostrophes correctly?
- Did I vary the length of my sentences?
- Did I capitalize "I" whenever I used it?
- Did I use commas when I wrote lists?

Instructional delivery: Model editing strategies and teach students to check their work against their checklist.

Instructional delivery: Explicitly teach one editing skill at a time.

Instructional delivery: Teach students how to proofread others' work and provide corrective, supportive feedback.

Publishing Stage of Writing

Publishing is the last stage of the writing process. Minor changes might be necessary because in writing there are usually a number of revisions and edits that can be made. Now students are ready to publish their work, which consists of creating a written product that is easy for the reader to read. If it is handwritten, it should be neat and legible.

WORKING TOGETHER

TAKING ON TECHNOLOGY

Many teachers are uncomfortable working with technology, especially sophisticated technology such as speech-to-text or text-to-speech. We encourage you to get to know and collaborate with your AT specialist. Not every school has an expert in AT in the building. Many school districts or regional service centers hire itinerant professionals who move from school to school and provide consultant services with classroom teachers and special educators. If you need help with AT devices or services, contact the AT specialist and arrange for a meeting to discuss your students who have special needs.

Skills. Teachers should be able to rate the student (weak, average, or strong) in the following skills:

- Applies capitalization rules.
- Spells correctly.
- Writes neatly with little difficulty.
- Uses appropriate grammar.
- Edits/proofs well.
- Writes well conceptually.
- Applies a sense of audience effectively.
- Demonstrates overall writing skills.

Setting demands. The teacher should also share the extent to which the following tasks are accomplished in the classroom:

- Writes test answers.
- Writes papers (reports, term papers).
- Writes stories/essays/poems.
- Copies from the chalkboard/text (words and numbers).
- Takes notes.
- Spells words correctly (in isolation and in continuous text).

Having this information available will give the AT specialist some of the information they require to help you work with your students who have special needs. You will probably be asked many more questions. Also, be sure to ask questions that you have regarding how AT devices and services can help you meet the needs of your struggling students. Together, you can examine the student ratings and the writing requirements of the classroom setting.

Questions

1. Think about students you have worked with or observed. What are their AT needs, if any, and what resources might you use to learn more about AT devices and services? Knowledge about AT will help you discuss your students' needs with the AT specialist.
2. Role-play with a classmate a conversation concerning a hypothetical student. One of you will be the teacher, the other the AT specialist. What questions would be asked? What information would you require to answer the questions?

Characteristics of Students Who Struggle With Publishing

Penmanship is important for handwritten work, but it can be a struggle for some students. Cecil Mercer and Paige Pullen (2009) described a variety of handwriting difficulties:

- Slowness
- Incorrect direction of letters and numbers
- Too much or too little slant
- Inconsistent spacing
- General messiness
- Inability to stay on a horizontal line
- Too much or too little pencil/pen pressure
- Mirror writing
- Closed letters
- Closed top loops that should be open (forming *e* like *i*)
- Open loops that should be closed (forming *i* like *e*)
- Omission of parts of letters

Strategies for Teaching During the Publishing Stage

Graham (2009–10) stressed the importance of handwriting in writing improvement, noting that "early handwriting instruction improves students' writing. Not just its legibility, but its quantity and quality" (p. 20).

Instructional content: Establish desirable habits such as short daily learning periods.

Instructional content: Do not accept poorly written work.

Instructional delivery: Have students overlearn skills, that is, continue to practice them beyond mastery. Apply this strategy to letter formation and alignment in isolation and then use the skills in meaningful contexts and assignments.

Instructional delivery: Have students evaluate their own handwriting.

Instructional delivery: Teach handwriting skills explicitly.

WAYS TEACHERS CAN PROVIDE EFFECTIVE INSTRUCTION AND ADAPTATIONS FOR WRITING

Reading and writing can be taught separately, but opportunities exist to teach them together as part of integrated literacy lessons. For example, students can create a story map to go along with their reading comprehension and prewriting instruction. The map components become a writing outline describing the story elements.

In the next example for teaching reading and writing together, word identification, reading comprehension, and drafting or revising instruction are taught. The teacher selects a passage from the text, deletes certain words, and creates a maze for students to complete. By providing three word choices, only one of which fits the sentence semantically and syntactically, instruction is provided in word selection, which is an important skill in drafting or revising. Taking the preceding sentence as an example, we have the following:

By ________ (provide, provided, providing) three word choices, only one of which ______ (fitting, fits, fitted) the sentence semantically and syntactically, _______ (illusion, instruction, illustrate) is provided in word selection, which is an important skill in drafting or revising.

UNIVERSAL DESIGN FOR LEARNING IN ACTION

USING UNIVERSAL DESIGN FOR LEARNING PRINCIPLES TO DESIGN AND INTEGRATE LITERACY LESSONS

Note: This UDL-based lesson was developed, in part, using the CAST UDL Lesson Builder: http://lessonbuilder.cast.org/

The UDL framework (version 2.2) consists of three main principles (I. Representation, II. Action and Expression, and III. Engagement; CAST, 2018). Each principle has three guidelines and several checkpoints that define them in greater depth. In this lesson plan, we delineate how various instructional strategies meet the UDL checkpoints.

Lesson Overview

Title: Writing Lesson: PLEASE
Subject: Prewriting and Drafting
Grade Level(s): 4
Duration: 45 minutes

Unit Description

This lesson is designed to help students plan and write paragraphs.

Lesson Description for Day

Prerequisite skills: Ability to identify a topic, generate ideas, and transfer thoughts and ideas to print.

Goals

Unit Goals: Develop a coherent paragraph that contributes to a longer passage.
Lesson Goals: The purpose of this lesson is to teach students to identify a topic, generate ideas that contribute to the topic, and draft a main idea and supportive sentences.

Methods

Anticipatory Set:
Tell the student(s) that the purpose of the day's lesson is to help them write paragraphs about the character they identified in *To Kill a Mockingbird* during their reading period.

Introduce and Model New Knowledge:

1. Make copies of all five character maps for *To Kill a Mockingbird* that were created during the reading period. (Note: The students worked in small groups and created character maps for Atticus Finch, Scout Finch, Jem Finch, Tom Robinson, and Mayella Ewell.) Tell the students that today they will be using character maps to write a paragraph about the character from *To Kill a Mockingbird*.
2. Allow students to identify the character they want to write about. Have them select the associated character map. (*Checkpoint 7.1: Optimize individual choice and autonomy.*)
3. Introduce the PLEASE strategy to the students. Project a copy of the strategy onto the whiteboard. For any students with dyslexia, provide a digital recording of the strategy's steps. (*Checkpoint 1.3: Offer alternatives for visual information.*)
4. Read aloud each step of the strategy. Direct students to echo each step after your reading.
5. If needed, define/give examples of *evaluate*, *activate*, and any other words that may not be in students' vocabularies. (*Checkpoint 1.1: Clarify vocabulary and symbols.*)
6. Have students write each step separately on index cards. Afterward, have them shuffle their decks. Then ask how they can remember the strategy steps (PLEASE) and have them place the step cards in order on their desks. Ask, "What does the P represent in the PLEASE strategy? (*Pick a topic.*) What is your topic? (*The character each student selected.*) What does the L represent in the PLEASE strategy? (*List your ideas about the topic.*) Where will you get your ideas from? (*The entries in the character map.*) What does the E represent in the PLEASE strategy? (*Evaluate your list.*) For this writing assignment, we evaluate our character maps in two ways. First, we decide whether we have enough information on our list to use in a paragraph. Second, we have to organize our ideas so that they will flow logically in our paragraph. For example, if we are using Mayella Ewell and we want the paragraph to be about her living in poverty, we'll have to focus on the character map that contains that information." It might be useful to have students create a sentence strip for each entry into the map. These can be used later.
7. Continue with remaining steps, providing examples and scaffolds as needed. (*Checkpoint 6.3: Facilitate managing information and resources.*)
8. Have students work in pairs (those who selected the same character) to repeat and practice reciting the steps as a means to memorize the strategy components. (*Checkpoint 8.3: Foster collaboration and community.*)

Provide Guided Practice: *(Checkpoint 5.3: Build fluencies with graduated levels of support for practice and performance.)*

1. Direct the students to work in pairs to activate the paragraph with a topic sentence. Work with each group as they generate their sentence. Check for understanding and provide error correction as needed.
2. As you move about the room, ask pairs the steps of the strategy. Allow them to peek at cards if they are unable to remember a step.
3. Once a topic sentence is written, have students work on the next steps of the strategy (e.g., supply supporting sentences and end with concluding sentence). If they made sentence strips

earlier, they can use these for this step. As with the previous step, move about the room, check for understanding and effective sentences, and provide support as needed.

Provide Independent Practice:
Once the students have completed their paragraphs, model how to evaluate the quality of the paragraph. (*Checkpoint 6.4: Enhance capacity for progress monitoring.*) This can be done by asking three questions. First, does the topic sentence provide the main idea of the paragraph? Second, do the supporting sentences connect to the main idea, or are there sentences that provide tangential information (i.e., "sorta kinda" related to the main idea but seem to move a bit off topic) or provide nonrelated information (i.e., information that is intrusive)? Finally, does the concluding sentence wrap a bow around the paragraph (i.e., ties the supporting sentence together to remind readers of the main idea and/or introduces the next paragraph)? If the answer to any of these questions is, "No," work with the students to improve the paragraph.

UDL Guidelines are available at http://www.udlcenter.org/aboutudl/udlguidelines/downloads

Source: Adapted from Welch (1992).

SUMMARY

Successful writers engage in a multistep process that includes five stages: prewriting, drafting, revising, editing, and publishing. In the prewriting stage, students generate a topic, develop ideas about the topic, determine the purpose for their writing, select an audience who will be the reader, organize their thoughts and the paper, and determine the form and tone for what they will write.

During the drafting stage, students write down the ideas they generated in the preceding section. Little attention is paid to mechanical and grammatical errors. This is a free-flowing stage wherein the writer is relatively unencumbered by the rules of writing.

The revising stage allows the writers to return to their first drafts and improve what they have written. Care is taken to consider the reader, whose understanding of what is written will be enhanced by the author's choice of words, grammar, and paragraph structure. Corrections of spelling and other mistakes of mechanics and grammar can be made during the revising stage, but they are more likely to be made during the editing stage. In this writing stage, the writer serves as their own editor, but they also might enlist the aid of a peer.

In the final stage, the publishing stage, the writer prepares a final draft that will be read by the intended audience. The paper should be free of errors and neatly written.

Throughout each stage, struggling writers confront a variety of challenges that can greatly reduce the quality of their written product. Specifically, struggling writers display numerous problems (e.g., organizing their thoughts, generating sentences and paragraphs, adjusting vocabulary and syntax based on the reader's ability, correcting mechanical errors, and writing a legible document) that, if not dealt with, result in short, hollow writings that are full of errors of all types. However, teachers can use the ADAPT Framework to identify the tasks associated with each writing stage, determine the requisite skills that are needed to complete the tasks, examine the student's strengths and struggles with regard to each requisite ability, and propose and monitor adaptations to help the student create and write a decipherable document.

REVIEW THE LEARNING OBJECTIVES

Let's review the learning objectives for this chapter. If you are uncertain and cannot talk through the answers provided for any of these questions, reread those sections of the text.

12.1 Describe issues that are related to writing instruction.

During every stage of the writing process, teachers expect students to come to class with requisite skills that some may not have. Through all of the writing stages, some students will lack the requisite skills expected by the teacher, skills that might or might not have been taught in previous years. When prerequisite skills are missing, teachers are challenged to adapt their instruction so that all struggling students can achieve success.

12.2 Name the stages of the writing process.

Prewriting, drafting, revising, editing, and publishing.

Prewriting: Review the purposes for writing and ways to select from the various purposes; discuss audience sense, the process for determining the probable reader; and review the way the purpose and audience will affect form and tone.

Drafting: Present a sentence pattern (beginning with simple sentences and moving to compound sentences, complex sentences, and then compound-complex sentences), use examples and nonexamples to illustrate the critical features of a particular sentence pattern, and provide students opportunities to practice identifying parts of sentences and the associated sentence patterns.

Revising: Students should decide whether their writing tells the reader what the writing is about, whether the purpose is clear, and whether any part of the writing does not help achieve the purpose.

Editing: Have the writer serve as the first editor of their own work, using checklists and other strategies. Model editing strategies and teach the students to make appropriate comments, and then have the students use peers as editors. Briefly edit students' writing and confer with students about one or two editing skills.

Publishing: Teach handwriting skills explicitly, establish desirable habits in short daily learning periods, and have students overlearn skills in isolation and then apply them in meaningful contexts and assignments.

12.3 Discuss ways teachers can provide effective instruction and adaptations for writing.

The ADAPT Framework can help make instructional adaptations to ensure that students attain the instructional writing objectives. Teachers can examine the instructional task of the lesson and any prerequisite skills students need and, if students lack one or more prerequisites, make lesson adaptations such as providing an alternative activity, changing the instructional content or materials, or using flexible grouping strategies. Once the adapted lesson has been taught, teachers conduct lesson-related assessments to ensure the student attained the instructional objective, that is, learned what was taught.

REVISIT THE OPENING CHALLENGE

Check your answers to the Reflection Questions from the Opening Challenge and revise them on the basis of what you have learned.

1. What specific difficulties might students in both teachers' classes exhibit in the writing stages?
2. How can the teachers effectively work with their students during each stage of the writing process?
3. How can these teachers provide lessons adapted to students who require additional instruction?
4. How can writing assessments (see Chapter 9) be used to identify struggling students and to monitor their Response to Intervention?

KEY TERMS

audience
audience sense
brainstorming
drafting
dysgraphia
editing
form
generalize
legibility
mirror writing

mnemonic
modeling
nonexamples
overlearn
peer conferencing
prewriting
publishing
purpose
recursive
revising
self-writing
tone
writing conferences
writing process

PROFESSIONAL STANDARDS AND LICENSURE

For a complete description of Professional Standards and Licensure, please see the appendix.

CEC Initial Preparation Standards

Standard 1: Learner Development and Individual Learning Differences

Standard 3: Curricular Content Knowledge

Standard 4: Assessment

Standard 5: Instructional Planning and Strategies

INTASC Core Principles

Standard 1: Learner Development

Standard 2: Learning Differences

Standard 4: Content Knowledge

Standard 6: Assessment

Standard 7: Planning for Instruction

Standard 8: Instructional Strategies

Standard 9: Professional Learning and Ethical Practice

Praxis II: Education of Exceptional Students: Core Content Knowledge

I. Understanding Exceptionalities: Characteristics of Students With Disabilities

III. Delivery of Services to Students: Curriculum and Instruction

COMMON CORE STATE STANDARDS

Writing

Text Types and Purposes

Production and Distribution of Writing

Research to Build and Present Knowledge

Range of Writing

PUBLICATIONS THAT FEATURE STUDENT WRITING, POETRY, AND ART

Once the paper is publishable, you might want to make the student aware of places where a particularly outstanding paper can be widely shared. Here are a few that are available online.

New Moon Girls (https://newmoongirls.com) was created by girls and women and publishes works that are pro-girl and that deal with female issues. New Moon Girls encourages submissions that encompass a variety of literary genres and artwork.

Polyphony Lit (https://www.polyphonylit.org) is an international magazine that is run by and intended for high school students. High school writers submit their work, which then goes through a multistage review process; all reviews are conducted by high school students.

Potato Hill Poetry (https://www.potatohill.com) appears bimonthly except in July and August and is for teachers and students in kindergarten through 12. The magazine publishes poems by students, along with writing exercises, interviews with poets, book reviews, contests, and other poetry-related material. Its staff is also interested in submissions of cartoons, writing exercises, artwork (black ink on plain white paper), essays on the writing process, and black-and-white photographs.

Skipping Stones (https://www.skippingstones.org), an award-winning resource in multicultural education, is published bimonthly during the school year and encourages cooperation, creativity, and celebration of cultural and environmental richness. It accepts art and original writings in every language from students of all ages; non-English writings are accompanied by English translations. Each issue also contains international pen pals, book reviews, news, and a guide for parents and teachers.

Stone Soup (https://stonesoup.com) is a magazine made up entirely of the creative work of children. Young people from all over the world contribute their stories, poems, book reviews, and artwork to *Stone Soup.*

Storybird (https://storybird.com) allows prospective authors to select artwork from their archives to inspire them to write original books, novels, and poetry for a family-friendly audience. The site's global community is available to provide swift feedback for drafts and completed work, and writers can engage with readers within the community throughout the writing process.

Teen Ink (https://www.teenink.com) is a national magazine, book, and website featuring writing, art, photos, poetry, information about issues of interest to teens, and more. All articles are by teenage authors.

The Concord Review (https://www.tcr.org/) is a quarterly journal of exemplary history essays, approximately 5,000 words in length, by high school students.

iStock.com/track5

13 TEACHING MATHEMATICS

LEARNING OBJECTIVES

After studying this chapter, you will be able to meet the following learning objectives:

13.1 Explain the characteristics of students with mathematics difficulties and attributes of effective instruction.

13.2 Describe early number development and how it is it taught.

13.3 Name the number combinations and describe how they are taught.

13.4 Explain place value and describe how it is it taught.

13.5 Explain whole-number computation and describe how is it taught.

13.6 Explain rational numbers and describe how they are taught.

13.7 Explain algebra and describe how it is taught.

13.8 Explain problem solving and describe how it is taught.

Opening Challenge

Helping Struggling Students Access the Mathematics Curriculum

Elementary Grades. Mr. Jamison is a third-grade teacher in a large urban school district. His class of 23 is culturally and linguistically diverse (CLD) and includes several students who have reading and mathematics problems. Three—one from Turkey, one from Chile, and one from Taiwan—are bilingual. After administering the district's curriculum-based assessment in mathematics, Mr. Jamison learns that one third of his students do not perform at the competent level on end-of-second-grade skills and concepts; several are performing closer to the first-grade level in fundamental concepts and skills such as numeration. Third grade is the year his students take the state's assessment in reading and mathematics. He realizes he must focus extra attention on the Common Core State Standards for Mathematics (CCSSM; Council of Chief State School Officers & National Governors' Association, 2022; Common Core State Standards Initiative, 2021), Operations and Algebraic Thinking, the part of the standards that presents the greatest challenges for his students. *"I have to begin teaching the third-grade mathematics curriculum to all my students. But I must provide extra instruction on fundamental skills and concepts to my struggling students to give them the support they will need to learn more advanced mathematics. I'll use word problems so students can apply what they learn to a problem situation. I know what I need to do, but how am I going to find time for the extra instruction in mathematics and reading? How can I use peer-mediated strategies, such as PALS, to support my teaching? What should I do about monitoring the students' progress in mathematics?"*

Secondary Grades. Ms. Kellogg is reviewing her sixth-grade students' papers from today's quiz on problem solving. She is using a problem-based approach to teaching the CCSSM (Council of Chief State School Officers & National Governors' Association, 2022) required by her school district. She starts lessons with a quick vocabulary assignment, a review of what was taught the previous day, and an introduction of materials for the day's exercises. Her students work in small groups to generate solutions to problems that require the use of measurement, geometry, and pre-algebra skills and concepts. Ms. Kellogg reflects on the quiz results. *"Most of my 140 students got the majority of the problems correct. They used different strategies to solve the problems, which suggests that their group work helps them identify ways to solve problems correctly. But I have 32 papers in which most of the answers are incorrect. Many mistakes are due to inaccurate calculations and faulty strategies. I've spent weeks on problems that focus on specific skills, yet some of my students aren't getting it. I am stumped about what to do next."*

Mr. Jamison and Ms. Kellogg share a similar concern: A significant number of students in their classes lack prerequisite skills to perform grade-level mathematics. These teachers must decide how to provide extra intervention for their students, what interventions to implement, and how to monitor student progress to determine whether the interventions are working.

Reflection Questions

In your journal, write down your answers to the following questions. After completing the chapter, check your answers and revise them on the basis of what you have learned.

1. What mathematical learning characteristics might be contributing to the students' learning difficulties?
2. How can Mr. Jamison and Ms. Kellogg use the features of effective mathematics instruction to structure their lessons?
3. What instructional adaptations can be implemented to help students access the mathematics curriculum?
4. What suggestions do you have on ways in which these teachers can monitor student progress?

Mathematical literacy is the ability to use skills and concepts to reason, solve problems, and communicate about mathematical problems in the classroom and in everyday life (National Mathematics Advisory Panel [NMAP], 2008). According to the National Council of Teachers of Mathematics

(NCTM, 2000) in their *Principles and Standards for School Mathematics*, "The need to understand and be able to use mathematics in everyday life and in the workplace has never been greater and will continue to increase" (p. 4). NCTM noted, "Those who understand and can do mathematics will have significantly enhanced opportunities and options for shaping their futures. A lack of mathematical competence keeps those doors closed" (p. 5). The development and application of mathematical competence are important educational goals for all students. The CCSSM (Council of Chief State School Officers & National Governors' Association, 2022) provide guidance for states and school districts in their development of mathematics curricula, instruction, and assessment. States, school districts, researchers, higher education teacher preparation faculty, and textbook publishers have acknowledged the importance of the CCSSM.

We know mathematics instruction should include approaches, activities, and interventions to teach mathematical skills and concepts that promote mathematics literacy for all students. Adaptations help students with mathematical difficulties and disabilities participate in classroom discussions and learn mathematical skills and concepts emphasized in the CCSSM.

In this chapter, you will learn about these students and ways to provide effective mathematics instruction using the ADAPT Framework. We begin with information about students with mathematics difficulties; we use the word *difficulties* to encompass students with and without disabilities who demonstrate problems learning mathematics.

CHARACTERISTICS OF STUDENTS WITH MATHEMATICS DIFFICULTIES AND ATTRIBUTES OF EFFECTIVE INSTRUCTION

About 5% to 8% of school-age students are identified as having a mathematics disability (Geary, 2011), and in some cases students have difficulties in both reading and mathematics instruction. About 5% to 10% of school-age students have persistent low performance in mathematics. Taken together, these percentages show that mathematics difficulties are prevalent and could have long-term consequences as students move through the grades with increasingly more difficult mathematics curriculum (Bryant, Bryant, Kethley, et al., 2008; Jordan, Glutting et al., 2009; Murphy et al., 2007). Clearly educators and researchers need to pay attention to the mathematical needs of these students.

In preschool, parents, educators, and researchers notice that some students have problems learning basic mathematical ideas such as counting, telling how many objects are in a group, and naming numbers.

Research findings have shown that 5% to 8% of school-age children have a mathematics disability.

Ariel Skelley/Getty Images

These students could be exhibiting problems with number sense. Number sense is an awareness and knowledge of concepts related to numbers, measurement, data, and algebraic thinking (Berch, 2005). You might have worked with a student whose answer to an arithmetic problem was off the mark. Through multiple opportunities to use representations to show and talk about numbers, students can develop number sense to help them reason mathematically. Now, we examine mathematics difficulties and disabilities.

Mathematics Difficulties and Disabilities

According to the Individuals with Disabilities Education Improvement Act of 2004 (IDEA, 2004), a LD can be identified in mathematics calculation and/or mathematics problem solving. Sometimes, mathematics difficulties are referred to as dyscalculia, which refers to problems in learning mathematics skills and concepts. However, the terms *LDs in mathematics* and *mathematics disability* are more widely used today.

Students with mathematics calculation difficulties might demonstrate problems with some or most of the following skills:

- Identifying the meaning of signs (e.g., +, −, ×, ÷, =, ≥, Σ)
- Remembering answers to basic number combinations (e.g., 8 + 9 =?, 7 × 7 =?)
- Using effective counting strategies to calculate answers to arithmetic problems
- Understanding the commutative property (e.g., 5 + 3 = 8 and 3 + 5 = 8)
- Solving multidigit calculations that require regrouping
- Misaligning numbers
- Ignoring decimal points
- Difficulty solving word problems as observed in any of the following skills:
  - Reading the problem
  - Understanding the meaning of the sentences
  - Understanding what the problem is asking
  - Identifying extraneous information that is not required for solving the problem
  - Developing and implementing a plan for solving the problem
  - Solving multiple steps in advanced word problems

Mathematics difficulties are persistent across the elementary and secondary levels and into adulthood. Mathematics difficulties are cumulative and get worse across the grade levels (Jordan, Glutting et al., 2009).

Gersten, Jordan, and Flojo (2005) examined the results of research comparing the abilities of young students in kindergarten through Grade 2 who demonstrated mathematics difficulties as compared to their typically achieving peers. Learning difficulties are evident in number combinations (basic facts), counting strategies (counting all, counting on), and number sense (basic counting techniques, understanding of size of numbers, number relationships). Gersten and colleagues found that, over a period of time, limited mastery of number combinations (basic facts) was a "hallmark of mathematics difficulties" (p. 296). Apparently, difficulties learning number combinations are a characteristic of a developmental difference that is connected to memory or cognitive problems (Geary, 2011).

Bryant, Bryant, and Hammill (2000) asked a group of teachers who taught students with LDs and mathematics difficulties to rate the frequency of mathematical skills that were problematic for their students. These mathematics skills were then analyzed statistically to determine whether they actually predicted mathematics difficulties. Table 13.1 shows the results of this analysis of mathematics skills, indicating which were most predictive of mathematics difficulties of second- through eighth-grade students.

In the case of students with LDs who receive mathematics instruction in inclusive classrooms, teachers must be aware of their students' mathematical difficulties in order to plan ways to provide much-needed support, for example by making adaptations to instructional delivery, instructional activities, and instructional materials (review the ADAPT Framework presented in Chapters 2 and 7). Support can also be provided working collaboratively with the special education inclusion teacher to assist struggling students during mathematics instruction. (See Co-Teaching Approaches in Chapter 3 for ways professionals can collaborate.)

For students with autism spectrum disorder (ASD) and students with intellectual disability (ID) ranging from mild to severe, different mathematics profiles appear. Some researchers believe some of these students can have average mathematics abilities (Wei et al., 2015), while others have noted that about 25% of students with ASD have a mathematics LD (Williams et al., 2008). Depending on the student's intellectual cognitive profile and mathematics difficulties, treatments for students with ASD can be similar to those for students with mild to severe cognitive disabilities or LD (Gevarter et al., 2016). Table 13.2 shows a sampling of behavioral strategies that were part of research studies focusing on students with either ASD or severe cognitive disabilities.

TABLE 13.1 ■ Mathematics Skills That Are Most Predictive of Mathematics Difficulties

- Has difficulty with multistep problems
- Makes borrowing (i.e., regrouping, renaming) errors
- Cannot recall number facts automatically
- Misspells number words (writes 13 as *threeteen*, 20 as *twoty*)
- Reaches unreasonable answers
- Calculates poorly when the order in which digits are presented is altered
- Cannot copy numbers accurately
- Orders and spaces numbers inaccurately in multiplication and division
- Does not remember number words or digits

Source: Bryant et al. (2000).

TABLE 13.2 ■ Behavioral Strategies for Teaching Mathematics to Students With ASD or Severe Cognitive Disabilities

Skills	Students With ASD	Students With Severe Cognitive Disabilities	Mathematics Material
Calculations	x	x	Manipulatives, virtual manipulatives, TouchMath
Prompting: Verbal, gestural, or physical assistance given to learners to assist them in acquiring or engaging in a targeted behavior or skill. Reinforcement: An event or activity occurring after a learner engages in a desired behavior that leads to the increased occurrence of the behavior in the future.			
Money	x	x	Coins and bills
Prompting: Verbal, gestural, or physical assistance given to learners to assist them in acquiring or engaging in a targeted behavior or skill. Reinforcement: An event or activity occurring after a learner engages in a desired behavior that leads to the increased occurrence of the behavior in the future.			
Purchasing	x	x	Items to purchase
Prompting: Verbal, gestural, or physical assistance given to learners to assist them in acquiring or engaging in a targeted behavior or skill. Constant time delay: A learner engages in a behavior or skill; a brief delay occurs between the opportunity to use the skill and any additional instructions or prompts.			
Word Problems	x		Problems
Reinforcement: An event or activity occurring after a learner engages in a desired behavior that leads to the increased occurrence of the behavior in the future. Task analysis: An activity or behavior is divided into small, manageable steps to assess and teach the skill. Video self-modeling reinforcement: A visual model of the targeted behavior or skill is provided via video recording and display equipment to assist learning in a desired behavior or skill.			

Sources: Browder et al. (2008); Gevarter et al. (2016); Wong et al. (2013).

Students with severe cognitive disabilities typically are taught functional skills, which means skills they need to be involved in daily living activities, such as counting money, purchasing, basic calculations, time, and measurement (Browder et al., 2008). Although most of these skills are identified in the CCSSM, purchasing is not; it is a functional skill that students must learn. Students with severe cognitive disabilities will need a curriculum to help them learn the skills that will help them function successfully in a job and in the community.

Factors Contributing to Mathematics Difficulties

Several factors contribute to mathematics difficulties. Language difficulties can interfere with understanding the vocabulary of the curriculum. For example, students must comprehend the meaning of terms and symbols related to mathematics instruction. Years ago, Wiig and Semel (1984) referred to mathematics as conceptually dense, which means that students must understand the meaning of each mathematical symbol and word because context clues, such as those that appear in reading, are limited or nonexistent. Wiig and Semel's idea is critical because students must understand the meaning of abstract symbols such as =, $\sum$, π, and $\geq$ to solve problems. Students must understand each symbol to decide whether a number statement is true or false.

Second, students with mathematics difficulties may explain the equal sign (=) as an operational symbol meaning "I have to find the answer" (Powell & Fuchs, 2010). But they need to understand that the equal sign is a relational symbol—meaning both sides of the equation must be the same or there is a relationship between them—to be able to solve different equations: $6 \times 8 = 48$, $48 = 6 \times 8$, $6 \times 8 = 40 + 8$, and so forth (Powell, 2014). Teachers can teach and review the symbolic language pertaining to mathematics. The Considering Diversity section on language and symbols of mathematics provides ideas for teachers to think about as they work with students from culturally and linguistically diverse backgrounds, including those from other countries.

Considering Diversity: Focusing on the Language and Symbols of Mathematics

Although mathematics can be called a universal language, there are some important differences among cultures with respect to terminology, algorithms, and solving strategies. We must not assume that learners have a low level of mathematical proficiency if they are interpreting terminology, performing algorithms, and using strategies that are different from those used in this country because they may be mathematically correct. For example, in Chinese, 14 is "ten four." In Eastern Europe, for example, the numeral 3,076 corresponds to the numeral 3.076 in the United States (Sorto, 2012).

The linguistic and symbolic features of mathematics have tricky spots because words can be used in unfamiliar ways (e.g., odd and even), structural relationships between words and syntax must be discerned (e.g., relationship of adjectives and nouns in sentence structure), and algorithmic formats (e.g., reading from left to right and from top to bottom) may be different. Therefore, teachers must be sure that all students have the necessary semantic, linguistic, and symbolic understanding of the mathematics concepts and skills presented for instruction.

Language difficulties can occur when solving word problems, for instance, because this requires understanding what the problem is asking and the sentence structure and identifying extraneous information (Van de Garderen & Scheuermann, 2014). Difficulties with syntax and word meaning can affect students' ability to solve problems successfully.

The language and symbolism of mathematics must be taught explicitly as part of a mathematics lesson. This is especially true for secondary students, who are often faced with abstract mathematical concepts, such as algebra and geometry, that require a solid foundation of mathematical skills (equations, formulae, mathematical properties) and language. Teaching ideas include the following: (a) identify prerequisite symbols, syntactic language, and word meanings for the lesson; (b) assess current student understanding of this language; (c) provide explicit instruction to teach the language; and (d) include sufficient practice and review.

Think back to Mr. Jamison's concerns about his students from culturally and linguistically diverse backgrounds in the Opening Challenge. Mr. Jamison needs ideas for helping his students learn the language of mathematics. Table 13.3 provides examples of the language or vocabulary associated with mathematics curricula. For struggling students, instruction in and review of new terms is critical.

TABLE 13.3 ■ Examples of Vocabulary Terms for Mathematics Instruction

addend	equivalent	logarithmic	positive	square
area	estimate	least common denominator	product	square root
circle	exponent	magnitude	proper fraction	sum
circumference	expression	matrix	proportion	symmetry
coefficient	fraction	minus	pyramid	theorem
commutative	function	minute	ratio	tomorrow
coordinate	greater than	month	rational	triangle
decimal	greatest common factor	negative	rectangle	variable
denominator	improper fraction	notation	regrouping	vectors
diagonal	integer	numerator	relationship	volume
diameter	inverse	pattern	remainder	yesterday
dividend	isosceles	percent	right angle	zero
divisor	length	perimeter	round	
equal	less than	place value	second	
equation	linear	polynomial	sort	

Consider using the instructional ideas for teaching vocabulary found in Chapter 11 for teaching the language of mathematics.

The third factor focuses on how problems with memory and executive functioning contribute to mathematics difficulties. Working memory is the function by which we process and store information simultaneously. Executive functioning is the ability to self-monitor by using working memory, inner speech, attention, and recall of recent information (Swanson & Jerman, 2006). Memory difficulties can influence the child's ability to remember the steps for solving more difficult word problems in the upper grades (Bryant et al., 2000), to remember the steps in solving algebraic equations, or to remember what specific symbols mean. It is common to hear a teacher say, "He knew the math facts yesterday, but he just can't seem to remember them today." Memory difficulties play an important role in how successfully students can perform mathematical operations (Shin & Bryant, 2015). Finally, mathematics difficulties can be a result of instructional issues. One instructional issue is the insufficient development of essential understandings of whole numbers, the relationships among the four operations, and whole number properties. Yet another issue is lacking an understanding of the arithmetic properties. Students may have a limited understanding of the commutative ($A + B = B + A$; $A \times B = B \times A$) and associative ($[A + B] + C = A + [B + C]$) properties of addition and multiplication and of the distributive property ($A \times [B + C] = [A \times B] + [A \times C]$). Knowledge about these properties can help students solve more accurately ($5 \times 3 = 3 \times 5$) and more effectively acquire answers for more difficult problems ($4 \times 8 = 4 \times 6 + 4 \times 2 = 24 + 8 = 32$; National Research Council, 2009).

Finally, another instructional issue is insufficient opportunities to learn, practice, and master effective and efficient strategies. Teachers must include validated principles of instructional delivery, including scaffolding instruction (Coyne et al., 2011; Doabler & Fien, 2013). Refer to Chapter 7 for additional instructional delivery practices that should be included as part of mathematics instruction. Now, we will focus on instructional practices.

Evidence-Based Instructional Practices

For students receiving Tiers 2 and 3 mathematics intervention in a response to intervention framework and students with mathematics disabilities, evidence-based instructional practices provide most mathematics concepts and skills. First, the concrete-semiconcrete-abstract (CSA) instructional routine helps students understand the abstract nature of mathematics and develop conceptual understanding. CSA was originally researched as a way to teach place value (Peterson et al., 1988) and number combinations (Miller & Mercer, 1993; Miller et al., 1992). With CSA, students learned the skills to the criterion level. CSA has also been used for the teaching of rational numbers such as fractions (Butler et al., 2003) and algebraic expressions (Strickland & Maccini, 2013). Table 13.4 shows the steps of the CSA instructional routine. The following instructional procedures should be used when implementing the CSA instructional routine:

1. The CSA teaching procedures begin with the teacher providing an advance organizer about the purpose of the lesson.
2. The teacher models how to solve the problem, while verbalizing the steps (e.g., thinking aloud). The teacher asks questions, such as, "What is the first thing I do?"
3. Next, the teacher implements guided practice. Students work on several problems, and the teacher provides prompts and cues. A prompt might go something like this: "You have the correct number of counters for the first number. Now which number do you look at?"
4. The teacher provides corrective feedback and assistance immediately.
5. Finally, students work independently to complete problems.

During guided practice, students use manipulatives in the concrete phase and tallies in the semiconcrete phase; in the abstract (symbolic) phase, students solve the problem only using numerals. It should be noted that multiple representations are used in the CSA routine. In this case, teachers can say, "Today we are going to represent 4 + 8 by using concrete objects." Concrete objects or manipulatives should be chosen carefully to represent or model the mathematics (Dougherty, 2021). Figure 13.1 provides examples of various types of manipulatives and materials.

Other evidence-based intervention practices include the following:

- Instruction during the intervention should be explicit and systematic. This includes providing models of proficient problem solving, verbalization of thought processes, guided practice, corrective feedback, and frequent cumulative review.
- Interventions should include instruction on solving word problems that is based on common underlying structures of the problems.
- Intervention materials should include opportunities for students to work with multiple representations of mathematical ideas, and interventionists should be proficient in the use of multiple representations of mathematical topics.
- Interventions at all grade levels should devote about 10 minutes in each session to building fluent retrieval of basic arithmetic facts.
- Progress monitoring should be employed with students receiving supplemental instruction if they appear to be at risk.

TABLE 13.4 ■ Concrete-Semiconcrete-Abstract Instructional Routine

Steps of the Concrete-Semiconcrete-Abstract Instructional Routine	
STEP 1. Concrete	Use manipulatives to physically represent a number concept or skill being taught, such as whole-number computation of addition with regrouping. Refer to Figure 13.1 for examples of manipulatives and materials for mathematics instruction.
STEP 2. Semiconcrete	After several lessons where students achieve 90% accuracy on problems using manipulatives, change the representation to semiconcrete. Use pictorial representations such as tally marks or pictures of base-10 materials for several lessons.
STEP 3. Abstract	After several lessons where students achieve 90% accuracy on problems using pictorial representations, change the representation to abstract. Have students solve problems that employ only numbers but are otherwise similar to those presented in Steps 1 and 2. Again, expect 90% accuracy for the problems presented.

FIGURE 13.1 ■ Examples of Manipulatives and Materials for Mathematics Instruction

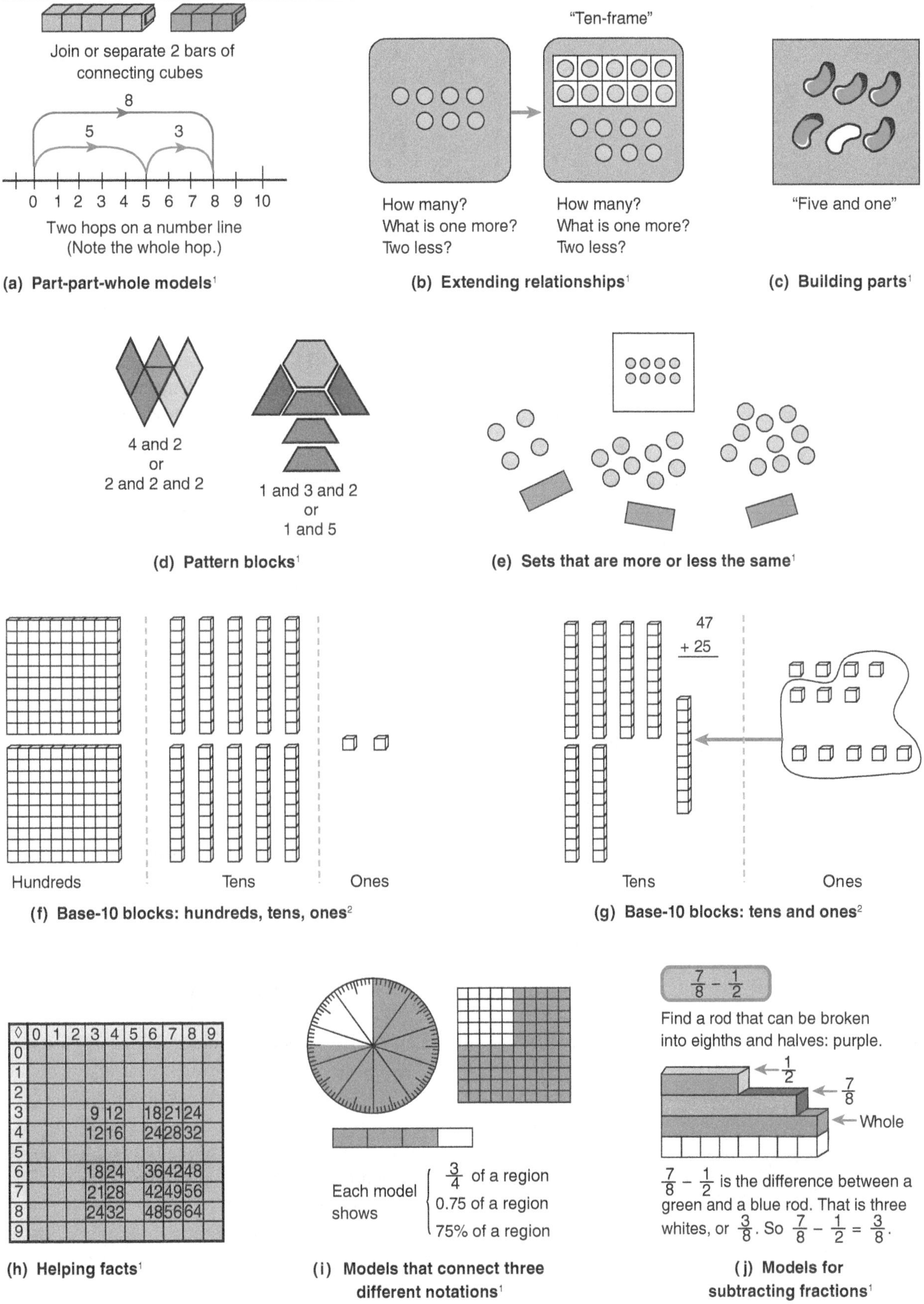

(a) **Part-part-whole models**[1]

(b) **Extending relationships**[1]

(c) **Building parts**[1]

(d) **Pattern blocks**[1]

(e) **Sets that are more or less the same**[1]

(f) **Base-10 blocks: hundreds, tens, ones**[2]

(g) **Base-10 blocks: tens and ones**[2]

(h) **Helping facts**[1]

(i) **Models that connect three different notations**[1]

(j) **Models for subtracting fractions**[1]

Sources: [1]Van de Walle et al. (2012); [2]Hudson and Miller (2006).

- Motivational strategies should be included in Tiers 2 and 3 interventions.
- Students should receive help in recognizing that fractions are numbers and that they expand the number system beyond whole numbers. Number lines can be used as a central representational tool in teaching this and other fraction concepts.
- Students should be assisted in understanding why procedures for computations with fractions make sense.
- Students' conceptual understanding of strategies for solving ratio, rate, and proportion problems should be developed before they are exposed to cross-multiplication as a procedure to solve such problems. (Gersten et al., 2009; Siegler et al., 2010)

Finally, practices to help students gain a better conceptual understanding of mathematical ideas should be included in instruction for all students. The following list provides examples of these evidence-based mathematics practices:

- Using the precise mathematical definitions for the content being taught; definitions should be developmentally appropriate while retaining the intended meaning of the concepts (Milgram, 2005; Wu, 2005, 2006)
- Providing a mathematical rationale that underlies algorithms, explaining why some algorithms are not generalizable, and applying logical reasoning to solve problems (Wu, 2006)
- Translating between verbal and symbolic statements (Wu, 2005)
- Having students explain their reasoning about solutions for problems
- Having students use multiple representations and describing how multiple representations are connected to the mathematics (NCTM, 2014)
- Providing reversibility problems; for example, rather than asking students to solve the equation $4 + 2 = \square$, give "6" and have students identify addends that equal "6" (Dougherty et al., 2015).

In each of the following sections, we present mathematics content from the CCSSM. We use the four categories of the ADAPT Framework to provide ideas for making adaptations to instruction. We use assessment ideas from Chapter 9 and understanding of the learning characteristics of individuals with mathematics difficulties and disabilities. We now focus on early number development.

EARLY NUMBER DEVELOPMENT AND HOW IT IS TAUGHT

Early number development consists of a variety of skills and concepts that are taught in preschool, kindergarten, first grade, and second grade (Chard et al., 2008; Clarke et al., 2016). The ability to count is a crucial skill that many young children develop before they enter formal schooling in kindergarten. Experiences at home, on the playground, and in the grocery store can expose students to counting principles (Bryant, Roberts, Bryant, et al., 2011). In their classic work on children's understanding of numbers, Gelman and Gallistel (1978) presented five counting principles important for early number development: (a) one-to-one correspondence, (b) stable order (i.e., counting words are stated in a consistent order), (c) cardinality (i.e., the last counting word indicates the number of objects in a given set), (d) abstraction (i.e., any group of objects can be collected to count), and (e) order irrelevance (i.e., counting objects in any sequence does not alter the count). Children require numerous examples and a lot of practice with these five counting principles as a foundation for later work with computation.

Furthermore, young children learn the vocabulary that describes mathematical relationships. For example, they use "more" to ask for another cookie and "all gone" when the cookies are finished. They may hear an adult ask, "Do you want another cookie?" or "Do you want one more cookie?" Children's experiences with objects teach the early language of mathematics via physical representations that

Experience with objects, such as the manipulatives these students are using, teaches the early language of mathematics through physical representations that children understand.

iStock.com/ktaylorg

children can understand. Finally, young children often know how to read and write some numerals, such as 1, 2, and 3 when they enter school.

Parents and teachers can create sets with objects so children are counting objects, saying how many, and selecting the numeral that represents the count. Although their writing may be elemental at the early stage, children are hearing, representing, seeing, and writing numbers (they can be asked to write the number 1). Young children develop their early understanding about mathematical concepts that leads to more formal instruction.

The magnitude of numerals is another important concept for students to learn for later mathematical content. For instance, students should be able to say that 51 is greater than 48 and 19 is less than 20. The ability to make these judgments relates to an understanding about quantity and knowing that five 10's is more than four 10's and one 10 is less than two groups of 10. Moreover, this ability depends on understanding place value or the base-10 system, which is the decimal numeral system that has 10 as its base.

Difficulties With Early Number Development

Research results have shown that students with early mathematics problems show difficulties understanding number sense. They struggle to achieve conceptual understanding of counting principles; that struggle can affect their use of more advanced counting strategies (e.g., counting on: 8 + 2 = 11) to solve number combinations (Geary, 2004, 2011). Counting up two or three numbers from a given number and understanding "greater than" and "less than" in number magnitude are other important skills that can be problematic (Jordan et al., 2012; Jordan, Kaplan et al., 2009). Number reversals may persist long after instruction in writing numbers, and representing the teen numbers are consistently challenging for struggling students (Bley & Thornton, 2001). Consider that 11 and 12 sound very different from 13, 14, 15, and so forth. Students may have difficulty saying these numerals. Finally, Jordan, Kaplan, et al. (2009) found that students with mathematics difficulties scored lower on place value tasks than average students. Taken together, these findings support the ideas that students with mathematics difficulties need consistent instructional time on number knowledge, counting principles, and place value concepts in the early grades (Bryant, Bryant, Kethley et al., 2008; Doabler et al., 2016; Fuchs et al., 2010).

Teaching Early Number Development

We begin with some general notes on teaching early number development and then look more closely at several specific skills.

- Diagnosis: Conduct an informal assessment asking students to read and write numerals, count objects, identify which numeral or group has more quantity, and tell how many are in a group. Use the results to help you determine early number skills and focus beginning instruction on early number development.
- Instructional content—Comparing and grouping objects: Provide many opportunities for students to show set equivalency, to make groups based on problems, and to decompose (i.e., take apart) larger numbers into smaller sets. Pair number symbols with groupings to reinforce the connection between concrete representations and abstract symbols.
- Instructional content—Reading and writing numerals: Pair instruction on reading numerals with writing numerals. Writing proficiency may take longer to master as young children learn how to hold the pencil correctly and make correct stroke formations. Provide models of correctly written numerals, including directional arrows for stroke formation. Do not allow messy work because if you do, it will persist throughout the school years.
- Instructional materials—Place value and the 10-frame: Use the 10-frame frequently to help students make and see the concept of 10. Use two 10-frames to build the teen numbers. Use a 5-frame initially for students who struggle with the 10-frame.
- Instructional materials: Use counting cubes, number lines, 10-frames, and objects for counting, comparing, grouping, and decomposing activities, number magnitude, number sequencing, and number recognition.
- Language: Provide multiple opportunities for students to use the language of mathematics. Refer back to Table 13.3 for examples of the language to emphasize. Model the use of these terms, such as *same, equal, more*, and *less*, in early number development activities.
- Proficiency and progress monitoring: Build fluent responding for number recognition and number writing. Use flash cards for number facts, where students see the number and respond within 3–5 seconds (i.e., the look and say strategy). Focus instruction on numbers students cannot quickly name. Use the quick write strategy, in which students write numbers in sequence, beginning with 0, for 1 minute. Count the number of correctly formed numerals. Then focus instruction on those numerals that are not in order or not written correctly.

Counting

Develop basic counting skills. Conduct warm-ups by giving students a number and having them count up "two more" or count back "two less." Have students tap the count or show fingers so they get the count right. This procedure builds counting skills and reinforces the concepts of more and less. Give students two groups of objects. Have them count the first group and place it in a cup. Then, beginning with the last number named in the cup, have them count on the second group of objects. This develops the counting-on strategy. Have students count groups of objects and then ask, "How many?" This builds the counting principles of one-to-one correspondence and cardinality.

Teen Numbers

Teach 14, 16, 17, 18, and 19 first by emphasizing that you say the second number first, such as four-teen. Try "fast numbers" with these five numbers; that is, the student looks and says the number quickly (within 3 seconds). Once students know these numbers, move to 13 and 15. Tell students how to read thir-teen and fif-teen. Once students know these two numbers, mix them with the other five numbers. Next, teach 11 and 12. They are not teen numbers but fall in the 10 to 20 number range. Tell students they just have to learn these numbers by sight. Once they know them, mix them with the other teen numbers. Pair the reading and writing of the teen numbers with making the numbers in the 10-frame during instruction. Have students name the numbers out of order and write them when dictated. Conduct magnitude comparison activities (discussed next) with these numbers.

Magnitude Comparison

Give students two numbers and have them tell which number is greater than or less than the other number. At first, provide numbers that are somewhat far apart, such as 3 and 8, 22 and 36, or 105 and 116. Then provide numbers that are closer together, such as 9 and 11, 28 and 30, or 111 and 115. Focus on the teen numbers and on numbers with 0, such as 50, 106, and 207. For smaller numbers, have students use cubes to make trains or use the number line to show magnitude. For larger numbers, have students use the 100's chart to explain number magnitude. Connect magnitude comparison with place value activities (discussed later).

Numeral Recognition: Fast Numbers

Show students the number cards 0 through 5. Model the look and say strategy quickly. Correct errors if needed and provide the correct response right away. Put correctly named number cards in one pile and incorrectly named number cards in another pile. Spend more time on the incorrect pile. Have students say numbers quickly for 30 seconds to see how many they can get right. Increase the range of numbers gradually. Keep numbers that the students did correctly in a special pile and present them once a week to be sure students can still name them quickly.

Number Writing: Quick Write

Have students write numbers, beginning with zero, for 1 minute. At the end of the minute, have students count the number of numerals written. Numerals that are written backward, are very messy, or are not in sequence are considered errors. Correct errors by providing a number line for students to see how numerals are written correctly. Have students graph the number of numerals they can write correctly in 1 minute. This is a good warm-up activity and can be done several times a week.

Reversals

Reversals may occur with single-digit numerals, such as 6 for 9, and with multidigit numbers, such as 24 for 42. Give students many opportunities to practice writing numerals correctly using a variety of materials. Use stencils for tracing, models of correctly formed numerals, and models with directional cues showing where to start making the numeral and in what direction to go. Have students correct reversals.

Part-Part-Whole Relationships

Identifying ways to compose and decompose numbers is a foundation skill that helps students think about the concept of numbers. The part-part-whole and missing-parts relationships are the building blocks for learning number combinations and solving word problems. It is important for students to develop an understanding of these relationships. For example, have students show the parts of a number such as 5. Model the commutative property, showing $4 + 1 = 1 + 4$ by using colored cubes and the five-frame. Make 5 with $4 + 1$; then turn the frame around so students see that $1 + 4$ also equals 5. Use the five-frame to determine other parts of 5, such as $3 + 2$, $2 + 3$, $0 + 5$, and $5 + 0$. These activities can be done with other number quantities and should be an integral part of instruction. Number combinations are often difficult for students. In the next section we examine ways to teach this important foundation skill.

NUMBER COMBINATIONS AND HOW THEY ARE TAUGHT

Instruction in number combinations (sometimes called basic facts) consists of developing declarative and procedural knowledge and conceptual understanding (see Chapter 7 for explanations). In the elementary grades, students are taught strategies for learning these number combinations, so most remember the answers automatically. These students demonstrate computational fluency, which consists of knowing and using efficient methods for accurate computing (NCTM, 2000). Geary (2004) identified strategies that typically developing students use for solving number combinations.

When students are first learning addition, they use finger counting or verbal counting strategies (Siegler & Shrager, 1984). The counting-all and counting-on strategies are most commonly used (Fuson, 1982; Groen & Parkman, 1972).

The counting-all strategy means taking the quantity of each addend and then counting both quantities (2 + 3 is 1, 2 + 1, 2, 3 = 1, 2, 3, 4, 5). The counting-on strategy means taking the larger addend and counting on by the other addend (3 + 2 is 3 + 1, 2 = 3, 4, 5). The decomposition strategy means that students break down a fact into a partial sum and then add or subtract 1, for example (5 + 6 = 5 + 5 = 10 + 1 = 11 or 6 + 6 = 12 − 1 = 11). The direct retrieval strategy assumes students have learned the facts and can now retrieve the answer automatically. Eventually, as students master facts, the strategies they use become more memory based. However, for students who find mathematics challenging, computational fluency remains a persistent problem (Bryant, Roberts, et al., 2011; Geary, 2004; Jordan et al., 2003).

Difficulties With Number Combinations

Difficulty with learning and remembering number combinations is a typical problem among students who struggle with mathematics and students who are identified as having mathematics disabilities. Problems in retrieval of number combinations seem to inhibit the ability to grasp the more complex algebraic concepts taught in later years (Bryant, Bryant, et al., 2011; Geary, 2004). Lack of efficient and effective counting strategies is another problem commonly associated with number combinations and students who struggle with mathematics (Bryant, Bryant, Gersten et al., 2008; Gersten et al., 2005). These students require instruction to develop both conceptual understanding of number combinations and procedural knowledge to figure out the answers. We know that instruction for struggling students is most enhanced through the use of physical, pictorial, and abstract or symbolic representations of number combinations.

Teaching Number Combinations

Let's begin with general notes and then look more closely at some specific skills.

- Diagnosis: Assess to identify which number combinations students know as "fast facts" and which they do not. Use observation and clinical interviews to identify what strategies (e.g., counting on fingers) the students use to solve facts when a quick response is not provided. The **think aloud** procedure is used to examine a student's knowledge of and thinking about how to solve problems (Kritikos et al., 2018).
- Instructional content—Sequence: Teach number combinations systematically. Although there is no best sequence, you should generally teach easier strategies first (e.g., count on: + 0, + 1, + 2, + 3; and doubles: 4 + 4). Then teach commutative property combinations (e.g., 1 + 4 = 4 + 1) for addition. Teach fact families (e.g., 5 + 3, 3 + 5, 8 − 3, 8 − 5) once students have mastered some addition facts.
- Instructional content—Decomposition: Present multiple opportunities for students to practice decomposition of numbers to solve arithmetic problems. For example, students can use the doubles + 1 strategy to arrive at the answer for 7 + 8: "What double is in 7 + 8?" Answer: 7 + 7. "What is double + 1?" Answer: 7 + 7 + 1 = 15, so 7 + 8 = 15.
- Acquisition: For students learning facts, practice is an important component of instruction and should occur for about 10 minutes daily. Teachers, such as Mr. Jamison in the Opening Challenge, who are looking for ways to give students more practice can use apps to provide it. Recall from Chapter 7 the key features—such as multiple examples and response opportunities—to look for when making decisions about downloading educational apps.
- Proficiency: Conduct 1-minute timings (i.e., fast facts) on number combinations to build fluency. Show flash cards with combinations and give students up to 3 seconds to say the answer (no fingers). Facts that are not answered quickly remain in the practice pile.
- Generalization: Promote generalization by having students answer problems with mixed operations and whole-number computational problems.

Table 13.5 presents a list of strategies and gives examples of number combinations for each strategy.

Returning to our Opening Challenge, recall the issues Mr. Jamison faces with some of his students with mathematics. Now, you will see how he adapts instruction to address their needs. In ADAPT in Action, Mr. Jamison uses the ADAPT Framework to help students who have difficulty with some addition combinations. For many students, place value is a challenging concept. In the next section we discuss how to teach it.

TABLE 13.5 ■ Arithmetic Strategies and Combinations

Addition Strategies	Addition Combinations
Facts with zero Zero rule: "Any number + 0 is the same number."	(0, 1, 2, 3, 4, 5, 6, 7, 8, 9) + 0 and the commutative facts
Count on: + 1 One more than	(0, 1, 2, 3, 4, 5, 6, 7, 8, 9) + 1 and the commutative facts
Count on: + 2 Two more than	(0, 1, 2, 3, 4, 5, 6, 7, 8, 9) + 2 and the commutative facts
Count on: + 3 Three more than	(0, 1, 2, 3, 4, 5, 6, 7, 8, 9) + 3 and the commutative facts
Doubles Count by 2's	(3 + 3, 4 + 4, 5 + 5, 6 + 6, 7 + 7, 8 + 8, 9 + 9)
Near doubles Doubles + 1 Doubles − 1	(4 + 5, 5 + 6, 6 + 7, 7 + 8, 8 + 9) and the commutative facts
9, 8, 7: Make 10 plus more	(9 + 4, 9 + 5, 9 + 6, 9 + 7, 8 + 4, 8 + 5, 8 + 6, 7 + 4, 7 + 5, 7 + 8) and the commutative facts
Subtraction Strategies	**Subtraction Combinations**
Facts with zero Zero rule: "Any number minus zero is the same number."	(0, 1, 2, 3, 4, 5, 6, 7, 8, 9) − 0
Facts with the same number: "Any number minus the same number is zero."	$n - n = 0$
Count up +1, +2, + 3. Start with the smaller number and count up to the bigger number (e.g., 9 − 7, start with 7 and count up to 9, the answer is 2).	(12, 11) − 9 (11, 9) − 8 (9, 8) − 7 (9, 8, 7) − 6
(8, 7, 6) − 5	(7, 6, 5) − 4
Double, then "Fact Family" (4 + 4 = 8; 8 − 4 = 4)	(8 − 4, 10 − 5, 12 − 6, 14 − 7, 16 − 8, 18 − 9)
9, 8, 7: Up to 10, then add	(17 − 9, 17 − 8, 16 − 9, 15 − 9, 15 − 8, 15 − 7, 14 − 9, 14 − 8, 13 − 9, 13 − 8, 13 − 7, 12 − 9, 12 − 8, 12 − 7, 11 − 9, 11 − 8, 11 − 7)
Multiplication Strategies	**Multiplication Combinations**
Skip counting: 2's, 5's	(2, 3, 4, 5, 6, 7, 8, 9) × 2; (2, 3, 4, 5, 6, 7, 8, 9) × 5 and the commutative facts
Nifty 9's: Multiply, then check	9 × 2 = 18 (1 + 8 = 9), 9 × 3 = 27 (2 + 7 = 9), 9 × 4 = 36 (3 + 6 = 9), 9 × 5 = 45 (4 + 5 = 9), 9 × 6 = 54 (5 + 4 = 9), 9 × 7 = 63 (6 + 3 = 9), 9 × 8 = 72 (7 + 2 = 9), 9 × 9 = 81 (8 + 1 = 9) and the commutative facts
Zero rule: Any $n \times 0 = 0$	(0, 1, 2, 3, 4, 5, 6, 7, 8, 9) × 0

(Continued)

TABLE 13.5 ■ Arithmetic Strategies and Combinations (Continued)

Multiplication Strategies	Multiplication Combinations
Identity rule: Any $n \times 1 = n$	$(1, 2, 3, 4, 5, 6, 7, 8, 9) \times 1$
Same n: Count by the same factor	$3 \times 3, 4 \times 4, 6 \times 6, 7 \times 7, 8 \times 8$ Example: $3 \times 3 = 3, 6, 9$
Harder facts: Distribute, then add	$8 \times 7 = 8 \times 2 = 16 + 8 \times 5 = 40 = 56$ $8 \times 6 = 8 \times 1 = 8 + 8 \times 5 = 40 = 48$ $8 \times 4 = 8 \times 2 = 16 + 8 \times 2 = 16 = 32$
Division Strategies	**Division Combinations**
Any $n \div n = 1$	$9 \div 9, 8 \div 8, 7 \div 7, 6 \div 6, 5 \div 5, 4 \div 4, 3 \div 3, 2 \div 2, 1 \div 1$
Any $n \div 1 = n$	$(9, 8, 7, 6, 5, 4, 3, 2, 1) \div 1$
Related facts in division	Example: $72 \div 8 = 9$ and $72 \div 9 = 8$
Fact families divide/multiply	Example: $72 \div 8 = 9, 72 \div 9 = 8, 9 \times 8 = 72, 8 \times 9 = 72$

Sources: Bley and Thornton (2001); Bryant, Bryant, et al. (2011); Stein et al. (2006); Van de Walle et al. (2016).

PLACE VALUE AND HOW IT IS TAUGHT

The base-10 system is an important component of mathematics instruction that students must fully grasp (Van de Walle et al., 2016). Understanding place value helps students understand numerical relationships and the "how" and "why" of procedures used to solve problems. Yet evidence also suggests that students do not learn place value concepts sufficiently to understand procedures for multidigit calculations (Jordan, Kaplan et al., 2009). For example, they might see the numeral 63 as a single numeral rather than seeing each individual digit representing specific values in the number. Students might hear the number 205 and write 2005 because they do not understand that a "100's" number has three digits. Instruction in place value must be emphasized throughout instruction in whole and rational numbers (i.e., decimals). Teachers should ensure that students develop conceptual understanding of the base-10 system using concrete and pictorial representations.

Difficulties With Place Value

Students may demonstrate a variety of problems related to their conceptual understanding of place value. Insufficient time spent with concrete representations can result in poor understanding of place and value. According to Ross (1989), as cited in Van de Walle et al. (2012), there are five levels of place-value difficulties.

1. Single numeral: The student does not understand individual digits in numerals such as 52 as representing specific values in the number. Rather, the student regards 52 as a single numeral.
2. Position names: The student can name the position of the digits (in 52, 5 is in the 10's place and 2 is in the 1's place), but does not associate value with the position.
3. Face value: The student takes each digit at face value. For 52, the student selects five blocks to go with the 5 and two blocks to go with the 2. This indicates the student does not understand the value of the position.
4. Transition to place value: For 52, the student selects two blocks for the 1's place, and selects the remaining 50 blocks for the 5. The student does not demonstrate grouping of 10's.
5. Full understanding: For 52, the student selects five groups of 10 for the 5, and the two remaining blocks for the 2.

ADAPT IN ACTION

MR. JAMISON: NUMBER COMBINATIONS

Mr. Jamison is concerned about three students who have not learned addition combinations to 18. Through informal diagnostic teaching, he finds they can recognize and write numerals quickly. They can also solve simple addition combinations, including sums to 10 and doubles. However, more difficult combinations involving sums to 11 through 18 are challenging for the students. Mr. Jamison uses a clinical interview procedure wherein he asks each student to think aloud how they would solve problems such as 7 + 4, 8 + 6, and 9 + 7. Consistently, the three students read the first number and use their fingers to count on to arrive at the solution. Mr. Jamison recalls from his teacher preparation program that counting on is a good strategy when students are first learning some facts, particularly when one addend is 1, 2, or 3. But it is not an efficient strategy for solving harder combinations. He decides to teach the three students the make 10 plus more strategy. Keep in mind that Mr. Jamison has other students who have trouble with more-difficult addition combinations, so they too could benefit from the adaptations. Also, Mr. Jamison can use this lesson for any of his students who are still not proficient with addition combinations. Instructional Strategy 13.1 shows the make 10 plus more strategy.

Following the lesson, Mr. Jamison reviews the progress-monitoring data for his students. He learns they are missing an important concept of the make 10 plus more strategy and decides to use the ADAPT Framework to make decisions about the next steps for instruction.

A: Ask, "What am I requiring the student to do?" Mr. Jamison wants the students to add combinations with sums 11 to 18. He wants them to show the addition strategy using different representations (e.g., 10-frames and counters).

D: Determine the prerequisite skills of the task. "I know students need to decompose one number to make 10 and to know how much to add to get to 10. Students also need to be able to say the answer to, '10 plus *x* is the same as _____?'"

A: Analyze the student's strengths and struggles. The students did a good job of decomposing one number by using the 10-frames to make 10. But they could not tell how much to add to 10 to make it the same as or equal to 13. For example, it was difficult for the students to quickly say 10 + 3 = 13 or 10 + 6 = 16.

P: Propose and implement adaptations from among the four categories. Mr. Jamison decides to adapt the make 10 plus more lesson by teaching a lesson just on the make 10 plus more strategy (i.e., instructional content and activity). He will have his students use the 10-frames and counters (i.e., instructional materials) to show 10 + more and to tell what number. He will then put these combinations on flash cards and have students say the answers quickly.

T: Test to determine whether the adaptations helped the student accomplish the task. Mr. Jamison will continue to collect progress-monitoring data to determine whether the reduced instructional content helps the students learn the make 10 plus more strategy. Then he will return to make 10 plus more and add a fast-facts component for progress monitoring.

Benchmark. Use the "Benchmark" procedure to build fluency. For instance, given a worksheet of facts and working from left to right, designate a fact as the benchmark to reach by the end of the 1-minute timing. Students can star or circle the designated fact to identify it.

You can choose the benchmark fact by (a) identifying the number of correct problems answered in a previous 1-minute timing, (b) multiplying that number by 25%, and (c) adding the 25% figure to the original figure. This new number becomes the benchmark for the next 1-minute marathon. The benchmark strategy is very motivating because it promotes self-competition (i.e., to beat yesterday's score). Distribute rewards to students who reach their benchmark.

Timed drills. You can use periodic timed drills, distributed practice (over several days or across weeks), and data analysis of student performance to monitor automaticity abilities on lower-level, cognitive skills. Developing automaticity of such cognitive skills is particularly important at the elementary level because students are learning mathematical skills. At the secondary level, automaticity development must continue in life skills areas (working with money and time) particularly for students with intellectual disabilities. If students were already exposed to a strong proficiency-building program at the elementary level but are still struggling, review their educational goals, transitional needs, and curriculum. For some students with more severe learning problems or severe intellectual disability, automaticity in basic facts might be limited. In these cases, calculator instruction is the obvious choice. Examine Instructional Strategy 13.1 for examples of teaching procedures, progress monitoring, adaptations, prerequisite abilities and adaptations, and representations for procedural strategies.

ADAPT Framework: Mr. Jamison

A ASK "What am I requiring the student to do?"	D DETERMINE the prerequisite skills of the task.	A ANALYZE the student's strengths and struggles. Strengths	Struggles	P PROPOSE and implement adaptations from among the four categories.	T TEST to determine whether the adaptations helped the student to accomplish the task.
The students will add combinations with sums 11 to 18 showing the addition strategy using concrete representations (ten-frames and counters).	1. Decomposes one number to make 10.	1			
	2. Knows how much to add to get to 10.		2	2. Instructional content: Focus on 10 + 1, 2, 3, 4, 5, 6, 7, 8 in random order. Instructional delivery: Students start on the 10 on the number line and count on to solve the equation for each combination. Instructional material: Number line.	2. Give an equation (e.g., 10 + 6 =) and have students use the number line to solve it.
	3. Says automatically what "Ten Plus More" equals.		3	3. Instructional content: 10 + addends = 11 – 18. Instructional delivery: Provide multiple opportunities to practice. Instructional activity: Play "what number solves this equation?" Show students cards with different equations to solve by retrieving the answers automatically. Instructional material: Ten Plus More Cards.	3. Give students a number and have them make the number using cubes and the five-frame. Record the number of ways they can represent a number; all possibilities should be shown by students.

INSTRUCTIONAL STRATEGY 13.1

STRATEGIES TO TEACH NUMBER COMBINATIONS

Addition: Count On (+ 1, + 2, + 3)[1,2]

Teaching Procedure

1. Tell students to start big by selecting the larger of the two addends and then to count on by the amount of the second number.
2. Emphasize + 1, + 2, or + 3, depending on the number. For example, 9 + 3 = is computed by saying, "Start big"—9 add three more, 10, 11, 12 to arrive at 12. Have students verbalize the process to ensure accuracy in using the "count on" procedure.

Progress Monitoring: Monitor progress by conducting fast facts—containing facts with + 1, + 2, and + 3, where students have to say or write the response quickly (within 3 seconds).
Adaptations: Instructional materials, instructional delivery, instructional content
Representations: Concrete and pictorial

Prerequisite Skills	Adaptations
1. Ability to identify larger number to start big. **2.** Ability to count on a designated amount (e.g., 2, 3) from a designated number (7, 9).	**1.** Provide two numbers, one of which is 1, 2, or 3. Have students state which number is larger. Use the number line or concrete objects to represent each number if necessary. Have students tap + 1, + 2, or + 3 or show a finger for each number counted on.
3. Ability to write the last number spoken.	**2.** Conduct warm-up of rote counting from designated number (e.g., 7) and counting on by 1, 2, or 3. Use a number line as pictorial representation if necessary. **3.** Provide a number line or number strip with numbers as a referent.

Multiplication: Count By

Teaching Procedure

1. Tell students to identify a number in the problem they know how to count by.
2. Make tallies or hold up the number of fingers for the other number in the problem.
3. Count by the number from 1 until all of the tallies or fingers are accounted for; the last number named is the answer.

Example: $4 \times 8 = ?$

1. I know how to count by 4's.
2. I will hold up eight fingers.
3. I count by 4 eight times: 4, 8, 12, 16, 20, 24, 28, 32.
4. 32 is the answer.

Progress Monitoring: Monitor progress by conducting fast facts, where students have to say or write the response quickly (within 3 seconds) to a group of facts (e.g., the 3's, 4's, 5's, 6's, 7's, 8's, 9's). Then mix up the facts.
Adaptations: Instructional materials, instructional delivery, instructional content
Representations: Concrete and pictorial
Division: How Many Groups?[2]

Teaching Procedure

Prerequisite Skills	Adaptations
1. Ability to count by 2, 3, 4, 5, 6, 7, 8, 9.	**1.** Conduct count-by warm-ups. Use a chart to show the count-by number patterns.
2. Ability to keep track of how many counting by.	**2.** Have students hold up a finger for each number to be counted.

Prerequisite Skills	Adaptations
1. Ability to count by a number. **2.** Ability to keep track of how many counting by.	**1.** Show students pictorial groups of the number being counted by. **2.** Focus initially on easier count-by facts, such as count by 2's and count by 5's. **3.** Have students hold up a finger for the number counted by.

1. Tell students to read the division problem 81 ÷ 9 = x and then ask, "How many groups of 9 equal 81?"
2. Have students count by 9's until they reach 81.
3. Tell them that the number of times they count by 9 represents the number of groups of 9 that equal 81.

Progress Monitoring: Monitor progress by having students say answers for fast facts.
Adaptations: Instructional materials, instructional delivery, instructional content
Representations: Concrete and pictorial

Sources: [1] Bley and Thornton (2001); [2] Van de Walle et al. (2012).

Young children, of course, do not fully understand place value, and it should not be surprising that older students who struggle with learning mathematics have not achieved full understanding of the base-10 system. Diagnostic teaching—giving problems and asking students to explain how they solved them—can help teachers understand student reasoning about place value.

Teaching Place Value

The following techniques can be applied to teaching place-value concepts.

- Diagnosis: Using the clinical interview procedure and manipulatives, and having students write numbers to represent place values, assess their level of place-value understanding.
- Instructional materials: You can use a variety of manipulatives to teach place value and the concept of whole-number computation with and without regrouping: rods, cubes, base-10 blocks, and bean sticks help teach whole-number computation at the concrete level, as do base-10 mats and place-value charts. Figure 13.1 shows examples of manipulatives and other materials.
- Vocabulary: Teach and regularly use the vocabulary of place value. Students should use base-10 language such as "53 represents five 10's and three 1's. Other vocabulary should include regrouping to describe how ten 1's are regrouped to add to the 10's place, or how a 10 is "unbundled" to add to the 1's place during whole-number addition. Similarly, the vocabulary related to 100's and 1,000's should be used for larger place-value groupings. Refer to Table 13.3 for examples of terms to teach.
- Instructional content: The idea of zero as a placeholder is one of the most challenging concepts for many students, including struggling students. Provide multiple opportunities for students to use manipulatives to represent numbers containing zero as a placeholder to carry out whole-number operations.
- Multiple representations—Concrete, pictorial, and abstract representations: Pair the use of manipulatives to concretely represent the place and value of numbers with the use of written numerals to demonstrate how to write the numbers (abstract/symbolic representation). For example, base-10 blocks are used on the place-value mat to represent numbers; students then write the numbers to show how many in each place. Then move to pictorial representations paired with concrete along with abstract.
- Progress monitoring: Assess student understanding of place value by giving them numbers to represent with base-10 blocks, having them tell the numbers in two ways (base-10 number and standard number) and writing the number. Include numbers with zero as a placeholder on a regular basis because numbers with zero are the most problematic for students to understand.

Teen Numbers

Have students spend time on teen numbers. These numbers represent another area that is very problematic for struggling students to learn. Use two 10-frames to represent quantity for the teen numbers.

Provide a number. Have students build the number in the frames, read the number, and write the number. Ask questions such as the following: "How many more is 14 than 11?" "How many do I need to add to 12 to get 15?" "How many is 2 less than 17?" "How much is 10 plus 8?" Teen numbers should also be taught within the context of 100's. Repeat the activities described here by using 100's and teen numbers such as 215, 317, and 411. See Figure 13.1 for an example of a 10-frame. The 10-frame provides students with a visual representation of the concept of 10. It is a useful instructional tool that can be used, for example for counting, counting by 5, and solving simple addition and subtraction problems.

Need to Trade?

Need to trade is a prerequisite activity to renaming or regrouping in addition. Present a variety of addition problems with and without renaming and ask students to identify those in which renaming is required, that is, in which they need to trade ten 1's for one 10 (Bley & Thornton, 2001). Have students use base-10 blocks to represent numbers initially and then move to pictorial representation such as tally marks.

Are There Enough?

"Are there enough?" is used for subtraction problems with and without renaming. Give students different subtraction problems and have them decide whether the minuend number in the 1's place is large enough for them to subtract the subtrahend number in the 1's place. For example, $32 - 14 = x$: Can four 1's be subtracted from two 1's? Students must have multiple practice opportunities with renaming using concrete and pictorial representations. Numbers with various places up to 1,000's can be used, as well as numbers with zeros as placeholders. This activity focuses students' attention on the 1's place, number discrimination, and place value (Bley & Thornton, 2001). The "Need to Trade" and "Are There Enough?" activities prepare students for whole-number computation. The application of place value to whole-number computation is discussed next.

WHOLE-NUMBER COMPUTATION AND HOW IT IS TAUGHT

Solving problems that contain whole numbers requires an understanding of the relationship between numbers and place value, as well as skill in estimating, determining the reasonableness of answers, using a calculator, and using appropriate algorithms. Instruction in place value and whole numbers should occur throughout the curriculum. It is not necessary for students to master addition before being introduced to subtraction or to be proficient in basic number combinations before being introduced to whole-number problems.

Whole-number operations include addition, subtraction, multiplication, and division without and with regrouping. Students should understand the meanings of the operations and how they are related to one another. They should also be able to compute fluently. Place-value abilities are a fundamental skill for whole-number computations. Estimation and rounding strategies are important companion skills, particularly with advanced multiplication and division computation (Hudson & Miller, 2006). Whole-number computation should include the development of conceptual understanding, instruction in procedural strategies, and the application of computation in word problems (Hudson & Miller, 2006).

Difficulties With Whole-Number Computation

Bley and Thornton (2001) identified the process of solving whole-number computation as complex because it relies on symbols, multiple steps, and a level of abstraction that can be problematic for struggling students. Difficulty with number combinations can interfere with students' ability to attempt whole number computations. Students may view the task as too difficult because they lack fluency with basic facts. The multistep process of computing whole-number problems can be overwhelming to students who have difficulty remembering multiple steps and sequences for solving problems. Difficulties with understanding number relationships and place value can affect the ability to apply important fundamental skills, such as estimating, rounding, recognizing reasonableness of answers, and doing mental computation when solving whole-number computations. Finally, using **algorithmic** procedures to compute whole-number problems can cause difficulties for students well beyond the elementary school years.

Teaching Whole-Number Computation

The general steps involved in teaching whole-number computation follow. Note that calculators and other technology have an important role to play.

- Diagnosis: Provide three problems each of addition, subtraction, multiplication, and division computation, including problems with and without regrouping and division with remainders. Include problems with zero as a value in the 1's, 10's, and 100's place. Provide reasonable time for students to complete the problems. Correct the work, noting what types of errors are made. Refer to Table 13.6 for examples of error patterns identified in whole-number computation and remedial strategies to address these error patterns (Ashlock, 2010).
- Instructional materials: Use materials from place-value instruction to support the development of conceptual understanding of whole-number operations. Students should be asked to explain their reasoning for their solutions. Using materials without student explanations does not lead to strong conceptual understanding.
- Technology: Provide students with calculators to check their answers for whole-number computations.
- Vocabulary: Use visuals to demonstrate concepts such as regrouping and remainder.
- Instructional materials: Provide a facts table to support students who need help recalling number combinations. Pair number combinations instruction with whole-number computations.
- Instructional content—task analysis: Provide similar types of problems when initially teaching whole-number computation at the abstract/symbolic representation level. Similar types of problems include two digits + two digits with no regrouping, three digits – three digits with 0 in the 10's place, and two digits + one digit with regrouping. Then provide mixed-problem worksheets with the same operation, such as two digits + one digit with regrouping, two digits + two digits with regrouping, and three digits + three digits with regrouping. Finally, provide mixed-problem worksheets with mixed operations.
- Strategies: Teach students procedural strategies (examples are described later) to solve whole-number computations. Use invented strategies for those students who can benefit from representing whole-number computations in nontraditional ways. Refer to Table 13.7 for examples of invented algorithms. Choose judiciously which strategies to teach; too many strategies can confuse students. Work with students to determine the strategy that makes sense to them and that they can use independently, efficiently, and effectively.
- Generalization: Promote generalization by having students answer problems with mixed operation signs in whole-number computational problems.
- Technology: Software programs can be used to support the extra instruction that students may require to learn whole-number computation. Some programs offer excellent visualizations of the process using manipulatives, which is often the type of instruction that teachers do not have sufficient time to provide. In the Tech Notes, the Unifix® cubes software program is shown, illustrating how the cubes are partitioned for a simple division problem with a remainder.

TABLE 13.6 ■ Error Patterns and Remedial Techniques

Operations	Type of Errors	Remedial Techniques
1. $\begin{array}{r}76\\+49\\\hline 1115\end{array}$	No regrouping of the ones in the ones place.	• Use base-ten blocks to model regrouping. • Use grid paper so only one digit can be recorded in each box, "forcing" the need to regroup. Include highlighted grid boxes above the problem to cue the need to write a numeral from regrouping tens or hundreds.
2. $\begin{array}{r}34\\729\\+694\\\hline 1117\end{array}$	Work begins on left rather than right. Regrouping done backward.	• Insert ↓ above the ones place as the place to start. • Explain that in math, we start opposite from where we start with reading.
3. $\begin{array}{r}414\\\cancel{5}7\cancel{4}\\-268\\\hline 266\end{array}$	Work begins on left with taking 1 from 5 to "regroup" to ones place. Regrouping in the tens place ignored.	• Insert ↓ above the ones place as the place to start. • Use base-ten blocks and a base-ten mat to model the conceptual understanding of regrouping.
4. $\begin{array}{r}410\\\cancel{5}0\cancel{0}\\-268\\\hline 284\end{array}$	Regrouping for the ones place is partially conducted. No regrouping for the tens place.	• Use base-ten blocks to model the conceptual understanding of regrouping. • Use D + PM to teach the procedural steps. • Give examples of subtraction problems with the zero in the minuend and with it in the subtrahend. Have students circle only those problems that can be computed without regrouping.
5. $\begin{array}{r}534\\\times 24\\\hline 1068\end{array}$	Each column is treated as separate multiplication. The left multiplier continues to be used when the multiplicand has more digits than the multiplier. The 4 in the ones place for the multiplier is ignored.	• Teach the use of the distributive property as an alternative algorithm. • $532 \times 24 = (20 \times 532) + (4 \times 532)$ • Create a cover so that only one digit of the multiplier is revealed at a time. • Have students check their work using a calculator.
6. $\begin{array}{r}95\\4\overline{)3620}\\\underline{36}\\20\\20\end{array}$	The zero in the tens place is missing from the quotient. When the student "brings down" and division is not possible, the next digit is "brought down" with no zero used as a placeholder.	• Give students grid paper to help with placement issues.
7. $\begin{array}{r}\frac{1}{4}=\frac{1}{12}\\+\frac{1}{3}=\frac{1}{12}\\\hline \frac{2}{12}\end{array}$	The student can identify the lowest common multiplier but merely copies the original numerator.	• Explain the purpose of the equal sign—that it means the same fractional part. • Have students use manipulatives to demonstrate that fractional parts on either side of the equal sign are equivalent.
8. $\begin{array}{r}6\frac{1}{3}\\-2\frac{2}{3}\\\hline 4\frac{1}{3}\end{array}$	The whole numbers are subtracted. There is no regrouping when the subtrahend is larger than the minuend.	• Have students use fractional parts to work through the problem. Use a cue to signal the need to start working with the fractions before the whole numbers. Have students regroup the whole number unit for an equal set of fractional parts so the subtraction can be performed. • Have students use markings to signal regrouping of a whole into fractional parts. • Provide examples of mixed fractions that require regrouping for subtraction purposes.
9. $\begin{array}{r}6.8\\+5.5\\\hline 11.13\end{array}$	The decimal point is in the wrong place in the sum. The tenths are not regrouped as units.	• Have students use rods to show a unit for comparison. Have students use rods to show each addend as tenths as compared with the unit. Have students combine the tenths rods and trade for a unit. • Have students use grid paper with the instruction that only one digit can be placed in each box.

Source: Ashlock (2010).

TABLE 13.7 ■ Invented Algorithms

(a) Invented strategies for addition with two-digit numbers		
Add Tens, Add Ones, Then Combine	46 + 38 40 and 30 is 70. 6 and 8 is 14. 70 and 14 is 84.	46 +38 70 14 84
Move Some to Make Tens	46 + 38 Take 2 from the 46 and put it with the 38 to make 40. Now you have 44, and 40 more is 84.	46 + 38 76 + 4 → 80 80 + 4 → 84
Add on Tens, Then Add Ones	46 □ 38 46 and 30 more is 76. Then I added on the other 8. 76 and 4 is 80, and 4 more is 84.	2 46 + 38 44 + 40 84
Use a Nice Number and Compensate	46 + 38 46 and 40 is 86. That's 2 extra, so it's 84.	46 + 38 46 + 40 → 86 − 2 → 84
(b) Invented strategies for subtraction by counting up		
Add Tens to Get Close, Then Ones	73 − 46 46 and 20 is 66. (30 more is too much.) Then 4 more is 70 and 3 is 73. That's 20 and 7, or 27	46 > 20 66 > 4 70 > 3 73 27
Add Tens to Overshoot, Then Come Back	73 − 46 46 and 30 is 76. That's 3 too much, so it's 27.	73 − 46 → 46 + 30 → 76 − 3 → 73 30 − 3 = 27
Add Ones to Make a Ten, Then Tens and Ones	73 − 46 46 and 4 is 50. 50 and 20 is 70, and 3 more is 73. The 4 and 3 is 7, and 20 more is 27.	73 − 46 46 + 4 → 50 + 20 → 70 + 3 → 73 27
	Similarly, 46 and 4 is 50. 50 and 23 is 73. 23 and 4 is 27.	46 + 4 → 50 50 + 23 → 73 23 + 4 = 27
(c) Partitioning strategies for multiplication		
By Decades	27 × 4 268 × 7	4 × 20 = 80 4 × 7 = 28 > 108 7 × 200 = 1400 7 × 60 = 420 > 1820 7 × 8 = 56 1876

(c) Partitioning strategies for multiplication

By Tens and Ones	27 × 4	10 x 4 = 40 10 x 4 = 40 → 80 7 x 4 = 28 → 108
Partitioning the Multiplier	46 × 3	Double 46 → 92 138
Other Partitions	27 × 8	so 25 x 4 = 100 25 x 8 = 200 2 x 8 = 16 → 216

(d) Models and symbols used to solve division tasks

92 ÷ 4

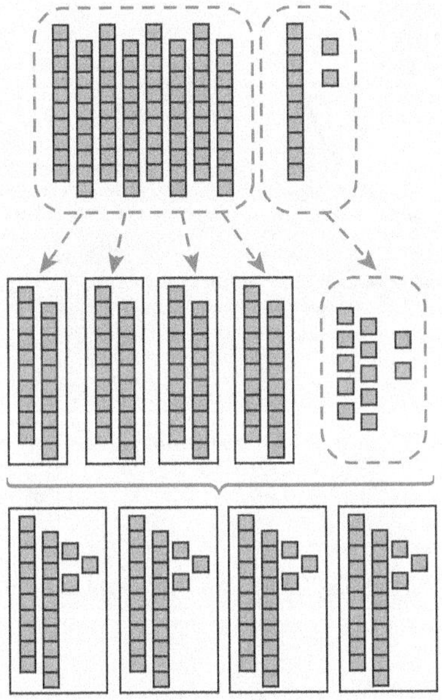

453 ÷ 6
(share with 6 kids)

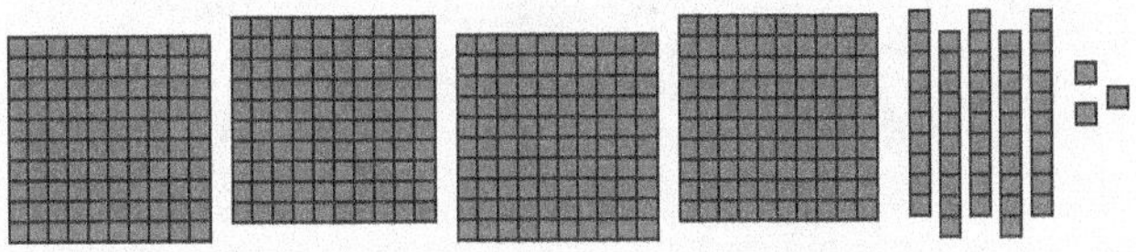

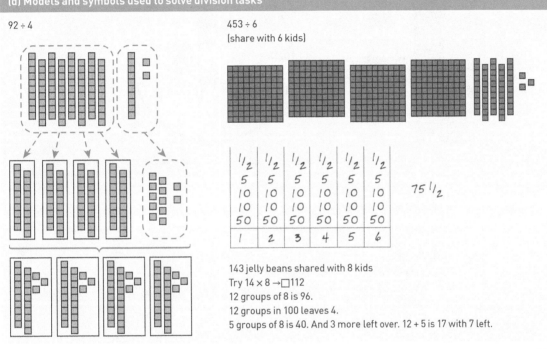

1/2	1/2	1/2	1/2	1/2	1/2
5	5	5	5	5	5
10	10	10	10	10	10
10	10	10	10	10	10
50	50	50	50	50	50
1	2	3	4	5	6

75 1/2

143 jelly beans shared with 8 kids
Try 14 × 8 →□112
12 groups of 8 is 96.
12 groups in 100 leaves 4.
5 groups of 8 is 40. And 3 more left over. 12 + 5 is 17 with 7 left.

Source: Van de Walle et al. (2012). Reprinted with permission.

TECH NOTES

USING SOFTWARE TO SHOW PICTORIAL REPRESENTATIONS OF MATH CONCEPTS

Unifix® Software (Didax Educational Resources, 2015) is a program that shows pictorial representations of abstract math concepts. The Unifix® are interlocking cubes that students can arrange to display patterning, counting, and operations. Unifix® Software supports switch access, which means that students with motor problems can use the software with switches that control movement in the software.

You can use the following procedures with the Unifix® cubes software to pictorially represent and solve the equation 17 ÷ 5 = x.

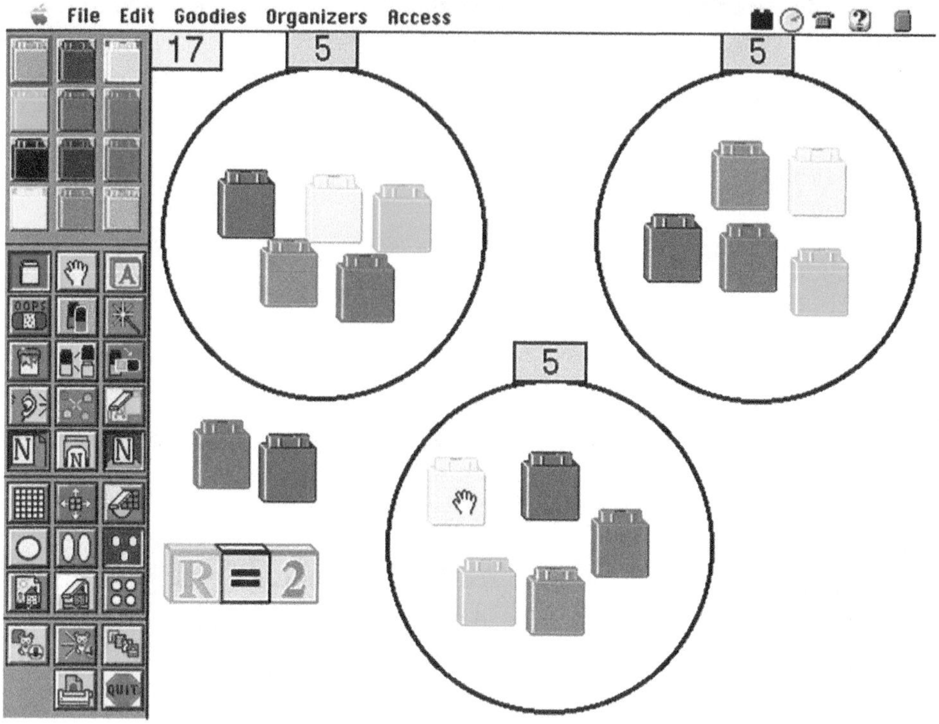

Unifix® Software can be used to provide pictorial representations and experiences with mathematics concepts.
Didax/Unifix

Teaching Procedure

1. Identify higher- and lower-performing students who can work together at the computer station.
2. Review the concept of division using the base-10 blocks.
3. Have students work in pairs at the computer with the Unifix® Software.
4. Monitor progress by having students complete four division problems independently, using paper and pencil.

Rounding

Have students round numbers up or down to the nearest 10 or the nearest 100 for whole-number computation, column addition, mental computation, estimation, and determining the reasonableness of an answer. Teach students rounding rules. Here is the rule for rounding: If the number you are rounding is followed by 5, 6, 7, 8, or 9, round the number up. Example: 148 rounded to the nearest 10 is 150. If the number you are rounding is followed by 0, 1, 2, 3, or 4, round the number down. Example: 32 rounded to the nearest 10 is 30. In the division problem, 286 divided by 72,286 can be rounded up to the nearest 10, 290, and 72 can be rounded down to 70 so $290 \div 70$ = about 4. To check their work, have students use multiplication (e.g., $70 \times 4 = 280$).

Estimation: The Front-End Strategy

Teach students the front-end strategy for computing column addition (Siegler & Booth, 2005). Provide students with a list of numbers to be added, such as 376 + 87 + 432 + 11 =?. Show the students how to first add the numbers in the front (i.e., the 100's column: 300 + 400 = 700). Then adjust the numbers in the 10's and 1's columns to form 100 (87 + 11 is about 100, and 76 + 32 is about 100, which makes 200). Third, add the front number (700) plus the adjusted number (200). Finally, estimate the answer (900 in this case). This strategy can be applied to adding money as well.

Estimation: The Clustering Strategy

Teach students to use the clustering strategy when all the numbers have about the same numerical value. For instance, the numbers of people who attended a football game during one month might be 15,833, 17,021, and 16,682. All the numbers cluster around 16,000, so a reasonable estimate is 16,000 × 3 = 48,000 people for three games.

Bean Stick Computation

Have students use bean sticks as manipulatives for addition and subtraction whole-number computation with and without regrouping. Sticks of 10 beans demonstrate place value for the 10's place, and remaining beans represent the 1's place. Demonstrate using the beans to trade ten 1's for a 10 for regrouping. The demonstration plus permanent model (discussed later) technique can be used for instructional purposes. Figure 13.2 shows an example of using bean sticks for addition with no regrouping. Because bean sticks are pregrouped with 10 beans per stick, they can be used for problems without regrouping or renaming. For problems that require regrouping, it is better to use groupable models. When using pre-grouped models, such as bean sticks, be sure to check student understanding that one bean stick of 10 is the same as 10 ones (Van de Walle et al., 2016).

FIGURE 13.2 ■ Using Bean Sticks to Solve Computational Problems

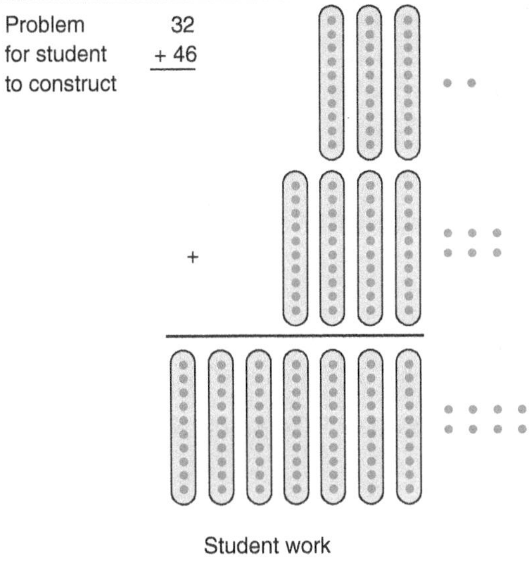

Alternative Algorithms

Teach students algorithms, which are routine, step-by-step procedures for computation. Examples of alternative algorithms include partial products and expanded notation, which are based on place value. Partial products can be used to teach division; they help students focus on place value and the quantity that is actually being partitioned.

$$
\begin{array}{r}
428 \div 2 = ? \\
400 \div 2 = 200 \\
20 \div 2 = 10 \\
8 \div 2 = 4 \\
\hline
214
\end{array}
$$

Expanded notation can be used for whole-number subtraction and division. The expanded-notation algorithm helps students show place-value representations of numerals and calculate answers, as illustrated in the following array. Below is an example of the expanded notation procedure.

	Subtraction	Division
457	400 + 50 + 7	428 ÷ 2 = ?
-35	-30 + 5	(400 + 20 + 8) ÷ 2 =
___	___	
	400 + 20 + 2 = 422	(200 + 10 + 4) = 214

For both types of alternative algorithms, model and think aloud how you solve a division problem. Students then compute and verbalize the steps in applying these algorithms, use manipulatives to represent the process, or work with a partner to solve problems.

Demonstration Plus Permanent Model

Have students use the demonstration plus permanent model (D + PM) intervention, which has proved successful in teaching students explicitly how to solve problems that include addition, subtraction, multiplication, and division of whole-number computation. This intervention takes only a short time to implement, is best applied individually or in small groups, and can greatly facilitate mastery of computation. Teachers using this intervention often report that students catch on very quickly and learn the steps efficiently. The D + PM intervention is at the level of abstract representation but can easily be adapted with pictorial representations (problems shown using base-10 models) and physical representations (problems completed using base-10 models). Thus, an instructional materials adaptation can help students who require additional conceptual development to understand place value, as well as computing with and without regrouping. The following steps make up the demonstration (D) + permanent model (PM) intervention:

- Demonstrate (D) how to solve a problem by thinking aloud the steps in whole-number computation. Stress place-value and regrouping language if regrouping is involved.
- Leave the demonstrated problem as a referent (PM) on the student's worksheet or the whiteboard.
- Have students compute the next problem, saying the steps out loud. If the problem is worked correctly, have students complete the remaining problems (Rivera & Smith, 1988).

Key Questions

Some students become confused when doing multistep whole-number computation (division, multiplication). Ask the following key questions to help students get back on track:

- What is the problem?
- What are the steps?
- What did you just do?
- What do you do next?

Mercer et al. (2010) recommended teaching students the following cue or family strategy to remember the steps required to solve division problems: Daddy (divide), Mother (multiply), Sister (subtract), and Brother (bring down). Students can be taught to use the family strategy or to ask themselves the key questions by referring to a chart or cue card, an approach that promotes more self-regulated learning. You can pair these techniques with the D + PM intervention to teach students how to solve division problems. It is important that students verbalize the steps and explain what they are doing.

Sequence of Instruction

Use the sequence of instruction approach to promote generalization. Traditionally, special education teachers present information to students in a task-analyzed, sequenced format, teaching the easiest skill first. Once that skill has been mastered, teachers present the next skill, and so on. Investigations have revealed, however, that students do not have to be taught whole-number computational skills in an easy-to-difficult sequence for learning to occur. Rather, they can be taught the most difficult skill within a group; most will generalize the algorithmic process to the easier problems. Concrete representations such as bean sticks and base-10 models can promote understanding of place value and renaming. However, it is important again that students verbalize their understanding of the whole-number computation.

We suggest the following guidelines:

1. Develop a task analysis of whole-number computation (two digits + one digit, two digits + two digits, three digits + two digits, three digits + three digits—all with no regrouping; two digits + one digit, two digits + two digits, three digits + two digits, three digits + three digits—all with regrouping).
2. Test students to identify the skills they have mastered and those that require instruction.
3. Group skills by no regrouping and regrouping.
4. Select the most difficult skill within a group as the instructional target (say, three digits + three digits with no renaming; three digits + three digits with renaming).
5. Teach this most difficult skill using the D + PM intervention.
6. Present problems representing all the skills within a group for practice (two digits + one digit, two digits + two digits, three digits + two digits, three digits + three digits—all with regrouping).
7. Collect student performance data on all the skills on the practice sheet. (Rivera & Smith, 1988)

We now talk about mathematical areas that can be challenging as students progress through the grades. Students need a solid understanding of the concepts and skills discussed so far to help them prepare for more advanced mathematics instruction.

RATIONAL NUMBERS AND HOW THEY ARE TAUGHT

Rational numbers are critical for more advanced mathematics success, especially in algebra (NMAP, 2008). They include the whole numbers and integers; numbers that can be written as the quotient of two integers, a ÷ b, where b is not zero (NCTM, 2000); and fractions, decimals, and percentages. Students should work flexibly with fractions, decimals, and their relationship to percentages, applying these rational numbers to real-life problems related to money, cooking, shopping, and measurement (NCTM, 2000). According to Van de Walle et al. (2016), developing students' understanding of fraction concepts is critical to their success in learning and understanding how to compute with fractions. Students should be taught to view fraction and decimal systems as representing the same concepts. Once they understand this relationship, they should be introduced to percentages and taught the interrelatedness of decimals, fractions, and percentages (Hudson & Miller, 2006).

Difficulties With Rational Numbers

Students encounter a variety of challenges as they work with fractions, decimals, and percentages. According to Bley and Thornton (2001), those who demonstrate problems with abstract reasoning have difficulties with rational numbers. Research findings from a longitudinal study of 147 students in sixth, seventh, and eighth grade with mathematics LDs, mathematics difficulties, and typical achievement showed that those with a mathematics LD performed poorly on ranking proportions with fractions and decimals (e.g., ranking smallest to largest decimals shown as numbers and fractions shown as

Students encounter a variety of challenges as they engage in work with fractions, decimals, and percentages.
Hero Images Inc. / Alamy Stock Photo

pictures) compared with the other two groups (Mazzocco & Devlin, 2008). Students with a mathematics LD manifested significantly more difficulties in identifying fraction and decimal equivalence (e.g., $0.50 = \frac{5}{10}$) than did students with mathematics difficulties and students who were typical achievers. Mazzocco and Devlin (2008) suggested poor conceptual understanding of rational numbers (weak number sense) as a possible explanation for low performance in basic tasks, which are associated with earlier grades' content. Students also have difficulties with understanding that a fraction is a number rather than two numbers making up the fraction. When comparing fractions, students might think that $\frac{1}{8}$ is greater than $\frac{1}{4}$ because 8 is greater than 4. Integers also can present challenges. Students have problems with integers, often due to rules learned in earlier grades that do not apply to the new material (Karp et al., 2014). For example, when we add two negative numbers such as −4 + −6, the sum (−10) is smaller than either of the two addends.

The vocabulary associated with these number systems can be problematic and thus require explicit instruction in the definitions and use of the terms. Number sense regarding the relative sizes of parts (e.g., thirds, 10ths, 0.60, and 25%) and their relationship to a whole unit could be difficult for some students. Problems of this nature will interfere with the ability to judge the reasonableness of answers to questions such as, "Is $\frac{3}{4}$ or $\frac{1}{4}$ closer to a whole?" Relating fractions, decimals, and percentages requires a sense of number size and relationship, and without a good sense of number size, even numeral relationships can be challenging. Difficulty remembering the meaning of symbols can interfere with interpreting how to solve problems. For example, −1 means negative one and not subtract one. Finally, understanding and recalling the procedural steps necessary in computations is yet another difficult area for students who are struggling.

Teaching Rational Numbers

Our overview of teaching these skills reflects the fact that many students, with and without unique learning needs or disabilities, need lots of help learning to work with rational numbers and integers.

- Diagnosis: Refer to Table 13.6 for examples of error patterns and remedial strategies to address them (Ashlock, 2010).

- Vocabulary: Teach terms related to fractions, decimals, percentages, and integers explicitly (Van de Walle et al., 2016). For example, with fractions, teach the terms *numerator* and *denominator*. Provide corrective feedback if a student says the "top" number and the "bottom" number.
- Instructional content: Make connections to money: Talk about and show how decimals such as 0.25, 0.10, and 0.05 are related to money. Make connections to telling time: Connect simple fractions ($\frac{1}{2}$, $\frac{1}{4}$) to telling time: half past the hour, quarter after an hour, or quarter to an hour.
- Instructional content: Teach the three types of questions and generate problems for students to solve (see Table 13.8).
- Instructional materials: Use rods, fraction tiles, grid paper, Geoboards, number lines, and pattern blocks to provide activities with quantities in different forms and shapes. Provide multiple exercises for students to represent similar values across the numeration systems using various materials. For example, use a paper strip to show $\frac{1}{4}$ of a region, a Geoboard to show 0.25 of a region, and grid paper to show 25% of a region. Number lines and integer chips are very useful for teaching integers.

  Figure 13.1 shows examples of manipulatives and materials that can be used for instruction in fractions, decimals, and percentages. See the National Library of Virtual Manipulatives (h ttp://nlvm.usu.edu/en/nav/vlibrary.html) for multiple manipulative tools for numbers and operations, algebra, geometry, measurement, and data analysis and probability.
- Strategies: Use the CSA or D + PM procedure for teaching addition, subtraction, multiplication, and division algorithms.
- Technology: Encourage students to check their work using calculators.
- Progress monitoring: On a weekly basis, conduct assessments on concepts and skills taught to assess whether students are benefiting from instruction. Error analysis can pinpoint misconceptions you can target for further instruction and review.

TABLE 13.8 ■ A Framework of Three Questions to Promote Algebraic Thinking

Type of Question	Fractions $\frac{1}{2} \times \frac{3}{4}$	Integers -3 + -8
1. Reversibility question	What are two fractions whose product is $\frac{3}{8}$?	What are two integers whose sum is -11?
2. Flexibility question	$\frac{1}{2} \times \frac{3}{4}$ $\frac{1}{2} \times \frac{2}{4}$ $\frac{1}{2} \times \frac{1}{4}$ How are these problems alike?	-3 + (-8) -4 + (-8) -5 + (-8) How are these problems alike?
3. Generalization question	If the factors of a multiplication problem are between 0 and 1, what can you predict about the size of the product?	What are two negative integers whose sum is negative? What are a positive integer and a negative integer whose sum is negative? What are two positive integers whose sum is negative? What do you notice about the integers that you found?

Source: Dougherty et al. (2015). Reprinted with permission.

Sorting Fractions and Decimals

Given a variety of fractions (or decimals) and the three choices close to zero, close to $\frac{1}{2}$, and close to 1, have students sort the fractions (or decimals) according to their relationship to the choices. To do this accurately, students must understand the relative sizes of the fractions (or decimals). Have them use manipulatives and number lines to demonstrate the accuracy of their choices (Bley & Thornton, 2001).

Fractions and Decimals to Sort					
$\frac{1}{9}$	$\frac{4}{5}$	$\frac{1}{20}$	$\frac{5}{8}$	$\frac{6}{7}$	$\frac{2}{3}$
.91	.01	.47	.87	.05	
Close to Zero		Close to $\frac{1}{2}$			Close to 1

Fractions as Equal to or Greater Than 1

Teach students a range of fractional representations when first introducing the concept of a fraction to help develop number sense about relative size. Rather than limiting instruction to $\frac{1}{2}$, $\frac{1}{4}$, and $\frac{1}{3}$, include fractions such as $\frac{5}{5}$, $\frac{3}{1}$, and $\frac{12}{4}$, using fraction strips and shapes such as squares, rectangles, and circles to illustrate physical representations of the fractional concepts. Students then learn from the beginning of fraction instruction that fractions represent relationships, not specific amounts.

Comparisons

Have students make comparisons to see comparative sizes of fractions and the relationship between the sizes. For example, students might state that $\frac{1}{3}$ is greater than $\frac{1}{2}$ because 3 is greater than 2; however, comparisons using manipulatives such as fraction strips or fraction bars can help students develop an understanding of relative sizes. Note that students must know the identity of the whole (e.g., a cake or a pizza) to discern that $\frac{1}{2}$ is indeed greater than $\frac{1}{3}$.

Number Combinations and Fractions

Combine instruction on number combinations with simple fraction problems. Build fluency in responding to problems, relying on number combinations, and then present fractions containing the combinations students have been practicing. If the targeted multiplication facts are factors of 8, fraction problems might include the following example:

$$\frac{8}{9} \times \frac{6}{8} = \frac{48}{72} = \frac{2}{3}$$

This technique helps students make the connection between learning multiplication combinations and computing problems with fractions, and it provides additional practice with multiplication combinations.

Money, Decimals, and Percentages

Teach money and decimals together because they have a natural connection. Mastery of money and decimals is a life skill; they may have more relevance for students if taught together. Use number combinations that have been taught and mastered during study of whole-number computation. Use the newspaper or advertising circulars to teach and reinforce money, decimals, percentages, and computational skills. Computing the prices of items, spending a designated amount of money by shopping the sales, and comparison shopping are all activities that require students to use money, decimals, percentages, and computational skills.

Algebra is an important area that requires careful attention. We take a look at it in the next section.

ALGEBRA AND HOW IT IS TAUGHT

Algebra uses mathematical statements to describe relationships between things that vary over time. Algebra is about finding the unknown. Algebra is identified as the gateway to college readiness; students must be prepared to be successful with algebraic content (NCTM, 2000; NMAP, 2008). Algebraic reasoning and the development of algebraic concepts require the use of models and algebraic symbols to represent problems and quantitative relationships and strategies to construct and solve simple to complex equations. Algebraic reasoning relies on patterns; variables, equality, and equations; symbolism; and relations, functions, and representations (Allsopp et al., 2018; Van de Walle et al., 2016). For students at risk and students with mathematics disabilities who find mathematics difficult, adaptations are critical to helping them succeed with algebraic content and developing their potential to pursue higher education.

Difficulties With Algebra

Difficulties with algebra stem from a variety of problems, including difficulties mastering number combinations and understanding the vocabulary used in algebraic reasoning. As noted in the problem-solving section later in this chapter, students who demonstrate mathematical difficulties typically exhibit poor performance in solving word problems, which are an important component of algebraic study. Another challenge is understanding equivalence. Students must understand the idea of equivalence to be able to interpret equations of the type $2x - 10 = 3x + 7$. Students also need to understand the roles of a variable such as a specific value and varying quantities. Finally, limited algebraic thinking impedes some students' success. Algebraic thinking means thinking about underlying mathematical structures to analyze, generalize, model, justify, or prove quantitative relationships (Byrd et al., 2015; Dougherty et al., 2015; Dougherty et al., 2021; Kieran, 2004).

Teaching Algebraic Reasoning

Students who are well on their way to mastering the concepts and skills addressed earlier in this chapter are ready for the exciting challenge of algebraic reasoning.

- Diagnosis: Use the think-aloud process with specific problems to assess the level of students' reasoning.
- Instructional content: Make connections in activities among patterns, functions, and variables. For example, students can identify and extend a pattern, represent the relationship in a table, identify the functional relationship formula, and predict the next response in a table by using the formula.
- Instructional content: Teach the mathematical properties presented in Table 13.9. These properties are part of algebraic reasoning and are important concepts for students to understand. Even if remembering the name of the property is an issue, students must develop conceptual understanding of how numbers are related and how values are influenced by the properties in this table.
- Instructional materials: Use a mathematics balance to help students visualize equalities. The pan balance allows for comparisons of numeric or algebraic expressions. Students can practice arithmetic and algebraic skills and investigate the important concept of equivalence (see Figure 13.3).
- Vocabulary: Check student understanding of the key vocabulary of algebraic instruction.
- Strategies: Provide specific strategies and teach using the think aloud procedure so students learn how to solve equations and word problems.

TABLE 13.9 ■ Mathematical Properties

Property	Formula
Identity Property of Addition: Any number plus zero equals the number; the value does not change.	$n + 0 = n$
Commutative Property of Addition: The order in which numbers are added does not change the answer.	$a + b = b + a$
Associative Property of Addition: When adding, the grouping does not change the answer.	$a + (b + c) = (a + b) + c$
Identity Property of Multiplication: Any number times one equals the number; the value does not change.	$n \times 1 = n$
Commutative Property of Multiplication: The order in which numbers are multiplied does not change the answer.	$a \times b = b \times a$
Associative Property of Multiplication: When multiplying, the grouping does not change the answer.	$a \times (b \times c) = (a \times b) \times c$
Distributive Property of Multiplication: The product can be written as the sum of two products.	$a \times (b + c) = (a \times b) + (a \times c)$

FIGURE 13.3 ■ Pan Balance: Representation of the equation 3k + 10 = 16

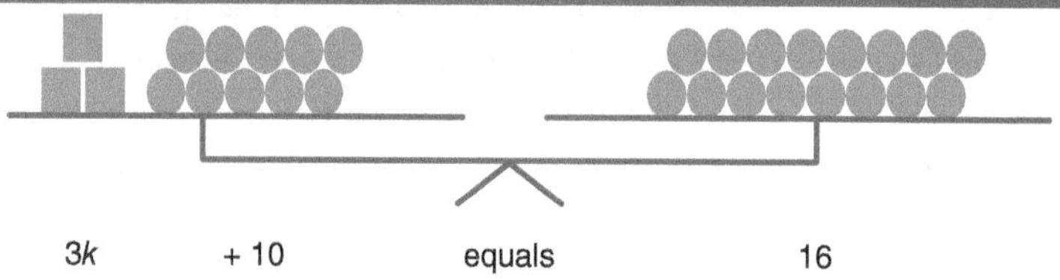

- Technology: Teach students how to use graphing calculators to plot points and draw curves when graphing patterns (Van de Walle et al., 2016). Refer to the applets on the e-Standards published by the NCTM. The applets feature the connection between word problems as real-life situations and graphs and equations. For instance, students can manipulate a situation involving runners and their speed, distance, and time from a starting point. As the students manipulate the variables, the relationship among these variables can be graphed. Finally, review the National Library of Virtual Manipulatives to determine how algebraic concepts can be represented using virtual manipulatives.

Fact Families

Explain to students that fact families are three numbers that are related, just as the people in a family are related. For example, the numbers 2, 5, and 7 can be used to make two addition problems (2 + 5 = 7 and 5 + 2 = 7) and two subtraction problems (7 – 5 = 2 and 7 – 2 = 5). Demonstrate with manipulatives the commutative property and subtraction as the inverse of addition. Provide students with many opportunities to create their own "families." Have them write equations for their problems. Use Figure 13.4 to convey the notion of family and to give students a place to write the number sentences for their fact families. Note that the family of facts in Figure 13.4 also can be used to teach fact families for number combinations.

Solving Algebraic Equations

Teach students a strategy for solving algebraic equations. The following strategy requires students to ask themselves questions to guide their thinking through the steps (Allsopp et al., 2018):

Solve: $5x = 25$

FIGURE 13.4 ■ Family of Facts

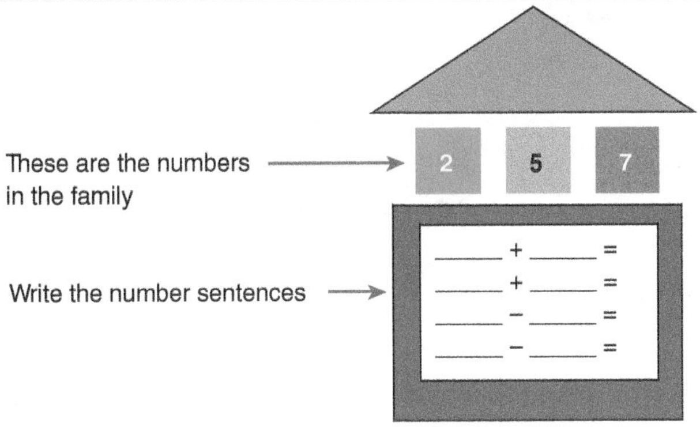
These are the numbers in the family
2
5
7
Write the number sentences
___ + ___ =
___ + ___ =
___ − ___ =
___ − ___ =

1. Is there a letter?

   "There is a letter that represents a variable. I need to figure out the value of the variable."

2. What is on each side of the equals sign?

   "There is $5x$ and 25, and $5x$ means 5 times x."

3. What is the value for x?

   "I know that 5 times 5 equals 25, so the value of x is 5."

Order of Operations

Teach students the order in which operations are used to solve equations. The standard order follows:

1. Perform all operations within parentheses and brackets.
2. Evaluate each power (exponent).
3. Do all multiplications and divisions, from left to right.
4. Do all additions and subtractions, from left to right.

Teachers frequently teach students to use the mnemonic "Please Excuse My Dear Aunt Sally" as a way to remember the order of operations. "Please" is a reminder for parentheses, "Excuse" stands for exponents, "My" refers to multiplication, "Dear" means division, "Aunt" is a reminder for addition, and "Sally" means subtraction.

Provide examples of equations for which students have to explain how to solve the problem using the order of operations rules. Create a poster and bookmark with the order information as a cue for those students who may need help remembering it.

Graphic Organizers

Use graphic organizers as a way to help students visualize mathematical relationships, vocabulary, and concepts. Venn diagrams can demonstrate similarities and differences between two concepts; hierarchical diagrams can show subordinate relationships to a superordinate concept; and mapping diagrams (see Figure 13.5) can depict how information about concepts can be organized (Maccini & Gagnon, 2005). Figure 13.5 shows the four operations and terms that convey each. Students must show they understand what operation each term represents as they encounter them in algebraic equations by explaining the meaning of each term.

The Working Together feature shows how individuals with different expertise collaborate to provide mathematics instruction to all students in an inclusive classroom and intensive interventions to those students who require additional support. You will see how teachers structure algebra instruction, making use of a block model to increasingly intensify instruction for struggling students.

FIGURE 13.5 ■ Graphic Organizer

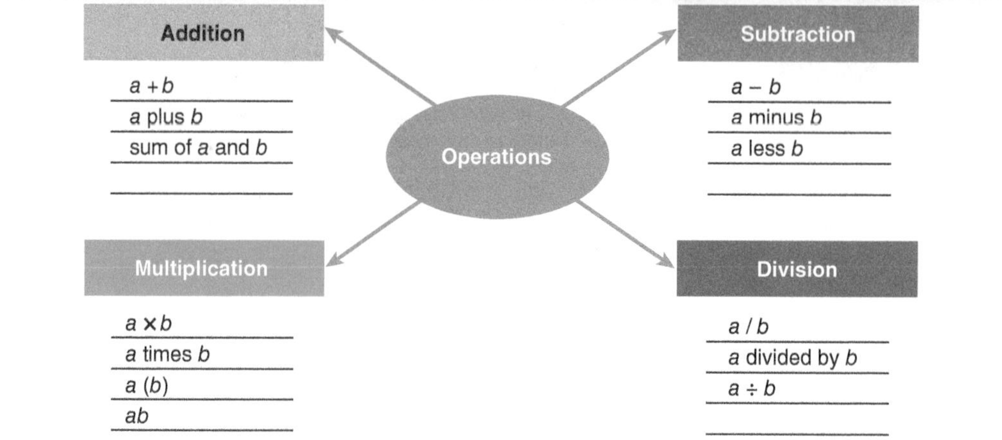

Source: Adapted from Maccini and Gagnon (2005). Reprinted with permission.

WORKING TOGETHER

COLLABORATING TO SUPPORT STRUGGLING STUDENTS IN ALGEBRA

Parkview High School is located in an urban school district in which a large percentage of students are eligible for free or reduced-price lunch. All students take algebra; those who require more intensive intervention have a double block of algebra each day. Approximately one third of the ninth graders need this type of model because of low performance and behavioral issues such as low attendance and low task completion. The principal and the mathematics department chair worked with the data management team to pull other sources of data to develop profiles of students' mathematics difficulties. Ms. Martinez, the mathematics teacher; Mr. Wilson, the mathematics interventionist teacher; and Ms. Rodriguez, the special education teacher worked together to provide differentiated and supplemental instruction when progress-monitoring data indicated a need to intervene.

The double block includes regular, Tier 1 intervention in the first part of class, taught by Ms. Martinez, and intensified Tiers 2 or 3 intervention taught by Mr. Wilson and Ms. Rodriguez, respectively, during the second part of the block class. Students are grouped into small homogeneous groups, based on progress-monitoring data related to algebraic concepts, and taught strategies for solving equations. The vocabulary of each lesson is carefully taught, and students are required to engage with the mathematics by explaining what they are doing, justifying answers, and problem solving. Students use multiple representations to model the mathematics. Ms. Martinez, Mr. Wilson, and Ms. Rodriguez use a three-station coteaching model for instruction. In one station, Ms. Martinez teaches the mathematics; in the second, Mr. Wilson teaches the strategies; and in the third station, Ms. Rodriguez works with students to provide individualized problems for practicing the content.

Depending on the day, Ms. Martinez can be reviewing, Mr. Wilson can be reteaching, and Ms. Rodriguez can be providing individualized instruction for students who continue to struggle with the concepts. During their planning time, the three teachers review each student's progress-monitoring data to choose next steps for the following day, which could include regrouping students and intensifying instruction.

Questions

1. Is there another coteaching model Ms. Martinez, Mr. Wilson, and Ms. Rodriguez could consider for the double block of algebra intervention? What might this other model offer that is different from the stations model?
2. What activities might Ms. Martinez, Mr. Wilson, and Ms. Rodriguez develop together for the stations model where students are working independently so they remain engaged?
3. How can Ms. Martinez, Mr. Wilson, and Ms. Rodriguez work together to help students who have struggled for years in mathematics deal with possible motivation issues?

Problem solving is one of the most important areas in mathematics. In the next section, we discuss a variety of ways to teach this subject.

PROBLEM SOLVING AND HOW IT IS TAUGHT

Problem solving is a basic life skill as well as an essential component of a total mathematics program (NCTM, 2000; NMAP, 2008; Woodward et al., 2012), emphasized in the CCSSM (Council of Chief State School Officers & National Governors' Association, 2010).

You can develop word problems from classroom and daily life situations that require problem solving. Connect conceptual and skill development to problem solving by integrating whole-number computation, fractions, decimals, percentages, and algebraic equations into word problems students can solve that reflect real-life situations.

Mayer (1998) identified five types of knowledge needed to solve word problems: (a) linguistic (English language and syntax), (b) semantic (understanding of the meaning of words), (c) schematic (knowledge of word problem types and recognition of irrelevant information), (d) strategic (ability to plan and monitor solution strategies), and (e) procedural (ability to perform a sequence of operations). As noted by Montague et al. (2011), good problem solvers use a variety of cognitive and metacognitive strategies to solve word problems, such as rereading, drawing pictures, identifying important information, and disregarding extraneous information.

Difficulties With Problem Solving

Students with mathematical difficulties struggle to solve word problems for a variety of reasons. They might not understand how to use the five types of knowledge or schema for solving word problems (Jitendra et al., 2007). They might not recognize the types of word problem structures or choose an appropriate solution strategy to solve the problem (Powell, 2011; Shin & Bryant, 2015). They might have problems applying multiple steps within word problems (Shin & Bryant, 2015) or selecting and using the correct algorithms (Hecht et al., 2003). Students might use the key word strategy in which they read a problem and interpret a key word, such as *together* or *less*, incorrectly and thus arrive at an inaccurate solution. In fact, teachers teach key words thinking that they will help students solve problems more accurately. But key words can be misleading. The takeaway message is, "Do not teach key words" (Powell, 2018). Moreover, students have been shown to have difficulties paraphrasing what they were being asked to do in the problem and visually representing the process and solution (Krawec, 2014).

Solving real-world word problems is a basic life skill and is recommended as a major component of the mathematics curriculum.

iStock.com/Maica

Types of Word Problems

The word problems typically found in elementary curricula require (a) join, part-part-whole, separate, and compare for addition and subtraction, and (b) equal-groups, multiplicative comparisons, combinations, and product-of-measures problems for multiplication and division (Van de Walle et al., 2012). Mayer (1998) indicated that interest, area, mixture, river current, probability, number, work, navigation, progressions, exponentials, triangles, distance/rate/time, averages, scale conversion, and ratio problem categories are typically included in secondary-level textbooks.

In some cases, students with limited reading abilities have difficulty solving story problems simply because they are unable to read the words. Adapting instruction might be the answer to this type of problem. For instance, story problems could be presented on audiotape as well as on paper so that difficult words are read aloud to the students. Another way to address low reading levels is to have students work in cooperative learning or peer-tutoring arrangements. A student with a more advanced reading level could be the designated reader for the other student or students. A third possibility is to have students work individually or in small groups with the teacher, a family member volunteer, or the paraprofessional. This individualized attention could easily address the reading-level problem and provide additional support in solving story problems. A fourth option could include controlling the reading level of the word problems to more closely match the reading level of the students. By carefully selecting words, teachers can address the reading level more adequately in some cases.

Teaching Problem Solving

The general steps for teaching problem solving follow:

- Diagnosis: Use clinical interview procedures to assess the reasons for difficulty solving problems. (These might include language, numbers that are too big, reading problems, extraneous information, or linguistic structure.) Rewrite problems accordingly. In some cases, someone might need to read problems to students who have serious reading issues.
- Instructional delivery: Include problems with too little or too much information; ask students to tell what is needed or what is extra.
- Instructional delivery: Have students write story problems for peers to solve.
- Instructional delivery: Have students substitute smaller numbers for larger numbers that may be troublesome. Students can (a) use manipulatives to depict problems, (b) use charts and tables to organize information, (c) solve problems containing more than one right answer, (d) devise their own story problems, (e) solve real problems (situations in the classroom or current events), and (f) focus on the language of the story problem by explaining problems with varying linguistic, symbolic, and extraneous information in their own words.
- Strategy instruction: Teach explicit strategies. Refer to Instructional Strategy 13.1 for ways to teach problem solving. Refer to What Works Clearinghouse (Institute of Education Sciences, 2012) for an evidence-based practice guide on problem solving.
- Calculations: Have students use calculators to check their work.
- Progress monitoring: Monitor student performance regularly. Provide several problems for students to solve independently. Ask them to show their work, including the ways they both make a plan for and perform their calculations.

Instructional Strategy 13.2 provides an example of teaching procedures that focuses on geometry instruction.

One of the most useful applications of algebraic reasoning is in using equations to solve word problems. Figure 13.6 shows three examples of strategies that teachers can use to help students become more

FIGURE 13.6 ■ Fast Draw

Fast

1. F ind what you're solving for.
2. A sk yourself, "What are the parts of the problem?"
3. S et up the numbers.
4. T ie down the sign.

Draw

1. D iscover the sign.
2. R ead the problem.
3. A nswer, or draw and check.
4. W rite the answer.

Questions and actions is a cognitive strategy with the steps spelled out. The questions help students to monitor their action and are an example of the metacognitive part to this strategy.

Questions and Actions

Step	Questions	Actions
Read the problem.	Are there words I don't know? Do I know what each word means? Do I need to reread the problem? Are there number words?	Underline words. Find out definitions. Reread. Underline.
Restate the problem.	What information is important? What information isn't needed? What is the question asking?	Underline. Cross out. Put in own words.
Develop a plan.	What are the facts? How can they be organized? How many steps are there? What operations will I use?	Make a list. Develop a chart. Use manipulatives. Use smaller numbers. Select an operation.
Compute the problem.	Did I get the correct answer?	Estimate. Check with partner. Verify with a calculator.
Examine the results.	Have I answered the question? Does my answer seem reasonable? Can I restate the question and answer?	Reread the question. Check the question and answer. Write a number sentence.

The math scene investigator is a cognitive strategy that has specific steps for students to follow as they work with word problems. It has been used with younger students but could be taught to middle school students who struggle with word problems, as well.

Math Scene Investigator[2]

Step	Actions Within Each Step
Inspect and find clues.	Read the problem.
	Underline the question and the unit.
	Circle important information.
	Cross out extraneous information.
Plan and solve.	Draw a picture to solve.
	Write the equation.
Retrace.	Write the related fact equation.

Sources: [1]Adapted from Mercer and Miller (1992); [2]Pfannenstiel et al. (2015).

skillful problem solvers: fast draw, questions and actions, and math scene investigator. Students with mathematics difficulties benefit from learning cognitive and metacognitive strategies to help them work with problems.

INSTRUCTIONAL STRATEGY 13.2

GEOMETRY, MEASUREMENT, PROBLEM SOLVING: BUYING SOD FOR THE BACKYARD

Instructional Objective: The student will use a strategy to solve a multistep problem.
Instructional Content: Problem solving, number and operation, geometry, measurement, algebra (conceptual understanding)
Instructional Materials: Graph paper, recording sheet
Instructional Delivery: Grouping: Small group of students; Vocabulary: area, square, foot
Before teaching the lesson, review the vocabulary terms. Have students define the terms in their own words. Use visuals for English learners.

Teaching Procedure

1. Provide directions to the whole class for the activity:
   "In small groups, you are going to work together to generate a solution to the following problem. You are going to lay sod in your backyard. Sod is sold in squares measuring 12 inches by 12 inches. The backyard is 50 feet by 72 feet. Draw on graph paper a diagram of the backyard area you wish to sod. Sod goes for $0.85 a square. How much will enough sod to complete the project cost? Solve the problem and record your group's answer and reasoning."
2. Tell students that each one of them should write, on their recording sheet, what the problem is asking, strategies for solving the problem, and the calculations.
3. Circulate among groups, asking questions to promote discussion and problem solving.
4. Have a speaker from each small group explain to the whole class how the group solved the problem.

Progress Monitoring (Independent Practice): After the lesson, give each student four problems to solve independently. Ask students to draw a diagram to represent each problem and to show all calculations.

Source: Bryant et al. (2006).

Fast draw 1 uses a mnemonic, FAST DRAW, for students to learn and then to apply to word problems. It is important that students memorize the mnemonic and the steps for each letter before using the strategy. The goal is that students can use this strategy independently, but they must learn the mnemonic first.

Think back to the Opening Challenge with Ms. Kellogg. ADAPT in Action provides information about how Ms. Kellogg approached problem-solving instruction with her students with mathematics difficulties and disabilities.

ADAPT IN ACTION

MS. KELLOGG: PROBLEM-SOLVING INSTRUCTION

Ms. Kellogg has students with identified mathematics disabilities who are having trouble, and other students are struggling as well. She decides to provide a problem-solving lesson that incorporates skills from the different areas of the curriculum. The problem will require the use of geometry, measurement, and algebra. She wants students to develop their strategies for solving the problems and to present their solution strategies to the class as a learning experience.

During group work, Ms. Kellogg will look for students' ability to read the problem, paraphrase what the problem is asking, identify relevant information, identify and use a strategy with visuals, and calculate the answer. She will also observe the students' engagement by sitting with each group for 10 minutes to observe who is participating, how frequently, and what they are discussing.

Following the lesson, Ms. Kellogg reviews her progress-monitoring data and learns that at least one student in each group makes infrequent or no contributions to the discussion of how to solve the problem. Her struggling students who did not perform well on the progress-monitoring problems need adapted instruction. She decides to use the ADAPT Framework to figure out her next steps.

A: Ask, "What am I requiring the student to do?" Ms. Kellogg wants the students to solve problems using strategies, including multiple representations. She also wants them to compute the calculations correctly.

D: Determine the prerequisite skills of the task. "I know students need to read the problem, figure out what it is asking (including identifying whether there is extraneous information and whether it is a multistep problem), set up a plan using visuals, and calculate the answer."

A: Analyze the student's strengths and struggles. At least five students in each class period had difficulty identifying a plan to solve the problem, did not show the work for each step of a multistep problem, and made calculation errors.

P: Propose and implement adaptations from among the four categories. Ms. Kellogg decides to use the questions and actions strategy shown earlier to help students work through each step of the problem-solving process. This strategy taps both the cognitive (steps) and metacognitive (self-questioning) aspects of problem solving.

T: Test to determine whether the adaptations helped the student accomplish the task. Ms. Kellogg will continue to collect progress-monitoring data and group observation information to determine whether students use the steps of the questions and actions strategy in their small group work and whether their independent performance improves.

ADAPT Framework: Problem Solving

A ASK "What am I requiring the student to do?"	D DETERMINE the prerequisite skills of the task.	A ANALYZE the student's strengths and struggles. Strengths	Struggles	P PROPOSE and implement adaptations from among the four categories.	T TEST to determine whether the adaptations helped the student to accomplish the task.
Solve problems using strategies, including visual representations.	**1.** Read the problem.	1			
	2. Figure out what it is asking.	2			
	3. Set up a plan using visuals.		3	**3.** Instructional activity:	**3.** and 4: Use progress monitoring and observations to determine progress and success.
	4. Calculate the answer.		4	**4.** Use the Question and Actions strategy.	
				5. Instructional material: Use a calculator to self-heck.	

UNIVERSAL DESIGN FOR LEARNING IN ACTION

UNIVERSAL DESIGN FOR LEARNING LESSON

Note: This Universal Design for Learning (UDL)-based lesson was developed, in part, using the CAST UDL Lesson Builder: http://lessonbuilder.cast.org/.

The UDL framework (version 2.2) consists of three main principles (I. Representation, II. Action and Expression, and III. Engagement; CAST, 2018). Each principle has three guidelines and several checkpoints that explain them in greater depth. In this lesson plan, we delineate how various instructional strategies meet the UDL checkpoints.

Lesson Overview

Title: Using grids to learn percentages.
Subject: Mathematics: Number and operation-percentage
Grade Level: 6
Duration: 45 minutes

Unit Description

This lesson is part of a group of lessons that focus on the relationships among percentages, fractions, and decimals.

Lesson Description for Day

Prerequisite skills: Ability to communicate verbally

Goals

Unit Goals: The goal of this unit is to understand the relationships among percentages, fractions, and decimals.
Lesson Goals: The purpose of this lesson is to introduce the concept of percentage using a 10 × 10 grid.

Methods

Anticipatory Set:
Tell the students that the purpose of the day's lesson is to help them become familiar with the concept of a percentage to prepare for further lessons about the relationships among percentages, fractions, and decimals. They will need to understand how these concepts are related and ways for representing similar quantities.
Introduce and Model New Knowledge:

1. Introduce the mathematical term *percent* and the symbol that denotes percent. Explain that percent means one part in a hundred. Show pictures from newspaper clippings that use percent and the % symbol to discuss sales (*Checkpoint 2.1: Clarify vocabulary and symbols*). Have students provide real-life examples of items that they and their family buy on sale and what bargains they look for, such as 50% off (*Checkpoint 3.1: Activate or supply background knowledge*).
2. Explain that they are going to use the concept of percent for planting a garden. Read the problem to the students:

   Ms. Sanchez is going to plant a garden this spring. She has a plot of land that she will divide into parts so that she can plant both flowers and vegetables. Ms. Sanchez knows that she wants more land devoted to flowers and that the remaining land will be for different types of vegetables. She decides to draw a grid to help her visualize what the garden might look like.
3. Using National Library of Virtual Manipulatives (http://nlvm.usu.edu/en/nav/vlibrary.html) grids, show students models of what Ms. Sanchez's garden might look like (*Checkpoint 5.2: Use multiple tools for construction and composition*).
4. Show a percentage and ask students what the grid would look like given the percentage, so that they can work from a number to shading a grid and from a shaded grid to providing a percentage to help students become comfortable with using the virtual manipulatives (*Checkpoint 3.3: Guide information processing, visualization, and manipulation*).

Provide Guided Practice:

1. Have students work in pairs at computer stations to use the virtual manipulative grid to create pictorial scenarios of what Ms. Sanchez's garden might look like.
2. Have student pairs share with each other their ideas and use the term *percent* as they describe their plot of land's partitions (*Checkpoint 7.1: Optimize individual choice and autonomy*).

Provide Independent Practice: At the end of the lesson, give students scenarios for the garden and have them show their gardens.

SUMMARY

It is important for teachers to challenge their students to achieve mathematical competence. It is equally important for teachers to provide appropriate instructional adaptations for those students who are most in need of academic assistance. For students with mathematics disabilities, adaptations are important to help them participate in classroom discussions and learn mathematical skills and concepts emphasized in the NCTM standards.

Instructional adaptations are necessary to help students benefit from instruction in the general education setting. This chapter offers ideas about adaptations for early number development; number combinations; place value; whole-number computation; fractions, decimals, and percentages; algebra; and problem solving. Keep in mind that other areas addressed in the Common Core State Standards (e.g., measurement, geometry, and statistics and probability) also require adapted instruction.

REVIEW THE LEARNING OBJECTIVES

Let's review the learning objectives for this chapter. If you are uncertain and cannot talk through the answers provided for any of these questions, reread those sections of the text.

13.1. Explain the characteristics of students with mathematics difficulties and attributes of effective instruction.

Students with mathematics difficulties can display problems with language processing, working memory and executive functioning, and cognitive development. Students with significant cognitive disabilities will need an alternative curriculum for mathematics with a focus on life skills, particularly as they get older. Students exhibit problems with a variety of math skills and concepts, including arithmetic and whole-number computation, place value, rational numbers, algebraic thinking, and problem solving. Attributes of effective instruction include instructional delivery features that are intended to help students learn mathematical content for their grade level or that is developmentally appropriate.

13.2. Describe early number development and how it is taught.

Early number development describes a variety of skills and concepts—which involve number sense—that typically emerge and are taught in preschool, kindergarten, first grade, and second grade. Teaching early numbers involves number and operation concepts.

13.3. Name the number combinations and describe how they are taught.

Instruction in number combinations consists of developing declarative and procedural knowledge and conceptual understanding. In the elementary grades, students are taught different strategies, such as counting on, for learning these number combinations.

13.4. Explain place value and describe how it is taught.

Place value refers to the base-10 system, which is an important component of mathematics instruction. Teaching place value involves the use of manipulatives and activities to promote the concept of regrouping and the base-10 system.

13.5. Explain whole-number computation and describe how it is taught.
Whole-number computation requires an understanding of the relationship between numbers and place value, estimating, determining the reasonableness of answers, and using appropriate algorithms. Teaching whole number computation involves error analysis to determine remedial strategies, the use of manipulatives, and strategies or algorithms for solving problems.

13.6. Explain rational numbers and describe how they are taught.
Rational numbers include the whole numbers and integers, numbers that can be written as the quotient of two integers, a ÷ b, where b is not zero; and fractions, decimals, and percentages. Teaching involves the use of manipulatives and opportunities to practice the concepts associated with rational numbers.

13.7. Explain algebra and describe how it is taught.
Algebra uses mathematical statements to describe relationships between things that vary over time. Algebraic reasoning and the development of algebraic concepts require the use of models and algebraic symbols to represent problems and quantitative relationships and strategies to construct and solve simple-to-complex equations.

13.8. Explain problem solving and describe how it is taught.
Problem solving is a process that involves understanding word problem structures and how to translate these structures into equations to solve the problem. Problem solving is taught through various cognitive and metacognitive strategies and should include real-world problems.

REVISIT THE OPENING CHALLENGE

Check your answers to the Reflection Questions from the Opening Challenge and revise them on the basis of what you have learned.

1. What mathematical learning characteristics might be contributing to the students' learning difficulties?
2. How can Mr. Jamison and Ms. Kellogg use the features of effective mathematics instruction to structure their lessons?
3. What instructional adaptations can be implemented to help students access the mathematics curriculum?
4. What suggestions do you have on ways in which these teachers can monitor student progress?

KEY TERMS

algorithmic
base-10
diagnostic teaching
dyscalculia
executive functioning
number sense
partial products
think aloud
working memory

PROFESSIONAL STANDARDS AND LICENSURE

For a complete description of Professional Standards and Licensure, please see the appendix.

CEC Initial Preparation Standards

Standard 1: Learner Development and Individual Learning Differences

Standard 3: Curricular Content Knowledge

Standard 4: Assessment

Standard 5: Instructional Planning and Strategies

INTASC Core Principles

Standard 1: Learner Development

Standard 2: Learning Differences

Standard 4: Content Knowledge

Standard 6: Assessment

Standard 7: Planning for Instruction

Standard 8: Instructional Strategies

Standard 9: Professional Learning and Ethical Practice

Praxis II: Education of Exceptional Students: Core Content Knowledge

I. Understanding Exceptionalities: Human Development and Behavior

III. Delivery of Services to Students: Background Knowledge

COMMON CORE STATE STANDARDS

Mathematical Practices

Make sense of problems and persevere in solving them.

Reason abstractly and quantitatively.

Construct viable arguments and critique the reasoning of others.

Model with mathematics.

Use appropriate tools strategically.

Attend to precision.

Look for and make use of structure.

Look for and express regularity in repeated reasoning.

Domains

Counting and Cardinality K.CC

Operations and Algebraic Thinking K, 1,2,3,4,5.OA

Number and Operations in Base Ten K, 1,2,3,4,5.NBT

Number and Operations—Fractions 3,4,5.NF

Ratios and Proportional Relationships 6,7.RP

The Number System 6,7,8.NS

Expressions and Equations 6,7,8.EE

Functions 8, HS.F

Measurement and Data K,1,2,3,4,5.MD

Geometry K,1,2,3,4,5,6,7,8, HS.G

Statistics and Probability 6,7,8, HS.SP

Number and Quantity HS

Algebra HS

Modeling HS

Troy Aossey/Getty Images

14 FACILITATING CONTENT-AREA INSTRUCTION AND STUDY SKILLS

LEARNING OBJECTIVES

After studying this chapter, you will be able to meet the following learning objectives:

14.1 Explain the difficulties students demonstrate with content-area instruction.

14.2 Describe how teachers can teach content-area vocabulary and concepts.

14.3 Explain how teachers can teach students to monitor their reading comprehension.

14.4 Describe how students can learn from textbook instruction.

14.5 Explain how teachers can promote student participation.

14.6 Describe how teachers can help students with difficulties in study skills.

14.7 Name ways to facilitate memorization and test taking.

Opening Challenge

Facilitating Content-Area Instruction and Study Skills

Elementary Grades. Mrs. Gonzales is in her 15th year of teaching fifth grade in a middle-class suburban school district whose demographics reflect a rich cultural diversity. Fewer than 30% of enrolled students are eligible for free or reduced-cost meals. Several of Mrs. Gonzales's 27 students have learning disabilities, and two are being referred for possible attention deficit hyperactivity disorder. Reviewing results from the survey she gave the class, Mrs. Gonzales found that few had time management skills or strategies to help them understand content-area expository texts. She notes, *"Most of my students have good decoding skills and can read fairly fluently. However, clearly I have to help them read their content textbooks successfully. Time management skills showed similarly poor results on the survey. My students did not identify a plan for taking notes or studying for tests, and few spend uninterrupted time studying. Those who have learning disabilities are extremely capable, but they need help to benefit from content-area instruction and to implement effective study skills. Some of my English learners also need help with vocabulary and comprehension strategies for textbook reading if they are to avoid being at a serious disadvantage when they go into middle school next year."*

Secondary Grades. Mr. Kim is in his ninth year of teaching honors and general history in the 10th, 11th, and 12th grades in an urban school district. His students span a range of academic abilities, and most are eligible for free or reduced-cost lunch. Several have reading disabilities, one has a mild developmental disability, and several are English learners. His classes range in size from 15 to 37 students and encompass many ethnic and linguistic backgrounds. Mr. Kim recognizes that students need strategies to learn the content and concepts in their history textbooks. He wants to prepare them to handle the demands of a postsecondary education, but many cannot describe what good note-taking and test-preparation practices look like or how to budget their time. He reflects, *"I use the textbooks as a starting point for my teaching and build on the information in them through lectures and hands-on activities. History has to come alive for my students, not just be a recounting of the past. But my students have to be able to grasp the concepts and learn the vocabulary from the text to understand what I am teaching."*

Reflection Questions

In your journal, write down your answers to the following questions. After completing the chapter, check your answers and revise them on the basis of what you have learned.

1. What difficulties might students in both teachers' classes exhibit with regard to content-area instruction and study skills?
2. How can the teachers effectively work with their students to help them become efficient learners in content-area instruction and study skills?
3. How can these teachers provide adapted lessons to students who require intensive intervention, while keeping the rest of the class busy with relevant work?
4. How can study skills assessment be used to identify how students, including struggling students, become more efficient learners?

As students progress from the upper elementary grades to middle school and to high school, teachers teach their content-area material and students use study skills such as taking notes. Students must now read textbooks at their grade level (or above their grade level or reading level); write reports and papers, using technology such as laptops, desktop computers, or tablets; take notes, often using portable devices such as tablets or smartphones in the classroom or the library; and participate in discussions and activities. Students must also complete homework, take tests, conduct research, and manage their time across subject areas. Because teachers have to cover a great deal of instructional content, instructional pacing might not align with the learning needs of struggling students who need a lot of practice to master material. Students with unique learning needs or disabilities are often challenged to keep up with their classmates.

Content-area instruction focuses on teaching students content-area knowledge in mathematics, social studies, science, and literature. Secondary teachers use instructional approaches for teaching content-area material to students. Content-area instruction involves teachers presenting lectures on textbook content and students reading their textbooks to identify important facts and concepts for weekly quizzes or tests (Bryant et al., 2015). Content-area instruction includes student-centered activities, which engage students in the learning process. Students solve problems, discuss issues, and work alone or in small groups to create products. Teachers facilitate student learning by providing hands-on activities, asking lower- and higher-order questions, and leading discussions. In content-area classes, students need to be able to read and understand textbooks and to engage in class discussions and questioning.

Effective study skills are needed for students to learn from textbooks, teachers' lectures, and class discussions. Additionally, students need to use effective study skills. Hoover and Patton (2007) explained, "Study skills are specific skills employed to acquire, record, remember, and use information efficiently" (p. 2). Time management is a very important skill. Students must be able to manage their time. Students must also be able to concentrate in class and at home as they study and complete homework. Effective listening skills are needed to listen to lectures and discussions so they can take notes on important information. Memorizing information is another skill needed to study. Additionally, students must take objective and short-answer tests to pass their classes. Study skills must be directly taught, but this doesn't always happen (Lavenstein, 2015). Rather, students may have to learn these skills from helpful teachers, peers, parents, or online resources.

Because of the problems many students show with literacy skills, there is an increasing focus at the state and national levels on the literacy needs of struggling readers to identify ways to help them learn content-area material. Teachers desire strategies to help their students understand material in textbooks such as key concepts and terminology (Vaughn & Bos, 2015). However, in our work with content-area teachers, we have found that many do not view themselves as reading specialists. Teachers may be frustrated and concerned when some students lack the basic skills needed to be successful in their classes (Bryant et al., 2015).

In this chapter, we provide an overview of content-area instruction and study skills, and we teach about the difficulties faced by students who struggle in these areas and the teachers responsible for meeting their needs. Instructional strategies and adaptations based on the ADAPT Framework are provided to help you teach students who need extra instructional support.

DIFFICULTIES STUDENTS DEMONSTRATE WITH CONTENT-AREA INSTRUCTION

Struggling readers are challenged by reading and understanding content in textbooks. Moreover, struggling older students often read well below grade level and have difficulty understanding the information from their textbooks (Bryant et al., 2015; Vaughn et al., 2010). Struggling readers do not have strategies for learning vocabulary, monitoring their reading, and dealing with content in print. In addition, activities that require discussion and small-group participation can be problematic because students have not learned the content well enough to help them contribute.

Students with challenges do not learn the meanings of vocabulary and concept knowledge at the same rate as other students. Students who have reading disabilities likely will have poorer vocabularies than better readers. This is so because vocabulary learning happens as students read various types of materials. Consequently, the gap between good and poor readers will grow larger over time (Stone & Urquhart, 2008). Another issue is that students lack strategies for learning vocabulary and struggle with the multiple meanings of words, word origins, or derivational meanings—which are meanings of words formed from other words, such as when prefixes, suffixes, or inflectional endings that are added to base words. Using a dictionary to look up the meanings of words and using context clues in text may not be useful strategies because dictionaries may be too difficult to comprehend, or the context may not provide clues for figuring out word meanings.

Understanding reading material requires us to think about and construct meaning before, during, and after reading by integrating information from the text material with our background knowledge (Lynch, 2014). Also, self-monitoring reading comprehension requires many skills. For instance, readers must activate their background knowledge about a topic, ask themselves questions, state main ideas and supporting details, paraphrase, and summarize information. Good readers monitor their comprehension of reading as they read, and they use strategies to foster comprehension and retention (Honig et al., 2012). We know that students who struggle with self-monitoring their reading comprehension lack the ability to establish a purpose for reading or activate background knowledge. These students do not have self-questioning abilities that ensure comprehension. Also, students' summarizing strategies are lacking (Schumaker & Deshler, 2006). Any one of these problems can seriously interfere with reading text and learning new concepts. Combined, they present serious reading challenges for struggling students, with and without disabilities.

When content-area instruction in science, history, and social studies focuses on the textbook as a primary source of information, the assumption is that students can read and understand **expository text**, which is explanatory or factual in structure and includes multisyllabic, technical words; various expository text structures (e.g., cause and effect, compare and contrast); and concepts and facts (Schumaker & Deshler, 2006). Research findings have shown a strong connection between students' understanding of text structure and their ability to understand their reading material (Butler et al., 2010). Students with reading difficulties who do not understand text structures likely will have difficulty deriving meaning from their content-area textbooks or other materials. Students may not use the **physical features of the text**, such as headings, tables, boldfaced terms, and chapter organizers and summaries.

Teaching the content-area vocabulary is a critical component of promoting reading comprehension. What method is this teacher using to teach vocabulary? What other methods might be helpful?

Compassionate Eye Foundation/Robert Kent/DigitalVision/Getty Images

Finally, in classrooms with student-centered activities, students with unique learning needs or disabilities may be challenged by instruction with group interactions, discussions, and product development. For instance, students may lack the basic reading and writing skills that are needed to contribute to group work assignments. Students may make connections to or recall previously taught material located in an earlier chapter or unit. Difficulty comprehending figurative and literal meanings and distinguishing between **connotative meanings** (i.e., associated meanings that enrich a word's primary meaning) and **denotative meanings** (i.e., dictionary definitions) can hinder students' ability to understand their readings and engage in discussions. Let's turn now to ways to teach content-area vocabulary and concepts.

TEACHING CONTENT-AREA VOCABULARY AND CONCEPTS

Good readers acquire vocabulary quickly during their school years (Honig et al., 2012). They learn about 3,000 new words every year as they read content-area materials and read independently. By the time they graduate from high school, most will have encountered more than 88,500 word families (consisting of a base word and its derivatives, such as *success* and *successfully*; Beck et al., 2013).

Each content area has its own concepts and technical vocabulary, the language students must learn if they are to comprehend specific information. A semantic concept is a general idea or understanding; it is a crucial word or phrase critical for grasping the content. Technical vocabulary includes words that relate specifically to each content area. For example, history students must understand the meaning of the technical term *transcontinental* as they read about westward migration and railroad expansion in the United States. They also need to understand the relationship between transcontinental and migratory patterns and the reasons people migrated west. To learn content-area material, students need strategies to develop an understanding of the meaning of concepts, in this case represented by the word *migration*, and their relationships to the content and the meaning of vocabulary words (Honig et al., 2012). Let's review some ideas for teaching technical vocabulary and concepts.

Teaching Technical Vocabulary and Concepts

Vacca et al. (2014) provided suggestions for helping students learn the meanings of new words and concepts that they encounter in content-area texts. We have blended these suggestions with the adaptation categories from the ADAPT Framework:

- **Instructional delivery**: Present new vocabulary in semantically related groups, which are groups of words with meaningful relationships.
- **Instructional delivery**: Teach students the meaning of the prefixes and the Greek and Latin roots used most frequently in specific content areas. For example, in social studies, teach *trans* (meaning over, across, beyond), *geo* (meaning earth), and *port* (meaning carry); in science, teach *bio* (meaning life), *ex* (meaning from, former), and *meter* (meaning measure).
- **Instructional activity**: Have students link new vocabulary with their background knowledge by describing what they already know about the topic (Beck et al., 2013).
- **Instructional activity**: Have students make up "kid-friendly" sentences using new vocabulary, such as "insisted means someone tells you strongly that you have to do something, like my mother insisted that I do my homework before watching TV" (Manyak et al., 2014, p. 16).
- **Instructional materials**: Have students develop word lists or banks.

- **Instructional materials**: Have students use typographic cues such as footnotes, italics, boldface print, and parenthetical definitions to define words. (See the next bullet for examples of parenthetical definitions.)
- **Instructional materials**: Have students use visual displays, including graphic organizers such as **hierarchical charts** (e.g., charts with broader concepts listed first, connected to supporting narrower concepts), **Venn diagrams** (i.e., intersecting shapes that show how concepts are similar and different), **semantic maps** (e.g., maps or webs of related words, vocabulary, concepts), and graphs.
- **Instructional delivery**: Help English learners by teaching academic language.
- **Instructional delivery**: Provide opportunities for gifted and/or talented students to work together to develop and expand their content vocabularies.

Now we examine specific instructional strategies to promote the understanding of content-area concepts and related vocabulary.

Considering Diversity: Teaching Students Who Are Gifted and/or Talented

Although secondary students who are gifted and/or talented may take advanced placement (AP) classes, you may find that your class includes students who are gifted or have special talents. Bauer et al. (n.d.) provided a number of recommendations that can be used to meet these students' unique needs. These suggestions are examples of good teaching and can be used with many students.

- **Compact the curriculum and provide enrichment activities**. Provide environments that are stimulating and address students' cognitive, physical, emotional, and social needs in the curriculum. Let the students move quickly through the required curriculum content and onto more advanced material. Allow for academic rigor.
- **Allow students to pursue independent projects based on their individual interests**. Assign independent projects based on your students' ability level. Encourage creativity and original thinking among gifted students. Allow them to explore ways of connecting unrelated issues in creative ways.
- **Teach interactively**. Have students work together, teach one another, and actively participate in their own and their classmates' education. Note: This example does not advocate gifted children being peer tutors in the classroom; the gifted student should be challenged as well. Emphasis should be on working together in the classroom. Cluster gifted children together at a table in your classroom and utilize advanced materials, as well as other suggested resources and modification, to meet their exceptional needs.
- **Explore multiple points of view about contemporary topics and provide students with opportunities to analyze and evaluate material**. Allow open forums and debates in the classroom about controversial issues. Utilize specialized training to ensure your ability to meet the needs of gifted students. Share personal interests with all students, to enrich and expand their world.
- **Do not assign extra work to gifted children who finish assignments early**. This is unfair and frustrating to them. Simply offering more of the same only restricts further learning. Instead, allow those children to work on independent projects or other unfinished work when they finish an assignment early.
- **Consider team teaching, collaboration, and consultation with other teachers**. Use the knowledge, skills, and support of other educators or professionals in the schools. In addition, attend professional development sessions that offer strategies to meet the needs of students who are gifted and/or talented.

Source: Adapted from Bauer et al. (n.d.).

INSTRUCTIONAL STRATEGY 14.1

SEMANTIC FEATURE ANALYSIS: CIVIL WAR BATTLES

Instructional Objective: The student will create a graphic display to connect a concept to related key vocabulary terms.
Instructional Content: Vocabulary from lessons
Instructional Materials: Concept, semantic feature analysis grid, vocabulary
Instructional Delivery: Grouping: Whole class for initial instruction; small groups for practice and sharing

Teaching Procedures

1. Identify the concept to teach.
2. Model how to complete a semantic feature analysis grid.
3. List the related vocabulary words down the left-hand column, and write the names of the features across the top row.
4. Review the vocabulary words to see whether they contain any of the features listed under characteristics; if so, have the students put a + in the corresponding box. If not, have students put a – in the box.
5. Have students provide a reason why they chose to put + or – in the box.
6. Have students work in small groups to complete a semantic feature analysis grid for a concept to be studied and related vocabulary words.
7. Have students explain their grids to the class.

A completed semantic feature analysis grid for some of the Civil War battles is shown in Table 14.1.

Progress Monitoring: Give students key concepts from a lesson, and have them generate related vocabulary.

Source: Vacca et al. (2014).

Evidence-Based Instructional Strategies

The following evidence-based instructional strategy provides effective ways to help students learn the meanings of technical words and concepts.

The semantic feature analysis grid is implemented as part of instruction (see Table 14.1). Returning to our Opening Challenge, recall the issues Mr. Kim faced with his class in terms of reading and vocabulary. The ADAPT in Action feature below shows how Mr. Kim can adapt instruction to address Cynthia's needs.

Now we focus on ways in which students can monitor their own reading comprehension.

TABLE 14.1 ■ Semantic Feature Analysis Grid

Concept: Civil War Battles	Characteristics			
	Fought in South	South Victories	1863	Ulysses S. Grant Involved
Vicksburg	+	–	+	+
Gettysburg	–	–	+	–
First Bull Run	+	+	–	–
Chattanooga (3rd)	+	–	+	+

ADAPT IN ACTION

CYNTHIA: ORGANIZING TO LEARN

Cynthia is a student in Mr. Kim's class. She was diagnosed as having learning disabilities that affect spoken language (with particular deficits in listening) and reasoning and thinking (executive functioning). This diagnosis explains in part why she gets confused with verbal directions and is extremely disorganized.

Mr. Kim finds Cynthia one of his greatest challenges: "She is so bright but seemingly doesn't care a bit about her schoolwork. I know that's not the case, because she often shares with me her frustration at not being able to get straight A's. She likes to read when she can find her books, but she is constantly missing assignment due dates and misplacing items needed for each assignment. She also loses her completed assignment when she does get something done. Her attention span is short compared with that of the other students, which affects her ability to listen to directions and her peers. Sustaining attention on reading varies; thus, her comprehension abilities vary. Tackling new vocabulary is also hampered by her difficulties focusing and keeping her attention on her reading. The referral for an attention deficit hyperactivity disorder evaluation may reveal why she has organization and concentration difficulties, which in turn affect her academics."

Following the lesson, Mr. Kim reviewed the progress-monitoring data for each student. Given Cynthia's difficulties with the reading assignment, Mr. Kim decides to use the ADAPT Framework to make decisions about the next steps in instruction for Cynthia. Consider the ADAPT Framework, and then identify adaptations that might be useful.

A: Ask, "What am I requiring the student to do?" Mr. Kim noted, "Students have to use the visual display, semantic feature analysis, to connect the concept of Civil War battles with related words and ideas in print."

D: Determine the prerequisite skills of the task. Mr. Kim comments, "The students need to be able to skim the chapter to find the battles and then read carefully to find out where and when the battles were fought, learn who won them, and determine whether General Ulysses S. Grant was a participant. So, they have to find key vocabulary terms (the names of battles) and comprehend what they read in the sections that describe each battle. Also, they need to have their materials (textbook, notebook, and semantic feature analysis grid) available, take notes, and then decipher what they have written so they can complete their grid. This will take some time, so they must stay on task and keep from being distracted, all the while attending to what they are doing as they work in small groups."

A: Analyze the student's strengths and struggles. All the students have the requisite skills except Cynthia. "She does well working in small groups, but she has trouble understanding the semantic features as we discuss them before moving into small groups. She has no problem reading the text, but she doesn't always have her book or notebook with her. She can take and read her notes. She stays on task for only about 5 to 10 minutes at a time. If she has her book, she should be able to complete part of the grid."

P: Propose and implement adaptations from among the four categories. Mr. Kim decides to pair Cynthia with another student before the small group work to help her understand the semantic features they will be discussing (instructional delivery). He will have Cynthia work on only one battle at a time (instructional content). The day before the lesson, Mr. Kim will make sure Cynthia records in her schoolwork diary that she needs to bring her history book to class (instructional material).

T: Test to determine whether the adaptations helped the student accomplish the task. After the lesson, Mr. Kim evaluated Cynthia's understanding of the lesson. He was satisfied, based on the progress-monitoring data he collected, that Cynthia understood semantic features and was able to complete a section of the grid successfully.

Let's take a look at the adaptations Mr. Kim chose to help Cynthia. He decided to continue using them.

ADAPT Framework: For Cynthia

A ASK "What am I requiring the student to do?"	D DETERMINE the prerequisite skills of the task.	A ANALYZE the student's strengths and struggles.		P PROPOSE and implement adaptations from among the four categories.	T TEST to determine whether the adaptations helped the student accomplish the task.
		Strengths	Struggles		
Create a visual display to connect Civil War battles with related words and ideas in print.	1. Be able to skim the chapter to find the battles.	1			
	2. Read carefully about the battles.	2			
	3. Find key vocabulary terms (the battles).		3	3. Instructional delivery: Cynthia will be paired with another student before the small group work to help her understand the semantic features they will be discussing and help her stay on task.	3. Check to see if Cynthia is understanding the vocabulary and semantic features in text.
	4. Comprehend what is read in the sections that describe each battle.	4			
	5. Have materials available.		5	5. Instructional materials: The day before the work is to be done, Mr. Kim will make sure Cynthia records in her "schoolwork diary" that she needs to bring her history book to class.	5. Check diary for reminder, and monitor her bringing text to class.
	6. Take notes.	6			
	7. Decipher what was written in the notes.	7			
	8. Complete the grid.	8			
	9. Stay on task and keep from being distracted.		9	9. Instructional content: Cynthia will work on only one battle at a time.	9. Monitor to ensure that Cynthia focuses on one battle at a time.
	10. Work in small groups.	10			

MONITORING READING COMPREHENSION

Good readers monitor their understanding of reading as they progress through the text and use strategies to understand and remember the material (Wright, 2013). Students who are able to monitor their reading comprehension know whether they are understanding and/or remembering what they are reading. Reading comprehension monitoring requires regulating comprehension during reading so students can prevent deficient understanding. Reading comprehension monitoring means (a) activating background knowledge, (b) clarifying the purposes for reading, (c) identifying the key information, (d) summarizing information, (e) focusing on self-questioning about the text, (f) using text structure formats to understand text, and (g) correcting problems when comprehension is weak. Students benefit from instruction on when and how to use different strategies to monitor their reading comprehension so they will be able to fix any comprehension problems. Let's review ways to teach students how to monitor their reading comprehension.

Teaching Students to Monitor Their Understanding

Students should undertake multiple activities before, during, and after reading to guarantee that comprehension monitoring is an ongoing process. You can use the following suggestions to teach reading comprehension monitoring. We have blended them with the adaptation categories from the ADAPT Framework.

Instructional delivery: Teach students to ask questions before, during, and after reading.

Questions before reading:

- What is my purpose for reading?
- What do I already know about this topic (activate background knowledge)?
- What do I think I will learn about this topic (make predictions)?

Questions during reading:

- Does what I am reading make sense?
- Is this what I expected? Should I revise my predictions or suspend judgment until later?
- How are the important points related to one another? What parts are similar and/or different?
- Should I read on, reread, or stop and use a fix-up strategy? Are there any words I don't understand?

Questions after reading:

- What were the most important points?
- What is my opinion? How do I feel? Do I agree or disagree?
- What new information did I learn? (Vacca et al., 2014)

Instructional delivery: Help students link background knowledge with topics to be studied before reading. For example,

- Students can make predictions about the reading based on such physical features of the text as pictures, graphs, and headings.
- Students can watch a video that depicts a time era or science concept to be studied. This is particularly important for students who lack background knowledge in the area being studied.
- Students can make a semantic map (see Figure 14.1) to activate their prior knowledge.

Instructional delivery: Teach students ways to think about the text during reading:

- Students can use paraphrasing strategies to help monitor their understanding of content in each paragraph.
- Students can use fix-up strategies to repair faulty comprehension, such as checking their understanding using the questions listed earlier, rereading difficult sentences, and paraphrasing sentences or paragraphs. (You can examine the fix-up strategies presented in Chapter 11.)
- Students can turn headings into questions and answer the questions as they read sections of the text.
- Students can complete graphic organizers (discussed in the next section) to organize their thoughts about the reading. For instance, Figure 14.2 shows a character map for Stuart Little that illustrates how a graphic organizer can be created during reading to examine character traits.

Instructional delivery: Help students think about the content after reading. For example,

- students can summarize text in small chunks, such as chapter sections, and then combine the smaller summaries into a chapter summary; or
- students can write reports to answer questions about what they read.

Now we review specific instructional strategies for comprehension monitoring.

FIGURE 14.1 ■ Semantic Map for Sharks

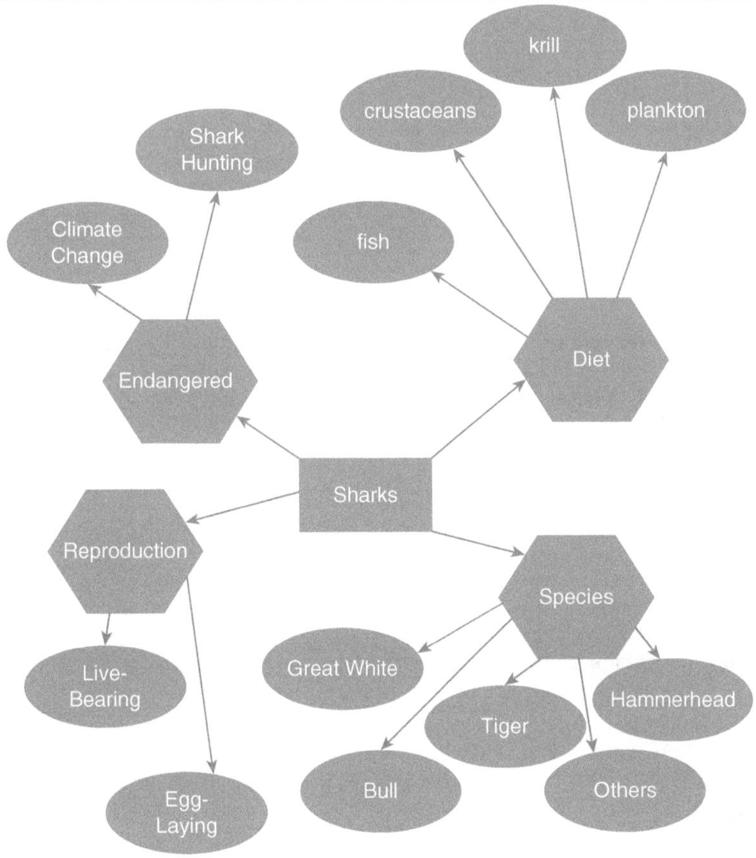

FIGURE 14.2 ■ Stuart Little Character Map

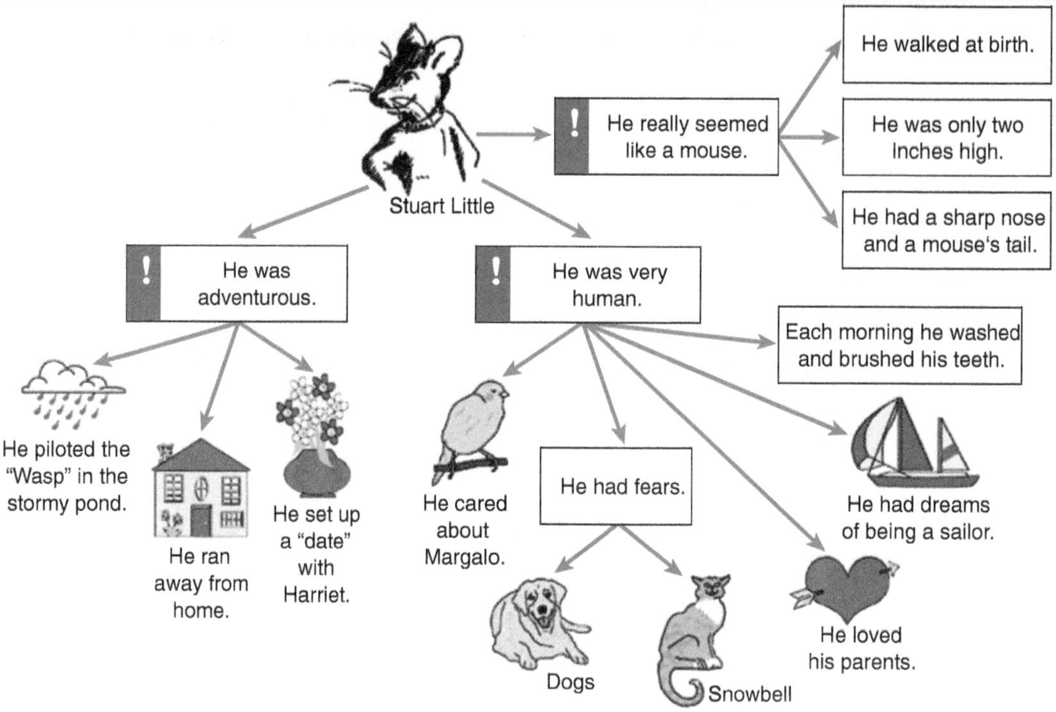

Source: Bryant and Bryant (2011).

Evidence-Based Instructional Strategies

The evidence-based practices in Instructional Strategy 14.2 provide effective means to help students learn how to monitor their reading comprehension.

INSTRUCTIONAL STRATEGY 14.2

KWLS

Instructional Objective: Before, during, and after reading, the students will create a KWLS chart to determine what they know about a topic and what they are learning as they read.
Instructional Content: Reading comprehension: Activating prior knowledge and acquiring new knowledge
Instructional Materials: KWLS chart, history text
Instructional Delivery: Grouping: Whole class group

Teaching Procedure

1. Determine the core concept.
2. Develop a KWLS chart with the core concept stated in question form.
3. Before they read the material, ask the students what they think they already *know* about the core concept. That information is to be recorded in the K column.
4. Ask the students what they *want* to find out while reading the material. That information is to be recorded in the W column.
5. After reading a portion of the text, return to the KWLS chart and confirm or deny the knowledge in the K (What I know) column.

6. Complete the L (What I Learned) column by writing the answers to the questions written in the W (What I want to find out) column and entering other pertinent information that students have *learned* from the reading.
7. Complete the S (What I *still* need to learn) column as they are reading. A sample of a completed KWLS chart is shown for the core concept question "What were the American colonists' attitudes toward England before the American Revolution?"
8. Repeat steps 5, 6, and 7 until the reading has been completed.

K What I Know	W What I Want to find out	L What I Learned	S What I Still need to learn
The American Revolution started in 1776. Years before the war, colonists were unhappy with British rule and taxation.	Why did the people in the colonies want to be independent? Was independence the original goal?	The desire for independence had a lot to do with the feeling of being overtaxed. For some, independence was the goal; for others, the goal was to make King George realize that the colonies needed to be treated fairly.	Why was King George unwilling to negotiate with the colonists? What compromises did the colonists offer to England in return for being taxed less?

Progress Monitoring: Review students' charts after they finish filling them in to determine the accuracy of the information. Provide a comprehension check to determine how well students are understanding their reading.

Sources: KWLS chart adapted from Casareno (2010); Ogle (1986).

LEARNING FROM TEXTBOOK INSTRUCTION

Textbooks are an important part of content-area instruction. Other than in classes such as English literature, textbooks typically consist largely of expository text (informational text), although stories (narrative text) are sometimes included to provide a humanistic perspective. For example, in a social studies text an explanation of events surrounding the Civil War can be personalized with stories about the effects of the war on soldiers and their families.

Teaching Students How to Learn From Textbooks

We provide suggestions for accessing textbook material that can help teachers promote student learning. We present the suggestions with the categories of adaptations from the ADAPT Framework.

Instructional materials: Considerations for selecting textbooks (can also serve as guidelines for textbook selection committees):

- Make sure textbooks have coherence (logical flow of ideas) and appropriateness (match between material to be read and reader's knowledge and skills). The relationships between main ideas and details should be clear and to the point.
- Look for signal words (words that serve as cues to text structure, such as *first, second,* and *finally* for sequence and terms like *on the other hand* for comparison and contrast).
- Ensure that visuals in the text, for example, photos or graphs, are informative and reinforce important content information.
- Check that graphic organizers such as flowcharts and diagrams support the text structure.

Textbooks are the materials used most often by content-area teachers as the basis for their instruction. What other kinds of materials in this classroom are helping students learn about geography and culture?

iStock.com/FatCamera

- Be sure there are sufficient practice activities that help students learn and apply concepts and ideas.
- Look for vocabulary words that are reinforced with activities to help students develop an understanding of concepts.

Instructional delivery:

- Divide reading assignments into meaningful segments and plan the lesson around these segments.
- Introduce topics by having your students think about what they already know about them (e.g., "What do you know already about . . .? What connections can you make?").
- Have students preview reading segments by examining the illustrations, headings, and other clues to the content.
- Ask students to make predictions about what they will learn. They may write individual predictions, write with a partner, or contribute to an oral discussion, creating a list of class predictions.
- Have students read the selection and evaluate their predictions. Were their predictions correct? Were they on the wrong track? What evidence supported or contradicted the predictions? Have them discuss their predictions and the content of the reading.
- Close each lesson by reviewing the reading content and discussing prediction strategies students used before reading the text. Review ways to make more accurate predictions using text features.
- Teach words that signal text structures:
    - Sequence—*first, second, next*
    - Cause/Effect—*causes, effects, as a result of*

- Problem/Solution—*the problem is, the question is, difficulty*
- Compare/Contrast—*is similar, is different, however, in the same way*
- Description—*for example, also, another feature*
- Enumerative—*includes the following*

- Teach text structures using graphic organizers. Model how to use the graphic organizers. Figure 14.3 shows an example of a graphic organizer that can be used as a study guide and as a source of information for test questions.

Source: Section 7: Instructional strategies that facilitate learning across content areas (Westchester University, n.d.).

Promoting students' participation is an important part of teaching. In the next section, we discuss how teachers can promote student participation in class discussions and activities.

PROMOTING STUDENT PARTICIPATION

Students learn by engaging in the learning process through discussions, questioning, and small-group activities. Students with learning difficulties should be actively involved to foster understanding.

Heather Walport-Glawron wrote an article for the Edutopia.org website in 2012 (updated in 2014) in which she summarized responses from middle-school students to the question, "What engages students?" Their answers follow:

1. Working with their peers
2. Working with technology
3. Connect the real world to the work we do/project-based learning
4. Clearly love what you do (as a teacher)
5. Get me out of my seat!
6. Bring in visuals
7. Student choice
8. Understand your clients—the kids
9. Mix it up!
10. Be human (as a teacher)

Source: Adapted from Walport-Glawron (2012).

Do you believe there are important items on this list? What might you add to the list?. Do you recall any of your teachers (or professors) offering any of these engagement activities or strategies? Are there any activities or strategies that you might use in your classroom to promote student engagement?

Using Class Discussions to Engage Students

All students can be included in class discussions through different activities and strategies. Questioning strategies can promote discussions by having students engage in asking and answering questions. Teachers should work with small groups to check for understanding, model how to respond to questions, and ask probing questions to foster student thinking. The following ideas can be conducted in all content-area classes. The categories of adaptations from the ADAPT Framework are incorporated.

FIGURE 14.3 ■ Question Exploration Guide

"How do problems with the ozone layer teach us about human effects on the environment?"

Effectiveness of Question Exploration

Text Reference chapter 7, pages 101-116 **Name:** Marie David

Course ____________

Unit x **Title** Our Environment

Lesson ____________ **Critical Question #:** 3 ____________ **Date:** 1-25-16

(1) What is the critical question?

How do problems with the ozone layer teach us about human effects on our environment?

(2) What are the key terms and explanation?

What is our environment?	All the things surrounding us (air, land, living things)
What is the ozone layer?	Invisible layer of gas that shields us from UV radiation
What is UV?	Ultraviolet radiation, or harmful rays from the sun
What are CFCs?	Chlorofluorocarbons-chemicals with chlorine

(3) What are the supporting questions and answers?

What has happened in the past?	In the past, a protective ozone layer was formed when UV rays hit the oxygen in the air around the earth.
What is a PROBLEM and its CAUSES?	The ozone layer is being destroyed by CFCs we may not even know about in everyday products (cleaning products, foam containers, refrigerator coolants and spray cans).
What are the EFFECTS?	The effects include: 1. physical harm (skin cancer & cataracts) 2. environmental harm (crops and ocean plants) 3. change in weather patterns 4. greenhouse warming of the earth
What are SOLUTIONS?	Solutions include: 1. voluntary cutbacks of CFC products 2. use of alternatives to CFCs (HCFCs) 3. world conferences to cut CFCs
What are other concerns?	Some people didn't know or still don't think it's a problem.

(4) What is the main idea answer?

People can harm the environment without intending it or even believing it.

(5) Explore and use the main idea.

How can we explore the facts ourselves?
(Experiments with balloons show that oxygen can be changed to ozone.)

(6) Extend the main idea to your world. What can an individual do?

(An individual can decide to do research on which products cause damage to ozone.)

Source: Bulgren et al. (2009).

- **Instructional materials/delivery**: Provide a discussion guide with questions students should answer alone, with a partner, or in a small group before class discussions begin. For example, in a small-group setting, each group could be responsible for summarizing content for an assigned element of a novel such as setting, characters, problem, and resolution. In social studies or science, you could assign students a specific part of a chapter to summarize or chapter headings to turn into questions and then answer.
- **Instructional delivery**: Provide a question stem card with stem questions such as "How are ________ and _______ alike and different?" "What explanation can you offer about . . .?" "Why do you think . . .?" "How would you describe . . .?" and a topic, character, event, or issue to go with the stem. Students should prepare an answer to the question before discussion, working with a partner or in a small group.
- **Instructional delivery**: Divide students into small groups and give them one question representing each level of Bloom's taxonomy: knowledge, comprehension, application, analysis, synthesis, and evaluation. Questions can be the same across groups, so when groups share their responses after the activity, the class can identify multiple perspectives about questions that require higher-order thinking, such as synthesis and evaluation.
- **Instructional activity**: Have students record their questions about content and put the questions in a box. Draw questions and have students answer the questions.

In another strategy, the "What's Old" and "What's New" technique provides another example of how teachers can foster engagement to help students self-monitor their comprehension.

1. Divide the class into small groups. Provide each group a chapter to review, telling students to peruse the topics and special features within their sections.
2. Ask the groups to think about the primary topics discussed and list them on a chart under the column headings "What's Old" and "What's New." To help them categorize the topics, ask students to consider whether the content has been covered in past classes. If there is some disagreement among group members, encourage students to develop unanimity.
3. Instruct students to return to the "What's Old" column after they finish the chart and place an asterisk beside topics they have reviewed several times. In the "What's New" column, ask them to circle items that are so new that they had never heard of them before this exercise.
4. Have each group come forward in turn to display the charts. Allow students to lead their classmates on a chapter walk, pointing out old and new concepts. Encourage them to seek feedback from the class about their lists.

Source: Garber-Miller (2006).

In the next section, we present information about anchoring instruction as a means for promoting student participation. **Anchored instruction** begins with an event or problem situation (the anchor) that is presented in a video or movie that serves as background information and creates a shared experience among students (Thomas & Rieth, 2011). The anchor can be the main focus or a supplement to facilitate student discussions (Kumar, 2010). Although more research is needed, the technique shows promise for teaching secondary students with academic problems (Bottge et al., 2014).

Instructional Strategy 14.3 shows how to use the technique.

Teachers can include all students in class discussions through various activities and techniques. What are some examples of techniques that may be useful in your classroom?

iStock.com/monkeybusinessimages

INSTRUCTIONAL STRATEGY 14.3

ANCHORED INSTRUCTION

Instructional Objective: The students will learn content using an anchor and present their knowledge in a group presentation.
Instructional Content: Expository or narrative text presented through a video
Instructional Materials: Video anchor, computers, writing materials
Instructional Delivery: Grouping: Whole class or small group

Teaching Procedures

1. Identify a video that corresponds with the text to be read. In this case, we will use *To Kill a Mockingbird* as the video anchor to teach human relationships, social studies events (post-World War I, World War II, the Great Depression), and themes such as racism, authority, power, and socioeconomic status. Students are divided into small groups, and each group will work to prepare a multimedia presentation about researched topics that will be presented to the class after the assignments are completed.
2. **Phase 1: Setting the Stage**. This phase consists of activities to help students develop interviewing and research skills for their final multimedia project. Students learn how to conduct interviews, ask questions to research a topic, and apply their background knowledge to new information learned about a topic. As an example, the jigsaw cooperative learning procedure (see https://www.jigsaw.org/) can be used, where members of one jigsaw group conduct research about the author of the text being read; in this case, Harper Lee is the author of *To Kill a Mockingbird*. Part of the multimedia presentation can include a video in which, after students return to their primary groups, one member of the group interviews "Ms. Lee" about her life and how her life experiences could have influenced her writing. Table 14.2 shows the three procedures employed in Phase 1.
3. **Phase 2: Watching the Anchor/Retelling**. This phase occurs over several days and introduces students to the themes of the story—for example, power, money, and human relationships in *To Kill a Mockingbird*. After watching the film, students retell the events and identify scenes

they think are important to the story. Retelling descriptions are written on sentence strips and ordered according to their place in the story. If students recognize that information is missing, additional strips are created and added to the descriptions. Students answer questions about the movie related to the themes, setting, characters, and events. Students then engage in a discussion to confirm conclusions and clarify misconceptions.

TABLE 14.2 ■ Anchored Instruction Procedures for Phase 1

Learning How to Interview

1. Ask students to bring in boxes that contain two to four objects they believe best represent them. Let them brainstorm possible items to include in their boxes.
2. Tell students that today they will work in small groups to learn more about each other by examining the objects each person brought in and by asking questions about the objects. They should ask different types of questions. These might be "why," "how," or "what" questions, or they might come up with other types of questions.
3. Divide students into groups of three. Assign students the following roles: recorder, interviewer (questioner), and responder. Students will be assigned a different role every time.
4. The interviewers are given about 10 minutes to question a student about his or her object box. Encourage students to ask questions that explore issues such as "Who is this person?" "What do these objects tell me about him or her?"
5. Once the small groups of three have finished questioning, join each group with another group of three. Ask this group of six the following:
   - What types of questions gave you the most information about a person? Why?
   - What types of questions didn't seem to give you much information? Why not?
   - Ask students to share their responses from the small group sessions, and record their responses on paper.

Learning How to Research a Topic

1. Show students a picture depicting a scene from the 1930s.
2. Ask students the following, encouraging them to discuss the photograph:
   - What's going on in this picture?
   - What do you see?
   - Who are the people in this picture?
   - What do you think they are doing? Why?
   - When do you think this took place?
   - Where do you think it took place?
   - How would you describe what is happening in the photograph?
3. Tell students to think of the photograph as similar to the object box they worked with earlier. Different elements of the photograph come together to provide a portrait of a particular time and place, just as different objects come together to give us a portrait of a person. Ask questions such as the following to stimulate student thinking:
   - What did the photographer want to capture when taking this picture? What is the photographer trying to show us?
   - What message is the photographer trying to convey?
   - What elements of the photograph are essential to understand that message?
   - What information is missing? (What are you wondering about that might help you better understand the photographer's message?)
4. Record students' questions on the board.

(Continued)

TABLE 14.2 ■ Anchored Instruction Procedures for Phase 1 (*Continued*)

Transitioning to the Anchor

Following student responses, return to the photograph. Ask students the following:

- Do you think this picture is typical of the 1930s? Why or why not?
- What have you learned about this time in history?
- What are you learning about the kinds of questions that provide you with the most information?
- What did you learn about people in the 1930s?
- Who had power? Who had money? How did people get along with one another?

4. **Phase 3: Segmenting**. In this phase, students segment the movie into scenes and label them for use during Phase 5, when they will conduct their research. Strategies used in this phase include looking for logical breaks between scenes based on plot, scene changes, and character appearances. For instance, if the students choose Mayella Ewell's courtroom scene as a segment, it might be labeled "Mayella's Testimony."
5. **Phase 4: Characterization**. In this phase, students conduct character analysis. Students work in small groups, and each group chooses one character to portray. The students create an acrostic for their character. For example, for Scout: S—secretive, c—curious, o—outward, u—unpredictable, and t— tomboy. Students identify scenes from the video that depict that character's personality and show how the character relates to the themes of power, money, and human relationships. Characterization activities are shown in Table 14.3.

TABLE 14.3 ■ Anchored Instruction, Phase 4, Characterization

Character Research Procedure

1. Explain to the students that they will use video segments to develop portraits of important characters in *To Kill a Mockingbird.* Ask the class to identify the main characters of the story.
   - What are the most important relationships in *To Kill a Mockingbird?*
2. Model how to create a character web and how to find scenes using film segments.

   For example:
   - Choose Mayella Ewell. On the board, create a character web around her name. Ask students to identify Mayella's qualities, her relationships with others, her power in Macon, and her financial situation.
   - Choose the scene from the movie that best illustrates Mayella's character in terms of money, power, and human relationships (Mayella's courtroom testimony).
3. Explain that students will choose a character and, working in groups, will find the most important scenes for that character that reveal money, power, and human relationships.
4. Have groups present their findings on characters to the class.

6. **Phase 5: Student Research and Presentations**. Students work in small groups to develop a research question on issues that stem from their discussions. Group members conduct research to gather information to answer their questions and create a multimedia presentation. Students must use library and Internet resources. For instance, one question might be, "How did the stock market work?" Students would research this question and relate it to the stock market crash that occurred during the Great Depression in the United States, the period of time depicted in *To Kill a Mockingbird.* The teacher helps students research their topic and develop their presentation; a group multimedia presentation is the final event.

As noted in Chapter 7, Universal Design for Learning (UDL) can be an effective means for fostering access to the curriculum for all students. Using anchoring instruction is presented as a way to foster group participation. Now we present a UDL lesson that focuses on using *To Kill a Mockingbird* and incorporates the UDL principles and checkpoints.

Source: Rieth et al. (2003). Adapted with permission.

UNIVERSAL DESIGN FOR LEARNING IN ACTION

UNIVERSAL DESIGN FOR LEARNING LESSON

Note: This UDL-based lesson was developed, in part, using the CAST UDL Lesson Builder (http://lessonbuilder.cast.org).

The UDL framework (version 2.2) consists of three main principles (I. Representation, II. Action and Expression, and III. Engagement; CAST, 2018). Each principle has three guidelines and several checkpoints that define them in greater depth. In this lesson plan, we delineate how various instructional strategies meet the UDL checkpoints.

Title: English I Lesson: Dramatic Structure
Subject: English I Lesson on Literature
Grade Level: 9
Duration: 45 minutes
Unit Description: This lesson is part of a group of lessons centering on Harper Lee's *To Kill a Mockingbird.*
Lesson Description for Day: Prerequisite skills: Ability to communicate verbally, attend to a short video clip, work collaboratively

Goals

Unit Goals: The goal of this unit is to understand the interplay of heroism and courage during the 1930s in the Deep South.
Lesson Goals: The purpose of this lesson is to teach students to complete a project that conveys the phases of plot: exposition, rising action, climax, falling action, and denouement.

Methods

Anticipatory Set: Tell students that the purpose of the day's lesson is to help them understand dramatic structure as it relates to literature. They will be working with print and digital copies of Harper Lee's novel *To Kill a Mockingbird*, as well as the film version that came out in 1962. The movie does a good job of following the events of the book, so the three can be used in conjunction with one another.

Introduce and Model New Knowledge

1. Introduce new vocabulary (exposition, rising action, climax, falling action, denouement) by saying the words, having students repeat the words, writing the words on the board, discussing definitions, and providing strategies for remembering the definitions (e.g., **d**enouement = **d**ecision or **d**one).
2. Read a section of *To Kill a Mockingbird* to the class and diagram the plot on the board using a plot diagram and the new vocabulary words. Provide a print copy of the text for students to follow along.
3. Play a short clip of the movie *To Kill a Mockingbird* (*Checkpoint 1.3: Offer alternatives for visual information*) that picks up from the material just read. Have students work in small groups to diagram the plot.
4. Provide scaffolds as needed (Checkpoint 4.2: Optimize access to tools and assistive technologies; Checkpoint 6.3: Facilitate managing information and resources).
   a. Demonstrate to students how they can change the fonts and backgrounds of digital text by copying and pasting to Microsoft Word; also, for students who are using text-to-speech technology, make sure they understand how to adjust the volume and speed of the audio (*Checkpoint 1.1: Offer ways of customizing the display of information*).
   b. Provide graphic organizers (e.g., word maps, semantic maps) to help struggling students better understand key vocabulary terms (*Checkpoint 2.1: Clarify vocabulary and symbols*).

Provide Guided Practice

1. Provide print, digital, and video versions of *To Kill a Mockingbird.*
2. Select a chapter that will be the focus of the activity.
3. Have students work in small groups to diagram the plot of the selected chapter (*Checkpoint 8.3: Foster collaboration and community*). Allow students to choose groupings for learning activities.

4. Allow students to choose what they will produce:
   a. Create a PowerPoint, Animoto, or Prezi presentation.
   b. Create a performance or scenes.
   c. Create a poster or diorama.
   d. Other (as approved by the teacher).
5. Be prepared to model, for example, PowerPoint procedures.
6. Check for understanding and provide corrective feedback as needed.
7. Support self-regulation skills by assisting students in setting and monitoring learning and behavioral goals (*Checkpoint 9.2: Facilitate personal coping skills and strategies*).

Provide Independent Practice

1. At the end of each day, students answer questions related to the new information as they leave the classroom (e.g., What is exposition?).
2. When student projects are completed, they will be evaluated using a scoring rubric designed for the product type.

Source: Johnson-Harris & Mundschenk (2014).

UDL Guidelines are available at http://udlguidelines.cast.org/.

Next, we talk about study skills, which are important for successful learning at all grade levels. Students should learn about effective study skills in the elementary grades and be required to maintain their use in the middle grades. As students move through the high school grades, they will refine their study skills and use them in other adult contexts (Hoover & Patton, 2007). Many students with learning difficulties demonstrate problems with study skills, consequently, teachers must be prepared to foster the development and use of effective study skills for their struggling students.

HELPING STUDENTS WITH DIFFICULTIES IN STUDY SKILLS

Students with special learning needs must be explicitly taught study skills because many have not learned how to approach academic tasks in a way that will help them gain and use information presented via text, lecture, and media (IRIS Center, 2015). Students need to be able to manage study and exam preparation time to be success in secondary and postsecondary classes. Students with unique learning needs or disabilities may show difficulties with time management because they organize their time poorly, are easily distracted from tasks or projects, lack stick-to-it-ness or persistence, and find it difficult to organize their ideas into a cohesive plan of action (Bryant et al., 2015). If students show difficulty in any one of these areas, they may have trouble completing a task.

Many students, including those who have unique learning needs, take classes in career and technical education. According to a 2013 paper written by the American Institutes for Research, career and technical education "is an educational strategy for providing young people with the academic, technical, and employability skills and knowledge to pursue postsecondary training or higher education and enter a career field prepared for ongoing learning" (p. 1). Career and technical education offer students opportunities to work with business and postsecondary education professionals. Relatedly, in 2014 the National Association of Colleges and Employers identified the main skills necessary for to succeed in the workplace. These skills include the ability to (a) work as a team member; (b) make decisions and solve problems; (c) communicate verbally with people inside and outside their company or organization; (d) plan, organize and prioritize work; (e) obtain and process information; (f) analyze quantitative data; (g) call on their technical knowledge related to their responsibilities; (h) be proficient with computer software programs; (i) create and/or edit written reports; and (j) sell and influence others. Spisak (2015) noted that few items on this list are directly related to what he termed "hard skills," that is, those that are specifically job-related, taught skills. The remaining "soft skills" include "study skills, listening skills, organization skills, and writing skills . . . which are essential to a student's success in school and in their careers" (p. 14). As you read this section of the chapter, consider how you might be able to include these skills as you teach to better prepare your students as they move on with their lives.

Study Skills

Students use listening skills to obtain meaning from spoken language, to foster efficient study habits, and to promote communication.

Research findings have shown that teachers spend minimal time on listening instruction despite its importance as a study skill (Hoover & Patton, 2007). The ability to listen, to receive and understand information, is a crucial skill that needs to be taught explicitly.

Listening instruction is important because students must listen to take notes during lectures or discussions and to follow directions (Hoover & Patton, 2007). Listening necessitates understanding spoken language, including sentence structure and vocabulary. Students must also be able to separate out the most important information from less important information.

According to Hoover and Patton (2007), students with special learning needs might show the following listening difficulties:

- Are unable to concentrate during listening activities
- Lose attention frequently due to visual distractions during listening activities
- Lose attention often due to auditory distractions during listening activities
- Are unable to identify primary and secondary points in verbal messages
- Are unable to follow verbal directions, even when repeated several times
- Are unable to state purposes of a listening activity. (p. 67)

Note taking is needed as students listen to lectures and discussions. Students with special learning needs may exhibit trouble taking notes for several reasons. First, they may not be able to select the most critical information or write quickly enough to keep up with the instructor. Even when students do take notes, they may have difficulties making sense of their notes following the lecture if they are illegible or unorganized (Boyle et al., 2015).

Related to listening skills, students with special learning needs may demonstrate difficulties with short-term, long-term, and working memory. **Short-term memory** is a temporary store of information that we tap for immediate use, like remembering two tasks to accomplish today or a short list of items to buy at the supermarket. Long-term memory is a permanent store of information whose permanence is aided by the way information is stored. Working memory is defined "as a processing resource of limited capacity that is involved in the preservation of information while simultaneously processing the same or other information" (Swanson & Fung, 2016, p. 1154). Memorizing information for class work and tests relies on all three types of memory.

Students with learning difficulties experience many difficulties related to memorizing and test taking. They may not have efficient memorization strategies such as **chunking**, rehearsing, and creating mnemonics for studying material that will be tested. Students might not make connections between new and learned material to help them memorize content. Students might not have efficient strategies for taking a test, such as managing time or dealing with multiple-choice questions methodically. Students might not access memory strategies to gather information to take the test. Finally, students could have problems reading and comprehending test instructions. With this list in mind, it is not surprising that many students have difficulties while taking exams.

We return to Mrs. Gonzales, who had her students complete a survey to help her learn about their content-area and study skills. The survey is shown in Table 14.4, which you may want to use with your students.

Next, we talk about ways to help students improve their time management skills.

TABLE 14.4 ■ Study Skills Questionnaire

The purpose of this survey is to find out about your own study habits and attitudes. Read each statement and indicate (by writing 1, 2, 3, or 4 in the blank) how well it applies to you.

1 = Sounds not at all like me	2 = Sounds a little like me
3 = Sounds quite a bit like me	4 = Sounds just like me

Reading Textbooks	____ **1.** I browse the headings, pictures, chapter questions, and summaries before I start reading a chapter.
	____ **2.** I make up questions from a chapter before, during, and after reading it.
	____ **3.** I try to get the meaning of new words as I see them for the first time.
	____ **4.** I look for familiar concepts as well as ideas that spark my interest as I read.
	____ **5.** I look for the main ideas as I read.
Taking Notes	____ **6.** I take notes as I read my textbooks.
	____ **7.** I take notes during class lectures.
	____ **8.** I rewrite or type up my notes after class.
	____ **9.** I compare my notes with those of a classmate.
	____ **10.** I try to organize main ideas and details meaningfully.
Studying	____ **11.** I study where it is quiet and there are few distractions.
	____ **12.** I study for a length of time and then take a short break before returning to studying.
	____ **13.** I have all my supplies handy when I study, such as pens, paper, calculator, etc.
	____ **14.** I set study goals, such as the number of problems I will do or the pages I will read.
	____ **15.** I study at least 2 hours for every hour I am in class each week.
Memorizing	____ **16.** I try to study when my energy is at its peak to increase my concentration level.
	____ **17.** I quiz myself over material that could appear on future exams and quizzes to ensure quick recall.
	____ **18.** I say and repeat difficult concepts out loud to understand them and recall them better.
	____ **19.** I change my notes into my own words, for better understanding.
	____ **20.** I try to create associations between new material I am trying to learn and information I already know.
Preparing for Tests	____ **21.** I study with a classmate or group.
	____ **22.** When I don't understand something, I get help from tutors, classmates, and my instructors.
	____ **23.** I do all homework assignments and turn them in on time.
	____ **24.** I can easily identify what I have learned and what I have not yet learned before I take a test.
	____ **25.** I anticipate the questions that may be asked on tests and make sure I know the answers.
Managing Time	____ **26.** I use a calendar to mark upcoming academic and personal deadlines and events.
	____ **27.** I use a "to do" list to keep track of academic and personal tasks I must complete.
	____ **28.** I start studying for quizzes and tests at least several days before I take them.
	____ **29.** I start papers and projects as soon as they are assigned.
	____ **30.** I have enough time for school and fun.

Source: Adapted from Red Rocks Community College, Connect to Success, T+ (n.d.).

Teaching Time Management Skills

Some students with learning problems have difficulties with organizational skills in general; managing and organizing time is one component of the bigger self-management picture. Time management requires students to (a) identify what they have to accomplish, (b) understand how long a task will take to complete, and (c) schedule blocks of time to get the job done efficiently. Time management involves making judgments and estimates about the time requirements of each task; your students may struggle with time management if they lack good estimation skills and conceptual understanding of time. For example, the student who does not begin a research paper until three days before the due date either has not demonstrated sufficient understanding of the demands of the task or lacks the time management skills to complete the task by the deadline. You can use the following activities to help students with their time management skills (Study Guides and Strategies, n.d.):

- Block out study time and breaks during the day.
- Dedicate study spaces.
- Conduct weekly reviews.
- Prioritize assignments.
- Get something done!
- Postpone unnecessary activities until the work is done.
- Identify helpful resources.
- Use free time wisely.
- Review notes and readings just before class.
- Review lecture notes just after class.

More than ever before, students are being held accountable to higher standards, as evidenced by the increasing number of states that have adopted the Common Core State Standards. With increased accountability comes an increased workload, and students are required to complete assignments on time for all of their classes. As shown in the Tech Notes feature, technology can provide students like Marta with time management options.

TECH NOTES

ELECTRONIC CALENDARS AS TIME MANAGEMENT TOOLS

For students like Marta, who habitually turn in assignments late, electronic calendars can be useful tools for time management. Programs such as Google Calendar or one of the many inexpensive smartphone calendar apps help students organize their schedules so that they can complete assignments on time. For example, Marta has a paper that is due November 15 for her English I class. Noting that date on a calendar is all well and good, but Marta is better served by breaking the assignment into manageable steps and placing each event into her electronic calendar. For example, she could enter the following:

- Begin research on topic on October 1.
- Create an outline based on the research by October 10.
- Annotate the outline by October 20.
- Write first draft by October 30.
- Revise the draft by November 10.
- Edit the revision by November 12.
- Turn in the paper on November 15.

Electronic calendars can send out alerts when a deadline is approaching, often in the form of an e-mail or text message. Of course, students must pay attention to the calendars as deadlines approach, and parents can help by entering important dates on their calendars as well. Numerous products are available for such purposes. To see a listing of the more popular family-based calendars, simply type "family electronic calendars" into your favorite search engine. Techdialogue (2013) offered these suggestions for using Google Calendar for the classroom, but they apply to any electronic calendar with similar features:

1. Lesson plans and objectives can be added quickly from any computer (and most mobile devices) with Internet access.
2. As teachers get more experienced using Google Calendar, they can embed their calendars on their classroom websites.
3. Advanced users can add their Google Calendar to their smartphones and help students and parents subscribe to the classroom calendar so that they can set up reminders on their devices.

4. Educators can use Google Calendars to share schedules with colleagues, from computer lab schedules to athletics practice.

Think about your needs as a student and how electronic calendars can help you develop more efficient study skills. Then project ahead to how you might use this technology in your own classroom to help your students plan schedules and become more efficient learners.

Have students keep a record of how their time was spent for one week. Then you can perform an analysis of their time management with them so you can set up a plan to address any problems the students are having with time.

Teaching Listening and Note-Taking Skills

According to Steimle and colleagues (2009), classroom lectures too often lead to passive listeners, but that does not need to be the case; notetaking requires students to be able to (a) listen actively, (b) recognize important points and supporting details, (c) utilize an organizational framework, (d) know some personal shorthand method for abbreviating information, and (e) write quickly. Taking personal notes can help students actively follow the lecture, select relevant information, and restate it in their own words. Given the importance of note taking and its relationship to higher quiz scores, test scores, and grades (Boyle, 2011; Boyle & Rivera, 2012), your students must know how to listen effectively to obtain the information for which you will hold them accountable.

If your students are encountering obstacles to effective listening, their learning may suffer. Here are some barriers that often impede learning from lectures (Hopper, 2016, p. 130, cited in Strang, 2016):

- Talking instead of listening.
- Thinking of what you're going to say instead of listening.
- Mentally arguing with the speaker.
- Thinking about something else while the speaker is talking.
- Getting impatient with the speaker.
- Giving in to a poor environment—too noisy, too hot, too hungry.
- Dividing your attention—texting, finishing homework, staring at someone else in the class.
- Not listening actively—not taking notes, not asking questions, and so on.
- Not being motivated to listen—thinking the subject is boring.
- Being distracted by the speaker's mannerisms, voice, or appearance.

Fortunately, Hopper (2016, pp. 131–132, cited in Strang, 2016) provided some suggestions you can make to your students to help them improve their listening skills:

- Before you even get to class, be prepared—complete all assigned readings and coursework, and bring all needed materials with you.
- Sit as close to the front of the room as you can.
- Get to class on time—if not early.
- Establish and maintain eye contact with the speaker throughout the lecture.
- Listen for verbal cues. These can be specific words, such as "first," "then," "however," or "my main point is . . ."—or, they can be found in the speaker's tone of voice or level of enthusiasm.

- Watch the speaker's gestures and other nonverbal behaviors.
- Have your notebook (and pen or pencil), tablet, or laptop ready at all times.
- Respond to and reflect on the lecture as it proceeds. As questions come to mind, jot them down to ask later.
- Eliminate distractions (such as those mentioned above), and steer yourself away from them!

Source: Hopper (2016). Reprinted with permission.

More than 30 years ago, Bragstad and Stumpf (1987) identified a five-step note-taking procedure that uses key words that students can learn to help them recall lecture and textbook material. Their method still remains popular with teachers and students. Model the steps that follow, offer examples of poorly written and well-written notes, and then allow students opportunities to practice with feedback. (Do not use your students' own work as examples of poor notes.) Students can take notes from a lecture or textbook and then work in small groups to discuss what they did for each step. You can use students' notes in the note shrink quiz box (see Step 2) to construct quizzes to test understanding of the lecture or textbook material. The following steps are recommended to improve students' note-taking skills:

These students are writing out notes as they listen. How can you help your students develop better listening and note-taking skills?

iStock.com/simonkr

Step 1: *Note-take*, which requires taking notes of important facts during the lecture.

Step 2: *Note shrink*, wherein students survey their notes, identify important points and thought chunks, and record chunks in a quiz box.

Step 3: *Note talk*, in which students put the content into their own words.

Step 4: *Note think*, which entails linking the new information to existing knowledge and experiences.

Step 5: *Note review*, which schedules 10 minutes a day for going over the notes.

Finally, Susan Vogel (1997), a leading researcher in postsecondary learning disabilities, offered the following suggestions, which remain useful today in helping students learn and remember information. You can put these steps in a handout for students to help them remember how to take notes more effectively:

- Color code, enlarge, underline, and highlight your notes to learn the material.
- Copy your notes over if writing helps you memorize.
- Rehearse, either orally or in writing, material to be mastered.
- Write out concepts in full.
- Read your notes, silently or aloud.
- Paraphrase or explain concepts to a friend.

Think about strategies you have used in the past to learn and remember information presented in text or during lectures. How are they similar to what has been presented here? What additional strategies have you used to help retain information that was presented? How might you share the information presented here, along with strategies that you have used successfully, to your students?

WAYS TO FACILITATE MEMORIZATION AND TEST TAKING

Memorization skills are needed to help students learn. For instance, students will be asked to memorize information in different subject areas and to remember that information when they take tests or participate in class discussions. Consequently, it is critical for students to have strategies for learning, storing, and retrieving information. Research findings have shown that students with learning difficulties exhibit problems with short-term and working memory resulting from ineffective information processing abilities (Johnson et al., 2010). Students' problems come from limited efficient memory strategies (chunking, organizing), a lack of automaticity with basic knowledge (computational facts, sight words), and inefficient self-regulation (meta-memory) strategies.

You can help students improve their memory skills by (a) teaching them how to create mnemonic devices to help them memorize and recall content, such as lists of information, important people, and steps in a procedure; (b) discuss how they can remember information with mental images—have them provide specific examples of images they create; (c) teaching them to chunk related information to memorize and recall information and (d) giving them opportunities to explain information with verbal rehearsal in small or whole groups. If your students with unique learning needs are to learn, retain, and recall content information, they must be able to apply strategies they know to help these cognitive, or thinking, processes. Now let's look at some ways to help students recall information and take tests successfully.

Teaching Memorization and Test-Taking Skills

Memorizing information for tests necessitates reviewing the material often and committing the information to memory. Memory strategies that foster recall, such as listing, categorizing, drawing, visualizing, alphabetizing, devising acronyms, applying mnemonic strategies, and creating associations, are procedures used by students with good study skills.

Teachers can help their students become better test takers through the following ways. Hoover and Patton (2007) suggested the following:

- Show students how to take different types of tests.
- Explain different methods of studying and types of materials necessary to study for objective and essay tests.

- Review completed tests with students, highlighting test-taking errors.
- Explore test-taking procedures with students, and explain different types of questions.
- Identify and discuss key vocabulary terms found in test instructions, such as *compare, contrast, match*, and *evaluate*.
- Teach students general strategies to use when taking tests: Review the entire test, know the time allotted for test completion, recognize the point values of specific test items, read and reread the directions and test questions, identify key words in questions, and respond to more difficult items after answering the easier items.
- Teach students specific strategies to use when taking multiple-choice tests: Know the number and kind of answers to select, remember the question, narrow down the possible correct answers by eliminating obviously incorrect ones, and record each answer carefully.

As previously mentioned, mnemonic strategies can be useful for preparing to take tests. PIRATES is one such strategy that has been researched greatly and shown to be effective. Table 14.5 details how PIRATES can be taught so students can develop efficient test-taking skills.

We provide an example of the application of study skills for students with visual impairment (VI). Students with a VI have to access the curriculum, including content-area material, and be taught study skills as well. To meet these objectives, educators must think about the individual needs of students and the adaptations that are necessary to foster successful learning. The Working Together feature details information about the technology considerations to plan for in ample time to ensure that the student is ready to start learning along with his or her peers.

TABLE 14.5 ■ The PIRATES Test-Taking Strategy

Step 1: Prepare to succeed	
Put "PIRATES" and name on the test. Allot time and order to sections.	Say something positive. Start within 2 minutes.
Step 2: Inspect the instructions	
Read the instructions carefully. Underline how and where to respond.	Notice special requirements.
Step 3: Read, remember, and reduce	
Read the whole question. Remember with memory strategies.	Reduce choices.
Step 4: Answer or abandon	
Answer the question.	Abandon the question if you're not sure.
Step 5: Turn back	
Turn back to abandoned questions when you get to the end of the test.	Tell yourself to earn more points.
Step 6: Estimate	
Estimate unknown answers using the ACE guessing technique.	Avoid absolutes. Choose the longest or most detailed choice. Eliminate identical choices.
Step 7: Survey	
Survey to ensure that all questions are answered.	Switch an answer only if you're sure.

Source: Hughes et al. (2005). Reprinted with permission.

WORKING TOGETHER

COLLABORATING TO TEACH STUDENTS WITH VISUAL IMPAIRMENTS

Most teachers need assistance when they are working with students who have sensory challenges. Access to the general education curriculum for these students is of great importance, so consultation about their needs is a critical part of a special educator's and general educator's job. Professionals collaborating in their work with students who are blind or visually impaired should address the following issues. Together, these professionals can make decisions about materials, braille text, and grading. Susan J. Spungin, an internationally renowned expert on the education and rehabilitation of individuals who are blind or visually impaired, offers suggestions to general education teachers who have students who are blind or visually impaired in their classroom.

- Consider the child as more like other children than different from them. Talk with the child about his or her interests and experiences and expect the child to follow rules that are appropriate to his or her developmental level.
- Always let a visually impaired child know when you are approaching or leaving. Identify yourself by name, especially if the child doesn't know you well. Never make a game of having a child guess who you are. To do so can be confusing, frightening, or frustrating to a child.
- Briefly describe aspects of the environment that might be of importance or interest to the child that he or she cannot see.
- Always ask before providing physical assistance. If the child cannot understand words, offer your hand or arm for assistance. If the child does not know you well, touch him or her only on the hands or forearms, as you might touch another person in a social situation. Reserve hugging and close physical contact for children who know you well, especially if the child is older than preschool age.
- Use words like *blind* or *visually impaired* in normal conversation with the child, but only when they are important to the topic being discussed. Feel free to use words like *look* and *see*, just as you would with any other child.
- When walking with a child, encourage him or her to hold your arm near or above the elbow and to use a cane, if he or she has one. A young child might hold your wrist or forefinger. Discourage hand holding as a means of providing travel assistance; help the child understand that it is a way of expressing affection and is different from travel assistance.

Questions

1. What are some considerations for teaching students who have visual impairments?
2. How should teachers collaborate to ensure students with visual impairments can access the curriculum?
3. Which of the items on this list did you already know? What information is new to you?
4. If you learn that you are to have a student who is blind or visually impaired in your classroom, where would you go for assistance? What questions might you have?

Source: Spungin (2013).

SUMMARY

Content-area instruction is the emphasis of upper elementary and secondary teaching. In these grades, students learn content from textbooks, listen to teachers' lectures, and participate in activities that help them use their knowledge. Study skills are important at the secondary level because students must (a) manage their time efficiently to study notes from class and the textbook, (b) memorize material, and (c) take tests that enable them to advance to the next grade level and eventually graduate from high school. However, we know that students with unique learning needs or disabilities exhibit a variety of problems in learning and studying content, which interferes with their ability to gain access to and master content-area material. As you recall, reading and understanding textbooks present challenges for students with reading problems. Acquiring information through listening to lectures and learning this information sufficiently to do well on tests are challenges for many struggling students. For content-area instruction, we discussed instructional techniques to foster student learning in the areas of content-area vocabulary and concepts, self-monitoring of reading comprehension, textbook reading, and student participation. For study skills, techniques were identified for time management, listening and note taking, and for memorization and test-taking.

REVIEW THE LEARNING OBJECTIVES

Let's review the learning objectives for this chapter. If you are uncertain and/or cannot talk through the answers provided for any of these questions, reread those sections of the chapter.

14.1 Explain the difficulties students demonstrate with content-area instruction.
Some students are slow readers orally and silently, have limited sight vocabularies, have trouble decoding words with inflectional endings and multisyllabic words, and/or have difficulty constructing mental images of text descriptions and structures. They have particular difficulty when they attempt to summarize text, generate and answer different types and levels of questions, draw inferences, and monitor their comprehension. They may also struggle to understand derivational, denotative, and connotative meanings and to apply word meanings across content areas.

14.2 Describe how teachers can teach content-area vocabulary and concepts.
When using textbooks, students can benefit from using graphic organizers and comprehension monitoring strategies. They should learn to identify the meaning of unfamiliar words through mapping, associations, and context clues. Teachers can foster student participation by providing class discussion guides and asking higher- and lower-order questions. Students can also participate in learning by conducting research, using anchors to promote understanding, and using technology to create multimedia projects.

14.3 Explain how teachers can teach students to monitor their reading comprehension.
Teachers can help students master the steps in comprehension monitoring. The monitoring steps include are (a) activating background knowledge, (b) clarifying the purposes for reading, (c) identifying the important information, (d) summarizing information, (e) engaging in self-questioning about the text, (f) using text structure formats to comprehend text, and (g) correcting problems when comprehension is inadequate.

14.4 Describe how students can learn from textbook instruction.
Students can benefit from explicit instruction that helps them recognize and use text structures and features that aid comprehension, such as introductions, outlines, objectives, headings, boldface type, graphics, and focus questions. Because textbooks continue to be the materials used most often by content-area teachers as the basis for their instruction, selecting textbooks is an important consideration for teachers and students.

14.5 Explain how teachers can promote student participation.
Teachers should include all students in class discussions through questioning strategies that facilitate discussions and by requiring students to write their responses and share their ideas within small groups. Teachers should spend time observing small group work and checking for understanding, modeling how to respond to questions, and asking probing questions to stimulate student thinking.

14.6 Describe how teachers can help students with difficulties in study skills.
Teachers can help students to audit their time by having them use electronic calendars and other useful devices. Students can also be taught how to learn content by color-coding, enlarging, underlining, highlighting, and rewriting their notes. Finally, teachers can suggest tips for being better test takers.

14.7 Name ways to facilitate memorization and test taking.

There are numerous ways to help students improve their memory skills, such as (a) teaching students how to create mnemonic devices to assist them in memorizing and recalling content such as lists of information, important people, and steps in a procedure; (b) discussing how some information can be remembered by creating mental images—have students provide specific examples of images they create; and (c) teaching students to "chunk" related information for easier memorization and recall—this necessitates discussing the concepts of compare and contrast, where students must attend to specific categorical features to be able to state how things are similar and how they are different. Strategies such as PIRATES can also be helpful.

REVISIT THE OPENING CHALLENGE

Check your answers to the Reflection Questions from the Opening Challenge and revise them on the basis of what you have learned.

1. What difficulties might students in both teachers' classes exhibit with regard to content-area instruction and study skills?
2. How can the teachers effectively work with their students to help them become efficient learners in content-area instruction and study skills?
3. How can these teachers provide adapted lessons to students who require intensive intervention, while keeping the rest of the class busy with relevant work?
4. How can study skills assessment be used to identify how students, including struggling students, become more efficient learners?

KEY TERMS

anchored instruction
chunking
connotative meanings
content-area instruction
denotative meanings
expository text
fix-up strategy
hierarchical charts
information processing
physical features of the text
semantic maps
short-term memory
signal words
Venn diagrams

PROFESSIONAL STANDARDS AND LICENSURE

For a complete description of Professional Standards and Licensure, please see the appendix.

CEC Initial Preparation Standards

Standard 1: Learner Development and Individual Learning Differences

Standard 3: Curricular Content Knowledge

Standard 4: Assessment

Standard 5: Instructional Planning and Strategies

INTASC Core Principles

Standard 1: Learner Development

Standard 2: Learning Differences

Standard 4: Content Knowledge

Standard 6: Assessment

Standard 7: Planning for Instruction

Standard 8: Instructional Strategies

Standard 9: Professional Learning and Ethical Practice

Praxis II: Education of Exceptional Students: Core Content Knowledge

I. Understanding Exceptionalities: Human Development and Behavior

III. Delivery of Services to Students: Background Knowledge

COMMON CORE STATE STANDARDS

Reading

- Literacy
- Craft and structure
- Integration of knowledge and ideas
- Range of reading and level of text complexity

Writing

- Text types and purposes
- Production and distribution of writing
- Research to build and present knowledge
- Range of writing

GLOSSARY

504 plan: An individualized educational plan outlining accommodations and other services to be delivered to children who do not qualify for special education services through IDEA because their educational performance is not affected by their disabilities but receive services through Section 504 of the Rehabilitation Act

academic learning time: The amount of time students spend on an academic task that they perform with a high degree of success

access to the general education curriculum: A requirement of IDEA 2004; gives students with disabilities the right to receive evidence-based instruction in the general education curriculum, to the greatest extent possible

accommodations: Supports to compensate for disabilities; adjustments to assignments or tests

acronym: A memory aid that consists of a word made from the first letters of the words that convey the information to be learned

acrostic: A memory aid that consists of a sentence wherein the first letters of the words stand for both the items to be recalled and their proper order

active listening: A method of listening that involves ways to listen and respond to communication partners more effectively

active participation: A form of learning in which teachers strive to directly involve students in the learning process

active process assessment: A type of assessment that helps children to be more involved and engaged in the assessment process, not passive recipients

ADAPT Framework: Steps used to differentiate instruction; provides questions to assist teachers in making instructional and evaluation decisions for individual students

adaptive behavior: Conceptual, social, and practical skills used in daily life

adequate yearly progress: The progress of students toward their end-of-year goals, as tracked by the use of assessment data

advance organizer: Activities to prepare students for the lesson's content

age equivalents: Derived developmental scores reported in years and months

algorithmic: Pertaining to solving a mathematical problem (e.g., finding the greatest common divisor) in a finite number of steps

Americans with Disabilities Act (ADA): Federal antidiscrimination legislation guaranteeing basic civil rights to people with disabilities

anchored instruction: An instructional technique that begins with an event or problem situation (a video or movie can be the anchor). The video is used to provide background information about the event or problem situation and to create a context that contributes to a shared experience among students to facilitate learning

anorexia: Intense fear of gaining weight, disturbed body image, and chronic refusal of or absence of appetite for food, causing severe weight loss (25% of body weight)

array of services: Constellation of special education services, personnel, and educational placements

assessment: Gathering relevant information to help make decisions

assistive technologist: A related services provider and member of multidisciplinary IEP teams who assists with the selection, acquisition, or use of assistive technology

assistive technology (AT): Equipment (devices) or services that help compensate for an individual's disabilities

Assistive Technology Act of 2004 (ATA, or Tech Act): Federal legislation that facilitates increased accessibility through technology

assistive technology device: Equipment and aids used to reduce the effects of disabilities

assistive technology services: Services delivered by a related services provider who is an expert in assistive technology

asthma: The most common chronic health condition among children, resulting in difficulty breathing

astigmatism: A refractive error, that is, a problem with how the eye focuses light

at risk: Students who have experiences, living conditions, or characteristics that have been shown to contribute to school failure

audience: In writing, the person(s) who will read the paper

audience sense: In writing, the process for determining the probable reader

audiogram: A grid or graph used to record a person's hearing abilities

audiologist: A related services provider and member of multidisciplinary IEP teams who diagnoses hearing losses and auditory problems

augmentative and alternative communication devices (AAC): Software and hardware used to facilitate communication

aura: A signal of an upcoming seizure

automaticity: Practicing skills until they require less cognitive processing of base words

basal textbook: A textbook adopted by school districts to serve as a primary source for subject-area content

base-10: Decimal numeral system that has 10 as its base

base word: The primary lexical unit of a word; also known as the root word

behavioral strategies: Techniques to increase or decrease targeted behaviors

behavior intervention plan (BIP): Part of an IEP for students whose behavior and/or social skills require intervention

bell-shaped curve: A symmetrical curve that represents the normal distribution of values, frequencies, or probabilities of a set of data

benchmark: In assessment, a predetermined standard for success or failure

braille: A system of reading and writing that uses dot codes embossed on paper; tactile reading; in 1824, Louis Braille created a precursor to the method used today

brainstorming: To think of several ideas related to a topic, write notes as one thinks, and use the notes to generate further ideas

bulimia: Chronically causing oneself to vomit or otherwise remove food to limit weight gain

check for understanding: During a lesson, periodically determining whether students are learning the content

child find: A requirement of IDEA 2004 in which educators help refer and identify children and youths with disabilities

chronic illnesses: Illnesses that last for an extended period of time

chunking: Organizing information by groups or topics

classroom management: Purposeful planning, delivery, and evaluation of techniques and procedures that ensure a classroom environment conducive to teaching and learning

clinical teaching cycle: Sequenced instruction, reteaching if necessary, and informal assessment procedures, including assessment of academic and conversational language proficiency

coexisting disabilities: The situation of having more than one disability; comorbidity

cognitive strategy instruction: Method of teaching techniques, principles, or rules that lead students through an instructional activity; may or may not involve mnemonics

collaboration: Professionals working in partnerships to provide educational services

collaborative consultation: A partnership between the general education and special education teachers, tapping the expertise of both to provide appropriate services to students with disabilities

community-based instruction: Teaching functional skills in real-life situations or in environments where they occur

concepts: A general idea or understanding; a crucial word or a few words that are critical for understanding the content

conflict: A disagreement of interests or ideas

congenital: Present at birth or originating during early infancy

connotative meanings: An associated meaning added to the primary meaning

construct validity: A form of technical adequacy in assessment that reflects whether tests provide results that are associated with the construct being measured

content-area instruction: Teaching students subject knowledge in areas such as social studies, science, and literature

content validity: A form of technical adequacy in assessment that reflects whether tests contain items that come from a legitimate source and meet basic statistical criteria

contingent observation: A behavior management approach in which a disruptive student is removed from an activity but is still able to observe the activity

continuum of services: Pattern in which each level of special education services is more restrictive than the one before, and services come in a lock-step sequence

convergent, lower-order questions: Questions that usually have one answer and start with *who, what, where*, or *when*

cooperative learning: A grouping practice in which small, mixed-ability groups work collaboratively to complete activities

core curriculum: Content that is taught to all students in the general education classroom

coteaching: Team teaching by general education and special education teachers

criterion-referenced tests: Assessment measures administered for purposes of comparing performance to standards that signal mastery of the content being tested

criterion-related validity: A form of technical adequacy in assessment that has to do with whether tests produce results similar to established tests, either presently (concurrent criterion-related validity) or in the future (predictive criterion-related validity)

criterion-specific rewards: A reward system in which students earn privileges only when they reach desirable levels of the target behavior

cues: Visual or verbal prompts provided to increase the likelihood of correct student responses

culture: A way of perceiving the world and of interacting within it

cumulative folders: A means of documenting and collecting a student's school activities across time

cumulative practice: Students practice skills that have been learned to that point

curb cuts: Now on almost every street corner, these inclines allow for easier access to cross streets, created for people who use wheelchairs and benefiting those with strollers, suitcases, and other rolling devices

curriculum-based measurement (CBM): A direct measurement system used to monitor students' progress mastering basic academic skills

data-based decision making: Using data to identify students who require additional instruction and to determine whether intensive intervention supports are effective

data-based individualization: A system of individualizing instruction by using data from students' performance to determine changes in instruction

decodable texts: Text that contains words made up of the sounds and patterns that students have mastered

decoding: Identifying unknown words by using knowledge of letter-sound correspondences

de minimis: Only meeting a minimum amount of performance change

denotative meanings: Literal, dictionary meaning

depression: Feelings of rejection, guilt, and negative self-image and worth

derived scores: Normative scores (e.g., age equivalents, grade equivalents, ratio IQs, percentiles, and standard scores) into which raw scores are converted

developmental delay: A condition that occurs with children who are less developed mentally or physically than their agemates; behind in developmental milestones

diagnostic measures: Assessments performed to confirm or determine the presence of a condition

diagnostic teaching: Giving problems and asking students questions to determine their thinking

differentiated instruction: Provision of an individualized array of instructional interventions

direct instruction: Teacher-directed instruction that focuses on using explicit, systematic procedures such as modeling, practice opportunities, pacing, error correction, and progress monitoring

disabilities: Results of impairments or medical conditions

distributed practice: Practice opportunities presented over time on skills that have been taught

divergent, higher-order questions: Questions that require students to make inferences, to analyze or synthesize information, and to evaluate content

Down syndrome: A genetic cause of intellectual disabilities resulting from a chromosomal abnormality

drafting: In writing, the stage in which the author attempts to put words on paper using the planning and organization information developed during prewriting

due process hearings: Noncourt proceeding before an impartial hearing officer, used when parents and school personnel disagree on a special education issue

dyscalculia: A disorder in learning mathematics skills and concepts

dysgraphia: A disorder in writing that involves problems with handwriting, spelling, and composition

dyslexia: A language-based reading disability

early intervening: Providing instructional intervention before special education services become necessary

echolalia: Repeating words and phrases over and over again

ecological assessment: An assessment approach that explores the student's relationship to his or her environment, rather than simply focusing on student strengths and deficits

editing: In writing, the stage in which writers focus on the mechanical aspects of spelling, capitalization, and punctuation

Education for All Handicapped Children Act (EHA): *See* Public Law (PL) 94-142

efficacy: The power to produce an effect

Emergency Care Plan: A document that provides instructions on what school personnel should do in cases of emergencies that also includes important contact information

engaged time: The amount of time that students are involved in learning

English language learners (ELLs): see English learners (ELs)

English learners (ELs): Students who are learning English as their second (or third) language; previously called English language learners (ELLs)

enrichment: Addition to the traditional curriculum of further topics and skills for the instruction of gifted and talented students

error-correction procedures: The teacher's provision of immediate feedback to correct error responses

event recording: An observational system to measure each occurrence of a discrete behavior (i.e., a behavior with an observable beginning and end, such as hand raising)

evidence-based practices: Instruction proved effective through rigorous research; also known as validated practice

executive functioning: Ability to self-monitor by using working memory, inner speech, attention, and rehearsal

exempt: In high-stakes testing, the status of a student who does not have to participate in testing

explicit instruction: Instruction in which the teacher specifically outlines the learning goals and provides clear, definitive explanations of the skills being taught and instructional procedures being used

explicit systematic instruction: Teachers model the task and provide extensive feedback as students work through multiple opportunities to practice and respond

expository text: Authentic and accurate information that is usually presented using clear, focused language and moves from facts that are general to specific and abstract to concrete

externalizing behaviors: Behaviors directed toward others (e.g., aggressive behaviors)

family systems approach: An approach in which families' needs and support are defined according to resources, interactions, functions, and the life cycle

fidelity: Following the protocol or lesson steps as developed for the instructional practice; ensuring the research measures are valid and reliable

fix-up strategy: In reading, a technique used to aid in comprehension by being able to identify unknown words or phrases

form: In writing, the type of written product (e.g., a letter, story, essay, shopping list, or poem)

fragile X syndrome (FXS): A genetic cause of intellectual disabilities

free appropriate public education (FAPE): Ensures that students with disabilities receive necessary education and services without cost to the family

frustration-level texts: In reading, the level at which the student has less than 90% word recognition and less than 90% comprehension

full inclusion: Special education or related services delivered exclusively in the general education classroom

functional behavior assessment: An assessment that defines the target behavior, determines its cause, and determines the consequences that maintain it; it is a required step in qualifying for special education services for students with emotional or behavioral disorders

functional capabilities: Student strengths related to specific tasks

functional skills: Skills used to manage a home, cook, shop, commute, and organize personal living environments with the goal of independent living; also known as life skills

generalize: To transfer learning from particular instances to other environments, people, times, or events

general vocabulary: Words that are used on a regular basis during conversation

gifted and talented: Students who are identified at the preschool, elementary, or secondary level as possessing demonstrated or potential abilities that give evidence of high performance capability

grade equivalent: Derived developmental score reported in years and tenths of years

graphic organizers: Visual aids to help students organize, understand, see relationships, and remember important information

guided practice: The teacher's provision of multiple opportunities to respond and practice

handicap: A challenge or barrier imposed by others, or by society, because of a condition or disability

hand over hand: Sign language for individuals with deaf-blindness wherein signs are conveyed through touch

hierarchical charts: Charts on which broader concepts are listed first and then connected to smaller, supporting concepts

high-frequency words: The most commonly occurring words in text

high-incidence disabilities: Special education categories with the most students

high-leverage practice: An educational practice that has proven effective across time

high-stakes assessments: State- and districtwide assessments to ensure that all students are making satisfactory progress

holistic evaluation: Evaluations in which a single, overall rating is assigned to achievement in learning the curriculum; contrast with the use of an analytical evaluation scale

home-bound/hospital instruction: Special education services delivered to the student's home or hospital setting, usually as a consequence of the student's fragile health

hyperactivity: Impaired ability to sit or concentrate for long periods of time

I-message: A communication technique that involves stating the behavior of concern, the effect of the behavior on the person sending the I-message, and the feelings that the person sending the I-message has as a result

impulsivity: Impaired ability to control one's own behavior

inattention: Inability to pay attention or focus

inclusive education: Educational setting in which students with disabilities have access to the general education curriculum, participate in school activities alongside students without disabilities, and attend their neighborhood school

independent practice: Practice that does not require direct teacher supervision or guidance; may occur in the classroom or as homework

individualized education program (IEP): Management tool to identify needed services and to specify and organize them in detail; developed through collaboration among general and special educators, administrators, medical professionals, related services providers, the student's family, and (if appropriate) the student who will receive special education services

individualized family service plan (IFSP): Management tool to identify and organize services and resources for infants and toddlers (birth to age 3) and their families

Individuals with Disabilities Education Act (IDEA): The special education law that protects the rights of students with disabilities to a free appropriate public education; originated with PL 94-142 in 1975

inferential thinking skills: Reasoning skills; the ability to understand meaning that is not explicitly stated

informal reading inventory: A unique reading test that consists of graded word lists and graded passages and for which test scores are reported in terms of grade equivalents

information processing: The flow of information that leads to understanding, knowledge, and the ability to act on information

input adaptations: How students access test stimuli and questions

in-school supervision: Removing a student from one or more classes and requiring him or her to spend the time in a designated school area

instructional objective: A statement as to what students should be able to do following instruction

instructional reading level: The reading level at which the reader has either 90% to 94% word recognition and 90% to 100% comprehension or 95% word recognition and 90% to 94% comprehension

intelligence quotient (IQ): Score on a standardized test that is supposed to reflect learning ability

intensive intervention: Instruction or behavioral procedures that are delivered individually or in small groups that are sustained and frequent

interdependent group contingency: Arrangement in which individuals earn reinforcement when they achieve a goal established for the group

interest inventory: An assessment of a person's likes and dislikes

interim alternative educational setting (IAES): A special education placement to ensure progress toward IEP goals, assigned when a serious behavioral infraction necessitates removal from current placement

inter-individual: Occurring between, or involving, two or more people

internalizing behaviors: Behaviors directed inward (e.g., withdrawn, anxious, depressed)

interval recording: A system designed to measure the number of intervals of time in which continuous, highly frequent behavior occurs during the observation period

intra-individual difference: In assessment, the strengths and weaknesses a person exhibits across test scores

irregular words: Words in which some or all of the letters do not make their common sounds

itinerants: Professionals who work in different locations

language delays: Slowed development of language skills; may or may not result in language impairments

language different: Students who are just beginning to learn a second language or are using nonstandard English

language impairments: Difficulty in mastering, or inability to master, the various systems of rules in language, which then interferes with communication

least restrictive environment (LRE): Educational placement of students with disabilities that provides as much inclusion in the core curriculum, and as much integration with typical learners, as possible and appropriate

legibility: The extent to which what is written can be deciphered or understood

letter combinations: Two or more consecutive letters that represent a single sound (/sh/) or multiple sounds (/bl/) in words

letter-sound correspondences: Associations of a common sound with specific letters or letter combinations in a word

level of concern: Amount of student interest in the instruction

life skills: Skills associated with living in a home, cooking, shopping, and other daily activities

limb loss: Loss of a physical appendage (e.g., foot, arm)

loudness: An aspect of voice, consisting of the intensity of the sound produced while speaking

low-incidence disabilities: Special education categories with relatively few students

mainstreamed: A term formerly used to signify including students with disabilities in school activities alongside students who do not have disabilities

manifestation determination: Determination of whether a student's disciplinary problems are due to their disability

medically fragile: A term used to describe the status of individuals with health conditions that require 24-hour supervision by a nurse

mirror writing: Writing in a direction that is the opposite of the typical manner

mixed-ability groups: Arrangement of students into groups whose members are performing at various levels on the skills targeted for instruction

mnemonic: A technique for aiding memory by forming meaningful associations and linkages across information that appears to be unrelated

modeling: A demonstration of how to perform the steps involved in solving a problem

morphemes: The smallest unit of language that conveys meaning

multicultural education: Instruction that provides students with ways to see themselves reflected in the curriculum, as well as to learn about others

multidisciplinary teams: Groups of professionals with different areas of expertise, assembled to meet the special needs of individual students

multiple means of action and expression: Encouraging students to respond in different ways, in accordance with their strengths

multiple means of engagement: Involving students in activities by using a variety of modes of representation and expression to address their interests

multiple means of representation: Presenting information in various formats to reduce or avoid sensory and cognitive barriers to learning

multi-tiered systems of support (MTSS): Tiered levels of increasingly intensive intervention at the primary, secondary, and tertiary levels to address problems with academic (RTI) and/or behavioral issues (PBIS)

No Child Left Behind Act (NCLB): Reauthorization of the Elementary and Secondary Education Act mandating higher standards for both students and teachers, including an accountability system

nonexamples: Information that is given, usually by a teacher, that is specifically not an example of what is being taught; intended to make meaning clearer

nonverbal communication: Information given to another through sending and receiving wordless cues

normal curve: Theoretical construct of the typical distribution of human traits such as intelligence; also known as a bell-shaped curve

norm-referenced interpretations: Interpretations of student's relative standing when his or her scores are compared to that of a normative group

norm-referenced tests: Tests that compare a student's knowledge or skills to the knowledge or skills of a normative group

number sense: Good intuition and understanding about numbers and the relationships among them

objective referral process: Specific, transparent procedures employed to make referral decisions

observations: In assessment, watching students do something, thinking about what they are doing, determining why they are doing it, and identifying what the behavior means to the students and those around them

occupational therapist: a related services provider and member of interdisciplinary IEP teams who directs activities that improve muscular control and develop self-help skills

on-task behavior: Behavior focused on the task at hand

orientation and mobility: Skills needed to move safely and independently at school and in the community

orthopedic impairments: The term used in IDEA 2004 for physical disabilities or physical impairments

other health impairments: A special education category that consists of health conditions that create special needs and disabilities but are not described specifically in any other category; also includes ADHD

overlearn: To continue to practice beyond the point of mastery

overrepresented: The assignment to a special education category of more students from a diverse group than would be expected on the basis of the proportion of that diverse group in the overall population of students

paraprofessional: Classroom assistant who is not a certified teacher but performs instructional duties to fulfill a child or children's IEPs

paraprofessionals, or paraeducators: Teacher assistants who work in a supportive role under the supervision of licensed professionals

partial products: Partitioning quantities to help students focus on place value

pedagogy: Instructional practices, teaching

peer conferencing: Students discussing each other's written products; considered an effective feedback and editing activity in the writing process

peer or expert consultation: Teachers observing their peers providing interventions to learners, such as English learners, who need supplemental instruction

peer tutoring: A grouping practice wherein pairs of students work on their skills, usually for extra practice

percentiles: Scores reported on norm-referenced tests that indicate the percentage of scores (determined from a normative sample) that fall below a person's raw score; percentile rank

perinatal: During birth

peripheral vision: The outer area of a person's visual field

phonograms: Parts of a word to which consonants or blends are added to make a word (examples include *an*, *ip*, and *un*); also known as rimes

phonological awareness: One's sensitivity to, or explicit awareness of, the phonological structure of words in one's language

physical features of the text: Headings, tables, bold-faced terms, chapter organizers and summaries, and the like

physical therapist (PT): A related service provider and member of multidisciplinary teams with expertise in improving individuals' motor functioning, movement, and fitness

pitch: An aspect of voice; its perceived high or low sound quality

planned ignoring: Deliberate, systematic withdrawal of attention by the individual from whom attention is sought

Positive Behavioral Interventions and Supports (PBIS): The type of schoolwide MTSS that seeks to prevent behavior problems and provide interventions through a tiered approach, with each tier providing more intensive interventions and support

postlingually deaf: Deafness that occurs after speech is developed

postnatal: After birth

pragmatics: Function or use of language within social contexts

preictal stage: Timeframe before a seizure

prelingual deafness: Deafness that occurs before speech is developed

prenatal: Before birth

prereferral: Steps taken before the actual referral of a child to special education

present levels of academic achievement and functional performance (PLAAFP): A part of all IEPs to ensure that the program outlined is of high quality and exceeds de minimus progress

prevalence: Total number of cases at a given time

prewriting: The writing stage that involves activities, such as planning and organizing, that are conducted by the writer prior to writing

prior knowledge: What a student already knows about a topic

process assessment: Procedures used to determine the manner in which students derive a particular answer when solving a problem

progress monitoring: The systematic and frequent assessment of students' improvement of the skills being taught

prosocial behaviors: Behaviors that are positive and that build relationships

Public Law (PL) 94-142: Originally passed in 1975 to guarantee a free appropriate public education to all students with disabilities; also known as the Education for All Handicapped Children Act (EHA)

publishing: In writing, the stage in which the author's work is complete and is publicly shared in some format

pull-in programs: Pull-in (or push-in) programs are those taught to all students in a mainstream or inclusive classroom

pull-out programs: Part-time special services provided outside of the general education classroom, such as in a resource room

purpose: In writing, the reason for writing (e.g., to convey a message, to make a request, or to express feelings)

reading comprehension: The ability to understand what is read

reading fluency: The ability to read text accurately, quickly, and (if reading aloud) with expression

reading vocabulary: Words a student recognizes in print

recursive: In writing, the act of moving back and forth between stages as one writes and polishes one's work

reinforcement: The application of an event that increases the likelihood that the behavior it follows will occur again. Thus reinforcement is functionally related to an increase in frequency of that behavior

related services: Special education services from a wide range of disciplines and professions

reliability: In assessment, the consistency of measurement results

residual vision: The amount and degree of vision a person has functional use of despite a visual problem

resistant to treatment: A defining characteristic of learning disabilities. Validated methods typically applied in general education settings are not adequate to bring about sufficient learning; the student requires more intensive and sustained explicit instruction

response to intervention (RTI): The type of MTSS that prevents academic failure and addresses students' academic performance with increasing intensity of data-based instruction

revising: In writing, the stage in which authors make changes to the sequencing and structure of the written work to refine the content

rewards: Representations of targeted improvement, including tangible items, privileges, free time, or honors

robotics: The design, construction, operation, and use of robots, which includes the technology that makes robotic action possible

same-ability groups: Homogeneous groups of students who have similar skills

scaffolding: Providing temporary instruction supports to help struggling students learn

screening: The use of assessment data to identify quickly and efficiently who is struggling in a particular area

seclusion time-out: For severe, out-of-control behavior, placement of the pupil in an isolated room

Section 504 of the Rehabilitation Act of 1973: First federal law to outline the basic civil rights of people with disabilities

self-advocacy: Capacity to understand, ask for, and explain one's need for accommodations; expressing one's rights and needs

self-determination: Ability to identify and achieve goals for oneself

self-regulation: When individuals monitor their own behavior

self-writing: Writing about the student's own experiences

semantic maps: Visual display of a map or web of related words, vocabulary, or concepts

semantics: The language system that controls the content, intent and meaning of spoken and written language

service manager: A case coordinator who oversees the implementation and evaluation of IFSPs

short-term memory: The temporary store of information that is tapped for immediate use

sickle-cell anemia: A hereditary blood disorder that inhibits blood flow; African Americans are most at risk for this health impairment

sight word recognition: The ability to read a word automatically when encountering it in text or in a list of words

signals: Visual, auditory, and verbal cues that teachers use to gain student attention

signal words: Words that indicate the use of a text structure (e.g., first, second, and third for sequence and on the other hand for contrast)

silent reading fluency: The number of words read at a certain comprehension level at a certain reading level

sociogram: A depiction of peer relationships in graphic form

special education: Individualized education and services for students with disabilities and sometimes for students who are gifted and talented

special education categories: System used in IDEA 2004 to classify disabilities among students

specialized vocabulary: Words that have multiple meanings depending on the context

specific praise: Complimenting or verbally rewarding others for their accomplishments

speech/language pathologist (SLP): a related service provider and member of multidisciplinary teams with expertise in speech impairments and language development

student-centered learning: Learning in which students are actively engaged in hands-on tasks, discussions, and decision making

student response systems: The manner in which students can interact with one another and the teacher

stuttering: The lack of fluency in an individual's speech pattern, often characterized by hesitations or repetitions of sounds or words; dysfluency; a speech impairment

survey batteries: Compilations of tests that assess different areas and provide an overview of achievement

syntax: Rules that direct the order of words and phrases

systems of support: networks of people and services to promote independence

target behavior: A specific behavior, either positive or inappropriate, that the teacher focuses on to increase or decrease that behavior

teacher assistance team process: A collaborative approach in which the team discusses a student's problem, identifies possible interventions, and assists the teacher as needed in implementing strategies

teacher proximity: The teacher positioning himself or herself close to a student to prevent or eliminate problem behavior

technical vocabulary: Words that are used in a particular content area

text: Textbook or what appears in print

think aloud: The teacher saying out loud the steps they are taking while solving a problem

time sampling: Recording the number of intervals in which a target behavior occurs during the period of observation

tone: In writing, the "voice" of a written product, which can be lighthearted, serious, optimistic, pessimistic, and so forth

traffic patterns: Paths that students frequently follow as they move about the classroom

transition component of IEPs: A part of IEPs for students age 16 or older to help them move to adulthood

traumatic brain injury (TBI): Head injury not due to a stroke, brain tumor, or other internal cause; not present at birth

typical learners: Students and individuals without disabilities

unexpected underachievement: A defining characteristic of learning disabilities; poor school performance cannot be explained by other disabilities or limited potential

universal design: Barrier-free architectural and building designs, as set forth in the Americans with Disabilities Act, that meet the needs of everyone, but built for people with physical challenges.

Universal Design for Learning (UDL): Uses the principles of universal design by using materials and/or technology that increases access to the curriculum and instruction for all students, particularly those with disabilities

universal screening: Testing of everyone, including newborns, to determine the existence or risk of disability

validity: The extent to which an assessment device measures what it is supposed to measure

Venn diagrams: Intersecting shapes that show how concepts are similar and how they are different

verbal rehearsal: The use of a student repeatedly practicing aloud (or silently, still using words) to learn information

visual acuity: Sharpness of response to visual stimuli

wait time: The amount of time (about 3–4 seconds) between when the student is asked a question and when the teacher provides the response if the student does not answer

with-it-ness: A teacher's awareness of what is going on in his or her classroom at all times

working memory: The simultaneous processing and storing of information

writing conferences: Meeting held between writers (student-student or student-teacher) to improve a manuscript throughout the writing process

writing process: A recursive process involving five stages: prewriting, drafting, revising, editing, and publishing

REFERENCES

CHAPTER 1

American Psychiatric Association. (2013). *Diagnostic and statistical manual of mental disorders* (5th ed.). American Psychiatric Association.

Americans with Disabilities Act of 1990, PL No. 101-336, 104 Stat. 327 (1991).

Americans with Disabilities Amendments Act of 2008, PL 110-325 (2009).

Anastasiou, D., & Kauffman, J. M. (2017). Social constructionist approach to disability: Implications for special education. In A. R. Sadovnik, P. W. Cookson, S. F. Semel, & R. W. Coughlan (Eds.) *Exploring education* (5th ed.). Routledge.

Arlington Central School District Board of Education v. Murphy, 548 U.S. 291 (2006).

Artiles, A. J. (2019). Fourteenth Annual Brown Lecture in Education research: Re-envisioning equity research: Disability identification disparities as a case in point. *Educational Researchers, 48*(6), 325–335.

Artiles, A. (2020). Inclusive education in the 21st century: Disruptive interventions. *The Educational Forum, 84*(4), 289–295.

Artiles, A. (2022). Interdisciplinary inequality research in the E/BD field: Animating intersectionality, reflexivity, and equity. *Journal of Emotional and Behavioral Disorders*. https://doi.org/10.1177/10634266221083922

Assistive Technology Act of 2004, PL 108–364 (2004).

Asthma and Allergy Foundation of America. (2022). *Asthma facts and figures*. https://www.aafa.org/asthma-facts/

Ballard, J., Ramirez, B. A., & Weintraub, F. J. (1982). *Special education in America: Its legal and governmental foundations*. Council for Exceptional Children.

Barczak, M. A. (2019). Simulated and community-based instruction: Teaching students to make financial transactions. *Teaching Exceptional Children, 51*(4), 313–321. https://doi.org/10.1177/0040059919826035

Biggs, E. E., Gilson, C. B., & Carter, E. W. (2018). "Developing that balance": Preparing and supporting special education teachers work with paraprofessionals. *Teacher education and Special Education, 42*(2), 117–131. https://doi.org/10.1177/0888406418765611

Branson, J., & Miller, D. (2002). *Damned for their difference: The cultural construction of deaf people as disabled*. Gallaudet University Press.

Brown v. Board of Education, 347 U.S. 483 (1954).

Brownell, M. T., Ciullo, S., & Kennedy, M. J. (2020–2021). High-leverage practices: Teaching students with disabilities—and all students who need a boost. *American Educator*. American Federation of Teachers. https://www.aft.org/ae/winter2020-2021/brownell_ciullo_kennedy

Burlington School Committee v. Department of Education, 471 U.S. 359 (1985).

Carter v. Florence County School District 4, 950 F. 2d 156 (1993).

Cedar Rapids School District v. Garret F., 106 F. 3rd 822 (8th Cir. 1997), cert. gr. 118 S. Ct. 1793 (1998), aff'd, 119 S. Ct. 992 (1999).

Center for Parent Information & Resources. (2019, February). *Q&A about Part B of IDEA: Parent participation*. https://www.parentcenterhub.org/qa2/

Centers for Disease Control, National Biomonitoring Program. (2021). *Environmental chemicals*. https://www.cdc.gov/biomonitoring/environmental_chemicals.html

Coyne, M. D., Kame'enui, E. J., & Carnine, D. W. (2011). *Effective teaching strategies that accommodate diverse learners* (4th ed.). Pearson.

Danielson, L., Marx, T., Sienko, J. D., & Gallo, G. (2017). *Is intensive intervention special education? Defining services for students with disabilities*. Presentation to 2017 Leadership Conference, Washington, DC. https://intensiveintervention.org/resource/intensive-intervention-special-education-defining-services-students-disabilities

Deno, S. (2003). Developments in curriculum-based measurement. *Journal of Special Education, 37*, 184–192.

Doe v. Withers, 20 IDELR 422 (1993).

Education for All Handicapped Children Act (EHA), PL 94–142 (1975).

Education for All Handicapped Children Act (EHA; reauthorized), PL 99–457 (1986).

Elementary and Secondary Education (No Child Left Behind) Act of 2001 (ESEA), PL No. 107–110 (2002).

Elementary and Secondary Education Act (ESEA), PL 107–110 (2001).

Elementary and Secondary Education Act (ESEA), PL 114–95. (2015).

Endrew F. v. Douglas County School District RE-1, 580 U. S. (2017)

Finn, C. E., Jr., Rotherham, A. J., & Hokanson, C. R., Jr. (Eds.). (2001). *Rethinking special education for a new century*. Thomas B. Fordham Foundation and the Progressive Policy Institute.

Florian, L. (2007). Reimagining special education. In L. Florian (Ed.), *The Sage handbook of special education* (pp. 7–20). SAGE.

Foegen, A., Jiban, C., & Deno, S. (2007). Progress monitoring measures in mathematics. *Journal of Special Education, 41*(2), 121–139.

Forest Grove School District v. T. A., 129 S. Ct. 987 (2009).

Friend, M. (2019). *Co-teach! Building and sustaining effective classroom partnerships in inclusive schools* (3rd ed.). National Professional Resources.

Friend, M., & Barron, T. (2020). *Specially designed instruction for co-teaching: Maximizing student outcomes by intensifying teaching and learning*. National Professional Resources.

Fuchs, D., Fuchs, L. S., & Vaughn, S. (2014). What is intensive instruction and why is it important? *Teaching Exceptional Children, 46*, 13–18.

Fuchs, L. S., Fuchs, D., & Malone A. S. (2017). The taxonomy of intervention intensity. *Teaching Exceptional Children, 50*(1), 35–43.

Gartner, A., & Lipsky, D. K. (1987). Beyond special education: Toward a quality system for all students. *Harvard Educational Review, 57*, 367–395.

Grossman, H. (2002). *Ending discrimination in special education* (2nd ed.). Charles C Thomas.

Honig v. Doe, 484 U.S. 305, 108 S. Ct. 592 (1988).

Individuals with Disabilities Education Act (IDEA), PL 101–476. (1990).

Individuals with Disabilities Education Act (IDEA), PL 105–17, 111 Stat. 37 (1997).

Individuals with Disabilities Education Act Regulations, 34 C.F.R. §300.226 (2022).

Individuals with Disabilities Education Act Regulations, 34 C.F.R. §300.322 (2017).

Individuals with Disabilities Education Improvement Act (IDEIA or IDEA), PL 108–446 (2004).

Irving Independent School District v. Tatro, 468 U.S. 833 (1984).

Katsiyannis, A., & Yell, M. L. (2000). The Supreme Court and school health services: Cedar Rapids v. Garret F. *Exceptional Children, 66*, 317–326.

Knitzer, J., Steinberg, Z., & Fleisch, B. (1990). *At the schoolhouse door: An examination of programs and policies for children with emotional and behavioral problems.* Bank Street College of Education.

Lemons, C. J., Vaughn, S., Wexler, J., Kearns, D. M., & Sinclair, A. C. (2018). Envisioning an improved continuum of special education services for students with learning disabilities: Considering intervention intensity. *Learning Disabilities Research and Practice, 33*(3), 131–143.

Longmore, P. (2003). *Why I burned my book and other essays on disability.* Temple University Press.

Marshall, A. T., Betts, S., Kan, E. C., McConnell, R., Llanphear, B. P., & Sowell, E. R. (2020). Association of lead-exposure risk and family income with childhood brain outcomes. *Nature Medicine, 26*, 91–97. https://doi.org/10.1038/s41591-019-0713-y

Mills v. Board of Education of the District of Columbia, 348 F. Supp. 866 (1972).

Morris-Mathews, H., Stark, K. R., Jones, N. D., Brownell, M. T., & Bell, C. A. (2020). Danielson's Framework for Teaching: Convergence and divergence with conceptions of effectiveness in special education. *Journal of Learning Disabilities, 54*(1), 66–78.

Office of Special Education Programs. (2017a). *Questions and answers (Q&A) on U.S. Supreme Court case decision Endrew F. v. Douglas County School District RE-1.* https://sites.ed.gov/idea/files/qa-endrewcase-12-07-2017.pdf

Office of Special Education Programs. (2017b). *39th annual report to Congress on the implementation of the Individuals with Disabilities Education Act, 2017.* U.S. Department of Education. Retrieved from https://www2.ed.gov/about/reports/annual/osep/2017/parts-b-c/39th-arc-for-idea.pdf

Office of Special Education Programs (2019). *41st Annual Report to Congress on the Implementation of the Individuals with Disabilities Education Act, 2021.* http://www.ed.gov/about/reports/annual/osep/2019/parts-b-c/index.html

Office of Special Education Programs. (2021, May 26). *OSEP fast facts: School aged children 5 through 21 served under Part B of the IDEA.* Retrieved on March 29, 2023 from https://sites.ed.gov/idea/osep-fast-facts-school-aged-children-5-21-served-under-idea-part-b-21/

Office of Special Education Programs (2022). *43rd Annual Report to Congress on the Implementation of the Individuals with Disabilities Education Act, 2021.* http://www.ed.gov/about/reports/annual/osep

Patient Protection and Affordable Care Act, PL 111–148 (2010).

Pennsylvania Association for Retarded Children (PARC) v. Commonwealth of Education, 343 F. Supp. 279 (E.D. Pa. 1972).

Rehabilitation Act of 1973, Section 504, 19 U.S.C. 794 (1973).

Roos, P. (1970). Trends and issues in special education for the mentally retarded. *Education and Training of the Mentally Retarded, 5*, 51–61.

Rowe, D. A., Alverson, C. Y., Kwaitek, S., & Fowler, C. (2020, February). *Effective practices in transition: Operational definitions.* National Center on Transition. https://transitionta.org/wp-content/uploads/docs/Description-of-EBPs_2020_02-02.pdf

Rowley v. Hendrick Hudson School District, 458 U.S. 176 (1982).

Sailor, W. (1991). Special education in the restructured school. *Remedial and Special Education, 12*, 8–22.

Skiba, R. J., Artiles, A. J., Kozleski, E. B., Losen, D. J., & Harry, E. G. (2016). Risks and consequences of oversimplifying educational inequities: A response to Morgan et al. *Educational Researchers, 45*(3), 221–225.

Smith v. Robinson, 468 U.S. 992 (1984).

Snell, M. E., & Brown, F. (2006). *Instruction of students with severe disabilities* (6th ed.). Prentice Hall.

Stecker, P. M., Fuchs, L. S., & Fuchs, D. (2005). Using curriculum-based measurement to improve student achievement: Review of research. *Psychology in the Schools, 42*(8), 795–819.

Swanson, H. L., Hoskyn, M., & Lee, C. (1999). *Interventions for students with learning disabilities. A meta-analysis of treatment outcomes.* Guilford Press.

TASH. (2022). *Mission statement.* https://tash.org/about/

Technology-Related Assistance for Individuals with Disabilities Act of 1988. PL 100–407 (1998).

TIES Center. (2023). *TIES helps educators, parents, and administrators create and support inclusive school communities.* https://tiescenter.org/

Timothy W. v. Rochester, New Hampshire, School District, 875 F. 2d 945 (1989).

Turnbull, A., Turnbull, H. R., Wehmeyer, M. L., & Shogren, K. A. (2020). *Exceptional lives: Practice, progress, and dignity in today's schools* (9th ed.). Pearson.

21st Century Assistive Technology Act, S. 2401, 117th Cong. (1st Sess. 2021–2022), Reauthorization of the Assistive Technology Act of 2004.

U.S. Department of Health and Human Services. (2022 February 4). *HHS issues new guidance for health care providers on civil rights protections for people with disabilities.* https://www.hhs.gov/civil-rights/for-providers/civil-rights-covid19/disability-faqs/index.htmlVanderbilt University. (2022). Special Education Resource Project. https://my.vanderbilt.edu/spedteacherresources/

West, J. (1994). *Federal implementation of the Americans with Disabilities Act, 1991–1994.* Milank Memorial Fund.

Winzer, M. A. (2007). Confronting difference: An excursion through the history of special education. In L. Florian (Ed.), *The Sage handbook of special education* (pp. 21–33). SAGE.

Wrightslaw. (2017). *Learn about a free appropriate public education (FAPE) under the Individuals with Disabilities Education Act.* https://www.wrightslaw.com/info/fape.index.htm

Zobrest v. Catalina Foothills School District, 963 F. 2d 190 (1993).

CHAPTER 2

Annie E. Casey Foundation. (2021). *Kids count data book: State trends in child well-being.* https://assets.aecf.org/m/resourcedoc/aecf-2021kidscountdatabook-2021.pdf

Bassetti, M. (2018, February 9). Academic inequality in urban school settings: Funding disparities that lead to educational disadvantages. American Society of Public Administrators, *PA Times Online.* https://patimes.org/academic-inequality-urban-school-setting-funding-disparities-lead-educational-disadvantages

Cardichon, J., Darling-Hammond, L., Yang, M., Scott, C., Shields, P. M., & Burns, D. (2020). *Inequitable opportunity to learn: Student access to certified and experienced teachers.* Learning Policy Institute.

Carver-Thomas, D., & Darling-Hammond, L. (2017, August 16). Teacher turnover: Why it matters and what we can do about it. Learning Policy Institute. https://learningpolicyinstitute.org/product/teacher-turnover-report

Center for Parent Information & Resources (CPIR). (2017). *Transition planning.* https://www.parentcenterhub.org/iep-transition/

Center on Positive Behavior Interventions and Support. (2021, December). *Installing a universal screening tool: Questions to consider.* https://www.pbis.org/resource/installing-a-universal-behavior-screening-tool-questions-to-consider

Colvin, M. (2021). The impact of COVID-19 related educational disruption on children and adolescents: An interim data summary and commentary on ten considerations for neuropsychological practice. *The Clinical Neuropsychologist, 36*, 45–71.

Couvillon, M. A., Yell, M. L., & Katsiyannis, A. (2018). *Endrew F. v. Douglas County School District* (2017) and special education law: What teachers and administrators need to know. *Preventing School Failure, 62*(4), 289–299. https://www.tandfonline.com/doi/full/10.1080/1045988X.2018.1456400

Education for All Handicapped Children Act (EHA; reauthorized). PL No. 99-457 (1986).

Endrew F. v. Douglas County School District RE-1, 580 U. S. (2017).

Galiatsos, S., Kruse, L., & Whittaker, M. (2019). *Forward together: Helping educators unlock the power of students who learn differently.* National Center for Learning Disabilities (NCLD) and Understood.

Harvey, M. W., Rowe, D. A., Test, D. W., Imperatore, C., Lombardi, A., Conrad, M., Szymanski, A., & Barnett, K. (2019). Partnering to improve career and technical education for students with disabilities: A position paper of the Division on Career Development and Transition. *Career Development and Transition for Exceptional Individuals, 43*(2), 67–77. https://doi.org/10.1177/2165143419887839

Hussar, B., Zhang, J., Hein, S., Wang, K., Roberts, A., Cui, J., Smith, M., Bullock Mann, F., Barmer, A., & Dilig, R. (2020). *The condition of education 2020* (NCES 2020-144). U.S. Department of Education. National Center for Education Statistics. Retrieved May 12, 2022 from https://nces.ed.gov/pubsearch/pubsinfo

IDEAs That Work. (2018, April). *High expectations and appropriate supports: The importance of IEPs.* IDEAs That Work Symposium Series. Retrieved from https://osepideasthatwork.org/osep-meeting/high-expectations-and-appropriate-supports-importance-ieps-2018

The IRIS Center. (2018). *RTI (Part 1): An overview.* Vanderbilt University. Retrieved from https://iris.peabody.vanderbilt.edu/module/rti01/

The IRIS Center. (2019a). IEPs: *Developing high-quality individualized education programs.* Retrieved from https://iris.peabody.vanderbilt.edu/module/iep01/

The IRIS Center. (2019b). *IEP team members, handout.* https://iris.peabody.vanderbilt.edu/module/iep02/cresource/q2/p03/#content

The IRIS Center. (2019c). *IEPs: How administrators can support the development and implementation of high-quality IEPs.* Retrieved from https://iris.peabody.vanderbilt.edu/module/iep02/

Individuals with Disabilities Education Act (IDEA). PL No. 105-17, 111 Stat. 37 (1997).

Individuals with Disabilities Education Act Regulations, 34 C.F.R. §300.34 (2022).

Johnston, W. R., & Young, C. (2019). *Principal and teacher preparation to support the needs of diverse students: National findings from the American educator panels.* Rand Corporation, Research Report. www.rand.org/t/RR29909

Kern, L., Baton, E., & George, H. P. (2021, November). *Strengthening family participation in addressing behavior in an IEP.* Center on PBIS, University of Oregon. www.pbis.org

Lee, S. W. (2018). Pulling back the curtain: Revealing the cumulative importance of high-performing, highly qualified teachers on students' educational outcome. *Educational Evaluation and Policy Analysis, 40*(3), 359–381. doi: 10.3102/0162373718769379

Levin, S. (2021, April 14). *Principals matter for schools and students.* National Institute for Excellence in Teaching. https://www.niet.org/newsroom/show/blog/principals-matter-for-schools-students

Martinez, S., Kern, L., Flannery, B., White, A., Freeman, J., & George, H. P. (2019). *High school PBIS implementation: Staff buy-in.* OSEP Technical Assistance Center on Positive Behavioral Interventions and Supports. www.pbis.org.

Mitchell, C. (2019, May 29). Most classroom teachers feel unprepared to support students with disabilities. *Education Week.*

Morris-Mathews, H., Stark, K. R., Jones, N. D., Brownell, M. T., & Bell, C. A. (2020). Danielson's Framework for Teaching: Convergence and divergence with conceptions of effectiveness in special education. *Journal of Learning Disabilities, 54*(1), 66–78.

National Center for Education Statistics. (2021). *Fast facts: Dropout rates.* https://nces.ed.gov/fastfacts/display.asp

National Center for Education Statistics. (2023). Concentration of public school students eligible for free or reduced-price lunch. *Condition of Education.* U.S. Department of Education, Institute of Education Sciences. Retrieved September 2, 2023 from https://nces.ed.gov/programs/coe/indicator/clb

National Center for Homeless Education. (2020, January). *Student homeless in America: School years 2015–16 through 2019–20: Education for homeless children and youth.* Greensboro: Author https://nche.ed.gov/wp-content/uploads/2020/01/Federal-Data-Summary-SY-15.16-to-17.18-Published-1.30.2020.pdf

National Center for Homeless Education. (2021, November). *Student homeless in America: School years 2017-18 through 2017-18: Education for homeless children and youth.* https://nche.ed.gov/wp-content/uploads/2021/12/Student-Homelessness-in-America-2021.pdf

Oates, W. P., Lane, K. L., Ma, Z., Sherod, R., & Perez-Clark, P. (2021, December). *Installing a universal behavior screening tool: Questions to consider.* Center on PBIS, University of Oregon. www.pbis.org

Office of Special Education Programs (OSEP). (2006a). Building the legacy of IDEA 2004. *Topical brief: Individualized education program (IEP), team meetings, and changes to the IEP.* Retrieved from http://idea.ed.gov

Office of Special Education Programs (OSEP). (2017). *A transition guide to postsecondary education and employment for students and youth with disabilities.*

Office of Special Education Programs (OSEP). (2022). *43rd Annual Report to Congress on the Implementation of the Individuals with Disabilities Education Act, 2021.*

Opper, I. M. (2019). *Teachers matter: Understanding teachers' impact.* Rand Co.

PACER Center. (2020). *Individualized Education Program (IEP) check list for parents.* https://www.pacer.org/parent/php/PHP-c183.pdf

Postsecondary National Policy Institute (PNPI). (2022, March). *Students with disabilities in higher education: Fact Sheet.* https://pnpi.org/students-with-disabilities-in-higher-education/

Rehabilitation Act of 1973. Section 504, 19 U.S.C. section 794.

Taylor, K. (2017, May 30). Poverty's long-lasting effects on students' education and success. *Insight Into Diversity.* https://www.insightintodiversity.com/povertys-long-lasting-effects-on-students-education-and-success/

Terada, Y. (2019). *Understanding a teachers' long-term impact: Fostering skills like self-regulation does more to improve students' future outcomes than helping them raise test scores.* https://www.edutopia.org/article/understanding-teachers-long-term-impact

U.S. Bureau of Labor Statistics. (2022, February 24). *Persons with a disability: Labor force characteristics.* https://www.bls.gov/news.release/disabl.nr0.htm#

U.S. Government Accountability Office. (2016). *Special Education: State and local-imposed requirements complication federal efforts to reduce administrative burden.* https://www.gao.gov/assets/gao-16-25.pdf

Witte, A., Singleton, F., Smith, T., & Hershfeldt, P. (2021 June). *Enhancing family-school collaboration with diverse families.* Center on PBIS, University of Oregon. www.pbis.org

Wrightslaw. (2015). *Inclusion: Answers to frequently asked questions from the NEA.* Retrieved from http://www.wrightslaw.com/info/lre.faqs.inclusion.htm

Wrightslaw. (2016). *School says "No related services on the IEP."* Retrieved from https://www.wrightslaw.com/blog/school-says-no-related-services-on-the-iep/

Yell, M. L. (2012). *The law and special education* (3rd ed.). Pearson.

CHAPTER 3

Bernal, C., & Aragon, L. (2004). Critical factors affecting the success of paraprofessionals in the first two years of career ladder projects in Colorado. *Remedial and Special Education, 25*(4), 205–213.

Chopra, R. V., Sandoval-Lucero, E., Aragon, L., Bernal, C., De Balderas, H. B., & Carroll, D. (2004). The paraprofessional role of connector. *Remedial and Special Education, 25*(4), 219–231.

Eaves, M. & Leathers, D. G. (2017). *Successful nonverbal communication. Principles and applications* (5th ed.). Routledge.

Every Student Succeeds Act (ESSA) of 2015, PL 114-95 (2015).

Friend, M. (2006). *Special education: Contemporary perspectives for school professionals.* Pearson.

Friend, M., & Cook, L. (2010). *Interactions: Collaboration skills for school professionals* (6th ed.). Merrill.

Friend, M., Cook, L., Hurley-Chamberlain, D., & Shamberger, C. (2010). Co-teaching: An illustration of the complexity of collaboration in special education. *Journal of Educational and Psychological Consultation, 20*(1), 9–27. doi:10.1080/10474410903535380

Garcia, S. B. (2002). Parent-professional collaboration in culturally sensitive assessment. In A. J. Artiles & A. A. Ortiz (Eds.), *English language learners with special education needs* (pp. 87–103). Center for Applied Linguistics and Delta Systems.

Gerlach, K. (2014). *Let's team up!* National Professional Resources.

Giangreco, M. F., & Doyle, M. B. (2007). Teacher assistants in inclusive schools. In L. Florian (Ed.), *The Sage handbook of special education* (pp. 429–439). SAGE.

Gordon, T. (1980). *Leadership effectiveness training.* Wyden.

Hallahan, D. P., Kaufman, J. M., & Pullen, P. C. (2019). *Exceptional learners: An introduction to special education* (14th ed.). Pearson.

Heron, T. E., & Harris, K. C. (2000). *The educational consultant: Helping professionals, parents, and students in inclusive classrooms* (4th ed.). PRO-ED.

Honigsfield, A., & Dove, M. (2010). *Collaboration and co- teaching: Strategies for English learners.* Corwin. http://www.nysed.gov/common/nysed/files/programs/ bilingual-ed/co-teaching-models_1.pdf

Idol, L., Nevin, A., & Paolucci-Whitcomb, P. (2000). *Collaborative consultation* (2nd ed.). PRO-ED.

Individuals with Disabilities Education Improvement Act of 2004 (IDEA). PL No. 108-446.

Lavoie, R. (2008). *The teacher's role in home/school communication: Everybody wins.* Retrieved from http://www.ldonline.org/article/28021#top

Murray, C. (2004). Clarifying collaborative roles in urban high schools. *Teaching Exceptional Children, 36*(5), 44–51.

Ortiz, A. (2002). Prevention of school failure and early intervention for English language learners. In A. J. Artiles & A. A. Ortiz (Eds.), *English language learners with special education needs* (pp. 31–50). Center for Applied Linguistics and Delta Systems.

Pugach, M. C., & Johnson, L. J. (1995). *Collaborative practitioners, collaborative schools.* Love.

Riggs, C. G. (2005). To teachers: What paraeducators want you to know. *Teaching Exceptional Children, 36*(5), 8–12.

Rivera, D. P., & Smith, D. D. (1997). *Teaching students with learning and behavior problems* (3rd ed.). Pearson.

Scruggs, T. E., Mastropieri, M. A., & McDuffie, K. A. (2007). Co-teaching in inclusive classrooms: A metasynthesis of qualitative research. *Exceptional Children, 73*, 392–416.

Smith, D. D., Tyler, N. C., Skow, K., & Smith, S. (2018). *Introduction to contemporary special education: New horizons* (2nd ed.). Pearson.

Turnbull, A., Turnbull, H. R., & Wehmeyer, M. L., & Shogren, K. A. (2016). *Exceptional lives: Special education in today's schools* (8th ed.). Pearson.

Vaughn, S., Bos, C. S., & Schumm, J. S. (2013). *Teaching exceptional, diverse, and at-risk students in the general education classroom* (6th ed.). Pearson.

Villa, R. A., Thousand, J. S., & Nevin, A. (2008). *A guide to co-teaching: Practical tips for facilitating student learning.* Corwin.

Walther-Thomas, C. (1997). Co-teaching experiences: The benefits and problems that teachers report. *Journal of Learning Disabilities, 30*(4), 395–407.

Weiss, M. P., & Lloyd, J. W. (2002). Congruence between roles and actions of secondary special educators in co-taught and special education settings. *Journal of Special Education, 36*(2), 58–68.

White, R. (2004). The recruitment of paraeducators into the special education profession: A review of progress, select evaluation outcomes, and new initiatives. *Remedial and Special Education, 25*(4), 214–218.

CHAPTER 4

Au, K. H. (1980). Participation structures in a reading lesson with Hawaiian children: Analysis of a culturally appropriate instructional event. *Anthropology & Education Quarterly, 11*(2), 91–115.

Au, K. H., & Blake, K. M. (2003). Cultural identity and learning to teach in a diverse community: Findings from a collective case study. *Journal of Teacher Education, 54*(3), 192–205.

Bardack, S. (2010). *Common ELL terms and definitions.* English Language Learner Center, American Institutes for Research.

Barshay, J. (2019, April). Is there a trade-off between racial diversity and academic excellence in gifted classrooms? *The Hechinger Report.* Retrieved from https://hechingerreport.org/is-there-a-trade-off-between-racial-diversity-and-academic-excellence-in-gifted-classrooms/

Bernstein, B. O., Lubinski, D., & Benbow, C. P. (2021). Academic acceleration in gifted youth and fruitless concerns regarding psychological well-being: A 35-year longitudinal study. *Journal of Educational Psychology, 113*(4), 830–845.

Bilingual Education Act (81 Stat. 816) also known as Title VII of ESEA of 1967.

Boulder Valley School District Office of Advanced Academic Services. (2010). *Identifying talented and gifted students from culturally, linguistically, and ethnically diverse (CLED) populations.* Retrieved from https://sue.bvsd.org/classes/Pages/tag.aspx

Brown, J. E., & Ortiz, S. O. (2014). Intervention for English learners with learning disabilities. In J. T. Mascolo, V. C. Alfonso, & D. O. Flanagan (Eds.), *Essentials of planning, selecting, and tailoring interventions for unique learners* (pp. 274–275). John Wiley & Sons.

Bryant, B. R., Bryant, D. P., Porterfield, J., Falcomata, T., Shih, M., Valentine, C., . . . Bell, K. (2014). The effects of a Tier 3 intervention for second grade students with serious mathematics difficulties. *Journal of Learning Disabilities.* Advance online publication. doi:10.1177/0022219414538516

Calvan, B. C. (2021, October). Schools debate: Gifted and talented, or racist and elitist? *AP News.* Retrieved from https://apnews.com/article/new-york-education-new-york-city-united-states-race-and-ethnicity-f8cbdb50edba9802fe9ad503cfe7d467

Celic, C. M. (2009). *English language learners: Day by day, K–6.* Heinemann. https://www.heinemann.com/shared/onlineresources/E02682/Celic_websample.pdf

College Board. (2019, February). *Student participation and performance in advanced placement rise in tandem.* Retrieved from https://newsroom.collegeboard.org/student-participation-and-performance-advanced-placement-rise-tandem

Comber, B. (2013). Schools as meeting places: Critical and inclusive literacies in changing local environments. *Language Arts, 90,* 361–371.

Davidson Institute. (n.d.). *IQ and educational needs.* Retrieved from http://presskit.ditd.org/Davidson_Institute_Press_Kit/ditd_IQ_and_Educational_Needs.html

Davidson Institute. (2021a). *Twice-exceptional: Definition, characteristics, & identification.* Retrieved April 10, 2023 from https://www.davidsongifted.org/gifted-blog/twice-exceptional-definition-characteristics-identification/

Davidson Institute. (2021b). *What is giftedness.* Retrieved April 10, 2023 from https://www.davidsongifted.org/gifted-blog/what-is-giftedness/

Davidson Institute. (2022, July). *Anxiety and gifted students.* Retrieved from https://www.davidsongifted.org/gifted-blog/anxiety-and-gifted-children/

Elementary and Secondary Education Amendments of 1967: P.L. 90-247. (1968).

Gay, G. (2010). *Culturally responsive teaching: Theory, research, and practice* (2nd ed.). Teachers College Press.

Gentry, M., Gray, A., Whiting, G. W., Maeda, Y., & Pereira, N. (2019). *Access denied/system failure. Gifted education in the United States: Laws, access, equity, and missingness across the country by locale, Title I school status, and race.* Purdue University & Jack Kent Cooke Foundation.

Goldenberg, C. (2008). Teaching English language learners: What the research does—and does not—say. *American Educator, 32*(2) 8–23, 42–44.

Gollnick, D. M., & Chinn, P. C. (2012). *Multicultural education in a pluralistic society* (9th ed.). Merrill.

Heath, S. B. (1983). *Ways with words: Language, life, and work in communities and classrooms.* Cambridge University Press.

Hernández, D., & Napierala, J. S. (2012). Children in immigrant families: Essential to America's future. *Child and Youth Well-Being Index Policy Brief.* Foundation for Child Development.

Individuals with Disabilities Education Improvement Act (IDEA) of 2004. PL No. 108-446.

Josephson, J., Wolfgang, C., & Mehrenberg, R. (2018). Strategies for supporting students who are twice-exceptional. *The Journal of Special Education Apprenticeship, 7*(2).

Klingner, J. (2014). *Distinguishing language acquisition from learning disabilities.* Division of Specialized Instruction and Student Support Office of English Language Learners.

Klingner, J. K., Boelé, A. L., Linan-Thompson, S., & Rodriguez, D. (2014). Essential components of special education for ELLs with LD: Position statement of the Division for Learning Disabilities of the Council for Exceptional Children. *Learning Disabilities Research & Practice, 29*(3), 93–96.

Klingner, J. K., Vaughn, S., Boardman, A., & Swanson, E. (2012). *Now we get it! Boosting comprehension with collaborative strategic reading.* Jossey-Bass.

Lockhar, K. & Mun, R. U. (2020). Developing a strong home-school connection to better identify and serve culturally, linguistically, and economically diverse gifted and talented students. *Gifted Child Today, 43*(4), 231–238.

Lubinski, D., & Benbow, C. P. (2021). Intellectual precocity: What have we learned since Terman? *Gifted Child Quarterly, 65*(1), 3–28.

Medina, C. (2010). "Reading across communities" in biliteracy practices: Examining translocal discourses and cultural flows in literature discussions. *Reading Research Quarterly, 45*(1), 40–60.

Naidoo, J. C. (2014). *The importance of diversity in library programs and material collections for children.* Association for Library Service to Children.

National Association for Gifted Children. (2019). *Key considerations in identifying and supporting gifted and talented learners.* Retrieved from https://files.eric.ed.gov/fulltext/ED600214.pdf

National Center for Education Statistics (NCES). (2014). *Nation's report card.* Washington, DC: U.S. Department of Education. Retrieved from https://nces.ed.gov/nationsreportcard/

National Center for Education Statistics (NCES). (2021). *Percentage of public school students enrolled in gifted and talented programs, by sex, race/ethnicity, and state: Selected years, 2004 through 2017-18.*

Retrieved from https://nces.ed.gov/programs/digest/d21/tables/dt21_204.90.asp

National Center for Education Statistics (NCES). (2023). *Enrollment and percentage distribution of enrollment in public elementary and secondary schools, by race/ethnicity and region: Selected years, fall 1995 through fall 2030.* Retrieved from https://nces.ed.gov/programs/digest/d21/tables/dt21_203.50.asp

National Center for Research on Gifted Education. (2015). *Our mission.* Retrieved from https://ncrge.uconn.edu/#

National Council of Teachers of English. (2008). *English language learners: A policy research brief produced by the National Council of Teachers of English.* Retrieved from http://www.ncte.org/library/NCTEFiles/Resources/PolicyResearch/ELLResearchBrief.pdf

National Society for the Gifted & Talented. (2018). *Giftedness defined.* Retrieved from http://www.nsgt.org/giftedness- defined/

Neuliep, J. W. (2015). *Intercultural communication: A contextual approach* (6th ed.). SAGE.

Nieto, S., & Bode, P. (2008). *Affirming diversity: The sociopolitical context of multicultural education* (5th ed.). Pearson.

Office of Special Education Programs (OSEP). (2014). *36th annual report to Congress on the implementation of the Individuals with Disabilities Education Improvement Act.*

Orosco, M. J., & Klingner, J. K. (2010). Bilingual first grade instruction. In D. Haager, J. K. Klingner, & T. Jiménez, *How to teach English language learners: Effective strategies from outstanding educators, grades K–6* (pp. 53–79). Jossey-Bass.

Piazza, S. V., Rao, S., & Protacio, M. S. (2015). Converging recommendations for culturally responsive literacy practices: Students with learning disabilities, English language learners, and socioculturally diverse learners. *International Journal of Multicultural Education, 17*(3), 1–20.

Reardon, S. F., Weathers, E. S., Fahle, E. M., Jang, H., & Kalogrides, D. (2022). *Is separate still unequal? New evidence on school segregation and racial academic achievement gaps.* Retrieved from https://cepa.stanford.edu/content/separate-still-unequal-new-evidence-school-segregation-and-racial-academic-achievement-gaps

Rinn, A. N., Mun, R. U., & Hodges, J. (2022). *2020–2021 State of the states in gifted education.* National Association for Gifted Children and the Council of State Directors of Programs for the Gifted. https://cdn.ymaws.com/nagc.org/resource/resmgr/2020-21_state_of_the_states_.pdf

Ryan, C. (2013). *Language use in the United States: 2011.* U.S. Department of Commerce.

Sgueglia, K., & Paul, D. J. (2022, April 14). New York revives gifted and talented program with major expansion. *CNN.* Retrieved from https://www.cnn.com/2022/04/14/us/new-york-gifted-talented-education-program-expansion/index.html

Shealey, M. W., McHatton, P. A., & Wilson, V. (2011). Moving beyond disproportionality: The role of culturally responsive teaching in special education. *Teaching Education, 22*(4), 377–396.

Shobo Y. A., Meharie A., Hammer, P., and Hixson, N. (2012). *West Virginia Alternate Identification and Reporting program: An exploratory analysis.* West Virginia Department of Education, Division of Curriculum and Instructional Services, Office of Research. https://wvde.us/wp-content/uploads/2018/01/EvaluationofAIR2011Final062812.pdf

Stewner-Manzanares, G. (1988). The Bilingual Education Act: Twenty years later. Occasional Papers in Bilingual Education, *New Focus, 6.*

Sullivan, A. L., & Bal, A. (2013). Disproportionality in special education: Effects of individual and school variables on disability risk. *Exceptionality, 79*(4), 475–494.

Szymanski, A. (2021). High expectations, limited options: How gifted students living in poverty approach the demands of AP coursework. *Journal for the Education of the Gifted, 44*(2), 149–170.

U.S. Census Bureau. (2010). *Census 2000 redistricting* (PL 94-171, summary file, tables PL1 and PL2). U.S. Department of Commerce.

U.S. Census Bureau. (2011, April 2). *U.S. Census Bureau, population division.* Retrieved from http://www.census.gov/population/www/cen2000/phc-t1.html

U.S. Census Bureau. (2012). *The 2012 statistical abstract.*

U.S. Department of Education. (2022, February 15). *U.S. Department of Education invites applicants for Javits Gifted and Talented Program.* Retrieved on April 10, 2023 from https://www.ed.gov/news/press-releases/us-department-education-invites-applicants-javits-gifted-and-talented-program

U.S. Department of Education, National Center for Education Statistics. (2017). *Common Core of Data.*

Vaughn, S., Cirino, P. T., Linan-Thompson, S., Mathes, P. G., Carlson, C. D., Hagan, E. C., . . . Francis, D. J. (2006). Effectiveness of a Spanish intervention and an English intervention for English-language learners at risk for reading problems. *American Educational Research Journal, 43*, 449–487.

Vaughn, S., Mathes, P. G., Linan-Thompson, S., & Francis, D. J. (2005). Teaching English language learners at risk for reading disabilities to read: Putting research into practice. *Learning Disabilities Research & Practice, 20*, 58–67.

Yaluma, C. B., & Tyner, A. (2018). *Is there a gifted gap?: Gifted education in high-poverty schools.* Thomas B. Fordham Institute. Retrieved from https://fordhaminstitute.org/national/research/there-gifted-gap-gifted-education-high-poverty-schools

CHAPTER 5

ADDITUDE. (2018). *ADHD, by the numbers.* Retrieved from https://www.additudemag.com/the-statistics-of-adhd/

American Psychiatric Association. (2000). *Diagnostic and statistical manual of mental disorders* (4th ed., text rev.).

American Psychiatric Association. (2013). *Diagnostic and statistical manual of mental disorders* (5th ed.).

American Speech-Language-Hearing Association Ad Hoc Committee on Service Delivery in the Schools. (1993). Definitions of communication disorders and variations. *ASHA, 35*(Suppl. 10), 40–41.

Asperger, H. (1944/1991). "Autistic psychopathy" in childhood (U. Frith, Trans. Annot.). In U. Frith (Ed.), *Autism and Asperger syndrome* (pp. 37–92). Cambridge University Press.

Autism Science Foundation. (2022). *Beware of non-evidenced-based treatments.* Retrieved on October 8, 2022 from https://autismsciencefoundation.org/beware-of-non-evidence-based-treatments/

Autism Speaks. (2022). *Autism statistics and facts.* Retrieved May 9, 2023 from https://www.autismspeaks.org/autism-statistics-asd

Barrio, B. L. (2017). Special education policy change: Addressing the disproportionality of English language learners in special education programs in rural communities. *Rural Special Education Quarterly,*

36(22), 64–72. https://doi.org/10.1177/8756870517707217

Bettelheim, B. (1967). *Infantile autism and the birth of self.* Free Press.

Bishop, D. V. M. (2006). What causes specific language impairment in children? *Current Directions in Psychological Science, 15*(5), 217–221. https://doi.org/10.1111/j.1467-8721.2006.00439.x

Blacher, J., & Christensen, L. (2011). Sowing the seeds of the autism field: Leo Kanner (1943). *Intellectual and Developmental Disabilities, 49*, 172–191.

Bondy, A., & Frost, L. (2002). *A picture's worth: PECS and other visual communication strategies in autism.* Woodbine House.

Briscoe, T. (2023 May 14). Plan allocates $67 million for Excide-are clean up. *LA Times.* Retrieved May 14, 2023 from https://www.latimes.com/environment/story/2023-05-12/california-offers-funding-to-clean-lead-from-toxic-parkways

Bryant, B. R., Seok, S., Ok, M., & Bryant, D. P. (2012). Individuals with intellectual and/or developmental disabilities use of assistive technology devices in support provision. *Journal of Special Education Technology, 27*(2), 41–57.

Bryant, B. R., Shih, M., Bryant, D. P., & Seok, S. (2010). The role of assistive technology in support needs assessments for children with intellectual disabilities [Special series]. *Exceptionality, 18*(4), 203–213.

Bryant, D. P., Bryant, B. R., & Hammill, D. D. (2000, March/April). Characteristic behaviors of students with LD who have teacher-identified math weakness. *Journal of Learning Disabilities, 33*, 168–177, 199.

Cardichon, J., Darling-Hammond, L., Yang, M., Scott, C., Shields, P. M., & Burns, D. (2020). *Inequitable opportunity to learn: Student access to certified and experienced teachers.* Retrieved May 22, 2023 from https://learningpolicyinstitute.org/product/crdc-teacher-access-report

Center on Positive Behavioral Interventions and Supports. (2022 July). *Positive, proactive approaches to supporting children with disabilities.* Retrieved May 21, 2023 from https://www.pbis.org/current/positive-proactive-approaches-to-supporting-children-with-disabilities

Center on Positive Behavioral Interventions and Supports. (2023a). About. Retrieved May 21, 2023 from https://www.pbis.org/about/about

Center on Positive Behavioral Interventions and Supports. (2023b). Supporting and responding to educators classroom PBIS implementation needs: Guide to classroom systems and data. Center on PBIS, University of Oregon. www.pbis.org.

Center on Positive Behavioral Interventions and Supports. (n.d.). *What is Tier 3 support?* Retrieved May 21, 2023 from https://www.pbis.org/pbis/tier-3

Center for Parent Information and Resources. (2021, November). *Emotional disturbance updated!* Retrieved January 9, 2023 from https://www.parentcenterhub.org/emotionaldisturbance/

Centers for Disease Control and Prevention. (2022a, March 31). *Autism spectrum disorder: Past, present, and future impact of SEED.* Retrieved from https://www.cdc.gov/ncbddd/autism/features/impact-of-seed.html

Centers for Disease Control and Prevention. (2022b, August 9). *Data and statistics: About ADHD.* Retrieved May 21, 2023 from https://www.cdc.gov/ncbddd/adhd/data.html

Centers for Disease Control and Prevention. (2022c, April 6). *Diagnostic criteria for autism spectrum disorders.* Retrieved May 9, 2023 from https://www.cdc.gov/ncbddd/autism/hcp-dsm.html

Centers for Disease Control and Prevention. (2022d, April 1). *Fetal Alcohol Spectrum Disorders (FASDs).* https://www.cdc.gov/ncbddd/fasd/index.html

Centers for Disease Control and Prevention. (2022e, January 6). *Fetal alcohol spectrum disorders (FASDs): Data and statistics.* Retrieved May 9, 2023 from https://www.parentcenterhub.org/ei-overview/https://www.cdc.gov/ncbddd/fasd/data.html

Centers for Disease Control and Prevention. (2022f, June 3). *Fragile X syndrome: Data and statistics.* Retrieved May 12, 2023 from https://www.cdc.gov/ncbddd/fxs/data.html

Centers for Disease Control and Prevention. (2022g, March 28). *Signs and symptoms of autism spectrum disorders.* Retrieved May 9, 2023 from https://www.cdc.gov/ncbddd/autism/signs.html

Centers for Disease Control and Prevention. (2022h, March 31). *What is autism spectrum disorder?* Retrieved May 9, 2023 from https://www.cdc.gov/ncbddd/autism/facts.html

Centers for Disease Control and Prevention. (2023a, March 28). *Data and statistics on autism spectrum disorder.* Retrieved May 9, 2023 from https://www.cdc.gov/ncbddd/autism/data.html

Centers for Disease Control and Prevention. (2023b, May 9). *What is Down syndrome?* Retrieved May 12, 2023 from https://www.cdc.gov/ncbddd/birthdefects/downsyndrome.html

Compton, D. L., Fuchs, L. S., Fuchs, D., Lambert, W., & Hamlett, C. (2012). The cognitive and academic profiles of reading and mathematics learning disabilities. *Journal of Learning Disabilities, 45*, 79–95.

Council for Exceptional Children. (2018). *Behavior disorders: Definitions, characteristics & related information.* Council for Children with Behavior Disorders.

Del Toro, J., & Wang, M-T. (2021, October 7). For Black students, unfairly harsh discipline can lead to lower grades. *APA Newsroom.* Retrieved May 16, 2023 from https://www.apa.org/news/press/releases/2021/10/black-students-harsh-discipline

Dyslexic Advantage Team. (2021, November 17). *Dyslexia and dyscalculia.* Retrieved May 8, 2023 from https://www.dyslexicadvantage.org/dyslexia-and-dyscalculia

Eunice Kennedy Shriver National Institute of Child Health and Human Development (NICHD). (2018, September 11). *About learning disabilities.* Retrieved May 8, 2023 from https://www.nichd.nih.gov/health/topics/learning/conditioninfo

Fisher, K. W., & Shogren, K. A. (2012). Integrating augmentative and alternative communication and peer support for students with disabilities: A social-ecological perspective. *Journal of Special Education Technology, 27*(2), 23–39.

Flannery, S., Gerber, E., & Bubrick, J. (2023 January 3). *Generalized anxiety disorder in kids.* Retrieved January 12, 2023 from https://childmind.org/article/generalized-anxiety-disorder-in-kids

Fuchs, L. S., Fuchs, D., & Malone, A. S. (2017). The taxonomy of intervention intensity. *TEACHING Exceptional Children, 50*, 35–43. https://doi.org/10.1177/0040059917703962

Fuchs, L. S., Fuchs, D., Sterba, S. K., Barnes, M. A., Seethaler, P. M., & Changas, P. (2022). Building word-problem solving and working memory capacity: A randomized controlled trial comparing three intervention approaches. *Journal of Educational Psychology, 114*(7), 1633–1653. https://doi.org/10.1037/edu0000752

Fuchs, L. S., Seethaler, P. M., Sterba, S. K., Craddock, C., Fuchs, D., Compton, D. L., Geary, D. C., & Changas, P. (2021). Closing the word-problem achievement gap in first grade: Schema-based word-problem intervention with embedded language comprehension instruction. *Journal of Educational Psychology, 113*(1), 86–103. https://doi.org/10.1037/edu0000467

Forness, S. R., & Knitzer, J. (1992). A new proposed definition and terminology to replace "serious emotional disturbance" in IDEA. *School Psychology Review, 21*, 12–20.

Gilmour, A., Fuchs, D., & Wehby, J. (2019). Are students with disabilities accessing the curriculum? A meta-analysis of the reading achievement gap between students with and without disabilities. *Exceptional Children, 85*(3), 329–346. https://doi.org/10.1177/0014402918795830

Harris, K. R., & Graham, S. (1999). Programmatic intervention research: Illustrations from the evolution of self-regulated strategy development. *Learning Disability Quarterly, 22*, 251–262.

Hart, S. L., & Banda, D. R. (2010). Picture exchange communications system with individuals with developmental disabilities: A meta-analysis of single subject studies. *Remedial and Special Education, 31*, 476–488.

Ikhnana, S. (2022, June 16). *The ultimate guide to tier 2 behavior interventions in PBIS*. Live School. Retrieved January 14, 2023 from https://www.whyliveschool.com/blog/tier-2-behavior-interventions

International OCD Foundation. (2023). *How is OCD treated?* Retrieved May 15, 2023 from https://kids.iocdf.org/what-is-ocd-kids/how-is-ocd-treated/

Kanner, L. (1943). Autistic disturbances of affective contact. *Nervous Child, 2*, 217–250.

Kauffman, J. M., & Landrum, T. J. (2018). *Characteristics of behavioral disorders of children and youth* (11th ed.). Pearson.

Lambert, D. (2022, January 10). Amid shortages, schools settle for unprepared special education teachers. *EdSource*. Retrieved November 6, 2022 from https://edsource.org/2020/amid-shortages-schools-settle-for-underprepared-special-education-teachers/621656

Lerner, J. W., & Johns, B. H. (2015). *Learning disabilities and related disabilities: Strategies for success* (13th ed.). Cengage Learning.

Marrus, N., & Hall, L. (2017). Intellectual disability and language disorder. *Child and Adolescent Psychiatric Clinics of North America, 26*(3), 539–554. https://doi.org/10.1016/j.chc.2017.03.001

Morris-Mathews, H., Stark, K. R., Jones, N. D., Brownell, M. T., & Bell, C. A. (2020). Danielson's Framework for Teaching: Convergence and divergence with conceptions of effectiveness in special education. *Journal of Learning Disabilities, 54*(1), 66–78. https://doi.org/10.1177/0022219420941804

National Alliance on Mental Illness. (2023). *Mental health conditions*. https://www.nami.org/About-Mental-Illness/Mental-Health-Conditions

National Association for Gifted Children. (n.d.). *Frequently asked questions about gifted education*. Retrieved May 21, 2023 from https://nagc.org/page/frequently-asked-questions-about-gifted-education

National Center for Education Statistics. (2022). Students with disabilities. *Condition of Education*. Retrieved from https://nces.ed.gov/programs/coe/indicator/cgg

National Institute of Neurological Disorders and Stroke. (2022). *Learning disabilities: Definition*. Retrieved from www.ninds.nih.gov

National Institute of Neurological Disorders and Stroke. (2023, January 20). *What is dyslexia?* Retrieved May 8, 2023 from https://www.ninds.nih.gov/health-information/disorders/dyslexia

Office of Special Education Programs. (2018). *2017 Annual Reports to Congress on the Individuals with Disabilities Education Act (IDEA)*. Retrieved from https://www2.ed.gov/about/reports/annual/osep/2017/index.html

Office of Special Education Programs. (2020, May 6). *OSEP fast facts: Children with emotional disturbance*. Retrieved May 15, 2023 from https://sites.ed.gov/idea/osep-fast-facts-children-IDed-Emotional-Disturbance-20

Office of Special Education Programs. (2022). *43rd Annual Report to Congress on the Implementation of the Individuals with Disabilities Education Act, 2021*. https://sites.ed.gov/idea/2021-individuals-with-disabilities-education-act-annual-report-to-congress/

PBS World. (2023). *Tier 2 Interventions*. Retrieved May 21, 2023 from https://www.pbisworld.com/tier-2/

Pineda, D. (2023 May 18). Lead in water at many day care centers: Testing reveals dangerous levels at 25% of licensed facilities. *LA Times*. Retrieved May 18 2023 from https://enewspaper.latimes.com/infinity/article_share.aspx?guid=4baabfab-9741-463d-8ea6-3e5afdc0fd22

Prezas, R. F., & Jo, A. A. (2017). Differentiating language difference and language disorder: Information for teachers working with English language learners in the schools. *Journal of Human Services: Training, Research, and Practice, 2*(1), Article 2. Retrieved from https://scholarworks.sfasu.edu/jhstrp/vol2/iss1/2/

Pyramid Educational Consultants. (2012). *PECS and the pyramid approach*. Retrieved from http://www.pecs.org.uk/general/documents/2011Infobrochure.pdf

Pyramid Educational Consultants. (2022). *PECS® IV+*.

Ramig, P. R., & Shames, G. H. (2006). Stuttering and other disorders of fluency. In N. B. Anderson & G. H. Shames (Eds.), *Human communication disorders: An introduction* (7th ed., pp. 183–221). Pearson.

Ros, R., & Graziano, P. A. (2018). Social functioning in children with or at risk for attention deficit/hyperactivity disorder: a meta-analytic review *Journal of Clinical Child & Adolescent Psychology, 47*(2), 213–235, https://doi.org/10.1080/15374416.2016.1266644

Ryberg, R., Her, S., Temkin, D., & Harper, K. (2021, August 9). Despite reductions since 2011–2012, Black students and students with disabilities remain more likely to experience suspension. *Child Trends*. Retrieved May 16, 2023 from https://www.childtrends.org/publications/despite-reductions-black-students-and-students-with-disabilities-remain-more-likely-to-experience-suspension

Schalock, R. L., Luckasson, R., & Tassé, M. J. (2021a). *Intellectual disability: Definition, diagnosis, classification, and systems of support* (12th ed.). American Association on Intellectual and Developmental Disabilities.

Schalock, R. L., Luckasson, R., and Tassé, M. J. (2021b, March). *Twenty questions and answers regarding the 12th edition of the AAIDD manual: Intellectual disability: definition, diagnosis, classification, and systems of supports*. American Association on Intellectual and Developmental Disabilities.

TASH. (2018). *Community living*. Retrieved from https://tash.org/advocacy-issues/community-living/

Torgesen, J. K. (2002). Empirical and theoretical support for direct diagnosis of learning disabilities by assessment of intrinsic processing weaknesses. In R. Bradley, L. Danielson, & D. P. Hallahan (Eds.), *Identification of learning disabilities: Research to practice* (pp. 565–652). Lawrence Erlbaum.

Vaughn, S., & Bos, C. S. (2020). *Strategies for teaching students with learning and behavior problems.* Pearson.

West, J. (2022, May 25). Tackling teacher shortages. *Testimony to House Subcommittee on Labor/HHS/Education Appropriations.* Retrieved May 27, 2022 from https://docs.house.gov/meetings/AP/AP07/20220525/114831/HHRG-117-AP07-Wstate-WestJ-20220525.pdf

Wehmeyer, M. L., Tassé, M. J., Davies, D. D., & Stock, S. (2012). Support needs of adults with intellectual disability across domains: The role of technology. *Journal of Special Education Technology, 27*(2), 11–21.

World Population Review. (2022a). *Flint, Michigan population 2022.* Retrieved May 12, 2023 from https://worldpopulationreview.com/us-cities/flint-mi-population

World Population Review. (2022b). *Vernon, California population 2022.* Retrieved May 12, 2023 from https://worldpopulationreview.com/us-cities/vernon-ca-population

Ylanan, A., Briscoe, T., & Garrison, J. (2023, February 10). Do you live near the old Exide lead-acid battery smelter? Check your property's clean up status. *LA Times.* Retrieved May 12, 2023 from https://www.latimes.com/california/story/2023-02-10/exide-lead-soil-cleanup-check-your-propertys-status

Zheng, S., LeWinn, K., Ceja, T., Hanna-Attish, M., O'Connell, L., & Bishop, S. (2021, August 11). Adaptive aged children of Flint. *Frontiers in Psychology.* https://doi.org/10.3389/fpsyg.2021.692330

CHAPTER 6

American Association of the Deaf-Blind. (2009). *Frequently asked questions about deaf-blindness.* Retrieved from http://www.aadb.org/FAQ/faq_DeafBlindness.html#communication

American Foundation for the Blind (AFB). (2018). *Assistive technology.* Retrieved from http://www.afb.org/info/living-with- vision-loss/using-technology/assistive-technology/123

Americans with Disabilities Act (ADA) of 1990. PL No. 101-336, 104 Stat. 327.

Asthma and Allergy Foundation of America. (2022, May 25). *Most recent national asthma data.* Retrieved May 30, 2023 from https://www.cdc.gov/asthma/most_recent_national_asthma_data.htm

Branson, J., & Miller, D. (2002). *Damned for their difference: The cultural construction of deaf people as disabled.* Gallaudet University Press.

Brown, F., McDonnell, J., & Snell, M. E. (2016). *Instruction of students with severe disabilities.* Pearson.

Bryant, B. R., Seok, S., Ok, M., & Bryant, D. P. (2012). Individuals with intellectual and/or developmental disabilities use of assistive technology devices in support provision. *Journal of Special Education Technology, 27*(2), 41–57.

Bryant, D., & Bryant, B. (2011). *Assistive technology for people with disabilities* (2nd ed.). Pearson.

Cawthon, S. W., Barker, E., Daniel, J., Cooc, N., & Vielma, A. G. (2023). Longitudinal models of reading and mathematics achievement in deaf and hard of hearing students. *Journal of Deaf Studies and Deaf Education, 28*(1), 115–123. https://doi.org/10.1093/deafed/enac033

Center for Parent Information and Resources. (2016). *Developmental delay.* Retrieved from http://www.parentcenterhub.org/dd/

Centers for Disease Control and Prevention. (2020a, September 30). *Epilepsy.* Retrieved April 27, 2023 from https://www.cdc.gov/epilepsy/about/fastfacts.htm

Centers for Disease Control and Prevention. (2020b, December 14). *Sickle cell disease (SCD): What is sickle cell trait?* Retrieved April 28, 2023 from https://www.cdc.gov/ncbddd/sicklecell/traits.html

Centers for Disease Control and Prevention. (2021a, December 29). *Percentage of diagnosed diabetes.* Retrieved April 28, 2023 from https://www.cdc.gov/diabetes/data/statistics-report/diagnosed-diabetes.html

Centers for Disease Control and Prevention. (2021b, March 25). *Quick statistics about hearing.* Retrieved April 29, 2023 from https://www.nidcd.nih.gov/health/statistics/quick-statistics-hearing

Centers for Disease Control and Prevention. (2022a, March 22). *Get the facts about TBI.* Retrieved July 30, 2022 from https://www.cdc.gov/traumaticbraininjury/get_the_facts.html

Centers for Disease Control and Prevention. (2022b, April 6). *Preventing abusive head trauma.* Retrieved April 26, 2023 from https://www.cdc.gov/violenceprevention/childabuseandneglect/Abusive-Head-Trauma.html

Centers for Disease Control and Prevention. (2022c). *Surveillance report of traumatic brain injury-related deaths by age group, sex, and mechanism of injury—United States, 2018 and 2019.* https://www.cdc.gov/traumaticbraininjury/pdf/tbi-surveillance-report-2016-2017-508.pdf

Centers for Disease Control and Prevention (2023). *What is spina bifida?* Retrieved September 6, 2023 from https://www.cdc.gov/ncbddd/spinabifida/facts.html

Child Advocacy Network of Disability Organizations. (2023). *Multiple disabilities.* Retrieved April 26, 2023 from https://www.arc.org.mv/arccando/multiple-disabilities

Cosgrove, N. (2023 April 11). *10 interesting service dog statistics: Updated in 2023.* Retrieved April 29, 2023 from https://www.hepper.com/service-dog-statistics-and-facts/

Education for All Handicapped Children Act (EHA). PL No. 94-142 (1975).

Epilepsy Foundation of America. (2020). *Seizure first aid: How to help someone having a seizure.* Retrieved from https://www.epilepsy.com/sites/default/files/upload/image/SFA%20Lockscreen.jpg

Girma, H. (2019). *Haben: The deafblind woman who conquered Harvard Law School.* Hachette Book Group.

Groce, N. E. (1985). *Everyone here spoke sign language: Hereditary deafness on Martha's Vineyard.* Harvard University Press.

Individuals with Disabilities Education Improvement Act of 2004 (IDEIA or IDEA). PL No. 108–446.

Jackson, R. M. (2014). *Curriculum access for students with low-incidence disabilities: The promise of universal design for learning.* Retrieved from http://aem.cast.org/about/publications/2005/ncac-curriculum-access-low-incidence-udl.html

Keller, H. (1988). *The story of my life.* Dover Thrift Editions.

Lentz, J. L. (2020, July 6). *USH2020: Usher Syndrome Type 1C research update: Transcript of presentation.* USH Talks on 1C. Usher Syndrome Coalition. Retrieved April 26, 2023 from https://www.usher-syndrome.org/what-is-usher-syndrome/presentations/ush-talks/ush2020-virtual-presentations/ush2020-usher-syndrome-type-1c-research-update.html

National Center for Education Statistics. (2022). Students with disabilities. *Condition of Education.* U.S. Department of Education, Institute of Education Sciences. Retrieved May 1, 2023 from https://nces.ed.gov/programs/coe/indicator/cgg.

National Center on Birth Defects and Developmental Disabilities. (2022, August 18). *What is Sickle cell disease?* Retrieved April 28, 2023 from https://www.cdc.gov/ncbddd/sicklecell/facts.html

National Center on Birth Defects and Developmental Disabilities. (2023, February 23). *11 things to know about cerebral palsy.* Retrieved April 27, 2023 from https://www.cdc.gov/ncbddd/cp/features/cerebral-palsy-11-things.html

National Center on Deaf-Blindness. (2022a). *National child count: National deaf-blind child interactive maps.* Retrieved April 26, 2023 from https://www.nationaldb.org/info-center/national-child-count/interactive-maps/

National Center on Deaf-Blindness. (2022b). *2021 National deaf-blind child.* Retrieved April 26, 2023 from https://www.nationaldb.org/products/national-child-count/report-2021

National Institute on Deafness and Other Communication Disorders. (2019, November 12). *Assistive devices for people with hearing, voice, speech, or language disorders.* Retrieved April 27, 2023 from https://www.nidcd.nih.gov/health/assistive-devices-people-hearing-voice-speech-or-language-disorders

National Institute on Deafness and Other Communication Disorders. (2021a, March 24). *Cochlear implants.* Retrieved April 29, 2023 from https://www.nidcd.nih.gov/health/cochlear-implants

National Institute on Deafness and Other Communication Disorders. (2021b, March 25). *Quick statistics about hearing.* Retrieved April 29, 2023, from https://www.nidcd.nih.gov/health/statistics/quick-statistics-hearing

Office of Special Education Programs. (2018). *2017 Annual Reports to Congress on the Individuals with Disabilities Education Act (IDEA).* Retrieved from https://sites.ed.gov/idea/2017-annual-report-to-congress-on-the-individuals-with-disabilities-education-act/

Office of Special Education Programs. (2021, May 26). *OSEP fast facts: School aged children 5 (in Kindergarten) through 21 served under Part B, of the IDEA.* Retrieved April 25, 2023 from https://sites.ed.gov/idea/osep-fast-facts-school-aged-children-5-21-served-under-idea-part-b-21/

Office of Special Education Programs. (2022a). *43rd Annual Report to Congress on the Implementation of the Individuals with Disabilities Education Act, 2021.* https://sites.ed.gov/idea/2021-individuals-with-disabilities-education-act-annual-report-to-congress/

Office of Special Education Programs. (2022b, May 23). *OSEP fast facts: Educational environments of school aged children with disabilities.* Retrieved April 25, 2023 from https://sites.ed.gov/idea/osep-fast-facts-educational-environments-school-aged-children-disabilities/

Office of Special Education Programs. (2023, March 30). *OSEP fast facts: Students with traumatic brain injury.* Retrieved April 25, 2023 from https://sites.ed.gov/idea/osep-fast-facts-students-identified-with-traumatic-brain-injury-23/

Rinze, A. & Tange, R. A. (2021). The deafness history of Martha's Vineyard. *Acta Scientific Otolaryngology* 3(2),78–82.

U.S. Dept of Education. (2023). *School age students served under IDEA, Part B, as a percentage of population, by disability category and state: 2021–22.* Retrieved April 25, 2023 from https://data.ed.gov/dataset/idea-section-618-data-products-static-tables-part-b-count-environ-tables11/resources

U.S. Department of Education, EDFacts Data Warehouse (EDW). (2021). IDEA Part B Child Count and Educational Environments Collection 21. https://data.ed.gov/dataset/71ca7d0c-a161-4abe-9e2b-4e68ffb1061a/resource/c515f168-be9c-4505-a6d7-d52a47b9b2b7/download/countandedenvironment2020-21.csv

Usher Syndrome Coalition. (2022). *Frequent questions.* https://www.usher-syndrome.org/resources/frequent-questions.html

World Health Organization. (2022, October 13). *Blindness and visual impairment.* Retrieved May 1, 2023 from https://www.who.int/news-room/fact-sheets/detail/blindness-and-visual-impairment

CHAPTER 7

Archer, A. L., & Hughes, C. A. (2011). *Explicit instruction. Effective and efficient teaching.* Guilford Press.

Brophy, J. E., & Good, T. L. (1986). Teacher behavior and student achievement. In M. C. Wittrock (Ed.), *Handbook of research on teaching* (3rd ed., pp. 328–377). Macmillan.

Bryant, D. P., & Bryant, B. R. (1998). Using assistive technology adaptations to include students with learning disabilities in cooperative learning activities. *Journal of Learning Disabilities, 31*(1), 41–54.

Bryant, D. P., & Bryant, B. R. (2003). *Assistive technology for people with disabilities.* Pearson.

Coyne, M. D., Kame'enui, E. J., & Carnine, D. W. (2011). *Effective teaching strategies that accommodate diverse learners* (4th ed.). Pearson.

Delquadri, J., Greenwood, C. R., Whorton, D., Carta, J. J., & Hall, R. V. (1986). Classwide peer tutoring. *Exceptional Children, 52,* 535–542.

Fuchs, D., Fuchs, L. S., Mathes, P. G., & Simmons, D. C. (1997). Peer-assisted learning strategies: Making classrooms more responsive to diversity. *American Educational Research Journal, 34*(1), 174–206.

Gersten, R., Carnine, D., & Woodward, J. (1987). Direct instruction research: The third decade. *Remedial & Special Education, 8*(6), 48–56.

Harris, K. R., & Graham, S. (2009). Self-regulated strategy development in writing: Premises, evolution, and the future. *British Journal of Educational Psychology Monograph Series, 11*(6), 113–135.

Heron, T. E., Villareal, D. M., Yao, M., Christianson, R. J., & Heron, K. (2006). Peer tutoring systems: Applications in classroom and specialized environments. *Reading & Writing Quarterly, 22,* 27–45.

Johnson, D. W., Johnson, R. T., & Holubec, E. J. (1994). *Cooperative learning in the classroom* (6th ed.). Association for Supervision & Curriculum Development.

Klingner, J. K., Vaughn, S., Arguelles, M. E., Hughes, M. T., & Leftwich, S. A. (2004). Collaborative strategic reading: "Real-world" lessons from classroom teachers. *Remedial and Special Education, 25,* 291–302.

Krathwohl, D. R. (2002). A revision of Bloom's taxonomy: An overview. *Theory into Practice, 4*(4), 202–218.

Lenz, B. K., & Deshler, D. D. (2004). Adolescents with learning disabilities: Revisiting the educators' enigma. In B. Wong (Ed.), *Learning about learning disabilities* (3rd ed., pp. 535–564). Academic Press/Elsevier.

Mastropieri, M. A., & Scruggs, T. E. (2009). *The inclusive classroom: Strategies for effective differentiated instruction* (4th ed.). Pearson.

Mastropieri, M. A., & Scruggs, T. E. (2014). *The inclusive classroom: Strategies for effective differentiated instruction.* Pearson.

McMaster, K. L., Fuchs, D., & Fuchs, L. S. (2006). Research on peer-assisted learning strategies: The promise and limitations of peer-mediated instruction. *Reading & Writing Quarterly, 22*(1), 5–25.

Montague, M., & Dietz, S. (2009). Evaluating the evidence base for cognitive strategy instruction and mathematical problem solving. *Exceptional Children, 75*, 285–302.

Montague, M., Enders, C., & Dietz, S. (2011). The effects of cognitive strategy instruction on math problem solving of middle school students with learning disabilities. *Learning Disability Quarterly, 34*, 262–272.

National Governors Association Center for Best Practices and Council of Chief State School Officers. (2010). *Common Core State Standards.*

Pintrich, P. R. (2002). The role of metacognitive knowledge in learning, teaching, and assessing. *Theory into Practice, 41*(4). doi:10.1207/s15430421tip4104_3

Price, K. M., & Nelson, K. L. (2003). *Daily planning for today's classroom* (2nd ed.). Wadsworth-Thomson.

Rosenshine, B. (1987). Explicit teaching and teacher training. *Journal of Teacher Education, 38*(3), 34–36.

Schumaker, J. B., & Deshler, D. D. (2006). Teaching adolescents to be strategic learners. In D. D. Deshler & J. B. Schumaker (Eds.), *Teaching adolescents with disabilities: Accessing the general education curriculum* (pp. 121–156). Corwin.

Schumm, J. S., Moody, S. M., & Vaughn, S. (2000). Grouping for reading instruction: Does one size fit all? *Journal of Learning Disabilities, 33*(5), 477–488.

Slavin, R. E. (1991). Synthesis of research on cooperative learning. *Educational Leadership, 48*(5), 71–82.

Stowitschek, J. J., Stowitschek, C. E., Hendrickson, J. M., & Day, R. M. (1984). *Direct teaching tactics for exceptional children.* Aspen.

Swanson, H. L., & Deshler, D. (2003). Instructing adolescents with learning disabilities: Converting a meta-analysis to practice. *Journal of Learning Disabilities, 36*, 124–135.

Swanson, H. L., Hoskyn, M., & Lee, C. (1999). *Interventions for students with learning disabilities. A meta-analysis of treatment outcomes.* Guilford Press.

Tieso, C. (2005). The effects of grouping practices and curricular adjustments on achievement. *Journal for the Education of the Gifted, 29*(1), 60–89.

Vaughn, S., & Bos, C. (2011). *Strategies for teaching students with learning and behavior problems* (8th ed.). Pearson.

Vaughn, S., Hughes, M. T., Moody, S. W., & Elbaum, B. (2001). Instructional grouping for reading for students with learning disabilities: Implications for practice. *Intervention in School and Clinic, 35*, 131–137.

CHAPTER 8

Americans with Disabilities Act (ADA) of 1990, PL No. 101-336, 104 Stat. 328 (1991).

Assistive Technology Act of 2004 (ATA, or Tech Act), PL 108-364 (2004).

Bryant, D. P., & Bryant, B. R. (1998). Using assistive technology adaptations to include students with learning disabilities in cooperative learning activities. *Journal of Learning Disabilities, 31*(1), 41–54.

Bryant, D. P., & Bryant, B. R. (2011). *Assistive technology for people with disabilities* (2nd ed.). Pearson.

CAST. (2011). *Universal Design for Learning Guidelines version 2.0.*

CAST. (n.d.). *About Universal Design for Learning.* Retrieved from http://cast.org/udl/index.html

Deussen, T., Autio, E. Miller, B., Lockwood, A. T. & Stewart, V. (2008). *What teachers should know about instruction for English language learners.* Education Northwest.

Edyburn, D. (2010). Would you recognize universal design for learning if you saw it? Ten propositions for new directions for the second decade of UDL. *Learning Disability Quarterly, 33*, 33–41.

Hall, T. E., Cohen, N., Vue, G., & Ganley, P. (2015). Addressing learning disabilities with UDL and technology: Strategic reader. *Learning Disability Quarterly. 38*(2): 72–83. doi:10.1177/0731948714544375

Higher Education Opportunity Act of 2008 (HEOA). PL No. 110-315.

Individuals with Disabilities Education Improvement Act of 2004 (IDEIA or IDEA), PL 108-446 (2004).

International Business Machines (IBM). (1991). *Assistive technology training manual.*

Kennedy, M. J., Thomas, C. N., Meyer, P., Alves, K. D., & Lloyd, J. W. (2014). Using evidence-based multimedia to improve vocabulary performance of adolescents with LD: A UDL approach. *Learning Disability Quarterly, 37*(2), 71–86. doi:10.1177/0731948713507262

King-Sears, M. (2009). Universal design for learning: Technology and pedagogy. *Learning Disability Quarterly, 32*, 199–201.

King-Sears, M. E., Johnson, T. M., Berkeley, S., Weiss, M. P., Peters-Burton, E. E., Evmenova, A. S., . . . Hursh, J. C. (2014). An exploratory study of universal design for teaching chemistry to students with and without disabilities. *Learning Disability Quarterly, 38*(2), 84–96. doi:10.1177/0731948714564575

Lemons, C. J. (2000). *Comparison of parent and teacher knowledge and opinions related to augmentative and alternative communication* (Unpublished master's thesis). The University of Texas at Austin, Austin, TX.

Mace, R. (1998). *A perspective on universal design.* Excerpt of a presentation made by Ronald L. Mace, FAIA, at Designing for the 21st Century: An International Conference on Universal Design, June 19, 1998, Hofstra University, Hempstead, New York. Retrieved from http://www.ncsu.edu/ncsu/design/cud/about_us/usronmacespeech.htm

Ok, M. W., Kim, M-K, Kang, Y. J., & Bryant, B. R. (2016). How to find good apps: An evaluation rubric for instructional apps for teaching students with learning disabilities. *Intervention in School and Clinic, 51*(4), 244–252. doi:10.1177/1053451215589179

Ok, M., Rao, K., Bryant, B. R., & McDougal, D. (2017). Universal Design for Learning in pre-k to grade 12 classrooms: A systematic review of research, *Exceptionality, 25*(2), 116–138, doi:10.1080/09362835.2016.1196450

Rao, K., Ok, M. W., & Bryant, B. R. (2014). A review of research on universal design educational models. *Remedial and Special Education, 35*(3), 153–166.

Raskind, M., & Bryant, B. R. (2002). *Functional evaluation for assistive technology.* Psycho-Educational Services.

Rieth, H. J., Colburn, L. K., & Bryant, D. P. (2004). Trends and issues in instructional and assistive technology, In A. M. Sorrells, H. J. Rieth, & P. T. Sindelar (Eds.), *Critical issues in special education: Access, diversity, and accountability* (pp. 205–225). Pearson.

Rose, D. H., Harbour, W. S., Johnston, C. S., Daley, S. G., & Abarbanell, L. (2006). Universal Design for Learning in postsecondary education: Reflections on principles and their application. *Journal of Postsecondary Education and Disability, 19*, 135–151.

Rosenberg, J. Z. (2017). *22 best mobile apps for kids with special needs*. Retrieved from https://www.care.com/c/stories/6621/22-best-mobile-apps-for-kids-with-special-nee/

Technology and Media. (n.d.). *The AT quick wheel*. Council for Exceptional Children.

CHAPTER 9

Boulder Valley School District Office of Advanced Academic Services. (2010). *Identifying talented and gifted students from culturally, linguistically, and ethnically diverse (CLED) populations*. Retrieved from http://aea11gt.pbworks.com/w/file/fetch/116124529/CLED=20Identification.pdf

Bryant, B. R., Kim, M. K., Ok, M. W., Kang, E. Y., Bryant, D. P., Lang, R., Son, S. H. (2015). A comparison of the effects of reading interventions on engagement and performance for 4th grade students with learning disabilities. *Behavior Modification, 39*(1), 167–190.

CAST. (2011). *Universal design for learning guidelines version 2.0.*

Conners, C. K. (2008). *Conners rating scale* (3rd ed.) (Conner-III). The Psychological Corporation/Pearson.

Cuillos, S., SoRelle, D., Kim, S. A., Seo, Y. J., & Bryant, B. R. (2011). Monitoring student response to mathematics intervention: Using data to inform Tier 3 intervention. *Intervention in School and Clinic, 47*, 121.

Deno, S., & Mirkin, P. (1977). *Data-based program modification*. Council for Exceptional Children.

Dumont-Williams. (n.d.). *Score conversion tables for commonly used tests*. Retrieved from https://www.ritenour.k12.mo.us/cms/lib/MO01910124/Centricity/Domain/69/Psychometric_Conversion_Table.pdf

Every Student Succeeds Act (ESSA) of 2015, PL 114-95 (2015).

Flower, A., McKenna, J., Muething, C., Bryant, D. P., & Bryant, B. R. (2013). Effects of the good behavior game on classwide off-task behavior in a high school basic algebra resource classroom. *Behavior Modification, 38*, 45–68. doi:10.1177/0145445513507574

Hadaway, S. M., & Brue, A. W. (2016). *Practitioner's guide to functional behavioral assessment*. Springer.

Hammill, D., Brown, L., & Bryant, B. R. (1992). *A consumer's guide to tests in print* (2nd ed.). PRO-USDE.

Idea Partnership. (n.d.). *Functional behavior assessment*. Retrieved from http://www.ideapartnership.org/documents/ASD-Collection/asd-dg_Brief_FBA.pdf

iParadigms, LLC. (2012). *Rubric for narrative essay*. Retrieved from https://www.wlwv.k12.or.us/cms/lib/OR01001812/Centricity/Domain/1382/Rubric=20for=20Narrative=20Essay.pdf

Kritikos, E. P., McLoughlin, J. A., & Lewis, R. B. (2018). *Assessing students with special needs* (8th ed.). Pearson.

McMillan, J. H. (2018). *Using assessment mistakes and learning deficits to enhance motivation and learning*. Routledge.

Miller, M. N., Linn, R. L., & Gronlund, N. E. (2013). *Measurement and assessment in teaching* (11th ed.).Pearson.

National Center on Educational Outcomes (NCEO). (2013). *Alternate assessments for students with disabilities: Overview*. Retrieved from http://www.cehd.umn.edu/nceo/topicareas/alternateassessments/altassesstopic.htm

National Center on Intensive Intervention. (2013). *Data-based individualization: A framework for intensive intervention*. Office of Special Education, U.S. Department of Education.

National Governors Association Center for Best Practices & Council of Chief State School Officers. (2010). *Common core state standards*.

Overton, T. (2011). *Assessing learners with special needs: An applied approach* (7th ed.). Pearson.

Partnership for Assessment of Readiness for College and Careers (PARCC). (2013). *Expanding access: Accessibility features and accommodations for students with disabilities in PARCC assessments—A parent's guide*. Retrieved from https://osse.dc.gov/sites/default/files/dc/sites/osse/service_content/attachments/Parent%20PARCC%20Brochure%20for%20Students%20with%20Disabilities.pdf

Pearson Assessments. (2007). *Stanford achievement test*.

Rashotte, C., Torgesen, J. K., & Wagner, R. W. (2012). *Test of word reading efficiency* (TOWRE-2). PRO-USDE.

Rehabilitation Act of 1973. Section 504, 19 U.S.C. § 794.

Reynolds, C. R., Livingston, R. B., & Willson, V. (2009). *Measurement and assessment in education* (2nd ed.). Pearson.

Salvia, J., Ysseldyke, J., & Witmer, S (2017). *Assessment in special and inclusive education* (13th ed.). Cengage Learning.

Schrank, F. A., McGrew, K. W., Mather, N., & Woodcock, R. (2014). *Woodcock-Johnson IV* (WJ-IV). Riverside.

Seton Testing Services. (2016). *Iowa tests*.

Smith, D. D., Tyler, N. C., Skow, K., & Smith, S. (2018). *Introduction to contemporary special education: New horizons* (2nd ed.). Pearson.

Taylor, R. L. (2003). *Assessment of exceptional students* (6th ed.).Allyn & Bacon.

Thompson, S. J., Johnstone, C. J., & Thurlow, M. L. (2002). *Universal design applied to large scale assessments*. National Center on Educational Outcomes.

Torgesen, J., & Bryant, B. R. (2005). *Test of phonological awareness* (2nd ed.) (TOPA-2+). PRO-USDE.

Wagner, R. W., Torgesen, J. K., Rashotte, C., & Pearson, N. (2013). *Comprehensive test of phonological processes* (CTOPP-2). PRO-USDE.

Wiederholt, J. L., & Bryant, B. R. (2012). *Gray oral reading test* (5th ed.). Pro-Ed.

Woodcock, R. (2011). *Woodcock reading mastery test* (3rd ed.; WRMT-III). The Psychological Corporation/Pearson.

CHAPTER 10

Alberto, P. A., & Troutman, A. C. (2017). *Applied behavior analysis for teachers: Interactive edition* (9th ed.). Merrill.

Allen, K. E., Hart, B. M., Buell, J. S., Harris, F. R., & Wolf, M. M. (1964). Effects of social reinforcement on isolate behavior of a nursery school child. *Child Development, 35*, 511–518.

American Psychological Association. (2014). *Classroom management*. Retrieved from http://www.apa.org/education/k12/classroom-mgmt.aspx

Barrish, H. H., Saunders, M., & Wolf, M. M. (1969). Good behavior game: Effects of individual contingencies for group consequences on disruptive behavior in a classroom. *Journal of Applied Behavior Analysis, 2*, 119–124.

Belgrave, F. Z., & Brevade, J. (2015). *African American boys: Identity, culture, and development.* Springer.

Canter, L. (2010). *Assertive discipline: Positive behavior management for today's classroom* (4th ed.). Solution Tree Press.

Corrol, E., Tynan, D., & Lines, M. M. (2009). *Planned ignoring.* Nemours Foundation. Retrieved from https://www.nemours.org/content/dam/nemours/wwwv2/filebox/service/health/parenting/tips/13plannedignoring.pdf

Council for Children with Behavioral Disorders. (2009). *CCBD's position summary on the use of seclusion in school settings.* Retrieved from http://www.casecec.org/pdf/seclusion/Accepted,=20CCBD=20on=20Use=20of=20Seclusion,=207-8-09.pdf

Diallo, I., & Maizonniaux, C. (2017). Policies and pedagogies for students of diverse backgrounds. *International Journal of Pedagogies and Learning, 11*(3), 201–210, doi:10.1080/22040552.2016.1279526

Dreikurs, R. (1968). *Psychology in the classroom: A manual for teachers* (2nd ed.). Harper & Row.

Dreikurs, R., & Cassel, P. (1972). *Discipline without tears.* Hawthorn Books.

Education Portal. (2015). *Applying the Premack Principle in the classroom.* Retrieved from http://education-portal.com/academy/lesson/applying-the-premack-principle-in-the-classroom.html#lesson

Emmer, E., & Evertson, C. M. (2017). *Classroom management for middle and high school teachers* (10th ed.). Pearson.

Florida Association for Behavior Analysis. (2018). *Behavior can change.* Retrieved from http://behaviorcanchange.com/Assessments-commonly-used-in-ABA.php

Flower, A., McKenna, J., Muething, C., Bryant, D. P., & Bryant, B. R. (2013). Effects of the Good Behavior Game on class-wide off-task behavior in a high school basic algebra resource classroom. *Behavior Modification, 38*, 45–68. doi:10.1177/0145445513507574

Gordon, T. (2003). *Teacher effectiveness training.* Three Rivers Press.

Haydon, T., & Musti-Rao, S. (2011). Effective use of behavior-specific praise: A middle school case. *Beyond Behavior, 20*(2), 31–39.

Individuals with Disabilities Education Improvement Act of 2004 (IDIEA or IDEA), PL 108-446 (2004).

Intervention Central. (n.d.). *Jackpot! Ideas for classroom reward.* Retrieved from http://www.interventioncentral.org/behavioral-interventions/rewards/jackpot-ideas-classroom-rewards

Klingner, J. K., Boelé, A. L., Linan-Thompson, S., & Rodriguez, D. (2014). Essential components of special education for ELLs with LD: Position Statement of the Division for Learning Disabilities of the Council for Exceptional Children. *Learning Disabilities Research & Practice, 29*(3), 93–96.

Lane, K. L. (2007). Identifying and supporting students at risk for emotional and behavioral disorders within multi-level models: Data driven approaches to conducting secondary interventions with an academic emphasis. *Education & Treatment of Children, 30*(4), 135–164. doi:10.1353/etc.2007.0026

Lopez, I. (2017). *Keeping it real and relevant: Building authentic relationships in your diverse classroom.* ASCD.

Lovitt, T. (2000). *Preventing School Failure: Tactics for Teaching Adolescents* (2nd ed.). PRO-USDE.

Neo, M., Neo, K. T.-L., & Tan, H. Y.-J. (2012). Applying authentic learning strategies in a multimedia and web learning environment (MWLE): Malaysian students' perspective. *Turkish Online Journal of Educational Technology, 11*(3), 50–60. Retrieved from http://www.tojet.net/articles/v11i3/1135.pdf

Office of Special Education Programs (OSEP). (2004). *26th Annual Report to Congress on the implementation of the Individuals with Disabilities Education Act.* U.S. Department of Education.

PACER's National Bullying Prevention Center (2018). *Bullying and harassment of students with disabilities.*

Parsonson, B. S. (2012). *Evidence-based classroom behaviour management strategies.* Retrieved from https://files.eric.ed.gov/fulltext/EJ976654.pdf

Powell, M. (2013). 5 ways to make your classroom student-centered. *Education Week Teacher.* Retrieved from http://www.edweek.org/tm/articles/2013/12/24/ctq_powell_strengths.html

Raskaukas, J., & Scott, M. (2011). Modifying anti-bullying programs to include students with disabilities. *Teaching Exceptional Children, 44*(1), 60–67.

Rose, C., & Gage, N. (2017). Exploring the involvement of bullying among students with disabilities over time. *Exceptional Children 83*(3), 298–314. doi:10.1177/0014402916667587

Rose, C. A., Swearer, S. M., & Espelage, D. L. (2012). Bullying and students with disabilities: The untold narrative. *Focus on Exceptional Children, 45*(2), 1–10.

Ryan, J. B., Pierce, C. D., & Mooney, P. (2008). Evidence-based teaching strategies for students with EBD. *Beyond Behavior, 17*(3), 22–29.

Skinner, B. F. (1938). *The Behavior of organisms: An experimental analysis.* Appleton-Century.

Smith, D. D., Tyler, N. C., Skow, K., & Smith, S. (2018). *Introduction to contemporary special education: New horizons* (2nd ed.). Pearson.

Sugai, G., & Horner, R. H. (2009). Defining and describing schoolwide positive behavior support. In W. Sailor, D. Dunlao, G. Segai, & R. Horner (Eds.), *Handbook of positive behavior support* (pp. 307–326). Springer.

Swearer, S. M., Wang, C., Maag, J. W., Siebecker, A. B., & Frerichs, L. J. (2012). Understanding the bullying dynamic among students in special and general education. *Journal of School Psychology, 50*(4), 503–520.

Thompson, J. D. (n.d.). *What is your level of classroom "withitness?"* Retrieved from http://www.burtbooks.com/What=20Is=20Your=20Level=20of=20Classroom=20withitness.pdf

University of Nebraska–Lincoln, Office of Graduate Studies. (n.d.). *Twenty tips on motivating students.* Retrieved from http://www.unl.edu/gradstudies/current/teaching/motivating

White, N. A., &, & Loeber, R. (2008). Bullying and special education as predictors of serious delinquency. *Journal of Research in Crime and Delinquency, 45*(4), 380–397. doi:10.1177/0022427808322612

Wolfgang, C. H. (2009). *Solving discipline problems* (7th ed.). Pearson.

Zakrzewski, V. (2012, September 18). *Four ways teachers can show they care.* Greater Good Science Center at UC Berkeley, Berkeley, CA. Retrieved from http://greatergood.berkeley.edu/article/item/caring_teacher_student_relationship

CHAPTER 11

Bryant, B. R., Bryant, D. P., Hammill, D. D., & Sorrells, A. M. (2004). Characteristic reading behaviors of poor readers who have learning disabilities. *Assessment for Effective Intervention, 19*, 39–46.

Bryant, B. R., Wiederholt, J. L., & Bryant, D. P. (2012). *Gray Diagnostic Reading Test* (2nd ed.). PRO-USDE.

Bryant, D. P., Bryant, B. R., Langley, J., Flower, A., Hou, V., McKenna, J., . . . Tausiani, J. (2011). *Secondary special education observation and intervention study: Technical report.* Meadows Center for Preventing Educational Risk, College of Education, University of Texas at Austin and Texas Education Agency, Austin, TX.

CAST. (2018). *Universal design for learning guidelines version 2.2* [graphic organizer].

Cunningham, P. M. (2017). *Phonics they use: Words for reading and writing* (6th ed.). Pearson.

Dolch, E. W. (1948). *Problems in reading.* The Garrard Press.

Elkonin, D. B. (1973). U.S.S.R. In J. Downing (Ed.), *Comparative reading* (pp. 551–579). Macmillan.

Grantham, T. C., & Ford, D. Y. (2003). Beyond self-concept and self-esteem for African American students: Improving racial identity improves achievement. *High School Journal, 87*(1), 18–29.

Hasbrouck, J. & Tindal, G. (2017). *An update to compiled ORF norms* (Technical report No. 1702). Behavioral Research and Teaching. University of Oregon, Eugene, OR.

Honig, B., Diamond, L., & Gutlohn, L. (2012). *Teaching reading sourcebook* (Updated 2nd ed.). Arena Press.

Johnson, D. (1971). Dolch word list reexamined. *The Reading Teacher, 24*, 455–456.

Kim, M. K., Bryant, D. P., Bryant, B. R., & Park, Y. (2017). A synthesis of interventions for improving oral reading fluency of elementary students with learning disabilities. *Preventing School Failure: Alternative Education for Children and Youth, 61*(2), 116–125. doi:10.1080/1045988X.2016.1212321

Klingner, J., Vaughn, S., Dimino, J., Schumm, J. S., & Bryant, D. P. (2001). *Collaborative strategic reading.* Sopris West.

National Assessment of Educational Progress (NAEP). (2023). *The nation's report card.* National Center for Educational Statistics.

National Reading Panel. (2000). *Teaching children to read: An evidence-based assessment of the scientific research literature on reading and its implications for reading instruction.* National Institutes of Health, National Institute of Child Health and Human Development.

Office of Special Education Programs (OSEP). (2014). *Annual report to Congress on the Individuals with Disabilities Education Act.* U.S. Department of Education. Retrieved from https://www2.ed.gov/about/reports/annual/osep/2014/index.html

Office of Special Education Programs (OSEP). (2017). *Annual Report to Congress on the Individuals with Disabilities Education Act.* U.S. Department of Education. Retrieved from https://www2.ed.gov/about/reports/annual/osep/2017/index.html

Raskind, M., & Bryant, B. R. (2002). *Functional evaluation for assistive technology.* Psycho-Educational Services.

Reading Rockets. (2017). *Phonological and phonemic awareness.* Retrieved from http://www.readingrockets.org/helping/target/phonologicalphonemic

Torgesen, J., & Bryant, B. R. (2013). *Phonological awareness training for reading* (2nd ed.). PRO-USDE.

Vaughn, S., & Bos, C. S. (2015). *Strategies for teaching students with learning and behavior problems, enhanced Pearson e-text with loose-leaf version.* (Access card package, 9th ed.). Pearson.

Wanzek, J., & Roberts, G. (2012). Reading interventions with varying instructional emphases for fourth graders with reading difficulties. *Learning Disability Quarterly, 35*(2), 90–101. doi:10.1177/0731948711434047

Welcome Centre Human Genetics. (2017). *Dyslexia.* Retrieved from http://www.well.ox.ac.uk/dyslexia-2

CHAPTER 12

Atwell, N. (2010). *Writing in the middle—reading in the middle: DVD bundle.* Heinemann.

Berninger, V. W., & Wolf, B. J. (2009). *Teaching students with dyslexia and dysgraphia: Lessons from teaching and science.* Brookes.

Bryant, D. P., & Bryant, B. R. (2011). *Assistive technology for people with disabilities* (2nd ed.). Pearson.

CAST. (2018). *Universal design for learning guidelines version 2.2* [graphic organizer].

Finn, C. E., Petrilli, M. J., & Julian, L. (2006). *The state of state standards 2006.* Fordham Foundation.

Graham, S. (2009–10). Want to improve their writing? Don't neglect their handwriting. *American Educator, 33*(4), 20–40.

Graham, S., & Harris, K. R. (1988a). Instructional recommendations for teaching writing to exceptional students. *Exceptional Children, 54*, 506–512.

Graham, S., & Harris, K. R. (1988b). Research and instruction in written language: Introduction to the special issue. *Exceptional Children, 54*, 495–496.

Graves, D. (1983). *Writing: Teachers and children at work.* Heinemann.

Haager, D., & Klingner, J. K. (2005). *Differentiating instruction in inclusive classrooms.* Pearson.

Hammill, D. D., & Bryant, B. R. (1998). *Learning disabilities diagnostic inventory.* PRO-USDE.

Harris, K. R., & Graham, S. (2013). "An adjective is a word hanging down from a noun": Learning to write and students with learning disabilities. *Annals of Dyslexia, 63*(1), 65–79. doi:10.1007/s11881-011-0057-x

Harris, K., Graham, S., & Mason, L. (2002). POW plus TREE equals powerful opinion essays: Improving writing in the early grades. *Teaching Exceptional Children, 34*, 74–77.

Johnson, A. P. (2008). *Teaching reading and writing.* Rowman & Littlefield Education.

MacArthur, C. A., Philippakos, Z. A., & Graham, S. (2016). A multicomponent measure of writing motivation with basic college writers. *Learning Disability Quarterly, 39*, 31–43. doi:10.1177/0731948715583115

Mercer, C. D., & Pullen, P. C. (2009). *Students with learning disabilities* (7th ed.). Prentice Hall.

Shapiro, E. S. (2004). *Academic skills problems.* Sattler.

Tompkins, G. E. (2011). *Teaching writing: Balancing process and product* (6th ed.). Pearson.

Vaughn, S., & Bos, C. S. (2015b). *Teaching strategies for students with mild to moderate disabilities* (9th ed.). Pearson.

Welch, M. (1992). The PLEASE strategy: A metacognitive learning strategy for improving the paragraph writing of students with mild learning disabilities. *Learning Disability Quarterly, 15*, 119–128.

CHAPTER 13

Allsopp, D., Lovin, L., & van Ingen, S. (2018). *Teaching mathematics meaningfully: Solutions for reaching struggling learners* (2nd ed.). Brookes.

Ashlock, R. B. (2010). *Error patterns in computation: Using error patterns to help students learn* (10th ed.). Pearson.

Berch, D. B. (2005). Making sense of number sense: Implications for children with mathematical disabilities. *Journal of Learning Disabilities, 38*, 333–339. doi:10.1177/00222194050380040901

Bley, N., & Thornton, C. (2001). *Teaching mathematics to students with learning disabilities* (4th ed.). PRO-ED.

Browder, D. M., Spooner, F., Ahlgrim-Delzell, L., Harris, A., & Wakeman, S. (2008). A meta-analysis on teaching students with severe cognitive disabilities. *Exceptional Children, 74*, 407–432.

Bryant, B. R., Bryant, D. P., Kethley, C., Kim, S., Pool, C., & Seo, Y. (2008). Preventing mathematics difficulties in the primary grades: The critical features of instruction in textbooks as part of the equation. Special series, *Learning Disability Quarterly, 31*(1), 21–35.

Bryant, D. P., Bryant, B. R., Gersten, R., Scammacca, N., & Chavez, M. (2008). Mathematics intervention for first- and second-grade students with mathematics difficulties: The effects of Tier 2 intervention delivered as booster lessons. *Remedial and Special Education, 29*(1), 20–32.

Bryant, D. P., Bryant, B., & Hammill, D. D. (2000). Characteristic behaviors of students with LD who have teacher-identified math weaknesses. *Journal of Learning Disabilities, 33*(2), 168–177.

Bryant, D. P., Bryant, B. R., Roberts, G., Vaughn, S., Hughes, K., Porterfield, J., & Gersten, R. (2011). Effects of an early numeracy intervention on the performance of first-grade students with mathematics difficulties. *Exceptional Children, 78*(1), 7–23.

Bryant, D. P., Kim, S. A., Hartman, P., & Bryant, B. R. (2006). Standards-based mathematics instruction and teaching middle school students with mathematical disabilities. In M. Montague & A. Jitendra (Eds.), *Teaching mathematics to middle school students with learning difficulties* (pp. 7–28). Guilford.

Bryant, D. P., Roberts, G., Bryant, B. R., & DiAndreth-Elkins, L. (2011). Tier 2 early numeracy number sense interventions for kindergarten and first-grade students with mathematics difficulties. In R. Gersten & B. Newman-Gonchar (Eds.), *RTI mathematics* (pp. 65–83). Brookes.

Butler, F. M., Miller, S. P., Crehan, K., Babbitt, B., & Pierce, T. (2003). Fraction instruction for students with mathematics disabilities: Comparing two teaching sequences. *Learning Disabilities Research & Practice, 18*, 99–111.

Byrd, C. E., McNeil, N. M., Chesney, D. L., & Matthews, P. G. (2015). A specific misconception of the equal sign acts as a barrier to children's learning of early algebra. *Learning and Individual Differences, 38*, 61–67.

CAST. (2018). *Universal design for learning guidelines version 2.2* [graphic organizer].

Chard, D. J., Baker, S., Clarke, B., Jungjohann, K., Davis, K., & Smolkowski, K. (2008). Preventing early mathematics difficulties: The feasibility of a rigorous kindergarten mathematics curriculum. *Learning Disability Quarterly, 31*, 11–20.

Clarke, B., Doabler, C. T., Smolkowski, K., Baker, S., K., Fien, H., Cary, M. S. (2016). Examining the efficacy of a Tier 2 kindergarten mathematics intervention. *Journal of Learning Disabilities, 49*(2), 152–165. doi:10.1177/0022219414538514

Common Core State Standards Initiative. (2021). *Mathematics standards.* Retrieved from http://www.thecorestandards.org/Math/

Council of Chief State School Officers & National Governors' Association. (2022). *Common Core Sate Standards for Mathematics [CCSSM]. Common Core State Standards Initiative.* Retrieved from https://learning.ccsso.org/wp-content/uploads/2022/11/ADA-Compliant-Math-Standards.pdf

Coyne, M. D., Kame'enui, E. J., & Carnine, D. W. (2011). *Effective teaching strategies that accommodate diverse learners* (4th ed.). Pearson.

Didax Educational Resources. (2015). Retrieved from https://www.didax.com/math/virtual-manipulatives.html

Doabler, C. T., Clarke, B., Kosty, D., Kurtz-Nelson, E., Fien, H., Smolkowski, S. & Baker, S. (2016). Testing the efficacy of a tier-2 mathematics intervention: A conceptual replication study. *Exceptional Children, 83*(1), 92–110. doi:10.1177/0014402916660084.

Doabler, C. T., & Fien, H. (2013). Explicit mathematics instruction: What teachers can do for teaching students with mathematics difficulties. *Intervention in School and Clinic, 48*, 276–285.

Dougherty, B. (2021). Effective mathematical practices for mathematics instruction and developing mathematical reasoning. In D. P. Bryant (Ed.), *Intensifying mathematics interventions for students who struggle learning mathematics.* Guilford Press.

Dougherty, B., Bryant, D. P., Bryant, B. R., Darrough, R. L., & Pfannenstiel, K. H. (2015). Developing concepts and generalizations to build algebraic thinking: The reversibility, flexibility, and generalization approach. *Intervention in School and Clinic, 50*, 273–281. doi:10.1177/1053451214560892

Dougherty, B., Bryant, D. P., & Lee, J. (2021). Algebra. In D. P. Bryant (Ed.), *Intensifying mathematics interventions for students who struggle learning mathematics.* Guilford Press.

Fuchs, L. S., Geary, D. C., Compton, D. L., Fuchs, D., Hamlett, C. L., & Bryant, J. D. (2010). The contributions of numerosity and domain—general abilities to school readiness. *Child Development, 81*, 1520–1533. doi:10.1111/j.1467-8624.2010.01489.x

Fuson, K. C. (1982). An analysis of the counting-on solution procedure in addition. In T. P. Carpenter, J. M. Moser, & T. A. Romberg (Eds.), *Addition and subtraction: A cognitive perspective* (pp. 67–81). Lawrence Erlbaum.

Geary, D. C. (2004). Mathematics and learning disabilities. *Journal of Learning Disabilities, 37*, 4–15. doi:10.1177/00222194040370010201

Geary, D. C. (2011). Consequences, characteristics, and causes of mathematical learning disabilities and persistent low achievement in mathematics. *Journal of Developmental & Behavioral Pediatrics, 33*(30), 250–263. doi:10.1097/DBP.0b013e318209edef

Gelman, R., & Gallistel, C. R. (1978). *The child's understanding of number.* Harvard University Press.

Gersten, R., Beckmann, S., Clarke, B., Foegen, A., Marsh, L., Star, J. R., & Witzel, B. (2009). *Assisting students struggling with mathematics: Response to intervention (RTI) for elementary and middle schools* (NCEE 2009-4060). National Center for Education Evaluation and Regional Assistance, Institute of Education Sciences, U.S. Department of Education.

Gersten, R., Jordan, N. C., & Flojo, J. R. (2005). Early identification and intervention for students with mathematics difficulties.

Journal of Learning Disabilities, 38(4), 293–304.

Gevarter, C., Bryant, D. P., Bryant, B. R., Watkins, L. Zamora, C. & Sammarco, N. (2016). Mathematics interventions for individuals with autism spectrum disorder: A systematic review. *Review Journal of Autism and Developmental Disorders, 3*(3), 224–238. doi:10.1007/s40489-016-0078-9

Groen, G. J., & Parkman, J. M. (1972). A chronometric analysis of simple addition. *Psychology Review, 79*, 329–343.

Hecht, S., Close, L., & Santisi, M. (2003). Sources of individual differences in fraction skills. *Journal of Experimental Child Psychology, 86*(4), 277–302.

Hudson, P., & Miller, S. P. (2006). *Designing and implementing mathematics instruction for students with diverse learning needs.* Pearson.

Individuals with Disabilities Education Improvement Act (IDIEA or IDEA) of 2004. PL No. 108-446 (2004).

Institute of Education Sciences (IES). (n.d.). *Improving mathematical problem solving in grads 4 though 8.* What Works Clearinghouse. Retrieved from http://ies.ed.gov/ncee/wwc/PracticeGuide.aspx

Jitendra, A. K., Griffin, C., Haria, P., Leh, J., Adams, A., & Kaduvetoor, A. (2007). A comparison of single and multiple strategy instruction on third grade students' mathematical problem solving. *Journal of Educational Psychology, 99*, 115–127. doi:10.1037/0022-0663.99.1.115

Jordan, N. C., Glutting, J., Dyson, N., Hassinger-Das, B., & Irwin, C. (2012). Building kindergartners' number sense: A randomized controlled study. *Journal of Educational Psychology. 104*(3), 647-660. doi:10.1037/a0029018

Jordan, N. C., Glutting, J., & Ramineni, C. (2009). The importance of number sense to mathematics achievement in first and third grades. *Learning and Individual Differences.* Advance online publication. doi:10.1016/j.lindif.2009.07004

Jordan, N. C., Hanich, L. B., & Kaplan, D. (2003). Arithmetic fact mastery in young children: A longitudinal investigation. *Journal of Experimental Child Psychology, 85*, 103–119.

Jordan, N. C., Kaplan, D., Ramineni, C., & Locuniak, M. N. (2009). Early math matters: Kindergarten number competence and later mathematics outcomes. *Developmental Psychology, 45*, 850–867. doi:10.1037/a0014939

Karp, K., Bush, S., & Dougherty, B. J. (2014). Avoiding rules that expire. *Teaching Children Mathematics, 21*(1), 18–25.

Kieran, C. (2004). Algebra thinking in the early grades: What is it? *Mathematics Educator, 8*, 139–151.

Krawec, J. L. (2014). Problem representation and mathematical problem solving of students of varying math ability. *Journal of Learning Disabilities, 47*(2), 103–115. doi:10.1177/0022219412436976

Kritikos, E. P., McLoughlin, J. A., & Lewis, R. B. (2018). *Assessing students with special needs* (8th ed.). Pearson.

Maccini, P., & Gagnon, J. C. (2005). *Math graphic organizers for students with disabilities.* The Access Center: Improving Outcomes for All Students K–8. Retrieved from http://www.k8accesscenter.org/training_resources/documents/ MathGraphicOrg.pdf

Mayer, R. E. (1998). Cognitive, metacognitive, and motivational aspects of problem solving. *Instructional Science, 26*, 49–63.

Mazzocco, M. M. M., & Devlin, K. T. (2008). Parts and "holes": Gaps in rational number sense among children with vs. without mathematical learning disabilities. *Developmental Science, 11*(5), 681–691.

Mercer, C. D., Mercer, A. R., & Pullen, P. (2010). *Teaching students with learning problems* (7th ed.). Macmillan.

Mercer, C. D., & Miller, S. P. (1992). Teaching students with learning problems in math to acquire, understand, and apply basic math facts. *Remedial and Special Education, 13*(3), 19–35, 61.

Milgram, J. (2005). *The mathematics preservice teachers need to know.*

Miller, S. P., & Mercer, C. D. (1993). Mnemonics: Enhancing the math performance of students with learning difficulties. *Intervention in School and Clinic, 29*, 78–82.

Miller, S. P., Mercer, C. D., & Dillon, A. (1992). CSA: Acquiring and retaining math skills. *Intervention in School and Clinic, 28*, 105–110.

Montague, M. M., Enders, C., & Dietz, S. (2011). Effects of cognitive strategy instruction on math problem solving of middle school students with learning disabilities. *Learning Disability Quarterly, 34*(4), 262–272. doi:10.1177/0731948711421762

Murphy, M. M., Mazzocco, M. M. M., Hanich, L. B., & Early, M. C. (2007). Cognitive characteristics of children with mathematics learning disability (MLD) vary as a function of the cutoff criterion used to define MLD. *Journal of Learning Disabilities, 40*, 458–478. doi:10.1177/00222194070400050901

National Council of Teachers of Mathematics (NCTM). (2000). *Principles and standards for school mathematics.*

National Council of Teachers of Mathematics (NCTM). (2014). *Principles to actions: Ensuring mathematical success for all.*

National Mathematics Advisory Panel (NMAP). (2008). *Foundations for success: The final report of the National Mathematics Advisory Panel.* U.S. Department of Education.

National Research Council. (2009). *Mathematic learning in early childhood: Paths toward excellence and equity.*

Peterson, S. K., Mercer, C. D., & O'Shea, L. (1988). Teaching learning disabled students place value using the concrete to abstract sequence. *Learning Disabilities Research, 4*(1), 52–56.

Pfannenstiel, K. H., Bryant, D. P., Bryant, B. R., & Porterfield, J. A. (2015). Cognitive strategy instruction for teaching word problems to primary-level struggling students. *Intervention in School and Clinic, 50*, 291–296. doi:10.1177/1053451214560890

Powell, S. (2011). Solving word problems using schemas: A review of the literature. *Learning Disabilities Research & Practice, 26*(2), 94–108.

Powell, S. (2014). The influence of symbols and equations on understanding mathematical equivalence. *Intervention in School and Clinic, 50*, 266–272.

Powell, S. (2018, February). *How to help students with mathematics difficulties become expert problem solvers.* 2018 RME Research-to-Practice Conference, Dallas, TX.

Powell, S. R., & Fuchs, L. S. (2010). Contribution of equal-sign instruction beyond word problem tutoring for third-grade students with mathematics difficulty. *Journal of Educational Psychology, 102*, 381–394. doi:10.1037/a0018447

Rivera, D., & Smith, D. D. (1988). Using a demonstration strategy to teach middle school students with learning disabilities how to compute long division. *Journal of Learning Disabilities, 21*, 77–81.

Ross, S. H. (1989). Parts, wholes, and place value: A developmental view. *Arithmetic Teacher, 36*(6), 47–51.

Shin, M., & Bryant, D. P. (2015). A synthesis of mathematical and cognitive performances of students with mathematics learning disabilities. *Journal of Learning Disabilities, 45*, 96–112. doi:10.1177/0022219413508324

Siegler, R. S., & Booth, J. L. (2005). Development of numerical estimation: A review. In J. I. D. Campbell (Ed.), *Handbook of mathematical cognition* (pp. 197–212). CRC Press.

Siegler, R., Carpenter, T., Fennell, F., Geary, D., Lewis, J., Okamoto, Y., . . . Wray, J. (2010). *Developing effective fractions instruction for kindergarten through 8th grade: A practice guide* (NCEE No. 2010-4039). National Center for Education Evaluation and Regional Assistance, Institute of Education Sciences, U.S. Department of Education.

Siegler, R. S., & Shrager, J. (1984). Strategy choice in addition and subtraction: How do children know what to do? In C. Sophian (Ed.), *Origins of cognitive skills* (pp. 229–293). Lawrence Erlbaum.

Sorto, A. (2012). *Mathematics instructional strategies for English language learners.* Meadows Center for Preventing Educational Risk, University of Texas.

Stein, M., Kinder, D., Silbert, J., & Carnine, D. W. (2006). *Designing effective mathematics instruction.* Prentice Hall.

Strickland, T. K., & Maccini, P. (2013). The effects of the concrete-representational-abstract-integration strategy on the ability of students with learning disabilities to multiply linear expressions within area problems. *Remedial and Special Education, 34*(3), 142–153.

Swanson, H. L., & Jerman, O. (2006). Math disabilities: A selective meta-analysis of the literature. *Review of Educational Research, 76*(2), 249–274.

Van de Garderen, D., & Scheuermann, A. M. (2014). Diagramming word problems: A strategic approach for instruction. *Intervention in School and Clinic.* Advance online publication. doi:10.1177/1053451214560889

Van de Walle, J. A., Karp, K. S., & Bay-Williams, J. M. (2012). *Elementary and middle school mathematics: Teaching developmentally* (8th ed.). Pearson.

Van de Walle, J. A., Karp, K. S., & Bay-Williams, J. M. (2016). *Elementary and middle school mathematics: Teaching developmentally.* Pearson e-text. (9th ed.). Pearson.

Wei, X., Christiano, E. R., Yu, J. W., Wagner, M., & Spiker, D. (2015). Reading and math achievement profiles and longitudinal growth trajectories of children with an autism spectrum disorder. *Autism, 19*(2), 200–210. doi:10.1177/1362361313516549

Wiig, E. H., & Semel, E. M. (1984). *Language assessment and intervention for the learning disabled* (2nd ed.). Macmillan.

Williams, D. L., Goldstein, G., Kojkowski, N., & Minshew, N. J. (2008). Do individuals with high functioning autism have the IQ profile associated with nonverbal learning disability? *Research in Autism Spectrum Disorders, 2*, 353–361.

Wong, C., Odom, S. L., Hume, K., Cox, A. W., Fettig, A., Kucharczyk, S., . . . Schultz, T. R. (2013). *Evidence-based practices for children, youth, and young adults with autism spectrum disorder.* The University of North Carolina, Frank Porter Graham Child Development Institute, Autism Evidence-Based Practice Review Group.

Woodward, J., Beckmann, S., Driscoll, M., Franke, M., Herzig, P., Jitendra, A., . . . Ogbuehi, P. (2012). *Improving mathematical problem solving in grades 4 through 8: A practice guide* (NCEE 2012-4055). National Center for Education Evaluation and Regional Assistance, Institute of Education Sciences, U.S. Department of Education. Retrieved from http://ies.ed.gov/ncee/wwc/publications_reviews.aspx#pubsearch/

Wu, H. (2005, September). *Key mathematical ideas in grades 5–8.* Retrieved from http://math.berkeley.edu~wu/NCTM2005a.pdf

Wu, H. (2006, October). *Professional development: The hard work of learning mathematics.* Presentation at the fall southeastern section meeting of the American Mathematical Society, Johnson City, TN.

CHAPTER 14

American Institutes for Research. (2013). *How career and technical education can help students be college and career ready: A primer.* Retrieved from https://files.eric.ed.gov/fulltext/ED555696.pdf

Bauer, S., Benkstein, P., Pittel, A., & Koury, G. (n.d.). *Gifted students: Recommendations for teachers.* Retrieved from http://www.education.udel.edu/wp-content/uploads/2013/01/GiftedStudents.pdf

Beck, I. L., McKeown, M. G., & Kucan, L. (2013). *Bringing words to life: Robust vocabulary instruction* (2nd ed.). Guilford.

Bottge, B. A., Toland, M. D., Gassaway, L., Butler, M., Choo, S., Griffen, A. K., & Ma, X. (2014). Impact of enhanced anchored instruction in inclusive math classrooms. *Exceptional Children, 81*(2), 158–175.

Boyle, J. R. (2011). Thinking strategically to record notes in content classes. *American Secondary Education, 40*(1), 51–66.

Boyle, J. R., Forchelli, G. A., & Cariss, K. (2015) Note-taking interventions to assist students with disabilities in content area classes, *Preventing School Failure: Alternative Education for Children and Youth, 59*(3), 186–195. doi:10.1080/1045988X.2014.903463

Boyle, J. R., & Rivera, T. Z. (2012). Note-taking techniques for students with disabilities: A systematic review of the research. *Learning Disability Quarterly, 35*(3), 131–143. doi:10.1177/0731948711435794

Bragstad, B. J., & Stumpf, S. M. (1987). *A guidebook for teaching study skills and motivation* (2nd ed.). Pearson.

Bryant, B. R., Bryant, D. P., Kim, M.-K., & Hou, F. (2015, April). *High school English I support for students with learning disabilities.* Paper presented at the Council for Exceptional Children Annual Conference, San Diego, CA.

Bryant, D. P., & Bryant, B. R. (2011). *Assistive technology for people with disabilities.* Pearson.

Bulgren, J. A., Marquis, J. G., Lenz, B. K., Schumaker, J. B., & Deshler, D. D. (2009). Effectiveness of question exploration to enhance students' written expression of content knowledge and comprehension. *Reading & Writing Quarterly, 25*, 271–289. doi:10.1080/10573560903120813

Butler, S., Urrutia, K., Buenger, A., & Hunt, M. (2010). *A review of the current research on comprehension instruction.* RMC Research Corporation.

Casareno, A. B. (2010). When reading in college is a problem. In S. C. Brown & M. A. Fallon (Eds.), *Teaching inclusively in higher education.* Information Age.

CAST. (2018). *Universal design for learning guidelines version 2.2* [graphic organizer].

Garber-Miller, K. (2006). Playful test previews: Letting go of familiar mustache monologues. *Journal of Adolescent & Adult*

Literacy, 50(4), 284–288. doi:10/1598/LAA L.50.4.4

Honig, D. L., Diamond, & Gutlohn, L. (2012). *Teaching reading sourcebook* (2nd ed.). Consortium on Reading Excellence.

Hoover, J. J., & Patton, J. R. (2007). *Teaching students with learning problems to use study skills* (2nd ed.). PRO-USDE.

Hopper, C. H. (2016). *Practicing college learning strategies* (7th ed.). Cengage Learning.

Hughes, C. A., Schumaker, J. B., Deshler, D. D., & Mercer, C. D. (2005). *Learning strategies curriculum: The test-taking strategy: PIRATES.* Edge Enterprises.

IRIS Center. (2015). *Study skills strategies (Part 1): Foundations for effectively teaching study skills.* Retrieved from http://iris.peabody.vanderbilt.edu/module/ss1/

Johnson, E., Humphrey, M., Mellard, D., Woods, K., & Swanson, H. L. (2010). Cognitive processing deficits and students with specific learning disabilities: A selective meta-analysis of the literature. *Learning Disability Quarterly, 33*, 3–18.

Johnson-Harris, K. M., & Mundschenk, N. A. (2014). Working effectively with students with BD in a general education classroom: The case for universal design for learning. *The Clearing House: A Journal of Educational Strategies, Issues and Ideas, 87*(4), 168–174. doi:10.1080/00098655.2014.897927

Kumar, D. D. (2010). Approaches to interactive video anchors in problem-based science learning. *Journal of Science Education and Technology, 19*, 13–19. doi:10.1007/s10956-009-9154-6

Lavenstein, H. (2015). Not happy with your teenager's midterm grades? Start now with these steps toward better grades. *Rhode Island Tutorial & Educational Services.* Retrieved from https://www.ritutorial.org/happy-teenagers-midterm-grades-start-now-steps-toward-better-grades/

Lynch, E. (2014). *Strategies for helping readers: Activating prior knowledge.* Retrieved from https://www.sadlier.com/school/ela-blog/reading-strategy-activating-prior-knowledge

Manyak, P. C., VonGunten, H., Autenriett, D., Gillis, C., Mastre-O'Farrell, J., Irvine-McDermott, E., Baumann, J. F., & Blachowicz, C. Z. (2014). Four practical principles for enhancing vocabulary instruction. *The Reading Teacher, 68*(1), 13–23. doi:10.1002/trtr.1299

National Association of Colleges and Employers. (2014). *Employers: Verbal communication most important candidate skill.* Retrieved from http://www.naceweb.org/career-readiness/competencies/employers-verbal-communication-most- important-candidate-skill/

Ogle, D. M. (1986). A teaching model that develops active reading of expository text. *Reading Teacher, 39*, 564–570.

Red Rocks Community College, Connect to Success, T+. (n.d.). *Study skills questionnaire.* Retrieved from http://www.rrcc.edu/sites/default/files/instructional-services-step_5.pdf

Rieth, H. J., Bryant, D. P., Kinzer, C. K., Colburn, L. K., Hur, S.-J., Hartman, P., & Choi, H.-S. (2003). An analysis of the impact of anchored instruction on teaching and learning activities in two ninth-grade language arts classes. *Remedial and Special Education, 24*(3), 173–184.

Schumaker, J. B., & Deshler, D. D. (2006). Teaching adolescents to be strategic learners. In D. D. Deshler & J. B. Schumaker (Eds.), *Teaching adolescents with disabilities: Accessing the general education curriculum* (pp. 121–156). Corwin.

Spisak, D. (2015). *Soft skills: The foundation for academic and career success.* Retrieved from https://www.careereducationreview.net/wp-content/uploads/2015/12/Soft_Skills.pdf

Spungin, S. J. (2013, August 15). *For teachers: Basic tips for when you have a visually impaired student in your class.* Retrieved from http://www.afb.org/blog/afb-blog/for- teachers-basic-tips-for-when-you-have-a-visually-impaired-student-in-your-class/12

Steimle, J., Brdiczka, O., & Mühlhäuser, M. (2009). Collaborative paper-based annotation of lecture slides. *Educational Technology & Society, 12*(4), 125–137.

Stone, B., & Urquhart, V. (2008). *Remove limits to learning with systematic vocabulary instruction.* McREL.

Strang, T. (2016). *Tips for students: Become a better listener.* Retrieved from http://blog.cengage.com/tips-students-become- better-listener/

Study Guides and Strategies. (n.d.). *Time management.* Retrieved from http://www.studygs.net/enews/

Swanson, H. L., & Fung, W. (2016) Working memory components and problem-solving accuracy: Are there multiple pathways? *Journal of Educational Psychology, 108*(8), 1153–1177. doi:10.1037/edu0000116

Techdialogue. (2013, January 3). *An intro to using google calendar for the classroom.* Retrieved from https://techdialogue.wordpress.com/2013/01/03/an-intro-to-using-google-calendar- for-the-classroom/

Thomas, C. N., & Rieth, H. J. (2011). A research synthesis of the literature on multimedia anchored instruction in preservice teacher education. *Journal of Special Education Technology, 26*(2), 1–22.

Vacca, R. T., Vacca, J. L., & Mraz, M. E. (2014). *Content area reading: Literacy and learning across the curriculum* (11th ed.). Pearson.

Vaughn, S., & Bos, C. S. (2015). *Strategies for teaching students with learning and behavior problems* (9th ed.). Pearson.

Vaughn, S., Cirino, P. T., Wanzek, J., Wexler, J., Fletcher, J. M., Denton, C. A. . . . Francis, D. J. (2010). Response to intervention for middle school students with reading difficulties: Effects of a primary and secondary intervention. *School Psychology, 39*, 3–21.

Vogel, S. (1997). *College students with learning disabilities: A handbook.* Learning Disabilities Association of America.

Walport-Glawron, H. (2012). *Kids speak out on student engagement.* Retrieved from https://www.franklinschools.org/cms/lib2/IN01001624/Centricity/Domain/101/Kids%20Speak%20Out%20on%20Student%20Engagement%20_%20Edutopia.pdf

Westchester University (n.d.). *Section 7: Instructional strategies that facilitate learning across content areas.* Retrieved from https://www.wcupa.edu/education-socialwork/assessment Accreditation/documents/Instructional_Strategies.pdf

Wright, J. (2013). *How to: Improve reading comprehension with a cognitive strategy: Ask-read-tell.* Retrieved from http://www.interventioncentral.org/sites/default/files/pdfs/pdfs_blog/cognitive_strategy_reading_comprehension_ART.pdf

INDEX